Selected works of Jawaharlal Nehru

JAWAHARLAL NEHRU, APRIL 1957

Selected works of Jawaharlal Nehru

Second Series

Volume Thirty Seven

(22 February – 30 April 1957)

A Project of the
Jawaharlal Nehru
Memorial Fund

Enquiries regarding copyright
to be addressed to the publishers

PUBLISHED BY
Jawaharlal Nehru Memorial Fund
Teen Murti House, New Delhi 110 011

ISBN 019 568450 6
ISBN 978–019568450–6

DISTRIBUTED BY
Oxford University Press
YMCA Library Building, Jai Singh Road, New Delhi 110 001
Mumbai Kolkata Chennai
Oxford New York Toronto
Melbourne Tokyo Hong Kong

TYPESET BY
Digigrafics
D-69, Gulmohar Park
New Delhi 110 049

PRINTED AT
Lordson Publishers Pvt Ltd
C 5/19, Rana Pratap Bagh
Delhi 110 007

Editor

Mushirul Hasan

FOREWORD

Jawaharlal Nehru is one of the key figures of the twentieth century. He symbolised some of the major forces which have transformed our age.

When Jawaharlal Nehru was young, history was still the privilege of the West; the rest of the world lay in deliberate darkness. The impression given was that the vast continents of Asia and Africa existed merely to sustain their masters in Europe and North America. Jawaharlal Nehru's own education in Britain could be interpreted, in a sense, as an attempt to secure for him a place within the pale. His letters of the time are evidence of his sensitivity, his interest in science and international affairs as well as of his pride in India and Asia. But his personality was veiled by his shyness and a facade of nonchalance, and perhaps outwardly there was not much to distinguish him from the ordinary run of men. Gradually there emerged the warm and universal being who became intensely involved with the problems of the poor and the oppressed in all lands. In doing so, Jawaharlal Nehru gave articulation and leadership to millions of people in his own country and in Asia and Africa.

That imperialism was a curse which should be lifted from the brows of men, that poverty was incompatible with civilisation, that nationalism should be poised on a sense of international community and that it was not sufficient to brood on these things when action was urgent and compelling—these were the principles which inspired and gave vitality to Jawaharlal Nehru's activities in the years of India's struggle for freedom and made him not only an intense nationalist but one of the leaders of humanism.

No particular ideological doctrine could claim Jawaharlal Nehru for its own. Long days in jail were spent in reading widely. He drew much from the thought of the East and West and from the philosophies of the past and the present. Never religious in the formal sense, yet he had a deep love for the culture and tradition of his own land. Never a rigid Marxist, yet he was deeply influenced by that theory and was particularly impressed by what he saw in the Soviet Union on his first visit in 1927. However, he realised that the world was too complex, and man had too many facets, to be encompassed by any single or total explanation. He himself was a socialist with an abhorrence of regimentation and a democrat who was anxious to reconcile his faith in civil liberty with the necessity of mitigating economic and social wretchedness. His struggles, both within himself and with the outside world, to adjust such seeming contradictions are what make his life and work significant and fascinating.

As a leader of free India, Jawaharlal Nehru recognised that his country could neither stay out of the world nor divest itself of its own interests in world affairs. But to the extent that it was possible, Jawaharlal Nehru sought to speak objectively and to be a voice of sanity in the shrill phases of the 'cold war'. Whether his influence helped on certain occasions to maintain peace is for the future historian to assess. What we do know is that for a long stretch of time he commanded an international audience reaching far beyond governments, that he spoke for ordinary, sensitive, thinking men and women around the globe and that his was a constituency which extended far beyond India.

So the story of Jawaharlal Nehru is that of a man who evolved, who grew in storm and stress till he became the representative of much that was noble in his time. It is the story of a generous and gracious human being who summed up in himself the resurgence of the 'third world' as well as the humanism which transcends dogmas and is adapted to the contemporary context. His achievement, by its very nature and setting, was much greater than that of a Prime Minister. And it is with the conviction that the life of this man is of importance not only to scholars but to all, in India and elsewhere, who are interested in the valour and compassion of the human spirit that the Jawaharlal Nehru Memorial Fund has decided to publish a series of volumes consisting of all that is significant in what Jawaharlal Nehru spoke and wrote. There is, as is to be expected in the speeches and writings of a man so engrossed in affairs and gifted with expression, much that is ephemeral; this will be omitted. The official letters and memoranda will also not find place here. But it is planned to include everything else and the whole corpus should help to remind us of the quality and endeavour of one who was not only a leader of men and a lover of mankind, but a completely integrated human being.

New Delhi
18 January 1972

Chairman
Jawaharlal Nehru Memorial Fund

EDITORIAL NOTE

When asked by Derek Holroyde, a BBC correspondent in Delhi, about the outcome of the second general elections held from 24 February to 14 March 1957, Jawaharlal Nehru replied:

> Of course, there are many surprises in the elections as there always are, but broadly speaking, the elections were always entirely in favour of the Congress so far as Parliament is concerned, and the surprises came in the States, which shows that the broad policy of the Congress is approved of by the people, whether foreign or internal or economic but that, there is a good deal of discontentment about local causes and local organizations.

On the future plans of his government, the Prime Minister said:

> The first problem for our Government is obviously, the economic problem—the Second Five Year Plan, and all that goes under it. There are problems of foreign exchange, of development of internal resources, because the Second Five Year Plan puts a heavy burden on us, which is increased due to subsequent happenings, and we hope to shoulder that burden and we propose to do so.

And on disarmament, especially in the context of the nuclear tests by Soviet Union and Great Britain, he observed:

> It is very curious, that almost every country that possess it, says that if you are sure, the other party will not do it, we won't do it. Well, surely if that is so, let them all meet together and say we won't do it.

These views sum up the scope of this volume. It is an important collection of speeches and correspondence for understanding the evolution of Indian democracy, the coverage of the second general elections, the foregrounding of governance issues at the Centre and the States, and the articulation of India's foreign policy.

Three themes are salient in the coverage of the elections; one, the scale and depth of campaigning, and the wide variety of issues raised, national and international, before the electorate; second, Nehru's unswerving commitment to democratic structures and parliamentary processes; and lastly, his vision of a united India that he had so creatively expounded long years ago in 1945. Thus, he stated in Vijayawada on 22 February:

> People talk of North India and South India, East India and West India. But, to me, there is only one India and it is neither North nor South. It is one great India in which all of us, whether we live in the Himalayas or in Kanniyakumari, or right here, belong to one great big family. And it is only when all of us realize that fully and have that sense of complete integrated nationalism for Bharat, then India will be strong and will go ahead faster.

On the outcome of the elections, particularly in Uttar Pradesh, he commented:

> About a year ago I remember discussing the UP situation with some friends from my Province. I said then that the Congress was likely to lose a good number of seats in the coming elections and that, more particularly, Muslims, as a whole would not vote for the Congress. Many others also who had previously voted for the Congress will not do so for a variety of reasons. That was my appraisal of the situation long before the elections. This was not based on any careful survey but, if I may say so, was an instinctive reaction to what I had felt in the course of my visits to the UP or what I had heard. The fact that Muslims were drifting away from the Congress was obvious. For us to think that the fault does not lie with us but with others, is surely a wrong way of approach. In a democracy one has not only to be right but to make others feel that he is right, or else the others go their own way and leave us in the lurch.

In Jammu and Kashmir, for the first time, elections were held under the new State Constitution in March 1957. This volume offers vital information on the emerging democratic process in the Valley.

Nehru's principal concern was: How are 37 crores of human beings going to progress to emerge out of the mire of poverty in which they had struggled for so long? The remedial measures he proposed are set out in his speech at the Federation of Indian Chambers of Commerce and Industry in Delhi. In the opinion of Frank Moraes, Nehru's biographer in 1956, 'in the confused and complicated texture of thought of Congress, Nehru's economic thinking runs consistently like a firm thread.'

History, according to Nehru, had selected India as one of democracy's chief testing grounds, and he found tangible expression of the democratic spirit at work in the Community Development Programme that covered 220,000 out of a total of 500,000 villages and the National Extension Service. He called them 'revolutionary and perhaps the most significant thing that we are doing in India at present.' Earlier, he had proclaimed: 'All over India these are now centres of human activity that are like lamps spreading their light more and more in the surrounding darkness. This light must grow and grow until it covers the land.'

In the section on 'National Progress' letters and speeches on Food and Agriculture, Education and Culture, and Science communicate Nehru's commitment to the building of a modern, prosperous and secular India. There is no ambiguity over what he stood for. In fact, the clarity of his thinking invited opposition and created consternation among his detractors in political and bureaucratic circles.

Section three covers administrative matters, some of which relate to the implementation of Nehru's nation-building project. His knowledge and grasp of details is truly amazing. So also is his awareness of the weakness of the administrative structures that India inherited from the Raj.

The range of the Prime Minister's engagement is astonishing. For example, he comments on the cruelty towards monkeys, intervene in the case of unauthorized settlements and the uprootment of farmers near Delhi's Palam airport, and expresses his opinion on the upkeep of Delhi's Jama Masjid. When Rajkumari Amrit Kaur informed Nehru on 4 April 1957 that the Cabinet had decided that 'the slum area around Jama Masjid should be cleared and the matter taken in hand on a priority basis', he replied: 'I had myself visited this area and discussed it with many people there, including the shopkeepers, and most people agreed. Indeed, there is no help for it if we want to clear up this badly infested area, which spoils the Jama Masjid approach and has become a terrible slum.' The fact is that it was not possible to make any progress in the matter because Maulana Abul Kalam Azad had instructed at a meeting held on 9 February 1957 that 'the question of shifting of the shops should be held over until after the election.'

In the section on the Indian National Congress, the letter to Jayaprakash Narayan sums up the differences between the Prime Minister and the veteran Socialist leader. In a rather detailed exchange, he observed:

... I have had a feeling for many months, if not more, that there was a widening gap between our views about various matters. Almost everything that I thought important and emphasized, was criticized by you in strong language. I do not object, of course, to that criticism. But, I am merely pointing out that this difference in our viewpoints had grown so much that there were not many points of contact left. In fact, I was left in some state of amazement whenever I read your reported speeches or statements. Frankly, I felt that you had completely lost grip of the situation in India as well as in the world, and what you said had no reality at all. Also, I felt that your governing motive was hardly a positive or constructive one in so far as these elections were concerned, but much more so and active and bitter dislike of the Congress and a desire to see it defeated, whatever the consequences might be. With that attitude, it was difficult to deal with at all, and there was little room left for argument. We spoke different languages or the Communist language or most other languages, even though I may not agree with them, as often I do not. But, your language seemed to be a special one, which I could not make much of. It seemed to me the result of being cut off from reality and a result of woolly thinking.

Nehru continued:

Apart from opposition parties in the legislatures, everyone knows that in India there are all kinds of disruptive and reactionary forces. There is also the inertia of ages. And it is very easy for this inert mass to be roused by some religious or caste or linguistic or provincial or like cry, and thus to come in the way of all progress. That is the real opposition in the country, and it is a tremendously strong one. And that is what you seem to ignore completely. We have constantly to battle against it, as we have to battle against various world forces which threaten us. Whether in the domestic sphere or the international sphere, we fight for survival, and when I say that, I am not referring to the Congress only.

Evidently, you are not of this opinion. As you say, you are not worried by the cry of political instability in the country. I could not disagree with you more. I think that there is grave danger of political instability in this country and of disruption. Whatever the failings of the Congress, and they are many, it has done, I think, inestimable service to the country in checking these tendencies to disruption and instability and trying to bring about cohesion in the country. This has nothing to do with the Congress being good or bad, important as that is. What I am referring to is the grave danger of disruption and political instability which we have to face. The various courses you have suggested, might harm the Congress, but they would certainly tend to produce this instability in the country and, therefore, injure the country as a whole.

This volume, like the previous one, furnishes rich information on foreign affairs. He was guided, as always, by the principle of enlightened self-interest. Speaking in the Constituent Assembly in December 1947, he had given some indication of this trajectory:

> Whatever policy you may lay down, the main feature of the foreign affairs of a country has to be to find out what is most advantageous to her. We may talk about international goodwill and may mean what we talk. We may talk about peace and freedom and earnestly mean what we say. But in the ultimate analysis a government functions for the good of the country it governs and no government dare do anything which in the short or long run is manifestly to the disadvantage of that country. Therefore whether a country is imperialistic or socialist or communist, its foreign minister thinks primarily of the interests of that country.

At the same time, his responses to worldwide events were influenced by his upbringing and training and the influence of socialist and Marxian ideas. He fervently believed in decolonization, non-alignment, peace and nuclear disarmament, and India's prominent place in the emerging world order. His views are best summed up in the following excerpts drawn from a speech in Washington in October 1949:

> ... We have to achieve freedom and to defend it. We have to meet aggression and to resist it and the force employed must be adequate to the purpose. But even when preparing to resist aggression, the ultimate objective, the objective of peace and reconciliation, must never be lost sight of, and heart and mind must be attuned to this supreme aim, and not swayed or clouded by hatred or fear.

> This is the basis and the goal of our foreign policy. We are neither blind to reality nor do we propose to acquiesce in any challenge to man's freedom, from whatever quarter it may come. Where freedom is menaced, or justice threatened, or where aggression takes place, we cannot be and shall not be neutral. What we plead for, and endeavour to practice in our own important way, is a binding faith in peace, and an unfailing endeavour of thought and action to ensure it. The great democracy of the United States of America will, I feel sure, understand and appreciate our approach to life's problems because it could not have any other aim or a different ideal. Friendship and cooperation between our two countries are, therefore, natural. I stand here to offer both in the pursuit of justice, liberty and peace.

On Kashmir, he reiterated India's stand during his talks with Gunnar Jarring, the UN Security Council representative. Summarizing India's policy to Habib Bourguiba, the Tunisian Prime Minister, he wrote :

> Our case is and has been throughout these nine years that the Jammu and Kashmir State acceded to India legally and constitutionally in October 1947. Subsequently a Constituent Assembly, elected in the State under adult suffrage, drew up a Constitution and gave effect to parts of it in the course of the last four or five years. This was finalized some months ago. No other step has been taken since then, except that the Constituent Assembly dissolved itself. Therefore, the question of our not acting up to the Resolution passed by the Security Council does not arise.

Let me conclude this introduction with Nehru's foreword to the second Hebrew edition of *An Autobiography*:

> This book was written when we in India were in the middle of our struggle for freedom. That struggle was long drawn out and it brought many experiences of joy and sorrow, of hope and despair. But the despair did not last long because of the inspiration that came to us from our leader, Mahatma Gandhi, and the deep delight of working for a cause that took us out of our little shells.

> All of us are older now and our days of youth are long past. Yet, even now, when we face the troubles and torments that encompasses, something of that old memory of our leader gives us strength.

We thank various individuals and institutions for their help in publishing this volume. Shrimati Sonia Gandhi granted permission to consult and publish the papers in her possession. They are referred to as the JN Collection. We have also had access to important collections at the Nehru Memorial Museum Library, the Secretariats of the Prime Minister, the President and the Cabinet, and the Ministries of External and Home Affairs, Planning Commission, National Archives of India, and the Press Information Bureau. The All India Radio allowed us to use the tapes of Jawaharlal Nehru's speeches.

For their scholarly assisstance in the collection of archival material and its subsequent organization, I am indebted to Ms Geeta Kudaisya, Ms Shantisri Banerji and Dr Jawaid Alam. Equally my thanks to Ms Malini Rajani and Ms Saroja Anantha Krishnan for their editorial assistance.

29 April 2006   MUSHIRUL HASAN

CONTENTS

1. Second General Elections and After

I. The Campaign

II. Results and Analysis

III. Education and Culture

IV. The Nagas

8. Kashmir

I. In the UN

II. Assembly Elections

9. External Affairs

I. Foreign Policy

II. Pakistan

III. China and Tibet

IV. Iran

ILLUSTRATIONS

ABBREVIATIONS

AFPFL	Anti-Fascist People's Freedom League
AICC	All India Congress Committee
AIR	All India Radio
CPI	Communist Party of India
CS	Commonwealth Secretary
CSIR	Council of Scientific and Industrial Research
FS	Foreign Secretary
HAL	Hindustan Aircraft Limited
IAC	Indian Airlines Corporation
IAF	Indian Air Force
I & B Ministry	Information and Broadcasting Minstry
ICAR	Indian Council of Agricultural Research
KMPP	Kisan Mazdoor Praja Party
MEA	Ministry of External Affairs
MHA	Ministry of Home Affairs
MP	Member of Parliament
MWP	Minister Without Portfolio
NAI	National Archives of India
NATO	North Atlantic Treaty Organization
NEFA	North East Frontier Agency
NES	National Extension Service
NMML	Nehru Memorial Museum and Library
NR&SR	Natural Resources and Scientific Research
PCC	Pradesh Congress Committee

PEPSU	Patiala and East Punjab States Union
PIB	Press Information Bureau
PMS	Prime Minister's Secretariat
PPS	Principal Private Secretary
PSP	Praja Socialist Party
P&T	Posts and Telegraph
PWD	Public Works Department
RSS	Rashtriya Swayamsevak Sangh
SEATO	South East Asia Treaty Organization
SG	Secretary General
TA	Travelling Allowance
TCM	Technical Cooperation Mission
TTNC	Travancore Tamil Nad Congress
UK	United Kingdom
UN/UNO	United Nations Organization
UNCIP	United Nations Commission for India and Pakistan
UP	Uttar Pradesh
UPCC	Uttar Pradesh Congress Committee
US/USA	United States of America
USIS	United States Information Service
USSR	Union of Soviet Socialist Republics
WH&S Ministry	Works, Housing & Supply Ministry

SECOND GENERAL ELECTIONS AND AFTER

I. THE CAMPAIGN

1. Unity and Hard Work Vital to Progress[1]

Friends and comrades,

Although I have come here because of these general elections,[2] it is really some other reason that has brought me here, and I am not at all worried as to what you and the people of Andhra Pradesh will do about the elections. I know that you will stand firmly in support of the Congress and the Congress candidates. But I came here because I like coming to the South. I like coming to Andhra Pradesh because recently Andhra Pradesh has enlarged itself and has become much bigger.[3]

People talk of North India and South India, East India and West India. But, to me, there is only one India and it is neither North nor South. It is one great India in which all of us, whether we live in the Himalayas or in Kanniyakumari, or right here, belong to one great big family. And it is only when all of us realize that fully and have that sense of complete integrated nationalism for Bharat, then India will be strong and will go ahead faster. I know that you all know that India is one on the map politically and there is one Government and we all have many bonds together. I want these bonds to become so strong, so intimate bonds of the mind and the heart, so that our nationalism can become a rock which can never break down whatever happens.

---

1. Speech at a public meeting, PWD Maidan, Vijayawada, Andhra Pradesh, 22 February 1957. AIR tapes, NMML. N. Sanjiva Reddy, the Chief Minister, later translated the speech into Telugu.
2. Nehru launched the election campaign of the Congress at Mumbai on 20 January 1957 for the second general elections which were held from 24 February to 14 March 1957. Some election speeches, delivered from 22 February 1957 onwards, in Andhra Pradesh, Mysore, Kerala, Madhya Pradesh, Punjab and Uttar Pradesh appear in this volume.
3. The new State of Andhra Pradesh, constituted by the merger of Telengana area of former Hyderabad State with Coastal Andhra and Rayalaseema as a result of the reorganization of states, came into being on 1 November 1956.

3

Many of you know something about our past history of Bharat or India. It was a history which had very fine periods, and it was also a history of bad periods that saw the fall of our country from time to time. And you will see in that history that our chief weakness in the past had been the division, the lack of cohesiveness, fissiparous and separatist tendencies and numerous wars which divided India into different parts in the past.

Sometimes people quarrelled in the name of religion, sometimes in the name of different provinces, sometimes on the caste basis, and sometimes on the question of language. So we quarrelled, weakened ourselves, lost our freedom and foreigners came and took possession of our country. Now we have learnt the lesson, that there can be no progress for India until India is completely united and until we all feel that our future lies with the whole of India and that every separatist tendency is bad and should be curbed. There are, of course, differences and variations in India. You have your own beautiful language, and other parts of India have their own languages. You have your ways, you have a different climate from the North and these different manifestations of India are welcome. But, the important thing is that India is one and that you and I, and all of us, have inherited this great country and this great country belongs to all of us; not bits of it. The Andhra Pradesh is yours, of course, but it is mine also. Even so, the Himalayas and all that is in the north is not mine only, it is yours also. All this is our joint inheritance and our joint home.

Now, you know that the British came here and established a Raj because we were all divided. About 72 years ago, some great people in India started the Indian National Congress. It was a small organization then, but it grew, and that organization spoke always for the whole of India, not for one province, not for one religion, not for one caste, and not for one language. The Indian National Congress became the organization of the Indian people wherever they lived, whatever their religion or caste or language. And the Indian National Congress took up the first thing in its programme, the unity of India, and the integration of India, and for last 50 or 60 years, it had worked for that. In the latter years, we had our great leader Mahatma Gandhi and the Congress under his leadership became very strong and spread into all our villages from North to South. What did he teach us? He taught us that India was one; that everyone in India, whether he was in the North or South, had equal rights. And that an Indian, whether he was a Hindu or Muslim or a Christian or a Buddhist or a Sikh, was equal to another Indian. He taught us that we should put away our barriers, and he taught us that the caste system had oppressed so many of our brethren. Well, we must raise our people who had been put down, the Harijans and others, and that every one should have equal opportunities in this country.

So, this Congress under Gandhiji's leadership and guidance built up this united

India not only on the map but in the minds and hearts of the people. And it built them up as an organized strong community which could give battle peacefully to the British Raj. Ultimately the Indian people, organized by the Indian National Congress, won Swaraj for this country. And so, Swaraj came and then we had to work even harder for the next step in our journey.

The next step is to put an end to the poverty, unemployment, unhappiness and misery of the Indian people. Now, that is a very big task and we undertook it. Now, if we have to solve this problem of India's poverty and make India prosperous, then we must again remember Gandhiji's lessons. We must be united, we must work together, we must be disciplined, and we must go forward together. That is why we had the First Five Year Plan to fight poverty and to make India go ahead. In that Five Year Plan we succeeded and we laid the base for further progress. Then we had the Second Five Year Plan which is now going on. Now, this Second Five Year Plan deals with the whole of India. It deals with the peasants in their fields, the production, agriculture and the industry because we have to increase our production everywhere, if we are to get rid of our poverty.

So, we are trying to organize the peasants to produce much more and also to strengthen big industries and small. Our peasants in our country do not produce as much as the peasants in other countries. In fact, in other countries, they produce double and three times more of what we produce here per acre. That is bad, why should we not produce more? We can do so if we follow others' example, if we use better tools, better seeds, better manure, fertilizer etc. It is easy to do it provided we set our minds to it. Therefore, it has become very important for us to increase our agricultural production greatly because that will be the base of every other advance. Then we want to start many industries, big, middle and small and as well as cottage industries so that we can produce everything that we require in the country and that people may have employment. Now, we have to balance agriculture with industry and we have to balance heavy industry with small industry and cottage industry. All these have to march together in a balanced way and then only we bring benefits to all the people.

You know about the Community Development Schemes and Blocks and this is something which, I think, is revolutionary and I believe, it is the biggest thing which we are doing in India. This was started four and a half years ago and has already covered 220,000 villages benefiting a population of, I think, nearly 140 million rural population. We hope, in the next five years, to cover all the remaining villages in India so that the whole of rural India with its five hundred thousand villages will have these Community Schemes, benefiting especially the peasants of India. But, remember this that we have to work hard in order to progress. It is not by shouting slogans that we are going to do it. We do not build anything by shouting slogans. If we have to build a bridge over the river we do not build it by shouting slogans but by working in a trained way, as engineers do before a bridge is built. Now, we have to build something much more than a bridge. We have to build the new India, the new Bharat, and that requires hard work of everybody in India, men and women, and it is only by the measure of hard work and unity that we shall go ahead fast.

Now, you have got this great Andhra Province with its fine historical traditions and great potentialities for progress. I hope that you will be inspired by the old traditions and inspired even more by the will to work to bring out these potentialities and thus raise the standard of all our people. But, remember this that you will only do so if you have unity and if you respect the minorities in your Province. Most of you here naturally are Hindus. You must respect and honour and give every facility to the minorities, the Muslims, the Christians and others. And this province and indeed the whole of India will only advance if the women advance. It is not the question of only men going ahead. We want the whole of 37 crores of India to go ahead and India is not going ahead unless the women of India go ahead.

When we attained Swaraj we completed a political revolution but that is not enough. We want in this country two other revolutions—an economic revolution and a social revolution. Just as we brought about the political revolution peacefully and largely with cooperation, so we hope to bring about the economic and the social revolutions also peacefully. After Swaraj, you will remember that we put an end to the princely states in India. That was a tremendous thing and yet we did it quickly and peacefully. I do not think in any other country in the world such a big revolutionary change has been brought about so quickly and peacefully as in India.

Then we undertook the land reforms and put an end practically all over India to the zamindari, *jagirdari*, *taluqdari*, and like systems. In most countries this also has brought trouble but we did it in India peacefully and with people's cooperation. And then we advanced on the industrial front and a great public sector is growing, controlled by the State. We want to encourage private enterprise also because we want every one to work for greater production. But the importance of the public sector is growing and all the big industries are controlled by the State. The old Imperial Bank has become the State Bank of India.[4]

---

4. The State Bank of India Bill, which sought to nationalize the Imperial Bank of India and transform it into the State Bank of India, was passed by the Lok Sabha on 30 April 1955. After its passage in the Rajya Sabha on 4 May 1955, the Bill received the President's assent on 8 May 1955.

Insurance has become nationalized[5] and so firmly, step by step, the State is controlling the economic life of the country, not for the benefit of any individual but for the sake of the country and its people. Thus we are laying foundations for the growth of socialism.

In the social sphere you know that we have abolished by law untouchability[6] and the like and we have passed laws giving certain rights to women—Hindu women.[7] These are big changes; revolutionary changes. In the economic field and in the social field, step by step, we hope to forward peacefully without any conflict by carrying all the millions of people with us.

It is important to remember that we must do our activities peacefully just as we carried out our fight for Swaraj peacefully because if we forget this big lesson then we break up into factions, and our unity is disturbed. Therefore, we must remember that all our activities must be peaceful. If we differ in our opinion, as we have every right to, we must argue, try to convince each other and not indulge in violence. It is only the immature who indulge in violence and we are a mature country and we must act in a mature way.

I am very glad to find that among the candidates put up by the Congress, there are some women. I should like more and more women to stand and be elected and come to our Parliament and to the local Assembly because I attach the greatest importance to have women representatives.

I hope, of course, that you will support the Congress candidates—all of them, and get them elected. But, I would particularly like to draw your attention to minority candidates because we owe a duty to those groups or religious communities which are in a minority. The majority always owes a duty to them, to help them and not to crush them by the weight of its majority.

5. The process of nationalization of insurance started with the President's promulgation of an Ordinance of 19 January 1956 bringing all life insurance companies under Government management. The Life Insurance (Emergency Provisions) Bill was passed by the Lok Sabha and the Rajya Sabha on 3 March and 15 March 1956 respectively, and the Life Insurance Corporation Act came into force on 1 July 1956.
6. The Untouchability (Offences) Act, passed by the Lok Sabha on 28 April and by the Rajya Sabha on 2 May 1955, came in force on 1 June 1955. It provided penalties for preventing a person on the ground of untouchability from entering a place of public worship, offering prayers therein or taking water from a tank or well etc.
7. The following Acts were passed by the Parliament: (i) Hindu Marriage Act (1955), (ii) Hindu Law of Adoption and Maintenance Act (1956), (iii) Hindu Minority and Guardianship Act (1956), (iv) Special Marriage Act (1956), and (v) Hindu Succession Act (1956).

One thing more about these elections. Sometimes, I find that people are lazy and they do not take the trouble to vote. They think that the Congress candidates will get through and why we should trouble ourselves. That is bad. It is everyone's duty to vote. If you have got a vote, you must exercise that vote. Not to exercise it shows that you are not performing your duty. Therefore, I hope that everyone who has a vote will vote.

And now my time is up and I am going and I wish you well. I am very happy that this great State of Andhra is progressing and is doing well. And I am sure that you will do better still and bring prosperity to all the people of Andhra. And now, you must say *Jai Hind* with me three times.

2. Issues before the Electorate[1]

The US military aid to Pakistan and Britain's continuing support of Pakistan on the two-nation theory can lead to a dangerous situation and bring conflict in its wake. We have to remain fully prepared to meet any challenge to our freedom or any efforts to reverse the course of history. Our Army is quite strong. We have weapons too and these weapons will be used when the time comes to use them to defend ourselves. But more important than that is to develop the unity of hearts and to bring about an emotional integration of the people.

The Kashmir question has acquired special importance in the context of US military aid to Pakistan and Britain's old attitude to India's freedom. Be prepared to meet any danger that might arise. We can prepare ourselves fully by not getting perturbed and at the same time developing unity. India in no circumstances will allow foreign troops to step on her soil.

Military pacts and military aid have increased the danger of war. Leaders of Pakistan have openly stated that the military aid, including atomic weapons received from the USA, will be used against India. I do not understand with what intentions these arms are being sent to Pakistan. Is it to maintain peace in Asia? I have not understood fully these new ways of keeping peace.

The US Government has assured India that the military aid being given to

1. Speech at a public meeting, Fateh Maidan, Hyderabad, 22 February 1957. From *The Hindu* and *The Hindustan Times*, 23 February 1957.

Pakistan will not be used against India. We do not doubt the genuineness of this assurance. We have respect for the USA, which is a great country. We have friendly ties with them. But I want to ask: who is going to check whether the military aid sent to Pakistan is at any time used against India or not? Will this investigation start after they are used? Wherever this method of giving military aid has been followed, conflict and war have come in its wake. War cannot be prevented by warlike means.

Pakistan is an independent country and has a right to receive military aid from the USA. What right have I to tell Pakistan what to do or what not to do? But, I certainly have a right to say what the result of that will be, what dangers arise from such a step and what we have to do to meet any contingency flowing from these dangers.

The military aid to Pakistan has caused India anxiety and has forced her to divert funds for strengthening her Armed Forces. We do not like to do so, but we are forced. We are busy in building up our country and removing poverty from our midst. But this military aid to Pakistan has forced us to tighten our belts and stop some of our nation-building work in order to divert funds for buying armaments.

Britain had encouraged the propagation of the two-nation theory in India in pre-Independence days. The British Government did it to weaken the nationalist movement and sow disunity. India ultimately accepted Partition, because we were tired of internecine conflict engineered by the British. I, however, want to make it quite clear that we accepted Partition not on the basis of the two-nation theory but on the basis of a political settlement. The issue was decided mainly in the legislatures of Punjab and Bengal in undivided India. That was done through voting. Whether it was done rightly or wrongly is a different matter, I do not want to get into that.

Pakistani leaders took no part in the freedom movement. They were with the British and that was one reason why Britain is today so friendly and closer to Pakistan. The people of Kashmir, the majority of whom are Muslims, had repudiated the two-nation theory all along. The Hindus and Muslims of Kashmir have many common bonds and they opposed the two-nation concept. It is very strange indeed that even after ten years of India's freedom, Britain shall still support the two-nation concept. Pakistan has always been a great supporter of the two-nation theory, but what is odd is that this theory is sometimes also supported in subdued language by certain foreign countries, particularly Britain. It is really strange that Britain should try to adopt the old tactics of pre-Independence days and support the two-nation theory and try to revive the old conflict. Were these last ten years of freedom a dream, that Britain should today again harp on the two-nation theory and place this old conflict before us, as if nothing had changed in all these years? We will never accept the two-nation theory whatever be the consequences.

I do not wish to say anything about the leaders of Pakistan. They are leaders of a big country. But I will say with all respect that when India—and Pakistan was also included in it then—was in the throes of the freedom movement, these leaders of Pakistan did not take part in that movement. Not only this, these leaders, to some extent, opposed it. Our rulers at that time, the British, supported these leaders of Pakistan. This was done when our country was thirsting for freedom. It is, therefore, understandable that Britain has closer relations with Pakistan because of this old association. This is understandable. But I thought the world had changed a little during all these years, and it had started thinking in a new way on these questions. I am deeply pained to know that people in Britain, not all people but people generally, should continue to think on these matters in the same old way as was the case before India's freedom.

It appears that India's going out of the possession of Britain has dealt a severe blow to their hearts. Nobody can reverse the course of history. If, however, any effort is made to bring about a reversal of history, then storms will arise. So, this Kashmir question is important. But much more important than this are the things behind it.

I do not want that you or anyone in India should get perturbed over this matter. But I do want you to realize that it is a complicated matter, and there are dangers inherent in it. Apart from that, we have to consider the flow of the most modern weapons into Pakistan. Pakistan Army officers have openly stated that they have got atomic weapons also. Those are not atom bombs but atomic artillery, which can fire small atomic bombs. It is really very strange that these weapons are being sent to Pakistan.

I am of the firm opinion that instead of changing the atmosphere in favour of peace, SEATO has worsened it and made it more tense. The Baghdad Pact too has given birth to a thousand problems in West Asia and created disunity among Arab countries.

When Egypt failed to get arms from the West she got them from Czechoslovakia and Russia,[2] which angered Britain and the United States. Then there is the Suez crisis. The Anglo-French and Israeli forces invaded Suez.[3] All

2. In September 1955, Czechoslovakia supplied arms to Egypt, and it was known that the USSR was the original supplier. See also *Selected Works* (second series), Vol. 31, p. 380 and Vol. 34, p. 248.
3. On 29 October 1956, the Israeli Army attacked Egyptian positions in the Sinai Peninsula. And on 31 October 1956, the British and French air forces, began attacking Egyptian airfields from Cyprus.

these things arose because of the race for armaments. The general complaint is that there is Russian interference but Russia complains that these pacts threatened her security. There is no peace either in South, East or West Asia as a result of these pacts.

The atmosphere has also worsened especially when atomic weapons were placed in the hands of irresponsible nations. Certain scientists have predicted that grave harm can be caused to humanity even by the atomic tests. Rajagopalachari's[4] strong advocacy against these tests is praiseworthy.[5]

In Kashmir, the tribesmen with military equipment came first, crossing the Pakistan territory, on buses and by other means without notice and behind them was the Pakistan Army.[6] It was at that juncture that an appeal was made to India for help from Kashmir. It was our duty to help because if there was destruction in Kashmir, its effect would have been felt in India. Kashmir was acceded to India[7] and it was also our duty to protect that State from aggression.

So, the Kashmir question arose as a result of aggression by Pakistan on Kashmir. That basic fact has not yet been realized by certain big powers. Those aggressors are still sitting in parts of Kashmir. But a lot of extraneous factors are brought in, and the two-nation theory is trotted out in regard to the Kashmir question. That is done when the whole world knows that the Kashmiri people, the vast majority of whom are Muslims, had rejected the theory outright. The people of Kashmir, including Muslims, Hindus and others, participated in the freedom movement and did not lean towards the Muslim League in pre-Independence days.

Kashmir has made great progress in the last nine years. There were elections[8] and the State is making all round progress. The percentage of the educated has

4. Rajagopalachari was Congress Chief Minister of Madras, 1952-54; he later founded the Swatantra Party in 1959.
5. Nehru refers to Rajagopalachari's appeal to the western nations for an immediate moratorium on atomic test explosions. For more details see *Selected Works* (second series), Vol. 28, pp. 211-212 and Vol. 33, p. 148.
6. On 22 October 1947.
7. On 26 October 1947.
8. In October 1950, the General Council of the National Conference of Kashmir passed a resolution asking for elections to a Constituent Assembly for drafting a Constitution and simultaneously functioning as its legislature. In May 1951, Yuvraj Karan Singh in his capacity as the Regent, issued a proclamation convoking a Constituent Assembly on the basis of adult franchise. Accordingly, elections were held and the Assembly met on 5 November 1951.

increased admirably in a State[9] which was educationally far backward than other states before. Economic reforms have been introduced.[10] There is a peaceful atmosphere in the State. Seventy thousand tourists had visited Kashmir last year. But in the area of Kashmir forcibly occupied Pakistan, the story is altogether different. There is chaos there, and the people in that area have revolted a number of times against the Pakistan Government. Even now voices are being raised against the Pakistani Government.

The people of Kashmir had waited for a decision from the Security Council for two years.[11] It was then that a Constituent Assembly was elected and the work of framing the Constitution began.[12] The Maharaja was removed,[13] zamindari system was abolished largely benefiting the peasants.[14] A few months ago, the Constitution was completed and Kashmir reiterated that it was an integral part of India.

Pakistan talks a lot about democracy in the UN. A reference is sometimes made to what is known as the "free world", and an accusing finger is pointed

9. The percentage of the educated had increased due to certain measures taken by the Government. For example, tuition fees right from the kindergarten to the post-graduation were abolished in 1953. Primary schools for boys had increased from 1,064 in 1953 to 1,671 in 1956 and for girls from 175 in 1953 to 199 in 1956. There was 34 per cent increase in enrolment in this period for boys and 197 per cent for girls. Enrolment in degree colleges increased by 80 per cent from 2,687 in 1953-54 to 4,615 in 1956-57. There were twelve colleges in 1957 as against seven in 1954.

10. In accordance with The Big Landed Estates Abolition Act of 17 October 1950, all land holdings in excess of 125 acres were confiscated for distribution among the tillers of the land to whom the proprietary rights not exceeding the limit of 20 acres per head were given. Sections 13 and 14 of the Jammu and Kashmir Constitution directed the State to promote the welfare of the people by establishing a socialist order of society and laying stress on protecting the public sector.

11. The Government of India had formally called upon the United Nations Security Council on 1 January 1948 to deal with the Kashmir issue. The Council appointed the United Nations Commission for India and Pakistan and gave it the responsibility of investigating India's complaint. Due to the efforts of the Commission only a ceasefire agreement was signed on 1 January 1949. During the years 1950-53, the Security Council appointed three mediators—A.G.L. McNaughton, Owen Dixon and Frank Graham—and their efforts did not meet with success.

12. The Jammu and Kashmir Constituent Assembly met for the first time on 5 November 1951 and adopted the Constitution on 17 November 1956, which was brought into force on 26 January 1957.

13. Hari Singh abdicated the throne in favour of his son Yuvaraj Karan Singh on 20 June 1949.

14. The issue of compensation to the zamindars was referred to a ten-man committee of the Constituent Assembly. By March 1952 the Assembly adopted its report, recommending abolition of landlordism without compensation.

against India for suppressing democracy. What reply shall I give to all this? I am ready to say that there are very few countries in Asia and the world where there is more freedom and democracy than in India and Kashmir. You can see it— nothing is hidden. A lot is also said about plebiscite, but it is forgotten that one of the big conditions attached to it is that Pakistan must remove all her forces from Kashmir territory. That has not been done.

India's foreign policy is one of non-alignment with power blocs and friendship with all nations. The Communists want India to join the Russian four-squares and ensure safety, while others think that India should join hands with the United States. But our policy is to be friendly with all and follow an independent path. If we align ourselves with any bloc, then we have to swerve from our path.

I do not want that votes should be asked for, by the Congress in the name of Kashmir. I know it well that everyone in India will be with us. I do not want to make Kashmir an election issue. But the foreign policy pursued by the Congress Government is attacked on the issues of Kashmir, Goa or others. Therefore, it is necessary that the electorate should demonstrate in a strong voice to the world, particularly at this juncture, what the policy of India is.

The record of the achievements of the Congress are an open book and can be examined by anyone. Other parties build castles in the air. They give an excuse that they have had no opportunity so far to work. Firstly, they have to create confidence among the public about their capacity to work. The PSP has aligned itself with communal parties like the Muslim League in some places and made alliances with the Communists in other areas, whom they had opposed.[15] Communal parties have no relations to the present day world. The difficulty in India is that even in this twentieth century we have people with views and methods of all periods, even that of a thousand years ago. India will be ruined if communal parties are allowed to hold sway. The ideals of Communism are high but the policy of the Communist Party is bound up by violence and disorder. They always think that something favourable might arise from disorder.

I refute the statement made by an Opposition leader that if the Congress returns to power, it will be the end of democracy.[16] I want to ask in which country

15. In Kerala, the PSP reached an electoral understanding with the Muslim League. In Bombay, they had an electoral alliance with the Communist Party and the Jana Sangh. The three parties did not have much in common, but they united on the issue of Samyukta Maharashtra. In Bengal, the PSP allied itself with the Communist Party, Revolutionary Socialist Party, Forward Bloc and the Marxist Forward Bloc forming a Leftist Election Committee.
16. Addressing a press conference at Nagpur on 20 February 1957, Jayaprakash Narayan, the Praja Socialist Party leader, said that the ruling party had enjoyed "absolute power" for the last ten years and if their rule was not broken, it would be a "grave peril to democracy, good government and the public weal."

13

is there so much democracy in reality and also legally, other than in India. Democracy is in danger in countries where no single strong party existed. The traditions of countries like Britain and the United States are different. But, in new democracies, where there is no single strong party, difficulties arose.

In a big organization like the Congress, there may be some defects. But the Congress is the only organization capable of running the Government now. It is trying to uplift the people. The communal parties have no political strength but they have enough energy to rouse the people to take to wrong paths. They do not exercise their mind on economic problems. We will not allow a situation to develop, where the country would be divided into bits. The Congress is a strong organization. But it should be further strengthened in the interests of the country. India is in a dynamic state making an earnest effort to improve the lives of its people. Under the British, our economy was stagnant, though there were some external changes here and there. Now, it is a great task for the Congress to lift the country from the mire. The electorate should vote the Congress to power to enable it to fulfil this task. I became a regular member of the Congress 45 years ago though earlier, I attended some of its meetings.

Gandhiji had converted the Congress into a dynamic organization. The poor *kisan* found a ray of hope in Gandhiji. Slowly the intellectuals also got attracted to him and followed the path shown by him. Gandhiji found that the people of India resented foreign rule but had no courage to express it. They were haunted by fear. The problem before Gandhiji was to infuse life into these lifeless bodies and collect the scattered strength of the nation. Gandhiji was a doctor who cured the old disease afflicting people. His key message was that the people should give up fear. People began to lose fear and there was brightness on their faces. They walked with their head erect.

I apologize to Mr H.P. Mody, former Governor of Bombay, for having criticized him on the presumption that he was contesting the elections from Rajasthan on a ticket of the Ram Rajya Parishad. I have received a telegram from Mr Mody stating that he was contesting as an independent and not as Ram Rajya Parishad candidate.[17] I ask everyone of you to exercise your vote in favour of one or the other but not to be so lethargic as not to exercise your franchise.

---

17. On 23 February 1957, Nehru also wrote to H.P. Mody giving the reason for making such a mistake. He mentioned that he had received an official paper which gave the names of the candidates with their party symbols. In that Mody's name was mentioned with the Ram Rajya Parishad symbol and that made him think that Mody had come to some arrangement with the Ram Rajya Parishad.

3. Parliamentary Democracy Best Suited for India[1]

Friends and comrades,
First of all those of you who can hear my voice will you please raise your hands?

I am sorry I cannot speak to you in Kannada. So, I am going to speak in English. Perhaps for a few minutes at the end, I shall say a few words in Hindi.

You know that I have come here to Bangalore in connection with the general elections which are going to begin very soon. Naturally, I have come here on behalf of the great Congress Organization of which I have been a member for the last 45 years. And I have come to you to tell you what I feel about these elections, about the work in this country and also to suggest to you that at this time, more specially, it is desirable to strengthen and support the Congress and to vote for the Congress candidates in these elections. But, I should like to say something about broader issues. You are an audience here in Bangalore which, if I may say so, is an intelligent audience. I should like you, therefore, to consider certain basic questions. But one thing I should like to begin with. In this election, I hope and earnestly trust that all our candidates, the candidates of other parties and as well as independent candidates will carry out all their campaign at a high level, by not indulging in personality abuse or by not lowering the levels of our public life and to do everything peacefully and without malice. Naturally, in an election campaign, one party criticizes another. That is the virtue of the campaign so that people may hear all sides of the arguments, may discuss them among themselves and then come to a decision. I would like to call this general election some kind of a university for 37 crores of people in India. It would be an educational process, if it is properly conducted. I say so, because reports reach me of some little trouble here and there and of something said that should not be said. Sometimes, reports come to me from Congress candidates and sometimes from persons opposed to the Congress. Yesterday, at Hyderabad, I was shown a poster of a candidate opposing the Congress, the poster had my big picture on it as if I was supporting that candidate. It is an unfair exploitation of my picture and of me.

I hope that this election will be carried out peacefully and with good humour so that it may not leave any traces of ill will behind and whatever be the result of the election, we shall accept that result with good humour. That is necessary for democracy.

1. Speech at a public meeting, Bangalore, 23 February 1957. AIR tapes, NMML.

Now, why do you want these elections ? We say that we have what is called a parliamentary system of government. That is true. What are our objectives? Well, broadly speaking, obviously, the objectives of every Indian must be the betterment of India, the strengthening of India, the raising of the Indian people to have higher living standards, putting an end to poverty and putting an end to unemployment.

All these are common objectives. But the question arises as to how we attain them. Then again, there is a question of the domestic policy of the country and a foreign policy of the country. Both affect each other. One is the projection of the other. You cannot have a foreign policy entirely unrelated to domestic policy. Now, we have said that the objective of our Congress is to establish a socialistic pattern of society. We have also said that we will not lay down rigid doctrinaire rules for this purpose. But, we accept the broad conception of socialism and we hope to attain that. There are other parties which are socialistic; there is a Praja Socialist Party; there is the Communist Party which is socialistic in another sense and which goes further in a different direction. Now, what do we mean by calling ourselves Congress Socialists. Sometimes, people complain that we do not define our socialism. I admit that. I do not define it precisely because I do not want to tie up the people of India into a rigid pattern. It is enough for us to have a fairly clear idea about our broad objectives and the method to reach them. Gradually, the rest develops with experience.

Remember this, that the word socialism is a relatively modern word in the West, maybe it is 100 years old, 125 years old, perhaps the word may have been used earlier. Socialism in the West has been the child of the Industrial Revolution. That is when the Industrial Revolution came to the West, the people began to think more scientifically about socialism. Of course, even earlier people talked broadly about equality and about some kind of utopian socialism, but what is called the scientific approach to this matter came within the last hundred years or less.

Now, the scientific approach to any matter is a good approach. Because, it means thinking logically, thinking precisely and not vaguely and loosely. Suppose, all of us said that we want the good of India. That is good. But that is not precise thinking. Everybody wants the good of India. But that does not help in clarifying our minds. Therefore, approaching any question scientifically or with a scientific temper is a good thing.

I would like the scientific temper to spread in India, in regard to everything that we do. Many of us accept blindly the beliefs and dogmas which we cannot reasonably justify. It is not a good thing to do that. It is true that there are many things which we cannot measure scientifically. How do we measure goodness? We know when a thing is good and when a person is good but we cannot measure it. How do we measure truth? How do we measure beauty? How do we measure so many artistic things? Some things are not capable of measurement easily. I do not say that science answers all our questions. It does not. It stops somewhere, although the boundaries of science are ever-widening. Nevertheless, our temper and our approach should be that of science.

In this connection, I would like to remind you of a very great son of India, Gautama Buddha, whose Jayanti was celebrated last year, 2500 years of his *Mahanirvana*.[2] I have found it very fascinating to read the records of this great son of India because although he dealt with matters of the spirit, he always laid stress on a person by not accepting anything blindly. He was not in favour of blind belief or rituals. His approach even to the mysteries of the universe was one, if I may say so, of science. If science does not go far, he did not ask any one to believe it. He said experience it. If you are satisfied with your experience, then you believe it; accept nothing, because I say, or Buddha says or anybody says. So, you see, it has been our tradition in the past in India from the oldest times to bring in an element of scientific temper even to the most abstruse problems of philosophy. As I said, you cannot apply mathematics or physics or chemistry to the abstruse problems of philosophy. That is a different matter. But the temper of mind which refuses to accept anything on grounds of blind belief is the right temper. I say that because, in spite of the Buddha, we have been asked in India to accept too much on blind belief. We forget the scientific methods of approach. In fact, we have nothing to do with the modern developments of science and modern means during the last 100 years or so. We became a backward country in our thinking, in our action and we were ruled by others because of that. It is essential therefore that in whatever we do, whatever we think, we should try to evolve scientific methods of approach.

Here in Bangalore, this should not be difficult for you because Bangalore has become one of the principal scientific centres of India. So, I think that one of the biggest things that we have done in the last ten years of Independence is to establish all over India great scientific laboratories or institutes not only for practical work but for research work where thousands of our young men and women are doing very fine work and laying the foundation of scientific progress in India.

---

2. The 2,500th Buddha Jayanti celebrations were held in India from 26 to 30 November 1956. As part of the celebrations, an international symposium was organized at Vigyan Bhawan, New Delhi, from 26 to 29 November 1956. For Nehru's valedictory address at the symposium on Buddhism's contribution to arts, letters and philosophy, see *Selected Works* (second series), Vol. 35, pp. 619-624.

Now, I was talking to you about socialism. Scientific socialism came about a hundred or even less years ago. First of all, they started studying textbooks on Industrial Revolution in England. It was a great Revolution and it upset life in that country. It brought progress on the one hand and great misery on the other. Among the persons who have made an acute study of this was Marx who was supposed to be some kind of a father of communism. Now, Marx was a great man undoubtedly and anyone who reads Marx will see his keen insight into the social phenomena. But nevertheless, Marx studied something that happened 120 years ago in England. Now, to take that as a parallel for something that is going to happen in India today is obviously neither scientific nor logical nor right. Because ever since then, tremendous changes had taken place in the world, tremendous changes due to science and technology. The productive apparatus of humanity has become colossal. Marx never imagined, possibly he could not. It is today one can easily say, logically if you like, that the world can produce everything that every human being in the world needs and more so, if you have a scientific temper. It is not a part of science itself to believe rigidly in any theories propounded in a certain set of circumstances in the past. And therefore, I think that while I may respect Marx, it is quite absurd for any one to tell me that what Marx said applies to India today. I say that is sheer reaction. It is not revolution. It is pure reaction going back to 100 years to understand the world of today. Ridiculous. So, socialism became rather rigid and too much theoretical. Whether it was a communist or whether it was the other socialist in Europe, all of them are basing their theories on the experience of Europe in the 19th century. They are good theories. One can learn much from them. But the point is their rigidity comes in the way of posterity adapting itself to reality. Reality is of many kinds. I am not talking about the presence of metaphysical reality, but the reality in the world. Physical reality is changing. Conditions change. Conditions 1000 years ago are no longer present in India today. One thousand years ago, two thousand years ago, or even 100 years ago, practically you used to travel on foot or on chariot or on a horseback. There was no faster way of travelling. The fastest method of travel was possibly on horseback. Whether it was in the time of the Buddha or whether it was 150 years ago, the fastest method of travelling was by horse. Now, suddenly, the Industrial Revolution comes and changes everything—all our human relationships. You travel today by train, by automobile, by air and by steamship. All kinds of communications—telegraph, telephone, radar and radio have come into existence. I can give you a number of instances to show that the whole structure of life has changed in the last 100 years or a little more. How can, therefore, the theory built on the structure of life 200 years ago apply today? It cannot be. Therefore, we have to think of the facts of life today in India. It is no good of my taking the theory from America or from

Russia or from Germany, except to understand what it is and what I may learn from it. Therefore, what I am driving at is this, that many of our friends, Communists and Socialist friends, tend to become rigid in their approach, in their theory and somehow, lose sight of the facts of life in India. They talk about, let us say, nationalization; let us say, expropriation, a word which has been in common use in Europe in the last 100 years or so, and imagine, that is the pure milk of socialism. Now, I reject that approach. That may not be right in the present circumstances. We nationalized; we did other things too. But to approach that with a rigid doctrinaire mind, if I may say, is not scientific nor it is scientific socialism.

We must take into consideration facts and behind the facts is the background of the people. The background of the Indian people is an important fact. Nowhere in the wide world, I imagine, would there have been a Gandhi except in India. Please understand what I am talking. Now, I say the kind of teaching that Gandhiji gave us, the kind of path he showed us, the policy he laid down for us, has brought success to us in India, I am quite sure that nowhere else in the world would the people have accepted that policy. Why? Not because we are better but because Gandhiji's policy was attuned to the Indian mind, Indian spirit, Indian culture and inheritance. It has fitted in with India, with Indian mind, the peasant mind as well as the educated mind because it was something ingrained in our bones. If he went to Europe and America, he might have been a misfit, and his voice might have been a voice in the wilderness. He is respected today in Europe and America. Why? Because, he achieved success in India. It is this success that is respected there. Therefore, I say that one has to take into consideration the background of a country. The actual physical conditions of a country, the capacity of a country and a hundred and one things before we lay down the path of that country to go ahead. We have, in fact, not only to understand the problem intellectually but that should be in tune with the masses of India. I say these simple things to you because my friends, in the Socialist Party and the Communist Party with their rigid ideas, easily write long thesis to discuss these problems, each one of their resolutions is a book, and they discuss and argue but quite forget India and her problems, quite forget the Indian natural philosophy. They work hard for them and yet they miss the lesson that Gandhiji taught. Therefore, to talk about scientific socialism rigidly is, I think, not wise. We debated repeatedly on the Five Year Plan, we discussed these matters, we showed the practical steps that we are taking and that we intend to take. Only we do not tie ourselves up because we want to learn from experience. We must learn on the one side, from the experience of India, the capacity of India and on the other hand, we have to adopt all these things so that we realize the tremendous revolution that is going on in the world either as a result of science or technology.

19

We live on the threshold of the atomic age, a terrific thing, and all these theories which have been propounded in the last century or in the early years of this century by these Communists and Socialists, are theories which do not take into consideration, the tremendous advances of science. Marx lived before electricity came on the field. The steam power also came on the field and has brought a revolution. Another revolution came, the atomic revolution, today changing the whole fibre and texture of human life and relation. Therefore, we have to be wide awake about these changes and to adapt ourselves to some basic facts.

What do we want in India? Well, to put in one word, we want to eliminate, wipe out and put an end to poverty in India. True, everybody will agree. We want to put an end to unemployment and etc., in India. We want every human being in India to have certain essential basic necessities of life to begin with. After that we can think of other things. What are the basic necessities of life— food of course, clothing, housing, education, health and work—creative and productive work. If everybody in India have that in a proper measure, that would be a tremendous thing. After that, of course, people on that basis could advance further. You cannot limit a nation's advancement at all. You can go ahead. We want this general well-being in India and we do not want the ups and downs that we see today, the very rich and the very poor. We do not suggest that everybody can be alike, can be levelled to one pattern and regimented . That is not possible, at any rate, nor in the foreseeable future because people differ, people differ in their ability, and people differ in their physical strength or power. There are geniuses and well, there are fools; you cannot bring everybody to the same level. What is essential is that everybody should have the same chance to grow physically, mentally, morally and educationally. Then those of us who are geniuses, will grow further. A man may be a great artist; a man may be a great engineer; a man may be a great doctor; they all can grow. Every one should have equal opportunity of growth, both men and women.

Now, if you can ensure all this, then the next step after that can be thought of later. It is a big enough job to get 37 crores of people to this level. How are we to do this? Apart from the details, I suggest to you and I am prepared to say that whatever methods we may adopt should be peaceful methods always. Having achieved our freedom by peaceful methods, there is no reason why we should not achieve other things by peaceful methods. And they are peculiarly suited to us. But apart from that, the moment you go in for violent methods, you bring about an element of conflict and violence which is bad at any time. But today, when the world is on the threshold of an atomic age, violence is something terrible. We dare not play about with violence, even in a small way. We should not produce an atmosphere of violence. It is a bad thing. And that thing comes in the way of growth and in India if we encourage the atmosphere of violence, it will inevitably lead to disruptive tendencies, to disunion, to the break up of our unity and to weakness. Therefore, from every point of view, violence should be ruled out. Apart from that fact, democracy and violence do not go together. You cannot have a democratic structure working violently. That is not democracy. That may be something else. So, there are two basic propositions I wish you to consider. One is to rule out violence. I hope not only in our own country but also in the world too. But we do not know about the world. And whatever programme or policy we have, should be a peaceful one. Remember, do not imagine that revolutions are brought about by violence only. That is a wrong conception. It is true that violence has brought about some revolutions. But peaceful methods have also brought about revolutions and some times bigger ones. Our own political revolution was a peaceful one. After that, we put an end to all these Indian princely states, a tremendous thing. In no country has it been done peacefully. Peacefully and cooperatively, we put an end to the landlord system, the zamindari, the *jagirdari* and the *taluqdari* and all that. In other countries there have been violence in it. But we put an end to it peacefully. So, you see how even in our economic sphere or in our social sphere, we are bringing about revolutionary changes step by step, peacefully, and I have no doubt that we can bring in any number of changes right up to the final change to establish socialism, in all its fullness, by peaceful methods. Why then should we indulge in violence and split up the country and spend our energy in futile conflicts? More especially now, when violence is much more dangerous than it ever was in the past. So, we must accept this. The Socialists and Communists say that there is class conflict. Of course, there is class conflict. I do not deny that. There is a conflict between the landlord and the tenant. There is a conflict between the owner of the factory and the worker. The point is not to deny class conflict. I do not deny it. But how to cure it? How to get rid of it? Indeed how to get rid of parties? I say that the old method of breaking heads is not the right way to do it. We can get rid of them but maybe a little more slowly and much more soundly by peaceful methods. How? Well, largely by the democratic apparatus of Government, where everybody has a vote and ultimately that vote counts. There are other ways, other methods too. So, we must be clear in our minds about the peaceful method of approach.

Secondly, there is this broad idea of equality, not absolute equality, but I would say equality of opportunity. If we have equality of opportunity, then it is good enough. Those who can run faster, can run faster, but nobody's feet and hands should be tied as they are today. The poor man's feet and hands are tied. He gets no education, nor do his children. He gets no proper food. He may be a genius. He has no chance to progress. Therefore, everybody must have equal opportunities to progress.

21

And to that, you must know that there should not be great differences in the economic level of human beings. I cannot make them all same, but it is not proper, I think, it is even a little vulgar, for some people to be very rich and some to be poor. It is not decent. It hurts essentially a human being so, we should gradually equalize, gradually, I say. You cannot break it. And any attempt at doing it quickly produces conflicts and produces also possibly a stopping of the machine of production, which is bad, because if we are to get rid of poverty, our machine of production should function efficiently and must grow bigger and bigger. There is no other way. We do not get rid of poverty by getting money from abroad. We have to produce the money and money means we have to produce the goods. Goods is money and not gold and silver. So, we have to produce the goods—the goods from the fields, the goods from the factory and the goods from every kind of thing. And this is a big machine of production. The faster we grow, the more wealth we get for the country and for the individual. America is rich because her machine of production works at a tremendous pace both on the land and in the factory. I should not mean to say that we should copy America or Russia. But our production apparatus must increase not three-fold or ten-fold but twenty-fold and thirty-fold. And only then, we can be able to meet all our needs. Now, any step that we might take which may be justified logically but which stops the machine of production at present is a harmful step because it comes in the way of our progress. Therefore, you have always to remember that in all the steps that you may take in the land or in the industry, they should not stop or lessen the machine of production. All these are factors to be borne in mind.

Suppose when we had to face the problem of the Indian princely states, how did we solve it—cooperatively, with the consent of the princes. It is true that the consent was given under the pressure of circumstances. In a democracy, the pressure of the people is always there. Anyhow, we got their consent and we gave them large, very large pensions, I think, much too large, several lakhs and all that. Now, people complain that too much money was given as privy purses. But they forget that we settled their problem very very cheaply. If we had a conflict, we must have spent infinitely more. Apart from spending more, we would have had bloodshed and ill will lasting a generation or two. All kinds of disruptions must have taken place in India and we would not have settled down in independent India for many years. Imagine, the huge loss there. Well, we paid that loss in goodwill, what if we paid a few crores more. A few crores is just a dust in the balance compared to what we gained by it.

Take again what the Communists say, expropriate foreign capital from India. Thereby you will get, I do not know how much, 100 or 200 or 400 crores, whatever it may be. Apart from the fact that it is opposed to our Constitution, do you think that that gain of a few hundred crores is a very great gain to India when it is done at the cost of certain moral stature that we have got, and a certain goodwill of the world, of other countries. It is obvious, is it not? A hundred or a thousand crores are nothing to the goodwill and good repute of India and again the machine of production must go on. Suppose, if I suddenly upset the production by pushing out this man or that man, the immediate result is that production apparatus goes down. You have certainly in a country some accumulated wealth. There is much in the rich countries, less in the poorer countries. But essentially, the wealth of a country is what it produces year by year. India's wealth is what it produces in this year 1957. Naturally, we have also our old wealth, but essentially to calculate the national wealth of a country, the national income has to be taken into consideration. If we are to become a rich nation, our national income has to go up year by year. Now, there is another way of saying that our production has to go up year by year, that is, the national income has to go up which include production from land and industry.

So, I am merely giving you some example of how this application of some rigid theory, socialist theory, which may have been applicable 50 or 100 years ago in Europe does not apply to India today. Also remember that in Europe 50 years ago or less, there was no real democracy and the adult franchise. The democracy of England till 20 or 30 years ago or more was limited. Take adult franchise—it was very limited in the 19th century and only a small number of people had votes; the common people did not have votes. But when democracy spreads out, every adult has got a vote. Therefore, conditions today are quite different from what they were all over the world. Secondly, conditions are different in India to what they were and we must be bound by our own policies in tune with our country's genius and with the facts of life in India, keeping always in view our objective, that is the progress in production and secondly, equal opportunity for everybody.

I hope I have made you understand what our broad conceptions of socialism are and I see no reason why I should sit down and scratch my head and evolve theories. I am a practical man who have achieved something not as a professor who might have to consider some theoretical aspects of the question. Even a professor has to be practical and our laboratory today is the whole of India and the working in that laboratory may be seen in a hundred ways. But more especially our five year plans are not limited. We are prepared to change them if necessary. They are not based on theory but evolved after consulting all kinds of people in India. Don't imagine that the five year plan is a product of the imagination of the Congress Working Committee or the All India Congress Committee. Certainly, the Congress Working Committee and the All India Congress Committee considered it, gave their suggestions and discussed it. We discussed

23

it with Socialists, Communists, engineers, doctors, lawyers, panchayats and villagers; and we discussed it with everybody and then we drew up a five year plan. We discussed it in Parliament; we discussed it in the State Assemblies, so that the five year plan is the result of the joint wisdom, if I may say so, of the people of India. I do not say it is perfect. But, I do say that the Second Plan is more carefully thought out than the First. We are growing, we are getting more experience from difficulties, the problems and the realities, we are getting more sophisticated. We cannot plan academically. Every planner must know what is happening and what is being produced. Now, we are coming up. I have no doubt that the Third Plan would be better still. So, that is the way we approach the matter and it is not a doctrinaire way, not a party way. The party comes in only in this sense. The Congress party, having prepared it after consulting everybody, accepted it and threw its full weight for its realization. We invited Socialists, Communists and others. It is a common plan. We cannot help it. We asked them to help us. Generally, they don't do so. They criticize the plan after it is made. They say it is bad here or it is not socialistic. They rather keep away. That is not my fault. I want to treat it as a national plan and I consider it so.

Now, I will speak to you about something entirely different. I really began with that and then I shifted to some other subjects. We have a parliamentary system of government. I think that it is a good system. No system of government is perfect. So long as human beings are not perfect, no system of government can be perfect. Therefore, we have to devise methods, good methods. One can consider the quality of human beings. It is possible that one system may be suitable to one country and another to another because human beings are different.

Now, our system of government and our Constitution are largely based on the British system of parliamentary government. We have taken something from the American system, but in the main, it is British. But remember this that the British system of government applies to a tight little island, England, Scotland and Wales. It is a small country like a state of ours. It is easy to have a government in that area. It is far more difficult in a big country like India, with the great variety, variety of language, climate and all kinds of things. Therefore, it is inevitable for us to have the federal system of government and rightly because we want to preserve the variety of India. To give people of each state the sense of doing things by themselves and not to be tied down to a distant Centre too much is necessary. At the same time it is impossible today for a country to grow without centralization and every big thing is centralized. You cannot have a railway system in India with every state having its own railway and in the same manner the communication system, the currency, and the defence; you cannot have even industry, and centralization is inevitable in industry.

I regret to say that we are not fully and emotionally integrated into one nation.

Intellectually, we are to some extent integrated, but we divide on small matters; we fight on issues of religion, caste or language or something. It shows we are not integrated. We have fallen because we are never a united nation politically. Now, we can take no more risks about it. We are not going to allow India to become a weak nation again by disruption. Therefore, we have to have a strong Central Government. We have to have at the same time a large measure of autonomy in the states, and if you like, I could say even at the panchayat level. I want to give them powers because while on the one hand I consider centralization inevitable, I think that too much centralization is not good and therefore we must balance it by as much decentralization as possible subject always to the unity of India and to the economic progress of India. For that, we must have centralization in a large measure, a Central Planning Commission and all that. All these factors come in. So, we draw up our Constitution based partly on the American model but very much more so on the British model of parliamentary government. It could not be exactly the same as I said because the country is too big, a federal country.

Now, in the British model of parliamentary government, there are parties. You cannot maintain democracy in the parliamentary way without the party system. Suppose, there were no parties and 500 persons were elected to Parliament, each thinking as he liked with no discipline. Well, they may be very able persons and very interesting individuals. But nothing will be done in Parliament. They will be always quarrelling with each other. There will be no common plank—each takes his own stand in his head. Absolutely nothing can be done. It is a huge debating society and debating and doing nothing. Therefore, it becomes essential to have parties. Also, the people would not be properly educated if individuals come like this because each individual takes his own stand and there will be no common plank on which people could think and vote. If there are parties, parties put forward election programme and the like. There are rival programmes. They are discussed and that is the education for the masses. Democracy does not break down because of the discipline of the party system. If there is no strong party system, democracy would break down completely and probably you have a military dictator or some authoritarian government. In fact, it is surprising that there are few countries in the world which have real democracy. There are very few. I won't name them. You can find out yourself. Many countries which talk greatly about democracy, have no atom of democracy. Many of them are feudal absolutely. So, if you want to preserve democracy, especially parliamentary type of it, you must have the party system. In a parliament of 500, if there are, let us say, 10 parties of 50 each, what would happen? I do not quite know. But there probably would not be a very stable government. There will be shifts all the time, quarrels all the time, a coalition is seldom a very stable government, it pulls in different directions, all kinds of forces. The result would be instability in government, instability in policies and with the result no big programme could be undertaken. You see that in some countries, highly developed countries in Europe, there is no stability of government because there are innumerable parties. Therefore, in order to succeed, the parliamentary form of democracy must have the party system and normally must have a strong party forming government. If there is no strong party, the government would be changing all the time. Today, it becomes all the more important to have a strong party for a stable and strong government because we are still in the formative state. We are not like England with 200 or 100 years of experience and discipline behind them. We are developing and we dare not take risks. Now, I have given you this analysis not because I happen to be a Congressman but because I want you to realize that many of the criticisms advanced today about the Congress being a very big party are based on a complete misunderstanding of what democracy and the two-party government is. Though we find even today in a country, like Indonesia, considerable trouble because no prominent party can control the Government there. And the President of Indonesia has proposed even that the system of parliamentary system of government is not suitable to Indonesia and they should have some other form of government.[3] They are considering it. We in India are not faced with these difficulties simply because we have a strong party, the Congress which forms the strong Governments. We made, no doubt, many mistakes. Who is free from mistakes? But the point is we should consistently follow a certain policy and go ahead. We are not hampered by lack of strength. But even now, we are not fully and emotionally integrated. You know what happened last year in connection with the states reorganization. It is bad. It showed that we lacked unity, and we give more importance to our district or state than our national unity. That was bad. And what was amazing was that our so-called revolutionary parties, the Communist Party and the Praja Socialist Party took the leading part in these disturbances. What has the states reorganization got to do with socialism or communism? It is a political matter and an administrative matter. We may be wrong or right; but it has nothing to do with basic issues of communism. After all, it is an administrative division of India. So we see, our unity is not deep enough.

Secondly, I do not say that the Five Year Plan is a Congress Plan and only the Congress will look for it, of course not. It is a national Plan. Everybody is concerned with it. Take again foreign policy. Our foreign policy is not a party

3. This refers to Ahmed Soekarno's proposal for "guided democracy." For details, see *post*, p. 521.

matter and I believe it is undoubtedly a national policy in the sense that a very great part of the nation approved of it. But you know we are being bitterly criticized for our foreign policy because of Kashmir or because of Goa or because of something else. They merely criticize us but they don't tell us what to do. But on the whole our foreign policy aimed at not being aligned ourselves to any of the Great Power blocs, not going into any military alliances, but try to be friendly with every nation and judging everything on the merits. Maybe, the Communists want us to align ourselves more firmly with the Soviet Union in a military way; maybe some other party wants us to align ourselves with American group in a military way. Now, that is a clear issue on which I should take the electorate of India to express an opinion. They want us to align ourselves with some group of nations and go in for military alliances. I am entirely opposed to it for a variety of reasons. I think if we do that, it will be the ruination of India. I think, if we do that, we lose our independence of action. I think, if we do that, we lose something which is of infinite value to us, our soul of India.

So, now people say that a strong opposition is necessary. I agree. I want people in the country, in the legislatures, sharp enough to criticize the Government. I think, it is dangerous for a Government or for a party to become complacent on that issue. And I would submit that we have a strong opposition. If you look at the proceedings of the Parliament, you will find that we have got a strong opposition. Every bill is opposed. It has been helpful to us and I welcome that type of opposition even though I may consider it sometimes silly. But opposition may not necessarily be in terms of large numbers. If you bring in large numbers, then you weaken the Government and you do not know which is the Government and which is the opposition, practically speaking.

But apart from that, the real opposition in the country I should like you to understand is not merely the people in the Legislatures, but it is spread out in our own failings, in our lack of unity, in our reactionary tendencies, social, economic and the rest, in our general backwardness and in our inertia. That is the real thing we have to fight. But we forget it. That is, we have to be alert all the time. Some little thing happens in the economic plane and that might upset and lead to fighting or something else. We must always be on the alert. We have to pull out India from the quagmire of centuries. We have to pull it out; it has stuck there economically and socially for centuries. People as a whole have to pull it out. It is a terrific job and you cannot compare this to the conditions in a country which has been functioning with their democratic apparatus, and which is industrially and economically advanced. You can compare it if you like to a country like China which is trying to pull the Chinese people out of their quagmire and inertia. But there is a difference. China has done it by authoritarian methods and we are doing it by democratic methods. Yes, it is a great test. Our friends who criticize us and say that the Congress Party is powerful, have they thought of consequences of our lack of strength in the Government? Then they might arrive at the conclusion that democracy will then be in peril. It will be in peril if it cannot deliver the goods. Then people may think of totalitarian methods and military dictatorship; not that it is likely in India; but all those thoughts will come. I mentioned the country of Indonesia, a great country which is in difficulty where military had also played a game of constitution-making. We do not want this to happen in India. People do not realize how difficult it is to keep this equilibrium between the various forces. There are enough reactionary elements in India that exploit religion. And if we do not take care and are not wide awake, I tell you that it is not impossible that the reactionary elements of India may pull us in the wrong direction. As we saw, take the country like Germany, a very advanced country, and the strongest party in Germany was the Socialist Democrats, 25, 30 years ago. Now, they developed technically and scientifically and yet that German Nation grew into Nazism. These are the dangers that our friends of the Socialist Party and others seem to think that all these things automatically happen. They criticize the Government and the Congress which has laid strong foundations for democratic progress and at the same time to go ahead on the economic plane. Let the country hear the persons who criticize the results of our policies. Nobody denies them freedom of speech and writing. Let them criticize. The other day, a well known English correspondent of an English newspaper wrote about India. He said that it is surprising all these things happening in India. Great things are being done in agriculture, industry, river valley schemes and Community Projects. Tremendous things are happening in India and yet the greatest industry in India is the criticism of the Government.[4] The great professors indulge in it; lawyers indulge in it; intellectual people indulge in it; several parties indulge in it; even some Congressmen indulge in it; that is the greatest game in India and the Congress and the Government puts up with all this. I am surprised, he said, to find such terrific criticism and vilification of Government here in spite of tremendous achievements. Nowhere, in no other country have I found it. I don't mind the criticism. The real test of a democracy is not how many people are elected and not elected. But the people have the chance to elect and the people have the chance to express their opinion and criticize. Those tests are there. In these basic tests, you have every chance to criticize in writing and speeches etc. You have every chance to elect anybody you like. Anybody can stand in the elections. Is it my fault that I am elected or

4. For extracts of this *Manchester Guardian* article, see *Selected Works* (second series), Vol. 35, p. 586.

that my colleague is elected? Is it an argument? It so happens that I or the Congress have the goodwill of the people. Why do we have the goodwill of the people, I do not know. It may be that the people are wrong in giving their goodwill and affection to me. How am I to judge? I can only feel infinitely grateful for them. But am I to go and tell them to speak against my own organization and myself? The whole thing is some dirty game. I don't understand them.

Then it was said the other day by an eminent person who has taken up some strong dislike to the Congress that Congress has been and is being corrupted by power. And he quoted Lord Acton[5] that power corrupts and again, absolute power corrupts absolutely.[6] Now, I do submit that something has gone wrong with people's thinking if they use these words and phrases loosely without the least application to reality. What is absolute power? What is the power of the Congress? Are we an authoritarian Government? We are an elected Government with just a big majority. Is getting a big majority absolute power? Or is getting a big majority in two or three elections absolute power? What about the Tory Government in England which was returned after two or three elections? Do they say it has got absolute power? President Roosevelt was elected three or four times as President in the United States. Did anybody say that democracy has failed in the United States? You see some lack of clear thinking on these issues and this is due to absolute frustration. Because of frustration, instead of finding out the reasons for one's own failure, you go about criticizing and blaming others. That is not the way to carry on in politics.

So, I come there. Personally, I think that in this imperfect world, the system of parliamentary democracy or government is the best. It is my opinion although I can point out many failings. But, I think, it is the best for India. And I would go a step further and say that in the last few years we had it, and it has justified itself.

Ultimately, every system of government depends on the quality of the people; the system is something; it is the people who count; if Indian people go to pieces, every system will go to pieces. And I would submit my deepest respect for the

5. John Emerich Edward Dalberg Acton (1834-1902); Appointed a Deputy Lieutenant of Shropshire, 1855; Royal Commissioner on Historical Manuscripts and Trustee, British Museum; Lord-in-Waiting to Queen Victoria till 1895; Member of Parliament from Carlow, 1859-65; and from Bridgnorth, 1865-66; Professor of Modern History, Cambridge, from 1895; Created Baron Acton, 1897; Romanes Lecturer, Oxford, 1901; Publication: *Lecture on the Study of History*, 1895.
6. Jayaprakash Narayan said at a press conference in Nagpur on 20 February 1957 that Lord Acton's dictum that "power corrupts absolutely", though hackneyed, yet represented one of the most profound political truths. He said, "let no one imagine that corruption expresses itself only in nepotism and monetary forms." See also *post*, p. 366.

29

quality of Indian people, the average person in India, average peasant in India and the training they have got during the last 30 or 40 years under the Congress, and under Gandhiji, who had disciplined them. The services of the Congress organization have been of tremendous value not only in attaining Swaraj but in maintaining it and strengthening it and giving it a direction. What would happen if we have a number of parties like in some countries of Asia fighting for mastery. We had one or two states in India where we have no majority of a single party. What has been the result? Confusion, no proper government; Presidential rule and all kinds of difficulties. You know what happened where there have not been solid majority and stable government. Now, think of India. It will be a disaster if there is no majority for any single party in the Central Government. Therefore, it is of utmost importance for India to have a stout and strong party and to have a stout and strong Government at the Centre and in the States. At the same time if India is to hold together firmly and to progress stoutly—all that will depend on the maintenance of the whole democratic practice and tradition, freedom of expression, freedom of writing and freedom of election. That is essential. If that is there, it does not matter how big the majority is, because a big majority itself is bad sometimes and may produce conflict inside it. I have taken up a lot of your time in discussing the theory of government and democracy. But I want to say something about it because there is so much of loose thinking on the subject. What worries me today is this. In this election I would like each party to stand four-square before the electorate with its programme. Well, each party has got its election manifesto and the like. So far as the Congress is concerned, it has 10 years of Government. You can judge it by what it has done. Apart from its policies you have got not only its Election Manifesto but also the Five Year Plan, etc., which shows you the direction of its thinking.

You have got something which I consider the most revolutionary of all, the Community Development Projects in India. I think that is a terrific undertaking. I repeat the word in the biggest sense. Four and a half years ago, we started it in a relatively small way. Today after four years, five months and ten days, it covers 220,000 villages in India. Think of that, out of 500,000 villages in the whole of India it covers 220,000. Half of it covers 44 per cent of the rural population of India that is 130 million people. Now, is it not a terrific achievement? Covering does not mean merely appointing an officer there. It doesn't mean merely counting heads. It means keeping the whole project alive, making the people grow, grow in their agricultural methods, in their cultural methods, etc. In fact, a slow but steady revolution is taking place in our countryside which is not a revolution imposed from above but a voluntary thing growing from below. I talk to you about India being in this quagmire of 200 years of poverty, static all these years, but now something is happening there in the villages to pull it out of that. It is a remarkable thing. This has attracted perhaps more attention in other countries of the world than in India. Certainly, our friends in India seem to be almost ignorant of what is happening in India. They sit in their little offices and produce huge resolutions without knowing what is happening in India. This is the biggest revolution that is happening and now a lot of people coming from other countries to observe these, go back and do the same thing there. We are going to start huge institutions for training people. We have for our own purposes started over 200 institutes at present, training workers for the Community Centres. Now, all these things are happening here and no doubt quite possibly that our friends in the Praja Socialist Party might have done better. How can I say they would not have done better? But, they are writing about Community Centres. They say it has been a failure. Now, I do not like to use a strong language but anything more nonsensical I have never seen. This tremendous revolutionary experiment is certainly a success. To call it a failure is nonsense, nothing but nonsense. Obviously, I do not say that out of 220,000 villages, every village is a success; that is silly. Sometimes some villages are a failure; some are partly a success. But judging the experiment as a whole, it is a tremendous success. It is so great a success that we cannot catch up to that success. We are not keeping up to it. So, these factors have to be borne in mind.

But one terrific confusion is the kind of alliances that parties have made. The Praja Socialist Party which talks of socialism goes and joins up the Muslim League in Kerala. Now, I may say, there are two things with which I do not wish to deal with, rather I would like the country not to give them any quarter. The two things are, violence and communalism. I do not wish the country to give these two the slightest sympathy or quarter. Because, I think, they are utterly and absolutely bad for the country. You may discuss other theories. You may be right. I may be wrong. But so far as communalism is concerned and so far as violent methods are concerned, they are absolutely 100 per cent bad. If we adopt either of them, I have no doubt India will be ruined. But Praja Socialist Party goes and links up with the Muslim League which is a hundred per cent communal body. Of course, we have no Muslim League anywhere in India except in Malabar. They link up somewhere else with the Jana Sangh. The Communist Party links up with Jana Sangh which is a Hindu communal body. The other day, you must have seen, the biggest leader of the Communist Party, said bravely: "When we come to power, we banish and ban all communal organizations."[7] A very great

7. Ajoy Ghosh, General Secretary of the Communist Party, was reported to have said this in Lucknow. However, he denied this on 16 February in Hyderabad saying that he actually spoke about protection of minorities and ban of all propaganda inciting violence and against discrimination towards minorities.

statement. Within 24 hours, another leader of the Communist Party, as big as he, said; "I am cooperating with the Jana Sangh in Poona. And it is quite normal that we can always cooperate with them for separate objects." Of course, we are not in favour of Communists. If you start cooperating for one thing with somebody who holds a different opinion on vital matters, then your principle goes. I can give you so many instances of the Praja Socialist Party or the Communist Party making strange combinations all over India. In some place, I think it is in Banaras, a candidate standing for election is supported by the Praja Socialist Party, Communist Party, Jana Sangh, Hindu Mahasabha and two or three others. Look at this most extraordinary combination of all groups, communal, Socialist and Communist—all supporting him. Why? In opposition to the Congress. Their principle is not a principle, but the principle of just opposition to the Congress. And that is why I say it is a wrong thing. Let them come with positive principles in spite of their frustration. Is India going to be governed by such frustrated individuals? Is this great country going to be led by people who are just unhappy about everything and miserable? Have they lost touch with reality? That is a sorry state of affairs.

The Congress today is strong. Why? Because in spite of many failings it has done better. The Congress is a huge organization. It has many wrong people in it. Nevertheless, basically, it has aimed right, I think. It has some of the finest material in India. Its leadership is good, I am not talking about myself. Never. Nor about the Congress President, but others. The Congress is strong because it has trained a finest body of village workers in villages and that gives strength to the Congress. Because of these workers, the Congress is still in intimate touch with the real India. It is not cut off. I may be cut off sitting in Delhi. But Congress as an organization, in spite of its weaknesses, in spite of its failures, is still a more lively and more vital organization. It is more in touch with the Indian masses than any other party. That is why it has succeeded, otherwise it would fail. And the other people, sitting in their little committee meetings, losing touch with the Indian people and with the facts of life are producing huge resolutions.

Here in this election, am I going about driving people and say: "Look here, vote for the Congress." I reject it. I differ. I do hope that our friends there of the other parties will indulge in a little clear thinking and then criticize by all means. It will help us to think aright. It is important that the Congress should return strongly in a disciplined way and should work both in the domestic and international fields. Many independents may stand and socialist friends may stand and sometimes they may do good. Sometimes they are interesting, even though they may not do good. But from the larger point of view, in this parliamentary system of government, the independents have no place. In England, out of 667 members of Parliament, there may be one or two independents. They have no place really. They are a waste. They cannot think of any disciplined and good policy. Therefore, my advice to you is—you may take my advice or you may do what you like—you must strengthen the Congress and you must vote for the Congress candidates because of these considerations and in order to have a strong disciplined body to fight the nation's battle in India and outside.

Now, I want to refer very briefly to some outside events. And there is distress and despair not merely because of Kashmir. I had spoken so much about Kashmir. I am not going to say anything about it. I am disturbed and distressed at what, I feel, is happening in the world, more and more people indulging in arms and violence and military pacts and all that. If there is one thing of which I am convinced more than anything else is this: that out of war, only destruction will come, out of violence no good will come, and out of military pacts, you will not get more security, but less security and possibly ultimately war. I cannot imagine how great and wise countries think they will ensure peace and security by military pacts and by military armies, more especially when armaments today are the atomic bombs and the hydrogen bombs. The terrific thing that is happening in the world today is a kind of mental disintegration in thinking about simple matters. It is worse than physical disintegration. People are so full of fear of the other power that they have lost the capacity to consider logically what the consequences of a particular action is. As you know, we have been opposed to these military pacts. We have not joined them and we will not join them. We are opposed to those because they do not add to the strength of the country. I do not want the country to become weak. I cannot suppose anything so unrealistic. But having pacts with big countries, will result in reducing our Independence and bringing about a new form of influence into our policies. And that it will increase the insecurity.

You know very well that the two great countries that count in the world today, more than any, are the United States of America and the Soviet Union. The United States of America is probably the most powerful country in the world today, also the richest and the most highly developed country industrially. It has a tremendous responsibility to carry on its shoulders and the future of the world depends a great deal on the United States itself and what policies it pursues. The United States of America have a very great man as its President—Eisenhower—whom I had the honour of meeting two months ago.[8] I have no doubt that he is a man of peace. I have no doubt that he believes in strengthening democracy and the action he took in the crisis of the Middle East and Suez Canal—when the Anglo-French invasion and the Israeli invasion took place in Egypt—was the action of a bold and courageous man.

8. Nehru was in the United States from 16 to 21 December 1956. For his talks with Eisenhower, see *Selected Works* (second series), Vol. 36, pp. 539-543.

33

Yet I am despaired at the courage and perseverance in the military outlook and military methods in the Middle East or elsewhere. I would beg President Eisenhower and the leaders of the American people to consider that these military methods have not succeeded in the past and they are not likely to succeed in the future. The people of Asia want peace and the opportunity to grow. America is the richest country and is in a position to help the Middle Eastern countries to grow economically and otherwise. But all the help it may give is counterbalanced by this military approach, and most of the benefit will be washed away. There is the Soviet Union, a great country that came out of great revolution which was cruel, caused a lot of suffering and presented a terrific upheaval of human spirit. Soviet Union has gone through great sufferings in the last 20 or 30 years and it has become, as you know, one of the most powerful countries in the world. Again, the Soviet Union has a tremendous responsibility. The other day some events took place in Hungary[9] which deeply grieved us and many people, because they seemed to us to be a contradiction of the principles of the *Panchsheel*, to which so many countries including the Soviet Union have subscribed. You will find that most of the troubles arise whether in the Middle East or in Central Europe, because of the intervention of one country in the affairs of another. I think, the only wise course is that all these interventions and foreign armies and foreign forces should be withdrawn peacefully and gradually leaving the countries to work out their own future. Even if they fail, let them fail, they learn from their own experience. Today, we are always under the threshold of a great world war because something or the other happens in one country, in the Middle East or in Hungary or somewhere else. I earnestly hope, therefore, that the policy of withdrawal of foreign forces from these countries should be pursued.

The other day, the Soviet Union made a proposal in regard to the Middle East.[10] The proposal basically was that this Middle Eastern Area should be left

---

9. See *Selected Works* (second series), Vol. 35, pp. 450-484.
10. On 12 February 1957, Dmitri Shepilov, the Foreign Minister of Soviet Union, announced a six-point peace plan for the Middle East. The six principles, handed to the American, British and French ambassadors in Moscow were: (i) maintenance of peace in the Near and Middle East through settling disputed questions by peaceful means and negotiation, (ii) non-interference in the internal affairs of the Middle Eastern countries and respect for their sovereignty and independence, (iii) renunciation of any attempt to include these countries in military blocs, (iv) liquidation of foreign bases and the withdrawal of foreign troops from the Near and Middle Eastern countries, (v) mutual renunciation of the supply of arms to these countries and (vi) cooperation towards the economic development of these countries without making any political, military or other conditions incompatible with the dignity and sovereignty of these countries.

out of Great Power politics, should not be interfered with, and foreign forces should be withdrawn. That will mean, of course, that the Baghdad Pact itself should go. Now, I can very well understand the difficulties of countries who are committed to the Baghdad Pact or committed to any other policy to agree to this kind of thing. They criticized the Soviet policy and said that this is just a manoeuvre, just to put the other in the wrong and just a kind of a game of chess. It may be, I don't know. They constantly put others on the wrong. But, essentially, if I may say so, the proposal to make the Middle Eastern region free from all these outside arms interference, giving economic assistance free from military alliance and leaving them to develop on their own lines, seems to me to be a good proposal. In fact it is entirely in line with what we say in *Panchsheel*. If you suppose that there is some evil motive behind it, it may be so. How can you judge motives of individuals or countries? Anyhow, on the face of it, it is a reasonable proposal. I do believe that this is worthy of consideration. To reject such a proposal would be unwise. It is worthy of consideration and discussion and this very troubled area of the Middle East may find peace and some of the problems might be solved. I do not say this is a quick remedy, but anyhow, it points towards the right way and I would earnestly suggest to the Great Powers and to the lesser powers too, who have to deal with these matters, to give consideration to the proposal which on the face of it, is reasonable and, I think, points in the right direction.

Friends, I am afraid, I must have exhausted your patience. So, I am now going to stop. Thank you. *Jai Hind!*

4. Strengthen Congress for Stability of the Nation[1]

It is high time that the people of Kerala think in terms of having a strong Congress organization and a strong Government. You have already suffered enough from

1. Speech at a public meeting, Kottayam, Kerala, 24 February 1957. From *The Hindu*, 25 February 1957 and *National Herald,* 26 February 1957. This was Nehru's first election speech in Kerala, where he addressed more election meetings than in other states. Besides Kottayam, Nehru addressed election meetings at Ernakulam, Trichur, Kozhikode and Tellicherry. His speeches at Ernakulam and Kozhikode are also printed in this volume.

lack of cohesion and lack of stable Government.[2] In Kerala much harm has been done to the people because of an unstable Government, not a single party holding the reins of power. There were frequent changes of Government and also President's rule for some time. We cannot carry on Government as if it was just a debating society. We cannot have a stable Government when there is no strong party and when there is a fall or change constantly of parties, because of lack of majority. It is for you, the people of this new Kerala State, to make up your mind to have a stable Government backed by a strong party. Then you can go ahead as fast as you can. It is obvious that there is no chance of a stable Government in Kerala except on the basis of a strong Congress Party representing the people of Kerala and having the confidence of the various religious groups.

Here in Kerala, you have a variety of religions. We want you to have a beautiful garment in which all parts and religions of India will find an honourable place and cooperate with each other in furtherance of the progress of India and put an end as far as possible to all caste barriers which have been an evil and a menace to Indian society. I feel, we must have in this State as well as in other States and in the Centre, a strong Congress Party and Government. Otherwise, you will be weak again and not be able to take a step forward and you will have only arguments and talks between different groups and you will waste precious time and energy which you might have devoted for the furtherance of the State.

I have no time to talk about international affairs. You know that they are difficult. We face many difficult situations. So, whether you consider the position in India today internally, that is the problem of our rapid progress or you consider the world outside, it is necessary that we should have a strong Government at the Centre and in the states, which can speak with confidence for the Indian people and which can take strong action, knowing the confidence the Indian people reposed in it. Therefore, in these elections, it seems to me to be very necessary and desirable for you to consider this aspect, that is to say, in these elections the votes you give should be a challenge and an answer to those who say that India is divided, weak and split up into numerous groups. Thereby, you

2. After the first general elections in 1952, Congress formed the ministry under A.J. John with the support of Travancore Tamil Nad Congress. Six months later on a vote of no-confidence, the TTNC brought the government down. The Assembly was dissolved, and the A.J. John ministry continued as a caretaker ministry until the mid-term elections were held in February 1954. The PSP ministry headed by Pattom A. Thanu Pillai took office in March 1954 with Congress support. On 8 February 1955, this was brought down by the Congress through a no-confidence motion and a Congress ministry headed by P. Govinda Menon assumed office with the support of the TTNC. But Menon's government also fell when TTNC withdrew its support and, consequently, President's rule was imposed in March 1956 which continued until the 1957 elections.

should impress upon the world that we all stand together in the big task we have undertaken.

We, in India today, face one of the biggest and most exciting tasks of raising the standard of living of the 37 crores of people peacefully and democratically. Remember that our Constitution is based on democratic methods and on individual freedom. It is important for you to remember that, some parties which may appeal to you for votes do not believe much in individual freedom or in the ways of democracy. It is for you to decide what path you have to pursue in achieving the goals of economic and social revolutions. So far as we are concerned, I feel the first thing to remember is that we want democratic methods or rather, if I may say so, the peaceful methods including the maintenance of individual freedom. In these elections, everybody can say what he likes and some are even cursing and blaming the Government. We do not mind it. We want freedom of speech, except preaching of violence or indulgence in violence which is bad for the people. Short of that, complete freedom is guaranteed in our Constitution. We want to maintain it. We have faith in democracy and we believe in individual freedom. But keeping that in view, we believe in the urgent necessity of rapid advancement. We can only advance if we work hard for it. Nobody could push forward the 37 crores of people. They have to move forward themselves by their hard work.

We are trying to build up agriculture on the one hand and industries on the other and balancing them all. The task is great and it cannot be done by magic. It requires unity and hard work. I believe that this great work could only be carried through by our being united and by working through some great national organization like the Congress which has experience and a great tradition behind it. That is why, quite apart from individuals, it is necessary for the Congress to be strong keeping in view the future of India. That is why, I advise you to vote for the candidates put up by the Congress.

In a system of parliamentary government, an independent candidate has no meaning. He may be a good man but he cannot do much. In Kerala, I do not know the names of the various parties. But I certainly know the names of the Communist Party, the Praja Socialist Party and the Revolutionary Socialist Party, which apparently has found a little home here, having no shelter elsewhere in India. The Muslim League is a strange relic left here in Malabar, but which really should be in a museum. No doubt, ultimately, it will go to a museum. It is absurd to talk about the Muslim League in India. It is unfortunate that some in Malabar live in a past age. They have not woken up.

I find it a little difficult to deal with the Communist Party, because they shout so much, that it is difficult to understand what they are shouting about. They imagine that by shouting, they are brave and revolutionary and they can bring about revolution in the country. I think they are hopeless reactionaries and far from being revolutionary. Revolution does not mean shouting and violence. It means changing society, raising the standard of the people and changing them. The real thing is change and not violence.

The Communist Party simply repeats words, phrases and slogans from books written long ago and make all kinds of promises. I am told that the Communist Party had declared that when they were put in power in Kerala, they would double the subvention from the Central Government from Rs 90 crores to 200 crores. It is just childish nonsense and it shows the lack of serious thinking by the Communist Party. During the past one year, that Party has received many shocks. It looked to leadership elsewhere, in other countries and for advice and changes coming from other countries. You know what happened in Hungary. It was a shock to all of us. Basically, it was perhaps a greater shock to the Communists here, because it has upset all their theories and practices. The Communist Party is not capable of seriously advancing any independent argument. If by any mischance they win the elections in some states, I do not know what they will do with the promises they have made, which they cannot fulfil. My real objection to the Communist Party is that it seems to always live on the verge of violence. If they do not actually indulge in physical violence, they indulge in mental violence. The whole Communist creed, apart from economic contexts, seems to be based on hatred and violence. I am convinced that hatred and violence will fail in any country. I do not want people in India to indulge in or be misled by the cries of hatred and violence.

Our ideal is socialism. We want to establish a socialist order of society, not through bloodshed and violence but peacefully, cooperatively and with as much goodwill as possible.

The Praja Socialist Party in Kerala is a law unto itself and apparently is not even following its parent organization. I am told that it has come to an electoral arrangement with the Muslim League. That, I think, is quite enough to dispose it of from the mind of any reasonable person. It is quite absurd that any progressive and intelligent party should come to an understanding with a reactionary and communal organization with the hope of getting a few more votes.

I do not know the legal aspect of the curious agitation in Trivandrum about the Bench of the High Court.[3] It has come to some decision and it is not for me

3. An agitation for the establishment of a permanent bench of the Kerala High Court at Trivandrum had started in November 1956. An Action Committee was formed that launched direct action which took the form of picketing of courts and public offices throughout the Trivandrum district. As a result, 500 people were jailed. The agitation was called off temporarily due to elections.

to say whether it is right or wrong. But, to go about breaking heads and committing acts of violence on that issue is something which seems to be one of the most extraordinary things I have heard. Is this democracy? Is this the way to do a highly technical thing? But the PSP encouraged it presumably with the thought that they could get a few more votes. But it is not a responsible way of acting.

In the past, the country had produced many famous men and women. The history of India was full of great achievements but it also revealed one major failing of ours, our disunity. We went to pieces when we quarrelled; that was the first lesson we should learn from history, the lesson of unity. The country consists of varied climes and its people speak different languages and pursue different religions. But there is an amazing bond of unity which kept the people together for thousands of years.

The Congress is an all India movement; people from all parts of the country joined it irrespective of the language they spoke, the religion they followed and the community they belonged to. The Congress built unity among the people. Then came Mahatma Gandhi, under whom the Congress became bigger and more unified. He trained us to stand up peacefully against the British Empire and ultimately, the country became independent by following the path of non-violence shown by him.

5. Consolidate Parliamentary Democracy[1]

Friends and comrades,
I shall unfortunately speak to you in English, not in Malayalam. But my friend here will translate. I find his translation is so good that it is much better than my speech. I have been travelling about for a number of days because the general elections are upon us. And I have visited in the last four or five days a number of States in India and saw the various aspects of this great country of ours and more particularly met vast number of our people. The general elections are in some ways a bit of a nuisance—a troublesome affair. But there are some advantages about it. One is that it compels me to go about and come in contact

1. Speech at a public meeting, Ernakulam, Kerala, 24 February 1957. AIR tapes, NMML.

again with large numbers of my countrymen. I have always found that these contacts give me strength. Living too long in Delhi, I find, is rather depressing. So, I am happy to come so far from Delhi here to this very beautiful corner of India to meet you all again.

The general elections in India, more perhaps than in most other countries, seem to me to be a very exciting affair, by its very bigness. It is exciting to think that nearly 200 million people will go to the polls in the next few days—people of all kinds, of all parts of India, some from the hills, tribal folk and others. It is an example of faith in the people. It is for these people to vote and through their votes express their opinion on the policies of government and if they so like, change the governments. For, we have adopted a democratic structure and a parliamentary system of government in this country deliberately and consciously, as you know. And we intend fully to adhere to this because we believe intensely in individual freedom and democracy, even as we believe in the social structure which will bring up all our people and remove the inequalities. You know that our objective—economic and social objective—is socialist order of society. But you must remember two things with it—that that order is conditioned and allied to a democratic procedure, individual liberty and peaceful progress. I do not know if this particular combination exists anywhere else in this way and on this scale. Also, this time, as you know, we are struggling hard to raise the standard of our people, to increase our industry, advance our agriculture and increase our production and thus get rid of the curse of poverty. It is a tremendous task and no government can do it, no laws can do it; only the people themselves can do it, helped by the government, no doubt. No one can push 350 million people who do not want to be pushed. They can only move of their own accord, if they want to, and therefore it becomes necessary for the millions of our people to understand all these big problems, understand our policies, understand the five year plan, not in detail but broadly, and not only give their support to it but also their willing and enthusiastic cooperation to it. Only then can we go ahead. We had the First Five Year Plan and you know that we succeeded in reaching our objectives. That gave us strength and self-reliance. And now we have got a much bigger and more ambitious plan—the Second Five Year Plan and that will require all our effort and tremendous hard work from all of us. But still we are confident because we have seen that the people are moving, that the people understand and that the people want to get rid of this poverty. So, I have come here not merely because of this election but also to tell you a little about these great programmes and policies that we have and in which I want to invite you to take your full part.

So, our urgent and principal concern and occupation is to work in our country for the fulfilment of these great plans, and yet, we cannot quite forget what is happening elsewhere in the world. We cannot isolate ourselves. I would very much like for some time, at least for some years to be able to concentrate myself on our internal work but the world is too complicated today and no country can keep apart from the world's problems and so we are drawn into them and have to spend our time and energy over them, because what happens in the world is of the utmost consequence to us. If unfortunately war comes, we may not be in the war. But we, like any other country, will be affected by it, especially in any major war. So, in spite of our preoccupation with our own affairs we have to think of other matters too. During these last few days especially you must realize that my mind has been concerned a good deal with the Kashmir affairs and you will know that recently the Security Council has been considering this and has just, I believe two or three days ago, passed a certain resolution which you must have seen.[2] Now, I am not going to say much about this. I have said a great deal in the last few days but all I wish to say here first of all, is that our representative Krishna Menon there has placed India's case before the Security Council and the world in a magnificent manner and has reflected fully our own thoughts and feelings and passions in regard to this subject.

Secondly, you know that the Security Council has asked the President of the Council to pay a visit to India.[3] Naturally, if he comes we shall be courteous to him and hospitable because of his high position and we shall have talks with him. But because of the nature of the talks and of the high policies that he may deal with, it is difficult for me to say exactly at this stage what they will be. We are all much too busy with our elections and obviously till the elections are over, until we have had time to meet and consider these matters as well as till we have met our representative Krishna Menon when he comes back, and seen the various reports and statements made in the Security Council, only then we will be in a position to consider them and to decide our policies. But as I have said if the President of the Security Council comes to India he will be received as an honoured guest.

I have referred briefly to Kashmir. This itself shows how one issue leads to another and how they get entangled with each other. We see here the projection of other conflicts, the association of other pacts and alliances affecting the Kashmir issue. As you know, we are not in favour of military pacts and alliances, so far as we are concerned. We have not liked these alliances as they affect us directly or indirectly. Of course, it is up to the other countries, independent

2. On 21 February 1957. For more details see *post*, p. 416 fn 5.
3. Gunnar Jarring was in India from 24 to 28 March and from 6 to 9 April 1957. For his talks with Nehru see *post*, pp. 428–435.

countries, to have them or not. We do not and cannot interfere. But we have to consider their consequences and fight them out in so far as we are concerned. I have little doubt that in the consideration of the Kashmir issue, there was the projection of the Baghdad Pact upon it, although really it had nothing to do with it. And that is why issues become more complicated. I have no doubt that the principal originators of the Baghdad Pact did not have Kashmir in mind—it had nothing to do with it, but the fact is that step by step it leads in a particular direction which was perhaps not thought of by the originators and founders and affects, therefore, these other matters and creates grave difficulties.

So, whether we are in it or not, we get entangled in this depressing game of power politics. At any rate we are affected by it as we have seen recently, and I am very much distressed at the various developments that have been taking place in the last few months in the world. Some time ago, say a year ago or more, most of you perhaps took a hopeful view about world affairs. The whole cold war was toning down. There was a little hope that things were improving but suddenly other things happened and here we are back again in the—I don't know what I can call it—it is not the heat of the cold war but something like that. And the outlook is about as black as it can be. What has happened? Many things have happened, of course. There was the Anglo-French and Israeli attack on Egypt. There was the upheaval in Hungary which was sternly and cruelly repressed. And now the long shadow of all these pursues us. The problem of the Middle East, they say, is a very difficult one and all kinds of proposals are made. Apart from what happened in these countries which was so distressing, the effect has been to bring back that sense of fear and insecurity everywhere and an utter lack of confidence among the powers. Nobody trusts the other, because of this lack of confidence and fear, the pace of armament grows, atom bombs and hydrogen bombs get piling up and everything goes on to encourage a drift towards a disaster. No person who is sensitive can watch this with any comfort or contentment and it does not much matter who is in the right or who is in the wrong, if as a result of that, we all of us are consumed in some kind of war. Therefore, the outlook is depressing. I do not mean to say that a war is going to occur soon, not that, but the whole tendency is for some kind of mental disintegration in the world, in spite of the tremendous progress the world has made and can make. And it is terrible to contemplate this process of mental disintegration—all the old disciplines go away and only hatred and fear and violence take their place.

All of us have inevitably to play some little part in this tug of war in the world of ideas but obviously the greatest responsibility rests on two mighty nations, the United States of America and the Soviet Union. And unless they understand each other and have some little measure of confidence in each other, in spite of all that has happened, I suppose, these conflicts and deteriorating conditions will continue. Sometime ago, the President of the United States, a very great man and a man who loves peace and tries to work for peace made a proposal about the Middle East.[4] If I may venture to say, so many excellent things in that proposal were unfortunately associated with the military approach and I am, I say so with all respect, convinced that out of the military approach peace does not easily come. The other day, the Soviet Foreign Minister also made a proposal concerning the Middle East[5] and in the end many people said that this proposal was some manoeuvre in a game, maybe it was, how can I say? But it was a proposal, essentially, to keep the Middle East out of the struggle of the Great Powers in world politics, and to keep it out of entangling military alliances. I suppose it is no easy matter to upset all that has been done and accept that proposal; nevertheless there appears to me to be a good deal of reason behind the proposal to keep this area out of trouble and leave it to the people themselves to develop with the help, of course, of others—economic help. What motive there might be behind this or that move. I don't know and it may be that while the whole thing, the complete proposal is not easy of being acted upon, some steps may be taken to that end; it may be phased out; anyhow I would venture to say that the matter deserves consideration to see if some way out may be found. It does not help not to consider any proposal because after all there are only two ways of dealing with international problems; one is war which all sensible people rule out and the other is peaceful settlement even though it may be difficult, and even though it may take time. Therefore, I would in all humility suggest that all these methods should be considered by these two great nations, the United States of America and the Soviet Union, by their representatives; let them discuss them together with others, other Great Powers and I may say, I have no desire for India to be present or associated with these discussions—we do not wish to put ourselves in anywhere, we have enough of our own burdens to carry but anyhow— some kind of discussion on these issues may perhaps lead to a hopeful step or two. I don't say that all the fears of the world will vanish suddenly—that is too much to expect—but let us at least move in a direction of peace, in a direction of understanding and that itself would be a tremendous gain.

4. The proposal of Dwight David Eisenhower, placed before the US Congress on 5 January 1957, asked to authorize the use of American military forces to protect the territorial integrity and political independence of Middle East nations requesting such aid to resist "overt armed aggression from any nation controlled by International Communism." The proposal also asked to authorize the US to cooperate with any nation in the Middle East in the development of its economic strength.
5. See *ante*, pp. 34-35.

You will ask me what all this has got to do with the general elections. Well, perhaps not too much directly but I want to put before you what I have in my mind and to share my thoughts with you. Now, coming to this election, this State of Kerala, although it is a new State in its present shape, it is a very old State also. In the last few years this State which is said to be, I believe, the most highly educated in India, and which has its sons and daughters spread out all over India occupying very high posts, and not only all over India, but, if I may say so, a good part of the world too as our ambassadors. This State has put up a remarkable record of instability. While in other states, which are not blessed with so much education as Kerala, have carried on in a stable way and have worked hard, here it has been difficult to get a stable Government, and time and energy are spent by rival groups trying to push each other out. Now, the question is whether you and the people of Kerala are going to repeat this performance in this election also or not. Well, it is an interesting question; and I shall have to wait for your answer later on. But seriously, it is rather sad that people in Kerala should be, if I may use the word, so inarticulately inclined—going in different directions and unable to pull together. You have got here some parties which exist elsewhere too, some parties which are peculiar to your region, some parties which exist elsewhere take up a special colour here, like the PSP. The PSP is a socialist party but in Kerala it has an alliance with the Muslim League which is very extraordinary for any party thinking in terms of socialism, because a communal party is far removed not only from socialism but from any progressive politics. And it is an amazing thing that a progressive party, as the PSP claims to be, should go in for these manoeuvres and opportunist tactics in the hope of perhaps getting a few seats here.

We have, as I told you, a parliamentary democracy and I believe in that method of government. A parliamentary democracy requires, of course, peaceful processes, democratic processes and it can only function adequately if there are strong parties. If there are innumerable parties than there is no strength in the government. They all pull in different directions. If there are all kinds of odd independents—they are just waifs and strays, India would cease to function. There would be no policy, nothing—everybody pulling in a different direction. A parliamentary democracy requires organized parties. At the same time it does not require too many parties, when no party is strong enough to carry on the government. But at this particular juncture in India's history with great internal problems and great international problems, India must speak with a clear and strong voice, not be pulled in different directions, because of some internal party manoeuvring. Therefore, I feel, apart from other reasons, that the only Party that can be really strong is the Congress and it must and should be returned in strength during these elections.

Therefore, my advice to you is, and it is upto you to accept it or not, to vote for the Congress candidates.

Now, I mentioned the PSP, and in that connection I mentioned the Muslim League, which is some kind of an unhappy relic of some distant past age which we try to forget. Then there is in Kerala the Communist Party which has survived many shocks but in the process of surviving it has apparently lost the capacity to think. What the Communist Party stands for today, some people may know, but I am a little intelligent and I fail to understand what it stands for in India and when I put a straight question to them, I have no straight answer. The fact of the matter is that they represent in their thinking something again of the past day which has no relevance to the present day, which has no relevance to India, which has no relevance to parliamentary democracy, and which has no relevance to peaceful progress. They seem to go against all the basic things that I thought India stood for. And so they take refuge in loud slogans and louder promises. I am told that they promised here in their Manifesto that they will get an extra 100 crores out of nothing, I don't know. We should like to help Kerala to the best of our ability. We think it should develop greatly, industrially and otherwise. But to talk loosely of getting a 100 crores here and doing this or that, it has no meaning. It is utter irresponsible talk. There are many difficulties that I have with the Communist Party, but my major difficulty is its utter irresponsibility, its being always on the verge of trouble and violence, and thirdly, its looking outside for inspiration. That is not the way for India to grow. Of course, in the last few months, or last year, the Communist Party of India had suffered many nervous shocks. Because of developments elsewhere, because of what I just referred to you what happened in Hungary, which it is very difficult for them to explain away and yet they justify it, so that I cannot understand how any reasonable person in India can possibly support the Communist Party here.

I shall not talk about the other parties but I should just like to refer to the Kerala Socialist Party because I see it is present here with its flags. It used to oppose the Congress on the ground that it wanted a separate Kerala State and it wanted socialism. Now, the Kerala State has come and socialism is the objective of the Congress, there is no reason left why the Kerala Socialist Party should remain away and so I am glad to see, that it has returned to the fold and I congratulate it.[6]

Now, really if you look at the picture of India today, you will find this great exciting adventure of building up India, a terrific affair and an exciting thing.

6. In fact, some members of the Kerala Socialist Party, which was formed in 1947, joined the Congress, but others maintained its seperate identity.

You see great world problems surrounding us and if you want India really to make good, we have to do it with strength and a strong voice and not become a large debating society, constantly debating and pulling this way and that way by various small parties—that is not the way this country is going to survive these various crises. Therefore, apart from other reasons it becomes necessary to have the strong party, and the only strong party is this Congress which is 72 years old, a disciplined strong party with clear objectives, with fine band of workers everywhere and with, above all, an all India sense. Because right from the very beginning, we have always developed this all India sense, and all India unity, and the moment you or anybody forgets that lesson of unity, that moment you go back to chaos and disorder. Therefore, my strong advice to you, especially in Kerala, is to support the Congress; and certainly do not support any other party or any other individual that goes in for communalist or disruptive activities, like the Communist or the Muslim League or any like party or any allied party. Kerala has specially learnt some lessons during the last few years when repeatedly its constitutional structure of Government has broken down and President's rule has been introduced. We do not like the President's rule. It is only when we are forced to do it, it has been done. I want you people or your representatives to take the reins of the Government in your hands and go ahead here in Kerala. But if you can't make up your mind to come out with certain measure of unanimity, what is to be done? So, I hope you will learn this lesson and you stand strongly for the Congress and will build up the State on that basis.

And I am told that my time is up and I must go. So, now will you say *Jai Hind* with me. *Jai Hind!*

6. Equal Opportunities for All[1]

Friends and comrades,

I think I am happy to come back to Calicut. I came here about a year and a quarter ago, you will remember.[2] Since then changes have taken place and Calicut and Malabar have become part of the Kerala State.[3] And now, therefore, this great and historic city has slightly changed its geographical association. I hope that is good for you and for Kerala. It does not make much difference what internal changes we make in India, provided India remains united and strong. Calicut brings to my mind a train of historic memories. As you know Calicut was the first place which saw the intrusion of the West into India many hundreds of years ago.[4] That period is over. It ended ten years ago. And we started a new chapter in our history. Calicut also has been famous in past ages for its textiles which went from here to far off countries. So, first of all, I am glad to be here and I offer my greetings to you.

It was Calicut, as I said to you, which saw the first intrusion of Western power in India and from here it spread all over the country. Let this be a lesson to you and to all of us in India, a lesson so that we might remember that every little part of this great country is intimately connected with the rest, is united with the rest and if anything goes wrong in any corner of the country, it affects the whole body of India. And we can take no such risk in future. There is a very small part of the country that is still under foreign domination, that is Goa. And it is for this reason that we cannot tolerate any foreign foothold in this great country.

1. Speech at a public meeting, Kozhikode, Kerala, 25 February 1957. AIR tapes, NMML.
2. Nehru visited Kozhikode on 27 December 1955. For his speech see *Selected Works* (second series), Vol. 31, pp. 33-43.
3. Kerala was revived as a political entity under the States Reorganization Act of August 1956 and the new State of Kerala came into being on 1 November 1956. It comprises the Malabar District, the Kasargod taluk of South Canara District and the Part B State of Travancore-Cochin without its five Tamil-speaking *taluqas* in the South.
4. Kozhikode offered easy access to the western world by sea and its pepper, rice and other commodities brought Greek, Roman, Ethiopian and Arab traders during the 2nd century BC. The Arabs stayed and found colonies along the Malabar coast and their descendants are known as Malabar Muslims or Moplahs. The Portuguese, who arrived with Vasco da Gama in 1498, emulated the Arabs, whom they drove out wherever they could. The Dutch followed them in 1640 and benefited from Portuguese decline. The British dominated the scene after Cochin and Travancore became the subsidiaries of the East India Company in 1791 and 1795 respectively.

The main lesson is the unity of India, a unity which must be unshakeable and unbreakable.

In the past, India has suffered from disunity and therefore it fell, but now that we have built up this united India, we have to ensure that no walls of separation will divide us again. India today, as you know, is a secular State, which honours all its religions and gives them perfect freedom, in which men of every religion have equal opportunities and equal rights and equal obligations. All the great religions of India whether it is the Hindu religion or Islam or Christianity or Buddhism—they are all religions of India—where their followers have perfect and equal opportunity.

So, while each person may have his religion, but in national matters he is an Indian. Let us not mix up politics with religion because that means that we can never develop as a united nation. Therefore, we have not encouraged, and we will not encourage, in India this mixing up of politics with religion. This encouraging of communal organizations is not good because they separate a community from others, isolate and prevent it from taking full part in the rich current of India's national life.

We have in our Central Government, State Governments and in our Parliament and Assemblies respected members of all the religious communities of India. We have Muslims, Christians, Hindus and some others. There are Governors and there are our ambassadors abroad belonging to all communities because we want these avenues of service to the country to be open to all.

Therefore, we must remember that the great necessity for every person and every group in India is to realize the unity of India. You cannot in Kerala do any thing which will separate you from India. You will only suffer for the attempt. I cannot, according to the law, do any thing which can separate me from the South. That will not be India then. India has to hold together and we must have that sense of unity whatever our religion, whatever our state and whatever our language be. That is the first fundamental thing which everybody must remember because there is going to be no compromise on this issue. And if any person challenges that conception of Indian nation, Indian freedom and Indian nationhood, we shall not tolerate that.

For this reason the great organization that I represent, the Indian National Congress which was founded 72 years ago was meant for all the people of India—Hindus, Christians, Muslims, Jews and others whosoever live in this country, because it represented the idea of a united India. It was not a communal organization; it was a national organization and it grew step by step till it included the whole of this great country, and spread to towns and villages, and gained power, because it represented the organized strength of the Indian people of all religions and groups, till it wrested Swaraj from the British Empire.

Other organizations based on communalism came in the way of our attaining Swaraj because they joined hands with the British rulers in those days. Those organizations were the Muslim League, the Hindu Mahasabha and other communal organizations, whether Muslim or Hindu. They sided with those who wanted to prevent freedom coming to us. But we attained freedom and the Muslim League then departed and went off to Pakistan. But surprisingly, it has left a little bit of its tail in Malabar.

We are opposed to Muslim communalism and Hindu communalism—and there is plenty of Hindu communalism also in India, and we have to struggle against it—because both disrupt India, weaken India and are opposed to the idea of Indian nationalism. Now, if we have communalism—Hindu or Muslim—in any part of India—that does not serve the cause of that community even. We want the Muslims of India to play a great part in India, but if they separate themselves and live in their communal shell, then they will not take full part in our national life, and do not grow with it. That is why communalism, whether Hindu or Muslim, is narrow and prevents growth. Here in Kerala, you have three major communities; there are the Hindus, there are the Muslims and there are the Christians, all essential communities of Kerala State. Unless they live in peace and cooperate for the good of Kerala and themselves, there will be no great progress of Kerala. If they each keep apart in their religious groups, then Kerala will not go ahead fast.

Now, as you know, from today the general elections start in India—not here, but in other parts of India. These great elections in which every adult is entitled to take part and in which nearly 20 crores of people can vote—is a great and very significant event in our life and even in the world's life, because this great democratic experiment is conducted in this great country.

We believe in individual freedom. Anybody can see it if he likes. Even if he wants to talk arrant nonsense and folly, he can talk. Even if he wants to criticize the Government, he can do so. The only thing that he must not do is violence and the encouragement to violence. We believe in individual freedom and that is why we see people standing for elections—even people representing communal organizations which we thoroughly disapprove. They can do so. But by doing so, they injure their own cause.

These elections are not meant to give prizes to individuals we like, but for the people of the country, to give expression to their views, or their approval of policies and programmes put before the country. The programmes are put up by different parties. Independent people who stand can put forward no real programme because independents cannot function as a group. We have, therefore, in parliamentary democracy, parties which are formed and which can put forward programmes. Independents do not count. They are just waste, even though they

49

might be able men and might be helpful occasionally. The Parliament of independents will never go anywhere.

Therefore, we must have parties. Now, among the parties, we have the Indian National Congress, the Communist Party, the Praja Socialist Party and some communal parties. Let us examine these parties. Communal parties whether they are Hindu or Muslim or Sikh or Christian have no place in the world today. They might have had some place perhaps in Vasco da Gama's[5] time when he came to Calicut. But that was long ago. Today, they are relics of backward thinking, backward action and the repudiation of the fundamental principles of nationalism. Therefore, we cannot encourage communal parties. We want India to be a great, modern, progressive state, to be a welfare state and to remove poverty and unemployment and all that. We cannot remain stuck up in the mud of communal politics which prevents our growth. Therefore, I say, we must not encourage communal parties whether they are Hindus or Muslims or any other in this country. We allow them freedom, because our Constitution allows everybody freedom. But we must not encourage them, and those who encourage them are really, I am convinced, backward in their thinking and do not realize what they are doing.

There is the Communist Party, especially in Kerala, and the PSP. The Praja Socialist Party, called itself socialist, and allied itself here with a communal party, the Muslim League. This is a strange marriage of socialism with communalism, and out of such strange marriages there can only be illegitimate offsprings. So, one must stick to principles. The first two principles in India for any individual are, that he must stick to peaceful methods and unity and secondly, that he must not encourage communal politics. These are the things that every one must remember because if we go in for communal politics we disrupt India. We become a backward country as we have been and we still are to some extent. We cannot progress and we cannot form a strong united India. We cannot have democracy in India with communal politics. We cannot have socialism in India with communal politics. We cannot have peace in India with communal politics. Therefore, for any party like the Praja Socialist Party, to ally itself with a communal organization, whether Hindu or Muslim, means that it strays away both from democracy and socialism and a united India. In the same way, the Communists who call themselves very revolutionary, function in a very communal plane, putting forward communal-minded candidates and encouraging communal candidates.

5. (c. 1460-1524); a Portuguese navigator; discovered the sea route to India, and reached Calicut on 20 May 1498.

The most remarkable documents I have read recently is the supplementary Manifesto of the Communist Party which lays down, without thinking, all kinds of things which they propose to do here. We say, they can lay down anything they like. They can even promise the Sun and the Moon and the stars and everything. They say, they shall raise the quota for Kerala under the Second Plan to two hundred crores. Why they didn't put down one thousand crores, I don't know. They can put down any figure they like. And I would advise them to raise this figure. They say, they will have a survey of Kerala, geological survey of Kerala, for putting up industries. Wonderful! I wonder if they know the meaning of geology and geological surveying. I am a geologist, and I can tell them, I know much more about the geology of Kerala than the whole of the Communist Party put together. Just putting down in English things without understanding, and hoping to delude people, is not a responsible thing to do. Kerala is rich in minerals etc., and you very well know, even in atomic minerals. And Kerala is going to make great progress. But Kerala is going to the dogs if people who know nothing about industry or geology or anything like the Communist Party will be coming to power.

There are many other strange things in this Manifesto of the Communist Party. They said they will start a Thorium (Bar) Factory and attach it to a Rare Earths Factory. They will stop export of mineral sands. They will prepare irrigation-cum-electric plans. They will set apart sufficient funds for minor irrigation projects. They will do so many good things—which they will never be called upon to do. Let us have parties, certainly. Let us have parties with a sense of responsibility. Unfortunately, the Communist Party here, and in other parts of India, lacks sense and responsibility. It stopped thinking long ago. When it learned by heart a number of phrases and slogans in some books written long ago which have no relation to India, its mind stopped working. But the world does not stop, the world goes on. The clock of the world moves on whether you stop or not. And the clock of the world has moved on while the clock of Communist minds in India stopped long ago. And so they take refuge in loud shouting, in threats and in violence occasionally. Is this the way to build up India or Kerala?

I find here that even their gestures while teaching people, reflect violence. When I see a Communist crowd performing in the distance, they are always shaking their fists in the air. I do not know at whom. Does this denote any intelligent approach to any intelligent question? Has the Communist Party fallen so low that they have no argument left, except abuse and shaking fists at people? I think that the Communist Party is also a relic of the past now, so far as its intelligence is concerned. It is about time that it pulled itself up and tried to understand India as it is today, the world as it is today and not to remain in the rut.

So you see, these different parties ask for your votes here. Not one of them, if I may say so, has any touch with the reality today in India, and not one of them has the strength to do anything. All they do is to make big promises. In this Manifesto of the Communist Party they talk about the Five Year Plan in India— which has actually been worked out in consultation with all kinds of people, to the utmost of our present strength, and even beyond it. The fact of the matter is that the only national party in India which can take this country forward, in my opinion, is the Indian National Congress. And, therefore, if you want Kerala to line up with the rest of India and go forward fast, you must build up Kerala on a national basis, not on a communal basis, not on a basis of parties with narrow outlook, not on the basis of reactionary parties, and not on the basis of parties verging on violence. And my advise to you is, to support the Congress candidates because then you will at last have a stable government in Kerala.

To my Muslim fellow countrymen here, I should like to tell them that this Muslim League organization here is just ploughing the sand. What good does it bring to anybody, to the Muslims here or to India? They have sent some people, one I think, to our Parliament.[6] What good he has done to Kerala or to the Muslim Community here? He is just an odd singular person, lost in the Parliament House because he is isolated from everybody else. He cannot join in any big endeavour. He can occasionally deliver a speech—which hardly anybody hears. That is not the way to play a part in the Parliament. That is not the way to contribute to the great national renaissance that is going on. That is the way to remain in backwaters. If the Muslims of Kerala or Malabar want to live in backwater, I am sorry for that. I cannot raise you up, but I want you to consider how this is not at all good, either from the national point of view or even from the narrow point of view of Muslim interest. You will not protect Muslim interest in this way by remaining as an isolated community.

And now before I go over to any other subject I should like to remind you of the fact you must know. There has been a great deal of debate on the Kashmir issue in the Security Council. And in this debate our delegation there has worked hard with great credit. In particular the leader of our delegation, is a son of Calicut, V.K. Krishna Menon. And I am sure you will all agree with me in saying that he has performed with the greatest success and ability, served the cause of India and served the cause of freedom. And so we must send him all our good wishes more especially because in his effort to serve this great cause, he has suffered in health greatly.[7] We hope he will get well soon. I am told that the

---

6. B. Pocker was Muslim League member of the First Lok Sabha from Manjeri constituency in Malabar.
7. See *Selected Works* (second series), Vol. 36, p. 406.

President of the local Muslim League[8] has expressed himself on the subject of Kashmir and said that both Jawaharlal Nehru and V.K. Krishna Menon have mismanaged this Kashmir business. Well, I am grateful for his opinion. But he has not told us how to manage it. And I should like to know where he stands about this business and every business. We have serious problems in India and we do not want any doubters and quibblers about it. Where does the President of the Muslim League stand about the Kashmir business? Let us know clearly about it.

I would like to tell you a great deal about our Second Five Year Plan, about what has been done in India and what we propose to do, because after we attained Swaraj we embarked on a great enterprise—that is the fight with the poverty of India. The various people in India—36 crores of them—have to get rid of this curse of poverty which has persuaded us for ages past. That is a tremendous adventure for all of us. It is not an adventure for Hindus only, or the Muslims or the Christians, but for all of us. And unless we all pull together, we shall remain stuck in the mire of poverty. Therefore, we started the First Five Year Plan and we succeeded there and gained strength and self-reliance. And now we have the Second Five Year Plan which is a much bigger one and I want you to understand that Plan because we are bringing about great revolutionary changes in India in peaceful and cooperative method.

I should like you to understand this Second Plan. It deals with everything, with agriculture, with industry, with heavy industry, light industry, and cottage industry because all have to develop in a balanced way. We want much more food production, we want much more industry, much more employment and much more wealth production. And thus we shall gradually get rid of poverty. And we want to do this in a balanced way. We have seen recently in countries in Central Europe like Hungary and Poland how they, in their attempt to advance along one line, they forget the other. And there were great economic crisis. So, we have to be careful, we have to be wide awake about these matters. I cannot tell you all about these plans but I want you to read them because the burden of carrying them out is on you and on all of us. It cannot be carried out by Government decree.

On the one hand we are building great plants, steel plants and others. We are building reactors, atomic reactors. On the other we are spreading out a revolutionary scheme in the villages. This is the Community Development Scheme—Community Blocks which started four and a half years ago and today covers 220,000 villages of India out of 500,000. That is nearly half. That is a tremendously rapid growth. And I can tell you that this Community Scheme is

8. K.M. Seethi.

bringing about revolutionary changes in our rural areas. And it is one of the biggest and the most exciting things happening anywhere in the world today. I want you to realize what great things are happening in India. Many big things have already happened in the last two years. And much bigger things are going to happen. And I want you to become vital partners in this great enterprise of building new India—men and women both—and forget your little quarrels, your communal compartments and the rest, and join together in this tremendous enterprise which is for all of us in India. This is the main purpose of all these activities. Elections come and go, but this work, to build up a new united, integrated and progressive India, will continue. And I want you to be active partners in that work.

Meanwhile, these elections are coming upon us and my advice to you, for you to consider, is to vote for the candidates put up on behalf of the National Congress. And thus build greater unity and stability in the politics of Kerala, and make this State progress fast.

And now I am going on to the next stage in my journey. Thank you. *Jai Hind!* Will you say *Jai Hind* with me? *Jai Hind!*

7. Democracy and Socialism[1]

The idea of the general elections is that we should utilize it for two purposes—one to gain further contacts with people, and secondly to explain things to them. I want the general elections to be a kind of a vast university for the masses of the people to discuss political and economic subjects and domestic and international problems. Therefore, general elections, if properly and decently conducted with good humour, is good although it is a troublesome thing. In spite of its being troublesome, I think, it is important and certainly it is an essential part of the democratic process. But we should remember that when we talk about democracy or socialism, these words denote not only political or economic experience, but certain growth in the people. You cannot apply democracy or socialism in a feudal or backward society. Whatever you apply should fit in with the growth of the people. Socialism is a matter of developing contacts and relationships among

1. Speech at a public meeting, Central Maidan, Mangalore, 25 February 1957. From *The Hindu*, 26 February 1957.

various groups and individuals so that people think that they can bring about great changes.

I think democracy suits Indian people because Indian people are mature and can behave decently enough. We are a mature people with some wisdom of an old race. If we can only rid our failings and weaknesses we can do wonders. I am also surprised at the quality of the Indian people. I criticize them often and I get the reputation of losing my temper. I do not think it is just reputation. I do lose temper when things go wrong. I am anxious that India march faster. I lose my temper because of two reasons. I firmly believe in the quality of our people and when they relax, it hurts me, and also because the people of India have honoured me greatly with their affection and love. I love the people of India very greatly because there is an intimate relationship between us. I venture to treat them as friends and comrades and open my heart when necessary and even to grow with them when necessary, which I would not dare to do unless I did treat them as friends and comrades.

In India, I see a great variety of people and also in this diversity a stamp of unity which we have developed through the ages. I am sorry at the fate that has befallen us in the past because of poverty and misery. Then, I think of our failings and weaknesses, because after all if we did not have failings and weaknesses, we would not have fallen. Why did other people rule over us? It is a long and intricate question. But there are two aspects. Although we have fallen, nevertheless we have not lost something of the quality that we had, which has helped us to pull ourselves together. We failed for two reasons. One was the capacity to quarrel with each other, the capacity for disunity and split into factions, groups etc. I think, one of the major reasons is the caste system which has divided us into innumerable compartments. It came in the way of a close integration of the people, which a nation requires. It may be that the caste system which originated 2,000 years ago might have been useful at that time. But I am quite certain that in later years—for many hundreds of years—it has been very harmful to us and has weakened and divided us and prevented progress.

Gradually, we have become a static society. Any community or nation, which becomes static, soon becomes foolish and at any rate backward. So, we have lost the live force, which makes a nation great. We have lost dynamism. In Europe, people moved fast and made advances in science and technology. They were adventurous. Vasco da Gama came here. Columbus went to America.[2] You see a live force working as a spirit of adventure and daring. If you go to South East Asia, you see there the stamp of India in architecture, language, tradition, dance and everything. It was India that went there, not because of conflict or

2. Christopher Columbus (c.1451-1506) discovered Central America in 1502.

war, Indian culture went there 1000 or 1500 years back. Our people were full of the spirit of adventure. But then Indian society shrunk into its shell losing touch with the world. Our religion told us not to touch this or that or not to eat with other men. We became more and more rigid. Meanwhile, caste prevented the development of unity. And we became a subject people with our backs bent and heads low.

Then Congress came into being 72 years ago and changed the situation in India—sometime after the Indian revolution was crushed. The Indian National Congress was formed in a small way—but for the whole of India, for the people of every caste, every language and community.

The founders of the Congress had a broad vision. The Congress spread from the English educated class to the middle class in the days of Lokmanya Tilak. When Gandhiji came, then the Congress became a widespread national movement going down to the roots of society. The Congress especially Gandhiji had to face, a people cowed down and full of fear and a people who had lost the spirit of daring and adventure. It was for him to infuse life into the people, acting through the Congress. The problem was how to put life into the people.

The history of India from around the beginning of this century or about 1918 onwards was the process of infusing life into the people. The changes made by Gandhiji were not only amazing but also miraculous. He also did something more important, that was to instil hope and courage. He displayed and taught them the lessons of India's history. Gandhiji said that he wanted to wipe out the tears of millions. Irrespective of whether he was able to do so or not, his efforts definitely brought hope to every Indian heart. Gandhiji worked through the Congress because one could not work in the political field except through an organization. Gandhiji had to take this organization and make it into a peaceful and disciplined body of action in order to gain Swaraj. His primary object was not to gain Swaraj somehow but to strengthen the people of India and build unity. For thirty years he disciplined the Indian people. It was a terrific task to train hundreds and millions of people. How far did he succeed? He succeeded, of course, tremendously. But, he did not know whether he succeeded as much as he wanted. His last days were embittered because of the dreadful things that happened after Partition. Finally, he himself was killed at the hands of an Indian.

Our young men do not remember India's history of freedom. They read it in books. But they would never realize how privileged the people were to work under Gandhiji. He was a taskmaster but his approach was one of love. He had no pity for weakness. Gandhiji had changed the Indian people who were suppressed by foreign domination and who were divided among themselves by religious factions.

Independence has brought to us not rest but harder work and tremendous problems. When we became free we assumed that the rights we carry have no obligations. But obligations and rights go together. The immediate problem is to lift up the static society of India and make it dynamic. Gandhiji made our minds dynamic. But we have to make something else—make our economic structure dynamic because a poverty-stricken country is not dynamic. It is stuck in the shackles of poverty.

Planning cannot be done unless we have full particulars and data. We have made a fairly good plan particularly in agriculture because we are short of food. We must have a stable and sound agricultural economy. There are river valley projects both for food production and for generation of electric power. We have started numerous national laboratories because the modern world is a world of science. Unless we can keep up with science we will never make good progress. It is important for us to develop a temper for science.

We are building three new huge steel plants.[3] We cannot develop industries unless we have steel. A steel plant takes four to six years to be built. But it takes a longer time to produce trained men to be in charge of those plants.

When we talk about socialism, we do not accept any rigid socialism. We accept broad implications. It is for the people to give it a shape. We want rapid growth for the Indian people. That is why we are giving the broad framework of the socialist structure and step by step we develop the plan in practice.

The approach of the Communist Party is unfortunately vitiated in a spirit of hatred and violence. That has prevented the Communists from thinking straight. Many of the economic theories of the Communists may be good, but the method of approach and the way of action that the Communist Party has adopted is out of date and wrong.

The Communists have lost touch with life in India. The Communist Party says that it shall expropriate foreign capital and nationalize everything. But these are mere slogans which have no meaning unless we examine particular cases. My grievances against the Communists, many of whom are earnest and hard working, is their tendency to violence—violence in thinking and action.

You have to judge other parties not merely by what they are shouting but by understanding their background and capacity to do things.

The Praja Socialist Party has lost its foothold physically and mentally. There is no future for India unless we are united. We should have not only political unity but also emotional unity and psychological unity so that we may have the sensation of being closely linked together as a family.

Fifty years ago, young men were called revolutionaries when they threw

3. It was decided to set up three integrated iron and steel plants at Rourkela in Orissa, Bhilai in Madhya Pradesh and Durgapur in West Bengal during the Second Plan period.

bombs. But bomb-throwing was an immature and childish exercise. But, the courage of the young men was admired. For several years they went about throwing bombs on Englishmen or on Indians who served the British. They became heroes in the eyes of the public. Later when Gandhiji came, all this stopped. Bomb-throwers could not understand it, because their minds were so fixed and they could not get out of it. It was extraordinary how revolutionaries became unmoving and static. That is what is happening to our Communist friends. We have to think in terms of India's progress.

This business of Independents going to legislatures will bring no results. Look at the House of Commons. There are very few Independents there. Parties function because only they can deal with problems in a disciplined way. Therefore, parties are necessary. I do not claim that the Congress is an ideal organization. It has committed many mistakes. In a huge organization like the Congress, there are both good and bad people. On the whole it has kept up a remarkably high level of behaviour. You have to choose the best party you find.

I have grown up with the National Congress. The first session I attended as a boy visitor was in 1904.[4] I joined the National Congress a full 45 years ago and I am still in it. Naturally I have been associated with it during its ups and downs. But, in spite of all that, there are many things which I do not like. We discuss many matters and come to conclusions. Sometimes the decisions are not to my liking. But I cannot go on shouting that something has been done which is not to my liking.

In spite of its weakness and other things, Congress still remains the most stable weapon and organ in India's progress. That is why I am anxious that the reins of government should remain in the hands of persons who have close associations with the Congress. Therefore, in this election, Congressmen should be elected in large numbers to form a stable government. I can imagine nothing more unfortunate than this act of no party having a majority both in the Centre or in the State.

The misfortune of Kerala is that it did not have a stable government. I hope the people of the State will support the Congress so that they can have a stable government.

Remember we are living on the threshold of an atomic age. The whole world was changed by the Industrial Revolution 150 years ago and later by an electrical revolution. Now something more powerful than that has come. That is atomic energy. I have no doubt that in the next ten or twenty years this world will also

---

4. In 1904, Nehru along with his father Motilal Nehru had attended the Congress session at Bombay.

change very much if there is no war, which will destroy us. We have to go ahead and produce faster. If we are slow we will be overwhelmed.

The whole world is hard on us. Some admire us and some are jealous. Some dislike us. There are all kinds of people in the world. We have no malice against anybody. We want to be friends with everybody. The world is naturally looking at these elections in India a good deal and much can depend upon the results of these elections. If the world sees that India is united and stout and stands by the Congress Government and its policies, whether international or domestic, then India's status will be raised higher because they will see that India holds together and does not split up into numerous groups.

8. Unity Essential for Growth[1]

As you have just heard from Govind Dasji,[2] a small incident occurred when I was coming by plane today.[3] I left Bangalore in the morning and was on my way to Raipur when one of the engines failed. Anyhow, the other engine was fine and our pilot[4] decided that it would be better to land somewhere close by. The Raichur aerodrome was nearby and he landed very skilfully. That was the end of the matter. Another plane came from Hyderabad and took me to Raipur and now I have come to your city from Raipur. Except for the fact that there was some delay in my programme, in Raipur and here, no great damage was done. So, I do not want you to make too much of this trivial incident. Such things keep happening, there in no point in getting perturbed.

I have been touring for the last seven days. At the beginning of this election campaign I had said that I would not tour much, I would go to only a few places but I could not stress this and my colleagues put pressure. So, I have had to tour much more than I had intended to. The fact of the matter is that I too wanted, not

1. Speech at a public meeting, Jabalpur, Madhya Pradesh, 26 February 1957. AIR tapes, NMML. Original in Hindi.
2. Seth Govind Das was President, Mahakoshal PCC and Member of the first Lok Sabha.
3. Nehru's plane "Meghdoot", on a flight from Mangalore to Raipur in Madhya Pradesh, made an emergency landing at a deserted airstrip near Raichur in Mysore after its portside engine caught fire in mid-air.
4. Squadron Leader Reginald A. Rufus.

especially for electioneering, but to take advantage of the elections, to put some of my thoughts before the people. I am very anxious that the people in our country should understand the problems and issues facing us internally as well as externally. Neither India nor any other democracy can function unless people understand, at least broadly, what the issues are. It is not enough that you like me or someone else personally. Problems have to be understood in order to lay the firm foundations of the nation. Only then can a democracy function.

I have often said when people raise the issue of who should be the leaders at the top, and while that has to be considered, gone are the times when as in the olden days, there was one ruler or king at the top or some powerful leader who could lead the country. A democracy can function only when its foundations are solid. In fact I would say that it is only when all the assemblies in the country are strong and function well that democracy can be stable and we can build a strong nation. That would be such a strong foundation that nobody can shake it. Certainly other factors are also important. If there are good leaders at the top, that is a good thing. But if a country is dependent on a few leaders at the top, that is the nation's weakness, not strength. I accept that at critical junctures leaders can help a great deal and good leaders do so at all times. But there ought to be thousands of such leaders in the country, not all on the top rung perhaps, who will be backbone of the country.

As far as politics is concerned, as I said, its foundation lies in our Assemblies. Then there are other institutions above them. You have the State Legislatures and then the Parliament. Even as far as the economic issues are concerned, I feel that the roots should be firm and widespread through a system of cooperatives. Only then will the foundations be strong and we can take development in the direction towards socialism. I do not mean to say that cooperatives alone can bring about socialism. But they lay a tremendously strong foundation. That is what I mean. And we have to plan for all this.

It is obvious that in the ten years since India became independent, I feel that we have made a great deal of progress in many areas. But we cannot be complacent. We see how often we are led astray. For one thing, a sense of unity is still lacking in our country. Even today, people are led astray in the name of province or language or religion or caste, and the idea of India is lost sight of. Last year there was a great deal of debate over the issue of linguistic states. There should be debate over such an issue as redrawing the boundaries of states but it was accompanied by violence and clashes in many places.[5] That is wrong. Violence is always wrong but what I mean is that it was clear that people had lost sight of the real issue and had let other considerations take priority. Now,

5. See *Selected Works* (second series), Vol. 31, pp. 153 and 209 and Vol. 32, pp. 180-181.

this is a test, individually or as a nation, as to what our priorities are. If we let something of less importance take priority, then everything goes haywire.

What is the issue of foremost importance? It is obvious that for us it is India and its unity. If we lose sight of that and indulge in activities which lead to divisiveness in thought, and then in action, that is dangerous. We must realize that no matter what tall claims we may make, we have not really come to grips with our problems, nor have we rid ourselves of our old maladies. Divisiveness and lack of unity is a malady that has afflicted India for a long time. It is strange that in the entire history of India, political unity has seldom been achieved completely. We have had unity of a different kind, cultural unity and it is that which has kept India together. Otherwise we may have broken up into a thousand fragments. But lack of political unity has caused grave harm. We have to accept that we became politically united only under the British rule. I agree that it was unity in bondage, in slavery. But the unity that was forged enabled us to fight for our freedom. We had no other alternative except to wage the struggle on a united front.

The unity forced by colonial rule has had to be made stronger in our struggle for freedom. However, the unity for opposition to the British rule could not be complete. The moment that was removed, there were cracks in our unity. We must have the inner strength to forge unity. It is obvious that we are all Indians at heart to a very large extent. But we get carried away, we forget that unity and let other priorities hold sway. I mentioned linguistic provinces. Then there is religion. Caste divisions are always there. When the caste system first came into being in India thousands of years ago, I feel that it was appropriate for those times. Initially, a social organization came into being and the caste distinctions were not very rigid. It was based more on occupation which is to be found in all countries in some form or the other. But later the caste system became so rigid that it created great barriers in society. In a sense, we were no longer one nation. We became divided into many fragments. There is no doubt that it had an impact on political and social unity, which weakened the country.

Now, we are facing a number of issues, political, social and economic but at the core of all that is the issue of our identity—are we in reality one nation or not? We are one nation on the map, legally and constitutionally but are we so in spirit and emotion? What does it mean to be a nation? It means that there should be a close bond between the people of this country. All the millions of people living here should feel that they are part of one large family, irrespective of their religion, caste, language or province. It should be a bond that keeps us together. It should be strong and unbreakable, we can often find the chain being weakened. Until that continues to happen, our nationalism is not strong.

We have lacked unity in the past. But we got the opportunity to learn, to be

61

moulded into one nation. The young and the old alike in India got an opportunity. Gandhiji has become a mere name to the youth of today, they respect him but they do not have personal experience of seeing him, of the times that he lived and moulded the people of India. I want everyone to understand what he did because the task of moulding the country is not yet complete, it continues because we are a lively and vital nation. A nation which has vitality does not make a noise about its strength—that is what the weak do. A really strong nation does not need to do all this because it has confidence in itself and it progresses and faces challenges quietly.

I do not wish to give you the example of other countries. We are surrounded by other countries of Asia and other regions. If you compare them with India, you will find that India possesses an internal strength and vitality which is not to be found in the other countries. I am talking about the countries of Asia, not of Europe. I would say that this is a gift given by Gandhiji. If we had become free without Gandhiji being on the scene we would have been free but weak too. We would have quarrelled in the name of religion, caste or something else. There would not have been one single large party. There would have been innumerable parties, all making a noise. You can see what is happening in the other countries of Asia—they are good countries, with good people. But it is our good fortune to have been moulded by Gandhiji which has saved India and infused a new life into us and made us firm in our resolve and elevated our minds. This is one good fortune.

I am not here to make an election speech. I want to talk about more fundamental things which I want you to understand. I want India to go very far, be a great, strong and progressive nation. How is that to be done? We need planning, the five year plans, etc. This too is a part of that process, of infusing a new vitality into the nation. Or rather the vitality that it already has, must be enhanced. There are some who say that it would be harmful for the nation if the Congress becomes the single largest party and prevents other parties from growing. I accept that there is a great deal of truth in that. But I must mention that there are other things which go with that. For one thing, it would be harmful if the freedom to express different strands of opinions and ideas is suppressed, if dissent is not allowed or if criticism of the Congress is to be suppressed.

I am confident that the path that we have chosen, the path of democracy and parliamentary form of government, is the right one. There is no government in the world which is perfect. All of them suffer from some defect or the other. How can you have a flawless government until the entire population of a country becomes completely flawless? There is no way. But a democratic form of government is the best for our country because in a democracy, the government reflects the people. I feel that every individual should be free, and civil liberties should be protected on principle. That is the only way in which individuals can grow. I do not want merely to put up huge factories. Ultimately, the wealth of a nation is its people, not mere bricks and mortar. Therefore, human beings must grow.

I talked about civil liberties. But sometimes, when something wrong happens which causes the society great harm, then we have to interfere. Under a parliamentary form of government everyone has the chance to grow, the door is always open for opposition parties. But if that leads to many parties coming up and constantly at loggerheads with one another, instead of one strong party in opposition, then the parliamentary system breaks down, because no decision can be taken firmly and implemented. Fifty different voices and opinions are heard which is in a way right. But decisions must be taken and implemented firmly. When the decision-making process is weakened, then the system cannot function. Let me tell you once again, look at what is happening in the various countries of Asia. We see the example of a big country, its people are very good. They are troubled by the fact that no single party enjoys a majority, there are five or six different parties each pulling in a different direction. The result is that they are saying quite clearly that they want to abandon parliamentary democracy because it does not function well.

So, as I said I agree that opposition parties should have full opportunity to express their points of view. But to say that it is harmful to have a strong Congress Party or any other single strong party, is wrong. What has saved India in the face of grave challenges which arose in the ten years since Independence is a strong Congress Party. Nothing else could have saved this country except the organized strength of the Congress. Think of the grave challenges which we have faced. Right at the time of Independence, we had to face the terrible trauma of Partition, when millions of human beings were killed, millions fled from both sides of the border, and there was complete chaos and carnage everywhere. It was extremely difficult to control the situation. But we did. That situation had barely come under control when Gandhiji was assassinated. Terrible things happened which could have shaken the country from its roots and nobody knows what would have happened if the Congress had not been a strong force.

Then there are other problems and issues, economic and others. The Congress was the bulwark which has saved India during the last ten years. I agree that the Congress has taken many wrong steps, made mistakes. But it was the Congress which saved the country from the biggest mistake of being torn apart into fragments. At the root of these fissiparous tendencies lies the caste system which has kept people in separate compartments and prevented them from working as a united front. This is the biggest service the Congress has performed, the first big service to the nation. It was a historic task and the people of India became united under the banner of the Congress.

It is about 72 years since the Congress was formed but it is under Gandhiji's stewardship that it was forged into a strong force. He transformed the Congress from being a mere platform for making speeches into an active organization which got results. He taught the Congress to work quietly and face all challenges peacefully. He transformed it into an army in a sense which enabled it to perform a historic service. Now, the Congress is doing another great, historic service in striving to build a strong nation, to lay strong foundations which can withstand any kind of challenge. Our Armed Forces, our Army, Navy and Air Force are very good. But we do not have the military strength to challenge the Big Powers. I am fully convinced however that no matter how large or small our Armed Forces may be, the real strength of the nation lies in our unity and the courage of the people. I cannot ever lose sight of the fact that after all, we were able to oust the British rule from India without any weapons. And if we continue to have that strength, fearlessness and determination which unity brings, no force on earth can shake us, whether we possess military strength or not. We will certainly maintain our Armed Forces. That is different.

I am trying to lay before you some fundamental issues to show you how the work of the Congress has not been merely that of a political party, though that is also there. In fact, it functions basically as a political party. I do not know how long it will last, five years, ten years or more. But, this is a time for change as well as consolidation for our country. We have to follow the path we have chosen with determination. We can do that only if we have a strong government and in a parliamentary form of government, the government can be strong only when it is backed by a strong party with the organized strength of the people behind it. It is obvious that in the circumstances such a party is only the Congress. There is no other alternative.

So, I have come to the conclusion, and I have argued step by step before you, that it is very essential to strengthen the Congress, whether it is in the domestic sphere or in foreign affairs. I am aware of the innumerable shortcomings and weaknesses in the Congress. But there are defects and weaknesses in all the parties, though efforts are made in the Congress to keep things under control. But, somehow, it is fixed in my head that we cannot weaken the government or this large party of ours. Otherwise, we will get fragmented very easily, and India will speak in so many voices that it will not be heard in any world forum. At the moment it is heard loud and clear with respect—whether it will continue to be heard is a different matter. It is believed that the Government in India is strong enough to implement its policies. But when the government is no longer strong and there is a cacophony of voices in the country, nobody will respect us, especially if policies are changed all the time.

Yes, as I said, there is the other side of the coin too. The Congress must ensure that there is consensus about its policies, it must seek the cooperation of the opposition parties, as far as possible. They cannot be left out in the cold. They must have full freedom to express themselves in Parliament and the Assemblies, they should criticize stringently. I am fully prepared to accept that because there is often a danger that a majority party could easily become complacent and its thinking could stagnate. Their will to work is slackened. Therefore, it is very essential that there must be a vigilant opposition to point out when mistakes are made or policies go wrong. As far as possible major policies must be decided upon after a consensus has been arrived at. There must be discussions, debates and consultations. But once a decision is taken it should be implemented with firmness and determination. By consultations, I do not mean that there should be compromises and loopholes. That will dilute the decision-making process.

Now the question arises, how to hold on to the values that make our society strong and try to get rid of the evils which weaken it. There are complex questions which cannot be solved by mere slogan-mongering or mouthing ideological shibboleths, or by talking about socialism, communism and Gandhism. That is all very well in its place. But I want you to understand the complex questions that we face today in the country. We have to somehow pull millions of human beings out of the mire of poverty. We have to end the terrible poverty in the country. In order to do this we must take advantage of science and technology and understand the advances that are being made in this field. We must adopt new and improved techniques in agriculture. Farmers can benefit greatly by adopting even minor improvements. After all, why is it that in our country, we produce only one-fourth of what the other countries produce from one acre of land, whether it is wheat or paddy? If others can produce four times as much, why can't we? We can do it but our minds have got into a rut and it is difficult to get out of it and the mire of poverty is the most difficult to get out of. Poverty shackles thinking and the desire to progress. A society can grow only when its members earn enough. To eke out a living becomes extremely difficult if a human being does not earn enough to provide the basic necessities of life— food, clothing and shelter. A society can grow only if its members are able to take care of the basic necessities and have some savings to invest for the future. The developed nations have vast accumulations of savings and therefore, they can advance very rapidly. The poor countries have nothing to fall back upon and so they continue to stagnate in a mire of poverty.

Now, we must pull ourselves out of this mire. We have to do that through our economic policy but at the same time, we do not wish to lose sight of our ancient values and culture in our greed for material progress. We value our traditions and culture. I am not referring to any narrow religious traditions but of something far bigger and more inclusive. We must do all this quickly. Otherwise the country will be stagnant. These are all complex issues—I do not know if I have expressed myself clearly. But I want you to think about all these issues. During election time, there is a great deal of activity and noise with people demanding votes for this party or that. But the fundamental issues are seldom mentioned. I too wish to win the elections. I am a member of the Congress and I feel that it is very necessary for the country. So, it has to get a strong majority. Therefore, I would advise you to vote for Congress candidates. I do not even know the names of the candidates because I see them as part of our organization.

I do not wish to see India slacken. I do not want India to splinter into fifty small groups and parties, each singing its own different tunes. Even if they are good tunes, if there are innumerable different pulls and pressures, there can be no unity. Therefore, I want you to vote for the Congress. But over and above that, I am constantly thinking of how to uplift the 36 crores of human beings sunk in a mire of poverty. I think the First Five Year Plan has helped to shake them out of it a little. In a sense, the nation is on a knife's edge at the moment. There are countries which are mired in poverty. On the other hand, there are others where the society is beginning to move forward on its own steam. We are in the latter category. We will develop more but there are many difficulties in our path. No nation has succeeded till today in escaping from difficulties, whether they are capitalist countries or socialist countries. Please remember that ultimately, a country progresses, no matter what ideology it follows, through hard work. America is an extremely wealthy country. But please do not imagine that it has become wealthy without working hard. The American people are extremely hard working. The Soviet Union is a communist country. Do you think that they have become a Great Power by merely declaring adherence to communism? No other country in the world has worked so hard and borne as many hardships or paid as large a price as the Soviet Union has during the last forty years. It has not happened in a moment.

Take Germany, which was devastated during the Second World War with its cities in ruins. Within ten years, they have built up a strong edifice with their hard work. We talk about various isms—capitalism, socialism and communism— and so we should, for we have to decide where we wish to go. But beyond all isms, we have human beings, a society, and the vitality of a nation. A nation which has vitality will grow no matter what ideology it follows. The nation which lacks that vitality will go nowhere. A mere label of some ism is not going to work miracles. I often look back and think about India's history during the past 25, 30, 40 years, particularly since Gandhiji arrived on the scene and moulded the nation. He did great many things but one of the fundamental steps that he took was to make an incessant effort to infuse new life into a crushed nation. Please bear in mind that his concern was, first and foremost, not for the likes of you and me, the city-dwellers, but for the poor, downtrodden peasantry. He infused new life into them. He also gave a new vitality to the oppressed and downtrodden harijans and the tribals. He wanted that the entire country should come alive but his special concern was for the downtrodden. He breathed a new vitality into them and made a crushed nation come alive.

There is no yardstick to evaluate these things. But we have an invaluable heritage. Our country, our society is very ancient, they have existed for thousands of years. There is much that we can be proud of but at the same time many ills and weaknesses have also crept in. We have inherited the accumulated accretions, the good and the bad, over thousands of years. Perhaps no other country can boast of a history which dates back thousands of years. It is said that there was a very ancient civilization in Mesopotamia but even that is believed to have had its roots in the ancient civilization in Mohenjodaro 5,500 years ago, much before the coming of the Aryans. So, we have a very long and ancient history which gives us strength and our weaknesses too.

We have witnessed a great many ups and downs during this period and in fact, until recently, till just before we got our Independence, it was a period of downfall and degradation. It is not by some strange coincidence that we are coming out of that. Just think, if British rule had come to an end due to their weakness and not because we had struggled from a position of strength for freedom, we would have remained weak and could not have benefitted from that freedom. We would have fallen again in no time at all. We had to become strong and create a new vitality within ourselves, forge unity and learn to work hard and make sacrifices. That is what Gandhiji did—he led us by the hand. He was not so concerned about throwing out the British. He was more concerned that the people of this country should become strong and freedom would then follow automatically. You saw how he taught us discipline. If we strayed even a little bit from the right path he would immediately call a halt to the entire movement as he did in 1921. That was the first great movement, it had shaken the entire country out of its slackness and the world was watching in amazement. Millions of us were in jails, I too was in jail when suddenly we got the news that Gandhiji had called a halt to the entire movement. Why? It was because some peasants in Uttar Pradesh, in Gorakhpur, had attacked a police station and burnt it to the ground, killing or burning a few policemen. It was wrong. But we could not understand why the movement had to be called off in the whole country just because a few peasants in Gorakhpur district had misbehaved. We could not understand it all at that time. But we realized later that these were all steps towards training the people of India, to teach them not to swerve from the right path. Gandhiji's entire concentration was focussed on training India's millions—he was not after quick results or easy solutions. I have given you an example of how we were trained by Gandhiji and how he moulded us very ordinary human beings and make us strong and infused a new vitality into us. He ignited a spark in all of us.

One of the greatest evils is, of course, communalism. In fact, it was because of a communal party like the Muslim League that India had to be divided into two. But whether it is the Muslim League or a party of the Hindus or Christians or Sikhs, communalism is dangerous, it is anti-national and poisonous, it is divisive. We must understand this because people are often incited in the name of religion which leads them to forget the real values of life. A lot of harm was caused in India due to Muslim League's nationalism. It was not merely that a part of India was sliced off—that happened with our concurrence. We had to accept Partition and do not wish to see it reversed. But the tremendous harm that it caused us was compounded by the fact that it has given rise to communalism among the Hindus too. Hindu communal organizations have no goals like the Muslim League did. But it is the same thing and it drags us back from the nationalism of modern times to hundreds of years back when communalism and religious fundamentalism held sway. There is no place for it in these modern times. It is a different thing that some backward-looking individuals may believe in it but it has no place in these times. There is no doubt about it that if by some strange chance communalism spreads in our country, we will be ruined, we will break into fragments and we will no longer be one nation. Some things which may have been valid in other times can prove to be dangerous now. We put an end to the system of princely states because if we had not done so, India could not have been one united country. As you can imagine, India could not have functioned as one country if there had been 545 or 550 princely states, big and small, all over the country. Therefore, it was necessary to put an end to it. If you were to ask me why a system which had been appropriate for five hundred or a thousand years could not continue to exist, it is because even if they had been right for those times, they were no longer so. We abolished the zamindari, *jagirdari* and *taluqdari* systems. It was absolutely out of the question to let them continue if we wanted to progress. We had no enmity towards the zamindars, they were all our brethren, our kith and kin. It was not out of enmity towards them but the system had to be abolished because it was wrong. It might have been alright 500 or a 1000 years ago. What I mean to say is that to think that something which functioned well in one age could continue forever is not right.

Societies change, countries too change. There are a thousand different relationships in society, in trade or other activities. Once the relationship changes then the society too begins to change. I can give you thousands of examples but one concrete example which everyone can grasp easily is the mode of travel that was available to people upto a hundred and fifty or even a hundred years ago when the railways had not been established. What were the means of communication before the telegraph? People travelled by bullock carts or on horseback or carriages. The fastest mode of transport was on a horseback. You could not travel faster than that. This was the situation for thousands of years up to even a hundred and fifty years ago. It was the same for communications— messages and letters could be sent only through riders on horseback. Then there was a great revolution and new modes of fast travel appeared. The invention of the steam engine led to locomotives, then came motorcars and now aeroplanes and what not. The telegraph and the telephone revolutionized the mode of communications. I have only talked about two or three things. But there are thousands of such inventions.

Now, you will see that a link that binds a society is the mode of transport and communication. There has been a tremendous revolution in that area which has transformed the internal structures of society completely. Trade and commerce have been revolutionized. We often talk about the great revolutions which occurred in Russia, France and in China. But there has been no greater revolution than the Industrial Revolution which has transformed the relationship of people in society so completely. Science and technology have given us a thousand different inventions and discoveries.

Now, when society is changing so rapidly, it is important for our thinking also to keep pace with those changes. If we continue to stagnate in our old outmoded ways of thinking and refuse to change, then the world will go ahead and leave us far behind. This is what happened to a couple of centuries ago. The world was progressing rapidly while we stayed where we were, in our old ruts, full of pride that we were a great civilization. Our minds and thinking were set in rigid lines. The world progressed rapidly in every direction, other countries acquired new weapons and became militarily very powerful; taking advantage of advances in science and technology, they developed a thousand new ways to produce wealth from the land and from factories using new tools and equipment.

So, we must understand the importance of change. A society which refuses to change is heading for a fall. There is nothing unchangeable about ideas and ways of thinking. Everything changes and lives and dies and is rejuvenated. Anything that is static leads to rot. If flowing water gets separated from the river and stagnates, then it begins to get polluted. Our entire history teaches us that a society should not become static. Once we stagnate, we fall. The most important question before us today is how our society—and by that I do not mean a section at the top but the 37 crores of human beings in our country—is to emerge out of the stagnation of thousands of years and take our place in the modern world. It is difficult but it is happening slowly and all our efforts and circumstances are also propelling us in that direction. So long as our society remains stagnant and in a rut there is no progress possible, we cannot go ahead. We may talk about socialism and communism and other issues. But the basic thing is to get the society out of its rut—of rigidity in thinking, habits and ways of working.

Now, you will not accept it if somebody suggests that you travel to Delhi from Jabalpur by bullock cart. But you will accept a thousand other things which have no connection with the modern world. They belong to a bygone age of bullock carts. We continue to remain in a rut. I am not talking about the educated people living in cities but about the crores of people living all over the country. I am not blaming them for it—circumstances have forced them to stay in the old ruts and our society remained stagnant. However, it is wonderful that inspite of all that, there is something in our culture and the high ideals of our ancestors which has kept our society alive and strong from within.

So, we find both these things existing side by side. One is this inner vitality of our culture and civilization which can be seen even among the uneducated peasants. It would be wrong to say that being uneducated our peasants are uncivilized. I will not accept that. Our peasantry consists of people of high quality even if they are simple people. They are cultured because India's cultural heritage permeates their being, so that is very valuable.

On the other hand, there are many ills which keep us stagnant and in a rut. So, now the question is which way we lean. We are trying to make the Five Year Plan not merely of the Congress Party but a national Plan. We have had consultations with all the parties and apart from that with people from other streams—scientists and engineers and even members of the panchayat. We invited some experts from other countries, from Europe and the United States etc., but the final decision was ours, of the Planning Commission and the Government of India. Now, we have the responsibility of implementing the Plan.

Well, first of all, we must understand quite clearly that it is not enough to shout slogans or make a noise. The most important thing is to grasp the fact that we need a strong party at the helm of affairs to steer the country through the challenges it faces both in the domestic sphere and in external affairs, in order to keep the country strong and united, to mould the minds and thinking of the people so that the five year plans may be implemented smoothly and to make our foreign policy also vigorous. And that is possible only if the Congress is elected and forms the government. There is no other alternative.

Now, it is obvious that no matter which path we choose to take, there are bound to be some pitfalls. But the path that I have suggested is less risky. You will forgive me if I say something about myself. I have some strength left in me to work for the country, not that there are not several others who are also capable. But by chance I have worked for this country during the last 20-30 years and have established contact with the people of India who in turn have given me their love. They have placed their trust in me. Then later when we got Independence you elected me and made me the Prime Minister. That was a great honour and a great stature but I have an even higher status due to the love and confidence that the people of India have given me, and that is something nobody can take away from me whether I am Prime Minister or not. This has given a great boost to my spirit and inner strength because at this age, I do have to do a lot of running around.

There is no doubt about it that I derive my strength and my energy from the people of India, from their love which gives me a boost. Otherwise I would have been crushed under the burden of the load that I have to carry. But what I was trying to say was that by a strange coincidence I had the chance 25-30 years ago to join in the struggle for Independence when the people of India came to know me, to understand me and we established a close relationship. Then came Independence and I became the Prime Minister and somehow I have found the strength to contribute to forging unity in India. If I go to the South, the people give me their love, and so also in the North, in the East and West. So, I too have become a small symbol of united India. It is not so much because of any innate quality in me. It has happened through circumstances and I find myself in a position to serve the country. I will continue to do so till my strength lasts.

So, as I was saying, more than others, I am able to do what the country needs. It is the people who have been moulded by the past can do this in the best possible way. I don't know what will happen in the future. I mean that people may forget the story of the Gandhian era and adopt different ways of doing things which may be dangerous for India, that is why I want that India should become a stable and united country during the next 10-15 years. I am anxious that the country that we are trying to build should become firm on its axis. Once that happens, we will be carefree because the country will grow and progress on its own momentum.

Now, there are other parties in opposition. But who are the real opposition parties? Let me tell you that it is not the different political parties. The real opposition to the country's progress comes from the ignorance and stupidity of the people. You will forgive me for saying this but very often you find that the people are ignorant, their thinking is backward, they have lacked opportunity, and so some people take advantage of their backwardness and ignorance to incite them. For instance, take these elections. We bring out election manifestoes about the economic, political and social policies, all parties have done this. But what is it that wins the votes? I would say it is stupidity to ask for votes on issues like cow protection and I mean that in two ways. One is that these issues are raised merely to garner votes, it is not that they are greatly concerned about cow protection. That is one. Secondly, they resort to all kinds of lies. I was told just now by Dr Gadgil that in Madhya Bharat, an elderly member of some communal party was saying that Dr Gadgil was personally responsible for killing 65,000 cows. Poor Dr Gadgil. No, I was wrong, it was said that he has 36 thousand cows slaughtered every day. You can imagine that he wilted at the mere thought. As you are aware, there is a ban on cow slaughter in Madhya Bharat. So, you can imagine what a falsehood this is. There are similar laws in most countries today. It is a different matter that some people may do it clandestinely. Cow slaughter has become much reduced except in some big cities. But these canards are completely baseless and false.

The other aspect of this is that I remember I had said in Banaras and elsewhere that I am not prepared to worship the cow or any other animal.[6] Let people be in doubt about it, I have great love for all animals. But if anyone tells me to worship any of them, I will not do it. I believe that it is very important for us to take care of our cows, that is an economic necessity. The cow is not an object of worship but a very significant factor for our economy. Therefore, we must look after the cows in every possible way. I find that cows are much better looked after in countries where they are not worshipped than in India. This surprises me. There is no comparison between their healthy breeds and the cows we have in India. So, I want that we should follow a policy whereby our cows are protected and looked after well so that they and the people may benefit. I don't believe that you can look after cows merely by passing a bill banning cow slaughter. It has become a major issue in parts of northern Uttar Pradesh which are adjoining Punjab—the people of both States are complaining about it—a huge number of cows have become absolutely wild and dangerous because they are attacking people and destroying fields.

So, in short, issues which are relevant should be taken up so that they can be resolved. To take up issues and politicize them merely to pull down others is to deceive the people and it solves nothing. That is why I said that there is a great deal of stupidity in our country and that is the real obstacle. People take advantage of it and incite others to riots and other destructive acts. We have to be constantly vigilant. We can easily go astray so long as these things afflict us.

Well, anyhow, I have not said very much about our policies etc. Broadly speaking, as you know, we are implementing the five year plans to progress on many fronts, on the social and economic fronts simultaneously because if we

6. In Varanasi on 16 February 1957.

progress well on one front but lag behind on others, the balance is upset. We have to maintain a balance. We have to ensure that production keeps going up in agriculture and industries. If agricultural production does not keep pace, industry will suffer. Our first priority is to increase agricultural production not only for our own consumption but in surplus so that we can export foodgrains and be able to buy machinery and other things. As I have perhaps mentioned, in other countries, the production per acre is double, triple or even four times as much as what we produce. We can also do it. Just imagine, if we can double our food production, immediately the doors will be opened to enormous progress. The farmers will benefit and so will the entire country.

So, the first thing to bear in mind is that we must increase production from land rapidly. We can do it. Secondly, no matter how much we produce from land, until we increase industrial production we can neither solve the question of unemployment nor will there be enough wealth in the country to eradicate poverty. So, that also has to be done. Industries are of many kinds—heavy industry, medium industry and village industries. But unless we build heavy industries, the country cannot progress. We can import machinery from America but that is not real progress. We must produce those machines ourselves. Therefore, we have to set up heavy industries to produce machinery which will be used to set up other industries. It is a huge project involving heavy investment and requires people with know-how.

Now, to set up heavy industries, one of the basic requirements is of steel. So, we have to produce enough steel in the country to be able to progress. If you were to have an idea of the progress that a country makes, you should find out two things, how much steel and electricity are produced in that country. You can immediately gauge from that as to how far a country has progressed because electricity and steel are absolutely essential for a country's progress. That is why we are setting up river valley projects for producing power. As you know, three new steel plants are coming up and the old one at Tata Nagar in the private sector is expanding. One of the new public sector steel mills is in Madhya Pradesh.[7]

So, we are laying the foundations for development. We are also trying to set up heavy industries to produce machinery. But the problem is that all this imposes a very heavy burden. Whether we set up river valley projects or heavy industries or steel plants, it takes years, 7-8 years or even 10 years for them to be completed. That means that for 5-10 years we have to keep on ploughing in money without getting any returns. That imposes a very great burden on the country's exchequer.

---

7. An integrated iron and steel plant with an initial capacity of 10 lakh tons was set up at Bhilai with the help of the USSR.

Each of these steel plants require enormous investments—Rs 125 or 150 crores of rupees for one steel plant. The same thing applies to river valley projects, hundreds of crores of investment is needed. A poor country like ours in having to invest at least 400 crores in the steel plants without getting anything in return for years is rather difficult.

These are some of the problems that we are having to face today. Once the steel plants start producing steel, we will get a lot of wealth and many doors will open. Therefore, as I said, in the beginning, there are a great many difficulties in shaking a country out of its economic stagnation. Once it starts moving, it will gallop. So, these are the times we are living in today. The country has been shaken slightly. Once the steel plants and other projects are completed, we will no longer be dependent on other countries.

So, on the one hand, we are setting up heavy industries and facing great difficulties and shouldering a heavy burden. At the same time, we are paying a great deal of attention to village industries too because we are aware of their importance. Please do not think that we are repeating lessons learnt by rote or that we are paying lip service to village industries because Gandhiji believed in them or to merely please the people. That is not so. We consider village industries to be of tremendous importance. We are paying attention to heavy industries on the one hand and on the other we want that small industries, cottage industries like the Ambar Charkha should also improve, adopt new techniques and run on power etc. I will not go into the details because it is a long story but it is extremely essential for our economic policy. By adopting this policy, we can create more jobs which is very essential apart from the fact that we will produce a great deal of wealth quickly. On the one hand, since we can get no returns for at least 5 to 7 years from the heavy industries like steel plants, we must balance the situation by producing new wealth from our cottage industries. So, we are paying attention to that also.

Now, a genius has not yet been born in the world who can produce a foolproof blueprint for planning which is perfect for all times. That is not how it happens. When an engineer is asked to construct a bridge, he gives an estimate of the quantities of steel, cement, etc., which would be required. When we are engaged in the task of building a new India, we are having to mould 36 crores of human beings. Who can weigh 36 crores of human beings, like cement or steel, and gauge what their potential is? They are all different with different ways of thinking. Therefore, nobody can say anything with certainty and so we make plans, the five year plans, on the basis of which we can gauge from circumstances and what our own intelligence tells us. But there is always scope in that for us to make changes as we gain in experience. Therefore, we review the Plan every six months. The Second Plan is much better than the First one in the sense that more thought has gone into it because we have gained more experience, more knowledge, and we can use more statistics. So, it will go on.

One more thing that I wish to draw your attention to specially is our Community Development Projects. Of all the projects that we are implementing in the country today, I consider them the most revolutionary because they are shaking up the rural areas, changing and transforming them. It is not happening overnight but it is moving gradually in that direction. It is changing in a fundamental way and I feel that within the next five to ten years the face of our countryside would have been transformed. And when our rural areas change, it means that India will be transformed. 80% of our population lives in our villages and I was extremely worried about how to change them. It was just a little less than four and a half years ago that we started these Community Development Schemes, on 2nd October 1952 on Gandhi Jayanti day. Today, four and a half years later, it has spread to over 2 lakh 20 thousand villages out of the 5 lakh villages in India. 13 crores of human beings fall within their purview. I cannot imagine another country where such a scheme has permeated so rapidly on such a large scale.

I consider it revolutionary. It is not as if it is something superficial. The work is happening from within. I am not saying that the work that is being done in 2 lakh 20 thousand villages is uniformly good everywhere. It is obvious that there are ups and downs, in some places it is better than in others. But looking at the entire picture, good work is being done. In fact we are in great difficulties at the moment to fulfil the demand for skilled, trained workers to man the projects. We have set up a couple of hundred training centres to train people quickly to work as *gramsevaks* up to a higher grade. I would like to mention here that we need *gramsevikas* and there is some difficulty in getting them for training. Our sisters in the country must shake themselves a little because a country cannot grow until the women grow.

Well, I have placed various issues before you to draw your attention to some features and the basic tasks that we need to do. We have accepted socialism as our goal but mere ideology is not enough. We will work along those lines but the real test is to infuse new vitality into the people, to forge unity and to remove the factors which foment divisiveness—the most dangerous of them is communalism. That must be put an end to.

Now, as far as the elections are concerned, I have already told you what my views are. I consider it important that the Congress should be supported, as it is essential that the world hears us speaking in one strong voice and to let the world know where we are going. Therefore, my advice to you is that you should vote for the Congress. Please forgive me for holding you up for so long. *Jai Hind!* Please say *Jai Hind* with me—*Jai Hind!*

9. Do Not Vote on Parochial Considerations[1]

Sisters and brothers,

Partap Singh[2] mentioned just now that you and I have close emotional ties and so we should establish a mental rapport. Though emotional oneness is better in many ways, there ought to be a rapport of the minds too. We must understand how our minds work, understand especially the important issues before the country.

I want to talk to you about the country's affairs for a few minutes. As you know, we are having general elections in India, I am naturally interested in them. But elections will be over in a few days. I am interested in other bigger issues and want that you should try to understand them. We must understand one another because we have great tasks at hand. We have got an opportunity to do big things after a long time in India. But the Government cannot do anything alone. The people must participate in the task of nation-building. So, they must understand the issues and be prepared to shoulder the burdens. The Government must, of course, do its bit.

After all, when 37 crores of people are involved, how can a government or any other agency uplift them? The people must do it themselves. I cannot push 37 crores into making progress. It is obvious that the determination and push has to come from the people. No individual has the strength to push crores of people. Either they must make up their minds to go ahead or they will get nowhere. I want you to understand that we cannot tackle the tasks before us by a Governmental fiat from above. People are still in the habit of looking to the Government for every little thing, of regarding the collector as the *mai-baap*, begging and pleading and presenting petitions. At that time conditions were different and all the powers were centred in the hands of the Government. But in those days, all that the Government did was to maintain law and order and defend the Empire against external threats. The other function was tax collection. The Government performed other minor functions too. But today, the Government has innumerable functions because we want to progress. The British Government was interested only in maintaining the status quo. We can no longer afford to do that. So, we have to change our method of functioning if we want to progress.

---

1. Speech at a public meeting, Gurgaon, 28 February 1957. AIR tapes, NMML. Original in Hindi.
2. Partap Singh Kairon was Chief Minister of Punjab.

How were we to go about it? I agree that laws make a great deal of impact and there should be good laws. But how will laws help if we want to build a bridge? It will not be built until people go and work. Laws can help to finance the construction of the bridge. But ultimately it is the people who have to build it. Today, it is not a question of building one bridge in India but of thousands of tasks which need to be done. Neither law, nor slogans will do the work as some people seem to think. Can you till the field by merely shouting slogans? You have to work hard in order to produce a crop. At the moment our field is the whole of India. We have to sow the seeds to produce different kinds of crops which will benefit the country and its people. First of all, we have to sow the idea in the minds of the people. Once they are convinced about the need to do something, it would be a major step. Then other steps will follow.

I am telling you this so that you may not be under any misconception. We are going to have elections and the fever is mounting. Fiery speeches are being given. Now, I am no lecturer and certainly cannot make speeches like people do in the Punjab. I will only talk to you about the story of this country because my chief concern is to reach your minds and hearts and explain what is happening in India today and the kind of future we envisage. India had been in bondage for centuries and remained bogged down in a morass of poverty and degradation. To pull it out of that mire and set it on the path of progress is an extremely difficult task.

First of all, we must understand what India is all about. Once, a long time ago, I was passing through Rohtak in the evening and stopped somewhere. A group of peasants shouted: *Bharat Mata ki Jai*, so I asked them who this *Bharat Mata* was. Whether she was a woman or something else. They said it is the land. So I asked them which land? Was it the village land. This went on for some time. Finally they asked me to tell them what *Bharat Mata* was. I told them that *Bharat Mata* was all that they had said and more. *Bharat Mata* is a vast country of ours with its many provinces, rivers, fields, mountains, cities, villages and forests. But above all *Bharat Mata* is the people who live here which means all of us. They were surprised to hear that they too were *Bharat Mata*. I explained that all of us were parts of this vast land of ours and so when we shout *Bharat Mata ki Jai*, in a sense we are shouting victory to the people.

When we talk of India's progress it mans uplifting 37 crores of human beings in India. It is a pretty difficult task. Secondly, a nation which has been stagnant for a long time finds it difficult to move forward. I do not say that India was completely stagnant. There have been some changes no doubt. Yet the pace of change had slowed down over the past few centuries. People continued to work and some benefit might have accrued. But by and large, the country remained stagnant and poor. As you know, it is very difficult for a poor man to shake off

77

his poverty when he is trying hard for survival. He has no savings to better his condition. Similarly, a poor country has very little surplus capital to invest in tasks of development. So, progress is slow. It is a vicious circle. It is very difficult to tighten one's belt when even two square meals a day are not available. People want some relief. But on the other hand, if we want a better future, we must carry a heavier burden today. This is the dilemma that we are facing.

The affluent nations, like rich men, can go ahead very quickly because they have large surpluses. The United States is an extremely rich country. So, they can afford to spend a great deal and even waste. Yet there is a large surplus for development. Once a nation is developed, its progress gathers momentum on its own. But a poor country and society are stagnant and it takes time for them to move forward.

India is among the countries which have been stagnant for a long time. Our society and people's outlook have been stagnant too. We have to shake ourselves out of that mire of stagnation. Circumstances help to do so and Gandhiji came in our midst to shake the nation to its core. Things have changed a great deal even in the last ten years since Independence. But the pace of change is bound to be slow initially because, we have remained stagnant for too long. I am trying to point out how India can progress.

As I said just now, India had been stagnant for a long time. Our methods of production had become outdated and we closed our minds to the new developments taking place elsewhere. We have to change with the times in order to progress. The worst of it was that we had become mentally stagnant. Even today you come across a number of people who prefer to live in total mental darkness and ignorance. They behave as though nothing has changed anywhere including India becoming independent. I am amazed that such people are still around.

The communalist organizations are all full of such obscurantist people who have failed to understand what is happening in the world and in India. The Hindu Mahasabha, the Jana Sangh, the Rashtriya Swayamsevak Sangh, etc., belong to the middle ages in their mental outlook. What is to be done? It is difficult even to talk to such people. They are unable to grasp the changes that have taken place. As a result, they say things which have no relevance to problems in India today. They abuse the Government and the Congress constantly for which it is not necessary to be very intelligent. Or they foment discord and tensions in the name of religion. They do not know the first thing about Hinduism. Or, when they find nothing else, they raise the bogie of cow slaughter. We are concerned with solving the problems faced by human beings first, not of monkeys and cows. Is this relevant? Here is a country which has become independent after centuries, confronting great problems, political, economic and social. The eyes of the world are upon us to see how we fare and whether we have the intelligence and strength to solve our problems. India is an independent country. So, everybody, including the most foolish people, are free to abuse and rake up irrelevant issues. If we did not allow them that freedom, there is a danger that the intelligent people may be suppressed by mistake. The only restriction we have imposed is on violence and fissiparousness. Apart from that, everybody enjoys freedom of thought and expression.

In short, we have got freedom after years and years of struggle. Those of you who are very young may not even remember the freedom struggle. You read about it in books and of course, you have heard of Gandhiji, Lokmanya Tilak and other great leaders. Perhaps you also know that the Congress was born 72 years ago, 5 years before I was born. About 28 years before the birth of the Congress, a great rebellion had taken place against the British rule. It was crushed ruthlessly by the British and after that the country lay stunned. It was revived gradually and the Congress was established in 1885. It began as a very small organization of English educated intelligentsia. But they were far-sighted and soon the Congress had become a national party whose doors were open to the people of all provinces, religions and castes. Every Indian, irrespective of whether he lived in the Himalayas, or Punjab, Madras or Rameswaram and whether he was a Hindu, Muslim, Sikh, Christian, Parsee or Buddhist or Jain could join the Congress.

So, you can see that the Congress had a very broad base. Its doors were open to the rich and the poor alike and no distinctions of religion, caste and language were made. The emphasis was on national unity. We were already united by the yoke of foreign rule. Until then, India had been divided into various kingdoms and fiefs. To that extent I would say that even though it meant political bondage, India benefitted by British rule because we were united into one nation for the first time.

The Congress fostered the idea of nationalism further and to the extent it succeeded, and grew in strength. The British Government were concerned at the danger which the growth of the Congress posed. They knew that once the people of India were united their domination could not last long. So, they tried to isolate the Muslims though until then they had been against the Muslims due to the rebellion of 1857. With the growth of the Congress, the British began to throw out lures of special privileges to the Muslims to prevent them from joining the Congress. In spite of this as you know, Muslims flocked to the Congress in large numbers. The British tried to sow the seeds of dissension between the Sikhs and Hindus in Punjab because united, they posed difficulties for the Government. History shows how they succeeded in creating dissensions.

Anyhow the Congress worked for national unity. Then Gandhiji came on the scene and gave a great fillip to nationalism. Under his leadership the Congress spread to every village in India. As you know, Gandhiji was moved by the plight of the poor in India and he lived a life of great austerity. He was convinced that India could progress only when the poor, downtrodden millions were lifted out of the mire of poverty and degradation. He laid special stress on the uplift of the untouchables. In this way Gandhiji fostered national unity by laying special emphasis on removing disparities of wealth and social status. His argument was that we had no right to demand independence so long as three-fourth of the population was downtrodden. If we suppressed our own brethren, the British could suppress us easily. We must, therefore, have the courage to fight for the freedom of the poorest human being in India, for freedom from poverty and degradation, by ensuring equal opportunities for everyone. Gandhiji laid great emphasis on this aspect.

Apart from this, Gandhiji also laid stress on two or three things. One, as you know, he was an apostle of peace and non-violence. Two, he linked two things, conflict with non-violence. The common conception of conflict was to wield the lathi or gun. But Gandhiji's struggle was based on non-violence and love. People found it difficult to understand this in the beginning though his personality exercised a powerful influence on everyone. But gradually, we found that he was not talking in the air but was advocating a very deep and profound philosophy. In fact, we came to realize that there was no alternative before us. One, it was sound on principle. Two, it was the only idea which could truly unite us into one organized movement. Gandhiji's goal was to instil courage and confidence in the people of India. He worked step by step and over thirty years educated millions of Indians. He instilled discipline and taught us to conduct ourselves as soldiers. He gave us the opportunity to hold our heads high at a time when we were crushed and disheartened and full of fear. Even our great leaders were scared when charges of sedition were laid against them. They pleaded not guilty in the courts. It showed fear of speaking the truth. Gandhiji rooted out fear from the hearts of the people and infused a spark of vitality into them. He could not have given a greater gift to a poor and downtrodden nation. He infused a sense of confidence into the poor and enabled them to straighten their bent backs and hold their heads high. He fostered unity among us and organized us into a powerful force which challenged the might of the British Empire. His methods were unique and ultimately the world saw with wonder how he managed to free India in a civilized manner. India set a new example in the history of the world.

Well, India became free, and the chains of bondage were broken at last. But freedom did not make the country affluent. It merely paved the way to progress. It is up to us to utilize the opportunity to the full. Some people had foolishly imagined that now that we were free we could sit back and relax. Freedom has brought new responsibilities. Earlier our only task was to challenge British rule. Now, we have to combat against many things, nothing external but our own weaknesses, our laziness, stupidity, fissiparous tendencies, etc. It is a far more difficult job to uplift ourselves out of the mire of poverty. To put it in one sentence, we have to wage a war against India's poverty and unemployment. It cannot be done by passing laws alone. Laws merely pave the way. Poverty implies lack of essential goods, like food, clothes, houses, etc. Gold and silver are merely for trade. You need money to buy things with. But real wealth consists of essential goods. There is a shortage of essential goods in our country. The United States produces a large amount of goods and so it is extremely affluent. We have to work hard to produce what we need from land and industries as the people in the United States do.

This is the most urgent priority today. We must step up food production as well as other goods from industries. Until we do so we will remain poor. You must also bear in mind that whether we increase production or not, our population continues to increase. The number of mouths to be fed, people to be clothed and housed etc., keeps increasing every year by about fifty lakhs or so. So, it means that we have to find the means of increasing production in every sector, agriculture, industries and other crafts.

If you compare India with other countries, the first thing that strikes you is that the rate of production elsewhere is far more than ours. The average yield per acre of land is twice or thrice as much as it is in India. So, they are much more affluent. I think our average yield per acre is, ten or twelve maunds of wheat while elsewhere it is 20, 25 or more. The reason is that they have adopted modern methods of production like the use of fertilizers, good seeds and ploughs, etc. I am not suggesting that we should start using large tractors everywhere. Even without that, it is possible to increase production through hard work and little improvements. There is a greater degree of industrialization, of course, in other countries. Anyhow, our most urgent priority is to increase production from land so that everyone gets enough to eat. We must go beyond that so that we have a surplus which can be exported and machinery can be brought in lieu of it.

You may remember that we adopted planning six or seven years ago. The First Plan laid stress on increasing agricultural production and arrangements were made to take up big river valley schemes to build dams and ensure regular water supply for irrigation and power generation. Many such schemes have been taken up all over India in Bhakra Nangal, Damodar Valley, Tungabhadra, Mahanadi and elsewhere.

Power is extremely important for us. It is a source of energy which can be used for industrialization. You can gauge the strength of a nation by the amount of power and steel that it produces. You cannot go wrong. Steel and power are absolutely essential for industrialization. The First Plan laid stress on food production and steel and power generation.

Let me tell you one more thing which interests me in particular. How did the West advance so rapidly? The main reason is that those countries took advantage of the new inventions in science and technology. The world has been turned completely topsy-turvy by the new forces which have been discovered. Railways, motorcars, telephones, aeroplanes and a million other things are the result of these new discoveries. Ultimately came the atom bomb. The new sources of energy and technological know-how have contributed to the tremendous increase in wealth in the West. We will remain backward unless we too imbibe the new scientific knowledge and skills. It is not enough to import machinery and set up industries. We must advance on our own and do original research. We have set up huge National Science Laboratories all over the country to impart higher scientific and technical education. The science that is taught in schools and colleges is extremely elementary.

In short, we are trying to lay the foundations of a new India, self-reliant and strong, so that we need not be dependent on anyone for new skills and know-how. We succeeded to a very large extent in achieving our targets during the First Plan. As you know our food production has gone up and our initial difficulties were overcome. Though the problem has not been solved completely even now, the worst is over. The river valley projects and a number of industries are coming up. Once the First Plan ended, we had to think of the Second. In the Second Plan also we have laid stress on increasing food production because it is still an urgent priority. Once we solve that problem, all our other tasks become easy. We can go ahead with industrialization also with the surplus generated by agricultural production.

This is the first thing that you should bear in mind. Secondly, we are laying stress on industries of all types, small, medium and large; village and cottage industries. There is no competition between them. We are trying to produce more steel by setting up huge, steel plants. We want to produce four times the quantity of steel we are producing now within the next five years. Then we want to set up machine building industries. Ancilliary industries will come up all around them. We will not have to import machines and the spare parts from Germany or Japan. This is what is known as laying the foundation of future progress. We cannot progress, until we take these steps. How long can we keep importing machines? We become dependent on others for repairs and spare parts. We cannot become really strong economically and militarily unless we are completely self-reliant. So, we have laid stress on these fundamental issues.

In my opinion that is the only course open to us if we want to build a strong and powerful country. The only problem is that there is no immediate benefit. We have so far invested 150 crores of rupees in Bhakra Nangal. But we will not reap the benefit until it is completed. We have waited eight years already and it may take another two to three years more. The same thing is true of steel plants. It takes five to six years to build and enormous sums of money have to be invested during that time. When we take up huge projects like this, we have to keep pouring in money without getting any quick returns. Later, once the projects are complete, they will benefit millions of people for years to come. Something like Bhakra Nangal will benefit us for centuries.

That is why we have taken up these big projects. It required great courage because the returns are not immediate. It would have been easier for our Government to do something else which would have pleased the public, like reducing taxes. But India would have remained where it was which we could not accept. We must take India rapidly on the path of progress. So, we have adopted this path.

I am not going to tell you about the current Five Year Plan at length because it is a long story. But I want you to read it and understand what we are trying to do. It is not a rigid document which cannot be changed at all. We will change and modify it as we gain more experience. But it sets out broad guidelines of where we wish to go. The urgent priority before us is to increase agricultural production. Wherever we have tried, we have succeeded. We must set up industries wherever possible, small and cottage industries. Otherwise if we put up heavy industries without giving a fillip to small industries, the scales will be tilted and our economic condition will not improve. Therefore, it is extremely important to set up small industries in every village though that does not mean that we should stick to outdated methods of production. We must utilize new technology wherever possible. We have all spun a charkha. Now a new type of charkha called the Ambar Charkha is in the market. It is far more efficient than the old one. Why should we continue to use the old model when we spin four times as much yarn on the new one? If something better than the Ambar Charkha comes into the market, we will adopt that. There should be progress.

What I mean is that we are now engaged in a great war, not against another country but against the poverty in India. To win this war, we have to conduct ourselves like soldiers and march in step. How can we fight a battle if everyone pulls in different directions? Once a decision is taken, we must work hard to implement it. We have to make a multi-pronged attack on poverty by stepping up production from land, industries, village crafts, etc. But it takes time. There is no magic formula to put an end to poverty. People often run to astrologers to find a solution for their problems. But it is of no use. No nation has ever

83

progressed by looking to the stars. We need courage, hard work and pride in ourselves to progress. There are lengthy debates about ideologies and what not. But you can take it from me that no matter what ideology or policy we may decide to adopt, we will have to work hard. You will find that the Americans who are capitalists and Russians who are communists are all extremely hardworking people. The people in the Soviet Union have worked hard incessantly for the last forty years. They have had no breathing space at all. So, hard work is essential whichever path we choose to follow.

I want to draw your attention to the Second Five Year Plan because it is very essential that you should understand what it is all about. Passing laws in Delhi will not solve any problems.

Take Punjab, for instance. There are both good qualities and defects in the Punjab. The people of this state have great vitality and are capable of hard work. The farmers here are intelligent. Industries are coming up rapidly. On the other hand, they are quarrelsome too, and get carried away easily. Well, these things can be kept under control. I feel that the Punjab has a special opportunity to do something spectacular in the field of agriculture and small industries. In fact, there has already been considerable progress. I was amazed and happy too to hear that 27 thousand new units have been established during the last seven to eight years. Most of them have been set up by the refugees from West Punjab.

So, as I said, a nation with vitality will go far. We have great hopes from the Punjab because the people here have great vitality. You must march boldly on and set an example to the others. I have full faith that you will do so provided your attention is caught and your energies are not wasted in futile wrangles and disunity. You must fulfil these two conditions. I am going into small details in order to make you understand what we are trying to do. You must not forget that we are living in a revolutionary age of nuclear weapons and what not. A weak nation is bound to lag behind. Please do not be under the illusion that freedom is forever. At the slightest hint of weakness or complacence freedom can slip away. We must remain constantly vigilant and physically and mentally alert.

I want to mention one thing more which I consider extremely important. In my opinion, the Block Development and National Extension Schemes which are being implemented in the rural areas are revolutionary steps. I am not making an idle boast. I am saying this after considerable thought. A revolution is wrought not by violence but by social change. It is stupid and childish to equate bomb throwing with revolution. I feel that the Community Development Projects are transforming the five lakh villages in India. For a long, long time, India, particularly its villages, had remained stagnant and poor. It is up to us to pull the country out of that mire of poverty. 80% of our population lives in the rural areas. Until they progress, India will remain where it is.

84

The Community Development Schemes were started four and half years ago and within this short time two hundred and twenty thousand villages have been covered. It is a remarkable pace of development. I do not say that the rural areas have been completely transformed. But the seeds of change have been sown to a greater or lesser degree. On the whole change has been rapid and we are finding it difficult to keep pace with their demands. We feel that by the end of the Second Five Year Plan, we would have covered every single village in India. So, these are the various ways in which we are developing.

Above all this, however, there are two or three broad facts to be borne in mind. The most important thing is that all of us are citizens of this great country and in the same boat, whether we live in Madras or Punjab, we sink or sail together as a nation. We cannot progress in parts. Those days are gone. Freedom is for the country as a whole. We must keep the broader picture of the country before us if we wish to progress and foster national unity. If we allow the old vice of disunity and fissiparous tendencies to reign free, ruin is certain. There must be unity in the country, provincial and communal.

There are various provinces and religions in India. But everyone is an Indian whether he is a Hindu, Muslim, Sikh or Christian. All these religions have belonged to India for thousands of years. Christianity came to the shores of India 1900 years ago, before it reached Europe.[3] It was not brought here by the British. There are nearly one crore Christians in India. We must accord equal respect to all religions. Everyone must be free to follow his own religion without hindrance. Interference in another religion is absurd. Communalism and casteism has brought great ruin upon India by dividing the country into small compartments. Casteism is unique to India. Nowhere else in the world is this institution to be found. For centuries, our energies have been frittered away in these useless squabbles and disparities. There is no doubt about it that the caste system must go. Even if it takes time, we have to root out this extremely harmful and wrong institution. We must ensure equality for all the citizens of India and equal opportunities for progress. Then it is upto the individual to go ahead as far as he can. But there should be no lack of opportunity. This is what is known as socialism. There is no rigid code to be followed. But that is the direction in which we wish to go.

3. In the 1st century A.D., Jewish immigrants arrived in Kerala. The Syrian Orthodox Christians believe that St. Thomas, the Apostle, visited Kerala in the same century. The immigrants converted people from among the higher castes of Central Kerala who came to be known as Syrian Christians or Thomas Christians. Later, the Portuguese, who arrived in Kerala in the fifteenth century, introduced the Catholic Church.

The important thing is to do what we have set out to do in a peaceful manner. We are used to bringing about great revolutions in this country quietly without any fuss or violence. We got rid of British rule in that way, brought about the merger of the princely states and abolished the zamindari system immediately after Independence. There is no reason for us not to go ahead with our plans for development in the same way. But at the same time, it is absolutely essential that there must be complete unity in the country. All it requires is a little circumspection and forethought.

As I told you, the Congress has been functioning for the last 72 years. We fought for India's freedom under the banner of the Congress. Above all, it is an institution which stands for national unity. Take the other parties. Most of them are communalist organizations. The Muslim League is no longer powerful in India. But it did considerable harm to the national unity before Independence. The Hindu Mahasabha, Jana Sangh and other parties, like the Muslim League, have no particular economic or political goals. So, they harp on communal issues or of an undivided India and of going to war with Pakistan, etc. What they say is not only meaningless but absolutely wrong for they contain the seeds of fissiparousness. They are fully aware that they cannot do what they claim to. They say such things merely to incite the people. I am amazed that anybody can be so irresponsible as to talk of *Akhand Bharat* or *Hindu Rashtra*. Do they realize the implications of what they are saying? It means going to war with Pakistan which is meaningless. After all, we agreed to the Partition, rightly or wrongly. Taking everything into account, we bought India's freedom by agreeing to the creation of Pakistan. We did not want the tensions to continue. But now that Partition has taken place, we do not wish to interfere in the internal affairs of Pakistan. It only complicates matters and earns a bad name for us in world forums when the Hindu Mahasabha and the Jana Sangh say such irresponsible things. They make things difficult for us. After all, it is we who have to shoulder the burden while they talk in the air. This is not a sign of a responsible party.

What does a Hindu state imply? The Hindus are in a majority in the country and will have every opportunity for progress. But it is stupid to give a religious colouring to a government in this day and age. Pakistan is welcome to such stupidity. We do not accept it. The difficulty is that our comrades in the Hindu Mahasabha and the Jana Sangh are mentally three or four centuries behind the times. They refuse to get out of that rut. What I object to is that almost everything that they say is absurd and calculated to create divisions. Their propaganda is full of abuse. I have heard that they intend putting up a cow as a symbol to tell the people that Jawaharlal believes in cow slaughter. They resort to all kinds of lies to incite the people. After all, there is such a thing as intelligent debate. You cannot solve India's problems by putting up a cow for propaganda. It is really strange that in our country the best brains and every form of stupidity exist side by side.

Well, let us take the issue of cow slaughter. I feel that cows ought to be protected in a country like India. There is no doubt about that. I am not saying this on religious grounds but from the point of view of the welfare of the people and the country. I wonder why the countries, where cows are not worshipped, look after them much better whereas they are left to starve in India? We worship the cows but fail to look after them. It shows that we must look at these problems intelligently and find a solution. Slogans will not solve anything. Proper arrangements must be made to look after our cattle, to improve their breed and protect them well. Without taking these steps it is meaningless to ban cow slaughter for it leaves them in a pitiable condition. I have heard that on the borders of Uttar Pradesh and Punjab hundreds of cows have become wild which is dangerous to human beings. They roam around destroying crops. All this is because cow slaughter has been banned without making proper arrangements to look after the cattle. I am convinced that the people in the Hindu Mahasabha and Jana Sangh are less concerned about the cows and want to use them for vote catching.

These are the problems that we face in India today. It is up to you to decide who should hold the reins of power. These elections are held to ensure people's rule and it is up to the people to choose whom they want to send to the Parliament and the highest posts in Delhi and elsewhere. I am the Prime Minister of India, not because of my birth or something else but because I was elected by the people. The Congress Party won the majority of the seats in Parliament and I was elected as their leader. The President then invited me to form the government as the leader of the majority party. It shows that the people accept the policies of the Congress. If any other party gets the majority of seats in the elections, it will form the government. It is not my hereditary right to remain the Prime Minister. Presently, our President Dr Rajendra Prasad has been elected to this great post by the people's representatives in Parliament. There will be an election of the President after the general elections. Anybody in this land can aspire to these high posts if they have the merit and the qualifications. The doors are open to everyone.

We want people's rule in India, prosperity of the people and to reduce disparity between the haves and the have-nots. But that means a great deal of effort. We can increase our armed might for show. But the real strength of the economy will come by uplifting 37 crores of human beings. Once that is ensured, military might will follow automatically. But it is meaningless for a poor country to keep increasing its defence expenditure because armies cannot make a starving nation really strong. So, we are taking steps to raise the standard of living of the people of our country. But it takes time. I have seen some results in my own life time. Others after me will see more. Progress never comes to a standstill.

So, the question before you is which path you wish to take. I feel that fundamentally we should continue to follow the path shown by Gandhiji, the path of peace, non-violence and unity. Secondly, the path that we have taken in the last ten years is basically the right one. We can make alterations as we go along. Then who is to hold the reins of power? It is obvious that we want people to rule in India. Elections are held for that purpose. But every individual in the country cannot hold the reins. Other arrangements have to be made. The people choose their representatives to be in charge of administering the country. The important thing is not to choose your friends and relatives for it serves no purpose in the long run. We can function well only if you elect a strong organized party at the helm of affairs. We won the freedom struggle because we fought under the banner of an organized force, the Congress Party, which had spread to every village in India. We could have never won if everyone had pulled in different directions. Similarly, we will achieve our goals today only by organizing the people into a strong force. The government derives its strength from the people. I feel that the people have no alternative but to place their faith in the Congress. As far as the communal parties are concerned, they are useless. I do not think they are capable of even handling the administration of a village, let alone the entire nation. They will ruin the country by bringing to the fore all our vices and faults.

I would like to say a few words about independent candidates. I am sure they are good people. But what I cannot understand is how the great wars in the world can be fought by individuals. You need armies to fight and win a war. An independent candidate, however intelligent, cannot do more than making speeches. Take any of the advanced countries of the world. The system of independent candidates has been finished. In England, more than 600 members are elected to Parliament. There are only large political parties putting up candidates who go to the people with definite programmes and policies. The people then vote for the party they like. The Congress has a definite Manifesto and you can vote for the Congress candidate if you accept its policies. Other parties offer their own programmes. But independent candidates do not have very much to offer. So, it is meaningless for candidates to stand as independents. On the other hand, it has dangerous implications because often they tend to project their caste and look for support from other members of the caste. That is absolutely wrong and dangerous. It will break up the country and national unity will suffer. Each caste will look for its own aggrandizement. The entire concept is wrong and we must not allow such pernicious concepts to flourish.

So, at this critical juncture, in both the internal and external situations, it is necessary that we should be strong. We need to think clearly to carry the burden of this great country. I have no doubt in my mind that at the moment it is the Congress alone which is capable of taking on this task successfully. My advice to you is to vote for the Congress candidate. A great leader, Maulana Azad, is contesting the elections from this constituency. He has made a great place for himself in Indian history by playing a major role in India's freedom struggle. It would be an honour for everyone to elect him.

My advice to you would be to vote for all the Congress candidates who are contesting the elections from Punjab. I am happy that the Chief Minister, Sardar Partap Singh Kairon, has already won. It would be a good thing to strengthen his hands by voting other Congress candidates to power. You can imagine what will happen if various splinter groups come to power in Punjab or elsewhere in the country with no party enjoying a majority. There will be constant pushing and pulling and internal wrangling in the absence of a strong party in power. Therefore, I hope that the Congress candidates will be voted back to power in Punjab.

I would like to mention one thing more. We have always laid great stress on unity in the country. There has been some bitterness between the Hindus and Sikhs. As I said, the people of Punjab are easily swayed by emotions and a great deal of heat is generated over petty issues. There was a heated debate going on about where the borders of the PEPSU should be.[4] There had been riots over this. Our friends in the Jana Sangh resorted to stone-throwing when nothing else worked.[5] A committee was set up to make a demand for greater Punjab.[6] Anyhow, I am glad to say that the matter has ended.[7]

Now that the elections are round the corner, we want to make sure that everything should go off smoothly. It does not seem right that parties are formed on communal lines. There have always been great Sikh stalwarts in the Congress. As you know, we had aimed at an amicable settlement after talks with the Akali Dal and Sikh elders.[8] Unfortunately, after everything was settled, Master Tara Singh backed out though he had participated in the talks at every stage. I am

4. See *Selected Works* (second series), Vol. 33, p. 572.
5. See *Selected Works* (second series), Vol. 33, pp. 265, 299, 567 and 569 and Vol. 34, p. 267.
6. See *Selected Works* (second series), Vol. 33, p. 299.
7. On 1 November 1956, the new State of Punjab came into being after the integration of Punjab and PEPSU.
8. On 2 October 1956, the Shiromani Akali Dal's convention of 150 members, presided over by Master Tara Singh, had unanimously decided to join the Congress. For more details, see *Selected Works* (second series), Vol. 35, p. 240.

very unhappy that in his anger he is opposing the Hindu and Sikh candidates put up by the Congress.[9] He has every right to oppose anyone he likes. But it is regrettable that he is not willing to cooperate after all the talks that we have had. After all the Congress does not belong to the Hindus or the Sikhs alone but to the whole of India.

It is really sad that Master Tara Singh is again laying emphasis or the fact that he is opposing those whom he thinks are corrupt and dishonest. We have carefully scrutinized the candidates who are standing and tried our best to select good people. I am not saying that there have been no mistakes at all. But I can say with full confidence that the people whom Master Tara Singh is supporting also bear scrutiny. One of them was dismissed from Government service during British rule on charges of corruption. It is absurd to level charges of corruption at the Congress candidates. I have worked in the Congress for 45 years. It is a huge Party with good and bad elements in it. I do not claim that everyone of them is great. But I do not know of any other party in the world, let alone India, which has consistently made an effort to maintain a high standard. It has been due to Gandhiji's influence, though we seem to have forgotten Gandhiji's teachings.

Well, I have tried to explain some fundamental issues to you. I hope that you will vote for the Congress candidates and eliminate communalist tensions and casteism from Punjab. You have the vitality to go very far. Why should you weaken yourselves by getting bogged down in useless squabbles? You must progress and help India to progress too. *Jai Hind!*

9. At a press conference in Amritsar on 16 February 1956, Master Tara Singh, President, Akali Dal, charged the Congress High Command with breach of faith on four points: (i) he was not consulted at the time of the final preparations of the list of the Congress candidates from Punjab, (ii) merit was disregarded though it was used as a smokescreen, (iii) the Akalis had not been given seats according to their position in the Sikh community as proved in the last general elections and the Gurdwara elections in 1955, and (iv) the High Command had not disclosed to him at any stage during his negotiations that it had given some assurances to Gian Singh Rarewala, former Chief Minister of PEPSU. He also expressed surprise that the High Command refuted his charges of corruption against some Congress nominees and had not given him any opportunity to substantiate them.

10. India Wants Friendship with Pakistan[1]

There has been tension in West Asia. President Eisenhower, who is a great leader and a man of peace, has made certain proposals about the Middle East some time back. Later on another kind of proposals were made by the Soviet Union. It is not my business to criticize or praise any set of proposals. I feel that in both these proposals there are things worthy of consideration. I would like that serious consideration should be given to both the proposals not in the military way but in a peaceful way. If the leaders of the US and the Soviet Union discuss these two sets of proposals, then to some extent at least a way may be found for bringing peace to the Middle Eastern region. If efforts for a negotiated settlement continue, success will be achieved some day or the other. The two Big Powers who are trying to play from far off distances, should start direct negotiations immediately. This is necessary because a war cannot solve any problem. The only way left now is the way of negotiations. I hope that leaders of these two Great Powers will meet some time or the other, even though at the present moment they may be antagonistic to each other. I still hope that something will be done in this regard in the future.

The communal organizations like the Jana Sangh and the Hindu Mahasabha by raising the cry of *Akhand Bharat* are actually harming the cause of India. It is the height of stupidity to raise cries of *Akhand Bharat* which means Pakistan should be reunited with India. Only Pakistan benefits from such cries because it gets a propaganda handle to tell the world that the people of India want to undo Pakistan, after having accepted it. We accepted Pakistan although we were not happy to do so. We accepted it because we wanted to put an end to internecine conflicts which had become a feature of the political life of the country. In fact, this Partition is the price we paid for our freedom. It would have been possible to make the British quit India even without accepting Partition. But in that case this internecine conflict in the country would have been continued. We therefore, had no way out but to accept Partition. It was done with our consent. If now anyone raises a voice against it, it will only harm us.

If by chance Pakistan and India are to become one, the burden on India will increase manifold. It will be difficult to manage new responsibilities and new problems. India's Five Year Plan will be completely upset. India will be pressed

1. Speech at a public meeting, Meerut, 1 March 1957. From *The Hindu*, *National Herald* and *The Tribune*, 2 March 1957.

down under the weight of new burdens. So even from the selfish point of view, it is in India's interest that Pakistan should remain separate. We want Pakistan to be happy and prosperous and to make progress. We want friendship with our neighbouring country.

India has friendship with all countries but with Pakistan our relations have been a bit strained over the Kashmir issue and Canal Waters. But India has placed her point of view very clearly before the world in regard to both these matters and there should be no misunderstanding over this.

I have no doubt that except for some small mistakes India has basically followed the correct policy in regard to Kashmir. Out of her keen wish to come to a settlement with Pakistan through peaceful means, India had made certain proposals. But these proposals were not accepted. Later on, the other side had started saying that these proposals were some kind of commitments. Further, these proposals were subject to certain vital conditions which were not fulfilled. I have no doubt that the people of Kashmir have given their real opinion from their very heart about their future. Elections have been held in Kashmir a few years ago.[2] Elections will again be held in March there.[3] But in the so-called "Azad" Kashmir, there has been no election. Even in the whole of Pakistan there has been no elections. Moreover, Kashmir had made great progress during the last few years which it never had in her entire history. But conditions in one-third of Kashmir which is under Pakistan are miserable. There is great suffering there and there can be no comparison between the two sides.

The recent speeches on Kashmir of the Prime Minister of Pakistan shows that he has a very sharp mind. I do not want to enter into any debate over the points he has raised.[4] But I want to say again clearly that if anyone in Pakistan feels that India has designs on Pakistan, and wishes to attack and invade her, then he is absolutely wrong. Anybody can see what is happening in Pakistan. But we in India are devoting our entire strength and resources towards making the Five

2. In 1951 for Jammu and Kashmir Constituent Assembly.
3. Elections to the Lok Sabha were held on 25 March in Jammu and on 30 March in the Kashmir Valley.
4. Soon after H.S. Suhrawardy became the Prime Minister of Pakistan on 10 September 1956, his pronouncements became more and more strident. In his first policy statement of 12 September, Suhrawardy said: "Come what may we will not fail them (the Kashmiris)." On 2 December in Lahore, he said that neutralism for Pakistan would be "to keep us weak, so that we may not press our claim for Kashmir, so that we may not ask for a fair settlement of the Canal Waters dispute, so that we may not be in a position to settle any dispute with India in accordance with justice and fair play." He also stated openly that the US-Pakistan alliance was useful in dealing with India.

Year Plan a success and carrying out schemes like the Community Projects. Only a mad man can think of war and at the same time think of achieving progress in India. The two do not go together. The people of India will not allow themselves to be swept off their feet either because of anger or provocation or any sense of glory. India has, however, to remain fully prepared in the face of cries of war and jehad in Pakistan. India should not take any wrong step in anger or excitement.

India's policy of non-alignment is the correct policy. If all the countries joined one bloc or the other, then war is bound to come. In such an eventuality, no country will be left to help bring the two blocs together. The situation one year ago showed signs of the world moving towards peace. But during the last few months the position has worsened and nobody knows what may happen.

Without a strong united organization like the Congress, it is not possible to have a stable and effective government. The Communists have a violent approach to things and rely on what had been written in communist text books a hundred years ago. If the policies of the communal parties are accepted, India will be ruined.

There must be real unity in India to tackle big jobs. It is only when the nation can save and have a surplus to invest in big national undertakings, the nation is on the path of progress. If a nation has no surplus and leads a hand-to-mouth existence, she will remain in the morass of poverty. We are in the stage of pulling the people out of this morass and we will succeed provided we work hard in a cooperative united way.

11. No Yielding on Kashmir Issue[1]

The Kashmir question is important enough but more important than this is India's honour. I will challenge all these people who are trying to make out that India is the accused, to show us where we have not stuck to our commitments. I challenge that on the Kashmir question, we have not deviated even by an iota from any pledge or commitment we gave in the past. Mr Jarring is coming here.[2] We will

1. Speech at a public meeting, Kanpur, 4 March 1957. From *The Hindu*, *The Tribune* and *National Herald*, 5 March 1957.
2. Gunnar V. Jarring came to India on 24 March 1957 as the UN representative.

welcome him. But I want to make it quite clear that we are not going to deviate on the Kashmir issue under any threat from Pakistan or any other country.

You know about the US and the UK Resolution on Kashmir, which was vetoed by the Soviet Union.[3] These Powers tried to get the Resolution passed despite India's strong opposition to it. These Powers flouted every point put forward by India and backed a Resolution for sending a UN force to India. All these are pressures on India to deviate from her independent foreign policy. I am not going to sell India's honour and freedom under any pressure from even the mightiest power on earth.

The Pakistani Prime Minister, Suhrawardy in Lahore yesterday, has given certificates and testimonials to both the United States and the United Kingdom for backing Pakistan on Kashmir against India.[4] He has openly declared that this support of the US and the UK to Pakistan was a result of the latter's membership of the Baghdad Military Pact. This is open evidence that the members of the Baghdad Military Pact are siding with Pakistan.

You may remember that a sum of Rs 55 crores was given by India to Pakistan soon after the Partition.[5] At that time talks were going on between the representatives of the two countries over adjustments of certain dues. First, it was thought that this matter should be fully gone into before any payment was made. But ultimately India accepted to give this amount. Then Pakistan had invaded Kashmir which was a new factor to be taken into consideration. It was thought, since Pakistan also had to pay something to India, it was possible that India might not ultimately have to pay this big sum of Rs 55 crores. Further, the invasion of Kashmir was in full swing. Should India give such a big amount of money to the enemy which had attacked her? This was a question looming large in the minds of Indian leaders. We were in a dilemma and our first thought was that we should keep this matter pending because we know that this money would be used against India by Pakistan. But Gandhiji, who was alive then, insisted that once having given our word, we must fulfil it. So, we had to fulfil our pledge whether it was peace or war and we gave this amount of Rs 55 crores to Pakistan. This is our approach, which Gandhiji taught us. I want to tell you how we have stuck to our pledge and our word in the face of the most difficult circumstances. But certain Big Powers have found it convenient to forget all this and other basic facts and are now trying to put India in the wrong. India has stood firmly on every pledge and commitment she made in regard to Kashmir.

3. The Resolution was vetoed on 20 February 1957. For more details about the Resolution see *Selected Works* (second series), Vol. 36, p. 403.
4. See *post*, p. 432.
5. See *Selected Works* (second series), Vol. 4, p. 389 and Vol. 5, p. 7.

I challenge the whole world to show us where we have broken, in the slightest, any pledge that we gave.

It is very strange that on this Kashmir issue, certain Powers did not care to give any thought to the basic facts, like Pakistan's invasion of Kashmir and Kashmir's accession to India. India accepted the UNCIP Resolutions but Pakistan flouted them. Pakistan had violated the ceasefire line and had not removed her troops from Kashmir soil. No reference is made to these basic facts, and all the time efforts are made by certain Powers to put pressure on India, to show that she is in the wrong.

Coming to Suhrawardy's speech again, I do not want to give any special reply to all the "strange things" happening in Pakistan. I also would not like to enter into any argument over all this. But there are certain points in the Pakistan Prime Minister's speech which deserve to be noted. He has given a big certificate and testimonial to the British Government for lining itself behind Pakistan on the Kashmir issue. The testimonial is so blatant that it might have even embarrassed the British Government which is trying to maintain that it is not at all partial on the Kashmir issue but is keeping aloof and not taking sides. The Pakistan Prime Minister gave a similar testimonial to the United States also. Does all this not prove clearly that the people behind the Baghdad Military Pact, whatever its sponsors might have thought of it originally, are siding with Pakistan on the Kashmir issue? We also have to note that a lot of US military aid is flowing into Pakistan. It is because of this that Pakistan is speaking in a stronger voice against India.

The real thing is that certain powers who do not like India's independent foreign policy are trying to put pressure on her to change it. These pressures are being exerted from inside and outside. The idea behind these pressures is that if India does not change her policy of non-alignment, then she should be humiliated.

I find that many people in England and their newspapers have started to speak with the same voice which they used ten to fifteen years ago against India, that is, against the Congress, against our freedom and against our country. For many days, this voice was a little subdued. I do not say that the British Government is doing this but this anti-Indian tirade in Britain which was subdued has now erupted in all its fury. I am amazed to find what these people in Britain are saying and writing something which is obviously an open threat held out to India to change her independent foreign policy.

The unsuccessful attempt made by the "US and the UK" to get a Resolution passed in the Security Council, to send UN troops to India is nothing but a threat to India. But what I also want to tell you is that the sponsors of this Resolution did not reply to even one point raised by Mr Krishna Menon in the Security Council debates on Kashmir. These Powers tried to cover up the basic facts concerning Kashmir and tried to do something which was completely against the UN Charter and international law.

Certain critics of India's foreign policy want India to align herself with one bloc or the other. The Communists support India's foreign policy and maintain that it is not a bad policy, but they want India to come closer to the Soviet bloc. There are others who want India to align herself with the American bloc. This will go against the very foundation of India's foreign policy. Our policy is that we will not align ourselves with any bloc but will try to befriend all countries. If we lean on any one bloc, we will have to depart from our foreign policy. I have no doubt that if we want to retain our freedom, there is no other path for us to follow except the one we are pursuing now. If India deviates even a little from her foreign policy, she would be completely swept away.

The critics of India's foreign policy are also saying that because of it everybody is abusing India over the Kashmir issue. I would like these critics to come out with their own stand on the Kashmir issue. These critics have no other policy to put forward except this that India should come under the shadow of either the Soviet bloc or the American bloc. It should flatter either of the two blocs and seek its military protection. No one says this clearly and openly but this is at the back of their minds. That is why they say that India's independent foreign policy is not good.

At the present delicate juncture it is more than necessary that the people of India should tell the world where they stand. India must speak in a united voice and there must be a strong united party to run the administration effectively. This only the Congress Party can do. As for there being an opposition, there was a strong opposition even in the last Parliament. It was of course, not strong in numbers, but it was an effective opposition. The history of Asian countries, which have recently become free showed how essential it was for a strong party to run the administration and form the Government. Without it democracy cannot function.

The communal parties can only bring ruin to India. The other parties like the Praja Socialists and the Communists have no moorings in India. The Praja Socialists have thrown their principles overboard. The Communists even after the setbacks in Hungary, try to repeat parrot-like the old text book lessons of a hundred years ago.

India must develop the feeling of unity. The people have not been able to imbibe this feeling fully. They are swept away too easily by parochial considerations. The people in India are not yet emotionally integrated or united. This is a great danger and weakness which has to be fought and got over.

The Community Projects will slowly transform the face of the villages of India. This is a silent revolution which is being brought about in rural India.

II. RESULTS AND ANALYSIS

1. To O.V. Alagesan[1]

New Delhi
28 February 1957

My dear Alagesan,[2]

I have your letter of February 26.[3]

I am surprised and distressed to learn that some of your opponents in the election have tried to make political capital out of Ariyalur train disaster[4] and have even issued a poster on this subject. I think, this poster as well as the pamphlets issued on this subject are in very bad taste indeed and no decent person should approve of them. It is absurd to blame you for the Ariyalur train disaster or for your not resigning on that account. You offered your resignation to me at that time but I saw no reason to accept it.

You have all my good wishes for your election and I hope you will win and the voters will not be led away by these unfortunate and regrettable tactics.

This election, as I have laid great stress everywhere I have spoken, should be fought not only by maintaining high standards of propaganda and public utterance

1. JN Collection. Also available in AICC papers.
2. O.V. Alagesan (1911-92); participated in freedom movement; Member, Constituent Assembly and Provisional Parliament; Member, Lok Sabha, 1952-57, 1962-67, and again elected in 1971; Deputy Minister for Transport and Railways, 1952-57; Minister of State for Irrigation and Power, 1962-63, for Mines and Fuel, 1963, and for Petroleum and Chemicals, 1963-66; resigned from the Ministership during the anti-Hindi agitation in Tamil Nadu; India's Ambassador to Ethiopia, 1968-71.
3. Alagesan had written that posters and pamphlets in Tamil on the Ariyalur train accident were being distributed throughout the Madras State by the Dravida Munnetra Kazhagam. Their propaganda was that as Deputy Minister for Railways, Alagesan should have resigned along with Lal Bahadur Shastri after the incident. He also wrote that A. Ramaswami Mudaliar had been telling people privately that Nehru wanted his son A. Krishnaswami to win.
4. On 23 November 1956, 152 passengers were killed and several injured when the Madras-Tuticorin Express fell into a river near Ariyalur, 174 miles from Madras. Lal Bahadur Shastri, Union Railway Minister, accepted moral responsibility for the disaster and resigned on 25 November.

but also should be based on the principles of thé Congress, its past record and policies and programmes for the future. We are, I hope, a mature democracy and principles should be discussed. The Congress stands for certain programmes and principles and we seek suffrage of our countrymen for those principles and programmes.

You may use this letter if you so like.[5]

With all good wishes,

Yours sincerely,
Jawaharlal Nehru

5. Alagesan lost the general seat of the double-member Parliamentary constituency of Chinglepet in Madras State to A. Krishnaswami, an Independent supported by the PSP, by a margin of 1,728 votes.

2. To Barbara Wootton[1]

New Delhi
1 March 1957

Dear Miss Wootton,[2]

Thank you for your letter of the 18th February with which you sent me your articles on India. I have read them with great interest. It was a pleasure to meet you when you came here.

1. JN Collection.
2. Barbara Wootton (1897-1988); created Baroness of Abinger Common, 1958; Lecturer in Economics, Girton College, Cambridge, 1920-22; Research Officer, Trade Union Congress and Labour Party Joint Research Department, 1922-26; Principal, Morley College for Working Men and Women, 1926-27; Director of Studies for Tutorial Classes, University of London, 1927-44; Professor of Social Studies, University of London, 1948-52; Nuffield Research Fellow, Bedford College, University of London, 1952-57; Governor of the BBC, 1950-56; Deputy-Speaker in the House of Lords, 1967; Member, Interdepartmental Committee on the Business of the Criminal Courts, 1958-61, Council on Tribunals, 1961-64, Penal Advisory Council, 1966-79; author of *End Social Inequality, Social Foundations of Wage Policy, Crime and Criminal Law* and *Contemporary Britain*.

98

Our elections are going on and it is premature to say anything definite yet about the result though, broadly speaking, the trends are fairly clear. I must say that I am more and more astonished at the general level of intelligence of our electorate. They are by no means dumb voters. In a vast electorate there are of course all kinds of persons and peculiar difficulties arise because of symbols etc., on the voting boxes. There is some tendency for a voter becoming nervous and putting his paper in the nearest box he can see regardless of the symbol or who he is voting for. I remember a case when a totally unknown person who was one of those opposing me in the last election got a considerable number of votes simply because his box happened to be the first in the row and mine was somewhere further away. Then there are always local pulls or caste influences.

But, taking it all in all, it is really extraordinary what good sense the voters exercise. I am not saying this because of the vote for the Congress. If they do not approve of a person, they vote against him or her regardless of other matters. Generally speaking, one might say that a great majority of voters are in favour of the broad policies of the Congress and vote for it except when there are strong local influences against this or the candidate is persona non grata with the electorate. Thus far our elections have been conducted with decorum. There have been some petty incidents in some odd places chiefly due to the old linguistic province agitation. The Communists have toned down very much in their propaganda and even have many good words to say for the encouragement of private enterprise. They are chiefly relying on some local factors and on the linguistic province agitation which has nothing to do with communism.

Yours sincerely,
Jawaharlal Nehru

99

3. To Vijaya Lakshmi Pandit[1]

Anand Bhavan
Allahabad
12 March 1957

Nan dear,[2]

I came here this morning to perform my civic duty of voting. My vote was in Lal Bahadur's constituency, the city of Allahabad. The voting took only a few minutes. Then I had nothing to do the whole day. There could be no engagement when the whole city was in a state of high excitement about these elections, and almost everyone was engaged in some way or other. Indu was wandering about from polling booth to polling booth and had no time to eat at all. And so, after a long time, I had practically the whole day to myself with nothing very special to do. I slept and wrote some letters.

The polling for the general elections is now practically over all over India.[3] Only West Bengal remains. Polling there will take place in two or three days' time. Also parts of Himachal Pradesh, which are at present inaccessible owing to the winter snows. This will take place some weeks later.

Although polling is over, the actual announcement of results will take another two or three days. On this occasion, we have improved our electoral arrangements since last time, five years ago. But still it is a tremendous burden, and we really have not enough people to do it adequately.[4] Constituencies are huge. In my constituency, that is, largely the rural area of Allahabad District, there are over seven hundred thousand voters, men and women. Unfortunately, harvesting has begun and many peasants did not want to leave their fields. Counting has already taken place in a greater part of my constituency, and this gives me a provisional majority of about one hundred and fifty four thousand. Although voters are more experienced now, still they become nervous in the polling booths and tend to put in their voting papers in the first box, whichever it might be. Thus, one person opposing me, who has no influence at all and has done no work, got

---

1. JN Collection.
2. India's High Commissioner in UK at this time.
3. The polling for the second general elections started on 24 February 1957.
4. For Lok Sabha, the total number of constituencies were 403 at this time which returned 494 members including 91 from double-member constituencies. Elections were also held simultaneously for the 2906 State Assemblies covering 13 states and 4 Union Territories. 220,478 polling stations were set up for a total of 193,652,068 electors who used 3 million ballot boxes to cast their votes.

several thousand votes merely because his box was the first. On the whole, however, the voters exercise their vote intelligently.

It is amazing how these elections shake the whole country up. Apart from the vast number of polling booths, agents, candidates' representatives, there are thousands of workers in each constituency, and cars and especially jeeps rushing about. Even in Allahabad, the number of people working for various candidates is very large indeed. Here there has been a good deal of tension and momentary expectation of trouble. Fortunately, no major incident took place, and the police arrangements were good. Perhaps you will remember Chhunnan Guru,[5] an Allahabad panda, who is quite a gangster type. His brother[6] is a notorious goonda here. Chhunnan Guru is standing on behalf of the PSP and he is a regular terror in his mohalla. He threatens everybody, even the Muslims. He struts about the city with a group of hefty persons with lathis shouting often filthy slogans or some couplets. It may amuse you to know one of his couplets:

हमारे गुरू की क्या पहचान।
हाथ में डंडा मुँह में पान ।।[7]

The PSP candidates here have behaved badly and very vulgarly. They have already lost some of their seats and they may lose all of them.[8]

Indu has not only travelled about all over India, but has spent a good deal of time in Allahabad, and has set up a widespread organization here. This was not so much because of me, but more so because of Lal Bahadur and our other candidates. As I think I have written to you, Radhe Shyam Pathak opposed Lal Bahadur.[9] This was rather fortunate for us because this led to the PSP losing some of their Assembly seats also which they might have got if Lal Bahadur had been returned unopposed.[10]

In another three or four days' time, we shall have ninety per cent of the results, and this will give a clear picture of the States as well as of Parliament. Probably,

---

5. Kalyan Chandra Mohiley *alias* Chhunnan Guru (1900-1968); Praja Socialist Party Member of the UP Legislative Asembly, 1953-68.
6. Kamla Prasad Mohiley *alias* Kunnan Guru (1904-1993); a PSP member at this time.
7. "Our leader is known to carry a stick in his hand, chewing betel leaf."
8. Out of a total of 430 seats in the UP Legislative Assembly, the PSP got 44. In the Lok Sabha, they got 19 seats of which only 4 were from Uttar Pradesh.
9. Lal Bahadur Shastri secured 124,896 votes while R.S. Pathak of PSP got 68,864 votes.
10. PSP won only one Assembly seat from this area, i.e., Allahabad City South, secured by Chhunnan Guru. Congress bagged the Allahabad City North and the adjoining areas of Soraon East, Soraon West and Phulpur.

in Parliament we shall have a very big majority, bigger even than last time, though I am not sure yet. In the states we shall also have majorities everywhere except Kerala, Orissa and possibly Bengal. Kerala is heading for a Communist majority. If so, there would presumably be a Communist Government there. This will be the first occasion anywhere in the world when a Communist Party wins an election through democratic means. Of course, they cannot do very much in the State because the ultimate authority in most matters is with the Centre. Also they have toned down very much, and the programme they have issued is quite moderate. Nevertheless, this is an intriguing development.

Although we shall have substantial majorities in most of the states, quite a number of important Congressmen have been defeated, chiefly for local reasons. You know about C.B. Gupta.[11] Here is a couplet about him, which was heard much in Lucknow:

गली गली में शोर है।
सी.बी. गुप्ता चोर है।।[12]

This couplet has been varied in other places with some other name being put in, for instance, Lal Bahadur's in Allahabad.

Here is another couplet, of the PSP:

ये सरकार निकम्मी है।
इसको हमें बदलनी है।।[13]

I return tomorrow morning to Delhi and stay there. There is no more touring in prospect for me. In Delhi we have now to face a multitude of problems. Within four or five days, Parliament meets and I have to prepare the President's Address. In Parliament there will be discussions on foreign affairs, etc., and Jarring will also be in Delhi.[14]

Then there is the question of a new Government, which is never an easy matter and is peculiarly difficult now. The economic position in India, though not alarming, is giving us a good deal of trouble, especially the tendency of prices to rise. We are very much averse to slowing down our developmental plans of the Second Five Year Plan, but to some extent we are compelled to do so because of the lack of foreign exchange. It may be that we shall speed them

11. C.B. Gupta was Minister of Planning and Health in the UP Government.
12. "It is common knowledge that C.B. Gupta is a thief."
13. "This government is inefficient, we have to change it."
14. Gunnar V. Jarring, the UN Representative, held discussions in Delhi from 24 to 28 March and 6 to 9 April 1957, on the Kashmir issue.

up later if circumstances are more favourable. All this involves hard and continuous thinking and work. To begin with, Parliament, the new Ministers and the State Governments will have to settle down after these elections.

Then there is Kashmir, of course. I never cease to wonder at the indecency and vulgarity that emanates from Pakistan. Feroz Khan Noon issues some kind of a threat almost every day, saying that there must be a plebiscite or war.[15] It passes my comprehension how any decent Government can support this kind of thing. The wise gather at the SEATO meeting and Menzies is reported to have said that SEATO should guarantee a thousand years of peace.[16] Really, how people go mad. You remember Hitler saying that the Nazi regime has come for a thousand years.

Hansen, the Danish Prime Minister, spent three days in Delhi.[17] He was greatly pleased with his welcome there, apparently also with me. He seemed to think that he had found a kindred spirit in me, and paid me a compliment which, from his point of view, was a very high one. He said that he felt quite at home with me as I was like a Scandinavian, Scandinavia, of course, representing the height of culture and civilization and restrained behaviour. That may be so, but you will see that vulgarity and loud shouting and lies, such as Pakistan indulges in, seem to affect many people.

After many long years I am going to a dinner tonight given in my honour by all the lawyers attached to the High Court.

When voting finished today, large numbers of our Congress workers turned up at Anand Bhavan, including many women. Indu has especially shaken up the women and every Muslim woman came out. Indu has indeed grown and matured very greatly during the last year and especially during these elections. She worked with effect all over India but her special field was Allahabad City and District which she organized like a general preparing for battle. She is quite a heroine in Allahabad now and particularly with the women. Hardly eating and often carrying on with a handful of peanuts and a banana, she has been constantly on the

---

15. At a public meeting in Lahore on 11 March, Pakistan's Foreign Minister, Feroz Khan Noon, said that the alternative to plebiscite in Kashmir was "war between India and Pakistan with India in the Communist camp." He declared that Pakistan would accept nothing short of plebiscite as a solution of the Kashmir problem even if it had to wait for a few more years. He also said: "People in Kashmir can act like those of Cyprus who are fighting for freedom from British rule with bombs. But they (the Kashmiris) are waiting for the UN to decide first. We cannot say what will happen if the UN fails."

16. Opening the third session of the SEATO Council in Canberra on 11 March, the Australian Prime Minister, R.G. Menzies, said that it would be a great triumph if it ushered in a period of 1,000 years of peace.

17. H.C. Hansen arrived in Delhi on 7 March on a three-day goodwill visit.

move, returning at midnight, flushed, slightly gaunt but full of spirit and with flashing eyes.

Love,

Yours,
Jawahar

4. To M.C. Chagla[1]

New Delhi
13 March 1957

My dear Chagla,[2]

Thank you for your letter of the 12th March.[3] I quite agree with you. I think the general elections in India have demonstrated the success of this democratic experiment on a vast scale. Further they have shown that the people exercise this right on the whole as they want to and are not to be pushed in any direction against their will.

Yours sincerely,
Jawaharlal Nehru

---

1. M.C. Chagla Papers, NMML. Also available in JN Collection.
2. Chief Justice of Bombay High Court.
3. Chagla wrote that he felt proud to belong to a country where "democracy functions so effectively and efficiently. I only wish we had invited observers from all over the world to see what free elections really mean and how every voter was free to exercise his democratic choice.." He referred to the Kashmir issue and stated: "when people spoke glibly, almost dishonestly—at the Security Council of our denying Kashmir the right of free choice, they forgot that they were speaking of the largest democracy in the world where democratic processes are a reality and not a sham."

5. To Vijaya Lakshmi Pandit[1]

New Delhi
17 March 1957

Nan dear,

I wrote to you from Allahabad. On my return I received your letter of the 9th March.[2] I shall bear in mind what you have written. But at the present moment, everything is in a rather fluid condition and I do not know how many things will shape themselves.

The polling in the general elections is over all over India, except in Himachal Pradesh, where it cannot take place till the snows melt. But in many places where polling has taken place, the counting of votes has not been done. They are taking an unnecessarily long time over it. It has taken longer than I thought and probably we shall not have the final figures for another week or so. There have been so many surprises in these elections that one hesitates to take anything for granted. One thing is certain that the new Parliament will have a very large number of new faces.

In Maharashtra proper and in a good part of Gujarat, Congress has been very badly beaten by a mixed crowd on the states reorganization question.[3] Maharashtra has come as a great surprise because we thought that the big

---

1. JN Collection.
2. Vijaya Lakshmi Pandit had enclosed a report from *Daily Telegraph* dated 5 March 1957 about the discontent among the staff of the Indian High Commission in London. She wrote that the locally-recruited staff in the High Commission had been paid the British Civil Service scales since 1947 including the occasional pay awards or increases given by the UK Government to British Civil Service officers mainly for increased cost of living. However, the pay awards in 1955 had been withheld by the Indian Government despite the High Commissioner's recommendations to the contrary. The dissatisfaction of the local staff had assumed alarming proportions since the last pay award was announced in 1957. Vijaya Lakshmi also considered reducing the staff.
3. Out of 66 Lok Sabha seats from Bombay, Congress won only 38. In the 396-member Bombay State Legislative Assembly, it secured 234 seats, PSP 36, Communists 13, Jana Sangh 4, Independents and others 109. Owing to discontent against the administration, State Government's handling of the situation during the agitation for Samyukta Maharashtra, especially firing and the like incidents, caused a deep undercurrent of resentment through Maharashtra which went against the Congress. Gujarat denounced the decision for a bilingual Bombay State as an affront to democracy where the people were not taken into confidence about the decision.

bilingual State of Bombay was by and large acceptable to them. There has been a wave of excitement or passion if you like, which has carried everything before it. In reality it is not the provincial arrangements that have mattered so much, but the firings and the deaths due to them. Election propaganda in these areas has been largely confined to gruesome posters about these firings and people's deaths. In some of them, poor Morarji Desai has been shown firing or bayoneting some people. I suppose this wave of passion will pass, but for the moment it has done a good deal of harm.

Among our Central Ministers who have been defeated are Khandubhai Desai, the Labour Minister, Shri H.V. Pataskar, Minister for Legal Affairs, Alagesan, Deputy Minister for Railways, Maragatham Chandrasekhar,[4] Deputy Minister for Health, and Bhonsle, Deputy Minister for Rehabilitation. They are all good people and I am sorry to lose them, more especially Maragatham, who has done very well. She is modest, capable and very well behaved.

Kerala will probably have a Communist Government.[5] Perhaps it is as well to have this experiment. Apart from Kerala and these linguistic parties in Maharashtra and Gujarat, the Communists have not done well. In Orissa, the parties are evenly balanced, that is the Congress and the ex-Rulers' Party, the Ganatantra Parishad.[6]

Among the good results have been the defeat of N.C. Chatterjee and H.V. Kamath. Raja Mahendra Pratap, the mad man of Brindaban, has been returned to the Lok Sabha. It is evident that the Lok Sabha is going to be an exciting place in the future.

In Allahabad we won all the seats except unfortunately one of the Assembly seats in the City which Chhunnan Guru, the goonda type, won for the PSP.[7]

This electioneering business has been a very hard one for many of our candidates. If anybody thinks that the Congress has an easy time, they are very much mistaken. Feroze returned this morning after two months of continuous and intensive electioneering in his constituency of Rae Bareli. We do not know

4. Maragatham Chandrasekhar (b. 1917); Member, Lok Sabha, 1952-57, 1962-67; Union Deputy Minister, for Health, 1952-57, for Home Affairs, 1962-64, for Social Welfare, 1964-67; Member, Rajya Sabha, 1970-84; General Secretary, AICC, 1972.
5. In the 126-member Legislative Assembly in Kerala, Communists secured 60 seats, Congress 43, PSP 9, Independents 6 and others 8.
6. Congress won 56 seats in the 140-member Orissa Legislative Assembly and Ganatantra Parishad secured 51 seats.
7. Kalyan Chandra Mohiley alias Chhunnan Guru of PSP secured 21,600 votes while Baijnath Kapoor of Congress won 19,584.

the result yet.[8] I am afraid the standards have not been good. I do not say that Congressmen had behaved, but on the whole they had behaved better than the others. To some extent, the Communists have not behaved very badly. But the PSP and the Lohia Socialist Party have been the worst offenders in this respect. Do you know that Lohia, in the first number of a magazine[9] he brings out, wrote about us that our grandfather was a peon in Delhi and our father a junior vakil. Of course this has done him no good. In an address to Law College students in Hyderabad, he said that some people feel completely frustrated because the Congress is a strong monolithic party and cannot be defeated, so long as Jawaharlal is alive. Therefore, they wait for his death. Lohia dissociated himself from this view and said something to this effect that this will not be good enough. We must kick him out while he is alive.

Even Indu has not been spared and some highly objectionable things were said about her by the PSP candidates.

After putting up with this kind of personal mud-slinging for some time, chiefly about him, Feroze decided to retaliate and he told his supporters that if any such personal aspersion was made, they should give a beating to the man who makes it. So, there were a number of petty rows and I believe some complaints have been filed with the police.

Tomorrow the old Parliament is meeting in its last session which will last probably about ten days. Many of those people who will come tomorrow will fade out from Parliament. I am in a rather peculiar position because a new Government will have to be formed after the elections. This Government cannot be formed of course till all the elections are over and the majority party has elected a Leader.

I am sorry to read in your letter about the attacks being made on Dickie and Edwina. Unfortunately both of them, and chiefly Dickie, have not been dealt with very kindly in some of the Indian newspapers. Dickie is accused of having led us astray in the Kashmir issue in the earlier stages and about Edwina some of the Communist papers say that she comes here at a moment of crisis to put wrong pressures upon me. I suppose one has to put up with this kind of thing.

Malcolm MacDonald[10] arrived this evening. I have not seen him, but he sent

8. Feroze Gandhi secured 162,595 votes for the general seat from Rae Bareli defeating his nearest rival Nand Kishore, an Independent, who got 133,342 votes. The reserved seat from this double-constituency also went to the Congress candidate Baij Nath Kureel.
9. Rammanohar Lohia edited *Mankind*, an organ of the Socialist Party. It was started in August 1956 from Hyderabad.
10. Malcolm MacDonald was the British High Commissioner in India.

me two letters he had brought from Dickie and Edwina. I enclose a copy of Dickie's letter which might interest you.[11]

Suhrawardy, Feroz Khan Noon and his crowd continue to behave like the gangsters they are. It is really difficult to know how to deal with people of this type.

The Prime Minister of Poland arrived here today. He is going tomorrow to Burma and other countries and returning later for a longer stay.[12]

Love,

Yours,
Jawahar

11. Mountbatten wrote about MacDonald's efforts to improve an appreciation of India's case in the UN. MacDonald saw the British Prime Minister twice; appeared to have a real success in the Commonwealth Relations Office; addressed sixty Conservative MPs in the House of Commons, who had a complete misconception of the situation but were completely sympathetic by the end of the meeting; addressed another eighty Members of all parties with equally strong results; saw most influential editors etc. Mountbatten wrote that this marked a turning point to the good after so many terrible misunderstandings and friction. He also wrote that the UK was going through an awful time in recasting the armed forces as a result of their financial crisis but felt confident that they would somehow keep their head above water.

12. Josef Cyrankiewicz, the Polish Prime Minister, returned to India on 24 March for a ten-day visit. He led a high-level official delegation to Asia.

6. A Review of Election Results[1]

The Congress reverses in Maharashtra and Gujarat are mainly influenced by emotionalism and linguistic feelings. These reverses should not be treated as "shocks". We should treat them as factors which should goad us to work still harder and win the confidence of the masses. The greatest danger to the Congress Party which has emerged victorious in the elections is too many successes which

1. Address to the outgoing Congress Parliamentary Party, New Delhi, 18 March 1957, *The Hindu*, 19 March 1957.

108

make them complacent. It is from that point of view that we want you not to treat the Congress reverses in Maharashtra and Gujarat as "shocks". The importance of elections in these two regions where the Congress has suffered serious setbacks should not be ignored. I feel that what has happened there is a temporary phase.

The Second Five Year Plan and other developmental works represent the dynamic aspect of the Congress and the Government and stress should be laid on them and not on election reverses in Maharashtra and Gujarat.

The large majority of the electorate has sided with the Congress. That is a clear indication that the Congress is still a very strong and united body functioning effectively. It is, however, essential that in the interest of the country the Congress should function still more effectively and tackle all the problems boldly and in a dynamic way. It should effectively guard against fissiparous and separatist tendencies. Any party or Government which cease to be effective and dynamic will ultimately pass away. The Congress, therefore, must have a dynamic approach to all problems.

Parliament and the State Assemblies are not the only forums for doing public work. The services of those defeated at the polls can be utilized in several other important fields. Those who have not been returned should, therefore, have no cause for frustration and disillusionment. They should engage themselves in other development activities and should not think that their services are not required by the country.

The two-nation theory had been rejected long ago. Communalism of every type should be deprecated. This malady was given birth to by the Muslim League in the old days. So long the evils of communalism, casteism and parochialism continue, the country's progress will suffer. Congressmen should put up an effective fight against these. The elections have amply demonstrated that a large majority of the people are not in favour of parties which are trying to perpetuate these evils.

The world situation has recently deteriorated. A foreign affairs debate will be held before the end of the current session of Parliament.

Political upheavals in some countries are the result of non-existence of strong and stable political parties. It is, therefore, all the more essential that the Congress organization should become stronger and more stable and capable of effectively shouldering the big task facing the country. Congressmen should remember that the Congress is not a mere Party, it represent much more than a Party.

7. To V.V. Giri[1]

New Delhi
20 March 1957

My dear Giri,[2]

Thank you for your letter of the 19th March.[3] I was surprised and distressed to learn of your defeat at the elections.[4] I have no doubt that what you say in your letter is correct, that is, many votes go inadvertently to the first box.[5] In my own election, both five years ago and now, the first box belonged to a person who was almost wholly unknown and who did not try at all to canvass. Nevertheless, he got many thousands of votes. It is clear to me that they were put in there simply because it was the first box.

Your second point is also valid.[6] The general seat and the reserved seat boxes should be kept separately. In this present election, there were 32,000 invalid votes in my box, that is, votes which really should have been put in the reserved seat box. As a matter of fact, this made no difference and both the Congress

1. File No. 16(11)/57-PMS. Also available in JN Collection.
2. Giri contested for a Lok Sabha seat from Parvathipuram double-constituency in Andhra Pradesh as a general candidate.
3. Giri had written that he was defeated in spite of winning 7,000 votes more than the candidate for the general seat, owing to certain technicalities in declaring results for double-member constituencies. He enclosed his letter to G.B. Pant of 19 March that contained suggestions for preventing certain anomalies in the system.
4. From Parvathipuram constituency, B. Satyanarayan (ST) of Congress and Dippala Suri Dora (ST), an Independent, were elected with 126,792 and 124,604 votes respectively. The remaining two contestants—V.V. Giri of Congress and Vasireddy Krishnamurthy Naidu, an Independent—secured 124,039 and 118,968 votes respectively.
5. Giri wanted that the result of the general seat should be confined to the general seat candidates only. Thus the success of a candidate for the general seat was not to be affected by the votes secured by the reserved seat candidate.
6. Giri suggested that separate boxes for the general and reserved seats be placed in separate enclosures and the voter be asked to go to both enclosures for casting vote. Alternatively, the general seat boxes were to be placed on one table and the reserved seat boxes on the other.

candidates got in,[7] but I know this kind of thing happened in many cases and sometimes to our great disadvantage.

Yours very sincerely,
Jawaharlal Nehru

7. Nehru was elected on 14 March 1957 from the Phulpur double-member Parliamentary constituency of Uttar Pradesh by a majority of 193,119 votes. He secured 227,448 votes, while his opponents for the general seat lost their deposits. Nehru's running mate for the reserved seat from Phulpur, Masuriya Din (SC), also won by 137,108 votes.

8. To U Nu[1]

New Delhi
20 March 1957

My dear U Nu,[2]

A letter from you is not only always welcome, but gives much pleasure, and so I am happy to receive your letter of the 18th March, although it is a brief one.[3]

I am glad that you have taken charge of the Premiership again. I well realize that these burdens are heavy. But, sometimes, one cannot escape them.

Our elections are not completely over yet. It is clear, however, that we shall have a substantial majority in our Parliament and in a number of our States.[4] In

1. JN Collection.
2. Prime Minister of Myanmar.
3. U Nu had written that he had resumed his duties as Prime Minister from 1 March at the request of his colleagues. He had earlier relinquished the position after winning the elections of 27 April 1956 to deal with various organizational problems of his party, AFPFL. U Nu also congratulated Nehru on the "high success that the Congress Party has achieved."
4. The Congress Party won 371 seats in the 494-member Lok Sabha and a clear majority in 11 of the 13 State Assemblies. Owing to adverse weather conditions, voting was postponed in Himachal Pradesh for four seats. Six members from Kashmir were to be elected indirectly by the Jammu and Kashmir State Assembly for which elections were due in March-April.

111

one State, Orissa, we are rather weak, although ours will be the largest Party. The other big party consists of ex-rulers of petty States. These areas are very backward and the old rulers have still a good deal of influence.[5]

The most interesting development, however, is in the far South of India, in the small State of Kerala. There, the Communists appear to be getting a clear majority and, thus, will form the State Government.[6] This is a significant and rather unique event, because nowhere else in the world has any Communist Government been formed as a result of democratic elections. Of course, the State Government is very much under the control of the Central Government, and cannot go too far away from our broad policies. The Communist leaders in Kerala have declared that they will follow the Constitution strictly and all that. Probably, they will function, to begin with, moderately so as to gain goodwill. But, obviously, one never knows what kind of intrigues they might be up to. Kerala is, from the point of view of literacy, the most advanced area in India. I think the average literacy is somewhere between seventy and seventy-five per cent. It is also an area where there is a very considerable Christian population, dating back to the first century. They are mostly Roman Catholics or Syrian Christians, both rather orthodox. In spite of this, Kerala has gone Communist. I suppose, partly at least, the fault is ours, that is, of our local organization which became unpopular.[7]

We have lost a number of seats on the issue of reorganization of states. This issue has nothing to do with our international or domestic policy. But, it excited people, and we have suffered because of that. The Communists cleverly exploited the situation and profited by it. This is so especially in the Bombay State. Even so, we have a fair majority there.[8]

---

5. The Ganatantra Parishad, led by former Maharaja of Patna, R.N. Singhdeo, was formed in 1950. Described as a party of "right-wing feudalists with a left-wing programme", the Parishad won 51 seats in the Orissa Assembly.
6. In the 126-member Legislative Assembly, the Communists won 60 seats and five out of six Independents supported them. This gave them a clear majority. The President's rule ended in Kerala when a Ministry headed by E.M.S. Namboodiripad was sworn in on 5 April. This was described as the formation of "the first Communist Government in the world through the ballot box."
7. Various factors contributed to the defeat of the Congress in Kerala, such as widespread unemployment especially among the educated, transfer of territories between Tamilnadu and Kerala under the States Reorganization Act, incomplete agrarian reforms, frequent change of Ministries and subsequent imposition of the President's rule in March 1956, and dissension in the Congress organization.
8. Although the Congress secured an absolute majority by winning 234 seats in the 396-member Bombay Legislative Assembly, it suffered serious reverses on the linguistic issue, both in Maharashtra and Gujarat. Five Ministers lost their seats as the Opposition parties jointly fought the elections against the union of these areas in a bilingual state.

In the other States, we are likely to have fairly good majorities. But, the opposition parties have grown in strength. They are a mixed lot. We shall have plenty of difficulties in the future.

Two or three days ago, I came across a rather extraordinary document. This was reproduced in the *Pakistan Times,* a daily newspaper of Lahore, from some German paper. It is said to be a letter from Nelson Rockefeller[9] to President Eisenhower.[10] In the German newspaper, a photostatic copy of a part of the original text had been reproduced. I think the letter is genuine.[11]

As it might interest you, I am sending you a copy of this, taken from the *Pakistan Times*. The enunciation of American policy is very significant. Nelson Rockefeller was till recently specially attached to the President.

I shall give your message to Indira.[12] During our elections, she worked terribly hard and travelled all over India. I was very anxious about her health, as this is seldom satisfactory. But she ignored my advice and astonished everybody by her vigour and hard work. I think that she helped us in the elections more than almost anyone else. She has now gone to the Kashmir State because elections are going to be held there in about a week's time.

With all good wishes,

Yours sincerely,
Jawaharlal Nehru

9. Nelson Aldrich Rockefeller (1908-79); American public servant, oil magnate and politician; Coordinator, Inter-American Affairs and member, National Foreign Intelligence Advisory Board; 1940-41, 1969-74; Under Secretary of Health, Education and Welfare, 1953-54; Director, Rockefeller Center Inc., 1931-58; Chairman, President's Advisory Committee on Government Organization, 1953-58; Special Assistant to the President, 1954-56; Governor of New York State, 1959-73; Vice President of USA, 1974-77.

10. *Pakistan Times* published a confidential letter from Rockefeller, Special Assistant to the US President on cold war strategy and foreign policy till the end of 1956, to Eisenhower. Rockefeller criticized the US policy in Asia of building up military alliances and proposed that the US aid policy should be global and total i.e., covering all the parts of the world and combining political, psychological, economic, military and special methods into an integral unit. This meant utilizing all possibilities for one purpose. He cited the example of Iran where economic aid was used for accessing Iranian oil. He wrote: "We are now well established in the economy of that country. The strengthening of our economic position in Iran has enabled us to acquire control over her entire foreign policy and in particular to make her join Baghdad Pact."

11. A Berlin newspaper, *Neues Deutschland*, published his letter with the photostatic copy, which was reproduced in the *Pakistan Times*.

12. Maung Nu had promised to write to Indira Gandhi about Buddhism but was not able to do so.

9. An Introspection[1]

What has happened in Maharashtra and parts of Gujarat, I attach great importance to that than what has happened in Kerala. It is not merely a defeat in the election but the violent outburst of hostility, emotional bitterness, anger etc., that has to be taken serious note of. You may rightly condemn the people who displayed inciting posters. But the point is that an atmosphere has been created which enable them to do it. Some people do it, but that means the public was with them.[2]

2. We have talked about sabotage and the rest. Maybe, that may be there. We should take that into consideration also. But the basic fact is that all these things grow when respect for the Congress goes or lessens greatly or something happens. I have heard the President or just somebody saying something about administrative failings.[3] But unless it is stated definitely, in particular context, I do not think it has too much value. But it is evident that something has happened and something has happened remarkably rapidly. We have failed somewhere. The Governments, Central or local, may have failed; the PCCs and the Working Committee may have failed. In fact it is the failure that is writ large. We should examine our failures than to think so much of the mischief the other parties did. It is our failure. Unless we had completely failed, they would not have done. It is not a passing phase. We should change our approach to the problem. But it is something deep-seated, slowly growing which we should have met and it is likely too, unless some miracle happens, to petrify itself into violent hostilities to the Congress. It is something more than political differences of opinions. It is something frightening, the way we have become hated by the vast number of people. Maybe they do not question us, but the point is whether we are hated as an organization or as an individual or the Government, more especially in

1. Remarks at the Congress Working Committee Meeting, New Delhi, 23 March 1957. U.N. Dhebar Papers, NMML.
2. According to the assessment of the Party spokesman, the reverses in Maharashtra were ascribed to the opposition's ability to play not only upon the linguistic sentiments but also on the people's emotions against the frequent police firings during the linguistic agitation in Bombay. The opposition parties distributed in Maharashtra the photographs of victims of police firings.
3. After the announcement of the States Reorganization Commission's Report on 30 September 1955, Bombay city and other areas witnessed mob violence, large-scale riots and arson. Mass resignations were sent by local bodies.

Maharashtra or Gujarat. We should deal with this question along with Gujarat. Where we have erred, have we discussed that? How are we going to put it right? That thing may happen anywhere in India. This could only happen when we have lost roots. We are subsisting on artificial things. It is a grave situation. It is the peasantry which support us and not the intelligentsia. We have lost the intelligentsia. All that class we have lost and ultimately it is that class which affect the lower strata. We have in Maharashtra very strong groups opposed to Congress. What has happened to give them that power? My impression is that it is essentially the firing that did it and secondly, it is the refusal to enquire into that firing. The refusal may be justified[4] but we lose the living touch with the human hearts. I do not rule out firing. But I do feel that the consequences of firing are so bad that it is under the gravest and the most serious provocation that it can be resorted to. The situation may arise which may lead to firing. But it should be dealt with long before we reach that stage. Secondly, I would say, where there is firing, there should be a proper enquiry. Normally, I would not do that. But the whole background goes against us. Also there is a tendency in us of a certain complacency to accept the things as they are.

3. That is one major thing. All the organizations in the world would meet the situation like this. We should look at this broad picture. Normally, parties function on the political or economic levels. They fight elections. In both the points, whether domestic or international policies, we can see that there has been an overwhelming support in the country for our policies, say Five Year Plan, Community Projects and others. But the people may be annoyed because they want to get over their suffering. It is impossible to give relief immediately. We cannot change by magic. We have deliberately taken up certain fundamental planning which will get us results later or you do not progress at all. That gives some general discontent. But I am convinced that if you take your people into confidence, they understand. They are reasonable people. But they will only question if they have faith. The moment that faith goes, they do not listen.

4. So everything that has been suggested about the administration and organization are good and can be dealt with as far as we can. But there is something which overthrows everything. This thing is quite new and it can spread all over India.

5. Another thing—take for instance Kerala. The biggest problem is that the Communists will do things which will become examples for others because they will want to justify themselves. Another thing in Kerala is the defeat and a

---

4. Nehru's view on judicial enquiry into these disturbances was that it would lead to charges and counter-charges, tension and bitterness. See *Selected Works* (second series), Vol. 32, pp. 186-187, and 202.

very positive defeat for the Congress.[5] This defeat, I think, we should not have earned and there is no doubt about it that it is the defeat of local Congressmen. They are grossly unpopular there. The people in Kerala are angry with local Congress leaders and we are getting reports that resentment has taken place because of local leaders. Kerala newspapers (32 dailies in number)—the kinds of headlines they give is amusing—accusing all the time Congress for failures, corruption and all that. There must be some way of checking or proving what is going wrong. I am quite sure that in Kerala we should never lose. Either we have lost them because of wrong candidates being chosen or because of the general feeling against the local Congress.

6. There is a limit to the discipline. Discipline comes in either through emotional adjustment through the organization or fear of consequences. In other words, discipline does not take you further when you talk of discipline again and again.

7. Take other cases. Some people, important and prominent leaders have lost. I have examined their cases. For instance, in Lucknow, there was jubilation all round the city when one of the most prominent leaders of the Government and the Congress lost heavily.[6] Indeed, it is a defeat of the person. UP students have celebrated his defeat in London. Congressmen have lost simply because there is public resentment against them. They function too much as bosses. They wanted to keep down the people who joined their group or such things. There is no doubt about it that there is a public feeling against certain important Congressmen who were defeated in Bihar too.[7]

8. Whenever serious charges are made against Ministers or Congressmen, if these are not promptly enquired into and you do not create an impression in the public that you deal fairly with any charge made, then it does tremendous harm to the Government and the people. It is a very difficult matter, no doubt. But the fact is that it is carried on for months and years. For instance, in the Punjab there was a Ministry headed by Dr Gopichand Bhargava and the Working Committee asked him to resign. He resigned and the Congress prestige went up and we won.[8] Election has been a demonstration of how people do not like bosses, however big they may be. Now, we have been functioning because of the prestige

---

5. Intensive work done by the Communists, the anxiety of the people to have a stable government and shortcomings of the local organization of Congress were cited as reasons for the Communists' victory in Kerala.

6. C.B. Gupta lost his seat to Triloki Singh, General Secretary of the PSP, by 11,000 votes in a Lucknow constituency.

7. Three ministers of Bihar Government, Mahesh Prasad Sinha, K.B. Sahay and A.Q. Ansari, were unseated.

8. In June 1951. For details, see Selected Works (second series), Vol. 16 Pt. I, pp. 296-307.

of the Congress organization, because of Gandhiji's freedom struggle. But we have lost our roots and we are losing rapidly.

9. I think the less money we have, the better we can function. My experience is that money is a disadvantage both in the elections and to the man. Money is important in every organization but it is the least of the thing. We are in an amorphous organization. The fact is that money or membership, all kinds of people pay lip service to these things and who do not do anything than personal advancement. All our old records have got to be forgotten. The first thing is to think of this. Matters will not settle down and they would not settle down because they want the people to keep at the boiling point. Apart from all these things, all these problems are psychological. You cannot treat a man except by some soothing treatment, a friendly approach. Hostility increases hostility. Nobody can deal with it when the whole India thinks like that. It is the indirect approach that works in war. It is only a foolish General who bangs his head against another or in the course, the indirect approach which does not appear to be in conflict can so undermine deficiencies that have arisen. Take for instance, Maharashtra or Gujarat. I am not thinking in terms of political changes. It is important that we should have dealt with the emotional approach and not merely denouncing and cursing. We have lost the human touch. In politics human touch is more important than anything else. I want you to appreciate this point. There must be an attempt at friendliness and you must realize that you have the pot boiling. It is always dangerous to appraise the situation according to your wishful thinking. It is fundamentally a wrong analysis of the picture. Analysis should be correct and whatever steps you take should be in terms of that analysis and then it may possibly improve. But let us at least face it in a way thinking that we are on the right path to deal with it.

10. One thing more about UP. In certain parts of UP and Bihar, the Muslims in a body voted against the Congress, even against the Muslim candidate. Nevertheless, I saw that quite a large number of Muslims in UP have actually got an idea that the Government is against them. Urdu language was the simplest thing to deal with the whole thing. There are certain basic causes functioning. People expect big things to happen when the Government changes. So, all these are causes that function. They can be faced in a changed way.

11. Sabotage is of various types. They can be dealt with in a disciplined manner. But sabotage occurs when there is no fear of consequences. When a person thinks that he is not afraid of any action, then the sabotage takes place. True, you deal with it as best as you can. No organization in the wide world takes so much care about the candidates as we did. Nevertheless, we did, no doubt, a large number of mistakes and I think that we have to consider the local facts. Local administration is no good at all. The candidate chosen must essentially

be a person agreeable to the local area. It is really the Provincial Congress Committee which get its way and the PCC is the worst. There should be more proper recommendations.

10. Election Results in Kerala[1]

Jawaharlal Nehru: The results of elections in Kerala represent discontent with local matters, and local irritations, and not so much a positive support to Communism. I do not think the election results have anything to do with broad policies—economic, political or international.

Since this is the first time Communists have come to power through the ballot box, it may have some effect on International Communism.

Question: Mr Bevan[2] said if the Kerala Communists were to work out parliamentary democracy, theirs would be a Socialist Government with a Communist label and not a Communist Government. What do you think?

JN: You can give any name, but according to the declaration of the Communist Party itself about their functioning within the Constitutional framework, it can hardly be a pure Communist Government. It is not communism that is functioning there.

Q: There is markedly less radicalism in the States than at the Centre. Is it possible that the Kerala results can fill the gap.

JN: In some States less radicalism, yes. But, I think, what people are concerned with are not broad things but local difficulties and local irritations.

Q: Will the results have any impact on International Communism?

1. Informal talk with Pressmen, New Delhi, 29 March 1957. From *The Hindu*, 30 March 1957.
2. British Labour leader and Shadow Foreign Secretary of the Labour Opposition in Britain, Aneurin Bevan was touring India at this time.

118

JN: They might have.

Q: Do you think the land tenure reform effected by the Praja Socialist Government had something to do with the Communists getting into power?

JN: As a matter of fact, the principles of land legislation were formulated even before the PSP came into power. The land problem in Kerala is completely different from other places and I have not heard of the land problem being a major issue in these elections.

The number of votes cast for the Congress in Kerala is greater than last time. It should also be noted, that the number of seats won by the Congress is disproportionately small compared to their votes.

11. Issues after the Elections[1]

So this business is over.[2] We had to decide to meet informally to discuss the elections today and if necessary tomorrow, the new and the old Members participating. The proceedings begin now. We have to see what lessons these elections have taught us, what our weaknesses were and the mistakes that we made. That is very important. We may talk about our opponents, their misdeeds and their weaknesses, but we won't profit very much by that. We have to strengthen ourselves, try to rectify our mistakes. It is not enough to say that we lost because of the rascality of our opponents. You have to understand that there will be some rascality. To look for excuses is hardly the way to go about this. Our strength is our own, no one can snatch it away from us. So, we have to analyse deeply as to why we lost in some places and won in the others in the election. You like to mention that the number of Congress Members in this new Parliament is more than it was previously—how many more are there? (Three

1. Speech at the meeting of the Congress Parliamentary Party, New Delhi, 29 and 30 March 1957. Tape No. M-23/c and M-23/c(iii), NMML. Extracts.
2. Nehru had just been re-elected leader of the Congress Party in Lok Sabha. For his speech on this occasion, see *post*, pp. 146-151. The Party had now reassembled with both old and new Members to discuss the problems of organization as well as those arising from the elections.

more) Anyhow, 3 or 4 more, whatever it is. All the results have not been announced. That the number has increased is in itself surprising because normally if a Party runs the government for too long, its number in the Legislature should gradually fall. This is common sense, people get tired. But in spite of this, I feel that this election has shown up some of the organizational defects in the Congress. As a Congressman, I am not at all happy with these elections. Not because some of our candidates, big or small, may have lost. Of course, I feel sorry that some of our colleagues have lost, especially in Parliament and we will miss them because they were our trusted helpmates in our work. But it is not that. The picture that this election has thrown up all over the country, inspite of our overwhelming victory, is not a good one. It is bad for India and bad for the Congress. And if any Member feels that this is a passing phase, and that matters will right themselves, they are very much mistaken. What you have seen happening in Maharashtra and in some parts of Gujarat is dangerous, that will not go away so easily unless you use drastic measures. I do not agree that time will heal. Time may heal matters to some extent but the fact of the matter is that Congress is losing its hold, others are taking over. I am not worried about that opinion. The people who were involved, their methods were wrong. Suddenly the entire atmosphere changed and men, much respected and liked in their constituencies and their States, were uprooted not because of any personal animosities but simply because it was an ill wind that bode good to no one. This can happen again anywhere in India. We have to think how to contain this storm and prevent it from breaking us completely. I attach a great deal of importance to this. And I won't accept it if people come and tell me that we got a majority etc., etc. Those things are of no importance. You must remember that people can start up trends which can uproot your good men. Why does it happen? Why is our organization weakening? Why can't we stem this tide? These are matters to be pondered over. I know what publicity is being done over this business, big posters are everywhere showing corpses, shooting etc.[3] We have to think of ways of preventing such incidents. That is different. But more important is the fact that this ill wind can blow at any time, anywhere in the country, uprooting and upsetting lives, unless we are careful and guard against such a contingency and strengthen ourselves.

You have to remember one more thing. I have not looked at the list very carefully but I think perhaps most of the Congress candidates who have won, may be from the villages, from the rural areas. This shows that our impact has been somewhat less on the urban areas; our opponents have done better. In the

---

3. Some members had drawn attention to the distribution of posters in Maharashtra carrying pictures of corpses described as victims of police firing.

villages, anyhow, it is a good thing. We have to bear in mind the fact that India is a country of villages. But it has also to be remembered that an ill wind might blow in the villages more easily. In a manner of speaking, the intellectual classes are beginning to oppose us. This is also wrong. I mean to say, it is wrong in the long run because it is the intellectual classes who influence the masses, if not today, tomorrow or the day after—they are a link. And if the student community in the universities etc., are against us, we may abuse them, but we will be finished. So, it is not enough to keep saying that they are making a mistake. After all, in a democracy, it is the voice of the majority that counts, so we have to keep that in our favour. I am not prepared to say that the majority is always wise. But that is what decides the issue, whether it is wise or not. This is a matter for thought. We may make an effort to see that the majority takes a wise decision, but ultimately, it is the majority that decides.

These are matters to be pondered over. So, I put it to you that a tremendous weakness is stealing over us, a weakness that comes with being in power for too long. We think that we are in the right and our opponents are under a misconception and so they are wrong. We do not examine ourselves dispassionately, honestly. Self-introspection is extremely important for any party at all times. I do not care if in the elections, some people win or lose. What does cause me anxiety is the atmosphere behind it. There has been a different Government in Kerala. I am not prepared to believe that the voters of Kerala voted for the Communists. I feel that they voted in anger against the Congress there. This is what we have to prevent. If a voter is genuinely of the different conviction, that is another thing. Now I hear that in Bihar, inspite of our election reverses, we are again busy kicking one another. Now when such things happen in our organization, what should it do? I don't think it need do anything at all, it buries itself. There is hardly any necessity for you, for me to do anything—it will bury itself and nobody would shed a tear, who is right, who is wrong— these are different issues. The picture of an organization is seen from outside as to how it is functioning. When it lacks ability, cohesiveness and there is in-fighting, it goes to prove that it has outlived itself. And in these five years, this is the question that faces the Congress, in spite of its majority, whether it is an organization that will survive or whether it has outlived itself. And this is the problem that we have to solve in the next five years, in each province, whether we can give new life to the Congress or we are going to remain in the old ruts while the ground slips from under our feet and the organization becomes lifeless.

Now, let us start the discussion. I would suggest that as far as possible it would be preferable for Members of the Lok Sabha who have been fighting election to speak rather than the Members of Rajya Sabha, who have been witnesses. Well, I cannot force them but certainly even among them preference might be given to those who have been defeated in the election. Some people say things which they should not and others don't say openly what is in their minds. Perhaps it would be better if Members, both old and new, wrote out their opinions and sent them. They should be carefully read and analyzed. Dhebar Bhai tells me that even now some letters have come to him—not many, about a thousand. When more come in, we will analyze them. But that does not mean that you should stop all oral discussions. This is apart from that. Alright, you must start now.[4]

Have you understood me, that is, it is suggested that all Members or those Members who so wish should send a note about their experiences and any suggestions that they may have to offer in regard to these past elections. They can send them to us and we should forward them to the AICC office where they have already received a considerable number of these and no doubt will receive more. They can be analysed and points noted down. But that does not mean that we should put an end to this discussion. There is a certain value always in open discussions which cannot be obtained from notes. I do not mean to say that we should shout out everything from the house tops, but our policy has been in the past, and it is a good policy, not to be ashamed of confessing mistakes or faults or errors. Only by bringing them out can you face them and solve them. Therefore, I suggest that those of you who so wish should send these notes and so far as this meeting is concerned we shall continue it, not now because there is a reception or party, tea party, given on behalf of the Congress Party to all the Members of Parliament at 5.30, old and new, so we shall go to that party. This meeting will continue tomorrow at 10.30 morning, here.[5]

...I think the discussion yesterday and today has been very helpful and no doubt that as more people speak, it will be more helpful. I do not suppose anything has been said which by itself is very new, because all of us, to some extent, or other, are acquainted with these various aspects of these questions. Nevertheless, many points are brought out with emphasis here which might escape attention or notice. So, it has been helpful and it is a good thing that we have met in this way. I asked you yesterday to send your own notes and suggestions if you so wish. That will be very helpful indeed in another way, in a more concise and precise way but our jointly considering these matters means that each one of us hears what the other says, not merely each one of us communicates with an office when others do not get the benefit of his speech.

Now, it is important that we should analyze this election and try to profit, profit by the lessons we got from it, but let us do that also by realizing a certain

4. Speech in English begins here.
5. Speech on 30 March follows.

broad approach to the entire problem first, then go down to the details. One broad approach might be called a certain historical approach. That is, how the history, if I may use that word, is developing in India in regard to political, economic conditions, organizations and the rest. It is obvious that this approach varies, as we get away, from the after-effects of the struggle for Independence. As we get away from the purely political aspects of the problem to economic and other aspects we come up against something which is somewhat different. We had those problems before in view too. Always, I am talking about a broad policy now, always you have to consider two aspects of a problem; in broad policies, economic policies, what will lay the foundations of rapid progress in - the future and what will bring relief to the people in the present. You cannot ignore either aspect, because in giving relief in the present if you forget the future there will be no real progress in the future; and you will not, I think, be serving the country or the people, well, in thinking only of the future, that is not right or fair when people are suffering from so many disabilities. Always one has to balance that.

Now, this election produced one thing which is rather remarkable that there was no major issue in the election, that is to say, the broad policies of the Congress or the Government were broadly accepted by everybody, whether they were national policies or international, whether they were economic policies or social. It is an important thing to remember. There is an amazing amount of acceptance of these broad political and domestic, national and international policies. Now, people oppose them, people criticize them no doubt, the Communists, the Jana Sangh, the PSP, but they really did that more for show than anything and they could not say very much about them. It may be said, therefore, broadly speaking, that the broad policies of Government have been a success in the sense that they are generally accepted. Then come the policies at a slightly lower level of the State Governments and finally, of course, the implementation of policies. There is a governmental side. I am not referring to the Congress side yet. I do not think it can be said that the policies of the State Governments have always been popular and certainly it cannot be said as Members have pointed out that the implementation of policies has been very satisfactory.[6]

Now, that is one aspect. The other aspect of these elections is that Independents have surprisingly played a greater role than before. That is a bad sign politically speaking. It is a sign partly of the Congress hold lessening or if you like, the

6. Feroze Gandhi had pointed out the administrative lapses at the lower levels, such as the unattended common needs of the people because of official bungling; failure to pay compensation to those whose lands came under irrigation schemes; faulty collection of land revenue; and poor condition of roads.

whole organized party's hold lessening, but more specially the Congress hold. It is a sign of political immaturity, in a parliamentary system for Independents to come in large numbers, because Independents do not represent and cannot represent broad policies or any really big policies. They only come in either on the personal basis, because they want to take advantage of their personality or popularity if they have any, or to lay stress on negative aspects, on the badness of the administration etc. Now, an Independent may be a very good man. I do not say, it is bad but it is a sign of political immaturity for a country to have too many Independents. It shows that broad policies are not being considered by the public and they are thinking more about petty local things. That is an aspect of these elections which is not good. Insofar as a country, our Party has to deal with broad policies, and of course, including their implementation, that is important, you educate the electorate and bring it up to a higher level. I do not know how many people, our candidates or others, talked about these policies, broad policies or the next stage of policies and how much they merely talk in terms of personalities or brought my name in or somebody else's name in to trade on that name. Now it must be realized that this kind of trading has no future. It is obvious. Apart from the fact that what Mr Patil[7] said that we are an aging people and we will pass off by a flux of time, it will have no effect. But apart from the flux of time, this election itself shows that you cannot trade much on these things. You have always, of course, to have broad policies on which you stand, it is important. You have also to have, more specially, in regard to State elections, Assembly elections, the second grade of policies which govern that State and which affect the people even more than the broad policies and you have finally the implementation of those policies and the removal insofar as possible of grievances. Now, I am not going into details, I am merely drawing your attention to the major aspects of approach. People have spoken about other matters too, like the selection of candidates, the functioning of the Election Commission, the way voting is done and how confusing it is and how sometimes unfair results come out by the present system of double-member constituencies and the like.[8] These are matters to be considered. I myself think that the double-member constituency has had its day and it is far better to have single member constituencies. Whatever may be the future of reservation of seats, that I am not prepared to say, we may continue reservation or we may not, that depends, but the double-member constituency, I think, requires revision.[9]

7. S.K. Patil, President, Bombay Pradesh Congress Committee.
8. For example, V.V. Giri's defeat. For details of his case, see *ante*, pp. 110-112 and *post*, p. 141.
9. The double-member constituencies were scrapped in 1961.

Also it has been astonishing, as many members have pointed out, how the type of propaganda that was indulged in under the very noses of the Election Commission or the electoral officers was permitted—which certainly, I think, should not be permitted in any fair election which should be, I suppose even under the existing laws, considered to be a malpractice or a corrupt practice. I do not speak as a lawyer but a common decent approach to these problems shows that it is a malpractice. We object and I believe we have rules and laws to that effect to an appeal to religious bigotry. Whether that law or rule has given effect to or not is another matter, but this type, this other type of bigotry and raising people's passions by posters showing bloody corpses are even worse than religious bigotry. And if this kind of thing is permitted, then it is not a fair election whatever else it may be, apart from encouraging the worst urges and sentiments in a people which is a bad thing. We have talked in the last two or three days of democracy, of parliamentary government without being self-disciplined and restrained and spirit of compromise and all that. Well, this is a very, not only the reverse but ultimate limit of the upset of this. If this approach is made, this bloody approach, I may call it so, how it has to be checked I do not know exactly, but the matter which requires earnest consideration. We have to deal with people as they are. We may talk bravely of ourselves or our people as paragons of virtue. But we are not all paragons of virtue. We have to deal with them as they are and make rules and regulations and conventions which prevent us as far as possible from going in a bad direction. So, all this question of election methods, publicity, etc., should be considered.

Now, I have talked about the governmental aspect and I shall talk about it a little more. But we are meeting as a Congress Party and we are interested in the organization, which gives birth to the government and it is important that we consider that aspect. Much has been said and it is always said about the organization, the weakness etc., the contacts with the government, the cooperation between the organization and government and so on and so forth. In spite of all the efforts we have made, we have not been remarkably successful. We may make further efforts and perhaps we may do a little better in future about these contacts and cooperation. But all these things depend ultimately on a certain vital urge in the people or the organization and all the rules in the world do not take us very far if that is absent. In the 20s or the 30s, if I may say so, our organization was remarkably weak and yet it was very strong. I mean to say organizationally it was weak but behind it was a living urge of the people which made it strong. Our membership was probably far less than it was subsequently, but it was carried on a wave of emotion of urges and aspirations of the people and some great leaders and all that, so it made good. But I would not call our organization in the 20s, at the height of the struggle, a strong organization. But it was very strong because of being a living organization, because it was in touch with the aspirations and urges of the people and that gave it life. If you lack life, all the rules of the world will not give you life. We go on thinking about the rules and we should think of course, we have to go a little deeper down. We shall also have to find out how far we are—shall I say, rather as an organization, I am not talking about individuals—a somewhat exhausted organization, mentally speaking, somewhat in the ruts, I do not think we are, I am not merely mentioning that, I do not think we are an exhausted organization and, I think, the record of the last few years even shows that there is a good deal of life in this organization. We have taken steps forward and we are continually looking into this matter, that is important. We try to be vigilant, we may fail because the problem is a very big problem for any country and however good we might be, we cannot get out of these historic processes that are working.

Well, we should examine all these things no doubt. Obviously, so long as Congress Governments function in this country, then the general prestige of the organization will depend greatly on the prestige of the Government and the work that the Government does, it is obvious. We have not got a good organization because we have not got district committees functioning, and Pradesh Committees do not function properly and all that. And the simple thing which a political organization should do, is to see to it if it is interested in elections. It should see to it long before the election, it should think about the voters and all, think about all these things which every political organization does, which our people do not, because of this idea that if we get a ticket all is good, why should I worry. Or I may not get a ticket, why should I worry for the next person. Now, that of course is an entirely personal, self-centred and selfish approach. And if people in an organization do not have something more than the self-centred approach, do not have some measure if not much, some measure at least of an idealistic or crusading spirit, the organization becomes a mere machine, pure machine with, well, if I may use the word, I apologize for it, with a considerable proportion of people aiming at opportunist stand or self-seekers if you like. Then it loses grip gradually and all the credit you may have, goes.

Those are obvious things but what I mean to say is that we have to consider all these various points that have been raised and many more, both from the governmental point of view and the organizational plus also the electoral point of view. All require consideration but behind it all, two major facts stand out— the broad policies of a country and the implementation of those policies, at the lowest level. Broadly speaking, I think, the broad policies of the country, as I said, are generally approved and good, they may be varied, they are not rigid but broadly. So, for the moment we need not worry about that, although we should always be thinking about it. What we should worry about are the policy at the lower levels, at the State levels and although both are mixed up of course and the Planning Commission and all that comes in. And more particularly implementation and I think much has been said more particularly about the lowest level, the *lokpals* and the petty revenue and other officials. Now unfortunately, my experience has never lain there, I cannot speak from experience except what I have seen from a distance right from the beginning about 45 years ago of my political career, it has been unfortunately, very unfortunately it was somewhat higher level. So I never got personal acquaintance of this crowd of *lokpals* and others. Although naturally I met them, I heard about them, I cannot speak from experience, you know more about it. Pantji no doubt knows a great deal about it but it is true that it is these people at the bottom which are the visible emblems of a policy or a government to the general public—the policemen and such, and these petty revenue officials—these are the visible emblems of power. It is not very easy to deal with these all but I have no doubt, the problem is always before us and it should be dealt with. I cannot suggest a remedy but I do agree that it is of great importance.

Some members talked about panchayats. Again I cannot imagine any real democracy in this country unless democracy exists at the lowest levels. Therefore, panchayat in theory is of vital importance. In practice if it goes wrong how are we to correct it, I cannot immediately say. And it may be also I would say that even a wrong-doing panchayat is better than no panchayat. That, out of that they will learn and gradually improve possibly, we should try to see that they improve now, because after all, all these things—whether it is a panchayat whether it is a District Board, whether State Assembly or Parliament—reflect and necessarily must reflect the failings and virtues of the people. We do not come out of the air and an individual leader might be back or not but when you have these large-scale representations we have all these failings naturally of the people. If the panchayats have those failings they are there in our village folk. It is no good praising the village folk and blaming the panchayat. They are reflections of what they are, if they, whether it is the caste difference coming up or other differences or petty things which come up—whether it is panchayat, whether it is the Congress Party—they come up, we have to deal with our people in that way and we have to accept them as they are and try to improve them and get rid of these things constantly. They will be got rid of, well apart from our general approach, social outlook, laws etc., propaganda whatever it is, but really by the changing nature of society that is the basic thing that changes them. You talk about untouchability and I have no doubt that the Congress and later on, the Government has done a great deal in putting an end to untouchability. But in the final analysis, untouchability goes because the social structure has changed by different occupations coming in. You have, let us say, the person who is in a

127

social scale considered to be, well, very low down, the sweeper, the *mehter*, the *kowah*? Now, first of of all, everybody travels together in the railway train, everybody works together in a factory, more or less, they do not observe untouchability in a factory, in a tram and this and that, in an hundred ways they come together, you cannot observe it, these things change. Gradually, you get in your sanitation and drainage system, all kinds of plumbing and this and that where some of these processes are done automatically. You see these changes are really more important than all the propaganda you may do, because they change the nature of the work of the individual. If you keep the same social structure intact, all the advice that you may give, it does not really affect it except at the surface. You may tone down something. But the major thing is happening, it is happening and will continue to happen, the social structure will change because of new occupations, new methods of production, new methods of distribution and all that. I want to draw your attention, that these things—social habits and castes and everything—depend on a social structure. Our social structure got rigid and remained rigid. It is not so rigid now of course and I have no doubt that caste and other things will go, because of other things happening, not merely because reformers trying to reform. You had reformers all the time for thousands of years and they were good no doubt but the basic structure remained because the methods of production and distribution and living and all that remained what they were. They could not change them very much.

So, there are so many things one can talk about and publicity again was referred to. Yes, I suppose one of the Members referred to some posters about informing people, giving them the useful information that they will be taxed. I presume, I do not know, I presume that this was in Election Commission's poster, but was it done for the Election Commission. I know that I was wondering that those posters so far as I knew were organized, some of them at least, by the Election Commission and they asked the I & B Ministry, well whoever it was. Is this type of poster etc., really important and this type of publicity. And I think, it is correct to say that our publicity is capable of great improvement, that is to say it requires rather the mind that produces the poster and other requires some kind of intimate knowledge of the mind that will see it. I mean to say just like these advertising campaigns which I disapprove of very strongly, in other countries, specially in America. My own personal reaction to being told all the time to use a particular toothpaste is never to use it, I get very angry to be told all the time to use this toothpaste. But in America or elsewhere, it is always dinning it into the ear whether it is by radio, by broadcasting, by newspapers it is dinning in but that is a personal reaction. Anyhow the advertising experts know how to approach the American public, they do it because they know they can influence them. Well, I am not asking for this type of development of advertisement here but what I mean is rather it does not show any living touch with the people you are addressing. Apart from advertising if I address an audience what is my objective to get into the kind of the audience, not to deliver a literary address, if I could deliver a literary address, that I reserve for the literary society if I address it. It is to get into the mind of the audience even though I may speak very bad language which is not literary or correct but my purpose is served if I get at the mind of the audience. I am not sure if people remember that too often. I am not talking about elections because they want often to show off their knowledge of their language. They may use such difficult words that nobody understands. Though, the audience will be very pleased that I have addressed in a pure language. So, advertising has to reach the minds of the audience and their habits.

So, we have to consider all these big problems, governmental of course since we are still the Government in many places—not only big policies, five year plans—and may I say that it is very important. You must remember that we are passing through a very difficult phase in our planning and in our developmental work. The difficulty was partly inevitable it has not suddenly come on us, nothing has happened today. It has come on us in the course of these past three or four years. Partly it must come on a country which develops rapidly. It has to come, because you throw in a great deal of resources in things which do not produce results for years. You have to take that risk. Partly, it is due to factors entirely outside our control that is in other countries. Partly, maybe it is due to our own fault, whatever it may be. But we are passing through a very difficult period and this difficulty will last for some time, I should say a minimum of two years more. I think we should get over it after two years. Gradually, in a sense it will last because the faster you want to develop the more your difficulties will be. You have to choose whether you want to go fast or not. In the old days take the Indian States. I referred to the Indian States because as an example of static conditions—people were unhappy, poor, everything static and not many complaining either, there they were not in a very happy state of affairs. But you might say on the other hand, see how contented they are. The moment you move on, it is a sign of growth, the people's complaints you have to face and that is a good sign, of course that means that you have to be very vigilant all the time and you have to keep pace with that. That is a governmental side which would naturally have to be considered. But, I think it, is right to say that our Ministers, in the Central Government are also no doubt partly responsible or guilty but not so much, because the Central Government Ministers by virtue of being in the Central Government are rather high up in the layer of things. They do not go down deeply except they may go and deliver a speech. But our State Ministers are close to the ground, close to their people. And they have to be very close, if they lose that intimate contact, it is a bad thing. Central Ministers should also have it, of course, but I am saying and one thing I hope people forgive me for saying it because I am very guilty of it myself, all these petty pomp and splendour, is very irritating. It makes me very very unhappy that wherever I go, this pomp and splendour surrounds me and all this terrific security precautions, I do not know; it drives me crazy almost all this and I complain about it and something is done and much is not done, well, in the circumstance I accept. Security precautions, I do think that they should be much simpler and much more intelligent and not so obviously showy and not so expensive. Terrific lot of money is spent on them. But if I accept that by the compulsion of events, I accept it, I do not like it and some times I break through. But one must separate the idea of security and pomp. They are separate ideas and I do think we should endeavour to remove this element of show from Ministers' tours and whatever it is as far as possible and I do hope, I wish Ministers would not go about with a crowd of red-coated *chaprassis* about them. I think, the whole institution of *chaprassis* is a bad system. I cannot abolish them as they are today, but in reality, only a country where life is cheap can afford to have a *chaprassi*. In other countries whether they are capitalists or communists they do not have *chaprassis*. Why should we have these crowds of them, I do not understand. I will tell you I do not know what the figure of Central Government now here in Delhi is, not about the whole, before the last War I saw a figure, there were three thousand and some hundred *chaprassis*. After the War about 10 years back, when we came into power here, those three thousand some hundred has increased to 19 thousand and some hundred, this was 8 years, 9 years ago, I do not know what the figure is today, I have no idea. It creates difficulty throwing out people, out of employment and we did not want to create those difficulties but we made a rule then, let no fresh person be employed, that is, if there is need because our new department, new Ministries, all kinds of Government of India's work has grown, I do not know how much, but I should imagine a hundred times what it was before, you have no idea how it has grown, it may be that a part of it wastefully grown, but a great part of it has become essential. People talk about the Government of India functioning in pre-British times and now. I mean to say I should like some of you to go into the activities we have to indulge in. I am not saying that there is no waste, there may be a good deal of waste but the number of activities that the whole huge Ministries are creating is large. Take External Affairs, it did not exist previously, a huge Ministry spread out all over the world; take Rehabilitation, an entirely new and novel job, dealing with vast properties and vast numbers of people all over India. But all this whether it is Commerce and Industry, whether it is Finance, it is not only Independence but all these planning and growth that inevitably increases that bureaucratic element in Government. The more we go to our socialism the more bureaucracy we have.

You must remember that. There is no country which has such a tremendous bureaucracy as Soviet Union and China. You will be interested to learn that there are great complaints in China, tremendous complaints being raised at the size of the growing bureaucracy—and in China, of course, in countries like that, complaints do not normally come up at all. It is only when things become rather intolerable, that some voice is heard and the government itself starts denouncing it, not the voice I mean, but the bureaucracy and quite interesting I saw some notes there, saying that too many people have been engaged here and terrific waste and what we should do about these extra hands 50 per cent and, almost the same thing that we have been saying here, I read in their notes there. Because all these things look very good from a distance but when you examine them, you find all kinds of difficulties in these other countries. So, all these points arise and the problem is practical, of course, but the psychological problem too, our mental make-up, how we approach these questions. And then of course, how we translate that mental make-up into our governmental or organizational apparatus.

Well, one thing, I must say, I think Shri Feroze Gandhi referred to the NES, National Extension Service. I do not know if others referred to it or not.[10] Now these National Extension Service and the Community Projects have, you know, spread out to roughly at the present moment about 40 per cent of rural India, 220,000 villages and 129 million inhabitants, and it is proposed to complete this rural India by extending this to every single village in the course of the next 4 or 4 ½ or 5 years, terrific programme. I have been to some of these places. All of you must have seen some, and I get many many reports about them too. It is obvious that you cannot expect the same level in 220,000 villages where we are working, the level varies. But my own impression of what little I have seen and what more I get from reports, not the official types of report only but I get many types of reports, not merely statistical but other appraisals, is as I have said very frequently, that the most revolutionary thing that is happening in India is this Community Development. Basically revolutionary in the sense that it is changing the people there, apart from roads and buildings and all that, taking them out of their ruts and making them more self-reliant. The demand, if this is any test, the demand for this National Extension Service to go where it is not, it is terrific, the pressure on us, people see it functioning in the neighbourhood, they must have something to attract them. There is terrific demand—give it to us, give it to us, we see it there, we want something like this—this itself shows that it is appreciated. As I said there are various levels. First of all, the NES itself is on a lower level from the Community Project. Community Project is a more intensive

10. Members had criticized the huge expenditure on Community Projects and NES.

level and the NES is a lower level and a permanent level. The NES stage is transformed into the Community Project 40 per cent, for the simple reason that we cannot afford to make it for financial reasons hundred per cent. There must be many failings in the way it is working in a large number of places. We may make many improvements in it but basically it is something which is changing and revolutionizing the face of India and what is more it will gradually change all your lower structure of administration, that is, not only the NES but also what is going to be associated with it, that is cooperatives. You are laying stress on that. Small-scale and village industries, it really comprises almost every activity of the village whether social or agricultural or industrial in a small way. So, we have to improve it. We have to find out. Mr Feroze Gandhi said something about taking a few villages and making them sort of exemplars. Well, the exemplars are the Community Project area. I think, this taking a village or two is not a good idea or a few villages that in a sense, in a small way, was the British idea, having a so-called model village to show, which did not go very far, and which becomes an exhibition, this is not something which has grown out of the people. The important thing is that it should grow out of the people and they should know they have done it. What is very necessary I think is, and we are doing it—farms, demonstration farms, thousands of them, small farms for better agricultural methods and all that.

Certainly, let us try to improve this Extension Service etc., but I think, it is right for me to say that we have already shown how, not only how good but how successful the Scheme is and in fact we have become now a kind of world centre for the study of these methods. People come from all over to study them, to import them to their country, not the European countries, of course, because they are highly industrialized but other countries in Asia and even in South America, and now we are putting up, I forget what they are called, but schools of research, if I may call it, for these Community Centres work there. Because there, even more than elsewhere, it is the human-being that counts. There he comes in touch with the people, the people are with them and it is highly important that we should have people adequately trained by the hundred thousands at the village level and the researches and enquiries about the psychological approach it should be conducted apart from other. We are putting up some definite centres of scientific research for that purpose. It has many failings and anything which has grown so rapidly must inevitably have. But it is a very living organization, that is, if it is a living organization it will get rid of its failings and change that is a basic thing and you should help us, all of us should help it to correct those defects and make it more effective in its actual work.

Well, I suppose such discussions always end by being talked out when we can hardly do anything else but the Congress President is, I am quite sure, going to pursue these matters with the energy and earnestness and vigilance which he always applies to this. He is meeting Pradesh Presidents and Secretaries and others, and I believe he has in view a number of other approaches to this problem, which would gradually be disclosed to us.

12. General Elections and the Congress[1]

Broadly speaking, I would say that these elections have certainly their bad points and also some good points from the Congress point of view. The bad points can be divided into two parts—one is the actual injury caused that we see, and the other, which is more important, is certain trends which may affect this organization and affect the country a great deal in the future unless we understand those trends and deal with them.

There are certain disruptive tendencies inside the organization. No organization can survive these disruptive tendencies—the personal equation becoming more important than the organization, than the country. No constitution, no law that you may frame or rule can get over that basic undermining feature of an organization. In these elections many cases have come to me where people have hardly talked about the organization. They have talked about themselves—our own candidates. The man who does so, I think, should be ruled out completely here and now. We should not tolerate the individual approach in these matters. It is also my firm conviction that the more money you spend the worse it is for you. People are thinking that it is lack of money that counts.[2] I hold very strong reverse opinion. Of course, money is required for normal work. But the moment a person starts spending more money and thinking for more money, he is relying on a factor which shows that he has lost grip of the situation.

Then again we talk much about the administration and the relations with the

1. Speech at the conference of Presidents and Secretaries of Pradesh Congress Committees, New Delhi, 31 March 1957. JN Collection. Also published in *AICC Economic Review*, Vol. IX No. 1 (1 May 1957).
2. It was pointed out in the Congress Parliamentary Party meeting on 30 March that some Congress candidates received large funds to spend on their election and could engage cars and jeeps while others were handicapped for want of money and found it difficult to manage even bicycles.

organization. It is an important subject. Basically, what the Government does is far more important for the Congress organization than what the Congress does. This is obvious because the administration, if you like, is the Executive Branch of the Congress. It does not matter how good the Congress is if the administrative policies are not satisfactory—the Congress will suffer obviously, the organization will suffer.

It is a difficult question because we are somewhere between two stools, if I may say so. In Communist countries there is no difference between administration and organization. They are identical. That is not our position, nor does our Constitution give it, nor do we want it. In other countries, like say, England, it is the Government that is everything and the organization only comes in vaguely into the picture about some very basic policies. Take England, for example. The Labour Party has an organization standing for certain principles. The Conservative Party organizationally does nothing at all except efficiently to keep in touch with the voters. It keeps in touch with every voter and organizationally, from the electoral point of view, it is a good organization. They spend money, they have cars, they see that every man's name is put in the register. But the Conservative Party's annual function in England is the tamest affair imaginable. There is no vital discussion there. They just meet together and the Prime Minister, Foreign Minister and the Chancellor of Exchequer deliver speeches. Of course, there are certain limits beyond which no Government can go, that is against its own organization. But broadly speaking, the Conservative Government uses the organization and the organization is just a kind of electoral wing of it which does not shape the policies except in the broader sense. The Labour Party stands for certain principles and within the Party there are groups, there are some extreme and some more extreme. So, Labour Party conference is much more important. There is tussle not only between groups but for ideas and the conference lays down certain broad policies. But it is the Government that is everything and not the organization.

Now, therefore, we come somewhere between the Communist system and the normal working of the countries where there is parliamentary democracy. That is the essential difference of the situation. You cannot change it by passing resolutions. It is the human factor and, if the human approach is cooperative, well and good, if it is not then you suffer. One can, of course, try to help to make it cooperative. It is basically the Government policy and the implementation of that policy that affects the people. The Congress comes in not only in broadly effecting that policy or pushing it in this direction or that, but much more so in carrying the message of that policy to the people and thereby not only maintaining active contacts with the people but that link, the explanation what is being done and the difficulties etc. That becomes the major work of the Congress. Even our policy, apart from certain rather secondary matters, becomes broadly determined in our five year plans. It is not likely to be changed from year to year. You cannot change these big plans. It upsets everything. You may vary them here and there by setting something or dropping something as the five year plan itself is a thing which is not rigid. Within the terms of that broad determination of policy there is still plenty of room for variation, specially in the States and in that Congress can play a very important part. It is implementation of that policy again that is more important than its laying down. There again, the States play much greater part than the Central Government.

I think, in discussing these elections you must, therefore, adopt two lines of approach. One is, discussing each state as you are doing and analyzing the causes whether the administrative, governmental or organizational, what other party did, how far we or you were lacking or our organization is lacking. The second approach is a broader survey of the situation in regard to actual or potential forces that are at work. You can see them in Maharashtra,[3] you can see them in some parts of Gujarat;[4] you can see them in Kerala;[5] you can see another type at work in UP;[6] you can see a different type in Bihar—Hazaribagh or Chota Nagpur districts;[7] you can see something else in Bengal;[8] you can see something entirely

3. An election alliance against the Congress was formed even by the parties which differed from one another greatly. The Samyukta Maharashtra Election Committee, consisted of Communists, communalists and Praja Socialists, united on the single issue of Samyukta Maharashtra.
4. Similarly, all Opposition parties combined in the Maha Gujarat Samiti and the election became almost a referendum on the Maha Gujarat issue.
5. The PSP sought an electoral ally in Kerala but could not win one in Congress or the Communists. Therefore, it arrived at an understanding with the Muslim League and raised the issues of democracy and social justice.
6. While the strength of the Congress in UP Assembly declined from 390 to 226, the number of Opposition members grew. The PSP won 44 seats, the Socialist Party 25, the Communists 9 and the Jana Sangh 17.
7. The Janata Party of Raja of Ramgarh, Kamakhya Narayan Singh, won all the 16 seats from Hazaribagh in the Bihar Legislative Assembly. The PSP, the Janata Party and the Jharkhand Party won more seats in these elections at the cost of Congress.
8. In West Bengal, a united Leftist Election Committee comprising the five main Leftist parties, namely, the Communists, the Praja Socialists, the Revolutionary Socialists, Forward Bloc and the Marxist Forward Bloc was formed. It produced a minimum programme that opened the possibility of a coalition government should the Congress fail to secure a majority in the Assembly.

different in Tamilnad.[9] I should like you to consider these major forces at work. Before you find a remedy, you must diagnose the disease and understand it. That is because one thing acts and reacts on the other.

Organizationally, Congress is weak, not on the top but at the lower levels and even at the provincial level. In most cases it is not strong, at the district level it is very weak and at the levels below the district it is about non-existent in many places. Now, it is no good talking about what Congress should do and should not do if the Congress cannot even build up an organization and merely relies on public sympathy, relies on some kind of vague atmosphere of help from the public.

Unfortunately, we indulge in a great deal of, what I may call, tall talk about ahimsa and non-violence. The fact is that Indian people are more violent than most of the other people in the wide world. Violence and non-violence can be tested only in one's daily activities and not in expressions of high philosophy. In daily activities we get swept away. We have seen this in Delhi ten years ago after Partition. People had been swept away. You could see ten years ago—young men, reasonable people, intelligent people had been swept away and doing the most horrible things and yet we talk about ahimsa and non-violence. It is an amazing gap between what we say and what we do.

What happened ten years ago after Partition was a horrible thing, and yet it was something which did not directly, if I may say so, affect the inner structure of India or our organization. It did, of course, but not so much. There was a special reason for that which can be put on a different category, bad as it was. We see that kind of wave of violence and hatred attacking every part of India. That is, I think, the worst thing that has emerged from these elections. I do not attach much importance to your losing seats here and there. Of course, it does matter but not so much. It is sometime good thing to lose seats. Nothing is so bad as complacent outlook.

The Congress relied on mass enthusiasm. The moment that mass enthusiasm can be turned against it, the very thing on which it relied, it can suppress us. I am putting these things deliberately in an exaggerated way. I do not think the position is so bad. But I am putting it in an exaggerated way so that you may appreciate the danger of the situation. I think, on the other hand, there is a hopeful side of the situation too. The Congress would not have lost seats merely if some people were sitting at the top. It has lost because, in the final analysis,

---

9. Dissident Congressmen in Tamilnad formed the Tamilnad Congress Reform Committee, which criticized the manner of selection of candidates. They put up their candidates against those Congress nominees whom they considered undesirable. The caste sentiment amongst them was strong and widespread.

there are all over India considerable number of people, honest and hard working people, who worked for the Congress and were its backbone and strength, are not active today. But I warn you, I deliberately emphasize on this aspect because you should realize what we are up against. It may be the Communist Party in one place, it may be some other group in one place, it may be something else in another place. It may turn the very mass enthusiasm on which we relied all these years against you. A revolution, it is said, always swallows up those who create it—whether it is in France or Russia or elsewhere. Well, our revolution is a quite different one. We cannot draw that analogy. I would put it in this way— the very force that the Congress has created outruns the Congress and the Congress is left behind. Therefore, you have to always understand those forces, you have to keep pace with those forces.

We started the mass movements thirty-forty years ago. We directed them, we profited by them. Another type of movement comes and we are left behind. We complain so and so has done this or that. It may be true or not, but the fact is that we become out of date. Speed of youth, of mind and body goes from us organizationally and we go on struggling, trying to catch up something which is ahead of us. But, first of all, every organization and every major force depends on the quality of mind given to it. Without the mind, without the intellectual leadership, you may lose sometime, you may lose considerable time. In the final analysis, mind is the governing factor and the intellectual leadership it gives. Secondly, there is the spirit behind the organization, the crusading spirit, the belief in a cause and working for a cause. These are the two major things which rather overlap, which make up an organization. The rest is detail—though very important detail—but detail.

We find in India, our successes are largely due to the peasantry, to the rural masses. We are, by and large, losing the city folk. Well, comparatively the intelligent people did not matter very much. In the old days, in a struggle for freedom, it was far more important to have a disciplined army to fight. Naturally, you think of intelligent leadership. That matter is much more important.

It is no good seeking remedy unless you realize the nature and extent of a problem. It is a struggle for survival for the Congress. I think that the Congress has a great deal of actual and potential strength not only to survive but to go ahead, provided it is realized and utilized properly. If there is any inner failure— inner failure in an individual or an organization or a nation—there is no remedy for it. If one fails he loses his sense of direction and functioning and his crusading spirit and he just becomes dis-spirited and frustrated—that is what inner failure means. There can be inner failure for an organization too. I do not say that that has happened to the Congress but we should be warned that it might. But it has happened to many Congressmen.

Where the provincialist or communalistic approach is there, you can deal logically with people, you can reason with them, you can work with them. We have seen that the people can lose all sense of unity and cohesion. It is astounding. You see how disruptive tendencies have come out. We should not forget it since it is the major opposition that we have to deal with. I believe that if the Congress has any particular function, it is that of maintaining the unity and cohesiveness of India. I have no doubt in my mind that during the last five, seven, eight or nine years, the Congress Governments, by and large, have done a fairly remarkable work in the country. It is far more understood and appreciated outside India even by our opponents than inside the country. As one may remember, Dr Appleby, the American observer came here two or three times. He is a very strong critic and he looked at everything critically. But he also said that the amazing thing about India is that, in spite of the wonderful achievements in India, everybody is criticizing the Government.[10] In fact, it seems to be a major occupation in India to run down what we have done. It is easy to criticize because there is so much to criticize in India. We struggle against all kinds of powerful forces not created by this party or the other. But we have to struggle against the inertia of centuries, the habits of centuries, and the economic stagnation of centuries. We are getting out of that morass and deadlock. The Congress organization should explain all that to the people.

I should like to ask each individual Congress candidate what he has done and how far he has associated himself with the Community Development Programme in his constituency. I am afraid that a great majority of them have taken no interest at all. The implementation of the Community Development Schemes is most important and most vital and it is the most revolutionary thing that is happening in India. This is changing the face of India. Apart from that, it is in our interest to be associated with them and work with them. The new India is coming out from Community Development Projects and other things and not through resolutions.

No organization can live on its past record. We have to face a generation today which has no personal experience of our struggle for freedom. It is all history for them. They heard about it. It is not a personal experience which has impressed itself on their minds and hearts. In a way we are getting out of touch with this new generation. All over the world there is a strong tendency for the new generation to be out of touch with their forerunners. It is because the world is changing rapidly.

10. This refers to the second report on administration, by Paul H. Appleby. For an extract of his report on this subject, see *Selected Works* (second series), Vol. 35, p. 586.

There is another very important thing to be considered. It is how far the Congress is an old man's organization and how far is it something which provides fresh blood, fresh thinking, how far is it bearing those people who repeat phrases and ideas and have lost capacity to think afresh, and how far we have lost touch as an organization with the younger generation. To some extent we have, though not altogether. There are plenty of youngmen—there are Youth Departments and all that and they have done good work. But here and there, the students have also been, by and large, our most effective opponents—in canvassing, carrying on propaganda and accusing and all that. Now, one may call them foolish, and that they are not disciplined. But the point is that we have lost touch with them and, what is more, even though they may like the organization, they have no longer any respect for some of our people.

The Congress prospered in old times—I mean fundamentally and basically— because of the reputation of integrity of Congressmen, their reputation for service and sacrifice. I do not say everybody did it, but that was a reputation of the Congressmen—integrity, service and sacrifice for the nation. We do not have that reputation today to that degree. I am not talking about individuals. Individuals may have it. We get so many complaints in elections and others about lack of integrity. We see papers, cartoons, etc., and we receive complaints that Congressmen are hankering after office, quarreling with each other and are indulging in group formations. I do not mind ideological groups which may be there to discuss matters. But when one sees, these groups and conflicts based entirely on personal grounds, then naturally the respect of the public fades. The public has lost, by and large, respect for the integrity of the average Congressman. That is to say, individual Congressman may have that respect. That is individual matter. By and large, they have lost confidence in average Congressmen. Every Congressman wants to stick to offices—wherever it may be—and once that idea creeps in, then one of the basic things that gives strength to the Congress disappears. We have been in government for the last ten years and there is always reaction against the government in every country. People get tired of the same government, same faces. They just want a change and our argument against it and the necessity of the Congress for unity of India may not go far. Generally, people—great mass of people—require, what might be called, good government and honest government. Their chief sufferings are from lack of honesty at the lower levels. This lack of honesty is difficult to remove and do not imagine that we alone in India suffer from this. There are other countries also where petty dishonesty goes. In Europe, we see milk-man putting one, two or three bottles of milk in front of every door. Anybody can walk away with it. But they do not do so because milk is so cheap there. I do not know, if it is done here how many bottles will remain outside. Thus, when the living standards go up, the petty dishonesty disappears. Most people suffer from petty dishonesty because of poverty. One does not know here very much as to what happens in a country like China because there is no publicity, etc. But sometimes when we hear about it, then there is a flood of criticism—'see this is happening, that is happening, see these dishonest officials', etc. There is a little criticism now going on. Do not imagine that it is our peculiar failing. But it is there and there is no doubt about it. It grew during the last War. War upsets all canons of integrity and honesty in every country. We started this Government just after the War, facing that situation created partly by the old situation but made much worse by the War. A large number of people in every office, petty functionaries, used to do what they liked. We have been fighting against that. Naturally, we have fought with some success. But it is not an easy matter. We have very strict rules in punishing public servants, but you must have hundred per cent evidence and without that you cannot do anything. It is not easy to get that evidence always. In China it is different. There is no question of cent per cent, even five per cent evidence is enough. They do not mind punishing 90 innocent people to punish 10 guilty people. They want to create an impression, and they do create that impression. But we cannot do this in a democratic regime. We do not want to do it. There are all kinds of constitutional safeguards, civil liberties and Supreme Court. So in India while protecting the innocent, the guilty goes off. We have to face all these difficulties.

People criticize us why there is corruption. I think, there is less corruption in India than in majority of countries of Asia. India is, relatively speaking, a country where there is less corruption.

13. To N.C. Chatterji[1]

New Delhi
9 April 1957

Dear Shri Chatterji,[2]
I have your letter of April 9th.

We are all desirous of helping Shri V.V. Giri[3] and I respect your knowledge of the law of elections. But, you will appreciate that we have to rely on the advice we get. Our legal advisers have told us quite definitely that the law is quite clear and, indeed, there can be no other interpretation of it. We can change the law, and I hope something will be done to prevent this kind of anomaly from taking place in future.[4] There are any number of similar cases even during the last general elections, where two persons standing from the reserved seat have both been elected at the cost of a person standing for the general seat.[5]

We have already received a clear opinion from some of our advisers. We are asking for further opinion.

Yours sincerely,
Jawaharlal Nehru

1. JN Collection.
2. A prominent leader of the Hindu Mahasabha.
3. Giri was defeated in a double-member constituency inspite of securing more votes than the other general candidate owing to the procedure described below in footnote 5.
4. The double-member constituencies were scrapped just before the 1962 general elections by the Two-Member Constituency (Abolition) Act, 1961. The Act bifurcated the existing double-member constituencies to create two single-member constituencies, one reserved and one unreserved.
5. Such double-member constituencies had to be created where the regular formula of having 50% population of SC/ST was not feasible. A larger constituency, covering the population twice that of a single-member constituency, was created and two seats were allocated— one reserved and one general. The voter was given two ballot papers to be cast for two different candidates. The Scheduled Castes or the Scheduled Tribes were ensured a seat in the double-member constituency through a special procedure for the declaration of results. The result of the reserved seat was declared first confining the competition to the reserved candidates only. Then a pool was formed of all the remaining candidates which included SC/ST and non SC/ST candidates and the winner for the unreserved seat was declared.

III. FORMATION OF CENTRAL GOVERNMENT

1. To V.K. Krishna Menon[1]

New Delhi
11 March 1957

My dear Krishna,[2]

As you know, the President will address the Members of the two Houses on the opening day of Parliament, the 18th March. The President's Address has to be prepared. This session of Parliament is the final session of the old Parliament. It is rather odd that the old Parliament should meet when the new one has been elected. But we have to do so for various reasons.

The new Parliament will meet presumably early in May. The President will, no doubt, have to address them again. Thus we shall have two Presidential Addresses in the course of about six or seven weeks.

The last time the President addressed Parliament was a year ago. I suppose that in the Address to this outgoing Parliament some greater stress will have to be laid on past achievements. Something will, of course, have to be said about the present situation, more especially in international affairs.

I have been quite unable to apply my mind to it till the elections are over and we see the picture that emerges. I suppose by day after tomorrow, the 13th March, this will be fairly clear. This will give us only about two or three days to prepare this draft Address which will naturally have to be considered by the President and by Members of the Cabinet before it is finalized.

I should like you more particularly to draft something about international affairs. Some reference will presumably have to be made to the past year since the President last addressed Parliament. But what I am more concerned with is with reference to the present situation. I should like you to draft this. We have to make every effort to make the Address a short one, or, at any rate, not too long, and as we have to deal with a multitude of subjects, we cannot balance it too heavily on the side of international affairs.

1. V.K. Krishna Menon Papers, NMML. Also available in JN Collection.
2. Minister Without Portfolio at this time. He was sworn in on 17 April as Minister for Defence.

This is just to remind you of this. I shall speak to you about this matter when we meet.

Yours affectionately,
Jawaharlal Nehru

2. To Ram Subhag Singh[1]

New Delhi
18 March 1957

My dear Ram Subhag,[2]

The Congress Central Parliamentary Board has advised me to convene a meeting of the Congress Parliamentary Party as it will be after the new elections. This Party will consist of probably half of the present Members and about half new Members. It would be convenient to have such a meeting before the MPs go away from Delhi after the present session of Parliament.

It is desirable that the new Party should choose its leader at an early date. It is suggested, therefore, that a meeting of this new Party should be held on Friday, the 29th March at 3 p.m. in the Central Hall of Parliament. The business of this meeting will be short. After that, say at 3.30 p.m., we want all these newly elected Members plus the old Members, including those who will not continue in the Party later, to meet informally for full discussions about the elections, our organization etc. These discussions may well last for more than one day and may go on till Saturday, the 30th March.[3]

I am issuing a press note so that the newly elected members might know of this meeting. But, of course, an attempt should be made to send a separate notice to all those who have been elected and who are going to be elected in the next few days. Please see me tomorrow in my office in Parliament House after the Question Hour so that we can decide on the form of notice etc.

1. JN Collection.
2. Secretary, Congress Parliamentary Party.
3. See *ante*, pp. 119-133.

I enclose a copy of the press note I am issuing. Please issue the attached notice to all Members of the Congress Party in Parliament (both Houses) as well as to all newly elected Congress Members of the Lok Sabha. Where any old Member has been elected again, of course only one notice would be issued to him.

You should make arrangements to issue this notice to newly elected Members whose results have already been announced. As results come in, other successful candidates should get the notice.

With your notice, you will send a copy of my note to the press.

Yours sincerely,
Jawaharlal Nehru

3. Leader of the Congress Parliamentary Party[1]

Comrades and friends,
It would be wrong to say that I am surprised at being elected today by you because I knew this was in the air and it has been discussed before.[2] But though that may be so, yet it is of importance to me and affects me in a strange way, that you should elect an old colleague of yours unanimously in this way and show your confidence and trust in him. Secondly, being the leader of the Congress Party imposes a heavy burden of responsibility and many thoughts come to me. If you would forgive me, I would like to put them before you. Looking to the present-day conditions, an understanding of the Constitution leads to the presumption that the leader of the Congress Party would automatically become the Prime Minister. Now, in any country in the world today, being the Prime Minister means a heavy burden and in India, that burden is as heavy if not more so. And I am often troubled by the question as to how long an individual can carry this burden successfully. It is not merely a question of physical health—

1. Speech at the meeting of the Congress Parliamentary Party, New Delhi, 29 March 1957. Tape No. M-22/c(ii) and M-23/c(i), NMML. Nehru first spoke in Hindi and then in English.
2. Nehru was unanimously elected leader of the Congress Parliamentary Party. His name was proposed by Onkar Nath and seconded by Sharda Bhargava.

though that is also involved—but more of mental health, a freshness of the mind. To tackle the big problems that arise from day-to-day, the mind has to be fresh and when too many responsibilities and burdens are cast upon one individual, that freshness goes. This is not right. Normally I do not like it that one individual should continue for a long time in one post—I am not talking of the Prime Minister alone but generally about any position of great responsibility. I am fully aware of the constraints of the situation and for that reason only I am prepared to undertake this burden. No one should run away from responsibilities, merely for a more comfortable life. But if I had not had this in mind I would not have accepted it. Not that I am very tired or that I am not well. But no one can be objective about himself—his health or the state of his mind. A man can neither be his own doctor nor his own lawyer. He cannot gauge the state of his own physique objectively. Only others can tell if the mind is fresh or not. Often people tend to take a favourable view of themselves and divorce themselves from reality. Knowing this danger, as far as possible we must have traditions and rules whereby these difficulties may not arise. So, I want you to understand this because often I am faced with this problem. Not that I do not want to work—there is a great deal of work to be done in India—but I feel that it is not a good thing for one individual to occupy a position—and such a responsible one at that—for too long. It is neither good for him nor for the state. The fact is that you can look around all over the world—you will not find a single country, as far as I can see, where one individual has been the Prime Minister for 10 years, not only in the big countries, but in the smaller ones too. Whether it is England, America, France, Soviet Union or China or Japan—or take the smaller nations.

I am talking about the last ten years. You won't find any example of this anywhere. I am not talking of history. There may have been many Prime Ministers and Presidents. You mentioned Roosevelt—he stayed on against all traditions because a war was on and he paid for that with his life.[3] There can be no doubt about it that he died because he could not continue to carry that burden. Everyone knows that in the last few months and weeks, his health failed very rapidly. Some people even say that there is hardly anyone in the world capable of carrying on such a burden over a long period of time. A person may try to do so but it is foolhardy.

So, as I said, in the last ten years since we became independent and I became Prime Minister, no country has had one man as Prime Minister or President or a post of equivalent rank for such a long time. When I go to the Commonwealth .

3. Franklin D. Roosevelt, President of USA from 1933 to 1945, died of cerebral haemorrhage on 12 April 1945.

Prime Ministers' Conference, I see that all the Commonwealth countries have had change of Prime Ministers twice, thrice, even four times. I am the only constant factor. In England, there have been four changes in the last ten years, and these are changes in Canada, Australia, New Zealand, and South Africa. Pakistan has had frequent changes, Ceylon too. The face which is always to be seen in the Commonwealth Prime Ministers' Conference is mine. In all the other countries, whether of Europe or Asia, Communist or non-Communist, everywhere there have been changes. So, you should ponder on this question as to how long we can carry on like this here. I am not pleading a case on my behalf. But you should bear this in mind. Often the question is asked, in India and outside too, after Nehru, who? That is not the question. The question is in Nehru's life-time, what is going to happen? This is a more complicated question. Afterwards the force of circumstances will resolve the problem. But while I am alive, I do not want you to fall into a rut, get so used to my being here, that you may find yourselves in difficulties later. My mind is quite agitated over this problem. We face this problem in the Lok Sabha, Rajya Sabha and in all the States too. It is not for the Prime Ministership only. When we take up this matter in a few moments, we should, all of us, the old members and the new, reflect on this election. Many questions then arise, the main being that in many places people who had been entrenched for a long time have been ousted because people may have felt that they had been in power for too long. It is a very understandable feeling. We must not let this feeling take root, either in the Congress Committee, or in the Government—in the States and at the Centre. All these thoughts come to my mind but force of circumstances has compelled me to stay on. But you must remember that the same thing will not apply in future. So, you must not think that we have settled this matter once and for all. We will review the decision later.

You have come here, some new, some old—I don't know how many new Members are present. You will see that we have succeeded in trying to conduct the affairs of the Lok Sabha and Rajya Sabha with dignity, without hooliganism of any sort. Rules are observed and even people with differing viewpoints respect one another. We must remember this, firstly, because this is the right way and secondly, because the eyes of the world are turned towards us, to see how we function, what we say etc., and any misbehaviour would become known all over. Speeches of Members, if they have any relevance to any country in the world, is immediately publicized. If anything is said here, maybe thoughtlessly, or in a passion or even in fun, its effect is quite different. So, we have to remember that the work being in our Parliament is of historic importance, of building a new India. We have to lay very firm foundations, so your responsibility and mine is grave, a heavy burden, we may often be bogged down by small matters

ADDRESSING AN ELECTION MEETING, GURGAON, 28 FEBRUARY 1957

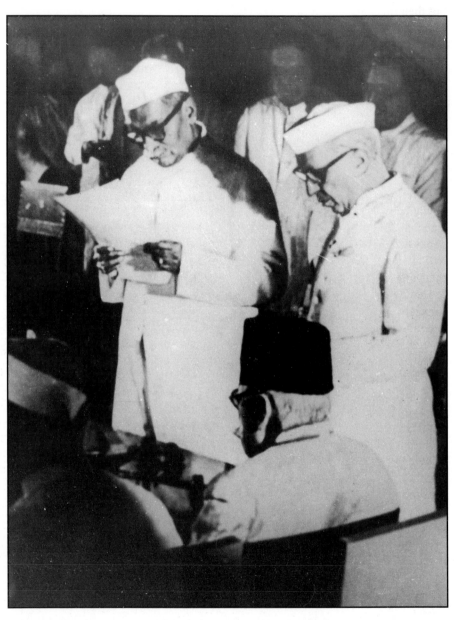

BEING SWORN IN AS PRIME MINISTER BY PRESIDENT
RAJENDRA PRASAD, NEW DELHI, 17 APRIL 1957

but then there are bigger issues behind them. I would like to mention another thing. Our Party is a large one, and to handle it is not an easy task. People have come together from all over the country. Many have complaints that they do not get an opportunity to speak or to ask a question or whatever. It is obvious that of 500 Members or 350, it may not be possible for everyone to speak though our effort is made to give as many as possible a chance. For the benefit of the new Members, I would like to explain that we have formed a number of committees on different matters so that people may be able to read and learn from experts about matters which interest them instead of everyone trying to interfere in everything. Well, I would now like to say a few words in English for those who do not understand Hindi.

Comrades, you have done me the honour of electing me as the Leader of this newly constituted and elected Congress Party for the Central Legislature. It is true that unlike, perhaps in some other places, there was no previous argument about this election, there was no canvassing and taking of signatures, etc., an evil habit which is growing in other places. There was a common expectation that you will elect me, so there was no element of excitement about this election. It seemed to be pre-determined, and so I recognize trying to look at this matter impersonally, that in the circumstances which we face today perhaps this election was almost inevitable. But because of that I want to draw your attention to certain important and basic aspects of these elections, and our working. Now, I have been Prime Minister for ten years. Ten years is a very long period for any person as a Prime Minister. Indeed, so far as these last ten years are concerned, I am the only survivor as Prime Minister. In all the other countries that I can think of there have been repeated changes whether of Presidents or Prime Ministers. That is the normal course. So, we have functioned somewhat abnormally in this country. I warn you, I am not complaining but I am merely drawing your attention to this fact and although we have functioned abnormally for these ten years which is a long period yet you have elected me leader presuming that will lead to my continuing as Prime Minister which it might for another period of years whatever that might be. Now that is a terrible ordeal for an individual. An ordeal in the sense not of hard work—one should work till one is just incapable of carrying on—but it is not a question of work, but the carrying of this tremendous responsibility which a Prime Ministership bestows on one. You know that the Prime Minister's position in a modern parliamentary democracy is rather unique. He is supposed to be the keystone of the arch of Government. If you follow the British parallel which we do more or less, a Prime Minister has a very great responsibility to shoulder and bear and very great decisions to make. Recent Prime Minister of England quite apart from what he did, being in agreement of our views or not, but his health completely broke down under the strain of that great responsibility.[4] So, it is not normally a good thing for persons who have to shoulder these heavy responsibilities, to be charged with them for long periods. We in India are getting into a bad habit and that is why I am venturing to place these words of warning before you. We are getting into a bad habit of continuing persons in high responsibility. It is a bad habit for a large number of reasons and it is worst of all for the persons so continuing. The strain is great on him. He cannot judge, no man can judge of his own capacity. No man can judge of his physical health failing him. A doctor might judge better. No man can judge of his mind not being as keen as it ought to be. No man can certainly judge of how far the mind is fresh or not and when great responsibilities have to be discharged, one ought to be at the top of one's physical form. Fitness is essential, physical and mental fitness, and for a Prime Minister who, in a sense, has to discharge the basic responsibility of Government, naturally together with his colleagues, must have this fitness of mind, alertness of mind, and freshness of mind. Now, I can't judge of my fitness. Broadly, I can say that I am generally well and fit, probably more fit than most people of my age, but it is something that creeps upon one, this staleness of mind. When people tend just to repeat what they have done, that fresh outlook goes when very much a fresh understanding of problems is necessary. We merely go on mumbling and repeating old phrases, old habits of mind. Therefore, it is not good I say, unless there are overbearing reasons to the contrary for the same persons to continue in places of high responsibility. Therefore, it is desirable to have conventions. They cannot be absolutely rigid but it is desirable to have conventions so that the personal equation does not come up. When a personal equation comes up you get into a difficulty. But if there are conventions to that effect then things are done with grace and without difficulty. I should like you to bear this in mind because looking round this picture of India today I find far too great a tendency for the same persons to continue in the same place doing the same things in the same way. That is an advantage, of course, but that has also grave disadvantages. And looking at it from the point of view of the development of democracy it is not a good thing. We have seen in these recent elections some important and valued colleagues being defeated. Not because that signified a defeat so much of the Congress because in the very area other Congressmen succeeded with the same voters, it was more a challenge to a person thinking himself indispensable and continuing in a way. The public didn't like it. One can understand their dislike of it. It is a healthy sign—a healthy sign

4. Anthony Eden resigned from Prime Ministership on 9 January 1957 and from Parliament on 10 January on grounds of ill health. Harold Macmillan took over as Prime Minister on 10 January 1957 and was elected Leader of the Conservative Party on 22 January.

of a healthy democracy and even though we may lose the valued colleagues we should appreciate the public's reaction and act up to it. Are we falling into the same habit, same rut? It is a serious matter for us to consider, because you do not see the consequences of it immediately. The consequences come afterwards and then you cannot remedy, it is better to be forewarned, it is better not to do something which is likely to lead to those consequences and unless there is the most dire necessity not to break a convention of this type of persons continuing. Just now President Roosevelt's name was mentioned, he carried on for a large number of years as the President of the United States. In the United States, there was a convention previously that there should be no third run for a President. Even second ones were not very usual. President Roosevelt had a third and fourth at least, he was elected a fourth time. Circumstances were very unusual because a Great War was being fought and they wanted a single leadership during that War but he paid for that with his life, it broke him completely and now I believe, because of what had happened then they have been warned and they have changed their convention and made it a law in the United States of America that nobody should stand, no President should stand for a third time,[5] the law of the State now, and a good law, I think, because the responsibilities on the President are terrific and no man can remain fresh after years of service. So, the responsibilities on the Prime Minister of India in the present context of things are also very great and you cannot expect that he will function with freshness as anybody who bears heavy responsibility should function and it is not a good thing for the same person to sit on the same chair. We in India are apt to be devoted to personalities. Well, to some extent there is no harm in that, but to some extent also there is a great deal of harm in that and this personal equation becomes more marked when the same person continues to occupy a high office for long, let there be changes, let there be something, let there be shake-ups, otherwise we tend to become static. And so, while I thank you in all humility for your electing me the leader of this great Party of this great organization, I can tell you in all honesty that I am not very happy at this continuation day after day, month after month, year after year. That does not mean that I am tired of work and therefore I wish to go and retire somewhere, not that. There are many many varieties of work in India which fascinate me, which draw me, wherever I am I shall work. The moment I do not work, well if I am dead to work and dead to functioning I ought to be dead to life too—I do not want to carry on like a miserable person lying in bed and not being able to walk and run and do whatever I normally want to do. But there it is. I do not feel

5. A constitutional amendment limiting the tenure of the Presidency to two terms was passed by the US Congress in March 1947.

happy at these things of this habit we are getting into in this country and that is why I have ventured to address these words to you. New Members and old will be meeting again here, of course later and new Members will learn the conventions we have developed in our work in Parliament. They will learn from old Members and otherwise too, because Parliament and any organization is based on a large number of conventions, forbearance, of mutual esteem, cooperation, self-discipline and restraint. We have to learn those. No doubt you will learn them, because we have great work to do in Parliament and I hope we shall do it worthily.

4. To Rajendra Prasad[1]

New Delhi
30 March 1957

My dear Mr President,

The general elections are now over for all practical purposes, although a few seats, chiefly in the mountains, still remain to be filled. These elections have resulted in the Congress Party in Parliament having a very large majority. The newly elected Members of this Party elected me as their leader yesterday.

It is proposed that the new Parliament should meet on the 11th May. The suggestion is that on that day, Members should be sworn in, and that the President may be pleased to Address the joint session of the two Houses on the 13th or the 14th May.

Some time during this interval, from now to the date of meeting of the new Parliament, the present Council of Ministers should resign and a new Council of Ministers should be constituted. I shall be glad to place my resignation, and with it the resignation of all my colleagues in the Council of Ministers, in your hands at any time that you may consider convenient and desirable. I shall be grateful to you for your advice in this matter as to when I should do this. The resignation of the present Council of Ministers should naturally be followed immediately with a new Council as there ought not to be any gap. It will be difficult to form a new Council for some time, and so, perhaps, the resignation

---

1. JN Collection.

of the present Council of Ministers might be deferred. But, in this matter, I seek your guidance.[2]

Yours sincerely,
Jawaharlal Nehru

2. Rajendra Prasad agreed and stated that there was no constitutional difficulty or impropriety in the present Council continuing in the meantime.

5. Resignation of the Cabinet[1]

The Prime Minister said that this was the last meeting of the present Cabinet and he proposed to offer the President in the afternoon the resignation of the Council of Ministers. If the President asks him for his recommendations regarding the new Council of Ministers, he would naturally have to propose some names. It was not his intention, however, to fill immediately all the posts of Ministers. He might add to them after meeting the newly elected Members.

2. The Prime Minister next referred to the evolution of proper conventions regarding the timing of resignation of the Cabinet and the formation of a new Government. This question might be conveniently examined some time after the new Cabinet assumes office.

3. The Prime Minister briefly referred also to the desirability of constituting a separate Ministry of Steel, Mines & Fuel, of separating 'Transport' from 'Railways' and combining it with 'Communications' in a new Ministry of Transport and Communications, abolishing the Production Ministry and dividing the work of that Ministry among other Ministries concerned and making certain other changes in the Ministries of Commerce & Industries, Education, Food and Agriculture.

4. Finally, the Prime Minister said that the country had faced very great problems, both internally and externally, during the last five years and he was thankful to all the Members of the Cabinet for the way in which they had shared the burden with him and for their cooperation and affection towards him.

1. Minutes of the Cabinet Meeting, New Delhi, 16 April 1957. JN Collection.

6. To Syed Mahmud[1]

New Delhi
16 April 1957

My dear Mahmud,[2]

We have already had a long talk and I explained to you my difficulties in this business of choosing a new Council of Ministers. Because of our old association and for other reasons, I have welcomed your being in the Council of Ministers as a Minister of State and, more especially, your association with the External Affairs Ministry. I realize that, in the circumstances, we were not able to take full advantage of your presence here, but I have no doubt that your association with this Ministry has been profitable to us and I hope to you.

I have had some hard decisions to make in regard to the new Council of Ministers and, as I told you, I have felt that I should not invite you to join this Council now. I indicated to you the many reasons for and against which I had to consider. It is necessary, of course, to have experienced colleagues. At the same time, there is a great criticism in new persons not being taken in and the same persons continuing. There is much force in both these aspects of this question, but the choice is always a very difficult one. I hope that you have appreciated my difficulties and realized that it is not for any lack of affection or appreciation of you and your work that I have come to the decision not to recommend your name.

This, of course, does not mean any break in our long association in common work. Both as a Member of Parliament as well as in any other capacity, we shall always be close to one another.

Thank you very much for your affection and for your long cooperation in our common tasks.[3]

With all good wishes,

Yours affectionately,
Jawahar

---

1. Syed Mahmud Papers, NMML. Also available in JN Collection.
2. Lok Sabha Member from Gopalganj, Bihar.
3. Similar letters were sent to Mahavir Tyagi, Arun Chandra Guha and M.C. Shah.

7. To Rajendra Prasad[1]

New Delhi
17 April 1957

Dear Mr President,

I have already submitted to you, in accordance with your directions, a list of the new Council of Ministers which I have recommended for your approval.[2]

2. This list of the Council of Ministers is divided into three parts:

(1) Members of Cabinet;[3]
(2) Ministers of State;[4] and
(3) Deputy Ministers.[5]

3. I am now enclosing a paper in which I have indicated the various Ministries and Departments to be included under each Ministry.[6] You will observe that the Ministry of Production is being abolished and the work handled in that Ministry is being allotted to appropriate Departments in other Ministries of which one is the new Ministry of Steel, Mines and Fuel. Transport has been joined with Communications in the new Ministry of Transport & Communications. The Ministry of Natural Resources and Scientific Research has been split up, Scientific Research going to the Ministry of Education while the work relating to Natural Resources has been included in the new Ministry of Steel, Mines and Fuel. There are some other changes also which have been proposed in the interest of rationalization of work.

4. I trust that these recommendations will meet with your approval.

Yours sincerely,
Jawaharlal Nehru

1. File No. 8/57, President's Secretariat. Also available in JN Collection.
2. On 16 April, Nehru submitted a list of 38 Ministers. The new Council of Ministers was sworn in on 17 April 1957.
3. Abul Kalam Azad, G.B. Pant, Morarji Desai, Jagjivan Ram, Gulzarilal Nanda, T.T. Krishnamachari, Lal Bahadur Shastri, Swaran Singh, K.C. Reddy, Ajit Prasad Jain, V.K. Krishna Menon and S.K. Patil were appointed Cabinet Ministers.
4. Satya Narayan Sinha, B.V. Keskar, D.P. Karmarkar, Panjabrao S. Deshmukh, K.D. Malaviya, M.C. Khanna, Nityanand Kanungo, Raj Bahadur, B.N. Datar, Manharlal Mansukhlal Shah, S.K. Dey, Ashok Kumar Sen, K.L. Shrimali and Humayun Kabir were appointed Ministers of State.
5. Surjit Singh Majithia, Abid Ali, A.K. Chanda, M.V. Krishnappa, Jaisukh Lal Hathi, Satish Chandra, S.N. Mishra, Bali Ram Bhagat, Mono Mohan Dass, Shah Nawaz Khan, Lakshmi N. Menon and Violet Alva were appointed Deputy Ministers.
6. Nehru held the charge of the Ministry of External Affairs and Department of Atomic Energy.

153

2
NATIONAL PROGRESS

I. ECONOMY

1. To B.G. Kher[1]

New Delhi
5 March 1957

My dear Kher,[2]

Thank you for your letter of the 1st March. I am sorry that you have not been keeping well. I hope that the rest in the Nursing Home has done you good.

I entirely agree with you on the desirability of issuing a cheap edition of Gandhiji's works in small pamphlet form. I would personally suggest that the price should be eight *annas* instead of four as you suggest. While it may be priced at eight annas for normal sale, it may be given at a reduced rate, say six *annas* or even four *annas*, to schools, panchayats, etc. This is a small matter, and you will, no doubt, decide as you think best.

One of the tremendous things happening in India today is the rapid growth of the Community Development Programme. This covers already 220,000 villages. In the course of the next five years or less, it will cover, I hope, all the 500,000 villages of India. We are thus building up an enormous apparatus for reaching the village people, apart from the other work that is being done there. Attempts are being made to start little libraries in connection with this Scheme. They have necessarily to be small, but I have no doubt that they will grow. It might well be possible for you to get a very large clientele for the cheap Gandhi book through these libraries.

I have glanced through the pamphlet called *Parishramalaya*. Broadly speaking, I agree with this approach. In fact this is more or less the approach that the Planning Commission has adopted. They are naturally thinking in terms of our Community Centres and Blocks being utilized for the development of cottage and small-scale industries. It would be a very good thing if parallel with this other ways of decentralizing industry were also adopted. But I would suggest that, in doing so, there should be cooperation with the Community Development Schemes.

1. JN Collection.
2. Chairman, Gandhi Smarak Nidhi at this time.

I am sending your pamphlet to S.K. Dey, our Minister for Community Development.

Yours sincerely,
Jawaharlal Nehru

2. Balance between Heavy and Light Industries[1]

I am happy to be here, friends. I have been reading, before I came here, the report which was sent to me of the progress of the work of the Khadi Board. Of course, we tried to follow it, more especially, in regard to the development and use of the Ambar Charkha, because the Ambar Charkha did promise substantial results in regard to some of the problems of village industries.

I should imagine that the results thus far achieved by the Ambar Charkha are promising. I will not, for a moment, say that they are entirely such as can be considered fully satisfying, but they are definitely promising and, therefore, I think that we should gain further experience in regard to not only carrying it out, but by its expansion. The Central Government have decided, have broadly accepted, if I may say so, the proposals made by the Khadi Board, subject always to periodic consideration of the entire problem every few months. We want to see exactly what is happening, what are the economic and other results.

You know very well that for a variety of reasons we are feeling great difficulties, financial I mean—internal, external, foreign exchange and all that. Though it is nothing to be surprised at, in a sense it is the obvious result of our attempting a rapid progress in a rapidly developing economy. It is only a more or less static economy that does not lead to any stresses and strains. The moment you venture out you face these factors. So, it is really these stresses and strains that indicate that the pace of our progress is much faster than it has been in the past. Also, because of foreign developments our progress is affected. If prices go up in America, England or Germany and we have to buy things from there, it affects us and we have to buy a good many things from others— machinery for instance;

1. Speech at a meeting of All India Khadi and Village Industries Board, New Delhi, 17 March 1957. PIB Files. Also published in *AICC Economic Review*, Vol. 8.

other things are very much little—in the main machines of various types. We want to manufacture them and we will, no doubt, do. But it takes more time. Every country has had to suffer this kind of circumstances. But in some countries like, say, England, or USA, they can spread the process out over long periods, generations, and even there they have to face very considerable difficulties. Other countries, who have industrialized rather rapidly, have done so under a different type of regime—the authoritarian apparatus of government.

Now, while I do believe that decentralization—whether it is in the political field or the economic field—is very desirable, we should always keep that in view, the fact remains that all modern tendencies in the world are towards decentralization whether it is the apparatus of government or political set-up or administration because bigger and bigger units come into play.

One of the main problems of the world is how to deal with this tremendous tendency to centralize? Compulsion of events makes us to decentralize. How to balance these two? I cannot give an answer to that. We have to be in touch with realities. So, this is a big problem of how having the need for centralization, yet to have decentralization to the largest possible extent. I have no solution to that except that one should go ahead and proceed by trial and error. Again we talk about finding a balance. A balance of what? Balance not in static conditions, but a balance in continually changing conditions and a balance today may be upset by something which happens tomorrow. You should remember that.

We have never lived in such a changing world, changing in accordance with the political, economic and other matters as we do today. We may give a forthright example. Take the atom bomb, atomic energy. It is likely to be used for some time but it has, in fact, tremendously changed the world. As you know, about this question of atomic energy—it has nothing to do with the Khadi Board—I would like to say something. It raises all kinds of political, economic and other problems, for one thing, for the first time in history something has come into being which can completely and absolutely destroy everything that history has created. We have had disasters in the past. We have had all kinds of catastrophes in the past too, but a great part of the accumulation of history, culture and energy survived and could survive.

Today, for the first time, we have got something in the world which can wipe out all history and culture. That is a terrific thing to remember. Whether in the political field or in the economic or anything, nobody knows exactly what might happen. All our schemes and everything that we might just do, might just be wiped out.

The second factor to be borne in mind is in relation to atomic energy and these explosions, experimental explosions, that are taking place from time to time. Thus far there are three countries, the USA, the Soviet Union and the UK.

No doubt a little later, there may be one or two more countries possible. Now, here again nobody knows really what the effect of these explosions is, not the immediate results, but the widespread effect in affecting the atmosphere and people for hundreds and thousands of miles. But everybody knows that it does have a bad effect. The result is that it may be that even with these explosions now the atmosphere is being poisoned not so as to kill a person immediately but gradually to enfeeble. It may be enfeebling the whole race gradually. Unfortunately, because these explosions are connected with military matters, full information is not given, they are secret, full information about the extent of damages is not for coming, and scientists have to keep silent about it. But it is, I think, a tragedy, a continuing tragedy, that even such things should happen when one knows that it is injurious to practically the whole race of humanity simply because one country is at the feet of another. I have said this about atomic energy although it has no relation.

The atomic bomb is a symbol of what is called scientific and technological progress. There are an infinite number of other things which are also remarkable symbols of technological progress, going ahead at a pace which is astounding. Everything that you make today is out of date by the time it is made. That is the world we live in. We cannot ignore it. We need not necessarily aim at getting everything or doing things as other countries do. There is no point in that. But there can be no doubt that a country even for survival has to be technologically advanced. Today, we talk about our five year plan and so many other things, but if you go further we really fight for survival. Advanced progress and unemployment are vital things to be dealt with. But in the final analysis in this world we like, other countries, have to fight for survival. People do not realize that. I do not mean to say that India will vanish; the country may remain, but the vital question is a question of survival. In the real sense it is a question of survival unless the people are strong enough. It is in that context that we have to be exceedingly alert, wide awake, always examining our successes and our failures, to see how best we can go ahead because in this process of survival, the economic aspect is of vital importance, the aspect of not only cresting a sense of contentment in our people to get the best out of them for their well-being but also for their advance in many other ways.

Now, the five year plan is an attempt at economic and other approaches, mainly economic. As you know, the Second Five Year Plan also lays very considerable stress on the agricultural economy and the like, that is basic, but apart from that we have laid stress on heavy industries in this Plan. We have not laid that stress on cottage industries for any economic or theoretical reasons, but this is our conviction that the survival of India depends upon that. Without our having heavy industries we do not survive as a nation in the long run. Today, the tempo of change in the world is so great that what took 100 years to achieve previously, is achieved in ten years now. We should build up heavy industries in the course of the next ten years if we are to survive. It is important and urgent for us to do that and let us not think in terms of atom bombs and all that. We are not going to make atom bombs. We, in this country, are more advanced in atomic energy than any other country in Asia and we are making good progress and we have had some very satisfactory discoveries of minerals in various part of India.

When I talk about heavy industries, I am not talking about atomic bombs. But without heavy industries we cannot remain independent, we become dependent, not only dependent but dependent in a bad way. Nor do I think we might be able to raise the standard of living adequately unless we have heavy industries at the back of us. I do not myself see any basic conflict in India, and certainly not at the present stage, between heavy industry or even other forms of mechanized industry and what are called village, household or cottage industries. I think, India offers opportunities for every type of advance provided they are coordinated, whether it is heavy or light industry, or village industries or cottage industries. Naturally, they have to be coordinated so as not to come in each other's way as far as possible.

But the problems that we have in India cannot be solved that way by any single approach. I cannot say today what 20 years later the picture of India might be. New forces come into play. You cannot ignore these forces. If the atomic energy comes we may use or we may not use it. I cannot say what the position might be 20 years later or 50 years later. I do not think anybody can really say in this changing world. What I am concerned with is today, the near future, and I am convinced that in this context of India we have to develop all these fronts simultaneously, that is to say, not only the front of heavy industry, but village and household industry. Furthermore, we have attached considerable importance to the work of the Khadi and Village Industries Board. It may be that some people in the Khadi and Village Industries Board view with some disfavour our stress on heavy industry or big industry, just as it may be that some people outside the Board view the cottage and small industries with disfavour and consider them a waste of energy and money. There are these obvious facts.

Both, if I may say so, tend to look at one side of the picture and in the context of this ever changing revolutionary situation in the world I can only say with some confidence that we have to explore and advance in all these fronts always keeping our eyes open, always be prepared to make adjustments to advance faster and maybe sometimes change our direction slightly, with no dogmas, but with certain objectives, of doing good to our people. Widespread advance and prosperity create employment and well-being and so on and so forth in the context of a peaceful existence. In fact, this desire to adjust makes it essential, even if there were no other reasons for doing so, to plan carefully and also to have a socialistic structure of our economy. Otherwise we cannot do it. If we leave it to purely competitive existence in an acquisitive society, this cannot be done. Therefore, we do attach importance to the work of Khadi Board but I wish you will appreciate when I say that we are going to consider this question with no dogmas but from the point of view of results, results judged not only in financial terms but in social terms. We can only proceed on that basis. There is no other basis on which we can proceed today. I do not consider results purely from the financial terms. We have to proceed both swiftly and with caution. There should always be caution so that in a difficult situation we may not suddenly land ourselves in greater difficulties. That is our general principle.

But even in a small thing, take the Ambar Charkha which is expanding its field of activities, we have to consider rather carefully the foreign exchange element involved in it. At the present moment it may not be very great but we have to consider it in relation to foreign exchange, every smallest bit of it. However, as I have told you, we want you to go ahead according to the Plan and subject always to our examining this every few months fully to see whether we can expedite on one aspect and not the other or slow down a little bit because we cannot afford today to take too grave risks with our money. It is so tight especially with anything involving foreign exchange.

In the final analysis, I have no doubt that all your programmes will depend on the techniques that you develop. Naturally, you cannot compare your techniques with the techniques of big industry. But the techniques of small industry are equally important because small industry or cottage industry have certain advantages, apart from the social side, we have seen even otherwise it has advantages which big industries do not have. Anyhow, ultimately your success depends on the techniques used. The moment your mind is closed you are doomed. Nothing is final in this world. Everything improves in techniques and I have no doubt that the Ambar Charkha can be improved and will be improved. It has to be a dynamic approach all the time constantly trying to make it better.

Therefore, in this task, which some of us are privileged to undertake and serve that is building up a new India, this question of cottage industries, village industries has to play a very important part and in that, if I may mention, your Board was cooperative and also receiving cooperation of all, not only of Acharya Vinoba Bhave and his colleagues in the Bhoodan movement but also in our Community Development Ministry. I consider the Community Development and the National Extension Service the most revolutionary thing which is being done in India today, revolutionary in the sense of changing human beings. We have given them opportunities to change themselves not by external pressure

SPEAKING AT THE DEVELOPMENT COMMISSIONERS' CONFERENCE, MUSSOORIE, 29 APRIL 1957

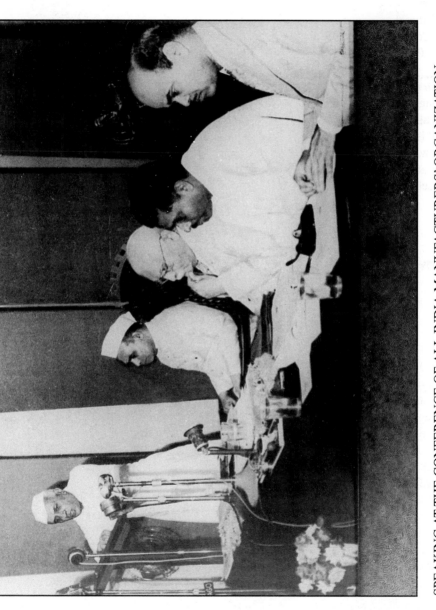

SPEAKING AT THE CONFERENCE OF ALL INDIA MANUFACTURERS' ORGANIZATION, NEW DELHI, 13 APRIL 1957

but really by creating new life in them. The speed of the advance of this movement is terrific. Broadly speaking, the Community Development movement in India and the Khadi Board came into existence round about the same time. I think, the Community Development movement has a few months seniority. It was spread to 220,000 villages covering a population of 129 millions. This may mean nothing at all. Nevertheless, the figures themselves are striking and such information as we have is also extraordinarily encouraging. I do not mean to say that 220,000 villages are forging ahead with flags waving and all that. I do not say that they are all on the same level. Some are rather backward.

It is, however, really something remarkable that is happening in India. As you know, we have asked the Community Projects Administration, particularly to pay attention to small and household industries. There should, of course, be the closest cooperation between your Board and them.

3. To Chief Ministers[1]

New Delhi
21 March 1957

My dear Chief Minister,
I have not written to you for a very long time, although events have followed one another thick and fast, both in India and in the outside world. I have not had much time for writing but, even more than that, I have not been in the mood to do so. I hope you will forgive me.

2. I hope to write to you a more comprehensive letter somewhat later. Today, I am writing to you about a particular matter connected with our Community Development Schemes.

3. In the course of my election tour, and otherwise also, I have laid very great stress on the importance of our Community Blocks and National Extension Service Scheme. I have called them revolutionary and perhaps the most significant thing that we are doing in India at present. That is no small praise, for we are doing very many significant things in India. I did not bestow that

1. File No. 17 (229)/57-66-PMS. This letter has been printed in G. Parthasarathi (ed.), *Jawaharlal Nehru: Letters to Chief Ministers, 1947-1964*, Vol. 4 (New Delhi, 1988), pp. 478-481.

praise on them lightly or without adequate reason. I do think that the waking up of the eighty per cent of our population living in the villages is a tremendous task. Also that, in the measure we have done this work thus far, it has been a great achievement. But the very success that we have met adds to our burdens and increases the complexities of the problem. Nevertheless, this rapid progress is most exhilarating.

4. Figures may mean much or very little. And yet, statistical figures give some idea of what has been accomplished. These Community Schemes now have spread out to two hundred twenty thousand villages in India, covering a population of one hundred and twenty-nine millions. It is our programme, as you know, that we should cover all the five hundred thousand villages of India by the end of the Second Five Year Plan. This does not mean some kind of superficial coverage, but intensive and organized work in these areas. It means training up a vast number of persons, young men and young women, to undertake this work. Indeed, the question of providing trained personnel has become the most important of all, because everything depends on them and the quality of their work. Essentially, this is not mere superficial building of roads or school-houses or hospitals and dispensaries or better agriculture, most important as all these things are. We aim at something bigger and deeper, that is, the building up of the innumerable human beings in villages. From that, everything else flows. Of course, all these things go together and cannot be separated.

5. We are laying stress in this programme on improved agriculture and more production and on the small-scale and village industries programme. I hope we are also laying stress on cooperatives and close contact with panchayats. Thus, we give a wide and firm foundation to the State and to the intricate working of its creative and productive apparatus at the ground level.

6. Soon, new Ministries will be formed in the States, and I am writing to you specially to keep this Community Development Programme in view at this juncture.

7. Some time ago, I requested all the Chief Ministers, as well as the Central Ministers dealing with the Community Development Programme, to be good enough to send me quarterly reports. I am grateful to them that they have sent these more or less regularly. But, I have often found that these reports contain a mass of detail. In effect, these reports are copies of the detailed statistical reports sent to the Ministry for Community Development. Such reports are very necessary for that Ministry, which goes into them carefully and analyses them, and then sends this analysis to the States as well as to the Members of the Central Committee.

8. To repeat this statistical material in the report sent to me personally, is hardly necessary and not of any particular help.

9. I would suggest to you not to trouble to send me this detailed report, which anyhow is sent to the Community Development Ministry. I would like you to send me a brief report of a page or two, just giving me your personal assessment of the progress in your State. This would be much more helpful to me and, perhaps, to you also. May I request you, therefore, to send this brief report containing your personal assessment of the progress made every quarter?

10. I have previously suggested that, owing to the importance of the Community Development Programme, the Chief Minister himself should be the Chairman of the State Development Committee and in charge of the portfolio of Community Development. I believe this is so in many of the States. I suggest that this practice should continue, so that the Chief Minister may remain in intimate touch with all these developments.

11. The State Development Committee should, I suggest, meet regularly and keep in close touch with developments. It should be a live body, making proposals and criticisms. It should make a proper assessment of what is being done every quarter. The Chief Minister, in his personal report to me, might mention what is being done by the State Development Committee.

12. There is another suggestion, which I should like to make to you. We have had, in Parliament, an informal Consultative Committee of Members of Parliament which keeps in touch with the Ministry of Community Development. I suggest that such a Committee might be formed in your State also. This would keep your State Legislature in touch with Community Development in the State.

Yours sincerely,
Jawaharlal Nehru

4. Ambar Charkha[1]

Jawaharlal Nehru: I think, Sir, the honourable Member would not have said what he has said if he had had all the facts etc. about the Ambar Charkha before him. It is not a question of approaching this, if I may say so, ideologically, for or against, but scientifically, in finding out what it can give and what it can do. The

1. Speech in the Lok Sabha, 21 March 1957. *Lok Sabha Debates*, Vol. I, Part II, cols. 302-303.

Ambar Charkha, I cannot say at the present moment, that it is final or a success, but I do say that it is one of the most promising things in this particular direction, that is to say, a higher technique in hand-spinning, a small cottage machine for hand-spinning. It is being improved day-to-day. As it is, it is undoubtedly a very considerable improvement on the old method of hand-spinning, and we believe that it is quite likely that it can become a very great improvement indeed, so that from every point of view, and looking at it purely from the scientific point of view, it is desirable to experiment and find out, because if this is a success it would mean, well, a petty revolution in a sense.

But, apart from that, one has to look at it also from another point of view; that is the social, the employment etc., point of view. One must remember that this has not taken the place of anything. There is no question of our thinking in terms of big industry being displaced by cottage industry. As things are in India, there is enormous room for both, and this is one of the most promising methods which has already yielded fairly good results and which is likely to yield, I think, much more substantial results. It is from that point of view that we are doing it.

5. Democracy and Economic Progress[1]

Mr President[2] and friends,
You invite me every year and I present myself, to listen to you and to say a few words. I think, all of us benefit by this exercise and at least it is essential that we should maintain close contact with one another. It is obvious that whether our views are similar or not, we must cooperate. There is no other alternative.

We have set ourselves some goals in this country and the broad picture is before you in the form of the five year plans. The First had envisaged a broad picture and it has been further defined in the Second. But we have decided upon one thing unequivocally and that is to take India on the path of progress as rapidly as possible. When I talk of India, I am not thinking of the two thousand

1. Speech at the 30th annual session of the Federation of Indian Chambers of Commerce and Industry, New Delhi, 23 March 1957. AIR tapes, NMML. Nehru first spoke in Hindi and then English.
2. Lakshmipat Singhania.

miles of territory but of the 37 crores of human beings. How are they to progress to emerge out of the mire of poverty in which they have struggled for so long? This is the question which haunts me constantly. India's problem is not one but 37 crores, as many problems as there are human beings. I am stressing this because very often our great scholars, pundits and professors quote statistics as though the people are not human beings but mere numbers. We have to look at everything from the point of view of how it will affect a human being.

This is right on principle in any case. But the other aspect of it is that whether it is a good principle or not, circumstances compel us to accept this norm. In a democracy in which every adult has the right to vote and give voice to his views, you open a door to something which will not be denied. If there is an attempt to muzzle freedom of expression, it will only lead to a great upheaval. In India, we have a true democracy. We have had adult suffrage at a time when we were facing grave economic and social problems. We have the task of bringing about a peaceful socio-economic revolution just as we have brought about a political revolution by getting Independence.

So, a combination of these two circumstances has made the problem more complex. It is more difficult and in another sense it could be easier too if we organize the strength of the entire nation into a great force. In other countries, you will find that they did not have to face the two problems together. Democracy, as we know it with complete freedom of expression, is a comparatively new phenomenon in the world. Many countries do not have it still. Even in those countries which talk a great deal of freedom there is not a trace of it.

So, the combination of these two things has made the entire problem of deciding upon the path that we should follow extremely complex. The Government of India or you and I sitting in this assembly may chalk out a policy. But ultimately it is the 37 crores of human beings who decide. Who can complain if a section among them decides that their present sufferings should be alleviated and that they should be able to live a life of greater ease and comfort. We can go to them and say that they are absolutely right. But we have a long way to go for we need new industries and investments have to be made in development work, and so we should wait. What we say may make very good sense. But it cannot satisfy the man who wants an easier life today. He has the right to decide in favour of that and to express his views freely. He can punish those who go against his wishes.

I think, we have not understood this matter fully yet. Very few of us think about democracy in its absolute sense. We seem to think that democracy means elections with all its accompanying noise and fanfare and candidates being chosen for Parliament or State Assemblies. Elections are only one aspect of democracy. The task of planning and laying the foundation of a strong economy that we have taken up arises not out of our wishes alone but from a compulsion of circumstances. We would have to do this whether we want or not. It cannot be stopped. So, the question is how to go about it. Our Government has adopted the path of planning. But the five year plans are not rigid documents. We have repeatedly said that we will make changes and alterations as and when we think they are necessary in the light of our experience, success and weaknesses. That does not mean that having drawn up a plan we can tamper with it constantly. It has taken years of careful thought in drawing up and we must adhere to it. But the doors are always open to make changes if circumstances change. Those who close their minds and divorce themselves from reality whether it is in politics or in economic matters are bound to come to grief. It is imperative to keep an open, clear mind in the modern times and be mentally agile in order to understand every move that takes place in the world.

Anyhow, we have chalked out a broad line of action in our five year plans. We will try to attain those goals not only because we think they are right for us but because there is no other alternative for India. Democracy cannot accept any other alternative. I have no doubt whatsoever on this score. A few changes here and there may be necessary. But that is a different matter. We want to implement the plans in such a manner that we can take advantage of our experience and in consultation with others. It is obvious that the same thing need not necessarily benefit everyone everywhere in the world. One man's gain is another's loss. So, there is constant conflict. Volumes have been written on this subject. How is this conflict to be resolved? It would be wrong to close one's eyes to it. At the same time, it would be equally wrong to aggravate the existing tensions. We must think of a way by which without closing our eyes to reality, we can resolve the tensions and create a climate of progress in the country. Our attitude to this problem is to try to find a way by which all the forces in the country can be mobilized into a united front.

I believe in a socialistic pattern of society. We have declared this as our goal. But even there, we have not adopted a rigid attitude which would prevent us from having any leeway or learning from our past experience or changed circumstances. At the same time we have allowed a very large margin within which other forces can also operate. The doors are open to all of you to function in your own way. In fact, we want to help you in that. There is no question of blind acceptance here. The basic question before us is to increase production of essential consumer goods and ensure their equitable distribution which will reduce the disparity between the haves and the have-nots. We do not want the new wealth to remain in the hands of a few people. That is not right.

What is the best way to implement the five year plans and attain the goals that we have set for ourselves? It is obvious that when a nation progresses very rapidly, it has to carry a tremendous burden and face innumerable problems and hardships. You complain, for instance, that the tax burden is so heavy that there is no surplus for investment. That is true. But at the same time, there are other factors which have to be taken into account. All of us are agreed on one thing and that is, there are grave problems facing us. But they are signs of our progress, our courage and daring. The faster a country progresses, the more difficulties we will have to face and our strength will increase in the same proportion to overcome them, so we must not panic. Nor should we close our eyes to the difficulties. There are grave problems and difficulties, particularly in the economic sphere. We want your advice on that. We cannot solve those problems very easily. The entire country will have to share the burden. We cannot run away from our responsibilities nor can we spread them out. There is no way in which we can increase the burden on the masses which is already staggering under the burden it is carrying.

We must keep this in mind. There is no point in our criticizing one another. I have no objection to criticisms. It is only through constructive criticism that we can keep ourselves on an even keel. I do not want that there should be any obstacle in the way of freedom of expression and criticism. Yes, you must also not complain if I reply to your criticisms just as stringently. It should be a two-way affair. There should be an open debate, devoid of malice or ulterior motives.

Let me give you an example. Some people often talk of free enterprise. Let them advocate it and I shall counter their arguments whenever I get the opportunity. I have an equal right to present my point of view. We want to allow free enterprise to flourish. But if they try to convert it into a philosophy and form organizations to back it up, I would say they are on the wrong track. In fact, I would go so far as to say that they cannot succeed. How can they take 37 crores of people with them? They are mistaken if they think they can. If they can point out the flaws in our way of thinking them their criticism will have some impact. But to condemn the five year plans and other economic policies as useless can do no good to anyone.

The fact of the matter is that the world is in a revolutionary ferment. India has changed. Today, in this revolutionary world of ours, it is only the nation which think along revolutionary lines, rightly or wrongly, can progress, understand the reality of the modern world and bring it under their control. Gone are the days when the world remained unchanging and stagnant. Today, we need human beings with agile minds and strong physique capable of running ahead in order to keep circumstances under control.

India is a vast country and I feel that in the last ten years we have achieved a great deal about which we can be justly proud. It is not that we have not made mistakes or there are no weaknesses in us. But ours is a great country and we must strive to uphold its honour, with our heads held high and confidence in ourselves, friendship towards all but ultimately relying on our own strength. We have not given in to outside pressure or threats, nor resort to sycophancy. We feel that this is the best way in a relationship between individuals or nations, an emphasis on equality and friendship, not a relationship of master and servant or superior and inferior. That is not right either for individuals or nations. Therefore, we have adopted a policy of friendship and cooperation with everyone while holding on to our freedom to follow the path that we think is right. We feel that this is the only way to maintain peace in the world.

You can compare the conditions in the rest of Asia and elsewhere with what we have done, the areas in which we have progressed or lagged behind, the mistakes that we have made. But at the same time we must bear in mind that the least bit of complacency can lead to grave danger. We can lay ourselves open to dangers in the economic or political field as well as in international affairs. But most important of all, we can solve these problems only when there is fundamental unity among us. Opinions may differ but there should be fundamental unity in the country.

You referred to the recent general elections. The results may not always have been to our liking. But that does not matter. We will accept the verdict of the people. However, these elections have brought to the fore an ancient malady of India, a dangerous aspect of our national character which decides the country and breaks up its unity. One, of course, is the caste system which has kept Indian society in fragments for centuries. It is bad enough to have these distinctions in the social sphere. But to bring casteism into politics is extremely pernicious. The other dangerous aspect of these elections was provincialism. You may say that there are two kinds of problems in the country. One is internal, the socio-economic problems, which includes the five year plan and our agricultural or industrial policies etc. It is obvious that our progress depends on the headway that we make in this area. The second category is in the area of international affairs and our foreign policy.

These are the two broad categories of national problems. I do not say that every man in India is of the same opinion. But, I think, by and large, there is a consensus of opinion on these two major areas—international and domestic policies. The picture that emerged during these elections was that while there was not much talk of five year plans or economic and other domestic policies, provincialism was the uppermost concern with many of the parties. There were complaints about decisions taken by the Government regarding territories which were to belong to different provinces. I do not say that the people do not have the right to question our decision. It is obvious that they have every right to express their opinions freely. We have a duty to take their views and emotions into account. But what I am drawing your attention to is that at a crucial moment when we have to think about major national and international issues of progress and India's role in maintaining peace in the world, if the people's attention is absorbed in different issues, it would mean that we are not capable of putting national interest or world peace before our own petty preoccupations. It is not wrong to be attached to one's own province. But to put that before the nation is wrong.

I am not criticizing anyone. I respect the opinions of others. I also agree that considerations other than merely provincialism tend to obscure issues. There is resentment against police firings or what is considered ill-treatment by the Government. It is obvious that it is regretted when people are killed in police firings. If I had my way, the question of police firing would not arise at all. But sometimes it has to be done. However, I am always upset by its consequences. What I want to point out is that it is wrong to focus attention solely on provincial issues when there are grave national concerns before us whether those provincial issues are justified or not. It shows how easily we get carried away by petty problems and forget the larger issues. Those who are totally preoccupied with petty issues to the exclusion of everything else have obviously not understood the significance of larger issues.

I am trying to draw your attention to the fact that we tend to get carried away too easily by casteism, provincialism and communalism. How can we hope to progress so long as we are steeped in such stupidity? As far as I am concerned, I will tell you quite clearly that you can elect whom you wish. But we cannot serve the nation if we throw away honour and dignity for the sake of a few votes.

So, these are the dangers that we face. We can sit here and pass resolutions, good resolutions. But if you look at the picture that India presents today, it is of a nation of 37 crores of human beings, a vital vibrant nation in ferment. It is in a fever of unrest and turmoil and we have to keep our finger on the nation's pulse constantly. It is not an easy matter to take on the responsibilities of a great nation like this. But we cannot run away from them. We have to shoulder the responsibilities bravely with determination to face any difficulties that may arise cheerfully and overcome them. We must not allow ourselves to go under. We have certainly learnt this one lesson in the last 30-40 years. But the difficulties that we face concern the entire nation. None of us can hope to solve our problems single-handedly. They can be solved only through cooperation and understanding. There are complex problems in the world of today. I hope that you will realize that the greatest danger to the nation is not economic difficulties but the fact that we have not yet fully grasped the need for national unity. We live in separate compartments creating barriers in the name of caste, religion, province and language. Unless we get out of these narrow grooves, we cannot go very far on the path of progress.

What is there for me to say about the rest of your memorandum? There is much in it about which there can be no two views. There are certain matters about which there can be two schools of thought. But it is quite evident that gradually, inspite of differences of opinion, the nation has started thinking along similar lines. I have no doubt about it. In a broad way, we are on the same track. The nation as a whole accepts the broad aspects of planning. We have to carry heavy burdens for if we fail to do so now, they will only grow heavier. We cannot escape them.

The nation has been going through a crisis during the last two-three years. There is no alternative except to tighten our belts and with cool, clear minds go ahead, and to face whatever difficulties may arise. I hope that we will have your wholehearted cooperation in this. We will certainly listen to whatever complaints you may have and tell you about our problems in return. We must try to find a way out by putting our heads together. But it must be borne in mind that it is not a question of your intellect or mine alone, but of the wisdom or stupidity of millions of human beings. We have to take them along with us because the journey that we have embarked upon involves 37 crores of human beings, not a handful of us alone.

It has become a tradition for me to speak in two languages on this occasion. I shall now say a few words in English.

Mr President and friends,

In the course of your address, Mr President, you said something which I underlined immediately. You said, it is not only machinery that becomes obsolete, one has to guard against the obsolescence of the mind. No truer word could have been said, and so far as I am concerned, I have ventured with great respect and humility to repeat that lesson. Because we, all of us, tend to become rather obsolescent in our thinking. We see the machine which is out of date, but it is not so easy to deal with minds that are out of date.

We in this country, more specially, who have high traditions, who have a great history, and who have also very heavy burdens, that a long tradition and a long past given us, customs and other things, and how they pull us back at every stage. So, we have always, always to remember, that the world is changing and we have to change with it. I do not mean to say that what might be called certain basic things about life also change, I do not know. But there are certain principles I believe, which have a certain changeless quality. But in the rest of the trappings of life, our political systems, our economic systems and so many social things, they change with the changing world. It is only, when we do not change with the changing world that we get trapped and left behind as we have been in the past, and we are trying to come out of that. Therefore, these letters of yours, Mr President, should be inscribed in prominent places wherever your organization works so that you may always remember that the one thing to guard against is obsolescence of the mind. It is a truism, for anyone to say as I say, and I go on saying, that we live on the threshold of the atomic age, and yet that is a terrible thing to remember. It is terrible, not terrible, I mean in the sense that we need be frightened about it. There is no need to be frightened about anything, and patently we need not be frightened because if this atomic age leads us to widespread disaster, we will not be there to regret it. But anyhow, it is a tremendous thing to consider in its social consequences, apart from its military consequences or destructive consequence, it is a tremendous thing we have before us. And that should shake us from all our previous limited thinking and convictions. I do not mean to say we should rush into all kinds of anticipations and speculations, but it is something which should shake us.

Now, you may have read even in today's papers, a reference was made and in the President's Address about certain rather remarkable finds of Uranium and other atomic minerals in India. That is, well, in a sense a good thing for us, because it is a valuable thing, and we even require it, but also it is another burden. All these things entangle us. And well, modern life is complicated and will become more and more entangled, but what I am driving at is this, that we have to consider all these problems in a changing dynamic world with dynamic and changing minds, and when people talk to me, or people talk about free enterprise, there is, I think, some truth in what they say. But also I think that there is a vast quantity of error in what they say. In the sense that you cannot fit in that thinking of the 19th century to the atomic age or to middle of the 20th century, and if you can fit in that, in some countries you may, you cannot fit it in India, and I am concerned with India, I am not out to offer advice to other countries, with different circumstances, different backgrounds, countries more developed or less developed than India. We have to do with India as it is today, and we have to learn from other countries and we must be humble enough to learn everything we can from every country, but we can never learn much or with profit if we allow ourselves to be uprooted from our soil. No country, I am quite convinced, can progress unless it has strong roots in its soil. If those roots are there, you can grow and branch out and flower and leaf will come, and they may be freshened by winds from outside, from other countries and everywhere, but without those roots you are doomed as a nation, it cannot progress. I am absolutely convinced of this and the more I see this world around me of this day-to-day, whether in Europe or Asia or elsewhere, I see that the nation which loses its roots does not prosper, will not prosper, and gradually fades. So, we have to learn and we have to keep our roots, and we have to find out our own policies, political, economic and social, learning again from others, but deciding for ourselves what is right for us, in view of the circumstances prevailing in our country.

So, I want you to think of these problems in that way and I promise you that in whatever we may do, our Government, we are not rigid, we are not dogmatic, if we have given up dogma in religion, at least some of us, surely don't expect us to become dogmatic, in other matters. We have open minds, we have firm minds, I hope, and we have convictions too. And we do not wish to wobble and remain in a fluid condition. We have to march, because apart from our own desire to march, there is the compulsion of circumstances which makes us march. As I was saying in my Hindi speech, democracy in the fullest sense has certain necessary consequences. We talk a great deal about democracy today, but there are exceedingly few countries, that have democracy in the wide world, I mean to say full democracy. Most just use the word, and have nothing resembling democracy, in the normal sense of the word. Certainly, and even this democracy that we see is a recent growth in the world, relatively recent, 30-40 years, whatever it may be. Previously, there were limited franchise. Now with this adult franchise, everybody having the right to vote, and if you have fair elections, an impartial one, giving them this right to express their opinions firmly, change governments and the like, quite a new state of affairs has arisen not only in our country, but elsewhere too. We cannot, like some wise men sitting somewhere, imagine that we are governing India, nor can you in your Chambers, in your Committee think that you are going to direct the economic policy of the country along lines that you consider proper. In the final analysis, it is the millions of India that determine, and that will determine, rightly or wrongly, you and I can try to convince them, to convert them, certainly, not only in determining policies, but what is far more important, in implementing them, because these vast social and economic policies cannot be implemented by some act of Parliament or by some Government decree, they are implemented in the factory, in the field and in the market place by millions of people. Only then can you get a nation on the move.

So, we have to face these vast and enormous problems and we have arrived at a stage, and it is, I believe, a critical stage, leading a country from a certain type of, well, underdeveloped economy to a better type, to a higher type. Now, this transition period is a difficult one. The difficulty means that somebody has to pay for it, the whole country has to pay for it, of course, and the question arises how far those burdens which necessarily have to be borne, and how are they to be spread out, that is the question that Governments have to consider.

You gentlemen complain, and with justification, of tax burdens. They are heavy in India. It is true. But what about the burdens of the 80 per cent of the population of this country? They are very heavy and they have been heavy all this time and those 80 per cent have got a powerful voice in shaping the country's destiny today. Quite rightly. So that we have to deal, we have to shoulder that burden. Are we going to say that the burden is too heavy for us, or our arms are too weak, or our legs are too weak for us to carry us forward? Is that a kind of thing, any man or any nation of spirit going to say that? We have assumed the burden and we shall carry it, whatever happens. We must take up that attitude not only because, if I may say so with certain pride, and we are a proud people, and I do not see why we should be frightened of any circumstance internal or external, that might arise. There is one lesson that many of us learnt, when we served under our Great Master, Gandhiji, and that was not to be frightened. It has served us well when crises and difficulties have faced us, when in this city of Delhi and in Punjab and in Pakistan, 9 or 10 years ago, blood was flowing all round, well, we did not run away from it. We faced those circumstances, in spite of the horror that we saw. And so, we shall face every circumstance, but it is not a question of pride, though pride in a nation is an important thing, and I want my nation to be proud, not in a bad sense, not overbearing, not conceited, but certainly self-reliant and proud and certain pride in ourselves, in our people. But, as I said, it is not a question of pride, it is a question of the compulsion of circumstances. You dare not let go, you have to go forward, you cannot sit down in the middle of a river or something. Therefore, one has to, if one has to carry on, then one must put all one's united energy into doing it as well as possible, and not pull in various and different directions.

I am sure all of you gentlemen realize that and, by and large, agree with what I say. Broadly speaking, we have accepted a certain pattern and a certain road along which we should advance. It is laid down, more or less, in the five year plans. We say, they are not rigid, we may vary them, we may change them, naturally we may add to them, we may subtract from them, according to circumstances. But broadly, it is there and broadly you have accepted it and the country has accepted it. So, let us then march along that path to the best of our ability and not argue too much about certain things which had been decided upon, not that I wish to stop argument, but I want to turn all our energies in surviving and overcoming the difficulties that have arisen rather than in philosophizing about them.

Now, I mentioned in my Hindi speech a fact, which I should like to repeat. I do not want any of us in India to hide our failings. It is a bad habit, because we have to get over the failings, we do not get over them by hiding them. I am quite prepared to shout them out even, and I do to our people.

One of our principal failings has been and is, a great tendency to disrupt, a great tendency to forget the unity, the basic unity of India and to get excited about secondary matters. Now, the moment you make these secondary matters primary matters, well, you are lost. Then you have lost the sense of perspective, the sense of proportion, and that is what we have seen in these elections which have taken place.

The elections have been very good elections, and I think, we can be proud of those elections, in spite of what things that may have happened here and there. But what I am trying to put before you is this, that the elections have brought up not only this business of caste again, but this provincialism and linguism, if kept in their proper place may be all right, and are all right, but if they get out of their proper sphere, are dangerous for India as a whole. Now, I am not entering into the merits of these arguments that have been raised in regard to this states' redistribution. These things have been finalized by Acts of Parliament, and it seems to me very foolish to upset things which have been decided, without giving adequate thought and time and experience being gathered. But, here we are, I want others to think of this. Here we are struggling politically, economically against grave problems, world problems, and some of our friends and colleagues having their minds completely occupied by the question of the boundary of a State being changed or not, certain internal administrative questions. Now, it passes my comprehension that these friends of ours do not see how this concentration on matters of very secondary importance injures our work in the primary fields of activity, national or international. It may be that many people are annoyed or angry at something that our Government did—annoyed and angry, let us say, that in certain circumstances firing took place. Some people were shot down and killed, others were wounded. Well, I can quite understand that. I do not think, anyone in India can dislike this firing business as I do, I have a horror of it. I think that it is a bad thing and I hope that it will be possible to put an end to this, except when one cannot possibly help it, and all my heart goes out in sympathy with those who may suffer from it, specially, if they are young people who are the hope of our nation, but having said that, let us not mix up sentiment, however justified the sentiment may be, with higher political considerations of the nation's welfare. Because after all, a nation and a people are judged, they are judged about their maturity, how mature are they, do they get swept away by tides of sentiment, or do they balance things and then they react. I hope we are a mature nation. And I hope, therefore, that we shall consider questions that come up now before us in a mature way, and not merely and purely in an emotional and sentimental way.

There are one or two minor matters that I should like to remind you, which might be helpful to you. There has been a reference in the President's Address to the technical manpower difficulty. Of course, we are very conscious of this, and we are taking, I think, I cannot say if they are completely adequate steps, I hope they are, or they will be, but certainly many many steps towards training people and we want your cooperation in that, and we want your cooperation in other matters, and in training the technical or managerial limited manpower that we have. You require it and Government requires it. We do not wish to deprive you of the people you may have when you may want, but at the same time we have to come to some understanding sometimes, if our need is great we shall talk to you and take some of your men and we may be able to give you some of our men, but the main thing is that we should train up these people, because we cannot progress, after all, it is human beings that count, and they take time to train up. You may have a steel plant built in, let us say, in five years, but it will take a much longer time to build up the man who is going to control the steel plant. It is far more important. Money is a troublesome thing in this world, but I do think still, it is the least important of things. And a certain contempt for money is a very useful habit of mind, I think. I do not mean that the contempt should spread to the possessor of money, unless that money is used for wrong and vulgar purposes, when one cannot help feeling rather irritated. But it is the human beings that count, and it is to the extent that we produce trained human beings so that our country will advance.

I might tell you in this connection that in our Army, quite a considerable number—according to our rules, why those rules have been framed that way, I do not quite know—anyhow, quite a considerable number of young officers and men, retire from our Army at a very early age, meaning in the 30s, or maybe in the early 40s. Quite good officers, men, having served their period, they retire. Now, they are fine material, and many of them are technical people. It seems to me very very unfortunate that this fine material should be wasted, apart from the question of their being thrown out of employment. So, we have made arrangements, our Planning Commission has gone into this matter, and both in Government employ and in other civil employ, if we want to utilize them, because we really think they are very good, of course, they are very disciplined, which is a good thing, but otherwise they are good too, and I suggest to you also too you may get in touch, I don't know, with our Planning Commission, but I think, I am not merely saying this to provide employment for our young officers and men who retire after their period of service, but because I think, they really are good and those who employ them will benefit by their work.

I thank you again for your having invited me today and permitted me to tell you what I have in my mind. Thank you.

6. To T.T. Krishnamachari[1]

New Delhi
25 March 1957

My dear T.T.,[2]

Babubhai Chinai,[3] the new President of the Federation of Indian Chambers of Commerce and Industry, came to see me this afternoon. He has already seen you and probably he told me what he had already told you. Nevertheless, I repeat it.

1. He suggested to me that in view of the difficult foreign exchange position, I might make an appeal for gold and jewellery. I am perfectly prepared to make such an appeal if you think it worthwhile. Indeed, I have had this in my mind for some considerable time. The question is how and when to make it and in what form.[4]

2. He said that the old idea of occasionally our meeting selected industrialists might be revived. I said I was quite agreeable to this.

3. He suggested that a strong delegation, presumably of industrialists, should go to Europe and America. He thought that this might help in the foreign exchange position. I told him that I had no objection to this being done, but the Finance Minister had better consider this.

Yours sincerely,
Jawaharlal Nehru

1. File No. 37(35)/56-59-PMS. Also available in JN Collection.
2. Union Minister of Finance.
3. Babubhai Maneklal Chinai (1913-75); Industrialist from Bombay; Member, Bombay Legislative Council, 1952-58; President, Federation of Indian Chambers of Commerce and Industry, 1957-58; Member, Rajya Sabha, 1958-70.
4. Nehru made the appeal at the annual conference of All India Manufacturers' Organization on 13 April 1957. See *post*, pp. 191-192.

7. To S.K. Dey[1]

New Delhi
5 April 1957

My dear Dey,[2]

I went this morning to the Najafgarh area to see the damage caused by the recent hailstorm which occurred last month. I stopped at many villages and met the people there. I was told that Najafgarh is an important centre of one of your Community Blocks. In Najafgarh itself apparently much has been done in the shape of particular improvements, but in the surrounding villages I was a little surprised to find that people were almost completely ignorant of the Development Schemes and the work done by this Najafgarh Block. Evidently, this work has not touched them at all or enthused them. Also, it seemed to me that your Development Officers, were not at all concerned with this hailstorm and its effects which has shaken up the people all over the area. I should have thought that any natural calamity which affected the people should become the immediate concern of the Developmental authorities. Otherwise, they simply work in the air without any direct link with what is happening to the people.

I had a vague idea also that the Development Officer, whom I do not know, functions rather as a superior officer without any real intimate touch with the people. Some people referred to him as a big officer coming occasionally.

The general impression that I got was not very satisfactory. There are several schemes roundabout there, and notably one to improve a certain waterlogged area around the Najafgarh Jheel and the old canal which has become waterlogged. I think, the PWD is going to take this up in hand. I was told that the Jats of the area consider it beneath their dignity to carry earth. I spoke to a little meeting about this. In other words, I did not find any real awakening in this area which I would have expected in a Development Block.

Yours sincerely,
Jawaharlal Nehru

---

1. File No. 17(28)/57-PMS. Also available in JN Collection.
2. Union Minister of State for Community Development.

8. To V.T. Krishnamachari[1]

New Delhi
11 April 1957

My dear V.T.,[2]

I have seen a note prepared in your Industry Division regarding the utilization of Russian aid offer.[3] I have not read this carefully, but on glancing through it, I have seen a reference in it to the proposed integrated drug industry.

I am much interested in this matter. Whatever our ultimate decision is, one thing should be perfectly clear. The drug industry must be in the public sector. That indeed flows from our policy decisions. Apart from that, I think, an industry of the nature of the drug industry should not be in the private sector anyhow. There is far too much exploitation of the public in this industry.

You will remember the great arguments we had at the time the Penicillin Factory was to be established in India. There was great pull in favour of some arrangement with an American firm. Fortunately, we resisted it and we have got an effective Penicillin Factory functioning now.[4] I think, this principle should apply to the entire range of all drug industry, subject to those private concerns which are functioning now.

The question of Russian offer has been disposed of rather hurriedly, it seems to me. It may or may not be accepted ultimately. That is a matter to be considered.

But if we proceed on the basis of the drug industry being in the public sector, every other consideration will have to fit in with this. I think that the Russian aid offer should, therefore, be considered in this context. It is possible that the amount of aid suggested by them might be increased for this purpose.

There is another aspect of this question of the drug industry, as to how far it is practicable or desirable to have an integrated drug industry rather than a spread out one.

1. File No. 17(48)/56-66-PMS. Also available in JN Collection.
2. Deputy Chairman, Planning Commission,
3. The USSR offered a long-term loan of about 500 million roubles to K.C. Reddy, the Minister for Production, during his visit to Moscow in October 1956 for purchasing industrial equipment for the Second Five Year Plan. This was announced by the Government of India on 15 November 1956.
4. The Penicillin Factory at Pimpri (Pune) started production in 1956. It was expected to produce 180 to 200 lakh mega units of penicillin annually.

As you know, I am also deeply interested in the machinery manufacturing project which, of course, must also be in the public sector.

I do hope that in regard to these basic industries, there is no weakening in favour of the private sector.

Yours sincerely,
Jawaharlal Nehru

9. To Chester Bowles[1]

New Delhi
13 April 1957

Dear Chester Bowles,[2]

Thank you for your letter of April 1st, which I have read with much interest, more especially, your account of your visit to the Soviet Union[3] and the new currents of opinion in the United States.[4] Your analysis is helpful in understanding many things in this complicated and changing world.

When Kenneth Galbraith[5] was in India, I met him and had an interesting talk with him. I have read a number of papers which he wrote then and to which presumably you refer.

1. JN Collection.
2. US diplomat and author, served in India twice as US Ambassador.
3. Regarding Soviet Union, Chester Bowles wrote: "I was deeply impressed with accomplishments in the Soviet Union in education. I was also interested and pleased to see the extraordinary friendliness of the people to the Americans (even after ten or twelve years of anti-American propaganda); and the healthy ferment among the young people."
4. Regarding the USA, he wrote: "In the United States we are now witnessing the gradual crystallization of two sharply conflicting views on world affairs. One is a true creative international view that will support positive efforts...for a long range meaningful peace negotiations...between the Soviet Union and the United States.... The other is a modern reflection of our traditional isolationism."
5. John Kenneth Galbraith (1908-2006); economist and diplomat; Professor of Economics, Harvard University, 1949-75; United States Ambassador to India, 1961-63; publications include, *The Great Crisis, The Affluent Society, The New Industrial State* and *Ambassador's Journal*.

I entirely agree with you about the importance of the three factors that you mention, namely, (1) increase in production, (2) a sense of participation among the people, in this work of development and production and (3) increasing justice in distribution.

Our elections are over, and now I have to face the headache of forming a new Government.

With all good wishes to you and your wife.[6]

Yours sincerely,
Jawaharlal Nehru

6. Step Bowles.

10. To C. Subramaniam[1]

New Delhi
13 April 1957

My dear Subramaniam,[2]

I have received a letter from Chester Bowles, in which he states that his wife spent a night with a family in Madurai in South India. This family, according to her, owned four thousand acres of land. Chester Bowles mentions this as extraordinary anomaly when we talk of land reform and the like. I am myself surprised to learn that anybody in Madurai owns four thousand acres of land. How does this come about?

Yours sincerely,
Jawaharlal Nehru

1. JN Collection.
2. Minister of Finance, Education, Information and Law in Madras Government.

11. Public and Private Sectors Not Contradictory[1]

Mr Chairman,[2] friends,
I am thankful to you for having invited me again to this Conference of the Manufacturers' Organization. I believe you represent more the smaller manufacturers than the bigger ones. Now, in the economy of our country, obviously, both are necessary in the nature of things. The big schemes and the big people and the big projects get a much larger measure of publicity than the numerous smaller ones and yet important as the big schemes are, I have no doubt that the backbone of the economy of the country depends and will depend on the multitude, the vast number of small manufacturing schemes all over the country. The other day a colleague[3] of ours went to the Punjab for some kind of a quick survey of the small industries that had been started there more or less recently. He came back very much impressed with what had been done since Independence in the course of the last 9 or 10 years both by, if I may call, the permanent residents there and those who had come from Pakistan as refugees, without much capital or anything but with a great deal of the real capital that a nation or an individual should possess, that capital is the ability to work hard, enterprise and all that. I believe this colleague of ours who came back listed as far as I remember 26,000 small enterprises that had grown up in the last few years in East Punjab with a relatively small capital but with a great deal of energy and enterprise. That is the kind of thing which heartens one and increases one's self-confidence so that it is of high importance that these vast number of our people engaged in all kinds of middle or small manufacturers should have openings to develop....
We seem to be living in a world of ghosts and spectres. Over a 100 years ago a Manifesto was issued by Marx in Europe which became rather famous in subsequent years. In this Manifesto was the phrase "the spectres haunting Europe, spectres of revolution". This was the Communist Manifesto issued by Marx and Engels over a 100 years ago. Well, today, the spectre of war and apart from that spectre, there are so many ghosts that fill our minds today, there are the ghosts of old time which keep us tied to a state of affairs which no longer exists, ghosts

1. Speech at the annual conference of All India Manufacturers' Organization, New Delhi, 13 April 1957. AIR tapes, NMML. Extracts. For other part of Nehru's speech see *post*, pp. 271-272.
2. K.N. Modi.
3. Gulzarilal Nanda.

of the past preventing us from thinking in the present or in the future, ghosts of Adam Smith[4], thinking, making us, trying us up to some kind of economic thinking which has no application today, ghosts of Karl Marx also limiting our minds and making us think of something that he said a 100 years ago about conditions that existed 130 years ago. All these ghosts and spectres prevent us from realizing that we live in a terrifically dynamic and changing world, and what may well have been clear thinking some time back is out of date today in view of these new developments in science, in technology and the like. How are we to get rid of these ghosts and spectres that haunt us? It is very difficult, we in India have also to carry the burden which is both good value and bad, a burden, I do not know, how many thousands of years of history and experience. Those thousands of years of the experience of our race give us certainly a certain balance, I hope a certain maturity, which a race with this long experience has developed. But it also puts us into ruts of thought to some extent. And so we live in this world, this most dangerous world and yet it is so full of unreality, unreality in our thinking, in our actions, and yet there is the major reality of the hydrogen bomb hanging over us. So, here is this mixture of reality and unreality of fact and ghosts and spectres which envelop us.

I have mentioned these facts to you although they may not have any immediate or direct relation to your business in hand, in your agenda, and yet indeed they have a very direct relation because what happens affects all our future, as well as the world's future. And all our fine schemes and the five year plans will be shattered to bits if this evil business of war comes in. War, I say, but now in recent years another phrase has been exploited and is bandied about—cold war. I do not know if previous to the last decade or so, people used these words. Maybe, I don't remember it, cold war meaning all the apparatus of war and the psychology of war and the hatred and the propaganda of war, without shooting, actual shooting and killing. Personally, I should have thought that bad as the shooting and killing is, it is better than this continuous propagation of hatred which eats into one's vitals and ultimately prevents us from either thinking or clear action. And if you look at this business of cold war in the context of these terrific powers exemplified by nuclear warfare, then you see the tremendous dangers that the world faces. We in India are called, not quite correctly, our policy is called a neutral policy. That again is a strange use of the word in this

4. (1723-90); Scottish economist and philosopher; Professor of Logic, University of Glasgow, 1751-52; Professor of Moral Philosophy, 1752-63; Tutor to Duke of Buccleuch, 1764-66; Adviser to Charles Townshend, 1766-67; Commissioner of Customs for Scotland, 1778-90; publications: *The Theory of Moral Sentiments* and *An Inquiry into the Nature and Causes of the Wealth of Nations.*

context. One had thought of neutrality and neutral policies in terms of war. If there is a war, some countries are belligerent and some are neutral. If India's policy is a neutral policy, am I going to call the non-neutral countries belligerent? That is the alternative to carry that argument. If you use terms of war in times of peace, it means not only that you are thinking in terms of war, conditioning your minds in terms of war but also conditioning your policies in terms of war. And out of our minds and policies, directed to war-like purposes, I do not understand how peace can emerge. Today, we do not follow a neutral policy nor do we follow a belligerent policy. We follow a constructive, positive policy, independent policy conditioned, I hope, to the ways of peace and cooperation. We refuse to look on any country as an enemy country even though our interests may clash, even though occasionally high words may pass about some matter because we feel that that way of looking at it is not the right way and if you spread that out throughout the world, the world becomes wholly a dense fog of hatred and violence and ill will in which some people can hardly breath. What policies, in regard to foreign policies whether they are political or economic and the two necessarily have to be coordinated. What are some of the major policies that countries follow? If you will examine them, they are rather negative policies, anti this and anti that, anti that country and anti this country. The countries do not agree. Few countries agree completely in their policies. Some may agree basically and yet disagree about small matters but there is no complete agreement between any two countries just as it is difficult to have complete agreement between two thinking individuals. Yet, they broadly agree and cooperate and try to convince each other but where a policy is based on being against or anti some individual or some country, then the basis of finding some common way is absent or at any rate, it is difficult to find that basis so that this business of having policies to provide any safe way of finding some escape from the dilemmas of the present day world. There is much in this world which most of us do not like. There is much in us which others do not like. What are we to do about it? Are we to break each other's heads or throw bombs at each other, atomic or hydrogen or other to convince the other of the right or the wrongness of his ways? That is neither the democratic way nor the way of peace nor indeed the practical way nor the way as things are today. Therefore, inevitably we come to the logical conclusion that in this world, we should recognize the right of each country to live its own life provided it does not interfere with another country.

That is the right of peaceful coexistence, not in words only—those words are bandied about often enough and not acted upon by even those people who use those words, the right of peaceful coexistence, of live and let live, because there is no other way except the way of conflict and destruction and absolute destruction, because remember that for the first time in human history something has happened that has never happened before. There have been great wars in the past, terrific wars, awful destruction, but all this was confined to an area, however big that area might be. Today, these forces released by nuclear energy, forces which can be used for the advancement of humanity, but if used for the destruction of people, they envelope the world and even the atom bomb has become a minor thing today. An atomic bomb may destroy a city like Hiroshima, I do not know how many hundreds, thousands of people, if the destruction was confined to the city of Hiroshima. Now, comes the hydrogen bomb which apart from that destruction throw out all kinds of things, materials, radioactive materials which go up twenty, thirty, forty thousand feet high, much more, and hang there and go about and wherever they may come down on the earth's surface and they will come down anywhere; they are not limited by boundaries and frontiers. And wherever they will come down, they will bring slow, creeping death with them, death direct, death indirect, death everywhere in the soil and if an animal takes them, it suffers. They have come in the soil and vegetable grows up with them and if a man eats the vegetable, the man suffers, he gets it. And thus puts out this wretched thing strontium which goes into your bones and gradually eats into the bones and there is no way of getting it out. And this kind of thing may go on for generations as a result of a few big explosions, and more particularly, it affects the growing generation. So, there is the possibility today which has never existed before the humanity and all civilization of being destroyed utterly if a war takes place and being destroyed slowly, even if the war does not take place but these explosions go on and on. That is the possibility we have to face and that is the overwhelming thing. Whether you think in terms of your industrial development in this country or any other, you cannot ignore this basic fact which may put an end to you and to your thinking, to your development and to your five year plans. Therefore, it is of high importance that all of us should keep in mind and somehow try to the best of our ability to exorcize these spectres and ghosts that surround us, first of all in our thinking and also in our small way try to influence the minds of the great people of the world who have the power and destiny of the future in their hands that they might restrain this terrific power, that they might come together and find some way out, however much they may dislike each other or dislike each other's policies. I have said this because it comes to my mind and yet you are concerned and I am concerned—not naturally with the burden of the world we don't and you dare not presume to carry the burden of the world, you cannot—it is more than enough for us to carry the burden of India. We have no desire to interfere in any sense elsewhere. We have no desire to carry about messages to the rest of the world and try to tell them, what they should do and what they should not do. We are humble folk, working hard to solve some of the great problems of this country which we love, to improve the conditions of the millions of our countrymen and countrywomen and we want to do it in peace and in cooperation. We want to learn from others humbly and in all humility and yet if there happens to be anything that others can learn from us, they can learn it. We don't go out in missionary zeal thinking that we are better than others. I do not think we are better than others, we are all in the same boat with some virtues and many failings. Anyhow, we are facing at the present moment in this country this tremendous thing, the building up of a new India. We had a Five Year Plan and now we have a Second Five Year Plan and it is patent that this Second Five Year Plan puts great burdens upon us, greater than we had imagined when we framed that Plan because conditions have changed in many ways in the world, to some extent in India, and the burden grows and yet we have to shoulder that burden.

There is no escape from it and we don't want to escape from it. We don't wish to face defeat because conditions are hard. It is only by fighting against hard conditions that nations and peoples are made, not in soft living, not in easy ways of growth. Such as we are today, if we had a measure of determination and some other virtues, we will develop them apart from our long past in generation or two of our struggle for Independence. Something of that spirit of determination, I hope, exists in this country to undertake a task, however big it is and to see it through whatever the consequences. That is true. Whatever the consequences I said but it is not an individual task and no individual however great and determined he might be, can achieve a national task unless the people of the nation, the people of the country cooperate as partners in that tremendous undertaking. Therefore, this Second Five Year Plan or any other plan that may come afterwards has long ceased to be something emanating from the Planning Commission or from the Government of India. It has to be and we made every effort so that it might be a joint effort of people's thinking, of people's cooperation and, more especially, a joint effort in the implementation of it by millions of people with nothing of rigidity in it. We cannot be rigid in this changing world, yet we cannot also be always in a state of flux. We have to have certain cohesion about a plan, about acting, working it out but that cohesion should not become so rigid that you become a prisoner of your own previous thinking and cannot adapt yourself to what the conditions demand.

You have pointed out Mr Chairman, some of the difficulties under which we labour, present imbalances in our payments abroad, tendencies which are not good, our foreign exchange position—we know, of course, and you all know them. It is no good thinking of hiding it—by hiding, it does not disappear. We have to face those and face them cooperatively with you, with others, so that we may get over those difficulties as I feel confident we will. But we shall only do so with an effort, with a considerable effort and thinking in the broadest terms, not in terms of individual advantage, individual profit but in terms of the nation because in the ultimate analysis individual advantage surely cannot be isolated from the advantage of the nation. If the nation suffers, the individual suffers. There has been much talk of the public sector and the private sector. I am not going into that matter. I do believe that the public sector inevitably must expand in this country but I do not want people to think as if the public sector and the private sector are mutually contradictory or coming in the way of each other, pulling each other back. If that was the outlook, then there is something fundamentally wrong in our planning. Planning has to be an integrated thing, every part of it helping the other part and the private sector being in the plan and not only in the plan but in our national life in a big way, it is there. It has necessarily to have not only a very important place but a respected place but always in the context of the plan, in the context of the broad policies that we pursue, much as we may say about the virtues of free enterprise exactly what it means I am not going into that, but it is normally thought of in a certain context. But I put it to you in another context: if India is to progress as India must, we have to develop a spirit of enterprise in the 370 million people of India. We are not going to regiment them and make them robots. That is not the way the country is going to progress. I am all for enterprise, I am all for enterprise in the millions of India. When free enterprise actually leads not to free enterprise but to huge accumulations of power, economic and the rest, it is not free enterprise in the right way, in the right sense of the word at all. It comes in the way of the real development of the spirit of that enterprise in the people which I should like to develop. I am not going to pursue this argument but I am surprised at the loose way in which words are used and I am only thinking of India for the moment, I am not talking of other countries because conditions are different in other countries and one must not apply a single rule to measure for different countries.

I think that one of the most basic things that is happening in India, one of the most revolutionary things in India, is the Community Development Scheme which has extended already in the course of just four years and seven months to 220,000 villages of India out of a total of 500,000. Well, in four and half years that represents a tremendous effort. I do not mean to say that the 220,000 villages are all working up to the mark. Indeed, as we are in Delhi, I might say that the villages roundabout Delhi are not good specimens of the Community Development Scheme. They are rather bad specimens of it, whether it is the effect of Delhi being near them or what, I don't know. I am disappointed in them. So don't judge from these things, these villages round about Delhi. Maybe the saying that there are too many leaders in Delhi for the average man to function properly. But by and large, this Community Development Scheme has, I think, worked with amazing success. You cannot measure that so much, you can to some extent, by statistics. To some extent you can say that, well, in the Community areas food production has gone up by 25 per cent—true. I hope in the Five Year Plan, it will go up anything from 35 per cent to 40 per cent. That can be measured but it is not that. The real thing that is happening there, apart from the increase in agriculture and food, more food production, more roads, more schools, houses, more dispensaries or little hospitals or maternity homes, more cottage industries, is to pull out our peasantry from the ruts they have lived for thousands of years. Anything more tremendous and more revolutionary I cannot imagine, pulling out these 300 million people in our 500,000 villages and pulling them out not by any external agency but showing them the way to pull themselves out of their own effort. Well, the history of this will be written in the future. But, I think, we have seen enough in these last four years to give us a certain measure of confidence at the way these fine people of ours, the peasantry of India are again standing up on their own feet and recovering their self-reliance and the spirit of enterprise which I want in them. So, you see this map of India before you, consisting of all groups and classes and professions and ways of working down from the vast number of the peasantry up to these great factories and heavy industries and huge plants that are growing up and we seek to coordinate all this and we seek to grow on this within the democratic structure of society. We go to the peasant, we want him very much to have cooperatives, we don't compel him to have the cooperatives, we argue with him, we try to convince him and then bring him on to a cooperative enterprise. In this connection, I might say that some integrated cooperative schemes in parts of Bombay State and parts of Madras State are most encouraging and only recently I have been reading a report which I received from the Reserve Bank of India about the development of these cooperative schemes in Bombay State and Madras State. I found that report extremely encouraging but of course even so, we have touched only the fringe of the problem. The vast ocean remains but we have to go ahead. There are many other things that are happening in India, recent discovery or whatever you might like to call it or which you might have heard, which is of great interest to us, is the development of the long staple cotton in India, what is it called the sea island variety or some such thing. Now, that is of very considerable importance from the point of view of the textile trade and from the point of view of foreign exchange situation and all that.

I believe, in certain areas, in Malabar and in a sense some other places and totally in another direction, you may have heard of very important and very significant discoveries of atomic ores in some parts of India, on big scale. And that connected with the fact that in spite of our general economic underdevelopment and backwardness, we are rather advanced, we are very advanced so far as Asia is concerned in our atomic sciences which are going to be the future power giving sciences of the country, not today but 10 or 15 years later. It is, therefore, of great importance that we have discovered this uranium, thorium and other minerals in substantially big quantities in parts of India. So, you see that in spite of our many difficulties and the problems that we have to face, we are making good and it is in a spirit of confidence as well as of determination that we should view this scene.

There is one idea that I should like to put before you. Our difficulties, I think, well in a sense are temporary, temporary meaning not immediately today but temporary in terms of years. The next two years, possibly the next three years are likely to be difficult for us. We have to pull ourselves up in these two or three years. The mere fact that we are trying to develop fast, and develop into heavy industries region, necessarily involves difficulties for us. In fact, the measure of our difficulty is the measure of the advance we are making, the measure of the development the country is making. You will have no difficulty at all if you did not build up, you will have no difficulties about foreign exchange if you sit tight and did not build up those industries but then you won't advance either. Why this foreign exchange difficulty? We are not getting luxuries from abroad; we have practically cut down to the bone every import except the most essential machinery which we have to import which after a few years we shall be manufacturing, I hope, our own machines. We shall be having quite adequate food supplies. We shall not require as we require today, importing iron and steel. The position will be completely different. But the mere fact that we are trying to produce iron and steel in larger quantities, building plants as well as huge river valley schemes, other factories, and trying to build up machine-making industry, that casts a tremendous burden on us. Money goes into the purchasing power but not enough commodities.

As you have said in your address Mr Chairman, that almost inevitably happens to a country developing faster but one tries and one must try to shorten that period and to lessen the hardships of that period. That, of course, we must try. We must try to prevent inflation and the like and you must try to find the best ways of doing all this. It is really because we are laying so much stress on the development of heavy industry that compels us to balance that by the development of small industry and cottage industry, both from the point of view of goods and the point of view of employment. Anyhow, there is this question of foreign exchange.

May I say one word before that in regard to the food situation. There is nothing to be alarmed about but it is clear that this tendency for food prices slightly to rise is not a good tendency.[5] It has to be countered, has to be checked, in particular in regard to rice. Well, I hope that this too is a short term difficulty as we produce more. Meanwhile, we have to make preparations for the short term two or three years whatever it may be. We are—I am sorry I did not want to but nevertheless—importing an adequate quantity of rice and some wheat too because we do not want these prices to rise.[6] In regard to rice, I would like to appeal to you and to others that first of all, we should all try to avoid wastage. There is great waste. Our social habits are wasteful. Our feasts are wasteful. I am not asking you to eat less but don't waste. In our hotels and other places there is waste. Now, this waste is bad. We are trying to live down to the bone and there must be an organized deliberate attempt to prevent waste. You must know that in England during War time when there were all kinds of controls about food and people complained about them, the health of the nation went up, the health of the British people went up because they had a more reasonable diet. I have no doubt that our health will go up if we have a more logical and more reasonable diet. Well, I don't want as far as possible to have controls in India. We are not thinking in terms of controls at the present moment but I would rather that this self discipline is exercized. First of all, no waste. Secondly, more especially in the wheat-eating areas of India, to abstain as far as possible from rice. Let it go to the rice-eating areas. I don't say absolutely abstain, but the proportion of consumption of wheat may be more than rice so that rice may be available more for the rice-eating areas. I put that to you for your consideration because it would be a tremendous thing to think if we can organize these things without much disadvantage and without any compulsory measure.

Then one other thing. We talk about this foreign exchange difficulty and the rest.[7] Why should not people who happen to have gold and jewellery part with it for consideration of course. I am not asking for free gifts. I think, we should think of them. When we are short of this it would be helpful if people who have

5. A spurt in food prices occurred in the very first year of the Second Plan.
6. According to the PL 480 agreement of 29 April 1956, India was to import 3.1 million tonnes of wheat and 0.19 million tonnes of rice over a period of three years from the US.
7. The external payments position had been strained from the beginning of the Second Plan owing to a rise in imports both on private and public account. The increase in imports during 1956-57 arose out of the requirements of development projects under the Second Plan, although the following factors were also responsible: (i) increased defence expenditure, (ii) larger imports of foodgrains, (iii) increased requirements of raw materials, components, etc., (iv) higher imports of consumer goods, and (v) increase in freight rates and prices.

any gold with them should give it up and take whatever the equivalent of that is and such jewellery as you can give up in gold also. I do not want to deprive every woman of all the jewellery she possesses but, nevertheless, if this was done on a fairly wide scale, it would be very helpful[8] and what is more, all these things generate a certain atmosphere of partnership in meeting difficulties, in working for big causes which is more important than the actual things done. A little realization that we are also contributing to the building up of a new India, to meeting a particular difficulty, rises us in our own estimation, makes us more self-reliant and self-disciplined. Therefore, I should like you to think about this also. Thank you.

8. Nehru received letters from Harish Chander Mallik, a Station Master from Ambala District, and Baljit Tulsi, a housewife from Ludhiana, offering their gold jewellery when this appeal was reported in the newspapers on 14 April. The Consul of Columbia in Madras, A. Tavera Garcia, sent several gold articles as donation on 19 April and insisted that he considered himself 100 per cent Indian.

12. To U.N. Dhebar[1]

Flagstaff House
Chakrata
25 April 1957

My dear Dhebarbhai,[2]

I am writing from Chakrata where I arrived today. I shall stay here till the 28th morning when I go to Mussoorie, where I shall attend the Development Commissioners' Conference[3] of the Community Development Ministry.

I have been looking through the agenda and various papers connected with this Conference. They are an interesting collection and they give some idea of the varied activities of the Community Development movement, the problems

1. JN Collection. Also available in AICC Papers, NMML.
2. President, Indian National Congress at this time.
3. It was held on 29 April 1957. See *post, pp.* 202-204.

they are facing and the methods they are adopting to deal with them. As you might be interested in these papers, I am sending them to you, so that you might have an idea of these various activities also.

S.K. Dey met Vinobaji some little time ago and had a long talk with him, He came back with the conviction that the Community Development Scheme should be associated with the future of the *Gramdans*. Broadly speaking, Vinobaji agreed with this.

It is not clear to me how far the individual bits of land received by Vinobaji can be dealt with by the Community Schemes, though, of course, much can be done there also. But, in so far as whole villages are concerned, which have been given as *Gramdan*, it should certainly be much easier for the Community movement to deal with them as cooperative enterprises. I rather doubt the capacity of the Bhoodan Movement to deal with these villages in the future. Therefore, I welcome the idea of the close association of the Community Development movement with the *Gramdan* scheme.

I have naturally been thinking about the talks we have had about the future of the Congress. I think that the system of individual membership, which we have thus far had, cannot by itself lead to any effective organization. We see in India today two major developments. One is in the rural areas which is symbolized by the Community Development movement. This may well include cottage industries and the like. The other main development is in the shape of big industry and specially heavy industry. More and more people will be brought into these two major developments. The problem is how to be in intimate touch with these two and how to bring them in into the scope of our organization.

Thus, we shall have to think of functional representation. We may, of course, and should, I think, have individual representation also. Gradually, the functional representation will play an ever increasing part as that will be a more living contact.

I have no clear ideas of how to bring all this about, but I am merely mentioning to you how my mind is working. The first thing, of course, is for leading people in the Congress to have a vivid appreciation of the present deplorable state of the Congress organization and the absolute necessity of doing something to pull it out of the old ruts which are leading nowhere. This appreciation is essential. I have little doubt that if our leading Congressmen have this appreciation and give a lead, it will be followed by the country. The second is, of course, the practical aspects of their lead.

Yours sincerely,
Jawaharlal Nehru

13. To Lal Bahadur Shastri[1]

Flagstaff House
Chakrata
26 April 1957

My dear Lal Bahadur,

I enclose a letter from Ram Narayan Chaudhury.[2] Also one from L.B. Roy.[3] Ram Narayan has a habit of interfering with all kinds of matters.

However, the point he has raised has some importance. Some two or three years ago, I raised this myself in the Planning Commission. After some kind of rather superficial enquiry, the Planning Commission people told me that this was not feasible.

I have not given up this idea yet, though of course, I cannot say how far it is feasible. It is patent that we cannot replace the bullock cart in the foreseeable future. If so, then the question arises as to whether we can improve it. There are two ways of improving it. One is a lighter and better cart; the other is rubber tyred wheels. A bullock cart with rubber tyres will be at least hundred to two hundred per cent more efficient than the present one.

One difficulty was pointed out to me then that a rubber tyred bullock cart will not be able to go on the *kutcha* village roads. I do not know how far this is so.

L.B. Roy rightly points out that there is no point in enquiring what the price of old tyres is in the American market. They are not in the market and no question of asking for tenders arises. Such old tyres are probably just thrown away in America. If we think that it is worthwhile encouraging these rubber tyres in bullock carts, we can then find out how we can obtain them. Probably they will hardly cost anything, the real cost being that of freight. This can be worked out.

Anyhow, I suggest that you might send for L.B. Roy and talk it over with him.

Yours sincerely,
Jawaharlal Nehru

---

1. File No. 17(142)/56-61-PMS. Also available in JN Collection.
2. Information Secretary of the Bharat Sevak Samaj.
3. A rubber technologist from New Delhi.

14. Community Development Schemes[1]

I have frequently drawn attention to the great importance of our Community Development movement. I have called it the most revolutionary thing that was happening in India today, something that was changing the face of the countryside, that is, eighty per cent of our population.

2. I hold to that view. At the same time it is far more important for us to realize the shortcomings of that movement than merely to rejoice at what we have done and be complacent.

3. Our very success has brought new and difficult problems for us. We have, I believe, shaken up a great part of rural India by this programme, we have talked a great deal about the new life among our rural folk, about their growing self-reliance, etc. I am glad that just on the eve of this Conference,[2] we have received the fourth Evaluation Report on the working of Community Project and National Extension Service Blocks. This Report gives us an objective survey of both our achievements and our lack of success in regard to some basic matters. It gives prominence to some of the fundamental problems that we have to face.

4. We must always remember that the test of our success is not the number of Community Blocks that we establish or the amount of money that we spend on them. These two are certainly important factors, but the real test is something which is partly material but much more psychological. It is the spirit of the people that counts, their awakening to new horizons, their getting some glimpse of this great adventure of building up new India and, more particularly their own villages, their desire to achieve and, above all, the spirit of cooperation without which success cannot come.

5. I do not propose to say much about the various criticisms that have been made in the Evaluation Report, important as they are. All I wish to say about them is that you should pay particular attention to them. They are not criticisms made in a carping spirit, but friendly appraisals.

6. I would draw special attention to some factors which I consider basic. The first is the necessity of securing the organized or collective will of the community with the planning of the programme and also, to the extent possible, with its actual implementation.

---

1. Note, Chakrata, 27 April 1957. JN Collection. Also available in File No. 17(28)/57-PMS.
2. Conference of Development Commissioners of the Community Development Programme was held at Mussoorie on 29 April.

7. Equally important is a change in social attitudes and a readiness to cooperate in the various organizations that are being set up. In this matter, it is said, there has not been much success.

8. It is further said that even the Project staff is not fully aware of the objectives and techniques of Community Development. Further that there is still reluctance of the official machinery to make full and positive use of the Advisory Committees. Unless this reluctance gives place to an active effort to bring about the cooperation of the public, our real objective will not be achieved and self-reliance and initiative will not grow.

9. Then there is the wide disparity in the distribution of the achievement and of the benefits of Community Project programmes. This disparity is between the Headquarter village and the other villages. Within the villages, between cultivators and non-cultivators, and within the cultivating classes between cultivators of bigger holdings and those of smaller holdings and lesser financial resources. The removal of these disparities is not only our declared aim of bringing about regional and social justice, but is also important from the point of view of political consequences.

10. The Community Development programmes are gradually permeating into almost every activity. Development is no longer an isolated branch of activity. It has become the business of the whole administration. Therefore, the whole administrative machinery of Government must fully understand and get permeated with the philosophy underlying Community Development.

11. There is always a danger that our specialized workers and *Gramsevaks* might be so full of their own ideas that they may ignore what the villagers feel. This may well happen even to our enthusiastic workers. If this is so, then there is a vital gap between the thinking of the worker and the villager. The villager will feel that all this high talk has really little relation to his own needs. There will be no reaction from him. It is important, therefore, that the Extension Worker is receptive to what the villagers feel and tries to understand their wants and, where possible, to supply them. The point is that there should be a basis of mutual understanding between them. Only this will lead to cooperation. In effect, the Extension Worker, whatever his grade, should not appear to be somebody imposed from above, but a living part of the village organism. He should think in terms of individuals in the village and establish contact with every individual family.

12. Perhaps, it is not possible to do so at present because of the large area served by the *Gramsevak*. This means that there should be more *Gramsevaks* and a smaller area allotted to each.

13. The panchayat and the cooperative should be the basis of both our political and our economic structure. I know of all the criticisms that have been made of

the panchayats as well as of the cooperatives. Nevertheless, we must realize that democratic progress depends on the development of these two organs. Every effort should be made, therefore, to put life into these and to use them for the purposes of development.

14. In our Second Five Year Plan, we have emphasized the importance of cooperatives, both agricultural and industrial. Indeed, our idea is to have a Cooperative Commonwealth. Democracy means or should mean cooperation at the political level. That democracy is incomplete till it is extended to the economic field. Cooperation, therefore, both organizational and in spirit is the essence of the structure we aim at. Our cooperatives thus far have been rather formal and without much life or enthusiasm in them. It is this life and common purpose that we have to put in them. We shall have many failures, but that does not mean that we should change our basic ideal.

15. Everyone, I think, agrees that our agriculture requires numerous types of cooperatives. Some disagreement, however, has been voiced in regard to what might be called farming cooperatives, that is, joint work in farming land. Some people mix these up with collectives, and authoritarianism. There is no reason to do that. The very fact that our political structure is democratic and that the progress in cooperation that we can make must be through democratic processes, that is, through the consent of the people concerned, prevents any wrong tendency. Nor will agrarian cooperatives be very large. In fact, I think they should be small, possibly comprising just a village, or even part of a village. We may have to proceed cautiously in regard to these because we cannot impose them on unwilling people.

16. But it should be clearly understood that progress in agriculture and the development of a sounder basic structure necessitate our going towards cooperative farming. The development of modern science cannot be brought to the individual small farmer easily. It would be much easier for a cooperative to take advantage of these developments which are ever growing. This does not mean mechanization of farming, that is, the use of tractors and the like. Tractors may be used occasionally with profit, but I do not think it is feasible or desirable to think of any widespread mechanization. We should rather aim at simple improvements of technique in farming and in processes associated with it. At the same time, we may well have some demonstration farms where we can experiment otherwise.

17. We have to deal with a people who have for many centuries or many millennia been used to certain traditional ways of doing things. We cannot uproot them. We have to convince them and bring them round to new thinking and new ways of action. In particular, attention should be paid to what might be called local culture and social life which should not be uprooted. Indeed, it should be encouraged except where it is obviously bad.

18. I should like to repeat here what the Evaluation Report says about cooperation. It is not "just a technique of economic organization. On the contrary, cooperation is a way of life, embodying a philosophy that requires both understanding, acceptance and positive action on the part of its individual membership. It is in this sense that cooperation goes together with democracy and gives that attention and permanence to the latter in the economic sphere."

19. In the world as it is today, the lack of cooperation between independent nations has brought us to the verge of disaster. It is recognized that even separate nations have to fall in line and cooperate. How much more is this necessary within a nation and in regard to the basic activities of that nation?

20. All this requires persistent education, firstly among the Extension Workers themselves and then among others.

21. I have welcomed the decision to bring about a close coordination in the activities of the Central and State Social Welfare Boards and the Community Development movement. I think, that this is essential. There is inevitably a lack of this approach to women and children in our Community programmes. Women are not only important in themselves, but are probably more important from the point of view of creating reactions in the public. Also, they are the mothers of the next generation. As for children, I do feel that the greatest attention should be paid to them. They can learn more easily and grasp this new spirit. It is probably easier to influence their parents through the children. And, after all, it is the children for whom we are working, and who will constitute tomorrow's India.

22. We are passing through a grave crisis in regard to food. This crisis is not of today. It is a continuing one. Therefore, first priority has to be given to increasing the production of foodgrains. This is vital from every point of view, including our industrial growth. It is out of our surplus in agricultural production that we shall build up the resources for industrial growth.

23. In this matter, it is not enough to lay down broad targets. Those targets have to be translated in terms of a village and a family, and progress has to be closely watched. I hope that we shall soon have proper scientific sample surveys of each crop which will give us more accurate knowledge than we possess today.

24. Then there are cottage and small industries which have now become an integral part of our Community Development Schemes. I need not point out the great importance of these both from the point of view of production and the removal of unemployment. Only in this way can we have a balanced economy.

25. In our Second Five Year Plan, we are laying stress on heavy industry and the production of heavy machinery. Without these there can be no real industrial growth. These, however, are outside the scope of the Community Development Scheme, though this Scheme will naturally be affected by them. This Community

Development movement must concern itself chiefly with agricultural production and cottage and small industries. But above all, it must devote itself to developing that spirit of a cooperative community life among our people. We are a people with many virtues, but also with many failings. We have a magnificent inheritance from the past. We have also inherited bad customs and disruptive tendencies. The greatest task before the nation is to achieve social cohesion. This is another way of saying that we must develop the cooperative spirit in all our undertakings.

15. Oil Exploration and Exploitation[1]

We have considered the question of oil exploration and exploitation repeatedly in the Cabinet as well as in the Planning Commission. From time to time some ad hoc decisions have been arrived at. A Special Committee was appointed to report on the location of the proposed refinery. The Committee consisted of a number of representatives of Government from various Ministries, namely, Railways, WH & S, Heavy Industries, NR & SR and Production; also, representatives from the National Institute of Petroleum of France and from the Romanian Institute for Refineries. The Assam Oil Company had also a representative.

2. At a recent meeting of the Planning Commission, no decisions were arrived at. It was suggested that the matter should be considered afresh in all its aspects, including our legal liabilities or commitments, to the Assam Oil Company.

3. It seems to me that we should consider this matter fully at an early date and come to certain firm decisions, as delay is obviously harmful. We have actually found the oil in Assam and any delay in exploiting it means loss to us.

4. There is also the broad question of oil exploration in other parts of India. The Cabinet came to a decision, I think, some time ago that, apart from any decision we may have arrived at in regard to the new discoveries of oil in Assam at Naharkatia, Government should, as far as possible, explore and exploit oil resources in other parts of India directly. In pursuance of this, drilling operations have been started at Jwalamukhi in the Punjab a few days ago.

1. Note to Cabinet Secretary, Flagstaff House, Chakrata, 27 April 1957. JN Collection. Also available in K.D. Malaviya Papers, NMML.

5. Cabinet had broadly approved of a programme involving an expenditure of about 30 crores of rupees for oil exploration during the Second Plan. This exploration must take place in Kutch, Rajasthan, the Punjab and Uttar Pradesh.

6. The immediate issues which require urgent decision relate to the negotiations which have taken place with the Burma Oil Company in regard to the exploitation of the recently discovered oilfields in Assam. Previously, Cabinet had agreed to a rupee company being formed with Government having 33 and 1/3 per cent capital. This, however, has not been finalized, though negotiations have taken place on this basis.

7. Then there is the question of the location of the refinery. The Experts Committee gave a definite opinion in favour of the refinery being situated round about Calcutta, and they have given their reasons for it. The other two places considered were Dhubri in Assam and Barauni in Bihar.

8. The Assam Government and people have been pressing with some passion to have the refinery somewhere in Assam. While we should naturally give full consideration to their wishes, ultimately economic considerations must prevail in this matter.

9. There is a proposal to have a refinery at Fakiragram in Assam and to have the oil brought by river to this place by barges. It is admitted that the cheapest way of transport is by pipeline. The question to be considered was whether from the point of view of time and initial capital involved, it might not be desirable to utilize river transport up to Fakiragram. I find that the Experts Committee considered this matter generally without going into detail and reported that "water transport for crude oil or for refined product has, therefore, to be ruled out at present and no comparative costs by river transport need, therefore, be studied". They ruled out rail transport also in so far as crude oil was concerned, but they said that rail transport would be suitable for refined products.

10. At the recent meeting of the Planning Committee, it was suggested that whatever our ultimate decision might be, we should engage a competent firm of consultants to draw up a project report for the entire scheme. Also a separate report by the same firm or others for the transport of oil in barges.

11. I have mentioned only some important points that have to be considered and decided upon. There are numerous other associated matters. In view of the urgency of this question, I think that it would be desirable to have a Special Committee of the Cabinet to consider this. Discussions in the Planning Commission have tended to be rather vague, and there are too many people present at Planning Commission meetings. The full Cabinet should certainly be kept in full touch, but a smaller Committee of the Cabinet can go more deeply into this matter and its recommendations will, no doubt, have considerable force.

12. I suggest, therefore, that a Committee of the Cabinet for Oil be constituted. This should consist of :-

1. Prime Minister
2. Home Minister
3. Finance Minister
4. Minister of Commerce & Industry
5. Minister of Steel, Mines & Fuel
6. Minister of Defence
7. Minister of Fuel and
8. Representative of the Planning Commission

13. The Minister of Fuel has already circulated some papers to some Members of the Cabinet. These papers can be sent to all the Members of the Committee mentioned above. It might be desirable for him to prepare a brief statement of points to be decided upon. This should also be circulated.

14. An early date should be fixed for a meeting of this Committee of the Cabinet. This may be done after my return to Delhi.

15. There is one other matter I should like to mention lest it may be overlooked. In view of the very strong sentiment in Assam on this question, the Expert Committee had suggested that Government might consider the manufacture of nitrogenous fertilizers, e.g., urea, from the natural gas produced in the oilfields as well as its utilization for the production of energy and other industrial applications in Assam. In their opinion, this appeared to be economically feasible to transport natural gas up to Gauhati by a pipeline, if the gas pipeline is built at the same time as the crude oil pipeline. Advantage could then also be taken of the natural gas moving by pipeline in the entire area through which it passes.

16. Cabinet Secretary will please circulate copies of this note to the Members of the Cabinet Committee mentioned above.

16. Cooperative and Scientific Farming[1]

It is essential to adopt cooperative farming, so that the country can advantageously make use of the latest farming techniques. The scientific techniques are developing so fast that unless India adopts cooperative farming, she would be left behind in the march to progress.

This approach is not rigid and its acceptance should, of course, be subject to democratic processes based on the willingness of the people. And that cooperative farming is the determined and definite goal and this has been positively and unanimously laid down by the Planning Commission.

The *Gramdan* villages are the best suited for adoption of cooperative farming because these areas present "a clean slate" in view of the fact that the usual difficulties arising out of individual ownership of land do not obtain there. The idea of cooperative farming is inherent in the Community Development programme and forms the basis of the new urges in rural areas.

The centralization has certain bad aspects and hampers individual initiative and the only "escape" is the way of cooperation.

I oppose the idea of redistribution of *Gramdan* lands amongst villagers keeping only ten per cent of them for cooperative management. *Gramdan* villages, are specially suited for complete pooling of land resources and offer the best chance of putting the idea of cooperative endeavour into effect.

It is of the highest importance that we succeed in rural India. With the democratic apparatus and political consciousness we just cannot wait and leave the rural areas, till we do something elsewhere and come back to them because in the final analysis it is the rural areas which elect Members of Parliament and State Assemblies. They can make governments and upset governments.

No doubt it is necessary to establish heavy industries, but we have to come back to the vast rural population and unless that moved, I do not think we will get going in India. Also the villages cannot be ignored, partly because resources come from rural India.

You should shed your official character in your dealings with the rural people. It is of the highest importance that you do gain their faith and you can do so only if you make them feel that officials are not different from them.

---

1. Speech at the Development Commissioners' Conference, Mussoorie, 29 April 1957. From *The Hindu* and *The Hindustan Times*, 30 April 1957.

No moralising approach or lecturing to people would ensure their cooperation, and don't irritate your audience and people whom you are training. Properly approached in a friendly and reasonable manner, the response of the people would be good. Agricultural people by nature are conservative, but they do change their minds when convinced of the reasonableness of any proposition.

The essential factor in the changing rural India is infusing a new spirit in the life of the people. My mind has always been struggling with this—how to do it. I look back as some of my older colleagues do on my early experience, what you call the Gandhian Era. When Gandhiji came into the field almost suddenly or within a very short time he electrified the countryside. He was a remarkable individual and we cannot compete with him. Nevertheless, we can learn from what he did.

One major experience in my life has been to notice the change that has come over in rural India. It is astounding to see the poor peasant who has absolutely no initiative, no life left except to carry on in a miserable way, suddenly changing although he might have been a bag of bones. He had a straight back and he looked you in the face. He had no training, but some spirit was infused in him.

During the freedom struggle, for Congress workers in those days, it was an astounding experience to be in communion with the people, though there might have been a guff in special classes and although we were different in mental training and background, which was as far removed as anything can be from the Indian peasant, yet somehow that gap is bridged to a large extent. You cannot work miracles and change India entirely in the course of five or ten years. But I think we can bring about the change faster than most people think and for that we must pull out the people from the rut of inaction and once you do that their pace will increase.

Regarding the Bhoodan movement, I have no doubt in my mind that it has great significance for what it achieves and for the new psychology it creates about land and landholdings and the terrific passion for private possession of land.

As for the controversy, referred to in the earlier debates of the Conference about participation of officials in the Bhoodan movement, it is obvious that no Government can go about asking people to donate land.

I do feel that the Community Development movement should cooperate so far as is possible with the *Gram* and Bhoodan movements. Our approach should be merely a cooperative one.

I do feel that without Government cooperation I cannot see what the Bhoodan movement could do with the land it got. In fact, the movement has been getting cooperation through legislation passed in some States. The Government acts in every step and so if one talks to me that villagers are apart from Government apparatus, it is something which I cannot understand. It is rather an anarchic ideal and I have not grown up to that.

I welcome the Bhoodan movement and in a distant way try to encourage it by sympathy. It would be "absurd" as Prime Minister to go about asking people to give up land, but I agree with Acharya Bhave's ideal that land should be held in common by people.

It is an extraordinary thing that the people of India who are the gentlest creatures on earth should behave in a different way when roused in the name of religion or caste. The killings that took place during Partition shows that there is some thing in the Indians which can "break loose", also as was seen recently during the linguistic agitation. I am not going into the merits of it but it is a bad sign that people could behave in that way over any question, however, important it might be. I do not know why that "weakness" has come. Lack of unity in India in spite of cultural and basic unity, is perhaps because of the innumerable divisions of caste. Slogans will not help in bringing about unity but we have to go down deeper into the causes of lack of social harmony.

I see no reason why agricultural production in the country cannot be doubled when other countries are able to obtain higher yields. I feel that agricultural production is of the highest importance. You should make clear to the village community what is proposed to be done and then invite suggestions. Let the people have the sensation of deciding for themselves.

17. To Morarji Desai[1]

New Delhi
30 April 1957

My dear Morarji,

Your letter of the 29th April[2] (it is wrongly stated to be 29th May).

For some time past, I have been trying to study the various aspects of our development plans for the manufacture of heavy machines. In fact, I took a number of reports with me to Chakrata and read them there.

I entirely agree with you that these questions are often not looked at objectively but rather influenced by emotional or ideological reactions. We have to consider them purely from the point of view of what is advantageous to us. I get the feeling that some of our members of our Steel Experts Committee, coming from big private firms, do not particularly approve of any deal with the Soviet Union.

In considering this matter, it is not enough, I think, to deal with it in separate bits. But we have to look at it as a whole and from the point of view of our capacity to build up a heavy machine industry in the course of the Third Five Year Plan. Indeed, it really will go beyond that. But we have to plan for these various stages from now on. Since we are industrializing, we want machines. To import these machines from abroad is a very heavy foreign exchange drain on us and this will continue till we manufacture our own machines. In fact, the cost of building up even a full sized heavy machine plant is really less than the amount we are likely to spend in foreign exchange in importing machinery. Therefore, it becomes incumbent to make ourselves independent as soon as possible in this matter, both from the point of view of foreign exchange and because of political considerations. The world seems to be going from one crisis to another and from one mess to another. We cannot, in the ultimate analysis,

---

1. File NO. 17(226)/57-61-PMS. Also available in JN Collection.
2. Morarji informed Nehru that, "we propose to develop the heavy machine building project on the lines of the Russian recommendations and also to accept their scheme for the mining machinery project. At the same time, we are going to seek the collaboration of the other countries, UK, Germany and Czechoslovakia, in some of the other projects in this group because we naturally wish in matters of technique to get the best in whichever country it may be available." He also wrote: "The attitude which I have asked my officers to take is to assess each scheme or proposal on its own technical and economic merits... If in a particular field, on technological considerations we prefer the collaboration of one country to any other, we should try to get it."

rely on any foreign country, whatever it may, to be benevolent to us. We want to be friendly with them and we would gladly accept the help they give. But the major fact is that we should make ourselves self-reliant as soon as possible in regard to the manufacture of heavy machinery.

Take even the proposal that in the Third Five Year Plan we shall increase our steel output considerably. If we have to import much of this machinery from abroad, it will be a terrific strain on us, far greater even than putting up a heavy machine plant, I think.

I think, therefore, that we should consider this matter fully again. The meeting of the Planning Commission which is going to be held for this purpose is useful for a general discussion, but I would like to suggest there that we should not finalize anything at this stage but give it further consideration. Planning Commission meetings usually consist of a large crowd of persons which is not very helpful in discussion. After this meeting, I suggest that a few of us meet together and discuss this matter.

Yours sincerely,
Jawaharlal Nehru

II. FOOD AND AGRICULTURE

1. Agriculture and Community Development[1]

Dr Deshmukh,[2] sisters and brothers,

As you heard just now this is the third year I am attending your function.[3] Dr Deshmukh told us about the various things I have inaugurated here. But as far as I remember, the faces here seem to be the same. The names are different. Perhaps you change your dress to suit the occasion. This is to be a seminar. Earlier it was something else. Anyhow, the important thing is that no matter what you call it, experienced agriculturists and farmers like you gather together every year. You meet one another and discuss various issues among yourselves. I am sure this would benefit everyone. Therefore, such gatherings are important.

You may not be aware of it but today is a particularly auspicious day. It is the beginning of a new year. There are different calendars in different parts of the country. As you know we want to foster unity in the country. But that does not mean that there should be dull and stifling uniformity. However, we want to ensure a greater uniformity in our working. Various calendars are in use, including the English one.[4] I have nothing against the English calendar. But it is an alien one. There are other Indian calendars. We have set up a committee to look for a calendar which is most accurate and would serve everyone in India.[5] We will continue to observe the English calendar particularly in Government and

1. Inaugural speech at a seminar organized under the auspices of the Farmers' Forum, New Delhi, 22 March 1957. AIR tapes, NMML. Original in Hindi.
2. Panjabrao S. Deshmukh was Union Minister of State for Agriculture.
3. The first national convention of farmers was held at New Delhi on 3 April 1955. For Nehru's speech see *Selected Works* (second series), Vol. 28, pp. 433-440. For his speech at the second convention, held at New Delhi on 3 April 1956, see *Selected Works* (second series), Vol. 32, pp. 7-15.
4. The English calendar, known as the Gregorian calendar, is recognized as the international calendar.
5. The Calendar Reform Committee, constituted in November 1952 under the chairmanship of M.N. Saha, submitted its report in 1954. It recommended that a unified national calendar using *Saka* era should be used for civil purposes in place of local calendars. See also *Selected Works* (second series), Vol. 32, pp. 82-83.

international affairs. But we want a certain amalgam of the innumerable Indian calendars. Accordingly, we are observing the start of a new year from the month of *Chaitra* which begins today. My greetings to you.

A great many things have happened since we met last year. The most important is that the First Plan has come to an end and the Second has begun.[6] Nearly ten months have gone by since then. As you know, the First Plan had laid great stress on food and agriculture. From the beginning we had been facing food shortages which is troublesome. Country which is not self-sufficient in food cannot progress very far. So, we laid stress on increasing food production and our efforts have paid off. We have succeeded beyond our hopes.

The Second Plan also lays stress on agriculture. But industrialization occupies a major place in it because it is extremely important. We are trying to set up heavy industries, machine building industries and steel plants etc. Small-scale industries can come up only when we begin producing steel and machines in large quantities. I want you to understand this picture. India will progress only when there is even development on both the fronts—agriculture and industrialization. Both are equally important. Agricultural production is important to the urban as well as the rural areas. Until we step up production, India will remain poor.

So, the urgent priority before us is to increase the national wealth of India. Wealth does not mean gold and silver but essential consumer goods which are produced from land and industries. Otherwise India will remain backward. But, we have made it quite clear that the first priority is agriculture. If we slacken our efforts even a little, all the industries in the country cannot save us. So, both these things are essential. We must learn to become self-reliant in every way and to stand with our feet firmly rooted in our own soil.

You belong to the select few who may be doing good work. But the fact is that our average agricultural production is lower than that of any other country in the world. We may preen ourselves on our various achievements. But our agricultural production is very low.[7] If a list is drawn up of the average yield per acre in all the countries in the world, India will be almost at the bottom of it. This is not a good thing. It is not that our people are not hard-working. You know better than I do that we had become somewhat stagnant. A nation or race has to imbibe new ideas and knowledge constantly. The moment it becomes stagnant, there can be no progress, no matter what it looks like from the top. This is what has happened in India.

6. The Second Five Year Plan covered the period from April 1956 to March 1961.
7. For example, wheat production during 1955-56 was 290.57 kilograms per acre.

So, it is obvious that on the one hand, we have to improve our condition and remove poverty. On the other hand, due to the outdated methods of agriculture we follow, our average yield per acre is extremely low. It should be easy for us to increase production and even to double or treble it by simple improvements. I have no doubt about it that it should be easy. I have no right to tell you this because I am not a farmer, nor have I ever done farming. I do not know very much about it. But I do know a little about Indian conditions in India and the world. Therefore, I am presuming to tell you that it should be a simple matter to increase production. We have seen that already in the last six to seven years when there has been considerable progress.

You are select farmers and if the matter were to be left to you, there will be rapid progress. The problem is to influence the thirty crores who depend on land. You are already aware of the improvements that can be made. The question is of the average. Some individuals may be able to produce 30 or 40 *maunds* of wheat per acre and win a prize which is no doubt a good thing. But it is not a question of a handful of farmers. We have to increase the average yield per acre which is about eight or nine *maunds* at the moment. It is slightly higher in the Punjab and a few other places. But, we want to double and treble the national average and not parade the achievements of a few individual farmers. The government cannot do it on its own though it helps in every possible way, particularly by giving demonstrations to show how production can be increased. Many of you might have such model farms. So, in a sense, you are already helping the average. But from every point of view, it has become imperative that we should increase the food production in the country. It is fundamental to our progress. We have to base our programme of industrialization on that. By increasing agricultural production, our economic condition will improve and there will be a surplus which can be invested in other tasks of development. Suppose, for instance, if our agricultural production doubles, not only the farmers but the entire country will benefit by it. There will be a surplus of hundreds of crores of rupees for development, to buy new machines, set up industries, etc. Therefore, from all these points of view, it has become imperative that we should increase agricultural production in India.

What does that imply? For one thing, we must bring more land under cultivation. But what it really means is that the existing average yield per acre of land must be doubled. This is not impossible because it is being done in other countries and even in India, wherever an effort has been made, it has been possible. In some areas there is a problem about irrigation or the lack of fertilizers and good seeds, etc. As you know, these are the difficulties which can easily be solved. I am not for a moment suggesting that everyone should have huge tractors though I have nothing against them. But we cannot use tractors everywhere. We

209

will use them wherever it is possible but our attention should be concentrated on small improvements which everyone can easily adopt. Even the poorest farmer ought to be able to undertake these improvements. We can use tractors in the model farms.

After a great deal of debate between the Planning Commission and the states, it was finally decided what our target at the end of the next five years should be.[8] Let me tell you quite frankly that I am completely dissatisfied with the decision because, I think, the figure is very low. In my opinion, it should be increased. I cannot understand all this hesitation and fear. We should be bold in our approach instead of haggling over one per cent here and there. We should take a more long term view. The moment we tell the States to do something, they start demanding money as though the treasury is bursting with gold and silver for them to squander. Nobody is going to get any money. That is quite clear. We have to achieve the target we have set before ourselves by blood, sweat and toil. Where are we to produce something which we don't have? If we had had the money, there would have been no problem in the first place.

Now, these are not things which some select individuals can do on their own. We have to bear in mind that there are 37 crores of people living in this country out of which 30 crores live in the rural areas. It is a very large number. We want to make an impact on all the 30 crores. Gone are the days when, during British rule, a model village used to be put up as a showpiece. That kind of thing may deceive a few but does not help anyone.

As you know we have taken up a big scheme in the country, the Community Development Scheme which is spreading rapidly. Already two lakh twenty thousand villages with a population of 13 crores have been covered. It is our intention to cover every single village in India by the end of the Second Plan. It is not enough to show on paper that all the villages have been covered. A successful implementation of the Community Development Scheme implies improvement in agriculture, education, health care, building of roads, schools and hospitals, setting up of small and cottage industries, etc. Above all what it means is the betterment of human beings, men, women and children. They must have greater vitality and become capable of shouldering greater responsibilities. In fact, it means changing the people to make them self-reliant and self-confident. No government can do everything. You can forget it if you think a governmental agency can do everything for you. It is the people who make a nation great by their hard work and effort. The Community Development Schemes aim at

8. One of the main objectives of the Second Five Year Plan was an increase of fifteen per cent in agricultural production.

AT A SEMINAR ORGANIZED BY FARMERS' FORUM, NEW DELHI, 22 MARCH 1957

LISTENING TO THE DIFFICULTIES OF FARMERS IN NAJAFGARH, DELHI, 5 APRIL 1957

transforming the rural areas and teach the people to change their thinking. We can guide and advise, but ultimately it is the people who must show a new spirit. That is why I regard Community Development as the most revolutionary step in the country. I want it to spread to the entire country gradually for it will strengthen the foundation of the nation.

We are laying special stress on two things though our goal is all round development. One is improvement in agriculture and two, setting up of small-scale industries and cottage industries in the villages. We want the people to be more closely associated with the decision-making bodies. After all if we want progress in India, it cannot be done by the progress of a few individuals. India's millions must progress and develop self-confidence and be able to take on the burdens of the nation upon themselves. Only then one can enjoy the full advantages of freedom. If millions continue to be in a mire of poverty, how can the progress of a few thousand help? If we place our dependence on a handful of people we will remain weak. If the millions who live in India change and grow in stature, nobody can beat them. The Community Development Scheme aims at strengthening the people from the grassroots so that India can become strong enough to weather any crisis.

As you know, the world is a dangerous place and nobody knows when war may break out. At a time like this unless a nation's foundations are strong, it can topple over at any time as we see it happening all around us. If the foundations are strong, nothing can harm us. Therefore, it is very important that you should participate wholeheartedly in the Community Development Scheme. We must develop in various ways. Innumerable tasks are waiting to be done. We had become stagnant for a long time and there had been no progress in the country. We had lost our vitality and spirit. Therefore, we must try to progress now as fast as we can. Of all the tasks that need to be done, the most important is agricultural production and improving the standard of living of the peasants. This is fundamental to our progress. After all, eighty per cent of our population lives in villages and until that 80% progresses, how can India get anywhere?

That is one thing. Secondly, if we want to eradicate poverty, agricultural production is of fundamental importance. We always come round to that again and again. There is an exhibition of various machines, etc., which is a good thing. We must learn about them and take advantage. But ultimately, you must remember that it is only things which benefit millions of people that are best in the long run. Selected people can achieve a great deal. But it is what the millions of farmers do which is of real value not what a few thousands do. The farmers must share their experiences and learn from others. In this way, they will participate in great national tasks. You must understand that whatever you gain personally by increasing the output from land and working hard, you will become soldiers in the national cause, in the process. You must take others along with you if we are to succeed fully.

Therefore, it is my firm opinion that we must give a boost to cooperatives. That is the trend all over the world and there is no alternative particularly for a country like ours. Cooperatives are very essential, not merely to give credit which is a superficial thing, but in other ways. So, we must pay attention to them.

I have tried to share some of my thoughts with you. I hope you will think about them and point out our mistakes whenever you see any. All of us make mistakes. The best of governments make mistakes. It is not as though just by being in government, we are alone making mistakes. But a good, democratic government must be able to rectify its mistakes, and not try to hold on to them. That is foolish. We must show one another by debates and consultations what is right and what is wrong. Gradually, we will learn to follow the right path from our experience. We must learn to pick ourselves up and go on even if we stumble and fall. This is what we have been doing in the past and will continue to do so. *Jai Hind!*

2. To Bakhshi Ghulam Mohammad[1]

Flagstaff House
Chakrata
26 April 1957

My dear Bakhshi,[2]

I am writing to you about the rice position. I have just had a letter from Ajit Prasad Jain[3] in which he has expressed something akin to despair at the fact that while he is facing a terribly difficult situation all over the country, little help comes from Kashmir. I realize your difficulties, but I wish you would also realize the extremely serious position we have to face in regard to rice in India. We may

---

1. JN Collection. Copies of this letter were sent to Vishnu Sahay, Secretary of Kashmir Affairs and Labour, and Ajit Prasad Jain, Union Minister of Food and Agriculture.
2. Prime Minister of Jammu and Kashmir.
3. See the next item.

have to go in for very strict control and we may practically stop the flow of rice to a great part of North India so as to conserve what we have for the South and East. In spite of this position, demands from Kashmir are not reduced and, in fact, have a tendency to increase. The price at which rice is sold in Kashmir Valley is much less than the price in Kishtwar, and both are very much lower than anywhere else in the world.

In view of our financial position, rice subsidies are a great burden. Even a greater burden is importing rice for foreign exchange. It is quite possible that in spite of the rice shortage we might have to give up part of our imports to save foreign exchange. But the real difficulty is the actual shortage of rice, and we cannot afford to supply as much as we might have done in normal circumstances.

Political difficulties have to be considered wherever they occur, but in the final analysis we cannot agree to something which is beyond our capacity and which may bring about a financial collapse. Such a financial collapse would raise far greater political difficulties.

I want you to consider all these. The rates of rice in Kashmir are very low and the consumption per capita is high.

We are going to consider the whole rice position very soon in our Cabinet and possibly take strong measures.

Yours sincerely.
Jawaharlal Nehru

3. To A.P. Jain[1]

Flagstaff House
Chakrata
26 April 1957

My dear Ajit,

Your letter of April 24.[2] I have written a letter to Bakhshi Ghulam Mohammad, copy of which I enclose.

We must certainly consider this entire question of rice and foodgrains in Cabinet. Perhaps, before we go to the Cabinet, we should consider it in a smaller Committee of the Cabinet. It will be desirable now or a little later to form a small Food Committee of the Cabinet.

Yours sincerely,
Jawaharlal Nehru

---

1. JN Collection.
2. A.P. Jain wrote that the imposition of ban on the export of rice from Orissa had adversely affected the prices in West Bengal, and B.C. Roy and Prafulla Chandra Sen, member, West Bengal PCC, were considerably upset about this. At the same time the prices had declined in Orissa due to the ban. It was not his intention to suggest any reversal of the policy but he wanted Nehru to be in touch with the developments so that the matter might be judged in the light of past experience when similar questions arise later on.

4. To A.P. Jain[1]

New Delhi
30 April 1957

My dear Ajit,

Keskar[2] has written to me about the proposal made by the ICAR to set up an independent unit for film production. It appears that this unit would function in cooperation with the TCM and would be financed by the latter.

2. This raises quite a number of important issues. The first is as to whether our different Ministries should have separate film production units. Obviously, this would be wasteful and probably inefficient. Our Films Division has turned out to be an efficient organization and has produced very good films. If every Ministry starts doing this kind of thing, we cannot expect them to be as efficient. I do not think it at all a good thing for this kind of internal rivalry in such matters between Ministries of the Government of India.

3. But what I am much more concerned with is that the TCM should come into the picture in this way. The TCM has apparently been anxious to produce its own films for some Ministry or other. They tried to do so for the Community Projects. I recognize that we accept help from the TCM. But we have to be very careful about all this foreign help and certainly I do not want foreign personnel to come attached to that help. The TCM inevitably has connections with the USIS and I would object very strongly to the USIS even distantly and indirectly coming into the picture.

4. But broadly speaking, it is undesirable for a foreign agency to get associated with any form of publicity by us. It may be said that this is publicity for agricultural processes and all that. But even this can be utilized in a wrong way. Once we permit this kind of thing, it will be difficult to draw the line. As it is, we have been much concerned about the various activities of foreign agencies in India and I am not at all anxious to extend them. In fact, the question arises whether we can restrict them.

5. Because of all this I am surprised to find the ICAR spreading out in a direction which appears to me undesirable and likely to create difficulties for us in the future. It is all very well for the ICAR to say that they are doing this with

1. File No. 43(92)/57-PMS. Also available in JN Collection.
2. B.V. Keskar was Union Minister for Information and Broadcasting.

money from outside. That is exactly the reason why I object to it. If money from outside is gradually to creep in and affect our policies here, then the sooner we stop this money the better. The ICAR may be a semi-autonomous organization. I do not quite know what the position is. But obviously it is intimately connected with the Government and it should follow Government's broad policies and not strike out its own.

I should like you to look into this matter.

Yours sincerely,
Jawaharlal Nehru

III. EDUCATION AND CULTURE

1. Land for an Educational Institution[1]

I am sending you a letter from the Southern India Education Trust, Madras, which has been forwarded to me through Maulana Azad. Will you kindly have this matter looked into?

2. As you perhaps know, my broad view is that the Defence Ministry should not hold on to large pieces of land merely because it might conceivably require them much later. If these lands can be utilized for the public benefit otherwise, we should take a generous view of it. During my travels all over India, a constant complaint is that our Defence Ministry holds on to vast tracts of land which they do not use at all and which they prevent others from using. If a question of selling it arises, they ask for an exorbitant price. We have got a bad reputation in this matter. I think, we should be more generous and help in encouraging public activities and institutions.

3. This, of course, is the general approach. In this particular matter, apparently only three acres are involved. They were pointed out to me during one of my visits to Madras. I can offer no opinion without knowing what the Defence view is about their requirements there. But, I would suggest that we should meet the wishes of this educational institution unless there is something very important involved.

4. The suggestion made is that we should give this land free. Perhaps, it would be better to give it on a long lease with some relatively small rental.

---

1. Note to Defence Secretary, New Delhi, 27 February 1957. File No. 40 (115)/57-PMS. Also available in JN Collection.

2. To B.C. Roy[1]

New Delhi
28 February 1957

My dear Bidhan,[2]

I suppose that you are full of election activities apart from your other normal work. I have had enough of touring and indeed the elections would also be over soon. I propose to go just for a day to Kanpur and part of Fatehpur (which is part of my own constituency) on the 4th. Tomorrow I go to Meerut and come back. Apart from this, I hope to stay in Delhi now.

I am writing to you about a small matter which Rajkumari Amrit Kaur[3] has referred to me. This is about the Chinese acrobats, who are scheduled to go to Calcutta sometime next month after their visit to Delhi and Bombay. I gather that you have written to say that you do not want them there because on a previous occasion when the Russian troupe came, there was too great a rush involving a lathi charge etc.

I hope that you will not cancel this visit. These Chinese acrobats have been to a large number of places in the South and various parts of India. During my tour I heard about them and was told that they were greatly appreciated. In fact, they were rather unique in their own way. I propose to see them in Delhi day after tomorrow. The fact that they attract people surely is not a reason not to have them. It should be easy to make adequate arrangements. This has been easily done elsewhere. I can understand, however, that they will be a nuisance during election time when the Police and others are otherwise engaged. It should be easily possible to send them to Calcutta after the elections are over. I hope you will consider this matter.

1. JN Collection.
2. Chief Minister of West Bengal.
3. Union Minister for Health at this time.

3. To Abul Kalam Azad[1]

New Delhi
1 March 1957

My dear Maulana,[2]

A few days ago, you wrote to me and sent me a letter from Justice Basheer Ahmed Sayeed.[3] This referred to some land adjoining the Southern India Education Trust for Women's College.

I have enquired into this matter from the Defence Ministry. It appears that this question has been thoroughly considered by the Defence Ministry. The Defence Secretary inspected the place with the Area Commander, Madras Area, on the 16th April, 1956. Both of them were of opinion that it was not possible to lease any more land in the locality to the Trust. Justice Basheer Ahmed was informed of this. Apparently, he then approached you and you forwarded his letter to Dr Katju. Dr Katju looked into this matter himself and wrote to you that in his opinion, it would not be possible to accede to the request made by Justice Basheer Ahmed.

The land that the Education Trust now occupies, measuring 11, 200 square feet, also belonged to the Defence Ministry. This was leased to the Education Trust. The premium fixed for it was Rs 7,000/- and the annual rental Rs 350/-. Justice Basheer Ahmed made a request for a reduction in these amounts. The Defence Ministry considered this matter afresh and agreed to reduce the premium from Rs 7,000/- to Rs 3,500/- and the annual rental from Rs 350/- to Rs 100/-. Justice Basheer Ahmed thereupon wrote to the Defence Secretary, expressing his deep gratitude for his sympathetic interest in the Women's College and thanking him for the favour done to the institution by reducing the premium and the annual rental. He agreed that the conditions imposed by the Defence Ministry would be strictly adhered to by the Trust.

You will see that this matter has been repeatedly examined by the Ministry as well as by the Minister himself. Whatever land could be spared has already been given to the Southern India Education Trust, which has been treated

---

1. File No. 40 (115)/57-PMS.
2. Union Minister of Education, and Natural Resources & Scientific Research.
3. (b. 1900); Member, Madras Legislative Council, 1926-37; Secretary, District and Provincial Congress Committee, 1923-30; Member, AICC, 1923-30; Member, Madras Legislative Assembly, 1937-46; Puisne Judge, 1950-60; Chairman, Southern India Education Trust, Madras; founded New College, 1951 and SIET Women's College, 1955.

generously in regard to premium and rental. In these circumstances, I cannot ask the Defence Ministry to reconsider this matter.

Yours affectionately,
Jawaharlal Nehru

4. To S.B.H. Zaidi[1]

New Delhi
2 March 1957

My dear Zaidi,[2]

Two or three days ago, Ali Zaheer[3] came to see me. In the course of our talk, he mentioned the case of three Aligarh students who had been chosen by some American organization to go to the United States for further study. The Education Ministry of the Government of India had agreed to this ultimately and they were on the point of going when they were sent for by the American Consul in Delhi and certain questions were put to them. Apparently, these related to their general attitude to the Kashmir question and other like questions. Their answers not being to the liking of the American Consul, they have been refused visas to go to the United States.

Ali Zaheer was interested because his nephew, I think, Nurul Hasan,[4] is one of these students.

I should like to have the facts about this matter. It is, of course, open to the Americans to give visas or not but it does seem odd and objectionable for them to enquire about a person's views on Kashmir and decide on this basis.

Yours sincerely,
Jawaharlal Nehru

1. JN Collection.
2. Vice-Chancellor, Aligarh Muslim University.
3. Congress Member of the UP Legislative Assembly from Lucknow City West at this time.
4. Syed Nurul Hasan (1921-93); Professor of History, Aligarh Muslim University for several years; Member, Rajya Sabha, 1968-78; Union Minister of State for Education, Social Welfare and Culture, 1971-77; Vice-President, CSIR, 1980-83; Indian Ambassador to USSR, 1983-86; Governor, West Bengal, 1986-89; later Governor of Orissa.

5. To Shriman Narayan[1]

New Delhi
11 March 1957

My dear Shriman,[2]

Your letter of the 11th March, with which you have sent a letter from the Soviet Embassy.

The proposal is for some of our publications, and I presume notably reports of the annual sessions, to be microfilmed by the National Archives of India, that is our own Government's concern. I would have hesitated to give these books to any outside authority but, since it is our own Government which will do it, I think, it is desirable to agree to this.

In fact, I think that we should ourselves have a microfilmed set of these volumes, because we have no other copy and these old volumes might gradually disintegrate.

I do not know what the exact request was of the American scholars, to which you refer. Did they want the National Archives to do this microfilm work or did they wish to do it themselves? If we agree to the Soviet people taking this, obviously we can have no objection to the Americans having it also. Presumably, both parties will pay.

I suppose that when this is microfilmed extra copies can easily be made. I do not know. Anyhow, you should have an extra copy for the AICC libraries, even though we have to pay for it.

I think, therefore, that you can agree to this proposal. Further, that you can inform the American scholars that we have reconsidered this matter and we are prepared to let them have microfilms prepared by the National Archives of India.

Yours sincerely,
Jawaharlal Nehru

1. File No. SN-19, AICC Papers, NMML. Also available in JN Collection.
2. General Secretary, Indian National Congress.

6. To Lakshmi N. Menon[1]

New Delhi
11 March 1957

My dear Lakshmi,[2]

Your letter of the 9th March about the Lady Hardinge Medical College.[3]

When this matter first came up before me, I took the trouble to enquire into it more fully. After this enquiry, it seemed to me that the proposal made by the Health Ministry and recommended by many other eminent persons to enlarge the medical college had a great deal of justification in it. I really do not understand what all this agitation is about. In fact, many women doctors and others have supported the proposal and expert opinion is in favour of it.

The financial argument is important and we cannot just afford now to be lavish with our expenditure.[4] But to me it seems much more important that women doctors should not be trained in purdah and should have some experience of others also in so far as their training is concerned. I should have thought that this is an important element in training, more especially for the medical profession. We do not have separate women institutes for engineers or separate universities for women. Why then should there be separate medical colleges for women. If it is said that we should pay particular attention to our social habits and customs, I agree to some extent. These women students live separately, have their separate lives but in regard to the actual training courses surely it is better to have joint ones than separate. I can understand also that first priority should be given to women teachers and women students. If we split up our institutions in this way, standards will go down.

Yours sincerely,
Jawaharlal Nehru

1. File No. 28(36)/57-59-PMS. Also available in JN Collection.
2. Member of Rajya Sabha at this time.
3. Lakshmi Menon informed Nehru that various women organizations in Delhi wanted that the move to associate Lady Hardinge Medical College with Irwin Hospital should be dropped and "the College should continue as a separate women's institution and be financed more adequately to expand the scope of its activities and train more women from implementation of the various health programmes under the Second Five Year Plan."
4. The Health Ministry argued that the financial resources did not allow them to have another medical college in Delhi for men.

7. To David Alfaro Siqueiros[1]

New Delhi
16 March 1957

Dear Mr Siqueiros,

Thank you for your letter of January 24th, which took about a month to reach me.[2] Apparently it came by ocean mail.

I am interested to learn of the reports you have made in Mexico of your visit to India.[3]

We would greatly welcome your cooperation in developing mural paintings in India, especially in Delhi. Your visit[4] here was of great help to our artists and architects and broadened their own vision. I hope that we shall have the opportunity of taking advantage of your offer in the future. I know that there has been delay in this matter. We have passed through a difficult time here and even now we are having general elections on an enormous scale. Our voters alone number nearly two hundred millions. After these elections are over, a new Government will have to be formed.

Apart from this, owing to grave financial stringencies and specially in regard to foreign exchange, we have unfortunately limited greatly our work this year and some of our major proposals have been postponed. We had intended constructing the National Theatre in Delhi. That too has been postponed because of these difficulties.

For these reasons, we would not like to trouble you to come here in the near future and I do not wish to come in the way of any other work or engagement

1. File No. 40(47)/56-70-PMS. Also available in JN Collection.
2. In his letter Siqueiros, the well known Mexican Painter, recorded his impressions of India as "the oldest and most powerful source of universal culture." He wrote that the people of India had set themselves for the consolidation of their "national independence and consequent social progress."
3. Siqueiros pointed out in a press conference in Mexico that Nehru had extended extraordinary attention to him and showed extensive knowledge of Mexico as well as a sound recognition of the importance of their contemporary pictorial movement. He concluded that through him Nehru had paid tribute to Mexico and to Mexican culture as a whole.
4. Siqueiros visited India in November-December 1956 for four weeks at the invitation of the Government of India to interact with Indian artists and deliver lectures on Mexican art.

223

that you might be offered. As soon as the situation here is somewhat easier and we can undertake some of our big schemes, we shall communicate with you.

With all good wishes to you,

Yours sincerely,
Jawaharlal Nehru

8. Jain Viewpoint on *Bhagwan Buddha*[1]

This question has been very fully discussed at a meeting of the Executive of the Sahitya Akademi. We came to the conclusions that (1) the book should not be translated into any further Indian languages, (2) that a note explaining the criticism made by some Jains, should be attached to all the copies of the book already published, and (3) that no further edition should be considered. You might reply as follows, to this letter.

"Dear Sir,

The Prime Minister has seen your letter of the 12th March.[2] He is unable to understand what the declaration of a holiday has to do with the greatness or the spirituality of a great religious leader. It is true that many of our old holidays are associated in this way and have become customary. The result is that India has more holidays than any country in the world, and all our progress suffers. The Government, therefore, came to the conclusion that no further holidays should be accepted and that, in fact, some attempt should be made to reduce the existing number of holidays, so that national work may not suffer. Buddha Jayanti was included in the list of public holidays for certain international reasons. Probably, even that would not be done now after the Government's decisions.

The book you refer to, namely *Bhagwan Buddha*, is a well known book by a great scholar who has shown his reverence for the great spiritual leader. It is written in a completely detached spirit, without any bias. We have had

1. Note to K. Ram, Principal Private Secretary, New Delhi, 18 March 1957. JN Collection.
2. Letter not available.

224

this examined by competent scholars and many important leaders among the Jain community and, though they do not agree with some things that this book contains, they have admitted that it is a book of high scholarship, objectively written. It would be an unfortunate state of affairs if books of scholarship which are dispassionately and objectively written, are suppressed because some people do not agree with them.

This matter has nothing to do with the Government. Some translations of the book were issued at the instance of the Sahitya Akademi. A meeting of the Executive of that Akademi has very fully considered this matter again. They felt that it would be undesirable to lay down any principle of suppression of books in this way. In view, however, of Jain sentiment, it was decided that no further translations of the book should be considered. Also, that the existing copies should have a note attached to them, which clearly signifies the viewpoint of the Jains. We understand that this is being done.

The Prime Minister further wishes me to tell you that he considers fasting for such a purpose a coercive method, entirely opposed to ahimsa".

2. Send a copy of your letter to the Secretary of the Sahitya Akedemi.[3]

3. Krishna Kripalani.

9. Preservation of Nagarjunakonda Town[1]

Jawaharlal Nehru: Mr Chairman[2], I venture to speak on this resolution[3] for two reasons. One is because I have been deeply interested in this matter ever since its inception[4] and secondly because I have visited the place and spent some time

1. Speech in the Rajya Sabha, 22 March 1957, *Rajya Sabha Debates,* 1957, Vol. XVI, cols. 393, 401-405, 408-410.
2. S. Radhakrishnan.
3. This resolution, moved by V.K. Dhage, an independent Member from Bombay, asked the Government to take necessary steps to preserve the Nagarjunakouda town, in view of its association with early Buddhist history and development of various schools of Buddhist thought.
4. The issue of preserving the Nagarjunakonda town had come up when the foundation of the Nagarjunasagar Dam on the Krishna river was laid by Nehru on 10 December 1955. See also *Selected Works* (second series), Vol. 30, pp. 220-221, Vol. 31, pp. 3, 9-14, 103, 106 and 108-109 and Vol. 32, pp. 95-96.

there. When the idea of this project was first broached, the immediate thought that came to me was that this ancient site of Nagarjunakonda should be preserved and it was with that strong urge that I approached this question and discussed it with all kinds of people connected with this matter in the Ministries here, the engineers and others. I went there and discussed it there. I discussed it with the Archaeological Department also. I came to the conclusion that one could not give up this major scheme which would bring relief to a very large number of persons even for this important consideration of preserving the site. Secondly, the site itself, unless you consider the site as a covered up place which should not be uncovered, was not going to be preserved by leaving it there and digging it up. It was going to pieces. Whatever had been uncovered was deteriorating and disintegrating with great rapidity as it always does. The question therefore, was of leaving it as a historical site with hardly any of the memorials visible or appearing. The moment you make them visible anywhere, they deteriorate, they disintegrate, unless of course, you build them up afresh. But the major consideration certainly was that one could not sacrifice the interests of vast numbers of people round about for this purpose. Then we examined what could be done about it and I wanted and I suggested not only that the special articles should be removed from there and put in a museum—that was not enough—I suggested that these ancient structures should be bodily lifted and rebuilt nearby. Now, the site is such that when this big lake comes into being, it will be a huge lake, there is a hill which becomes an island and the hill has got a flat area at the top. So a suggestion was made that this flat area should be converted into some kind of a park with all these excavated buildings being rebuilt there such as could be—one cannot do it with everything—plus a museum there, which really would probably preserve these places much better than merely leaving them where they are.[5] In fact, they will be built in a part of the site, you might say. It is part of the site which remains above the water. We told the Archaeological Department to go ahead with this. It was a very difficult task because these archaeological excavations have to be done with extreme care by experts. In fact, we made special provisions for engaging new staff, engaging young people who may be studying archaeology in the universities to go and work there and help in that and we made it clear that whatever extra expenditure was involved in this will be met. We gave them almost a free and open cheque for that because we attach so much importance to preserving these monuments. There really was no other possible way out of it. First of all, it seems to me in the balance,

5. Finally, the Archaeological Survey of India transplanted and preserved the monuments and antiquities in a museum named Nagarjuna Island Museum, located at a distance of eleven kms from the dam.

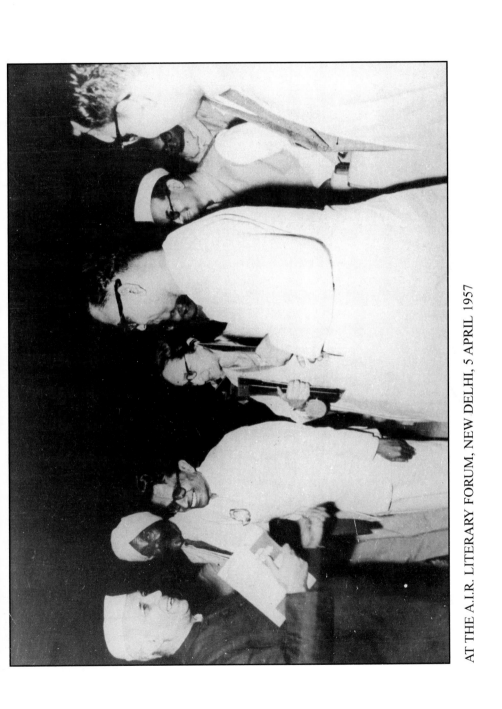

AT THE A.I.R. LITERARY FORUM, NEW DELHI, 5 APRIL 1957

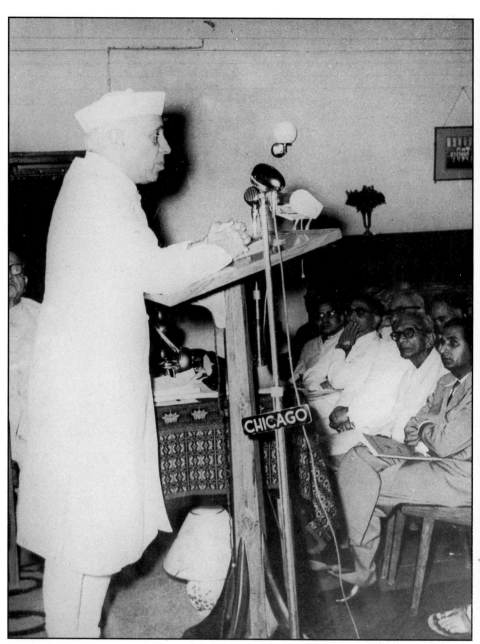

SPEAKING AT THE INDIAN INSTITUTE OF PUBLIC ADMINISTRATION, NEW DELHI, 6 APRIL 1957

however much you might have liked to preserve them, you could not go back on this huge scheme, giving benefit to vast numbers of people, merely to maintain something which is likely to disintegrate anyhow, and even from the point of view of preservation, this was a better way of preserving them, that is to say, first of all, taking the principal structure there which was disintegrating and removing it bodily, or rather removing it bit by bit, and reconstructing it in a part of the site itself which would be above the water level, and having a museum and a park there. That would really become a place, if you like, for some people, those who think that way, a place of pilgrimage, and for others a great site of historical and cultural interest. It has a tradition. I went there last year. It was very difficult at that moment, to see much there. Of course, they will be dug up, but the moment they are dug up, they go to pieces, they disintegrate. There is, for instance, a small amphitheatre, a small one, which is rather unique. I do not think there is any such amphitheatre existing anywhere, not in India certainly. I do not know what is going to happen. It is disintegrating. The moment it is reopened it disintegrates. We cannot do much except that after taking every possible care to preserve such of those structures by removing them, if you can do so, and having a museum and paying every attention to their preservation and proper upkeep. There is nothing more to be done about it.

There is a proposal, an amendment to this Resolution, about a committee going into it. What exactly was the committee to do? Honourable Members of this House, of course, are not only welcome to go there, we would invite them to go there and elsewhere also. There is no difficulty about their going there, about their being shown round there by the people in charge, and if they have any suggestions to make, we shall welcome those suggestions. But as for the appointment of a committee, is that committee supposed to consider whether this scheme is to go on or not? I submit that would be a very major decision and an unusual decision to make at any time, more especially, at this time when the scheme has gone pretty far, archaeologically and in the engineering way. Vast sums of money have been spent, after paying the fullest attention to this very aspect that has been raised here.

Humayun Kabir: May I make one suggestion to the Prime Minister at this stage?

There is, I believe, a committee already appointed which is looking into the question of preservation of these things and if one or two Members of Parliament of this House and of the other House can be associated with that committee, it would be useful. This could be done by an executive order of Government.

JN: That might be possible, of course. It is quite possible to add some people to that committee. They had formed a committee—I am not quite sure—and we made the Governor of Andhra[6] the Chairman of that committee. Of course, we wanted to give it considerable importance and we wanted the Governor himself to pay attention to its preservation. I am told the present committee is called a coordination committee. It is coordination between the engineering side and the archaeological side. The present committee consists of the Governor of Andhra Pradesh as chairman, the Chief Minister of Andhra[7] as member, the Administrator, Nagarjunsagar Project as member, Superintendent, Nagarjunakonda, Excavation Branch, Department of Archaeology, Guntur, as member-secretary. I think, it will certainly be possible for some additions to be made to this committee, from this House and the other House and people who are interested can be in this committee. But it should be clearly understood that we cannot go back on this project which has gone so far. That is neither feasible nor desirable.

The appointment of an *ad hoc* committee would be very unusual and much depends on what terms of reference you give it. If they give a report to go back on all that is done, that would produce a most embarrassing situation. First of all, as Prof. Humayun Kabir has suggested, we shall gladly add to this committee persons who are interested, from this House and the other House. Secondly, it does not require the appointment of a special committee. Honourable Members can always go there, individually or in a group, and if they inform us before of their going, arrangements will be made there for them to be shown round and explained everything. I submit, Sir, that both these, this Resolution and this amendment, should not be pressed.

xx xx xx

JN: That suggestion seems to be absolutely impossible of accomplishment. I cannot understand how in the middle of a lake to preserve the town a 500 feet wide wall could be constructed. I just cannot conceive of it.

V.K. Dhage: I have also made enquiries from the people concerned in this matter and I am told that it is possible to construct a wall for the purpose. I do not want to dispute what the honourable Prime Minister has to say, but what I am saying also is based on certain authority, namely, that we can construct a wall in the middle of the lake by pushing off the lake on one side and keeping the town on the other. Not only that, I have visited the site myself

6. C.M. Trivedi.
7. N. Sanjiva Reddy.

and I feel that it seems to be feasible. Though, of course, it means construction of a wall, it may probably mean another dam—I might probably be able to concede that point. But my point is no expenditure should be considered to be too big in order to preserve the town, and the town is a very ancient and historically important one. Now that is the point and I think, I should not insist upon my resolution being accepted but I would want the Prime Minister to say that if the Government of India invites a Parliamentary committee and makes them visit the place and see the site, etc., and if they make certain recommendations they would give due consideration to them. The point is as to whether or not the construction of the wall can take place irrespective of the consideration as to how high the cost will be, and if the Government will pay consideration to it, I will have no objection in withdrawing my resolution. Thank you, Sir,

Mr Chairman: Now, I shall put the amendment first.

V.K. Dhage: Sir, may I have the Prime Minister to say something with regard to the committee?

Mr Chairman: There is no committee. All that the Prime Minister said was that to that coordination committee presided over by the Andhra Governor, some representatives of this House and the other House might be added. (Turning to the Prime Minister) That is all that you said?

JN: What I said was two things. One was that in that coordinating committee, Members of this House and the other House can be added. Naturally, in adding them to the existing number the addition should be as small as possible and it is not convenient if such committees be big; as it is, it is a committee of four, I think. I would suggest that a Member of this House, and a Member of the other House be added. Apart from that, I said, I merely reminded the House, that it is completely easy for honourable Members of this House to visit the place and, if I may say so with all respect, it does not cost them anything because they can travel free, and we will arrange with the people there for any group of honourable Members or any single honourable Member to be shown round the place and they can discuss the matter with them. It does not require the appointment of a formal committee to consider all kinds of engineering and other problems. We cannot accept the particular thing that the honourable Member has referred to, about some walls being constructed. It has been considered by engineers, etc., and considered as not at all feasible.

These two things I submitted, Sir.

V.K. Dhage: Not feasible from the financial point of view or the engineering point of view.

JN: Purely engineering; the financial part did not come in. The engineers said that that was not feasible. So far as I remember the financial part was not considered—might have been, possibly, I don't know. Of course if you are prepared to spend enormous sums you can even create a new world; it depends on the sum completely.

10. To K.M. Munshi[1]

New Delhi
1 April 1957

My dear Munshi,[2]

Thank you for your letter of March 30.[3] I am glad you are preserving all those important papers in connection with our Constitution making. I think that it would be desirable for a proper selection etc., to be made and subsequently for this to be published. But I doubt if it is possible to get any money for this from the Wheat Loan Fund. I think this is completely earmarked for certain of our developmental projects.

So far as the Ford and Rockefeller Foundations are concerned, we have also approached them for various kinds of help in connection with our development schemes. I do not know if we can press them for additional help for this purpose.

We are in a difficult financial position and we are cutting down our expenditure

---

1. JN Collection.
2. Governor of Uttar Pradesh.
3. In this letter K.M. Munshi wrote to Nehru that he had "preserved most of the notes, memoranda, drafts and opinions which we exchanged with each other, as also minutes and other papers in connection with our work from August 1946 when you appointed me on the Constitution Committee of the AICC, till 26th January 1950." He suggested that if these materials were properly edited and published it would be "a valuable contribution to the literature on Constitutional law of the world." He also informed that Prof. Fowler Harper of the Yale School of Law assured him that, "his school would be able to cooperate in the project...." He further sought whether the Government of India "would help in securing pecuniary assistance from the Wheat Loan Fund or the Ford or Rockefeller Foundations."

very rigidly. Even some of our important schemes are being held up. I doubt, therefore, if it will be possible for us to make any special effort for new schemes such as you suggest. I have no idea how much it will cost. Much would depend upon that. Anyhow, I am consulting some of my colleagues here about your proposal.

Yours sincerely,
Jawaharlal Nehru

11. To S.K. Dey[1]

New Delhi
3 April 1957

My dear Dey,

Kailas Nath Kaul[2] has sent me the enclosed paper which I have read with interest.[3] It is a good note. I have myself seen his work and have found it good. In particular, I have found that he has great capacity for interesting people in the work they are doing and making them better at it. His open air school has been a success.

I think that we should profit by this example and try to introduce it elsewhere. But, of course, this requires the right type of person to do it.

Yours sincerely,
Jawaharlal Nehru

1. JN Collection.
2. Brother of Kamala Nehru and Director, National Botanical Gardens, Lucknow.
3. The note sent to Nehru on 1 April 1957, gave a brief and concise account of the success that Kailas Nath Kaul had attained in dealing with *usar* land.

12. Role of Language and Literature[1]

Dr Keskar, Men and Women of Letters,
I was not sure until today how this ceremony was going to be organized and which area was to be given special attention. Last year I found that the festival was theatre and poetry oriented. This year the emphasis seems to be on short stories. Whatever aspect we may take up, the question is what our goals are. As Dr Keskar pointed out[2] just now, it is pretty obvious what they are. In fact, most of the Indian languages have their origins from the same source and even in the cases where the source is different they have imbibed a great deal from the others. So, the question is what the correlation between these languages should be and in what way they can learn from one another and grow.

This is the issue which is vital, whichever way you look at it, politically or otherwise. We see in India and some times in other countries, the love that languages evoke. It is a good thing. We must encourage close contacts between the various languages and show that they are not antagonistic to one another rather they are cooperative and extend help to one another.

Europe has many famous languages. Most of them have emerged from under the shadow of Greek and Latin and flourished during the last 300 years or so. Before that Latin and Greek had suppressed them. English, French, Spanish, Italian all have their origins in Latin. They have grown and acquired prominence gradually in their own countries. But there is no antagonism between them. In a sense, an individual's education was not considered to be complete unless he knows two or three languages and this is true even now to some extent. There was no question of trying to impede the growth of another language in order to get ahead. The thoughts, ideas and poetry, prose etc., would percolate to other languages. There are excellent arrangements for translations in the West. But apart from that, large numbers of people know more than one language. Though every language has its roots in the soil of its own country, its progress has been greatly helped by the close give and take with other, European languages apart from Greek and Latin. Even today if you pick up a reputed journal in any

---

1. Speech at the second literary forum organized by the All India Radio, New Delhi, 5 April 1957. AIR tapes, NMML. Original in Hindi.
2. B.V. Keskar, the Minister for Information and Broadcasting, in his welcome address stated that the All India Radio had aroused a new hope in the cultural world of India but its more important role was to forge unity among regional languages and foster greater understanding.

European language you will find mention of the work being done in other languages, reviews of books published, and an attempt is made to show the impact they have made on their language. You can pick up any good journal in English, French, German, Russian or Spanish, you will find the same trend. This is how they have grown. There is no antagonism between them. The problems which we face in this country in connection with our languages do not arise in Europe to the same extent. Whether we look at it from the point of view of national unity or the growth of languages, it is extremely important to foster close links between various languages. People must be encouraged to learn more than one language well. This is very important.

Recently, a well known brain surgeon of Canada[3] was visiting India. He gave some talks on the radio. He said that perhaps many people may not be aware of the extraordinary fact that there is a corner in every child's brain for learning of languages. There are special cells which are renewed till the age of ten. After that the growth of new cells stops. The old ones may continue to exist but new ones do not grow. The conclusion that this surgeon has drawn is that until the age of ten a child can learn new languages very easily. The images which are imprinted on the mind then never fade away. Even when not in use, the memory is stored away in a corner of the brain.

What does learning a language mean? It is obvious to everyone that though adults also learn new languages, they cannot do so with the same facility as they learnt their mother tongue. There is some shortcoming in the syntax or the accent. You may learn thousands of words by heart and even speak a language fluently. But the accent will not be quite natural as in the case of one's mother tongue. When a child learns a language, upto the age of ten, he learns the correct pronunciation and accent instinctively, even if his vocabulary is not very extensive. He can build up his vocabulary at any time on the earlier foundations. This is not the case with grown-ups who learn a language even if they are able to speak and write well.

I have said this merely to show how mistaken the notion that some people have about children learning more than one language. It is a wrong notion that learning many languages casts a burden upon the child. Scientifically, it has been proved wrong. A child can learn many languages simultaneously. There are separate compartments in his brain and there is no question of any confusion. That does not mean that several languages should be taught in every school though in my opinion, two or three languages can easily be taught from the age of four or five. Children should be made to listen to the phonetic sounds of a

3. Dr Penfield.

language so that they are firmly imprinted on their brain. The method that we are following now in our schools of teaching only one language upto some class and then taking up the next, almost as though languages can be taught larger upon larger, is not borne out by modern scientific principles. If we want to teach two or three languages to a child, it is best to give a basic grounding in them before the age of ten. It is not necessary that they should have an extensive vocabulary. The child must have a basic grounding and learn to recognize the sounds and accents and the right pronunciation. We can easily build upon that later on.

I am saying this because whenever the question of teaching languages arises, it should be borne in mind that the sooner we start doing so the more successful we will be. It is wrong to feel that it will be too much of a burden for a child to learn two or three languages at the same time. Everything depends on the teacher. If he tries to make them learn everything, the child will feel frustrated and not learn anything. The child should be allowed to learn while he plays as far as possible, I do not know how far it is feasible. But this has been accepted. I have laid stress elsewhere too on the need to learn foreign languages. It is obvious that we cannot insist on everybody doing so. But people must do so in large numbers. In India the emphasis is on learning English which is but proper because it is the most widely spoken language in the world. Knowledge of a foreign language makes things easier in the field of literature, science, industry, business or foreign relations. So, seen from any point of view, it is necessary to learn a foreign language. Otherwise we will be cut off from the revolutionary events which are taking place in the world. It is not enough for a handful of people to learn foreign languages. We must lay the foundations for large numbers of common people to learn what is going on in the world.

As far as literature is concerned I consider it necessary for us to keep in touch with literary trends in the world. Literature cannot grow and flourish in isolation or through inbreeding. It must certainly draw sustenance from the soil in which it has roots. But two other things are equally important. First, the flow of ideas from the rest of the world. Second, a knowledge of the revolutionary changes which are shaping society and life styles in the rest of the world. The speed at which this is happening is amazing though we tend to take things for granted. We travel by train and plane, speak on the microphone, listen to the radio, etc. But I want you to remember that the world has changed completely in less than 150 years. It is modern science which has been responsible for these great changes. Science and technology and their off-shoots have changed our entire way of life and working, the structure of society, etc. It is obvious that something which is capable of changing the whole world and the structure of society is bound to have an impact on literature, for literature is not something apart from society or its innumerable functions. If it tries to remain in isolation, it begins to lose touch with reality and becomes vague and unsubstantial. A living, vital literature must be closely associated with this changing world. Otherwise, it may become ornate but will lose its vitality.

So, it is very essential that we should have close links with the world. India is changing rapidly though it may not be very evident. Soon the changes will gather momentum with the successful completion of the five year plans and other programmes. You may wonder what the connection between industries and literature could be. There is a link because industrialization changes people's life-style and way of working. It throws up new problems and challenges, new happiness and sorrow too. How long can you continue writing about the days gone by? I do not say that you should not write about that. But in order to grip the imagination of the people, you will have to write about the realities of modern life. Literature must throw light on the problems and dilemmas of our times. So, it is very important that literature should be closely linked to the changing world.

India is changing but still very far behind the advanced countries of the West. We want to catch up with the most advanced among them. But at the moment we are backward. The new trends and ideas in science and technology emanate from the West. There is no doubt about it. We must also contribute to the growth of ideas and so it is essential for us to learn foreign languages. We must learn them not superficially but go deep into the philosophy and thought which they advocate. That will help to generate new ideas in our country. We can progress not by copying anyone but only by imbibing new ideas and making them the foundation for new and original thinking and research in India. You cannot transplant a whole tree from somewhere. You can certainly plant the seed of an idea.

I have put some of these ideas before you. But I want you to be clear in your minds, specially about the kind of India and the world that we live in today. We are living on razor's edge today. That may be true at all times with the past on the one side and the future on the other, the present being poised on a razor's edge. But it is particularly so in this era of rapid scientific and technological advance. Strangely enough, the thinking of the people lags behind. Science is the product of the people's thinking. But it has not changed the thinking of the common man. So, there is a danger that while we grasp the ideas of modernity superficially, we do not imbibe them fully and we will fall between two stools.

What is the role of literature in all this? It is obvious that literature should be a bridge between the two. In order to do that, the builder of the bridge must be able to understand both sides of the picture. Writers must be able to draw the attention of the nation towards new ideas and developments to open the windows of the mind and let the fresh breeze of ideas flow in. The entire political, economic and social field is open to them and the edifice that we build must be full of vitality.

In my opinion, one of the areas of life in India which is full of vitality and spirit is that of folk dance and music. Many people look down upon them. But I feel that they are an image of the common man's vitality and hence I feel more reassured by that than by the intellectuals who write learned tones. Intellectual attainments may show ability but are not necessarily the symbol of progress of an entire nation.

Today, there is evidence of great vitality in India in every walk of life. It is obvious that that throws up new and difficult challenges. It is only the lifeless who ask no question. India faces difficult problems and challenges. Sometimes I feel deeply perturbed at some of the developments which are affecting the world today. I am not talking of what you read about in newspapers. It goes beyond that. It is not merely that preparations for war are constantly being made and the threat of war hangs like Democles' sword over our heads. But what perturbs me is that somehow there is a feeling of general uprooting of values and ideas. It is to be hoped that they will find fresh moorings. But the atmosphere is vitiated. We cannot take on the burden of the whole world upon us. But whether we like it or not, we have to face the challenges of the times in our country and make ourselves strong enough to tackle any problems that may arise.

So, our first duty is to defend ourselves. I do not mean militarily but in our thinking. We must build upon foundations of national unity among the diversities to face any challenges. How can we serve the world unless we are strong as a nation? We have to play a role on the world stage whether we like it or not because the world has shrunk today. No nation can live in isolation, fast travel and communications have served to make all nations close to one another. You can get to the other end of the world in a day. You get news from the far corners of the earth within seconds. The world has become a close-knit place. We have to do what we can to serve humanity.

So, we come round once again to the role of literature in all this. You will find that its parameters are extending more and more. But we must ensure that it does not become superficial in the process. At the same time, without a broad base, you can be cut off from the rest of the world which would be extremely dangerous specially in these times.

I have spoken at random. It is up to you to tell the people what is happening in India in this field.

13. To K.L. Shrimali[1]

New Delhi
12 April 1957

My dear Shrimali,[2]

I enclose a letter from Hayatullah Ansari.[3] The first part deals with elections and you need not trouble yourself about it. After this, he refers to his method of teaching Hindi in ten days. It seems that our Education Ministry has approved this method. I myself was rather impressed by it.

You will see that he is completely hard up and he cannot go ahead with the publication of his book or charts. I think that in the circumstances, when his method has been approved of, we should help him to publish these. We can even get them published on our own behalf by the Publications Division here.

You might consult Maulana Sahib about this matter.

Yours sincerely,
Jawaharlal Nehru

---

1. File No. 40(119)/57-PMS. Also available in JN Collection.
2. (1909-2000); Head Master, Vidya Bhavan, 1931-42; Principal, Vidya Bhavan Teachers' College, 1942-55; Deputy Minister for Education, 1955-57; Union Minister of State for Education and Scientific Research, 1957-62; Union Minister for Education 1962-63.
3. Secretary, Anjuman-i-Taraqqi-i-Urdu at this time and editor, *Qaumi Awaz*.

14. To Humayun Kabir[1]

New Delhi
12 April 1957

My dear Humayun,[2]

Your letter of the 11th April.

It would certainly be desirable if good biographies of our national leaders were prepared. I have found, however, that we in India, possessing many virtues as we do, have not yet developed the art of writing a good biography. Our idea of writing a biography is to use a string of eulogistic phrases.

I do not see how Government can sponsor any such biographies unless they are some short ones for, you might say, school use. The question of M.N. Roy's writings was a different one. It was not a biography. The idea was to preserve his manuscripts and possibly to publish a selection of them. I do not know what happened. So far as I remember, the proposal fell through.

I know Iswara Dutt[3] and he writes well, though I fear that he is also on the eulogistic side. But it will be a good thing if he writes a biography of Dr Sapru.[4] My difficulty is that I cannot sponsor it officially.

Yours sincerely,
Jawaharlal Nehru

---

1. JN Collection.
2. Congress Member, Rajya Sabha, from West Bengal at this time.
3. Iswara K. Dutt (1898-1968); eminent journalist and writer; worked as sub-editor in *The Hindu,* Assistant Editor in *The Leader* and Editor of *People's Voice*; author of several books.
4. The reference is to the Liberal leader, Tej Bahadur Sapru, also of Allahabad.

15. To Abul Kalam Azad[1]

New Delhi
15 April 1957

My dear Maulana,

I had a talk with Sanjiva Reddy[2] this morning about the Vice-Chancellorship of Osmania University. He will be seeing you also and speaking to you on this subject. I am putting down below what he told me.

As soon as the question of a vacancy arose in the Vice-Chancellorship of Osmania University, Sanjiva Reddy was anxious not to do anything without consultation with the Telangana people and the University leaders. He wrote to Ramkrishna Rao[3] for his advice. Ramkrishna Rao told him that he should not be in a hurry and suggested that he might make a temporary appointment pending the general elections. Further, he said that a really good man should be appointed and, if necessary, he could go outside the State for such a man. Thereupon he appointed a person named Doraiswamy, who is a senior professor there and who had always functioned as Vice-Chancellor in the temporary absence of Bhagawantam.[4]

Governor Trivedi recommended Syed Husain who is the Principal there now. But, in the past, Syed Husain had been repeatedly passed over even for temporary appointments as he was not considered quite up to the mark.

As for Abdul Haq, he is not a Telangana man, but if he was outstanding, there would be no difficulty. When Abdul Huq was professor in Madras, he was passed over repeatedly by Rajaji and others in regard to the appointment of the Director of Public Instruction as he was not considered quite good enough for it, although he was probably the senior-most person there. Ultimately, he was sent to the Public Service Commission more to get him out of the educational hierarchy. Rajaji did not have a high opinion of his capacity, although he is a good man.

Sanjiva Reddy has been consulting Gopala Reddi[5] and proposes to send for ten leading members of the Academic Council of the University to consult them

---

1. File No. 40(118)/57-PMS. Also available in JN Collection.
2. N. Sanjiva Reddy, Chief Minister of Andhra Pradesh.
3. B. Ramakrishna Rao, Governor of Kerala at this time.
4. S. Bhagawantam.
5. B. Gopala Reddi, Finance Minister, Government of Andhra Pradesh.

also. He is anxious that only a person who is acceptable to Telangana should be appointed.[6]

Yours affectionately,
Jawaharlal Nehru

6. Finally, D.S. Reddy was appointed Vice-Chancellor of Osmania University.

16. To B.V. Keskar[1]

New Delhi
19 April 1957

My dear Balakrishna,

K.A. Abbas wrote to me the other day about the film he is making in cooperation with the Soviet people.[2] His film relates to the visit of the Russian traveller in the fifteenth or sixteenth century to India. You will probably remember this.

Abbas said that he had proceeded very far with the film, but, at the last moment, they, that is the Indian side, were short of some money, and this had held up their work. He said that he could easily get this money from the Russians, but he did not like the idea of doing so, as it indicated that we could not even pay what we had agreed to do on this side. I think, the amount he asked for was rupees two hundred thousand which he said he would be able to begin paying back by the end of this year or earlier. An income was assured as the film had already been booked, and some advance payments were being received.

Abbas wanted a loan to be given to him from the Industrial Finance Corporation or a State Finance Corporation.

It seemed to me worthwhile to give him this loan as there is no doubt about re-payment, and there was every chance of the film being successful. Also, in this international matter, it did not seem to me good for the Indian side of the

1. File No. 43(56)/56-57-PMS. Also available in JN Collection.
2. The film *Pardesi* was the first Indo-Soviet co-production, co-directed by K.A. Abbas and Vassili M. Pronin in 1957.

contract to fail, especially at the last moment. I wrote, therefore, to the Finance Minister.[3] I enclose a copy of his reply.[4] You will notice that he says that, while it will not be proper for the Industrial Finance Corporation to grant a loan in this particular case, it would be possible to give a temporary accommodation asked for from the grants at the disposal of the Films Division of I & B if the I & B Ministry sponsors the proposal. The Finance Ministry will accept the proposal as the amount involved is small and the period is only some months.

I think, therefore, that you might sponsor this proposal and give the loan after you get the concurrence of the Ministry of Finance, which has already been promised.

You can send for Abbas, if you like to get further details. I think I have some papers about this. Should you want them, I shall send them.

Yours sincerely,
Jawaharlal Nehru

3. Nehru had written to T.T. Krishnamachari on 8 April and 16 April 1957 (not printed) regarding the loan K.A. Abbas had sought for making this film.
4. In his reply of 19 April 1957, T.T. Krishnamachari pointed out: "I understand that it will not be possible either for the Industrial Finance Corporation or a State Finance Corporation to grant a loan in this particular case as it is not covered by the relevant statutes." He added: "It may however be possible to give Shri Abbas the temporary accommodation he needs from the grants at the disposal of the Films Division of the I & B Ministry provided that Ministry sponsors the proposals."

17. To Jivraj N. Mehta[1]

Flagstaff House
Chakrata
26 April 1957

My dear Jivraj,[2]

Your letter of the 22nd April.[3]

It is true that we do not like any close association with the Asia Foundation. This Foundation undoubtedly is giving money for good purposes. At the same time, we have received definite and repeated information that sometimes, under cover of this good work, it has interfered with the internal politics of countries and indeed even with elections. This information has come to us from other countries. As with some other such organizations, it appears to have a dual object and a strong political bias.

This was why we had discouraged any close association with it. So far as we are concerned, even now it is not what you call persona grata with us. Nevertheless, when the Bombay University wrote to us repeatedly about a donation of ten thousand dollars from them for some purpose, we decided ultimately not to come in the way. It is difficult to go about explaining everything to the Senate of the Bombay University.

For the same reason we shall raise no objection to the acceptance of the offer made by the Asia Foundation to the Indian Conference of Social work to send one or two representatives abroad in connection with the work of the International Conference of Social Work. So far as this international organization is concerned, we have, of course, no objection to it whatever. Our only apprehension is that a semi-political organization like the Asia Foundation gradually develops contacts here which it might misuse.

Yours sincerely,
Jawaharlal Nehru

---

1. JN Collection.
2. Minister of Finance, Government of Bombay.
3. In his letter Jivraj Mehta wanted to know, "if the Asia Foundation is now persona grata with the External Affairs Ministry because I find from last Sunday's press reports that a donation of $ 10,000 has been accepted with thanks by the Senate of the Bombay University from the South Asia Programmes Department of the Asia Foundation, San Francisco, for providing amenities in one of the proposed University Clubs at the Bombay University."

18. To Y.B. Chavan[1]

New Delhi
30 April 1957

My dear Chavan,[2]

I am writing to you on a somewhat unusual subject, that is, what is called European music. Unfortunately, in a great part of India this has almost disappeared. The only big centre left is Bombay and, to a lesser extent, Calcutta.

While we are quite rightly encouraging all branches of Indian music in India, I think it is both necessary and desirable for European music to find a place here as a form of international art. This is good in itself but also it will be helpful in its inter-relation with Indian music. Both may well profit by this.

In Bombay there is, I believe, an organization called "Time and Talent" which has often sponsored first-class musical concerts. I understand that they want to start an Akademi of Fine Arts. I should like your Government to give them a pat on their back and generally encourage them. Perhaps, you might pass on this letter to your new Education Minister. If he wants particulars about this matter, I suggest that he might send for Miss Khurshed A.D. Naoroji, 78 Napean Sea Road, Bombay-6.

Yours sincerely,
Jawaharlal Nehru

1. JN Collection.
2. Chief Minister of Bombay.

IV. THE NAGAS

1. To Saiyid Fazl Ali[1]

Camp: Royal Cottage
Bangalore
23 February 1957

My dear Fazl Ali,[2]

Your letter of February 19th has reached me here at Bangalore.[3] You and I seem to have very similar opinions about the Naga problem and how to deal with it. I am clear in my mind, as you are, that we cannot continue the Naga Hills District as it is, fully under the Assam Government. I have indicated that to Medhi[4] and to some others. But I did not wish to pursue this matter further at this stage before the elections, as that might well have created an upsetting effect. As soon as the elections are over, I shall do it.

2. In the long run, I think that it is not desirable to have these small separate areas. The province of Assam should ultimately include these various areas round about. But that is the long run. In the short run, I have no doubt, as I have said above, that the Naga Hills District should be brought under the Centre and perhaps tagged on to the Tuensang Division or it may be kept separate.

3. I realize your difficulty in dealing with representative Nagas. If you make any commitment without reference to the Assam Government, they will naturally feel hurt. We do not want to bypass them in any way. But perhaps you could well say to any Nagas that see you that the Government of India is perfectly prepared to consider this matter, that is, the placing of the Naga Hills District under the Centre. In fact, I have clearly stated in public that we would like to consult the Naga leaders about the future arrangements for the Naga Hills District. We do not want to take any step without this consultation. Obviously, however, any

---

1. JN Collection.
2. Governor of Assam.
3. Nehru was in Bangalore conducting the election campaign in Mysore State and spoke at two public meetings on 23 January. His first speech is not printed in this volume. For his second speech, see *ante*, pp. 15-35.
4. Bisnuram Medhi was Chief Minister of Assam.

future step will depend on the state of law and order in their District, that is, on the ending of the present trouble.[5] Further, I am perfectly prepared to have an amnesty in the broadest sense of the word. That too is really dependent on these troubles ceasing. We have no desire to be vindictive even in serious cases. After all, we cannot treat the Nagas fighting for what they consider their freedom, as normal criminals in the settled part of India. I should imagine that in really serious cases we could refer them to some Council of their own which could recommend to us what action to take. These are rather vague ideas just to indicate to you how my mind is working.

4. The elections will soon be over, and so there is not much to be done meanwhile. You intend going to Patna. On your return from Patna, the situation might well have advanced enough for us to consider it both from the point of view of the elections and otherwise.

5. Any real change in the status of the Naga Hills District will presumably mean a constitutional amendment. I am not sure of this. You could look it up. I wonder if it is possible to amend the Constitution in such a way as to have these Centrally Administered Areas and at the same time to indicate that in future we hope that they will form part of a larger Assam. Also, is it possible to have them separate as Centrally Administered Areas and yet to have a link with Assam by asking them to send representatives to the Assam Assembly. Perhaps you could give thought to these matters.[6]

6. I hope to return to Delhi on the 27th forenoon.

Yours sincerely,
Jawaharlal Nehru

5. From March 1955 onwards the Naga extremists incited serious disorders in the Tuensang Division of NEFA for establishing an independent Naga State. There were brought under control in January 1956, but they resurfaced in the Naga Hills District of Assam bordering the Tuensang division. The District was declared a disturbed area on 31 January 1956, and in March 1956, Army units were sent to control the situation.

6. Finally, a separate administrative unit known as Naga Hills Tuensang Area (NHTA), under the Ministry of External Affairs and administered through the Governor of Assam acting in his discretion as the Agent of the President, was formed on 1 December 1957 by an Act of Parliament. This was an interim arrangement.

2. To Saiyid Fazl Ali[1]

Camp: Rama Nilayam
Trichur (Kerala)
24 February 1957

My dear Fazl Ali,

I have just received your letter of February 20[2] at Trichur.[3] As I have already told you, I entirely agree with your general approach to this problem. As the Nagas appear to be in a favourable mood to put an end to their violence, I agree that we should take advantage of it.

On the last occasion when they had a talk with General Thimayya, I had a feeling that they did not play fair with him and gained time so as to get out of a difficult position.[4] But I suppose we have to take some slight risk in this matter. I am prepared to take the risk.

I agree with you entirely that there should be no attempt to humiliate these people. If they seek our goodwill, we must also treat them with goodwill.

I am sending a copy of your letter to General Thimayya and asking him to write to you direct.[5]

Yours sincerely,
Jawaaharlal Nehru

1. JN Collection.
2. Fazl Ali wrote about a conference with the representatives of Ao, Sangtam and Phom areas in February where some vital decisions were taken. These were: (i) demand for political independence to be given up, stop violence and bring peace, (ii) free movement of hostiles to be allowed, (iii) regrouping of villages in Ao areas to be stopped, and (iv) warrants of arrest which were in force at the time to be cancelled or withheld. Fazl Ali suggested that if the above measures were adopted there would be complete peace and therefore Thimayya should be asked to issue immediate instructions accordingly so as not to produce the impression among the hostiles that they were going to be tricked. The word 'surrender' should not be used and instead the hostiles be asked to surrender their arms as a gesture of cooperation.
3. Nehru was at Trichur conducting the election campaign in Kerala. He spoke at a public meeting on 24 February (not printed).
4. On 26 October 1956, K.S. Thimayya, General Officer Commanding-in-Chief, Eastern Command, met Kughato Sema, representative of the underground elements, at Ghukiya and emphasized that there would be no talks till the arms were surrendered. Kughato wanted time to contact other tribal groups for talks. The General gave them ten days' time. Finally, on 4 November, the terms of surrender offered by the General were turned down by the representatives of different tribes, mainly under pressure from Kaito Sema, Commander-in-Chief and brother of Kughato.
5. Writing to Thimayya on the same day, Nehru asked him whether the steps they were contemplating (see the previous item) would come in the way of present operations and cause embarrassment in future or not. At the same time, he was hopeful that they would not harm, and might as well yield good results.

3. Development Activities in Naga Areas[1]

The first point to remember is that we cannot continue to make demands on the Air Force for lifting supplies by air. Apart from their difficulty to meet our demands, I do not think it is right for us to risk our trained officers in this way. I think that there was another aircraft disaster some weeks or months ago in airlifting.[2] The IAF will certainly take up any emergency task. But they cannot be expected, as a matter of routine, to carry out this heavy duty involving much risk to them.

2. I see that these airlift operations are being transferred to chartered aircraft from civil air companies. That is certainly better.

3. If there is urgent need for food or other necessaries, we have naturally to make some arrangements to send them by air if other methods are not available. But we should examine this matter fully from all points of view and we should not undertake responsibilities which we cannot easily discharge. [3]

4. In the note dated 16th October of Shri P.N. Luthra,[4] stress is laid on our redoubling our efforts for the planning and execution of development schemes, the building of schools, hospitals, etc., the addition of staff and so on. Does this note indicate that we are undertaking responsibilities which we cannot easily discharge and which, therefore, create grave difficulties for us? However great

---

1. Note to N.R. Pillai, Secretary General, Subimal Dutt, Foreign Secretary and B.K. Acharya, Joint Secretary (East), New Delhi, 2 March 1957. JN Collection. Also available in File No. 14(2)-NEFA, MHA.
2. In early February 1957, one of the IAF planes, used for airdropping essential articles for the Army, crashed near Ghaspani in the Naga Hills District. The crew was killed.
3. B.K. Acharya wrote on 1 March that the importance of opening up land communications by constructing roads and tracks and changing over to motorized or animal transport had been fully realized by the NEFA Administration. But the construction of roads had to take time in view of the mountainous terrain and shortage of engineering staff. But NEFA Administration endeavoured to tackle this difficulty by offering attractive emoluments to the staff. Acharya also wrote that it was not correct that the NEFA Administration assumed responsibility for feeding a large tribal population by air. Only the basic supplies like rice, sugar, and cooking oil, were carried by air. But at the request of the Defence Ministry, arrangements were being made to relieve the IAF from these NEFA airlift operations and to transfer the entire load to chartered civil companies.
4. Pran Nath Luthra was Commissioner in Nagaland.

our desire may be for development, we should keep within the bounds of our capacity.

5. Reference is made by Shri Luthra to our gaining a psychological advantage and intensifying development activities both in the Naga Hills District and the Tuensang Division. Quite apart from what I have said above, that is, our not undertaking too heavy responsibilities, there is another and an important aspect to be borne in mind. This has troubled me considerably during the past few months and, in fact, I spoke to FS about it some time ago.

6. This aspect is whether we are not going too fast in our developmental schemes and thereby upsetting and uprooting the tribal structure of life. We are dealing with a very difficult problem where we have always to remember that too rapid a change in the ways of life may lead to all kinds of new and difficult problems. In our enthusiasm, we may think that the more rapid the development, the better it will be for these tribal people. But experience in the past in other countries shows that the advance of "civilizations" in rapid strides has often led to disastrous results. The whole tribes have gradually succumbed and lost vitality in the new conditions created and have in fact almost died out. Some brief reference to this process was made by Shri Krishna Menon in his recent speech in the Security Council in regard to New Guinea.[5]

7. It is true that we have not forgotten this aspect and we are taking some precautions to prevent the influx of too many civilizers. We have protected the land and taken other steps. Nevertheless there is this grave danger. We have to deal with a people who, from civilized standards, are primitive and whose roots are in certain conditions and ways of living, which are completely different from ours. Schools, hospitals and an efficient administration will not give them new roots if the others are pulled out. The process has to be gradual and carefully watched. Generally speaking, the initiative must come from the people themselves for further changes.

8. It would be a disaster if we uprooted these people and sapped the vitality they possessed without giving any worthwhile alternative. Even in small matters, it has been pointed out how bad the effect of sudden changes is, such as clothes. We put these people in shorts and often introduced textiles from outside at the expense of their home weaving and artistry. Let us not be afraid if they wear too few clothes or none at all. There is no vulgarity in this or indecency. There is vulgarity and indecency in some dirty scraps of clothes being tied round them and making them ashamed of their bodies which they have never been before.

9. I remember, many years ago, reading an account of missionary activities in

5. V.K. Krishna Menon spoke in the Security Council on 23 and 24 January 1957.

the South Sea Islands. The bright and joyful life of these islanders was ruined by these missionaries. Let us not be missionaries of this kind.

10. Apart from the social and psychological aspects to which I have referred, there are political aspects also. The intrusion of too many outsiders and an administration, which appears to us to be efficient, but which may well be burdensome and troublesome to them, may well lead and perhaps has led to political unrest and then we come in with our armies and police. I almost feel that we should leave these people as they are and not try to improve them too suddenly. We cannot, of course, leave them completely as they are, but we can reduce the pace of translating our noble intentions.

11. I read somewhere, some time ago, a suggestion made that the boy scout organization or something like it could be introduced in these areas. Anything more absurd, I cannot imagine. It is this mental approach of trying to improve them by making them more after our own pattern that I consider dangerous and harmful.

12. Our first concern in regard to these areas is that there should be peace and order there and our frontiers should be well protected. In fact, it is the frontier that has made us very conscious of these areas. Because of the frontier, we have to build roads etc. To some extent that is to continue.

13. I want this whole question of development in the NEFA as well as in allied areas to be reconsidered with great care and the idea of rapid and enforced development given up. Let us go more slowly but more soundly. In particular, I think, it is bad to send too many outsiders to these remote areas. Every outsider there is a problem for himself as well as for others. It is not the senior official but rather the troops of others who follow, clerks and the like, that bring a disturbing influence and create problems. So far as senior officials are concerned, we pick them with some care. But it is not possible to exercise that care on all the others. Problems with women arise and we touch danger there so far as the tribe is concerned.

14. The recent troubles in the Naga Hills District[6] have compelled us to think

6. In spite of the successful breaking up of large rebel concentrations and destruction of their hide-outs by the Indian Army towards the end of 1956, the rebels regrouped and adopted the "hit and run tactics" in small groups. The hard core of hostile leadership in the Naga Hills District, with a fairly large number of followers and stocks of arms and ammunition, remained intact. Over 240 people, the vast majority of whom were loyal Naga villagers, were estimated to have been killed by the rebels. On 17 February, in Ghaspani in the Naga Hills District, the hostiles attacked the soldiers killing five and injuring nine, and took away a number of their arms. Even in the Tuensang Division, there was a marked increase in the activities of the rebels during the last week of December 1956 and throughout January 1957.

afresh about all these problems. I hope those troubles will settle down soon. But it is quite clear to me that we must not push ourselves too far and too fast and that we should allow these people to have a good deal of autonomy. Certainly we had to do something, build roads etc. Also we should proceed, I think, on the lines of Community Projects but fully adapted to the needs of the situation there and working with the full consent of the tribal councils etc. Above all, we must avoid sending many people there from outside. The fewer the better, subject to our essential requirements.

15. The whole Five Year Plan for the NEFA should, therefore, be revised from the point of view indicated above and we need not be in a hurry to show how many hospitals and schools and the rest we have build up. This approach will not only be a healthier one and more suited to these people, but will also reduce the burden we carry and lessen chances of conflict.[7]

16. As I have dealt with a number of issues in this note and have gone outside the scope of the particular subject in this file, I suggest that you send copies of this note to FS[8] and to our Adviser in the NEFA.[9] I think a separate copy should be sent to the Governor of Assam.

17. Some little time ago Dr Verrier Elwin[10] sent me a manuscript of a book he had written dealing with our approach to the tribal question in the NEFA. I wrote a foreword[11] to it in which I said that I entirely agreed with the approach commanded by Dr Elwin and I hope that all our officers in the tribal areas would read that book. I presume the book will be issued in the near future.

---

7. In response to Nehru's note, B.K. Acharya wrote on 6 March 1957 that the PM was right in drawing attention to the dangers of too fast a pace but the disadvantages of going too slow could not be ignored which were also pointed out by Verrier Elwin in his book *A Philosophy for NEFA*. In his recent tour of NEFA, Acharya elaborated that several tribal officers told him that this slow pace created discontent among the progressive and educated tribals who had now become "development-minded." Moreover, different tribes in NEFA were in different stages of development and a general and uniform pace of development for all would not meet their aspirations, so that some discretion had to be left in the hands of local administration.
8. Subimal Dutt.
9. KL Mehta was Adviser to the Governor of Assam for NEFA.
10. British anthropologist who worked amongst tribals in Central and North East India and became an Indian citizen in 1954.
11. For Nehru's foreword of 16 February 1957 to Verrier Elwin's book *A Philosophy for NEFA*, see *Selected Works* (second series), Vol. 36, pp. 251-252.

4. To Saiyid Fazl Ali[1]

New Delhi
3 March 1957

My dear Fazl Ali,

Yesterday, I had a talk with our Home Minister, Pantji, about the Naga Hills situation. Only recently he met you in Shillong and discussed this matter with you. He agreed with you about the approach we should make. I have already told you that I am in full agreement with you also.

I am convinced that we must take every step as soon as possible to put an end to this trouble. I am not afraid of trusting the Nagas, because I do believe that trust begets trust. Also I am not afraid of giving them any measure of local autonomy provided only that certain basic matters are clearly understood. The only thing that somewhat worried me was lest their hostile elements should be encouraged in their hostility in future and imagine that by violence and killing they can gain their ends.

I think that they must have realized by this time that they cannot coerce the Government of India into doing anything because of their violence. The time, therefore, appears to be ripe for a fresh attempt to be made of the kind you are making. We need not worry about small particulars nor indeed need we ask them to deliver up all arms. This surrender of arms is seldom successful as many go into hiding.

I shall be seeing Shrinagesh[2] and Thimayya this evening. Thimayya is taking charge as Chief of Army Staff in a couple of days.[3]

Should you think it necessary, I am prepared to come to Shillong at a somewhat later stage to finalize these matters. I am prepared to meet the Naga leaders also and have a straight talk with them. I cannot go there during this month or, at any rate, till the end of the month. Our Parliament will be meeting on the 18th and is likely to last about ten days or so.

Yours sincerely,
Jawaharlal Nehru

1. JN Collection.
2. S. M. Shrinagesh was Chief of Army Staff.
3. K.S. Thimayya officiated as Chief of Army Staff from 8 March to 8 May 1957. He took over as Chief of Army Staff on 8 May 1957.

5. Supply of Rifles to Home Guards in NEFA[1]

General Thimayya mentioned to me today that the present procedure for getting something done in the NEFA was very cumbrous and dilatory. Thus, he had been asked, I think, by the Adviser in NEFA to supply fifty rifles for the Home Guards or some other formation. He could easily do that immediately. In the case of the Naga Hills, all he had to do was to ring up Defence, get their permission and give the rifles. In the case of NEFA, the matter was referred to External Affairs Ministry and then to Defence and then back to the NEFA Administration. Usually this got hung up somewhere.

In the case in question, NEFA had asked for fifty rifles and General Thimayya had agreed to supply them, but this could not be done because orders were not forthcoming. In fact General Thimayya had got a telegram from our Adviser in NEFA asking him to expedite this.

I do not know where this matter has got delayed. Will you kindly enquire into this? You might get the exact facts from General Thimayya. It may be that I have not given them correctly.

Apart from this, I think, we should devise some method of dealing with such matters more expeditiously. In fact General Thimayya should be given authority to deal with such minor matters on the spot. Adjustments can be made later. I think that the Home Ministry also comes into the picture as probably they have to pay for the rifles given to the Home Guards.

1. Note to Secretary General, MEA, New Delhi, 3 March 1957. JN Collection.

6. Slow Down the Tempo of Five Year Plans[1]

I am glad to know that instructions have already been issued about slowing down the tempo of the five year plans and spread it out over a longer period of about ten years. I did not know this, otherwise I would not have laid special stress on it in my previous note. It is not necessary, therefore, to revise this Second Five Year Plan again. We may leave it where it is.

I agree with much that the Joint Secretary has written.[2] No hard and fast rule can be laid down about these matters and, in some respects, we may hasten development or in some areas the tempo can be in a somewhat faster pace. The real point is of the nature of development. Some types of development easily fit in and do not tend to create any marked upset. Other types do tend that way. More particularly, as I said, I am reluctant to push in large numbers of outsiders in these areas.

The building of roads and communications is important. But I am a little worried at the fact that the PWD, responsible for making these roads, might introduce a crowd of people from outside for this purpose and these people will have little conception as to how to deal with the tribals.

The Nagas vary greatly in education and general intelligence. Many of the Nagas are, I think, better material than most non-tribal people in India. At the same time they are much tougher and they will not easily put up with impositions. Some of the Nagas are much more backward in this respect. Apart from the Nagas, many of the tribes in the NEFA are very backward indeed. All these factors have to be kept in view and we should not try to apply some rigid uniform rule to everybody regardless of circumstances.

You may send a copy of this note also together with my previous one to the Governor of Assam, the Adviser, etc.

---

1. Note to Secretary General, Foreign Secretary, Joint Secretary (East), New Delhi, 6 March 1957. JN Collection. Also available in File No. 14(2)-NEFA, MEA.
2. For Joint Secretary B.K. Acharya's note see *ante*, p. 247.

7. To Saiyid Fazl Ali[1]

New Delhi
7 March 1957

My dear Fazl Ali,

I have just been reading your letter to the President dated March 5th.[2]

In this letter you refer to the general situation in the Naga Hills and the Tuensang Division. I have written to you about this previously and expressed my entire agreement with your approach. I need not say any more here. A few days ago I met General Shrinagesh and General Thimayya and we had a talk about this. Both of them agreed with this approach.

In your letter to the President you refer to Verrier Elwin's little book *A Philosophy for the NEFA*. Verrier Elwin had sent me a manuscript of this book and asked for a foreword for it. I wrote the foreword for it and sent it to him. I do not remember if I sent a copy of this foreword to you. If not, please get it from Elwin. In this foreword I expressed my agreement with the broad approach of Verrier Elwin to the problems of the NEFA and, indeed, to tribal people generally.

You write about the agricultural farms in NEFA and think they are not as useful as we thought they might be. I am inclined to agree with you. I think that small cooperative farms, as suggested by you, would be more suitable and would produce better results. I hope, therefore, that this matter will be enquired into

---

1. JN Collection. Also available in File No. 51(1)-NEFA/57, MHA.
2. After visiting a few places in NEFA, Fazl Ali wrote to President Rajendra Prasad, giving his views on various issues. These were: (i) agricultural farms in NEFA were costly, run at a loss and did not have practical approach to the food problem except providing some employment to the local people. It was, therefore, advisable to have a number of demonstrative and cooperative farms which would be successful with tribals who were accustomed to community life, (ii) it was important to provide the tribals with adequate stocks of yarn, introduce improved and economic methods of weaving and to have a number of Government or cooperative shops for this purpose, (iii) medical care was one of the greatest necessities and the tribals were gradually beginning to appreciate the value of modern treatment, (iv) Community Development or Extension blocks would not bring advantages to the tribals if they were run on conventional lines and the money set apart for employees and buildings should be used judiciously on the tribal people themselves, and (v) the present Naga problem could not be solved by military operations alone and what was needed was some kind of political approach; and the hostiles were bent upon carrying on their struggle if no solution which was satisfactory from their point of view, was reached.

more fully. In any event, it would be a good thing to start with some such small cooperative farms and see how they function.

About cloth, it is our policy to encourage local weaving. We should, of course, improve the methods without any major change which might not be agreeable to the people there. Cooperative shops appear to be desirable. But I am a little apprehensive of shops run by outsiders there. If you can induce the tribal people themselves to run them, it would be much better.

I agree with you about medical care. You say that the tribal people are afraid of bathing. This is unfortunately true. But I remember once camping somewhere near a river in the NEFA or the Naga Hills. Perhaps this was on the other side of the Burmese border. Anyhow, I saw a large number of these rather primitive Nagas going into the river for bathing.

It is, of course, desirable to have that approach. I imagine, however, that it is better to have no clothes at all than dirty clothes. In the course of time these tribal people have evolved some kind of a social structure and habits of living. Some of these habits are not good at all. And yet an attempt to change them rapidly may not have as good results as we want. Ever since I read about the efforts of missionaries in the Pacific Islands to clothe the people there, I have been rather alarmed. These missionaries succeeded in introducing skirts and other odd articles of clothing which were usually very dirty. A healthy people became addicts to skin diseases, apart from other rather unfortunate results.

There can be no doubt that the Community Development Schemes or Extension Blocks cannot be run in the NEFA on conventional lines. As a general principle, this has always been accepted. How to work it out is the question. I am writing to S.K. Dey on this subject.[3]

I entirely agree with you as well as with your officers that the amount spent in salaries of employees is proportionately very heavy in these Community Blocks.

Recently I have written two notes about the general approach to development in the NEFA.[4] I hope you have received copies of them.

Yours sincerely,
Jawaharlal Nehru

3. In his letter of 7 March to S.K. Dey, Union Minister of State for Community Development, Nehru wrote that Verrier Elwin and others viewed that the whole of NEFA should be regarded as one block and in each selected area such measures should be adopted as were suitable to it. For example, in the opium area, the use of opium should be restricted, in the food deficient areas measures should be taken to remove the deficiency, and in the dermatitis areas measures should be taken to control that skin disease.
4. See *ante*, pp. 247-250 & 253.

8. To Saiyid Fazl Ali[1]

New Delhi
13 March 1957

My dear Fazl Ali,

Thank you for your letter from Patna, dated March 10th. I am glad you are keeping me informed.

I do not at all like the idea of Phizo[2] being brought into the picture for talks. We may deal leniently with him if the issue of the talks is good. But, he is essentially a bad man, and to talk to him will mean acknowledging his influence and leadership and play into his hands.

There is an odd man who has given me a lot of trouble. His name is Triloki Nath Purwar.[3] I think he was for some time in Gandhiji's ashram and he is somewhat connected with Vinobaji. He went to these Naga Hill areas and became quite friendly with many of the Nagas. But he used to go a bit too far, and your Chief Minister disliked him. Once we arrested him, but released him soon after. I got very annoyed with him and for the last many months, I have refused to see him in spite of his efforts. I met him yesterday in Allahabad, and he again begged me to allow him to go to the Nagas and try to help. He said that he still got letters from them asking him to come and advise them.

I think, Triloki Nath is an honest man but not very responsible. And yet, sometimes, even such persons can be useful. I told him to see me a month later. If you like and if you think that he might perhaps be of some use, I could send him to you later.

Yours sincerely,
Jawaharlal Nehru

---

1. JN Collection.
2. A.Z. Phizo was President, Naga National Council.
3. A resident of Allahabad and a social worker who enjoyed the confidence of the underground Naga leaders and visited them unarmed.

9. To Saiyid Fazl Ali[1]

New Delhi
8 April 1957

My dear Fazl Ali,

Your letter of March 31st.[2]

I must confess that I view with some dismay the prospect of your leaving Assam.[3] We have been relying on your judgement, and I think that your coming away would be a considerable loss to our work which is so important.

I am sorry for the attitude that the Assam Government is taking. But, surely, you were not giving the Nagas any assurance about being taken under the Central Administration at this stage. It is true that I am convinced that this will have to be done, whatever the views of the Assam Government might be. But, anyhow, this will have to come a little later. The only promise I have made and repeated many times, is that we are prepared to consider a change in the set up there and the grant of a large measure of autonomy. Further, that we shall consult the Nagas before we finalize decisions.

You will remember my writing to you once and asking you to think over some possible Constitutional arrangement which could keep a link with Assam and yet, at the same time, give real autonomy to the Nagas.

In any event, whatever decision will have to be made, will be by the Central Government, no doubt in consultation with the Assam Government, and no burden of final decision should rest on you nor should there be any question of your action being criticized.

Yours sincerely,
Jawaharlal Nehru

1. JN Collection. A copy of this letter was sent to G.B. Pant.
2. In his letter Fazl Ali requested Nehru to send him to another state such as Bihar or UP as Governor. He cited two reasons for that. Firstly, the kindness and affection of people of Assam made a deep impression on his mind. They were expecting that Assam should derive all kinds of benefits during his Governorship. All this effusion was a great source of embarrassment to him because as a Governor he had very little power to mould the administration. Moreover, if the Naga Hills District was separated from Assam due to his intervention, he would lose all the goodwill and respect that he had earned so far. The second reason he mentioned was that his wife's health was declining as Shillong's climate and water did not suit her. Even for him, the present assignment had imposed severe strains.
3. In fact, Saiyid Fazl Ali continued as Governor of Assam till his death on 22 August 1959.

10. To Saiyid Fazl Ali[1]

New Delhi
8 April 1957

My dear Fazl Ali,

Thank you for your letter of April 5. I entirely agree with you that the proposal made in the note from the Intelligence Bureau to the effect that we should make large-scale arrests and have big concentration camps is out of the question at present.

Yours sincerely,
Jawaharlal Nehru

1. JN Collection.

11. To Saiyid Fazl Ali[1]

New Delhi
11 April 1957

My dear Fazl Ali,
Your letter of April 9.

It is obvious that this proposal for regrouping[2] has created a powerful affect on the people concerned.[3] Probably this is a more effective measure than any

1. JN Collection. A copy of this letter was sent to Subimal Dutt, Foreign Secretary, together with the letter under reply.
2. This was an idea taken from the British who tackled the Chinese insurgency in Malaya.
3. Regrouping meant joining together of a number of villages under the Army's protection. The regrouped villages were provided with ration and were not allowed to go out of the stockaded area even for cultivation. As a result of this the extremists were completely cut off from their bases in respect of supply of rations etc.

others that we have thus far thought of. Therefore, we should not give it up. At the same time, as you say, this may cast far too great a burden on us which we cannot easily carry. I take it therefore that some middle way has to be found. It is for you and General Thimayya to find out this middle way. It may be that a regrouping might begin in a small way with the possibility of its extension being always held out. Results may be watched.

This is a first reaction to your proposal. We are always between two stools. We do not want to be too harsh and if we are too soft, we fail.

Anyhow you and Thimayya are the best people to judge.

Yours sincerely,
Jawaharlal Nehru

12. To Saiyid Fazl Ali[1]

New Delhi
12 April 1957

My dear Fazl Ali,
Your letter of April 10th, enclosing a copy of a letter from Mrs Phizo etc.

I entirely agree with you that we should be courteous to them. Indeed, we should adopt that policy to everyone.

But, I do not quite understand what they want you to do. They complain of the repressive policy of Government. I think, they should be told that Government have every desire to cooperate and establish peaceful conditions which would enable the Nagas to live in dignity, according to their own ways. It is obvious, however, that Government cannot tolerate murder and violence, and as some sections of the Nagas have indulged in these, Government have been compelled to take action against them, as it would have done anywhere else in the country. We consider the Nagas as valued countrymen of ours, who should share in the freedom of the country, etc., etc.

1. JN Collection.

You might, perhaps, try to find out from the Deputy Commissioner[2] or somebody what exactly they aim at.

I do not see why any officers should object to this approach, and if they do, they should be told that they are wrong.

Yours sincerely,
Jawaharlal Nehru

2. S.J.D. Carvalho.

13. To Saiyid Fazl Ali[1]

New Delhi
15 April 1957

My dear Fazl Ali,

I had an interview today with Sashimeren Aier.[2] He did not tell me anything very new about the situation in the Naga Hills, except that he pleaded for the degrouping of the villages that had been grouped together. You will remember you wrote to me about this too, and I think I replied to you that we need not give up with procedure altogether as it was obviously something which exercised considerable pressure on the hostile Nagas. At the same time, I thought we should proceed very cautiously and in a slow way. The idea was that much inconvenience should not be caused and, at the same time, they should not think that we have given it up.

I have no idea to what extent this grouping has been done. Obviously, it must cause a great deal of inconvenience and, at the same time, cast a burden on us to feed and keep going all these people. You will be seeing General Thimayya soon, and you can decide as you think best. I shall probably also have a talk with Thimayya before he goes to Shillong. I think that if conditions appear favourable, there might be some de-grouping.

1. JN Collection.
2. I. Sashimeren Ajer was Assistant Commissioner, Scheduled Castes and Scheduled Tribes for Assam, Manipur and Tripura.

The second thing that Sashimeren Aier said was to suggest a free supply of books and food to Naga students in Government schools. He gave me a paper mentioning five schools and also the Gandhi Ashram. Altogether, there are apparently two thousand students. To feed them all as well as to supply books, etc., would amount to a considerable sum. As a broad policy, I am all in favour of giving at least one good meal to children attending schools anywhere in India. But, obviously, that is not practicable for us today. We could treat the Naga school children as a special case. Even so, it might involve us to a very considerable expenditure for any length of time. I do not know if any middle way can be found. I think, certainly, that books should be supplied to them and some help should be given in the way of food also. It is for you to consider how best this can be done.

I am sending you a cheque for rupees twenty-five thousand. This is not for any particular object and is to be used at your discretion, to help the students or otherwise in connection with the Nagas.

Aier further said that there were some three hundred Naga students in Shillong, who deserve to be helped.

Then, he came to his personal troubles. He told me of his difficulties, of his family, of his father and mother, of his brother who had been killed by the Nagas, and the brother's six children whom he had to support, and of the innumerable guests that were always coming to his house and whom he had to feed.

He joined service in 1954 at Rs 600/- per mensem in the grade of Rs 600-1,100. He was getting, I believe, Rs 720/- recently. Later, a special allowance of Rs 200/- was given to him. Altogether, with various allowances, he gets about Rs 1,000/- Out of this, he has to pay back a loan of rupees five thousand, which the Home Ministry had given to him. He has other payments to make also.

He had a debt of rupees fifteen thousand, of which he has paid five thousand, and rupees ten thousand still remain.

The Home Ministry has treated him well, and I hesitate to approach the Home Ministry again. Yet, I recognize his difficulties, and I think, he is a useful person, more particularly in connection with Naga troubles. He feels also that his service is temporary and might end at any time. Apart from this, he is in constant danger of being killed by the hostile Nagas.

You know all these facts, of course, and more. I should like your advice as to what we can do about him. For one thing, I think that he should be confirmed in his service. It may be that some financial help can also be given to him. Should you so wish, you can help him a little out of the money I am sending you.

Yours sincerely,
Jawaharlal Nehru

14. To Saiyid Fazl Ali[1]

New Delhi
18 April 1957

My dear Fazl Ali,

Your letter of April 16th with its enclosures. As desired by you, I am passing them on to Pantji....

I had a talk with Thimayya today, but there is nothing very special to report about this talk. Thimayya and I were in broad agreement about our general approach, but this, of course, necessarily depends upon developments. I told him that the grouping of villages had definitely produced a powerful effect on the hostile Nagas. We cannot give this up in theory. But, in practice, we should go very slow and see developments. The letter you have sent me from a young Sema officer indicates that this amalgamation of villages should be carried on with more vigour. These matters are for you to consider with Thimayya.

Yours sincerely,
Jawaharlal Nehru

---

1. JN Collection. Extracts. A copy of this letter was sent to G.B. Pant.

V. SCIENCE AND TECHNOLOGY

1. Both Heavy and Cottage Industries should be Developed[1]

Your Highness,[2] Your Excellency,[3] Chief Minister,[4] Mr Poonacha[5] and friends,

I am very happy to be here. I need not say that. But you will appreciate what pleasure it gives me to be present on any occasion which sees the accomplishment of any important project. It is given to us to labour but not always to see the results of our labours. So, when we see some results it gives us a thrill. As I wander about India and see sometimes new enterprises, new projects being started and to participate in their starting, I feel happy. But when I go to a place to see that completion of an enterprise, I feel happier still. Mr Narayanaswamy[6] just referred to the Hirakud Project. That is an instance when a number of years ago, in 1948, I performed the opening ceremony, not the opening ceremony— whatever it was—laying the foundation stone of that project,[7] which was a waste piece of Indian land then, and a month ago I went and saw this magnificent dam of 22 miles long—and I have seen in between also and then I pressed a button and the waters of the Mahanadi poured over that dam.[8] It was an experience which I should remember. Similar experiences in greater or lesser degree came to me, when I go to various parts of this great country and see this new India of our dreams gradually taking shape and so presently when I press this button in front of me and you see these gates go up and something else happen which I do not know. I hope you would share with me the thrill of achievement.

I am happy to be here for the reason I have stated and also because this

1. Speech at the inauguration of the high voltage insulator factory, Bangalore, 23 February 1957. AIR tapes, NMML.
2. Jaya Chamaraja Wodiyar, Governor of Mysore State.
3. Seijiro Yoshizawa, Japanese Ambassador to India.
4. S. Nijalingappa.
5. C.M. Poonacha, Minister for Home Affairs and Industries, Mysore Government.
6. K. Narayanaswamy (b. 1910); entered Government service, 1929; confirmation in the IAS, 1951; Director of Industries and Commerce, 1955; Chairman, Bangalore Water Supply and Sewerage Board, 1964.
7. For Nehru's speech on the occasion of laying the foundation of the Hirakud Dam in Orissa on 12 April 1948, see *Selected Works* (second series), Vol. 6, pp. 313-315.
8. For Nehru's speech on the occasion, see *Selected Works* (second series), Vol. 36, pp. 11-20.

enterprise has been a joint enterprise in its building up between India and Japan.[9] I need not tell you because you all know the great advance, the tremendous advance that Japan made when it once decided to enter the field of modern science and technology. It is one of the most remarkable episodes in history that their decision and the carrying out of their decision with determination and speed by the people of Japan. And now, we, who have been considerably backward in the development of science and technology in this country, although we have trotted about with them for a long time and produced good results and produced great men too in the scientific field. Now, we have also come to this determination to take advantage of science and technology for the benefit of our people so as to raise their standards, so as to build up a state where every one has a measure of welfare and happiness and there is no lack of the necessities of life. The way to this is complicated and long and there are many views as to how we should attain this. But, I think every one will agree in regard to certain primary requisites. We must have the basic things which science and technology give. We must have certain heavy industries. We must have the development of electricity and the various appliances that go with electricity and so on and so forth. That does not exclude our activities, our methods of creative work. The President of the Nippon Gaishi Kaisha[10] told us about the great industry being surrounded by medium industries and small industries in Japan. I think we have much to learn from that example and experience of Japan in this respect and I hope we should do so. It is curious that in our country we are being stressed on what might be considered two opposite poles. One is heavy industry; the other is cottage industry.

Some learned pundits argue about these matters as to which is better and which is not. I find no difficulty in having both and I see no essential conflict between the two. Where there is overlapping in future, it should be avoided or dealt with intelligently. At the present moment, I do not even see any marked overlapping. We have been using in past years, not the recent past, but previously, in developing our theories, economic or other, mostly from European or American text books. They are very good text books written by very able men. But all of them dealt with conditions in Europe or America and based their economic theories, whether they were capitalist or whether they were communist, on conditions which prevailed at the time in Europe. Also they were based almost

9. The Rs 85 lakh electro high-tension insulator factory which was to manufacture 2500 tons of insulators annually had been undertaken by the Mysore Government with the technical collaboration of the reputed Japanese firm Nippon Gaishi Kaisha Limited. The factory was the first of its kind in India and the biggest in Asia.
10. K. Yoshimoto.

always on the background of an industrialized community. Naturally, because, Europe or Western Europe and America were industrialized communities. Now, to apply those theories to India which is not an industrialized community, which in many other ways is very greatly different from Europe, seems to us, now at least not very wise. If we have to develop our economic theory and all our programme of industrial development, we can learn much of course, not only necessarily, from the analogy of know-how of those in other countries who possess it, not only from their experience, certainly, but in many other ways, but, we always have to remember that in the final analysis, we have to develop our own economic theory and our processes of development, keeping in view the particular conditions and problems we have to face in this country. Not by imitation though we should always be prepared to learn from others and if necessary even to copy from others where it is good. But the basic approach should be ours, and should be related to the facts of life in India. We have seldom in the past related them to these facts of life. Gandhiji was so terribly oppressed by the poverty of India, by the peasant in India as he was, that he based almost every theory or activity, keeping in view that peasant in India and how to raise his standard. Learned people in economics and other sciences doubted his approach, not realizing that he was not laying down any economic theory but he was dealing with a problem of the moment, by taking different facts of life as he saw them. As he dealt with reality he achieved a measure of success, a great measure of success in some directions. Now, we have to combine what might be called economic theory which, of course, is also changing. No old economic theory is absolutely valid today, though it throws light, a great deal of light on the working of various economic forces. So, we have to combine economic theory as we develop it, with the facts of life in India. We are concerned practically with those facts of life, with the raising of the human being in India and it would serve us little purpose if we put up a hundred or a thousand factories and yet the level of the common peasant, the common man in India remains much what it was. That would be a tragedy. Therefore, always we have to keep that in view. I suppose, today, the measure of a country's advance in the industrial field is the measure of how much steel and electricity a country produces. By that test, you can say, fairly accurately, how far a country has advanced industrially. We have realized that and so we are trying our best to increase the output of steel and electricity. It is clear to us that whether we think in terms of greater prosperity for the country, or of higher living standards for our people or even for the protection of our Independence and freedom, we must develop our industry. We must develop our heavy industry because that forms the base not only of our industrial growth but ultimately of the economic freedom. From that of course, lighter industries will grow. At the same time, we have to help in every way the growth of what are called household industries. What form or shape they may take is a matter for consideration. They may be various. They should use electric power at their disposal; and they should employ good techniques they can get at their level because we do not believe in perpetuating outmoded techniques. That is not wise. But it is another thing to help a household industry with the highest level of technique available because a higher technique can be employed in large-scale industry. The large-scale industry, of course, comes in and must come in, because some things cannot be done without it. There is no question of any objection to the growth of large-scale industry. But where we have to think in terms of human welfare, of employment and unemployment of the people of India as they are today, we have to think of encouraging household industry on a large-scale. So, we tried to balance these factors to produce some kind of stable equilibrium. To prevent disequilibrium and thus by trial and error, we proceeded. We have no rigid theory about these matters. We have a fairly clear objective in view and even that objective ultimately revolves round the growth of the average man in India. First, if you like the negative thing, although it is very positive for him to get rid of his disabilities, of his poverty and unemployment, and the more positive things to ensure him, some measure of cultural growth, because we do think that all the growth in the world would not carry us too far if somehow we miss the essence of culture that gives quality to life. I do not quite know why I have talked to you these matters on this occasion; perhaps, it is not too irrelevant. But anyhow, I am happy to be here to open this concern, to inaugurate it, and I am happy at this instance of Indo-Japanese cooperation. I hope that in future there will be many occasions of cooperation in various fields of activity between India and Japan. And now I propose to press the button and I expect you to feel the thrill of achievement.

2. To J.C. Ghosh[1]

New Delhi
22 March 1957

My dear Ghosh,[2]

I gather that you were the Chairman of a Special Committee consisting of you, Homi Bhabha,[3] Kothari,[4] Dewan Chand Sharma,[5] appointed to consider the recommendations of the Egerton[6] Committee[7] and to report to the Governing Body of the CSIR. Subsequently, Mahalanobis[8] was also appointed to this Committee. This Committee considered the draft Second Five Year Plan and presented a report which they called the first part of their report. In the course of this report, reference was made to the Second Five Year Plan and it was said that the Special Committee had not had time to consider all the proposals for the Second Five Year Plan in so far as the CSIR was concerned. The Committee was, however, of opinion that the proposed plan would require substantial revision and recasting if it was to conform broadly to the guiding principles outlined in the report. Therefore, your Committee said that they proposed to discuss this in the second part of the report.

I understand that the second part of the report was not prepared and, therefore,

1. File No. 17(231)/57-PMS. Also available in JN Collection.
2. Member, Planning Commission.
3. Homi Jehangir Bhabha was Secretary, Department of Atomic Energy, and Chairman, Atomic Energy Commission, Government of India.
4. Daulat Singh Kothari was Professor of Physics, Delhi University, and Scientific Adviser to the Ministry of Defence, Government of India.
5. Member, Lok Sabha at this time.
6. Alfred Charles Glyn Egerton was Director, the Salters' Institute of Industrial Chemistry and Emeritus Professor of Chemical Technology, University of London.
7. The Committee, comprising Alfred Egerton as Chairman, and Easton Dupony, S.N. Bose, Shri Ram, M.D. Chaturvedi, B.R. Batra and A.L. Mudaliar as members, was appointed by the Prime Minister to report on the activities of CSIR since 1949. The Committee, which submitted its report on 3 April 1954, pointed out the absence of better coordination among various wings of the research organizations and recommended appointment of competent liaison officers and strengthening of the National Research Development Corporation to facilitate a coordinated all round growth in industrial output. See also *Selected Works* (second series), Vol. 25, pp. 114-115.
8. P.C. Mahalanobis was founder and Director, Indian Statistical Institute in Kolkata and Member of the Planning Commission.

267

there was no reconsideration or revision of those proposals for the Second Five Year Plan as intended.

Apart from this, as you know, owing to various reasons, notably financial stringency, the Planning Commission have been revising many of the projects of the Second Five Year Plan. I think that it would be a good thing if the old proposals of the CSIR were reconsidered fully from the point of view of the situation now existing. This could best be done by the same Committee, that is, the Committee of which you were the Chairman. It is nearly two years when your first report was issued and since then many things have happened which have to be taken into consideration.

I suggest you might discuss this matter with Thacker[9] and then get your Committee together again for this purpose.

Yours sincerely,
Jawaharlal Nehru

9. Maneklal S. Thacker was Director, CSIR.

3. To Jagjivan Ram[1]

New Delhi
3 April 1957

My dear Jagjivan Ram,[2]
Some time ago, the Council of Scientific and Industrial Research appointed a Special Committee to consider the report of a Reviewing Committee which had been appointed to find out what our national laboratories were doing. This Reviewing Committee was presided over by Sir Alfred Egerton.[3] The Special Committee consisted of Dr J.C. Ghosh, Dr H.J. Bhabha, Dr. D.S. Kothari and Professor Diwan Chand Sharma. Later, Professor P.C. Mahalanobis was added to it.

1. JN Collection. Copies of this letter were sent to J.C. Ghosh and M.S. Thacker.
2. Union Minister for Transport and Railways.
3. See preceding item.

This Special Committee produced a report. But this report was in the nature of a preliminary report, and, in fact, they said in it that they would make a second report which would consider various proposals that had been made for inclusion in the Second Five Year Plan.

No second report was ever prepared or presented. I have, therefore, asked that Committee to consider this matter afresh and produce this second report.

It has been pointed out to me, however, that the Special Committee as it is constituted, might not be able to consider adequately all the matters that come up before them unless they had the help of an electrical engineer and a mechanical engineer. So far as the electrical engineer is concerned, I shall ask Professor Thacker to join the Committee. As for the mechanical engineer, I should like to ask the help of the Railway Ministry. If the Chairman of the Railway Board[4] could join this Special Committee, I would be glad. Otherwise, some other competent mechanical engineer might take his place.

I understand that it will not be necessary to give too much time to this Committee. Probably, there will be four meetings of two hours each, that is eight hours in all, spread out over a month or so, that is one meeting a week.

I might add that the Special Committee had drawn our attention specially to the slow progress in setting up pilot plants to test processes completed on laboratory scale. This matter will have to be examined specially. One of the reasons for the delay in setting up these pilot plants was the complicated procedure for the purchase of stores and equipment for scientific research. This might be varied. But, in view of our present difficulty in regard to foreign exchange, we shall probably have to put up the pilot plants ourselves.

Professor Thacker is at present in some foreign country. He will return in about ten days' time, and I shall discuss this matter further with him then. Meanwhile, I want to know if you can spare the Chairman of the Railway Board for this Committee's work.

Yours sincerely,
Jawaharlal Nehru

4. P.C. Mukherjee.

4. To Chief Ministers[1]

New Delhi
4 April 1957

My dear Chief Minister,

I am sending you a copy of a paper on "Science as a Factor in International Relations" which was read by Dr B.K. Blount[2] at a meeting of Chatham House in London.[3] This was published in *International Affairs* of January this year.

This paper is interesting and brings out vividly the basic changes that are taking place in industry, administration and international affairs because of the pace of scientific and technical advance.[4] It seems to me very important that we realize the nature of these changes so that we might adapt ourselves to them. Above all, it means special attention being paid to the training of scientific and technical personnel.

Yours sincerely,
Jawaharlal Nehru

1. File No. 17(232)/57-PMS. Also available in JN Collection. This special letter, in addition to the fortnightly letters, was sent to the Chief Ministers and the Prime Minister of Jammu and Kashmir State. Also printed in G. Parthasarathi (ed.), *Jawaharlal Nehru: Letters to Chief Ministers 1947-1964*, Vol. 4, p. 482.
2. Bertie Kennedy Blount (1907-1999); taught at Oxford University, 1931-38; Director, Science and Intelligence, Ministry of Defence, 1939-51; Deputy Secretary, Department of Science and Industrial Research, 1951-65; published papers in scientific journals.
3. On 23 October 1956.
4. Blount argued that the power of any country depends upon the technical advance in its administration, industry and military affairs. "Trade now follows the scientist and technologist, not the flag or the missionary." Those countries would advance rapidly which laid greatest stress on the learning of science and technology and their adoption in everyday life. Writing about China and India, he said China would soon be a leading nation but the future of India was uncertain.

5. Big Powers should End Nuclear Tests[1]

The Great Powers of the world should come together and find a way of stopping further test explosions of atomic and hydrogen bombs. It is the duty of all of us to try and persuade those Powers that they must find some way out of the present impasse, however much they might dislike each other or each other's policies. Humanity and civilization will be destroyed not only by a nuclear war but even if these explosions go on and on.

Eminent doctors are of the view that it is not a particularly good thing for children to wear watches with radium dials. From this one can well imagine the kind of danger that is involved in exploding bombs that are many times more powerful than the one which wiped out Hiroshima. These bombs, when explode may throw up all kinds of radio-active materials, twenty or forty thousand feet above the earth and wherever they come down on the earth's surface, they bring slow, creeping death. We seem to be living in a world of ghosts and spectres.

There is much talk about a hydrogen bomb test explosion in the Christmas Island by Britain.[2] There had been consternation in various parts of the world in regard to it and appeals have been made that it should not take place. While these appeals are continuing, three test explosions had taken place in rapid succession in some part of the Soviet Union[3] and so this extraordinary and mad contest goes on by some terrible freak of destiny.

If it was a matter affecting some individuals, one might regret it and no more, but when people realize that this is something which affects the world even though we may be outside the scope of the experiment, when they realize that it affects not only the present generation but it affects generations to come and no one knows, even the biggest scientists, to what extent the generations to come will be affected, the least that can be said is this; here is an unknown danger being let loose on the world. It may injure humanity perhaps a little—it may

---

1. Inaugural address to the annual conference of the All India Manufacturers' Organization, New Delhi, 13 April 1957. From *National Herald* and *The Hindustan Times*, 14 April 1957. Extracts. For other parts of Nehru's speech see *ante*, pp. Economy.
2. Three hydrogen bomb tests were conducted by the UK in and near the Christmas Island in the Pacific on 15 May, 31 May and 19 June 1957 respectively.
3. The British Defence Ministry and the US Atomic Energy Commission issued announcements on 20 January, 9 March and 6 April 1957 about tests of nuclear weapons by the Soviet Union on 19 January, 8 March and 3 April respectively. Moscow did not comment about these tests.

injure humanity perhaps a great deal. Nobody can say for certain, but everybody can say certainly that it does injure. In such a situation, it seems to be a terrible freak of destiny by which we are driven, countries are driven, to a course in spite of the obvious dangers involved....

6. Land to the Tata Institute of Fundamental Research[1]

I am sending you a letter from Dr Homi Bhabha. I think I wrote to you some time ago, after a visit to Bombay, about this matter of land for the Institute of Fundamental Research.[2]

It is clear that this Institute, dealing with not only highly important matters but also of the kind that are secret, should be compactly situated with most of its staff round about. The Reactors often work all night and other work is carried on till late hours. It is, therefore, prima facie desirable to give them this land which they have been asking for, for some time.

The only question that arises is to balance the needs of the Institute with that of our Navy. The Navy require this for aerials. Normally aerials do not cover large pieces of land in expensive localities. They are either placed in some other locality or even on tops of buildings etc. Apart from this, I presume that aerials can be so arranged as not to spread out over a large piece of land.

The balance thus appears to be very much in favour of giving 15 acres of land to the Research Institute.

I hope that this matter will be examined with speed and decisions taken soon. As Dr Bhabha has pointed out, on the last occasion there was great delay in taking decisions about the land which led not only to some years being wasted but also to unnecessary expenditure by Government.

1. Note to M.K. Vellodi, Defence Secretary, New Delhi, 14 April 1957. File No. 17(347)/59-PMS. Also available in JN Collection.
2. The Tata Institute of Fundamental Research was established in 1945 at Colaba, Mumbai, for advanced study and research in Nuclear Physics and Mathematics.

7. To A. Lakshmanaswami Mudaliar[1]

New Delhi
20 April 1957

My dear Dr Lakshmanaswami,[2]

I received today a letter from Professor S. Chandrasekhar[3] who is now in the University of Chicago.[4] This was about the Ramanujan Institute of Mathematics in Madras. I was surprised to learn that there was some danger of the disbandment or this Institute. Thereupon I enquired from Dr Thacker who assured me that this would not happen.

Dr Thacker has told me that this Institute will be handed over to the University of Madras. The Government of India would, however, be willing to give it financial support.

I was relieved to hear of this because, I think, it would be a tragedy for this Institute to cease to function. I am glad that the University of Madras will take it under its wing and I hope that it will prosper. You can rest assured that we shall not forget it and that we shall endeavour to help it.

As you might be interested in Professor Chandrasekhar's letter, I am sending you a copy.[5]

Yours sincerely,
Jawaharlal Nehru

1. JN Collection.
2. Vice-Chancellor, University of Madras.
3. Subrahmanyan Chandrasekhar (b. 1910); Fellow of Trinity College, Cambridge, 1933-37; Research Associate, University of Chicago, 1937-38; Assistant Professor, 1938-41; Associate Professor, 1942-43; Professor, 1944-46; Distinguished Service Professor of Theoretical Astrophysics, 1947-52; Editor, *Astrophysical Journal*, 1952-71; Marton D. Hull Distinguished Service Professor of Theoretical Astrophysics, 1952-86; Rumford Medal, American Academy of Arts and Science, 1957; Royal Medal, Royal Society, London, 1962; Nehru Memorial Lecture, 1968; shared Nobel Prize for Physics, 1983; R.D. Birla Award, 1984; Professor Emeritus, 1986- ; Publications: *Hydrodynamic and Hydromagnetic Stability, The Mathematical Theory of Black Holes, Aesthetics and Motivations in Science.*
4. Chandrasekhar wrote about the closure of the Ramanujan Institute of Mathematics, Madras, in April and expressed his anguish that it would be a matter of personal shame if the Institute was disbanded. He further wrote that to have an Institute at Madras, devoted purely to mathematical research, was both proper and necessary. The present staff was also competent and published fifty papers in various standard scientific periodicals, in 1950-56.
5. Nehru wrote to S. Chandrasekhar (not printed) on the same day that he would keep in touch with the matter and assured him that the Institute would be continued.

8. To Jagannath P. Chawla[1]

New Delhi
22 April 1957

Dear Shri Chawla,[2]

Your letter of October 9, 1956 reached me only four or five days ago. You had given this letter to Dr Homi Bhabha and, by mistake, his office had sent this on to someone else. So, your letter took nearly six months to reach me.

I have read it with great interest. Since you wrote it, I paid my brief visit to Washington and New York, but unfortunately I did not have occasion to meet you, unless I met you in some crowd at some party.

I agree with you that there is a tradition in India attaching greater importance and prestige to an administrative post than to a technical one. I think that this tradition is rapidly changing. This, of course, was inevitable as the industrial and technical side of India grew progressively more important. I agree with you also that technical people should be employed wherever the work is of a technical kind. Indeed, I have no objection to technical people taking administrative jobs also.

I have noted what you have said about the Indian Airlines Corporation. This matter has been troubling me also. I believe we have made some improvement since you saw it, but we are trying to overhaul the system now.

You refer to the large number of Indian engineers and scientists working in the United States and in Europe. We have tried to get some of these back in India, but often it has not been possible for us to offer the same terms which they were likely to get elsewhere. We have now constituted a Manpower Board here. One of its chief functions is to get in touch with our technical and scientific people in other countries.

I have noted what you have said about certain social problems of India. I am inclined to agree with you, to some extent at least. These changes, however, can hardly be imposed from above. They have to grow from below. I agree that there should be a love of life, but this love of life surely should lead to some kind of an integrated existence and not to a growing neurosis and unhappiness which comes to so many people even when their material wants are satisfied. In one of

---

1. JN Collection.
2. J.P. Chawla, an Indian aeronautical engineer, was a resident of Los Angeles, California.

my books I have referred to these opposing tendencies all over the world and at various periods of history.[3]

Yours sincerely,
Jawaharlal Nehru

3. Writing to the Cabinet Secretary, Y.N. Sukthankar, about the large number of Indian engineers and scientists serving abroad, Nehru hoped that the Manpower Committee or Scientific Board would take some steps.

9. Applicability of Central Health Service to Atomic Energy Establishment[1]

In my note of the 24th April,[2] I pointed out the specialized nature of this work in the Atomic Energy Department. Only doctors who had specialized in this particular matter would really be of help even in regard to the Central Health Service as applied to them. Thus the doctors for this purpose should be chosen on the advice of the Atomic Energy Department. For the rest, there might well be as much coordination and integration of health services as possible. Keeping the above point in view, the Health Ministry might discuss this with the Atomic Energy Department. In the final analysis, we should accept the views of the Department of Atomic Energy in this matter.

1. Note, Dehra Dun, 28 April 1957. JN Collection.
2. Nehru wrote to Amrit Kaur, Union Minister for Health, that Homi J. Bhabha asked him about the applicability of the Central Health Service to the Atomic Energy Establishment in Bombay. He was of the opinion that the Atomic Energy Establishments dealt with the effects of radiation which required specialized work and an average doctor was not suited to do it. Therefore, the Establishment should have their own arrangements for doctoring etc.

3
ADMINISTRATIVE MATTERS

1. To Jagjivan Ram[1]

Camp: Royal Cottage
Bangalore
23 February 1957

My dear Jagjivan Ram,

In a letter from the Governor of West Bengal,[2] reference is made to difficulties being experienced on the Railways due to the detention of trains while waiting for VIPs or high officials. I understand that the Railway Board has issued a confidential circular in order to minimize the inconvenience caused by detention of long distance trains on account of the entertainment of VIPs and high officials.

I think that we are completely wrong in upsetting the public because VIPs or high officials travel. I just do not see why this should be done at all. I doubt if it is done anywhere in the world. I am entirely opposed to any normal traffic, whether in Railways or on the roads, being held up because of VIPs. I think, the Railway Board should be informed.

Yours sincerely,
Jawaharlal Nehru

1. JN Collection.
2. Padmaja Naidu.

2. To Ashok K. Chanda[1]

New Delhi
28 February 1957

My dear Ashok,[2]

Your letter of 28th February with a note about pensions and gratuities to political sufferers, more especially in recent months.[3]

There appears to be nothing wrong about helping these people within reason and provided, of course, that each case is deserving of help. But it would certainly be wrong if this kind of help was utilized for election purposes. In particular, I think that scholarships for study to children or even others is a very desirable way of helping. It is not possible to say anything about individual cases without enquiry.

The fact that eight years have passed since Independence does not necessarily mean that this class of deserving persons is exhausted. I am getting such cases from time to time and I have sometimes helped them from some funds at my disposal, other than Government, or more frequently referred them to the State concerned.

I do not quite know what one can do about this without an intimate enquiry and that would hardly be desirable in these petty cases. Perhaps, the attention of the States concerned might be drawn to the fact that it was unfortunate that many of these grants were made on the eve of elections.

Yours sincerely,
Jawaharlal Nehru

1. JN Collection.
2. Comptroller and Auditor General.
3. A.K. Chanda had pointed out that large sums were being spent on political sufferers on the eve of elections by the Governments of Assam, Bihar, Uttar Pradesh and East Punjab which was likely to create misunderstanding.

3. To Sri Prakasa[1]

New Delhi
2 March 1957

My dear Prakasa,[2]

Thank you for your letter in which you referred to my aeroplane accident.[3] You mentioned in this also about your allowances, fairs, etc. I think, the Home Ministry must have sent their letter to you without consulting the Minister himself who had been travelling. I am enquiring into this.

I have just been reading your letter to the President dated March 1. In this you refer to Dr John Matthai's[4] very ungraceful and, I think, wholly uncalled for statement about the Governor. I had heard something about this the other day and at that time I had thought that he was objecting to some letter that your Secretary had written about the Rector's age. Now, I find that it was a matter dealt with by Mahtab.[5] However, this does not make much difference, but in a sense, it makes a little easier for you to say something about it.

Dr Matthai has a very definite trace of utter crankiness. He goes off the rail sometimes completely. He did that when he had to leave our Cabinet.[6] He did this again on a very silly occasion when I was made an honorary Member of the Bombay College of Surgeons, etc. Also in regard to the State Bank.[7] As he is retiring, it is difficult to pursue him. I met his wife in Trichur, and she told me how she was preparing their house where they would live in retirement.

But I definitely think that you cannot allow this matter to rest where it is. How best to deal with it is another matter, and will be for you to consider.

There are several points involved. I agree with you in regard to the autonomy of universities, but to call a suggestion by the Chancellor about the age an

---

1. JN Collection.
2. Governor of Bombay.
3. Nehru's 'Meghdoot' had to make an emergency landing at Raichur on 26 February 1957.
4. Chairman, National Book Trust at this time.
5. H.K. Mahtab was Governor of Bombay before Sri Prakasa.
6. John Matthai, the then Finance Minister, had resigned from Nehru's Cabinet in May 1950. On 2 June 1950, he alleged that Nehru himself supported the cause of many Ministers indulging in wasteful expenditure which had a demoralizing effect and made the position of the Finance Minister "unnecessarily difficult." He also criticized the setting up of the Planning Commission, a "parallel cabinet", and complained that he had to work under serious constraints in his exercise of control of expenditure.
7. See *Selected Works* (second series), Vol. 33, pp. 256-257.

interference is surely absurd. In any event, it is highly improper to condemn publicly such an action of the Governor. Apparently, they disagreed with the Governor's advice and reappointed the Rector, although he was over-age. I do not know if there are any other instances of Dr Matthai objecting to the Governor's interference. You might well write to him a letter enquiring from him what instances he has in view of the Governor's interference.

You should obviously see the new Vice-Chancellor[8] and explain the situation to him. Perhaps, you might write to him officially too, politely of course, but pointing out the impropriety of Dr Matthai's statement.

Yours sincerely,
Jawaharlal Nehru

8. T.M. Advani.

4. Problem of Foreign Exchange[1]

This question has put me in some difficulty. I do think that we must be very strict now about deputing people to go abroad. This should apply even to students, though, of course, we cannot apply it rigidly there or elsewhere.

2. I agree with the broad approach of the Finance Ministry in this matter. There is unfortunately not enough realization about the difficulties of the foreign exchange situation, and far too many people still continue to go abroad. At the same time, there is much force in the argument put forward on behalf of the Food & Agriculture Ministry. I would have liked this matter to be considered at the Cabinet meeting on the 13th March, but it appears that Rome meetings are being held from the 11th March onwards. Therefore, to postpone a decision to the 13th March will not be helpful. I would have gladly discussed this with the Food & Agriculture Minister and the Finance Minister, but both of them are out of Delhi and may not return for two or three days.

1. Note to Cabinet Secretary, New Delhi, 8 March 1957. Item No. XI/273, C-III, 1957, Confidential Section, Planning Commission.

3. In these circumstances, I feel that it may not be wise to rule out this deputation of Dr S.R. Sen[2] on this particular occasion. But the points raised by the Finance Minister, both in regard to this particular matter and other deputations, must be considered so that every Ministry might realize the great importance of limiting these delegations and deputations in order to save foreign exchange. These papers and this note, therefore, should be put up anyhow at the Cabinet meeting on the 13th March. But, I think, that it would be advisable now to agree to Dr Sen's going on deputation for this meeting in Rome.

4. You might discuss this matter with the Finance Ministry and let them see this note of mine.

2. (b. 1916); Indian economist; Deputy Economic Adviser, Government of India 1948-51; Economic and Statistical Adviser, Ministry of Food and Agriculture, Government of India, 1951-58; Joint Secretary, Planning Commission, 1959-63; Adviser and Additional Secretary, Government of India, 1963-69; Vice-Chairman, Irrigation Commission, Government of India, 1969-70; Ambassador, and Executive Director, IBRD, IFC and IDA, 1970-78; Chairman, International Food Policy Research Institute, Washington, D.C., 1979, and Government of India Committee on Cost of Production, 1979 ; author of *Strategy for Agricultural Development*, *Planning Machinery in India*, and *Politics of Indian Economy*.

●

5. To M.S. Patel[1]

New Delhi
9 March 1957

Dear Dr Patel,[2]

Thank you for your letter of the 4th March which reached me yesterday.

I have read the newsletter which you have sent me. I entirely agree with you that every effort should be made to stop corruption and leakage, particularly when large state schemes are being started by us. You are right in saying that

1. C.D. Deshmukh Papers, NMML. Also available in JN Collection.
2. A resident of Mumbai.

there is corruption. But my general impression is that this is being checked somewhat and is less than it was because of various steps that we have taken. However, that is not enough and we must be very careful about this.

You refer to what Mr Wells says about "overnight millionaires". I find from the newsletter that he is referring more especially to Thailand, Pakistan and Japan where American millions have been pouring in through US military expenditures. Fortunately, this has not happened in India. I think, there is a vast difference in this respect between India and some other countries of Asia which are receiving heavy aid from the United States. Such aid as we have received from abroad has been for specific civil schemes. There may be waste there and leakage. But the possibility is relatively limited. In the case of military aid there are hardly any checks and that is why the countries getting military aid are much worse off in this respect.

When you come to Delhi, I shall be happy to meet you.

Yours sincerely,
Jawaharlal Nehru

6. Introduction of Metric System[1]

On the 1st of April of this year 1957, a silent but far-reaching revolution is going to begin in India. This is the introduction of the decimal and metric system in our coinage. This will, no doubt, be followed by the extension of this system later to weights and measures.[2] For the present, however, we are introducing this system in the coinage only.

Many people will ask why this change should be made in a well established system and in something which affects the daily life and habits of all sections of the people. The question is relevant and deserves a full answer. No such change should be made unless it is obviously to the advantage of the nation and the people.

1. Message on the introduction of decimal and metric system of coinage in India, New Delhi, 9 March 1957. File No. 37(17)/56-59-PMS. Also available in JN Collection.
2. The metric system of weights and measures was introduced in October 1958.

I am convinced, however, that the change was not only necessary but essential, and any delay in it would have come in the way of our future progress. I have no doubt that some time or other this change would have become unavoidable. The later we made it, the more difficult it would have become.

Everything old is not necessarily bad just as everything new is not necessarily good. But, in a changing world, something that was good in the past may not fit in in present conditions. We have, therefore, to adapt ourselves to this changing world. The world today is one of science, technology and industry in their innumerable aspects. A cumbrous system of coinage and weights and measures is wasteful of time and energy and delays work. As our social life becomes more advanced and complex, these petty delays and waste mount up and add to a great deal. Therefore, it has become necessary to make this change now rather than at a later stage.

It is well known, I hope, that in adopting the decimal and metric system, we are not adopting something alien to India. Indeed, we are going back to something which was originally the product of Indian genius. India gave to the world long ago the great discovery of zero and numerals, and later the beginnings of what subsequently came to be known as the metric system that saw light through Indian genius. So we go back to our own.

Some of my colleagues have explained fully in speech and writing the significance of this change and the details of how the change is going to be made. Some inconvenience might well be caused, to begin with, because of this change over, as long established habits come in our way. But every effort has been made to avoid this inconvenience and to have a period of three years when both the old and the new coins will circulate side by side and be considered as legal tender. Thus any real inconvenience will be avoided and very soon the great convenience of this new system will, I am sure, be appreciated all over India. I seek the cooperation of our people in making this a success. I am sure this will be forthcoming.

It has been explained already that no one will suffer any loss by this change and indeed there may well be some gain, apart from the gain in using better and more expeditious methods.

I commend, therefore, the new coinage based on the decimal and metric system to our people.

7. To Govind Ballabh Pant[1]

New Delhi
15 March 1957

My dear Pantji,

Thank you for your letter of the 12th March.[2] I think you have been fairly generous in dealing with Governor's allowances in Bombay.

So far as the Nagpur Raj Bhavan is concerned, I have already expressed my opinion that it should be used for some other purpose, though keeping a few rooms for the Governor when he goes there. This should definitely reduce the expenditure for its upkeep.

I think, it is desirable for our Raj Bhavans to keep up certain standards and a certain efficiency. But, I think there is room for economy even there, more particularly in the number of staff employed. We must get used to fewer persons. Crowds of people moving about do not add to efficiency.

I do not understand why a grant of Rupees four lakhs eighty thousand should be given to Mysore for a Raj Bhavan. The Maharaja[3] has his own palace and his own staff which anyhow he keeps. I can understand his being given something for an additional secretary or clerks. But, surely, there is no point in giving him or any other Maharaja more or less the same grant as would be given to a non-Maharaja Governor. I think, we have got into a bad habit of doing so from the time of the Rajpramukhs. Gopalaswami Ayyangar had odd views on this subject with which I did not agree at all.[4]

Yours affectionately,
Jawaharlal Nehru

1. JN Collection.
2. G.B. Pant had informed Nehru that on Sri Prakasa's proposals for the revision of the Governor's allowances, a fresh order had been issued. He added: "We have made every effort to meet Sri Prakasa's wishes and I believe that he will find the amounts that are now being provided adequate and satisfactory."
3. Jaya Chamaraja Wodiyar.
4. Gopalaswami Ayyangar was chairman of the Committee on the Reorganization of the Machinery of Government in 1949.

8. Secularism and the Government of India[1]

Please acknowledge this letter from Acharya Swami Neminath Maharaj and tell him that I have read it with interest. I think, he is right in saying that certain difficulties arise in interpreting the secularism of the Government of India. The word itself is, perhaps, not too happy. But it is used in English for want of a more suitable word. What is meant by is that the State has no official religion and the Government as such is not committed to the upkeep of one religion. It does not, of course, mean that the State is against religion. It gives perfect freedom to all for their religious worship etc., provided this does not come in conflict with other religions.

2. That is clear enough. The question that the Acharya raises is about the behaviour of high officials. It is difficult to lay down definite directions about this. It is certainly open to them and they have every right to practise their own religion whatever it may be. It may not be, however, always right for them to propagate that religion while they occupy that high office.

3. Religion is rather a vague word and, in India especially, it covers all kind of cultural manifestations. That culture is part of the history and life of the people and has, therefore, to be welcomed, unless there is something bad in it.

1. Note to Principal Private Secretary, New Delhi, 15 March 1957. JN Collection.

9. To V.V. Giri[1]

New Delhi
16 March 1957

My dear Giri,

Thank you for your letter of the 15th March.

We have fully gone into this question of the United Press of India[2] and the matter is being considered afresh by the Minister of Information & Broadcasting.

I need not tell you that we consider it important to have news agencies and we would normally try to help the United Press. But it really has been quite extraordinary how badly this has been managed in the past and at the same time what heavy salaries it has paid. As things are, any help given to it does not ensure its continuance at all. Much of it goes in payment of its debt to Mr Karnani etc. I see absolutely no reason why Government money should go towards paying Karnani's debt.

You say that the United Press is trying to rehabilitate itself. No doubt, it has tried to do so for many years past without any satisfactory results. It might even be simpler for a new press agency to be started than to carry on with something which has got this terrible reputation of bad management and wasteful expenditure as well as debts.

I am merely pointing out to you some of the facts which have been before us. In spite of this, we have asked Dr Keskar, the Minister of I & B to consider what we can do about this matter.

I shall always be glad to meet you. But during the days you mention I shall be terribly busy with the Polish Prime Minister,[3] the German Foreign Minister[4] as well as Mr Jarring, who has come here on the Kashmir issue. I may, therefore, find it difficult to find time for an interview. But you should certainly see Dr Keskar who is dealing with this matter and who has had full talks with us.

Yours sincerely,
Jawaharlal Nehru

1. JN Collection.
2. United Press of India had to pay back a loan of Rs two lakh eighty thousand to Gopaldas Karnani, who had filed a petition in Calcutta High Court for liquidation of UPI. Karnani had also put forward certain conditions for withdrawal of this case.
3. Josef Cyrankiewicz. See *post*, pp. 545-547.
4. German Foreign Minister, Heinrich von Brentano, arrived in New Delhi on 27 March 1957.

10. Security Arrangements[1]

I have read the new letter you have addressed to Chief Secretaries about security arrangements. I do not think it is adequate. It is not enough to repeat, say, that security should be in conformity with instructions. Something much more precise should be said.[2]

2. In particular, two things have to be emphasized. The lining of routes by the Police must be abandoned completely. Only at a place where a crowd might be expected, some additional policemen might be placed. It is undesirable for large numbers of policemen to be brought from all over the state to a particular place because the Prime Minister is going to visit that place. In fact, as far as possible, except on very special occasions, no policemen should be brought from outside.

3. Traffic should not be stopped, that is, normal traffic should continue.

4. Guards of honour should be avoided.

5. It is not necessary for all the principal officials and others to collect together at the airport or the railway station, as the case may be, at the time of the arrival of the Prime Minister.

6. Every effort should be made to see that no inconvenience is caused to the public.

7. Apart from the Prime Minister, in regard to other Ministers, Central or State, who may be touring, the minimum arrangements should be made for reception etc., except on ceremonial occasions. It is not necessary for many officials or others to be present. This interferes with their work.

---

1. Note to A.V. Pai, Home Secretary, New Delhi, 18 March 1957. JN Collection.
2. Pai wrote on 18 March "that the main purpose of these instructions is to ensure the security of the Prime Minister and so, they should be applied intelligently... care being particularly taken to avoid excessive display of force and prolonged holds-up of vehicular or pedestrian traffic."

11. To P.F. Huss[1]

New Delhi
18 March 1957

Dear Dr Huss,[2]

Thank you for your letter of the 16th March. I received your letter of the 27th February also. I am sorry that no answer was sent to it. I received such a large number of letters and telegrams of congratulation that it became physically impossible for me to reply to them. I acknowledged all these messages in a message to the press.

In your letter of the 27th February, you refer to the Christians in India. Any person who knows Indian History or present conditions in India knows what an important part Christians have played in the life of India. Christianity came to India in the first century of the Christian Era, long before it went to Europe. In South India it is one of the major religions of the region. People in North India do not perhaps realize this. Christianity is as much a religion of India as any other.

There are, of course, narrow-minded individuals belonging to all religions who do not behave correctly. You refer to the Niyogi Enquiry Committee.[3] I confess I have not read this full report, although I have glanced through it. I can understand Christians not liking much that it contains. At the same time I should like to point out that unfortunately Christianity in North India especially was often utilized for political purposes by the British Government. It is this political aspect that we have disapproved of and not the religion at all which we respect. You can rest assured that Christianity will continue to be one of the respected religions of India.

Yours sincerely,
Jawaharlal Nehru

1. JN Collection.
2. A resident of Kolkata.
3. Christian Missionary Enquiry Committee worked under the chairmanship of M. Bhavanishankar Niyogi from 1954 to 1956.

12. Problem of Slums[1]

I am glad to know that a seminar on slum clearance is going to be held in Bombay.[2] I hope that it will produce practical results. I am a little afraid of seminars, which deal with questions in an academic and impersonal way. The slum problem is, above all, a human and personal one.

To visit a slum has been for me always a most painful experience which has pulled me out of my normal life. Many years ago, a visit to the Kanpur slums haunted me for a long time afterwards. In Bombay and here in Delhi I have also seen some of these slums and felt the same shock.

I know that this question, like any other, cannot be approached from the point of view of sentiment and we have to deal with it in a practical way. But I do think that sentiment in this matter and a feeling of anger that such things exist is important. It is not much good saying that this is the result of industrialization and factories and the like, or of giving some other reason for them. The point is that we should feel that these slums are a continuing disgrace to each one of us.

Some good work has been done no doubt, but a very great deal more remains to be done. Sometimes grandiose schemes are outlined and then, for lack of money, nothing or little is done. It is better perhaps to have a simpler approach which can be given effect to than to dream of big things which never take shape. In a country having cold climate, the problem of slums is more difficult than in the greater part of India. What people require in India, except for some time in the north, is not so much building but fresh air and fresh water and lighting and drainage. That appears to me far more important than heavy structures that may be put up. Structures and buildings are, of course, necessary, but they take second place in my thinking. What is much more important is fresh air, water, lighting and drainage. Buildings can grow gradually. I have sometimes found buildings put up with no adequate arrangements for water or drainage or latrines or lighting. That, I think, is the wrong way.

While we discuss and argue about the problems of the slums, the people living in them continue to face their miserable and unhappy existence. Are we to leave them where they are till we have finally evolved some major plans and till we have collected enough money for the purpose? I think that, apart from

1. Message for the seminar on slum clearance, New Delhi, 21 March 1957. File No. 9/2/57-PMS. Also available in JN Collection.
2. This seminar was organized by Hansa Mehta, President, Indian Conference of Social Work, in Mumbai from 14 to 20 May 1957.

these schemes, which no doubt are desirable, an immediate approach should be made to supply these first necessities, in so far as this is possible. Thus, water, latrines and drainage should be supplied even in existing slums, pending the implementation of a bigger scheme.

Here in Delhi, we have been trying to do something during the past year or more. There is a big scheme for the refashioning and replanning of the whole of Delhi. But we decided that we should not wait till then and that we should give such amenities as were possible immediately. The Health Ministry, the Delhi Municipality, the Improvement Trust and the Bharat Sevak Samaj cooperated to this end. So also the Rehabilitation Ministry, for there are many hundreds of thousands of refugees in Delhi. The work of these various organizations was coordinated to some extent by the special Delhi Authority that has been created.[3] I cannot say that this work has resulted in a great change, but it has brought considerable relief to the dwellers in the slums or to many of them. Meanwhile we are trying to plan for better days.

The Second Five Year Plan has put many heavy burdens upon us and we have to be careful about our expenditure. Nevertheless, the Government of India is very keenly aware of this slum problem and intends to help, in so far as it is possible for it, in the removal of these slums.

I wish the seminar on slum clearance success.

3. See *also Selected Works* (second series), Vol. 35, pp. 227-228.

13. Concern at Cutting Trees[1]

I am rather alarmed at the reports I receive of the cutting down of trees in various parts of the country. In particular, I am told that the Posts & Telegraph Department deals with trees in most ruthless manner. If at all any tree comes in the way of their alignment, down it goes.

2. I think it might be remembered that trees are not only very valuable for the nation but that a tree takes a generation to grow. It is easy to cut down a tree; it

1. Note to the Minister of State for Communications, Raj Bahadur, New Delhi, 22 March 1957. File No. 31(18)/56-PMS. Also available in JN Collection.

takes a long time for it to be planted and for it to grow. Perhaps, sometimes it is inevitable for a tree to be cut down. But no tree should be cut down unless there is no feasible alternative to it. It pains me to see how careless people are about trees and specially well-grown trees. I should like you to have instructions issued to all branches of the Posts & Telegraph Department to take particular care to preserve our trees.

I might mention that a case has been mentioned to me about a lovely avenue in Bangalore being ruined by the P & T Department cutting down the trees or one side of the trees.

14. The Case of Sajjad Zaheer[1]

Please read the attached letter from Shri Sajjad Zaheer.[2] On the whole, I have no objection to his going.[3] But I should like your advice.

Sajjad Zaheer, perhaps you may remember, is an old member of the Communist Party. He was in Pakistan in the early days after the Partition, was later arrested, I think, in connection with the big trial in which Military Officers were involved.[4] He spent some years in prison there and was subsequently discharged. We allowed him to come back.[5] But in our view, he was a Pakistani citizen. So, we did not consider him an Indian national. But, in view of the fact that his wife and all his

1. Note to Secretary General and Foreign Secretary, New Delhi, 23 March 1957. JN Collection.
2. (1905-1973); Communist leader and eminent Urdu writer; founded the Indian Progressive Writers' Association, London, 1935; elected member, Central Committee of the Communist Party at its first Congress in Bombay, 1943; Editor, *Qaumi Jung* in the 1940s and *Awami Daur* in the 1960s; publications include *Angare, Light on League-Unionist Conflict, Urdu Bazar, Nuqush-i-Zindaan, Zikr-i-Hafiz* and *Urdu, Hindi, Hindustani.*
3. Sajjad Zaheer had received an invitation from East Germany to attend a literary conference and had, for that reason, sought permission from the External Affairs Ministry.
4. After Partition, Sajjad Zaheer was sent by the Communist Party of India to Pakistan to organize the Communist Party there. He was elected as the first General Secretary of the Communist Party of Pakistan. He was arrested in the Rawalpindi Conspiracy Case on 9 March 1951 with the Chief of Pakistani Army, Major-General Akbar Khan, Air Commodore Juneja and Faiz Ahmed Faiz, a noted Urdu poet. The conspiracy was designed to overthrow the Government of Pakistan in favour of military rule and eventually set up a communist state.
5. After his release from Pakistan jail sometime in 1955, he came back to India.

family had all along been here, we allowed him to stay here. I do not quite know what kind of a permit he has got to stay, but broadly it was understood that we would not send him away.

I suppose he has to consider the risk of going out and not being allowed to come back to India. I do not know what kind of a passport he has got, if any, and on what kind of papers he would travel.

Since his experience in Pakistan, he has toned down considerably both in regard to communism and many other matters. He writes well in Urdu and knows French well. I think, he has recently translated for the Sahitya Akademi Voltaire's[6] *Candide* into Urdu.[7] He is the younger brother of Ali Zaheer.[8]

6. Voltaire (1694-1778); well known French philosopher and writer.
7. In 1957.
8. A Minister in the UP Government as this time.

15. To Gulzarilal Nanda[1]

New Delhi
30 March 1957

My dear Gulzarilal,

Your Private Secretary has sent me a copy of the address which you are delivering tomorrow at the All India Homoeopathic Medical Conference at Amritsar.[2] I have glanced through it. You have every right, of course, to hold your opinions. But it does surprise me a little that in a specific matter which is dealt with by a certain Ministry of the Government of India, namely, the Ministry of Health, another Minister should speak precisely and make a number of proposals, some

1. File No. 28(27)/56-57-PMS. Also available in JN Collection.
2. At the inaugural address to the twelfth All India Homoeopathic Medical Conference on 31 March 1957, Gulzarilal Nanda said that the homoeopathic , ayurvedic and unani systems of medicine were to be encouraged to extend medical relief to all the people in the country. He also said: "To those who assert that the indigenous systems and homoeopathy have no right to exist because they are outside the modern scientific systems, may well be asked ... whether they are able to extend their ministrations to all the people in the country, who are in need of medical help."

of which are opposed to the policy we have been pursuing. The matter has been discussed not only in Cabinet but also in Parliament.

I am all for a certain latitude in certain matters, but you will agree that it is most embarrassing for one Minister to take up a line opposed to the one adopted by another Minister in the latter's own subject.

Yours sincerely,
Jawaharlal Nehru

16. To Govind Ballabh Pant[1]

New Delhi
31 March 1957

My dear Pantji,

Maulana asked me today about the appointment of Governors. I suppose we shall have to deal with this matter fairly soon. The present position is that Governors have been recently appointed in the following States:

Assam,
Bombay,
Kerala,
Madras,
Mysore,
Orissa,
Rajasthan, and
West Bengal.

I take it that they continue even after the general elections.

In appointing some of these Governors, I think, I indicated that their period of appointment need not be the full term. Some of them indeed said that they would not like to be away for more than a year or two. However, nothing need be done about these States at this stage.

1. JN Collection.

Thus the remaining States, where the appointment of Governors has to be considered, are Andhra, Bihar, Madhya Pradesh, Punjab and the UP.

The dates of appointment of these Governors are as follows:

Andhra	..	C.M. Trivedi	..	1 Oct	1953
Bihar	..	R.R. Diwakar	..	15 June	1952
Madhya Pradesh	..	Dr Pattabhi Sitaramayya	..	2 July	1952
Punjab	..	C.P.N. Singh	..	11 March	1953
UP	..	K.M. Munshi	..	2 June	1952

You will notice that three of those, namely, Bihar, Madhya Pradesh and Uttar Pradesh, complete their five years in June or July next. I have, as a matter of fact, previously informed them that the change over will come some time after the elections. And so the exact date does not matter.

In the case of Andhra, Trivedi's five years will end on the 30th September 1958. But, of course, he was not sent to Andhra for a full five year term. He was in fact sent there for a year or two and we are entitled to change the Governor there on any date after these elections. Trivedi also has previously been Governor in Orissa and Punjab. In fact, he has been a Governor continuously from 1st of April 1946, that is, eleven years, except for minor periods in between when he was on leave.

C.P.N. Singh's five year term would expire on the 10th March 1953. Here again we can, if we so choose, ask him to resign after the elections.

Thus, in any event, we have to appoint Governors for Bihar, Madhya Pradesh and UP. I think, we should appoint them some time in May, so that they can take charge about the end of that month or the beginning of June.

In regard to Andhra, good as Trivedi is, I feel that we cannot continue him after eleven years of Governorship. About the Punjab, I am not quite clear in my mind as to whether we should terminate the Governorship soon or allow him to carry on till the end of his term, that is, March 1958.

We should indicate to these people fairly soon what our intentions are. The other day Munshi asked me how long he will have to stay there, as he wanted to make other arrangements. Should he go to Naini Tal etc.? I think, we should tell Munshi, Diwakar and Pattabhi that the change over will take place by the end of May.

Yours affectionately,
Jawaharlal Nehru

17. To K.D. Malaviya[1]

New Delhi
1 April 1957

My dear Keshava,[2]
Your letter of April 1st.

The Cabinet Secretary does not belong to any Ministry. He is supposed to be the senior most Secretary, and his function is to coordinate the work of all Ministries, to expedite their work, and he is often asked to take charge of important work himself, in association with other Secretaries. This has been done on several occasions during the last few years. When I took office, the Cabinet Secretary was an Englishman, Sir Eric Coates,[3] who was very much in the picture in every important matter. Coates had been previously a member of the Viceroy's Council.

This is the English practice too, where the Cabinet Secretary is supposed to have a supervisory function in regard to secretarial work in every Ministry. Naturally, this is done under the advice of the Minister. He does not come in the way of the Minister at all. Normally, in England, every Secretary whenever he is in difficulties, goes automatically to the Cabinet Secretary to ask him to help.

This oil matter is not only of great importance but is connected with several Ministries, and therefore it is peculiarly necessary for the Cabinet Secretary to be in the picture. In fact, that was why we appointed a Committee on the subject, of which the Cabinet Secretary was Chairman. Previous to Sukthankar, N.R. Pillai was Cabinet Secretary, and he functioned in the same way in regard to various matters. It is right that your Ministry should deal with this matter. But, we have often discussed the complications of the oil business and how it is spread out over two or three Ministries as well as, of course, the Planning Commission.

Apart from this, it is only right that Ramadhyani,[4] who is one of our junior Secretaries, should have the guidance of a senior Secretary. It is not a question of the senior Secretaries having anything different to say. The policy is laid down by the Cabinet or the Ministry concerned. But, there is such a thing as

1. JN Collection.
2. Union Minister of State for Natural Resources.
3. Eric Thomas Coates was Secretary, Viceroy's Executive Council, 1946-47.
4. R.K. Ramadhyani.

policy being carried out and another, and a very important thing, how negotiations are conducted. Here, experience tells a great deal.

Of course, you should talk to Sukthankar now and whenever you like and give him such directions as you think necessary.

Yours affectionately,
Jawaharlal Nehru

18. To Swaran Singh[1]

New Delhi
2 April 1957

My dear Swaran Singh,[2]

An Allahabad lawyer of some eminence, Pathak,[3] is our honorary Adviser on International Law in the External Affairs Ministry. He gives us a great deal of time. He has been a member of our UN Delegations and spends months abroad. He is a leading lawyer in Allahabad and has been offered a Judgeship in the High Court more than once, which he has not accepted. He has been of very great help to us and indeed continues to help us. We send for him frequently to Delhi and we do not pay him anything for this.

Our need for help from him continues and it would be of great advantage to us if he could remain more or less continuously in Delhi. He has a very fine library too on International Law, better than ours.

I am writing this to you, because he is perfectly prepared to come to Delhi and stay here provided he could have a house to stay. Do you think it is possible to provide him with a house?

Yours sincerely,
Jawaharlal Nehru

1. File No. 45(6)/57-PMS. Also available in JN Collection.
2. Union Minister of Works, Housing and Supply till 17 April 1957 when he took over as Minister of Steel, Mines and Fuel.
3. G.S. Pathak.

19. Concept of Good Administration[1]

The annual meetings on which I come to you are more or less of business character and they provide me with an opportunity of making some general remarks. A person who is not dealing in an expert way with a specific subject will evidently go in for generalizations on the various points. And as I am not taking any particular subject and I am no expert anyhow; so I say many things about many subjects. Looking at this Institute from a distance, sometimes looking at its publications on coming here every year, it seems to me that the Institute has been making good progress. One of our members said something about the lack of research. As a matter of fact, this Institute started functioning really only since a full-time Director appeared on the scene.[2]

We have been told that similar Institutes in other countries have begun to appreciate its work. There can be no doubt about the importance of the work which faces you today. Taking advantage of the presence of so many distinguished persons who have come here today. I am glad that from a small annual business session this gathering will spread out into a conference on a specific subject-matter, viz., recruitment and training for public services. We had a seminar on this subject some months ago. Now, this is something which I feel as really solid and worthwhile. I am quite sure that it will bear results. It may be that the results may not be very obvious, but it would anyhow be an earnest discussion of subjects of high importance. I often wonder how we have to approach these subjects. What I mean is that there are several approaches to them—the technician's approach, the professor's approach, the administrator's approach, and, maybe, the politician's approach and the man-in-the-street's approach. I believe that most of you who have gathered here at this meeting are, probably, people of either of two types: the administrator's type with actual experience behind or the professor's type. Both types are very important, both having a fund of knowledge at their disposal. It may be said, however, that neither of these two types represents the man-in-the-street approach. I do not think the man-in-the-street is likely to be well informed, or even very helpful. Whatever it may be, it is an important approach; obviously because it is the man-in-the-street or in the field who counts; because the administration is after all meant to serve him ultimately. You must always remember that aspect; if you do not, you

---

1. Speech at the third annual general body meeting of the Indian Institute of Public Administration, New Delhi, 6 April 1957. JN Papers, NMML.
2. V.K.N. Menon joined as Director of IIPA on 1 August 1956.

will have no solid relationship or ground. It is worthwhile repeating this, because the administration has not only to be good but it has also to be felt to be good by the people affected. That should be always so and it is all the more necessary in a fully democratic set-up.

I said a "fully democratic set-up", because a full democratic set-up is developing fast not only in this country but in many others too. Since the last generation or so democracy has spread out. This spreading out of democracy brings, and ought to bring, all kinds of changes in the relationship between the administrative apparatus and the people. Take the word which all the more used to be, and still is, usually looked down upon: that is "bureaucracy"or the "bureaucrat". During the British period it was considered to be a bad word by us, and something of that still hangs about it even now. It stood for government officials who considered themselves superior to the common man, the common human beings. There was something in that criticism, and I think, it is still somewhat true. Obviously, when there is a democratic set-up now, there must be a full realization of the implications of democracy—how it affects public administration, and how public administration affects it. After all, it should be one of the principal functions of public administration in its broader context to direct democracy into right channels. In fact, public administration, though necessarily requiring more and more things like training and trained service and experience, has become more and more allied to democracy, the democratic element, so that there appears to be no hard and fast demarcation line, in administration, between the trained public servant and the representative of the democracy. If there is no such reliance, or no such mixing together, there may be friction, and there will be hardships on both sides.

Now, what is self-government? We have a Parliament which is sovereign, which is elected every five years, normally speaking. It is obvious that the vast majority of the measures considered and passed by Parliament are in a way being considered by the 360 million odd people in the country. If I may say so, the peoples' representatives tend to function on the basis of a feeling of the general pulse of the people. The latter have got the power to kick out a Government, or a Member, after a certain period of time, as it is important to keep in check the Government or Parliament. Again, there also exists a general feeling or awareness in the people that things are being done according to their wishes or in consultation with them; in fact, they have begun to feel that they are functioning, that they are governing themselves. It is only partly true, but it is true enough in the sense that there is a check on the Government, and also on Parliament, that it would be kicked out if it went too far in any direction. Therefore, it behaves and tries to keep in line with public opinion. By and large, a Parliament or a Government does what is reasonable without really making a reference to the people. So long as it gives the impression that democracy has been preserved and that people are being consulted, that their wishes are being respected, it is all well. But whether they are actually consulted or not is another matter. If they get the impression that things are being imposed upon them, then friction arises.

Apart from doing his work, the administrator, whether he is low down or high up in the scale, must give the impression, even if that impression is not cent per cent correct, that he is working through public will and carrying out the public will. Of course, it cannot be done always, you cannot carry out everybody's will; but the broad impression that he is functioning in accordance with the public will, always thinking of public grievances, trying to remedy them, consulting the people and so on, must be given. I know it is big thing to consult everybody. Such an impression can be created or not created—it all depends upon the manner of functioning of the administration. It is quite essential in a democracy to create this impression both in the interest of the public and the administrator. Otherwise, democracy rebels; maybe not immediately but after a period of time; maybe a month later or a year later, it rebels and it creates trouble. This applies generally to all types of administrative activities but it applies more so to work of a social character, which affects the people at large. Therefore, it becomes all the more important that the administrator has his hands on the pulse of the people all the time, and the people feel that this man is one of them, that he is reflecting their wishes and will always reflect their wishes.

The administrator doing an honest man's job, and thinking that he is doing his utmost, often does not receive the recognition that is due to him. In fact, he meets with criticism and curses and feels irritated and hurt. An able administrator, however, will always do the right thing and make the people feel that he reflects their wishes. That sensation must come to the people, that he is reflecting their wishes to some extent. When a multitude of voices are advising the administrator or criticizing him, obviously he has to make his own choice and function according to his own decision. He cannot listen to and agree with each of the hundreds and thousands of voices which advise him in their own way. But by his manner of functioning he should make them realize that he has given due consideration to what they said and that he has been courteous not only to them but to their thinking. That way, by and large, he will be able to satisfy each of them to some extent.

In administration, as in most things in life, it is not only what one does, but the manner of doing it, that is exceedingly important, especially in dealings with large masses of human beings, as in a democracy. Of course, what you do is important enough but the manner of doing is of the highest importance—the manner of approach to the individual or to the group. I would like to stress this especially because it is of the highest importance, of course, for the politician, but equally so for the administrator. The politician realizes this normally, because he will have to go if he did not realize it quickly enough. The administrator, however, can continue much longer without realizing it fully; but there will be ill feeling against him and he would not be able to do his work adequately because most of it now involves the active cooperation of masses of people. The police functions no longer dominate the scene anywhere in the world. Each State wants to rise socially, economically, in all kinds of activities. As a matter of fact, in a way, all public administration is bureaucracy. The growth of socialism is the growth of bureaucracy. Bureaucracy will grow. It is very odd that the people who shout most loudly against bureaucracy are the people who want more and more of it. That is what is involved in the growth of socialistic avenues of work. The administrator's work is becoming bigger and bigger, not merely just keeping the peace in particular areas or collecting taxes. All this involves close contacts and touch with the people and winning over the people to his side. It involves, in fact, something of the approach of a politician, of a good politician, of an effective politician—not in the sense of the politician's approach when he tries to get votes, but the normal approach of a politician when he wants to win over the people to his side to do something with their help.

Incidentally, there is a mention in the report of the Director of a research project on local self-government. I think that it is of the highest importance that this Institute or any other should give consideration to the administrative problems of local self-government and even more particularly to those of panchayats. There are hundreds and thousands of panchayats in this country. They form the real base of our democracy. If that base is unsound, then we are not cent per cent stable democratically, even with the second base of our Parliament. We are told that panchayats have not succeeded because there are squabbles, there are parties, there is corruption and all that. It is true, I think, that our experience of panchayats has been distressing. But real democracy cannot be at the top, it can be only at the base; and in India, this is not something alien; it is something natural to this soil. The fact remains that the panchayat is the primary base of our democracy and we have to improve it.

We have to evolve ways and methods of doing things to combat faction and corruption in public administration. To take an instance, some kind of compensation is often given in the villages to a large number of people, or some relief work is taken in hand in some villages, and some petty official is put in charge of giving relief or compensation. There always are and there will always be great delays in giving it. Very often, by the time it reaches the recipient, either most of it disappears or by then the recipient has suffered a great deal. What are we going to do about it? Are we to wait till everybody is thoroughly honest and will not delay things? Of course, we should try to do that, but we cannot wait. Suppose we try another method of disbursing relief. Suppose the whole village is gathered together and the Government announcement about the scale of the compensation is made in public. The whole village will hear about it: "come forward, you take this much". You see, the chances of corruption would become lesser because the matter becomes too public. It is a very simple thing which is not done. Why can't we work through simple methods? I have suggested that instead of summoning the people, and their coming again and again, let the official go and sit in the village and call all the village people, announce publicly the Government's decision about compensation and say: "come along take it here and now". And where this is done immediately, the chances of somebody delaying it do not exist.

Unless some such methods are evolved, corruption will become serious. Of course, some may continue even with new methods, for its full elimination requires higher standards of integrity on the part of the people and other things. But we should make it more difficult for corruption to occur.

The biggest thing that leads to corruption is delay. The moment you give an officer a chance to delay matters, he can extort money in order to do something. Therefore, a method should be evolved which makes it impossible to delay. If there is no delay, there is no corruption. But we sit in rooms and form rules and regulations involving a great deal of delay. I do hope that the Director of this Institute will take in hand a study of panchayats. He may leave out municipalities and district boards for the time being. What is important is to start with the base, i.e., the panchayat, and examine what it can do and what methods it should adopt for its successful functioning.

I wonder if any or some of you have come across an address delivered by an Englishman, B. K. Blount, in October 1956 at Chatham House, London, on "Science as a Factor in International Relations". I think, it appeared in *International Affairs*.[3] It is a very interesting address and I would like to draw your attention to it in connection with the forthcoming discussions in your seminar on the question of training. I did not know this before, that a person who has gone in for purely technical studies is not allowed to enter the senior administrative services, for he is not cultured enough or an all-round educated person that a public administrator should be. In discussing other matters, I hope you will discuss this too.

Here, I am thrown back to the time when I was at school in England more than half a century ago. There used to be a great argument then in regard to the form and extent of introducing the subject of science in schools, i.e., as a

3. See *ante*, p. 270.

compulsory or as an optional subject. I suppose there have been some changes in the last 50 years; anyhow there is always this attempt, this pulling in two directions of what are called "cultural subjects" which presumably produce an integrated human being, and "technical and scientific subjects" which presumably produce a useful man. It may well be argued that too much stress on technology and other branches—specialist branches of physical sciences—has led to a certain lopsided growth of human beings in industrially and technically advanced countries. It has led to too great a power being placed in the hands of human beings without the corresponding moral capacity to use it rightly. But that is only one aspect of the problem. The other aspect, and an exceedingly important one, is that a country can only survive today if it has enough of scientific and technical personnel. There is no particular reason that the scientist should be an uncultured person; it may well be that the scientist is more cultured and more integrated than a person who has read, let us say, only literature.

I have already referred to Mr Blount's address. He brings out some points in a way which strikes your mind. Science itself is very old but scientific methods are about 150 years old. The application of the scientific methods, let us say, to industry, as everybody knows, makes a vast difference today. We all know of tremendous changes that science has brought in every field. And now we belong to the hydrogen bomb age, a tiny bit of mass converted into enormous energy which can be used for good or bad purposes. Blount humorously points out that if a country wants to progress it must have the capacity to get itself changed. Any country which is traditionally-minded in regard to various matters, including administration, is doomed in a rapidly changing world. Scientific methods help you, by collection of data, statistics and all kind of things, to assess the forces in action to control and watch them and to stop and remedy what is wrong. In fact, the scientific methods means planning. Planning is the scientific method; it is science in action. Planning has to be flexible, it has to be wide awake and alert. That applies not merely to industrial processes, it applies to administration as well. Administration has to adapt itself to the changing phases of society.

A second point which Mr Blount has stressed is that everything depends apparently on the number of technologists and engineers you have in the country. We cannot ignore it. Taking the big countries today, he adds, that by and large, it is now generally agreed that human beings given the same chance could produce the same results. And given the same chance, therefore, the bigger the countries and the more the population, the more the results. And that leads us to conclusion that China and India, being two countries with vast populations, are likely to forge ahead in technical and scientific fields. Their industrial productivity is naturally tremendously increasing. It seems all the more true of China. India is going in the right direction, but it has to struggle with traditionalism in the shape of some aspects of Hinduism, caste, etc. But, anyhow, India is going along the road. From the point of view of scientific technique, Western Europe appears to be somewhat at downgrade and the United States at the peak. The Soviet Union has, in the application, both in width and intensity, of their science and technology, gone ahead very fast and is likely to move faster still in the future.

The traditional concept of administration as something apart from the normal life of the community, is I think, completely out of date today. In fact, the administrator, who knows nothing of the other jobs, would not be a good administrator. In the highly complex society of today the integrating aspect of his role has become exceedingly important, and he must, therefore, keep himself fully informed not only of the developments in the social community he serves but also of those in the world at large. There are many problems but the general impression that I get of the world is an impression of disintegration, not of integration. It may be, of course, that this disintegrating process is connected with this transitional phase and out of this disintegration some bigger and deeper integration will come. Anyhow, we are all living in a disintegrating world, where standards have disappeared, moral values have been bidden goodbye, and people think more and more in terms of power over nature. It is obvious that all this technological and scientific progress in the world, unless it is balanced by some kind of moral standards and ethical values, is likely to lead to destruction. That is why we are so concerned over the basic question presented by atomic energy. Use it for evil, it will destroy the world; use it for good, it will raise the world to unknown standards of progress and happiness.

20. Popularizing Government Publications in Europe[1]

On returning from the annual meeting of the Indian Institute of Public Administration, I brought some of their publications with me, including their journal.[2] Shri A.C.N. Nambiar[3] saw this and was much interested. He said that this journal as well as the numerous other publications of the Government of

1. Note to Secretary General, Foreign Secretary, New Delhi, 6 April 1957. JN Collection.
2. *Indian Journal of Public Administration*.
3. India's Ambassador in the Federal Republic of Germany at this time.

India would interest many people in Europe if they could be made available to them. He suggested that we might make some arrangements for their sale through some recognized agency in various countries, such as, London, Paris, some centre in Germany, Berne or Geneva, etc. Perhaps, in some places some Indian might consider it worthwhile to open a bookshop and at the same time become agent for our publications. I told him this hardly appeared feasible. Of course, if there was such a bookshop, we would patronize it. Anyhow, some well known bookshop in these centres could be made our agent and it should be known throughout the country concerned that they were the agents for the Government of India publications.

Also, wherever we have a tourist office, they should receive all our publications for sale. At present they only get some publications for distribution to tourists.

I think that this idea is worth pursuing, not from the point of tourists but of serious students. A large number of publications are coming out either on behalf of the Government or by associated organizations. The Parliament Secretariat brings out some publications. The Parliamentary Reports themselves may be of interest to some people outside. There are various reports of committees and commissions as the Indian Institute of Public Administration and so on.

I suggest that this matter might be investigated and a beginning made. The I & B Ministry should be approached as well as others.

21. To Raj Bahadur[1]

New Delhi
9 April 1957

My dear Raj Bahadur,[2]

I enclose a copy of a letter which I have received from an English author of note.[3] Please read the last part of the letter, in which he refers to sending 150

1. JN Collection.
2. Union Minister of State for Communications.
3. In his letter of 4 April 1957 to Nehru, Dr Reginald Le May had written: "In June last I sent Dr Anand, at his request, 156 photographs of Buddhist objects to choose from for his numbers on South East Asia. Apparently, when they arrived he had to make a considerable deposit. Now, although he has posted them back in November last, they have not been received by me. On February 1st this year, Dr Anand informed me that the parcel had been held up in the Bombay P.O. because they had not yet refunded the deposit to Dr Anand."

photographs of Buddhist objects to choose from, to Dr Mulk Raj Anand of Bombay. They were required for the *Marg* periodical which is subsidized by the Government of India. These were held up to begin with and Mulk Raj was asked to deposit a big sum of money. Why, I do not know. However, he returned them, and now the Bombay Post Office has again held them up for the very odd reason that they (the Post Office) have not refunded the deposit to Mulk Raj. This really is very extraordinary. It does little credit to the Bombay Post Office or to our postal system. Will you please enquire about this matter and see that these things are sent back immediately to Mr Reginald Le May.

Yours sincerely,
Jawaharlal Nehru

22. Youth Delegations' Visits Abroad[1]

I agree that this matter and like matters should be dealt with by External Affairs, though the Education Ministry might well be concerned and have to be consulted. There is apparently a lack of clarity about these invitations, more especially those dealing with youth organizations. We should make the situation clear.

It is possible that the first reference by External Affairs Ministry on 15th November 1956 to the Ministry of Education, misled the latter. They were asked for their views, but they might have thought that they had to deal with it and they did so.

Anyhow, it should be made clear to them that these invitations from foreign countries raise a number of political questions which can only be decided by the Ministry of External Affairs and it is desirable, therefore, that this Ministry should deal with them, though they will do so, whenever necessary, in consultation with the Education Ministry.

If I had to deal with this matter, I would not have given it that importance and that wide extent which the Education Ministry has done by sending a circular letter to all Vice-Chancellors as well as Secretaries of youth organizations. Probably, they did so in a routine way without thinking of the consequences.

1. Note to Foreign Secretary, New Delhi, 13 April 1957. JN Collection.

But the consequences have to be faced by us now. The invitation was some kind of an ad hoc one, by some organization and we cannot raise it to the level of a major event in our contacts with the Soviet and address all Indian universities and the like in regard to it. It should be remembered that the Soviet youth delegation that came here, came rather casually and we did not like the manner of its coming. We decided ultimately to give it some kind of indirect help. In effect, nothing much happened except that they extended their invitation for an Indian youth delegation to go to the Soviet Union.

The Education Ministry have, by issuing their circular, made this a big affair. Also, I find that on the same date they issued another circular to the Vice-Chancellors and youth organizations for a delegation of Indian youth to go to China. I do not know how this second question has arisen.

It thus appears that the Education Ministry deal with this in some kind of a routine manner without considering the various implications and difficulties inherent in all such delegations. We cannot automatically accept them or organize them and, in any event, this can only be done by the External Affairs Ministry after full consideration of various aspects.

It is difficult to draw back on this now, as the matter has gone pretty far. External Affairs Ministry should, therefore, take charge of it and proceed in consultation with the Education Ministry wherever necessary.

This enquiry started because I sent a letter from Shri Hiralal Bose of the AICC to the External Affairs Ministry. I have not sent a reply to this yet. In the circumstances I see no objection to the Congress Youth Organization sending some people together with others. The question is, however, how many will be sent on the delegation. I do not like large and miscellaneous crowds going. The smaller the delegation, the better.

So far as the various youth organizations mentioned in Shri Azim Husain's[2] note are concerned, No. 5, that is, the All India Youth Federation, is definitely a communist organization, but in the circumstances we cannot leave it out.

I do not know what the financial aspect of this is, apart from the political aspect. We are trying to economize and as far as possible we should not encourage any delegations, unless they appear to be inescapable.

2. Joint Secretary, MEA, at this time.

23. Public Approach of Ministers[1]

I am addressing this note to my colleagues in the Government of India as I wish to share some thoughts with them and also to convey to them my concern at some developments that have taken place in the course of the past few years.

2. It seems to me that Ministers, both at the Centre and in the States, have gradually drifted in a certain direction which takes them away from the public, both practically and psychologically. In a democratic Government this factor of public contact and public approach is of great importance. Any barriers that come in the way are, therefore, harmful.

3. To some extent, it is inevitable that Ministers who are heavily occupied with their work have necessarily not much time or opportunity for, what I call, public contacts. Yet, I think, some measure of contact should be maintained so as to prevent that feeling of isolation and separateness which tends to grow up among people who function exclusively in offices. I do not mean to imply that our Ministers have isolated themselves, but there has been such a tendency and I should like this to be realized and checked.

4. There is the question of security, a topic that is painful to me because probably I suffer from this more than others. I realize the necessity for security precautions and I submit to them. Such security precautions have to be taken wherever necessary, not otherwise and not in excess of requirements. Even where they have to be taken, they should be unobtrusive and not obvious. I am not, however, discussing the aspect of security here, although that requires to be considered separately, so as to avoid unnecessary exhibitions which are irritating to all concerned and sometimes cause considerable inconvenience to the public.

5. What I should like to emphasize is that we should deliberately avoid the pomp and ceremony of office. We should function as normal citizens in our work and in our travels to the extent that this is possible. Unnecessary paraphernalia should be avoided. We have done away with a great deal of the unnecessary conventions of high office which existed in British times. Yet some remain, which can also be dispensed with.

6. In travelling, Ministers often have to do important work and even held conferences. They should have the facilities for doing this and, where necessary, a saloon might well be used. But unless this is necessary, it is better to avoid using a saloon. Also, it is not desirable to have any special arrangements for

1. Note to B.N. Datar, Union Minister of State for Home Affairs, New Delhi, 19 April 1957. File No. 2/4/57-SR (R), MHA.

security during travels, though some modest arrangements might be made, where considered necessary. There is no point in making this routine affairs. In particular, it is very embarrassing to all concerned and sometimes even rather irritating, for an armed policeman to march up and down in front of a carriage occupied by a Minister. The staff accompanying the Minister might also be kept down in terms of necessity.

7. One relic of British times is the red-coated *chaprassi*. The Central Secretariat abounds in them. I suppose nowhere else in the world are so many people employed in this way. When we came into office ten years ago or so, I was astonished to see the corridors full of them. They were good people and we did not wish to put an end to their employment. So, we kept them on, but we hoped that no additions would be made to them and gradually their numbers would decrease. But in spite of our directions, when new offices were opened, the old system continued to be followed. The number of *chaprassis* allotted to a Minister or an officer is supposed to denote the rank of that person. It is not clear to me on what logic this is based. Surely the only proper approach is that of necessity and not of rank or status. I think that the whole system of *chaprassis* carrying about files from one place to another is inherently bad. No doubt we require some messengers for this purpose. But they should be messengers attached to an office and not so much to an individual. I think also that it would be far more expeditious from the point of view of work that this system of perambulating files was greatly diminished. Many problems can be settled by quick conference with someone who is in an office a few yards away, instead of long noting on files, which are sent backwards and forwards. From the security point of view also, it is not desirable for secret papers to vender about in this way.

8. But I would refer in particular to these *chaprassis* accompanying Ministers. Where necessary, this should be done. Otherwise, this should be avoided. Certain old associations are connected with this business of red-coated *chaprassis* pursuing Ministers wherever they go, more for show than anything else.

9. We have certain rules about the display of National Flag on buildings and on automobiles. I think, these rules ought to be revised. Far too many people go about with Flags on their cars. The purpose of the Flag is essentially to enable quick movement in the streets so that a traffic policeman may not held up such a car. The Flag on an automobile is not meant to demonstrate the importance of the person inside the car. I do not think it is necessary for even Cabinet Ministers always to have that Flag. They can use it whenever considered necessary from the point of view of traffic convenience. I noticed that in Washington often when I travelled in a car with President Eisenhower, there was no flag at all. We might, therefore, in practice limit the use of the Flag, and we should revise the list of these who are entitled to the use of the Flag in their cars. I do not think it

is necessary to extend this so-called privilege to Deputy Ministers. This does not mean any attempt to lessen the dignity of a Deputy Minister. It is solely meant to avoid this psychology of pomp and show, which is not good from any point of view.

10. These are trivial instances that I have mentioned. But often it is the trivial instance that leaves an abiding impression on the mind of the public and gradually creates a wrong psychology. The main thing is that we should, while naturally preserving a certain dignity and decorum, avoid any showing off in anything that attracts attention.

11. I would suggest that even Governors should consider this matter and reduce some of the pomp and circumstance that is attached to their high office. I realize that there must be dignity and ceremonial about the Head of a State. But I notice a tendency to go too far or to continue certain conventions which may have been suitable to British times, but are not appropriate now.

24. To Lal Bahadur Shastri[1]

New Delhi
19 April 1957

My dear Lal Bahadur,[2]

I wrote to you about civil aviation today. I have since read some notes sent to me, at my request, by Shankar Prasada, Chairman of the IAC. There are two notes, one relating to the Viscount Project and the other to general aspects. There is also a covering note by my PPS. I enclose all these papers.

Obviously, I am not an expert and can express no opinion on the technical side. I recognize some of the difficulties pointed out by Shankar Prasada. But one thing troubles me greatly. It is stated in one of the notes that there is a serious pilot shortage. Because of this, standards have been lowered for Command training from a minimum of 3000 hours flying experience to 1500 hours. This results in lower standards of performance, neglect of training, low morale through fatigue etc. This also makes enforcement of discipline difficult as the Company

1. JN Collection.
2. Minister of Transport and Communications.

cannot afford to be too severe. It is also stated that nearly all the accidents which have occurred are attributable to pilot error.

Now, this is obviously a very serious comment and I do not see how we can take any risks in such a matter affecting lives of passengers and others. Surely, so long as this serious shortage of pilots exists, it is better to investigate some way of cutting down operations. We cannot expand at the expense of safety. To say that this is not possible is not a logical answer.

I know that if operations are cut down, they will result not only in loss but public criticism. At the same time I do not understand how we can carry on an airline by lowering standards of training and as a result, having lower standards of performance, low morale, fatigue, lack of discipline etc. I think this matter should be examined.

So far as the Viscount Project is concerned, you know that the Indian Air Force has been using Viscounts for over a year. They have flown me not only in India but have taken me all over Europe. It seems to me obviously desirable therefore that the advice of the IAF should be taken in regard to this Viscount Project. Indeed, I would say that the advice of the Indian Air Force should be taken in regard to other matters too and the difficulties that the Indian Airlines has to face.

Yours sincerely,
Jawaharlal Nehru

25. To Lal Bahadur Shastri[1]

New Delhi
19 April 1957

My dear Lal Bahadur,

I should like you particularly to look into the affairs of the Civil Aviation Department of your Ministry. I do not know what allocation of work you have

---

1. JN Collection.

made to your Ministers of State. You might, at least to begin with, ask Humayun Kabir[2] to go into this matter fully and report to you.

It is generally admitted that Civil Aviation is not functioning properly in India. There is no reason why it should not, because we have good material and our Air India International is certainly successful and well thought of. Personally, I think, the General Manager for Civil Aviation should always be a highly qualified technical man. At present you have a civilian officer, Jain. He might be good in his own way, but he obviously is not qualified technically. There is Shankar Prasada also who has plenty of push and energy. Again he is also not qualified. The result is that there is no technically qualified man at the top anywhere. There are, no doubt, various sections or departments which have engineers. But that does not appear to me to be good enough.

I was told that no technically qualified man of stature was available to take up the big job of General Manager. Even if that was so, we should have taken the trouble, in the last few years, to train up somebody so that after two or three years' training, he could take charge. We have apparently not done so. I do not know what persons might be available in India. But one thing I can do without much difficulty, that is, to get a competent man from our Air Force to be put in charge at least for the time being, say, for a year or two.

Some eight or nine months ago, International Civil Aviation sent us a Dutch expert, Weber. This man was good and he made numerous suggestions, but apparently nothing much came of these. He has now gone back a few days ago. He presented a long report to the Civil Aviation Department containing numerous suggestions. I have not seen this report, but I enquired about this some time ago from Civil Aviation. They said it was a very big report.

We have ordered some Viscount aircraft from England. I have enquired as to what steps are being taken to get people trained to use these aircraft. I am told that some people are being sent to England for the purpose. That is right, but I fear that enough time is not being given for training as well as other preparations for the use of these Viscounts which are highly delicate machines requiring special attention. I have a general feeling that the technical and training side is not properly attended to.

There are many other matters too about Civil Aviation which we have to consider. My present proposal to you is that Humayun Kabir should be asked to go into, Weber's report, the question of the Viscount aircraft coming here and the preparations made for it and other pending matters. He should then discuss

---

2. Minister of State for Civil Aviation at this time.

these with you and we may have a meeting to which we can invite Air Marshal Mukherjee[3] also.

Yours sincerely,
Jawaharlal Nehru

3. S. Mukherjee.

26. To Manu Subedar[1]

New Delhi
19 April 1957

Dear Manu Subedar,[2]

Thank you for your letter of 11th April.

I do not remember what exactly I wrote to you in 1953. But, I was sure then and, in spite of the experience of the recent elections, I am sure now that any proposal for the abolition of state autonomy is not feasible. I doubt if it is desirable from any long term point of view. In Indonesia, state autonomy was abolished about six years ago. They have never settled down since then, and trouble has continued. It is only in Communist States that there is a centralized administration. Even there, there is a constant pull towards decentralization, and both the Soviet and the Chinese Governments are being pushed in the direction of more powers for the states. In India, any attempt at having a unitary Centre would create an outcry, compared to which the trouble we had over the linguistic provinces agitation, would be petty indeed.

You must remember that there are limits beyond which a democratic government cannot go. Indeed, even an autocratic government has limits to its functioning.

1. JN Collection.
2. Economist, associated with Lotus Trust.

You suggest an indirect approach to this problem by a codification of all State laws. I am afraid that too is not feasible, though we may gradually approach some kind of uniformity.

Yours sincerely,
Jawaharlal Nehru

27. To K.C. Reddy[1]

New Delhi
22 April 1957

My dear Reddy,[2]

Owing to some changes among the Ministers and the possibility also of some further Deputy Ministers being appointed, your Ministry will have to consider the problem of giving houses. I do not think it is necessary for the junior Ministers to be given biggish houses. In fact, they might well stay on where they have been staying, unless for family reasons they require more accommodation.

What I mean to suggest is that it should not be considered an automatic rule that every Minister should be given a biggish house. We should proceed more on the lines of necessity than of status in this matter. As a matter of fact, it is often a nuisance to have a big house as it requires a larger staff for its upkeep and more expense. If people get accustomed to large houses, then they are much inconvenienced later when they may have to do without it.

Yours sincerely,
Jawaharlal Nehru

1. File No. 45(7)/57-PMS. Also available in JN Collection.
2. Minister of Works, Housing and Supply.

28. To Govind Ballabh Pant[1]

New Delhi
22 April 1957

My dear Pantji,

Thank you for your letter of the 22nd April[2] regarding the circular letter I sent on the 19th April[3] to Ministers.

In the course of this letter, you suggest that Ministers might surrender rupees one thousand a month out of their salaries and that existing scales of T.A. etc. might also be revised.

I agree with you about the latter proposal, that is, about T.A. being revised so as only the expenses actually incurred may be met by the State. As for the Ministers surrendering one thousand rupees, I presume you are referring to Cabinet Ministers. Cabinet Ministers get a salary now which works out, after the income tax deduction, at about, I think, Rs. 1,700/. I do not think this is by any means excessive, in spite of what some people might say, and, therefore, I do not quite see how a substantial reduction can be made in it. It may be possible to reduce it by some percentage, as we did once, say, ten per cent, which should amount to about Rs 250/- or so.

But, really it is not the salary that means much, but the very considerable overhead expenses. I think, we should be much stricter about these. I found that much money has been spent in Ministers' houses, both on considerable additional construction and in furnishing and in expensive equipment. The gardens cost a great deal in upkeep. Probably, it will be better to have more convenient houses built, but I imagine this is no time to do so.

It is really the extras that amount to a considerable figure. If we could come to grips with these extras, it might make a difference.

I mentioned something about flying a Flag on cars. I think, the best course would be for Ministers to be advised not to fly the Flag at all except on ceremonial and special occasions. I am trying to follow this now.

Probably, one of our most expensive items of all is the security arrangement

---

1. JN Collection.
2. G.B. Pant wrote about revision of rules concerning Ministers' salaries and allowances: "I welcome the proposals contained therein. They are appropriate and timely. Some of them call for a revision of the present rules and orders, and I am asking the Home Ministry to do the needful."
3. See *ante*, pp. 309-311.

for Ministers. I think, this could well be reduced and, at the same time, made much less obvious. In particular, I think, it is almost improper for lavish display of security.

Yours affectionately,
Jawaharlal Nehru

29. To Govind Ballabh Pant[1]

Flagstaff House
Chakrata
26 April 1957

My dear Pantji,

I came here yesterday. I found that some extensive arrangements had been made, presumably for security reasons, for my journey here as well as my stay. This house, where I am staying, is surrounded by a large number of policemen who have camps in the compound. In addition, there is a military guard. I gather that this was an act of courtesy of the Army.

On enquiry here I was told that about one thousand policemen of various kinds—armed police, civil police and plain clothesmen—had been deployed for my visit to Chakrata, Dehra Dun and Mussoorie for five days. Most of these persons had been placed along the long motor route from Saharanpur to Chakrata and probably beyond to Dehra Dun etc. Apparently, every culvert is so guarded apart from villages en route and sharp corners in the hills. Here in Chakrata, which is a military station with a very small civil population, there are large numbers of policemen in uniform and in plain clothes about.

Apart from other aspects of this super abundant security arrangements, the cost alone must be very high. I gather many have been brought from Meerut and some from other places.

I have come to Chakrata on a private visit with no functions. The only function I am attending is the Development Commissioners' Conference in Mussoorie.[2]

---

1. JN Collection.
2. For Nehru's speech at the Development Commissioners' Conference, see *ante*, pp. 195-199.

If even for a private visit intended for quiet and rest, all these extensive arrangements have to be made, then I wonder what would happen if there were public functions also. This is a remote corner of India where there is no possibility of large crowds even gathering.

The question arises as to what I should do in the future. I am becoming too great a burden on public money. You know how painful it is to me to have to put up with this enormous apparatus of security. I have never objected to security arrangements, but surely there is a limit to them, and there is a very important public aspect, apart from the private one. I have travelled much in various parts of the world as Prime Minister and every Government is concerned about security. So far as I am concerned, I have never seen anything like this elsewhere, certainly not for me. In London, I have a plain clothesman accompanying me when I go in a car, and I think, an extra policeman is put in front of our Embassy where I stay. I do not think any other arrangement is made. So also in most other places. It comes then that in my own country I have to face these masses of policemen wherever I go and whenever I travel. There is the cost of this, and there is the drawing away of these large numbers of policemen from their normal duties just for my sake.

If I have to face all this when I travel or go anywhere in India, then it is to be considered whether I should travel at all, publicly or even privately. Indeed, the choice appears to be either that I should give up all touring or give up the Prime Ministership. Something surely has to be done about this.

Yours affectionately,
Jawaharlal Nehru

I. BIHAR

1. To U.N. Dhebar[1]

New Delhi
8 April 1957

My dear Dhebar Bhai,

I sent you two days ago the papers[2] containing various charges against Jagjivan Ram. He came to see me yesterday afternoon. He denied all these charges vigorously and said that he was placed in a most embarrassing position because he did not know how to deal with these allegations. So far as withdrawal of his rival candidate was concerned, he said that he withdrew because a number of Harijan Panchayats called upon him to withdraw. I told him it was no good that such charges should be made and no clear denial should issue. He said that he would deal with them in public speeches he is supposed to deliver in Bihar soon.

Meanwhile, I have received more letters on this subject. As far as I can see, they repeat the same charges. In the context of Bihar politics today, it is difficult and indeed hardly possible to trust the impartiality of any person there. Indeed, in such matters even the bona fides of anyone are doubtful. It may thus be that all these charges have no foundation. Anyhow, I just do not know how to deal with them.

I am sending you the further papers I have received on this subject.

Yours sincerely,
Jawaharlal Nehru

1. JN Collection.
2. Some Congressmen from Bihar had written a letter to Nehru on 20 March 1957, drawing his attention towards the facts that, "Shri Jagjivan Ram, Railway Minister, during this election was opposed by a PSP Scheduled Caste candidate (Shri Chhathu Dusadh) whom he called to Delhi to his bungalow along with PSP candidate for the general seat (constituency Sasaram Bhabhua), Shri Shiv Pujan Singh. They stayed with Shri Jagjivan Ram...and entered into an unholy conspiracy against the Congress Party." They planned that Chhathu should withdraw and allow Jagjivan Ram to get elected unopposed. For this, a high job to the son of Chhathu had been promised. Shiv Pujan Singh suggested that "Shri Jagjivan Ram should pay Rs. 50,000/- out of which Rs. 10,000/- should be given to Shiv Pujan Singh to fight election against the Congress candidate Shri Ram Subhag Singh."

II. BOMBAY

1. To Sri Prakasa[1]

New Delhi
25 March 1957

My dear Prakasa,

Yesterday, at the meeting of our Working Committee, we discussed the elections and the lessons to be learnt from them. All the members spoke, giving their own impressions. I spoke also, and laid great stress on the significance of what had happened in Maharashtra and parts of Gujarat.[2] I dealt with many aspects of this. In the main, I said that it was not much good our blaming others, but we should see wherein we had erred ourselves. It seemed to me that it was not the bilingual State issue that had excited people so much, but rather the firings and the deaths and also the lack of any expression of regret and sympathy.

Today, Chavan came to see me, and I had a fairly good and frank talk with him. I told him that, obviously, the Samyukta Maharashtra Samiti[3] people will keep the pot boiling, as that was the only way for them to hold together. They will bring up all kinds of questions in relation to it and certainly a demand for an enquiry. What should our attitude be?

It was clear we cannot go back on the bilingual State. I also felt that an enquiry at this stage was neither feasible nor desirable, although I am firmly of opinion personally that firing should be banned except on the most serious occasions. Further, that there should be an automatic rule for an enquiry if any firing takes place. However, at this stage, to have an enquiry seemed to me wrong.

I mentioned to Chavan that one of the major difficulties we had to face was the strong feeling of a lack of sympathy. The Bombay Government apparently

1. JN Collection.
2. See *ante*, pp. 114-118.
3. The Samyukta Maharashtra Samiti was formed in January 1956 by Congressmen, Praja Socialists and Communists to oppose jointly the Central Government's decision to implement the recommendations of the States Reorganization Commission to divide the Bombay State into a bilingual Bombay and a separate Vidarbha State.

lacked the human touch and this hurt people even more than any actual occurrence. It was not much good going on blaming the people, including little boys and girls. This only irritated them further. My fear was that this anger and bitterness would sink deep down and it would be even more difficult to deal with it later, unless something was done.

I told Chavan that the approach to all these questions must be full of sympathy and there should be no hesitation in expressing regret. Further, that the matter should be approached from the human point of view, and an attempt should be made to soothe people. This will not solve any question, but it will tone down the bitterness.

Therefore, my advice to him was, first, to deal with these opposition members in a generally friendly manner, and second, when occasion arose, to say that he and his colleagues were naturally very unhappy at those incidents involving firing in Bombay, Ahmedabad, etc. Firing was always bad and should be avoided, except when there was absolutely no other alternative. It was particularly painful for them that young boys should have been inadvertently shot down, and their sympathy went out to their parents and relatives. He accepted the general principle that where such firing took place, an enquiry was desirable. But, to have an enquiry after a long period now, would be most unwise and would not help at all in our trying to develop normality and remove the bitterness in people's minds. We had very difficult tasks ahead and the economic situation was none too easy, nor was the international situation. At this moment, to dig up again all the old unfortunate incidents could only do harm to the national cause, and so on, etc.

I told him also that you had written to me, and that you felt rather isolated there.[4] Apparently, the Bombay Government had got used to the British Governors and, subsequently, Maharaj Singh and Girja Bajpai, both of whom were good men, but rather alien to Congressmen. In their time, this practice of keeping aloof must have developed, but this was completely wrong now, and the present Governor was one of our own old and senior colleagues. He could be of great help in many ways, and more especially in soothing people. He should, therefore, be encouraged to do this by meeting people of all kinds.

This is in brief what I said to him. He generally agreed with what I said. Possibly, he will speak to you about this on his return.

Yours affectionately,
Jawaharlal Nehru

4. In his letter of 21 March 1957, Sri Prakasa informed Nehru that in Bombay "the Governor is left more or less high and dry on his pedestal, and he has very little contact with his Ministers." He added that, "I feel that I cannot carry on here, you will perhaps agree to relieve me."

2. To Y.B. Chavan[1]

New Delhi
3 April 1957

My dear Chavan,[2]

You mentioned, I think, that in the course of the election, the American Consul[3] at Bombay paid you a visit in Poona to discuss the elections. Probably also he visited other persons including Leaders of the Opposition Parties. I shall be glad if you will let me have some particulars about the activities of the American Consul or indeed of any other foreign Consuls in regard to the elections.

Yours sincerely,
Jawaharlal Nehru

1. JN Collection.
2. (1913-84); Member, Bombay Legislative Assembly and later Maharashtra Legislative Assembly, 1946-62; Minister in the Government of Bombay, 1952-56; Chief Minister, Bombay State, 1956-60 and of Maharashtra, 1960-62; Union Minister for Defence, 1962-66, Home Affairs, 1966-70, Finance, 1970-74 and External Affairs, 1974-77; Deputy Prime Minister and Minister for Home Affairs, 1979-80.
3. William T. Turner.

3. To Govind Ballabh Pant[1]

New Delhi
4 April 1957

My dear Pantji,

Parulekar,[2] the Editor of the *Sakal*[3] of Poona, came to see me today. He discussed the general situation in Maharashtra and especially the elections. I suppose you know Parulekar. His paper commands considerable respect and he has built it up entirely himself. Throughout this tremendous agitation, he stood for a bilingual State.

1. JN Collection. Also available in AICC Papers, NMML.
2. N.B. Parulekar.
3. A Marathi daily.

He told me that what has happened in Maharashtra, and possibly elsewhere, should not be judged as if it was some sudden occurrence. Even the linguistic agitation was only a part of the situation. Gradually, during the past years, Maharashtra was drifting away from the Congress. Ultimately, the position was that it was "fed up" with the Congress for a variety of reasons. The chief of these apparently was the discontent of the so-called educated classes and the young men coming out of colleges and not finding employment. In this frame of mind, they voted for anybody who opposed the Congress.

Parulekar said that the greatest harm to the Congress during the past twenty-five years had been done by Gadgil,[4] Shankarrao Deo[5] and Jedhe.[6]

He said that it was astonishing how the Samiti, and that means chiefly the Communists, spent money in the elections in Maharashtra. According to him, they must have spent about Rs 1 crore in Maharashtra alone. They had vast numbers of vehicles, of posters, literature, etc. The Communist newspaper continues running at a great loss monthly. Parulekar wanted some enquiry made about these large funds.

He further suggested that the RSS organization had not only played a great mischief, but had percolated into all kinds of important places in the lower administration.

He wanted an enquiry into the Maharashtra elections, an enquiry not conducted by local Maharashtrians, but by outsiders.

Yours affectionately,
Jawaharlal Nehru

4. N.V. Gadgil, former Union Minister.
5. Congressman from Maharashtra and a Sarvodaya leader.
6. K.M. Jedhe, Member, Lok Sabha.

4. Protection of Strategic Areas[1]

I agree with your note.[2] But what is Dr Bhabha to do?[3] I suppose he cannot do much without the active cooperation of the Bombay Government. Anyhow, so far as he is concerned, we should take steps to prevent any further shrines and the like appearing.

2. So far as the beacon is concerned, the simplest thing would be for Dr Bhabha himself to have a beacon put there. I do not know who is responsible for the beacon.[4]

3. I suggest that you might write to the Chief Secretary of the Bombay Government on these two subjects.

1. Note to N.R. Pillai, Secretary General, New Delhi, 9 April 1957. File No. 57/68/57-Poll (1), MHA.
2. In his note of 9 April 1957, N.R. Pillai wrote about conversion of tombs into places of worship in Trombay: " I saw some of these shrines myself and agree with Dr Bhabha that we should take immediate steps to stop this mushroom growth of places of worship."
3. H.J. Bhabha, Secretary, Department of Atomic Energy, wrote to A.V. Pai, Secretary, Ministry of Home Affairs, on 6 April that during his visits to the Atomic Energy Establishment, Trombay, he was struck by the "rate at which tombs, or alleged tombs are being converted into places of worship in the entire area." He added: "As you know, the Trombay area has become a very strategic area for the country.... I suggest for your consideration, that some urgent action is necessary to protect the entire area, and ensure that no further so-called places of religious worship are allowed to be established in the area."
4. Bhabha also mentioned about a beacon on top of Trombay hill which was smashed by an alleged lunatic. He wrote that though the airlines had been informed about it, no risk could be taken.

III. DELHI

1. To T.T. Krishnamachari[1]

New Delhi
24 March 1957

My dear T.T.,

The recent violent hail-storm[2] in and around Delhi has done great damage in a large number of villages and ruined the bumper crop that we were expecting. This is most unfortunate. A rapid survey made by the Bharat Sevak Samaj together with some Revenue Official, disclosed a pitiful state of affairs. They sent me a report of this saying that thirty-one villages had suffered hundred per cent damage and another nineteen partial damage. I had these papers sent to the Chief Commissioner of Delhi[3] to find out what he proposed to do. His answer is not very helpful. I wrote to Ajit Prasad about making some arrangements to have cheap grain shops.[4] I do not know what he is doing.

As the need for immediate relief apparently is urgent, I am sending a cheque for Rs 15,000/- from the Prime Minister's Relief Fund to the Bharat Sevak Samaj. This will not go far of course, but something has to be done soon.

I should like your advice as to what we can do in this matter.

I am sending you the various papers in this connection, including a note from my PPS.

Yours sincerely,
Jawaharlal Nehru

---

1. JN Collection.
2. In early March 1957, Delhi and the neighbouring areas had been hit by a heavy hail-storm.
3. A.D. Pandit.
4. Nehru wrote to Ajit Prasad Jain, Minister of Food and Agriculture, on 23 March that he came to know that the people had neither foodgrains nor money to buy food and suggested that, "relief work and cheap grain shops should be opened."

2. Cruelty towards Monkeys[1]

You might briefly reply to this letter and say that an inquiry is being made into this matter.

2. I have read about these monkeys being thrown out near Purana Qila and dying in considerable numbers. The newspaper accounts say that someone brought them in a couple of trucks and left them there. Apparently, we have not found out who this person is. Also, it is stated that even if this person is found out, nothing much can be done to him except perhaps some small fine for cruelty to animals.

3. I am not, for the present, interested in the punishment to be given to such a person. But surely it is up to the Delhi Administration or the police to find out specifically who is guilty of this inhuman act. Is this done by any of the firms exporting monkeys? How we shall deal with them is another matter. This bringing in of the law every time irritates me. A Government can deal with a person in many ways apart from prosecuting him. Even a condemnation by public opinion is a deterrent.

4. Please, therefore, ask the Delhi Government to let me know who is responsible for this. They should take every step to find out.

1. Note to Principal Private Secretary, New Delhi, 30 March 1957. JN Collection.

3. Unauthorized Settlements[1]

I should like to have a meeting of the Slum Committee[2] in the course of the next two or, possibly, three weeks. Apart from trying to find out what has been done and what obstructions have come in their way, I am rather worried about three matters. One is that people continue to come from outside and put up shacks

1. Note to Principal Private Secretary, New Delhi, 5 April 1957. JN Collection.
2. See also *Selected Works* (second series), Vol. 32, pp. 163-65.

without any authority. Then, later, when asked to move, they demand alternative sites. Therefore, it is necessary to prevent the initial settling down of these unauthorized people. I gather that this is taking place still on a considerable scale, more especially on the Rajghat side.

2. Secondly, some slum owners are ejecting people on the plea that they want those houses for themselves.

3. Thirdly, the construction workers engaged in building operations are still living in the most unhealthy conditions in temporary huts. We discussed this matter previously and I gathered that some steps were going to be taken by WH&S or other authorities. These people have not got any proper sanitation, latrines, water supply etc. These amenities are not supplied to them because of the fear that if this is done these people will become permanent residents of those places which is undesirable. This is perfectly true. But something has to be done, preferably removing them to some place where they can later remain.

4. I should like the authorities concerned to look into these three matters as well as the general question of slum clearance and send me brief concise notes. I do not want long detailed notes. A note should not normally exceed two or three pages and it should deal with these points.

5. Then there is the question of the Master Plan for Delhi. I met some of these planners yesterday and they told me they were working out in great detail and this would take time. I told them that while this detailed working out was ultimately desirable, what was immediately necessary was that we should finalize the broad features of the Plan, so that we may know exactly what to do with each area of the city. This would help us in considering the problem of the clearance of slums and resettlement. In a sense, we agreed with the broad Plan with greater detail which they had produced. But we said at the same time that they should examine it afresh, consider the objections raised and suggestions made and then get this finally sanctioned by us. In particular, I have mentioned that Mr Mayer[3] of the USA had made certain definite proposals which should be considered. I gather that Mr Mayer is coming here within a few days' time. I want, therefore, our Delhi Planning authority to look into this matter in a broad way, apart from details, consult Mr Mayer and others and then put this up before us for final sanction. This will enable us to go ahead both with the slum clearance and other schemes within the ambit of that broad Plan.

3. Albert Mayer, architect and town planner.

4. To Abul Kalam Azad[1]

New Delhi
5 April 1957

My dear Maulana,

I enclose a copy of a letter from Rajkumari Amrit Kaur.[2] This relates to the clearance of the slum area around Jama Masjid, Cabinet decided to proceed with this immediately. I had myself visited this area and discussed it with many people there, including the shopkeepers, and most people agreed. Indeed, there is no help for it if we want to clear up this badly infested area which spoils the Jama Masjid approach and has become a terrible slum.

Yours affectionately,
Jawaharlal Nehru

1. JN Collection.
2. In her letter of 4 April 1957, Amrit Kaur informed Nehru that the Cabinet had decided on 2 September 1956 that, "the slum area around Jama Masjid should be cleared and the matter taken in hand on a 'priority basis'.... It has, however, not been possible to make any progress in the matter as I am informed that Maulana Sahib gave instructions at a meeting held by him on the 9th February 1957 that the question of shifting of the shops should be held over until after the election."

5. Uprooting Farmers Not Desirable[1]

These people from roundabout Delhi came to see me this morning and gave me the attached representation. I believe, their lands are somewhere between New Delhi and Palam. To some extent, it is perhaps inevitable that Delhi should expand that way. At the same time, I do not like the idea of a large number of people who have lived in those villages for almost ages past to be ejected and

1. Note to Principal Private Secretary, New Delhi, 21 April 1957. JN Collection.

330

made to fend for themselves. These people are good farmers. Also, in view of our food production programme, taking over of good cultivable land for housing expansion should be avoided as far as possible. There is, I believe, a good deal of stony land too in that direction which is not suitable for cultivation.

2. In schemes of expansion, it is not necessary or desirable to proceed in some logical way and take any land roundabout that adjoins the locality which is inhabited. In fact, it would be far better and healthier for tracts to be left open. Even in cities big parks are left open. Why should not most of these villagers be left with their lands and expansion to take place on the uncultivated land?

3. In recent years, these people had built a large number of wells and it gave them prosperity somewhat. They had a community life. All these factors are important and should be taken into consideration.

4. I do not know who is sponsoring this housing scheme, whether this is being done by some private organization or by the Government. In any event, I should like you to refer this matter to the Chief Commissioner and enquire from him what the proposal is and pointing out what I have said above. We should not sacrifice our farmer population roundabout merely to suit some exigencies of Delhi, unless there is absolutely no other way out. I suppose that compensation is provided for. But apart from compensation, where will these people go? It means uprooting them from places where they have lived for generations.

6. To Albert Mayer[1]

New Delhi
22 April 1957

Dear Mr Albert Mayer,
Thank you for your letter of the 22nd April.[2]

I quite understand that the working out of a Regional Plan for Delhi is a complex undertaking and will take time. I should not like to hurry things in any

---

1. File No. 28 (7)/56-65-PMS.
2. Albert Mayer informed Nehru that he had been closely working with the Health Ministry's Delhi Town Planning Organization, both directly on their work and to prepare the ground for the group of specialists who would be coming over later to assist and advise planners and specialists. He also pointed out that, "it must be borne in mind that working out a Regional Plan is a complex undertaking which has little genuine precedent anywhere, and particularly so in the case of a newly emerging and developing country. It will take time."

way, though naturally I would like this done as soon as possible. When I said that broad features of the Plan might be finalized soon, I had in view a number of things that are held up at present. It is difficult, in a big city, to put a stop to many activities. I do not want any of these activities to come in the way later, of the Plan we approve of. If we could, therefore, have some idea, as soon as feasible, about some broad features, if not all, of the Plan, it would help.

I did not know you were in Delhi. Otherwise, I would have asked you to come and see me. I am going away from Delhi for a few days.[3] I hope to see you early in May.

Yours sincerely,
Jawaharlal Nehru

3. Nehru visited Chakrata, Dehradun and Mussoorie from 25 to 29 April 1957.

7. To K.C. Reddy[1]

New Delhi
23 April 1957

My dear Reddy,

I have been in correspondence with your Ministry or rather with Swaran Singh[2] about the allotment of land in New Delhi to the Government Servants' Cooperative House Building Society. The last letter that Swaran Singh wrote to me on this subject was on April 6. In this letter, he mentioned that his Ministry had taken a firm decision to acquire nearly 1,100 acres of land adjoining the Ring Road.

He then refers to a proposal for the Health Ministry to acquire 3,000 acres of land for development purposes. It is presumably this that affects the Cooperative Society.

1. JN Collection.
2. Reddy took over the Union Ministry of Works, Housing and Supply from Swaran Singh on 17 April 1957.

Swaran Singh goes on to say in his letter that he would like to help those officers and non-officials who had no house of their own in Delhi and no other plot of land for residential purposes. He adds that cooperative societies as such could not be given any preference, as some of their members had houses of their own in Delhi or other plots of land on which they could build.

I agree with the broad approach of Swaran Singh in this matter, though I do not quite understand the conclusion he has arrived at. This question was raised by me in a letter I wrote to Swaran Singh some time previously when I learnt that profiteering in land by some Government employees as well as others was going on. Naturally, I objected to this. It was not my intention to stop bona fide procedures for Government employees to get small areas for building houses. Delhi is becoming almost an impossible place for people to live in unless they are very rich or unless they get some governmental assistance.

Some time back, that is in December 1950 and in November 1951, there were two Cabinet decisions on this subject and cooperative building societies of Government servants were encouraged. While I agree with Swaran Singh's broad policy as laid down in his letter to me, I do not understand why he prefers individual deals to dealing with a well-organized cooperative society. The reason he gives for this is a good one but not applicable. Thus, he says that cooperative societies as such should not be given preference as some of their members had houses of their own in Delhi etc. Of course, we must not give preference to any individual who has a house or a plot of land. That should be made perfectly clear. But subject to this proviso, I think that it is more desirable to deal with a cooperative society which is bona fide than with individuals where there would be difficulty to enquire always into the bona fide transactions.

Thus, I think that the principle we had approved of in Cabinet in December 1950, and in November 1951, should be adhered to and we should accept these Government employees cooperative societies as bona fide institutions for this purpose and deal with them. Care should, however, be taken that there is no profiteering, that the plots given are small and that the person asking for a plot has no other house or land in Delhi.

Yours sincerely,
Jawaharlal Nehru

IV. KERALA

1. To A.K. Gopalan[1]

New Delhi
11 March 1957

Dear Gopalan,

I have today received your letter of the 7th March.[2]

I see that a copy of this letter has been sent to the Chief Election Commissioner. I take it that it is really meant for him and not so much for me. You have made very serious charges against some Congressmen in your constituency as well as apparently in some other constituencies.[3] I can hardly believe that these charges are based on adequate information and proof. In any event, you have referred this matter to the Election Commissioner and it is for him to find out.

So far as I am concerned, I have always laid stress in public and in private on fair and impartial elections, and I would deprecate any malpractice, whoever commits it.

Yours sincerely,
Jawaharlal Nehru

1. JN Collection. Also available in AICC Papers, NMML.
2. A.K. Gopalan, CPI leader from Kerala, wrote: "I am pained to see that neither the authorities responsible for conducting the elections in a fair and free manner nor the Congress which as the ruling party has a special duty to maintain a high standard, are consciously observing even the rules and regulations of the People's Representation Act." He also complained that, "though polling was over in my constituency, in spite of the specific instructions of the Election Commission that counting should start as soon as physically possible. Counting in my constituency has been deliberately postponed by a week to 7th March."
3. Gopalan had pointed out that, "Congressmen all over the State are carrying on propaganda that I was defeated. If they are so sure of my defeat, why was not the counting done early enough?" He further complained that, "I have seen with my own eyes Congressmen transporting voters in hired lorries, cars and other vehicles. This was done in a widespread and organized manner in my constituency; this being done in other constituencies also."

2. To E.M.S. Namboodiripad[1]

New Delhi
17 April 1957

Dear Namboodiripad,[2]
Thank you for your letter of the 15th April.[3] I have been thinking of writing to you myself, but owing to heavy pressure of work, I have been unable to do so. I am feeling rather tired and stale and in about a week's time I am going away to the mountains for some rest for four or five days. I shall be back in Delhi before the end of the month.

2. I am writing to you rather briefly now. I shall be glad to have a talk with you when you come here.

3. In regard to the two specific matters that you have dealt with in your letter, there should be no difficulty. My purpose in suggesting that the Chief Minister himself should be in charge of the portfolio of Community Development was to lay stress on the importance of this work.[4] Also because, as you yourself realize, the work of development concerns almost every department and it was considered, therefore, desirable that the Chief Minister should be in charge and should coordinate all these activities. Further, the fact that the Chief Minister is in charge would necessarily lead our officers and others to think that it is of first importance. But, in view of what you say, there is no objection to your giving the portfolio of Community Development to one of your colleagues and for you to keep yourself intimately in touch with it.

4. So far as the suggestion made by the Deputy Chairman, Planning Commission[5] is concerned, that is, a State Development Committee of Ministers should be constituted, I have personally no objection to the whole Cabinet

---

1. JN Collection.
2. Chief Minister of Kerala.
3. In his letter, Namboodiripad stated: "I and my colleagues should do our utmost to establish such relationship with the Central Government as are not only correct constitutionally, but relations of sincere cooperation." He added: "I hope you will realize that certain attitude on the part of some important Congress leaders do not help the establishment of such relations of cooperation."
4. Namboodiripad informed Nehru that, "it will be too much for me to take anything more than General Administration, Law and Order, and Planning. It has, therefore, been decided to separate Community Development from Planning and to give the portfolio of Community Development to one of my colleagues."
5. V.T. Krishnamachari.

discharging the functions of the State Development Committee. It might have been better for a smaller body consisting of some members of your Cabinet to form this Committee. Of course, the matters would be discussed by your Cabinet as a whole whenever they feel like it. But, as far as I can make out, there need be no objection to your suggestion being followed.

5. Your third point is about the constitution of State and District Committees for purposes of rendering relief in cases of emergency. I do not quite know the background of this proposal which presumably must have been made by the Home Ministry. I imagine that ad hoc committees would be formed when necessary, but it would probably be desirable to have some continuing committee also.

6. You have made some general observations in your letter. These raise certain important considerations, as you yourself realize. Naturally, it is the Central Government's wish, as it must be yours, to see that the Governmental work in Kerala State functions smoothly and effectively and to the advantage of the people of Kerala. This can only be done successfully if there is genuine cooperation between the Central and State Governments. So far as the Central Government is concerned, they will gladly cooperate. This is not a matter concerning me personally, though, of course, I am interested in it. In some way or other, most of our Central Ministries have to deal with specific subjects concerning the States. More particularly, the Home Ministry deals with them. I am sure that all my colleagues would like to have this cooperation between the Central and the State Governments. This cooperation necessarily is a two-sided affair.

7. You refer to some action taken by the Home Ministry through the Governor. I do not know to what exactly you refer. I have seen references to three matters. One of these was the nomination by the Governor of an Anglo-Indian. The Governor has already explained the circumstances and I think that he acted correctly and without any trace of partiality in this matter. He had to nominate somebody at that time. In regard to nominations of Anglo-Indians, we have been guided by the one major organization of Anglo-Indians in India, the Anglo-Indian Association, or whatever the name is. These people, as a group, do not belong to any political party. Certainly, they do not belong to the Congress. You may perhaps know that the Anglo-Indian Association's recommendation was not approved of by certain Congress circles. The nomination, therefore, was in the ordinary course following the practice thus far followed and was in no sense a partial or party nomination.

8. You took exception also to the Governor sending for some Independent Members who had promised to join your Party. I really do not see what there was to object in this. It is a small matter and if the Governor felt that this was

desirable, it was entirely in his discretion to do so. He could then take action with a certain assurance. This had nothing to do with the Home Ministry.

9. The third matter, I suppose, related to the amnesty and release of prisoners.[6] I am not concerned with the legal or constitutional aspects of this matter, but rather the propriety of the method adopted and the action taken. Normally, the proper course is for such matters to be referred to the Central Government because any such action naturally affects other states, apart from its intrinsic nature. For a Party to release what are called political prisoners as a consequence of victory in an election, raises rather special issues, more especially when the prisoners concerned have been considered guilty by Courts of heinous crimes. There was also the question of a certain courtesy due to the President as well as the Supreme Court. When the Supreme Court had come to certain decisions and the President had separately also come to a certain decision after full consideration, it seemed to me very unbecoming to ignore all this and announce an amnesty covering even such cases. The question also arises as to what is a political offence. Is cold-blooded murder a political offence? Would it be a political offence if a communal organization, say the Hindu Mahasabha or the RSS, or the Jana Sangh, committed murders in the name of cow protection? Whatever rule is applied must be uniform.

10. Personally I am not in favour of the death penalty. But so long as that is there, some criterion has to be observed.

11. I think, it was mentioned somewhere that T. Prakasam, when he became Chief Minister of Andhra,[7] had a general jail delivery. That is true, although the cases covered there were of a different type and, so far as I remember, the question of so-called political prisoners did not arise. Even so, we took strong exception to this and informed both the Chief Minister and the Governor there of our views. Apart from the particular merits or demerits of a case, it is the procedure adopted that, I think, was very undesirable. We have to build up certain conventions. If every party adopts a new practice, then there is no convention and no uniformity and the procedure is rather anarchical. This cannot be good from the public point of view, even apart from the Government. Everyone will try to justify his own misdeed by giving it some political colour.

6. On 5 April 1957, following his election as leader of the Communist Legislature Party in Kerala, Namboodiripad announced that all political prisoners would be granted amnesty.
7. 1953-54.

12. I found in recent elections in some states that some notorious gangsters and goondas of no political complexion, allied themselves with some political parties just to get their protection and under that cover to indulge in all kinds of misdeeds.

13. You refer to certain attitudes on the part of some important Congress leaders. I do not exactly know to what you refer. I believe some statements were made. But I should like you to take into consideration the spate of statements and declarations that have been made by members of your Government as well as other leaders of the Communist Party in India in regard to the Kerala elections and the formation of your Government there. I confess that I have read them with some distress. They did not exhibit much sense of responsibility. Also, even while stating that there would be cooperation and adherence to the Constitution, hints were thrown out that if this did not succeed, other and violent courses might have to be followed. Veiled threats of this kind do not produce an atmosphere of cooperation.

14. The real difficulty, as you will no doubt realize, is that there is a good deal of suspicion on both sides. Quite apart from economic or other policies, the Communist Party in India has been closely associated with violent and like courses and has often declared in the past that they are out to break our Constitution. This is a challenge to the democratic process as well as peaceful methods, quite apart from the policies to be pursued. I shall not mention here the other grounds which give rise to a measure of suspicion and apprehension. It is this background atmosphere which comes in the way. I hope that it will improve and that your Government will not only in its declarations but in its policy, help to dissipate these apprehensions and thus make it easy for genuine cooperation. For my part, I shall work for this cooperation.

15. We are facing today a difficult economic situation, largely caused by our attempt to advance as fast as we can on the economic and industrial front. This will require every cooperative effort of ours.

16. I have written to you at greater length than I had intended, but even so I have only touched on the many important points that arise. I shall be happy to meet you when you come to Delhi and discuss some of these matters. You can rest assured that not only I but my colleagues have every desire to help.

Yours sincerely,
Jawaharlal Nehru

3. The Communist Government in Kerala[1]

I enclose a Top Secret note by the DIB.[2] I should like to draw your particular attention to a statement made in this to the effect that one of the top leaders of the P.B. proposes to go to Russia to consult Soviet leaders as to how to run the Government in Kerala in existing circumstances.[3]

2. I think that it would be desirable for you to meet the Soviet Ambassador here.[4] You can tell him that our policy in regard to the Kerala Government is to cooperate with it as we cooperate with other State Governments, so long as they function within the terms of our Constitution. We have noticed with some concern, however, that it is the intention of the Communist Party in India to send one of their leading representatives to the Soviet Union for consultation there as to how they should run the Kerala Government. Any such approach would be highly improper in our view and we are sure that the Soviet Government will not in any way, directly or indirectly, interfere in our internal affairs. When Mr Bulganin and Mr Khrushchev were here, the Prime Minister spoke to them about the activities of the Communist Party and the repeated visits of their leading men to Moscow for advice. Also the considerable funds that they managed to get from outside sources in various ways. Mr Khrushchev assured the Prime Minister that this kind of thing will not be encouraged in any way and they did not wish to interfere in the least with internal matters in India.[5]

3. You might consult Shri Krishna Menon about this matter. Also whether it would be desirable to make the same kind of approach, informally, of course, in Moscow by our Ambassador.[6]

---

1. Note to Secretary General and Foreign Secretary, New Delhi, 28 April 1957. JN Collection.
2. The note of 25 April 1957 by B.N. Mullik, Director, Information Bureau, contained the views expressed by A.K. Ghosh, the General Secretary of the Communist Party, Chandra Rajeshwar Rao, Politburo member, and M.N. Govinda Nair, Central Committee member, on the position of the Communist Party in Kerala and Andhra Pradesh during the meetings held in Andhra Pradesh between 10 to 20 April 1957. It gave an indication of the new trends in the Communist Party of India and its future plans.
3. Govinda Nair announced: "Very soon, either myself or Namboodiripad or A.K. Gopalan or Dange will be going to Russia to consult the Soviet Government as to how we should run the government in Kerala when the Central Government is under the Congress."
4. Mikhail A. Menshikov.
5. See *Selected Works* (second series), Vol. 31, 338-341.
6. K.P.S. Menon.

V. MADHYA PRADESH

1. Converting Ravines into Cultivable Land[1]

I presume that the Madhya Pradesh Government has been kept informed of all these developments.[2] The Chief Minister, Dr K.N. Katju, spoke to me only a few days ago about the importance and urgency of the problem of dealing with the dacoits who live in these ravines. This is thus a problem both of law and order as well as of higher production. If the ravines are properly dealt with, this means that erosion stops and a considerable area is brought under cultivation, apart from making it easy to deal with the dacoit menace. The importance, therefore, of this question is undoubted.

• 2. When I asked the Irrigation & Power Ministry to have a survey made and prepare a scheme, I did not suggest that this entire scheme should be taken in hand by either that Ministry or Food & Agriculture Ministry or, indeed, by the Central Government at all. All I wanted was that a proper scheme should be drawn up. As to who should give effect to it and at what pace is a matter to be considered separately. Naturally, the Madhya Pradesh Government is primarily responsible. It may be that the Central Government gives them a loan for the purpose, or of a part of it.

3. If the scheme prepared is really approved of, as appears to be the case, then steps should be taken, however gradual, in that direction.

4. I do not understand what is meant by the statement that "this work can be done by the local inhabitants in the course of time". The problem is an urgent one and cannot be left to local inhabitants, though the cooperation of the local people would no doubt be very valuable. It is really for the Madhya Pradesh Government to take this up and organize local cooperation.

1. Note to Principal Private Secretary, New Delhi, 17 April 1957. JN Collection.
2. The Ravines Reclamation Committee in its report of August 1956 proposed to convert ravines on the Madhya Pradesh and Uttar Pradesh border into cultivable land. The Standing Committee of the Central Soil Conservation Board considered it on 7 January 1957 and felt that although the scheme was good, work should not be taken up on such a big scale. It also viewed that demonstration work should be undertaken on a complete catchment basis and that a revised scheme should accordingly be prepared by the State Government and examined by the officers of the Ministry of Agriculture.

340

5. Nor do I understand why the Madhya Pradesh Government should draw up a revised scheme. If the scheme given in the report is considered good, the question of another scheme does not arise. The only question is of the time to be taken in implementing that scheme.

6. The whole point is that this is not merely a question of soil reclamation, but an important law and order problem, as the ravines are utilized by the dacoits.

7. All these aspects should be considered by the Madhya Pradesh Government. You might find out if they have seen the report of the Committee and are fully informed of the latest developments in regard to this matter. In any event, the pilot demonstration scheme should certainly be proceeded with.

VI. MADRAS

1. To U.N. Dhebar[1]

New Delhi
22 March 1957

My dear Dhebar Bhai,

Subramaniam,[2] the Finance Minister of Madras, has conveyed, rather indirectly, his views to me about the next Madras Ministry. He says that Kamaraj[3] should, of course, be the Chief Minister. As there was some talk of Subramaniam wanting to be the Chief Minister, he wanted to make clear that there was no such idea.

While he wants Kamaraj to be the Chief Minister, he is also equally clearly of opinion that in the interests of efficiency and good administration, Kamaraj should not take up any portfolio in the next Cabinet. I remember that Sri Prakasa also was of this opinion. Indeed Subramaniam says that if Kamaraj insists on taking up a portfolio, he, that is Subramaniam, would rather remain out of the Ministry.

---

1. AICC Papers, NMML.
2. C. Subramanium.
3. K. Kamaraj Nadar was Chief Minister of Madras from 1954 till 1963.

Subramaniam does not want his name to be mentioned in this connection, but he obviously wants us to talk to Kamaraj and make this proposal to him.

Yours sincerely,
Jawaharlal Nehru

2. To H.D. Rajah[1]

New Delhi
25 March 1957

Dear Rajah,[2]

I have just received your letter of the 23rd March in which you refer to a statement I issued.

It is true that I issued that statement. No one from Madras had asked me to do so, but when I saw the advertisement in *The Hindu* newspaper, I did think that it was not a very fair advertisement, and I decided to issue the statement I did on my own initiative.

I do not, of course, challenge your or your friends' right to issue that advertisement. Nor did I say that the references you had made were wrong, but it did strike me that odd quotations of a sentence here and there from some writing or speech twenty or thirty years ago were hardly appropriate in the present context. I issued my statement the moment I saw the advertisement. I was not aware of the fact then that the polling day was the next day, though I knew that it was in the near future.

I think there is a difference between people issuing notices under their signatures for a candidate, if they are contemporaries, and a notice in which some old quotations are given unrelated to the context.

You refer to illegal practices. I can say nothing about them not knowing the facts.

Yours sincerely,
Jawaharlal Nehru

1. JN Collection.
2. Republican Party Member of Rajya Sabha at this time.

VII. ORISSA

1. To Harekrushna Mahtab[1]

New Delhi
3 April 1957

My dear Mahtab,[2]

You told me, when you were here, that some American Consul or USIS Representative paid some money (I think you mentioned 68,000 dollars or rupees) to a Gantantra Party Press during the elections. You promised to send me particulars about this. Please do so. I should like to have as full information as you can give me about the activities of foreign representatives in India in connection with the elections or at the time of the elections.

Yours sincerely,
Jawaharlal Nehru

1. JN Collection.
2. Chief Minister of Orissa.

2. To U.N. Dhebar[1]

New Delhi
11 April 1957

My dear Dhebar Bhai,

I am returning Mahtab's letter to you.[2]

My reaction to his various proposals is that we should not have an understanding for the sake of forming a Government with either the Ganatantra Parishad or the Communist Party. As for winning over sufficient numbers of the Ganatantra Parishad people, I do not approve of trying to win over people who are not reliable and who may leave under pressure.

As Mahtab has already formed the Government, he should carry on till he is defeated. If he is defeated, it is for the Governor to find out if an alternative Government is possible. If the Ganatantra Parishad, with the help of others, can form such a Government, they should be given a chance. I doubt if that Government would last.

I do not see how a failure of Mahtab's Government immediately leads to President's rule. The possibilities are that Mahtab's Government functions till it is defeated. Normally the mere danger of this defeat brings a measure of discipline in the Party. If this is defeated, the Governor should send for the Ganatantra Parishad people and ask them to form a Government. If they do so, this Government functions till it is defeated. At that stage, the Governor should again try to find out if another stable Government is possible and in this process discuss the matter with Mahtab then.

My point is that every avenue should be explored before we plunge into President's rule. It will not be good for us to appear as if the Congress has

---

1. JN Collection. Also available in AICC Papers, NMML.
2. In his letter of 9 April 1957 to U.N. Dhebar, Harekrushna Mahtab apprised him of the strength of various political parties in Orissa Legislative Assembly and of the situation that was developing there with regard to the formation of government. He also informed that, "Four Independents and one from the Ganatantra Parishad came over and joined the Congress Party as regular members. Therefore, the strength of the Congress Party became 61. The support of the Jharkhand Party consisting of 5 members was assured to the Congress Party. Thus the strength of the Congress Party became 66. The strength of 8 or 9 other members were promised. In that way the Congress won the race."

forced the President's rule. Nor, of course, would it be good for us to go in for all kinds of intrigues in order to maintain office.

These are my initial reactions.

Yours sincerely,
Jawaharlal Nehru

VIII. PUNJAB

1. To Lal Singh[1]

New Delhi
6 March 1957

My dear Lal Singhji,[2]

I have seen your letter of the 6th March, together with a long letter attached to it, and I have read both. Thank you for writing to me.

I know very well the background of your work in the past and, of course, of what you have done in Parliament. I remember also well the straightforward and courageous attitude you took up when Master Tara Singh was attacking the Congress. For my part, I would have been happy to have you as a colleague.

I was not concerned with the choice of candidates from the Punjab. Indeed, I had little to do with the choice of candidates from other places also. But, I know that my colleagues in the Central Election Committee took a great deal of care in this matter. The fact that you were not ultimately selected, was certainly not meant to lower your credit. It is obviously not possible to select many good people. Why you were not selected and somebody else was, I do not know. The matter must have been carefully considered. I hope that the Congress will not

1. JN Collection.
2. Lal Singh (1896 -1963); educated at the California University Berkeley, USA; President, Hindustan Students' Association, California University, 1918-19; Professor of Agriculture, Khalsa College, Amritsar, 1923-1926; member, Advisory Board of Agricultural Research, 1947-51; Akali Dal Member, Lok Sabha, 1952-57.

enter into what might be called marriages of convenience. It is true, however, that every political party considers the situation in all its aspects and takes what, in the circumstances, is in its judgement the best course. This should not mean giving up any principle. In the Punjab, it was our earnest wish to put an end to communal outlook of both the Hindus and the Sikhs. Whether we shall succeed in this or not, I cannot say. But, we made an earnest attempt. You know that we insisted on the Akali Dal giving up politics, and this was agreed to. Unfortunately, Master Tara Singh did not act up to the assurances given to us.

However, what I wish to assure you is that, so far as I know, there is absolutely nothing against you and much in your favour. But, we tried to keep in view the larger considerations of promoting communal peace and amity and, in doing so, our choice became somewhat limited in certain cases.

My good wishes to you,

Yours sincerely,
Jawaharlal Nehru

IX. RAJASTHAN

1. To Mohanlal Sukhadia[1]

New Delhi
6 April 1957

My dear Sukhadia,[2]
I have received a letter in which it is stated that the Jal Mahal Palace Hotel is being acquired by the Rajasthan Government with a view to converting it into

---

1. JN Collection.
2. Mohanlal Sukhadia (1916-1982); Congressman from Rajasthan; imprisoned during the Quit India movement; Minister in Rajasthan for Civil Supplies, Agriculture and Irrigation, 1951-52, for Revenue and Famine Relief, 1952-54, and Chief Minister, 1955-70; elected to Lok Sabha, 1980.

Raj Bhavan for the use of the Governor. A number of arguments are used in this letter against this proposal and some of them appear to me valid.

But my primary reaction to such a proposal would be and is very definitely against it. Both the Home Minister and I have been thinking of trying to cut down expenditure on Raj Bhavans. We want, of course, a Raj Bhavan to be a place of dignity and properly run, but we do feel that we must get out of the habit of big palaces being used as Raj Bhavans. Not only is money spent on them far too much, but also the psychological effect on the people is not good. Certainly, a Governor should have an adequate residence, but that does not mean palaces and vast grounds. In fact, in some Raj Bhavans, I have actually suggested that a large part of the grounds should be separated from the Raj Bhavan and converted into a public park. I have suggested this even in Madras.

If this is our approach to the question of Raj Bhavans, then surely it would be very odd indeed for the Rajasthan Government to acquire a huge palace and grounds just to provide a residence for the Governor. I would object to it anywhere in India, more especially in Rajasthan which is not overflowing with money.

Apart from this, it is also to be considered that the Rajasthan Government wants to encourage tourist traffic. Why then do something which comes in its way?

Yours sincerely,
Jawaharlal Nehru

X. UTTAR PRADESH

1. To U.N. Dhebar[1]

New Delhi
1 March 1957

My dear Dhebarbhai,

I enclose a letter[2] which I received today, just for your information.

I went to Meerut today and had a very big meeting.[3] It was rather odd that while all the other candidates were present there, Charan Singh[4] was not present. Of course, one should not draw any inference from this as he may have been busy with canvassing for his own election.

There is little doubt that Charan Singh and Kailash Prakash[5] dislike each other and belong to what are called separate groups. But, I would not accept the charge made in the attached letter. I showed this letter to Shah Nawaz Khan,[6] who said that he did not believe this charge, although he agreed that Charan Singh was no friend of Kailash Prakash.

As you know, I have taken practically no part in the selection of UP candidates. I was sorry to learn, however, that one of the good men in Meerut was not chosen simply because Charan Singh objected to him. Another person was chosen at the instance of Charan Singh, and this man got defeated by a Communist. I am told that the idea was that Charan Singh should be "built up" in Meerut. This business of building up sometimes results in cracking the structure.

Yours sincerely,
Jawaharlal Nehru

1. JN Collection.
2. The letter was written to Nehru by Braham Prakash Rastogi, a Congressman from Meerut, in which he pointed out that, "Shri Charan Singh has been financing Khan Bahadur Aijaz Husain to fight against the Congress candidate Shri Kailash Prakash because the latter belongs to Gupta's (C.B. Gupta) group."
3. For Nehru's speech at Meerut, see *ante*, pp. 91-93.
4. Charan Singh was Deputy Minister in the UP Government at this time.
5. (1909-1998); Congress Member, UP Legislative Council, 1948-52, 1962-68 and 1970-76; Member, UP Legislative Assembly, 1952-62; Deputy Minister in the UP Government, 1956-57; Janta Party Member of Lok Sabha, 1977-79.
6. Deputy Minister for Railway and Transport at this time.

2. To Vijaya Lakshmi Pandit[1]

Circuit House
Kanpur
4 March 1957

Nan dear,

I have come here to Kanpur for a day for election work. This is my last election meeting[2] and I return to Delhi tomorrow morning. I shall remain there now except for a visit to Allahabad on 12th just in order to vote. I am tired of this touring.

I wonder if you have heard that Hariharnath Muttoo died some time ago.[3] This evening I paid a visit to Khima Didda.[4] She has become very old and weak.

The elections here are going on, though not always according to plan. The biggest blow that the UP Congress has suffered has been the overwhelming defeat of Chandra Bhanu Gupta in Lucknow. He and his colleagues were quite sure of winning, and yet he was defeated by a majority of eleven thousand votes by Triloki Singh.[5] What is more, there was a fairly widespread celebration of his defeat in Lucknow. This shows how unpopular he had become. It also shows that the electorate, though generally supporting the Congress, does not do so blindly, and expresses its will in no uncertain terms when it does not like a candidate.

The same kind of thing happened in regard to a Bihar Minister, Mahesh Prasad Sinha at Muzaffarpur. He suffered heavy defeat. Rawat,[6] Deputy Minister of UP, has also been defeated.[7] Charan Singh of Meerut has just scraped through by a narrow majority. Here in Kanpur, Beni Singh,[8] your old colleague, has unfortunately been defeated.

1. JN Collection.
2. For Nehru's speech at Kanpur, see *ante,* pp. 93-96.
3. Hariharnath Muttoo died on 13 January 1957.
4. Khimavati Muttoo, wife of Hariharnath, was the daughter of Bansi Dhar Nehru.
5. Triloki Singh, elected to the UP Legislative Assembly on Congress ticket, 1946; later left Congress and joined PSP; elected to the UP Legislative Assembly, 1957 and became Leader of Opposition in the House.
6. Jagan Prasad Rawat; Congressman from Agra; elected to the UP Legislative Assembly in 1937, 1946, 1952, 1962, 1967 and 1969; Parliamentary Secretary, 1946-52; Deputy Minister, 1952-57 and Minister in UP Government, 1963-67 and 1970.
7. He was defeated by S.K.D. Paliwal, an Independent candidate from Khairagarh.
8. Beni Singh of Congress was defeated by an Independent candidate, Moti Lal in Kanpur Rural.

SELECTED WORKS OF JAWAHARLAL NEHRU

I am not myself surprised at Chandra Bhanu Gupta's defeat, although the overwhelming character of it was rather surprising. He had become too much of a boss, and his general behaviour had irritated many people. The Muslims voted against him en bloc. So did the Kayasthas and the Banias.

Sampurnanand is having a fairly tough fight in Banaras, though probably he will win. In Allahabad, there was a very hard fought contest between Mangla Prasad,[9] UP Deputy Minister, and Saligram Jaiswal. Mangla Prasad won. I think, I wrote to you that Radhe Shyam Pathak[10] was opposing Lal Bahadur for Parliament from Allahabad City. Radhe seems to have gone off his head and is making a fool of himself.

Anyhow, in another week's time we shall have the final results.

Indira is not well, but is constantly moving about. Three or four days ago she was in Bengal. Yesterday she was in Ahmednagar. She is due to return to Allahabad tonight.

Yours,
Jawahar

9. Mangala Prasad (1898-1978); Congressman from Allahabad; took part in Civil Disobedience movement, 1930-31; elected to the UP Legislative Assembly, 1946, 1952 and 1957; served in the UP Government as Deputy Minister for Cooperatives, 1954-57; and Minister of State for Harijan Welfare and Legislative Affairs, 1957-61.
10. Praja Socialist Party leader from Allahabad.

350

3. To U.N. Dhebar[1]

New Delhi
5 March 1957

My dear Dhebarbhai,

I enclose some extracts from the local press. I would draw your attention particularly to page 2 which refers to a Saharanpur message appearing in the *Pratap*.[2] I think, it might be desirable for some enquiry to be made by the AICC office about the type of Congress propaganda alleged to have been carried on in Saharanpur in regard to Muslims.

Yours sincerely,
Jawaharlal Nehru

1. JN Collection. Also available in AICC Papers, NMML.
2. On 26 February 1957, the *Pratap* reported that, "according to a hand-bill issued by the Muslim Democratic Front, Saharanpur," the local propaganda jeep of the Congress Party announced in the Muslim *muhallas*: "(1) Maulana Manzurul Nabi has been given a Congress ticket to test (the loyalty) the Muslims. Any Muslim who did not vote for the Congress would be treated as a traitor, (2) no sooner Pakistan fired the first round in Kashmir, she (Pakistan) will be crushed, (3) Pakistan is mortgaged with the USA and in lieu of the interest on the mortgage, Pakistani women are offered to the Americans for their amusement." It also contained the replies of the Muslims that, "(1) to vote against the Congress is not a treachery but patriotism, (2) Indian Muslims do not want a war between India and Pakistan, and if war came, they would not fight to crush Pakistan, (3) it is a challenge to the self respect of Indian Muslims to say that women in Pakistan are offered to Americans for their amusement, because the mothers and sisters of a large number of Indian Muslims live in Pakistan."

4. To Jagjivan Ram[1]

New Delhi
13 March 1957

My dear Jagjivan Ram,

Anis Ahmed Abbasi, the editor of the Lucknow *Haqiqat* came to see me today. He spoke about the catering arrangements at Lucknow station. He was only concerned with the fact that some small shops or restaurants at the Lucknow station, which had thus far been run by Muslims and usually Shia contractors, were apparently now being closed. He gave me a letter which I enclose.

Whatever your broad policy may be in other places, which I understand is to do away with big contractors, I think, this Lucknow matter deserves some separate consideration. It concerns some small people. But the main thing is that Lucknow Shias, or most of them, do not eat food cooked by Hindus. Also, Muslims generally are terribly afraid that the meat supplied to them might be *jhatka* and not *halal*. The result is that they do not patronize Hindu shops. As a matter of fact, near the station, there are *jhatka* shops and presumably meat goes from there.

Apparently, Muslim meetings have been held in Lucknow over this matter, and the *Ulama* and *Mujtahids* have passed a resolution.

I do not want to encourage orthodoxy in food, whether it is Hindu or any other. But, I would prefer not to create difficulties for these Muslims of Lucknow in regard to food. Would it not be possible to allow them to have their little shop or restaurant at the station?

I am sending you a bundle of papers that he gave me, which includes a letter from the General Secretary of the All India Shia Conference.

Yours sincerely,
Jawaharlal Nehru

1. JN Collection.

5. To Charan Singh[1]

New Delhi
14 March 1957

My dear Charan Singh,

I have your letter of March 11th.[2]

From time to time, I have received letters from various parts of India, from Congressmen and others, in regard to the elections. Among these letters, there were one or two of complaints against you and making some rather ridiculous charges. It was my practice to send all these letters to the Congress President, and, I think, I sent those referring to you also, to him. I did not know and do not remember the names of the persons who sent these letters. Some days later, I was going to Meerut and Shah Nawaz Khan was accompanying me. In the course of conversation, I mentioned to him that I had received some letters about you, which, I think, accused you of helping anti-Congress candidates. Shah Nawaz replied that he did not believe such a charge. He added, however, that you were not in favour of Kailash Prakash, who was standing from Meerut City. That is all that he said to me, so far as I remember, about this matter.

In your letter, you mention a number of persons like Aijaz Husain, Vijaipal Singh and others, whom I do not know at all. Indeed, I am not acquainted with Meerut politics.

There is no question of my having an enquiry into anything. As is my practice, I shall forward your letter to the Congress President.

As you have written to me, I might tell you that I do not believe any such charges. But, I have certainly had an impression that you are rather narrow and rigid in your outlook, and have been associated with some grouping in the UP Congress. At the same time, my other impression is that your work in administration is efficient and, more particularly, that you have studied and paid a great deal of attention to agricultural classes.

1. JN Collection. Also available in AICC Papers, NMML.
2. Charan Singh refuted the complaints that were made against him by some Congressmen from Meerut that he had worked against the Congress candidates in the elections. He added that his suggestion for selection of candidates was ignored and "I must be excused for saying that I or those like me, have kept quiet, for we see no quarter from which redress can be expected."

I received your book on cooperative farming.[3] I am afraid I have not read it. I have little time for reading books.

Yours sincerely,
Jawaharlal Nehru

3. It is a brochure entitled *Whither Cooperative Farming*.

6. To Sampurnanand[1]

New Delhi
5 April 1957

My dear Sampurnanand,
The other day when you were here, you spoke to me about the activities of some Muslims in the elections. Some of these might have been Pakistan agents. You also mentioned the danger of these Pakistan agents or others being employed in positions demanding security.

I agreed with you that this require a measure of vigilance. But I hope that this does not colour our appraisal of the elections. I find some people in the UP blaming the Muslims for the defeat of the Congress candidates in many places. A number of these defeats might well have been due to the Muslims there voting against the Congress candidate.

If this was so, it deserves some enquiry and consideration. Why should they vote against the Congress candidates and sometimes even vote for a Jana Sangh man? Why have we lost their goodwill? This is a serious matter, because after all they are a large number in this country. Merely to blame them or imagine that most Muslims are pro-Pakistani and want to create trouble in India is not very helpful.

1. JN Collection. Also available in AICC Papers, NMML.

About a year ago I remember discussing the UP situation with some friends from my Province. I said then that the Congress was likely to lose a good number of seats in the coming elections and that, more particularly, Muslims as a whole would not vote for the Congress. Many others also who had previously voted for the Congress will not do so for a variety of reasons. That was my appraisal of the situation long before the elections. This was not based on any careful survey but, if I may say so, was an instinctive reaction to what I had felt in the course of my visits to the UP or what I had heard. The fact that Muslims were drifting away from the Congress was obvious. For us to think that the fault does not lie with us but with others, is surely a wrong way of approach. In a democracy one has not only to be right but to make others feel that he is right, or else the others go their own way and leave us in the lurch.

I mention this Muslim matter, but I am really thinking of broader issues. The recent elections are full of lessons for us. I do not propose to analyse them in detail, but I should like to mention some broad facts, as they strike me.

The biggest and the most painful surprise has been in Maharashtra and part of Gujarat. We see there a wave of sentiment or passion sweeping everything before it. I have no doubt that this is not peculiar to Maharashtra or Gujarat. It may happen in any part of the country. This indicates how superficial our position is anywhere and also a certain immaturity in the electorate. I do not mind the electorate going against us because they believe in some other policy. That would hurt us, but it is understandable. But for an electorate as a whole to forget major policies and to be swept away by a wave of emotion, is bad and shows great immaturity and instability. If that is so, then the future of India is full of perils.

What has happened in Kerala, though I dislike it, is something quite different and is understandable. Nothing upsetting has really happened there. It has been a gradual approach on fairly solid foundations. The Communist Party in Kerala has worked persistently for this year after year and has perfected its organization. It has built up a reputation for integrity and sincerity. The Congress, on the other hand, has had a feeble organization constantly splitting up. It has also a reputation for lack of integrity. The result when it came was, therefore, natural. There was a general feeling of dislike for and tiredness with leading Congressmen and desire for a change. The Communists with their far better organization going down to the villages and their general reputation for integrity, could easily take advantage of this. Even so, the actual voting was not so much against us.

An able and good observer in Maharashtra told me the other day that I was quite wrong in thinking that something sudden had happened in Maharashtra. This feeling against the Congress had grown in the course of years. The linguistic agitation gave it a fine opportunity for a common platform, but fundamentally it was a widespread feeling of being "fed up" with the Congress.

In the UP and Bihar, we have got considerable majorities, but we have been shaken up badly. It is quite conceivable, if things go on in the present way, that our majority itself may disappear. The defeats of some prominent Congressmen demonstrate that the public will just not put up with the people they dislike, whatever the high or any other command might say. In both these Provinces, while there are many Congressmen and Congress workers, there is practically no organization and there is a background of internecine quarrels among Congressmen.

It is clear to me that the Congress has lost its grip, generally speaking, all over India. We may win seats because of a certain prestige and for some other reasons, but we are not respected as we used to be and our organization has all gone to pieces. We have lost touch with the people. The nationalist appeal that we put forward still holds to some extent, but by itself it does not take us far and in any event other organizations can put that forward also perhaps in a more vigorous way.

Broadly speaking, the intelligentia is against us, the students are against us, and we rely mostly on a peasant vote. This peasant vote is unstable and is likely to be affected more and more by class and caste appeals. As it is, caste is breaking up the Congress. If you add to that a class appeal, the break up will be complete.

The outlook, therefore, is not at all good, in spite of our so-called victories. Unless we wake up and have the capacity not only to organize ourselves properly and not superficially and lose our sense of complacency, we have no future as an organization. We are now up against the full flood of democracy and the props that held us up in the past are no longer supporting us. Perhaps, the real explanation is that we have lost the crusading spirit that made us great.

Can we recover it or are we to see the gradual withering away of the Congress, attacked on the one side by Communism and on the other by a combination of fascism and communalism with castes coming in as an additional disturbing factor?

I have just jotted down some old ideas because I want people to think about the lessons of these elections. Frankly, I do not like them and I feel very far from complacent.

Yours sincerely,
Jawaharlal Nehru

7. To Munishwar Datt Upadhyaya[1]

New Delhi
7 April 1957

My dear Munishwar Datt,[2]

Now that the elections are over, all of us are naturally trying to understand what they mean and what lessons we can derive from them. I have given a great deal of thought to this matter, and the more I think, the more distressed I am.

I shall not refer to other parts of India. So far as the UP is concerned, it is clear to me that the Congress organization has for all practical purposes ceased to exist. It may function in the upper layers, but I do not call that a functioning organization. Secondly, it is clear that even the successes we had in the elections were not due to the organization, but to other factors. The way we have been functioning in the UP Congress in the past, stands condemned. Nothing could be clearer than this. I hope all of us realize this. I say so because I find attempts being made by some people to find scapegoats, as if the fault lay with somebody else. The first thing to realize is that the fault lay with us and with us alone, us meaning the Congress organization in the UP and, more especially, those who were running it. There is no hope for the Congress in the UP if we do not realize this fully and if we do not decide to function in a different way in future. We have had the clearest of warnings.

For my part, I feared some such development and even mentioned this fact many months ago. The whole way of our working appeared to me so wrong and so irritating to the public, that it would have been surprising if this had not produced an effect on the public.

The Congress Government and the Congress organization are closely tied up, and each suffers for the faults of the other. In these elections, however, I would say that it was the organization which was far more responsible for our unhappy condition than the Government. The question, therefore, is as to how this organization is going to run in future. If an attempt is made to continue to run it as in the past, then we are doomed. We have seen the excessive unpopularity both of some persons who have been defeated badly and of the methods of work adopted. We cannot, if we have the least wisdom, pursue those methods again or rely on those persons and give them any place of prominence in our organizational work.

1. JN Collection.
2. President, UPCC, at this time.

357

I am writing this to you because I want you to realize how I feel about these matters. There is no point in my being associated pro forma with a Committee whose methods of work I do not approve of.

Yours sincerely,
Jawaharlal Nehru

8. To Sampurnanand[1]

Flagstaff House
Chakrata
26 April 1957

My dear Sampurnanand,
I have been here in Chakrata since yesterday and naturally I have met a number of people and discussed the state of affairs here with them.

This, of course, is a very backward area from every point of view and, as you know, is very peculiar in regard to some customs that prevail here. I would suggest going rather slow in trying to change these customs here. They will, no doubt, change because of changing conditions, but I would not like the people here to feel that anything is being imposed upon them. In fact, I would like them to be treated as we are trying to treat the tribal folk in some parts of India.

I find that the work done by the Community Schemes here is appreciated, more especially, the arrangements made for water supply. It is in the development of these Community Schemes that I see the right line of progress here.

But, obviously, the outstanding need here is for roads. The construction of one or two roads will immediately open out wide areas and bring relief to them, especially in facilitating the export of potatoes, tomatoes, ginger, etc., which grow in abundance there. I think that this question of roads should be considered as one of high priority.

There are two roads about which there has been much discussion in the past. One is the Mussoorie-Chakrata road, and the other is the Chakrata-Tuini road.

I had a talk with the District Magistrate here today, and he showed me some

---

1. JN Collection.

correspondence he had had with your Government. I saw a letter which he had just received yesterday about these roads from the UP Government. From this letter it seemed to me that there was some misunderstanding as to what had been actually done already. In the letter there was talk of considering the question of building the Mussoorie-Chakrata road as well as a bridle path to Tuini.

As a matter of fact, I am told that the Mussoorie-Chakrata road is actually being built, at least on the Chakrata side of the Yamuna. The question that will arise is of connecting it with Mussoorie on the other side of the Yamuna. Having taken in hand this road from Chakrata to the Yamuna, it is obvious that it cannot be left mid-way, and has to be continued to Mussoorie. This will give a good outlet for the Chakrata region.

As far as the Tuini road is concerned, there has been for a long time past a bridle path from Mussoorie to Tuini, and in fact beyond Simla. I remember wanting to go along it from Mussoorie to Simla many years ago. The old Viceroys often went along it. So, there is no question of making a bridle path along this route; it is already there. The question is of a road. Merely broadening the bridle path will not be worthwhile, because the alignment of a road is often different from that of a bridle path. What should be done, I think, is to make the road up to Tuini. To begin with, this road need only be a jeepable road. This will not cost very much. Later, it may be made a pucca road. Even a jeepable road will partly open out this area and be of great use. Also it will not cost much. The Himachal Pradesh Government have already made, or are making a road to Tuini. If this road from Chakrata to Tuini is made, one gets a direct road from here to Simla. This is of advantage from many points of view, including strategic.

I should like you to consider this matter and help in removing the misunderstanding which appears to have arisen in some Department of your Government which deals with this matter.

Yours sincerely,
Jawaharlal Nehru

XI. WEST BENGAL

1. To B.C. Roy[1]

Camp: Royal Cottage
Bangalore
22 February 1957

My dear Bidhan,

I see from a letter from your Governor[2] to the President that there is a great deal of public feeling against the new constructions on the Calcutta Maidan. I share this feeling entirely and I am really grieved to learn that this one big open space in Calcutta is being restricted and spoiled. I gather that there are military buildings, bus stands, hawkers' market, All India Radio office, proposed art gallery etc. I do hope that all this will be stopped.

I have only recently objected very strongly to the Raj Bhavan grounds in Madras being handed over to a technical institute, important as the institute is. I have suggested that Raj Bhavan grounds there should be made into a public park for Madras. In Calcutta the need for open space is far more than in Madras. If I can help you in this matter, I shall gladly do so.

I learn also that there are many complaints in Calcutta about traffic stoppages when VIPs come. Again I sympathize with these complaints. I do not think any such stoppages are allowed in any of the great cities of Europe or America. I do hope that the Calcutta Police will behave more reasonably.

Yours affectionately,
Jawahar

1. JN Collection.
2. Padmaja Naidu.

5
INDIAN NATIONAL CONGRESS

1. To Gulzarilal Nanda[1]

New Delhi
31 March 1957

My dear Gulzarilal,

Your letter of March 27th.[2]

Recent developments in the country are, I think, very significant and disturbing. I have an idea that most people do not realize this fully. Certainly, it is the supreme obligation of every citizen to preserve the integrity of the country. But, merely repeating this does not take us far, as our repeating in the old days the slogan of Hindu-Muslim unity did not take us far. If we go about talking too much in public about the perils which beset us, that too is not good, although we should point out the dangers of disruptive tendencies etc.

In making our appeal, we proceed on certain assumptions which we accept. I am not sure that everybody accepts them or realizes what they are. Our unity is skin-deep and people get swept away by some momentary passion, or perhaps it is equally right to say that there are basic differences and even animosities which come up suddenly if something provokes them.

We can do propaganda and all that, and we should do it. But, I believe that it is really a diversion of interest that leads to people thinking less of the disruptive tendencies. The indirect approach, in war and in peace, is often much more effective than the direct approach. The indirect approach in our case would be the working out of the five year programme, the Community Schemes, etc., etc. I realize that that might not be enough. But, I do feel that any amount of speeches and propaganda of that type, to create what you call a suitable atmosphere for the growth of a deep sense of loyalty to the nation, will not take us very far.

---

1. JN Collection.
2. Gulzarilal Nanda, Union Minister for Planning, and Irrigation and Power, wrote: "The supreme obligation of every citizen is to help to preserve the integrity of the country and its capacity to secure the material and cultural advance for which we are striving." He suggested that the Bharat Sevak Samaj should be geared up for a concentrated attack on destructive forces and direct its resources for "creating a suitable atmosphere for the growth of a deep sense of loyalty to the nation." He proposed to initiate a mass campaign based on the realization that for the security and progress of the country, the entire community should be loyal to ethical and cultural values. He also pointed out: "I am wondering whether we should not link up this campaign with some slogan, 'Strong India' (Sushakt Bharat) is just one suggestion."

However, we should try. The Bharat Sevak Samaj may attempt this. But, I am a little afraid that it may thereby convert itself into what I would call a moralizing organization and not one which is doing creative and productive work. It is through work that people are made to think.

You may draw up some kind of a programme as you suggest, though it is not clear to me what it is likely to be. We should try, in a sense, to go slow so as not to rouse hostility and so as not to make people think that the Bharat Sevak Samaj, in the name of the unity of India, is trying to undermine them in some way.

I dislike the slogan 'Sushakt Bharat' or 'Strong India'.

Yours sincerely,
Jawaharlal Nehru

2. To Gulzarilal Nanda[1]

New Delhi
1 April 1957

My dear Gulzarilal,

I wrote to you yesterday in answer to a letter you wrote about the work of the Bharat Sevak Samaj. Today, I happened to meet Govind Sahai[2] who has recently been elected to the UP Assembly. I said to him that I hoped he would continue his work in the Bharat Sevak Samaj. He told me that recently some decision had been arrived at by the Bharat Sevak Samaj office that, because he had been elected on a party ticket, he had become a politician and, therefore, he could not take any prominent part in the Bharat Sevak Samaj work.

---

1. JN Collection.
2. (1907-67); joined Congress, 1930; participated in the freedom movement and jailed several times; Chairman, Jail Reforms Committee and Criminal Tribes Committee, 1946; left Congress in 1952 and elected to the UP Legislative Council as an Independent candidate; rejoined Congress in 1957 and elected to the UP Assembly from Nagina constituency in Bijnor district; Minister of State in UP for Jails, Relief and Rehabilitation and Youth Welfare, 1961-67; author of several books including *Imperialism in International Politics*.

I do not understand this at all. Are we not all politicians and party men? Is the Bharat Sevak Samaj to consist of pale and ineffective people who dare not take part in politics?

I do not know what exact instructions have been issued. But, if they at all imply that a man like Govind Sahai cannot function in the Bharat Sevak Samaj effectively, then there is something wrong about them.

As I wrote to you yesterday, I do not think moral lectures carry us far. We have to face a very difficult situation in the country, with all kinds of disruptive forces. Among these disruptive forces are the communal forces, the Jana Sangh, the RSS etc. Are we not to criticize them because that would mean politics?

Yours sincerely,
Jawaharlal Nehru

3. To Sankar Saran[1]

New Delhi
2 April 1957

My dear Sankar Saran,[2]
Your letter of the 2nd April.

It is not possible to express any kind of opinion which will cover all the students' movements of the world. They differ greatly and each case has to be considered separately. Many of these are propagandist and political both in Russia and the East European countries as well as in Western Europe and the United States. We have, therefore, to proceed cautiously. That does not mean that we should refuse to have contacts with them. Contacts which do not involve any commitment can always be made. Any closer association would require careful consideration in each case.

---

1. JN Collection.
2. (1893-1963); enrolled as an Advocate, 1919; Government Pleader, High Court, Allahabad, 1921; Deputy Government Advocate, 1937; Government Advocate, 1944; Judge, Allahabad High Court, 1946-53; Acting Chief Justice, 1952; Custodian General, Evacuee Property, Government of India, 1953.

This kind of question arises often for the Congress Youth organization. Perhaps you could get in touch with the AICC office on this subject and find out what they are doing.

Yours sincerely,
Jawaharlal Nehru

4. To Jayaprakash Narayan[1]

New Delhi
3 April 1957

My dear Jayaprakash,
I sent you a brief acknowledgement, on March 14th, of your letter of March 1st, which had reached me on March 13th.[2] I am sorry for the delay in answering it properly, but I have been terribly busy.

Even now, I do not know how exactly to answer it. If I attempted to deal adequately with the various points that you have raised, that would mean

1. JN Collection. Also available in AICC Papers, NMML.
2. Jayaprakash Narayan wrote that ever since the election campaign started, Nehru repeatedly called him a friend but his public references to him at Madras, Nagpur and other places indicated an utter lack of understanding of a friend. He reminded Nehru that three or four years ago he had spoken about the faults of the party system and had suggested that Nehru should encourage opposition to strengthen parliamentary democracy and also function as a national leader than a party leader because when anyone functioned as a party leader, he had to make compromises and look at every issue in terms of party gain. The huge majority that the Congress Party had enjoyed for the last ten years was harmful to the country's interests, and to reduce the Congress power he advised the opposition parties to avoid contests between themselves. And this he had suggested not out of dislike or hostility towards the Congress or its leadership but merely on account of certain political principles. In response to Nehru's criticism that he had given up politics but continued to dabble in it, Narayan wrote that he was not in competitive or party politics, but politics being all pervasive, no one could be out of it. Regarding Nehru's criticism of Sarvodaya workers, Narayan wrote that it was true that the workers eschewed party politics but they could always raise general political and ideological issues for the guidance of the electorate. Lastly, Narayan urged the leaders to find a better alternative to the present political system where Nehru's leadership was most needed.

discussing a multitude of internal and external problems. Indeed, that would mean writing something in the nature of a little book. Apart from the obvious difficulty of doing this, I doubt if it would help in producing any mutual understanding between us on these issues.

You say that while I have repeatedly referred to you as a friend, I have not tried to understand you as was due to you as a friend. Indeed, that in my public utterances referring to you, there has been, according to you, an utter lack of understanding.

Perhaps, you are right in saying that I do not understand much that you have said. But I do not think this is due to any want of trying to do so. I have read not only your letter carefully, but also the other papers you sent with it.

You say that I could have written to you to find out what you meant, or called you for a talk. I have always welcomed meeting you and shall do so in the future also. But, I do not quite understand this criticism. You make public references repeatedly condemning the Congress and our Government and criticizing most of our important policies. These are given considerable prominence in the press. And, at election time when I am also speaking frequently in public, I have to deal with criticism of my Government and the Congress and our policies, and naturally I had to refer to what you had said, as reported in the public press.[3] There was nothing personal about it. It would have been rather extraordinary if whenever what you had spoken was reported, I had asked you for explanations of what you had said, more especially when I was asked my reaction to it.

Apart from this, I have had a feeling for many months, if not more, that there was a widening gap between our views about various matters. Almost everything that I thought important and emphasized, was criticized by you in strong language. I do not object, of course, to that criticism. But, I am merely pointing out that this difference in our viewpoints had grown so much that there were not many points of contact left. In fact, I was left in some state of amazement whenever I read your reported speeches or statements. Frankly, I felt that you had completely lost grip of the situation in India as well as in the world, and what you said had no reality at all. Also, I felt that your governing motive was hardly a positive or constructive one in so far as these elections were concerned, but much more so an active and bitter dislike of the Congress and a desire to see it defeated, whatever the consequences might be. With that attitude, it was difficult to deal with at all, and there was little room left for argument. We spoke different languages. I hope that I can understand the Praja Socialist language or the Communist language or most other languages, even though I may not agree with them, as

3. For Jayaprakash Narayan's criticism of Congress and the Government, and Nehru's reply at election meetings see *ante*, pp. 13-14 & 29.

often I do not. But, your language seemed to be a special one, which I could not make much of. It seemed to me the result of being cut off from reality and a result of woolly thinking.

You were prepared to come to terms with the Communists, whose policy you actually disliked, in order to defeat the Congress. So also with other parties like an ex-rulers' group, the Gantantra Parishad in Orissa. I fail to find any logic in this thinking or advice, except a bitter dislike of the Congress. Dislike is hardly a subject on which one can argue.

You refer to what you had said to me some three or four years ago, about the faults of the party system. Of course, the party system, as indeed every system, has many faults. The parliamentary democracy that we have adopted, is also full of faults. Nevertheless, we adopted it because we thought that, in the balance, it was better than the other possible courses. Whatever system we might adopt, ultimately it depends on the human material available. The best of systems will fail if this material is not good enough for it.

I have quite failed to understand what you meant by my becoming a national leader, rather than a party leader. What exactly does a national leader do? If it is meant that he should collect a number of important people from different parties and form a government, surely this can only be done if there is some dominant common purpose. Without such a purpose, no government can function. Sometimes, such national governments are formed in wartime, when the only dominant purpose is winning the war and everything else is subordinated to it. Even so, they have not been much of a success in parliamentary democracies. Apart from a war, however, we have to deal with political and economic problems, national and international. There must be some common outlook and unity of purpose in dealing with these problems. Otherwise, there would be no movement at all and just an internal tug of war.

In view of the fact that you utterly disapprove of both our national and international policies, where does the common purpose come in? Are we to strike some kind of a golden mean which is neither this nor that? Surely, that is not a policy, and no government can function like that. Certainly also, I could have little place in a government which followed a policy with which I thoroughly disagreed. And I suppose that would apply to you also.

If you meant that by becoming a party leader, I was sacrificing some essential policy, which I would otherwise follow if I considered myself a national leader, then you are wrong. I may, of course, have made and might make in the future any number of mistakes. But, broadly speaking, we have tried to follow a policy that we considered correct for the nation. I do not know where the party comes in at all. Our international policy is not a Congress Party policy, although, of course, the Congress has approved of it. Nor is our general economic policy a party policy in any narrow sense. There may be differences about it. This general economic and development policy may be said to be contained in our five year plans. I do not pretend to say that everything in the Second Five Year Plan is rigid or perfect. We ourselves are always prepared to revise it. But, I do believe firmly in its basic right approach, having regard to the circumstances we have to face. No economic or any policy can come out of the higher atmosphere. It has to be related to the facts, resources, human material, etc., that we may have.

What, then, do you mean by this talk of a national leader or a national government? What compromise has our Government made in any basic matter? You might say that we ought to have gone further in some respect, and I might agree with you. The compromise is not because of the party, but because of the facts that encompassed us. We have to function as a Government dealing with these facts and not with theoretical propositions. What, again, I should like to know, have we done in terms of party-gain except, if you like, to set up candidates on behalf of the party?

You refer to your anxiety to lay soundly the foundation of parliamentary democracy. And yet, from much that you have said, it appears to me that your conception of parliamentary democracy is completely different not only from my conception, but from the normal conception of it.

Then again, when you say that I or the Congress should encourage the growth of an opposition, what exactly does this mean? So far as I understand parliamentary democracy, it means that every opportunity should be given for an opposition to function, to express its views by word or writing, to contest elections in fair conditions, and to try to convert the people to its views. The moment an opposition is given some kind of a protected position, it becomes rather a bogus opposition and cannot even carry weight with the people. I am not aware of any pattern of parliamentary democracy in which it has ever been suggested that the opposition should be encouraged, except in the ways I have mentioned above.

You say that the huge majorities that the Congress Party has enjoyed in the legislatures for the last ten years, have been harmful and have been fraught with serious danger to the country's interests. I do not and cannot say that everything that the Congress Party has done, has been the best in the best of all possible words. But, I do say with a measure of confidence and knowledge not only of India, but of the world, that what we have done in this country in the past ten years constitutes a remarkable and almost spectacular record of work for the progress of the country. Apart from general progress, I think, we have helped in strengthening the foundations of our infant democracy. I can, therefore, only disagree with you thoroughly on this subject.

I disagree with you also if you say that there has not been an adequate opposition in the legislatures or in the country. Opposition is not a question of the majority in a legislature. In the Lok Sabha, the opposition consisted of about one hundred and fifty persons out of a total membership of nearly five hundred. That opposition was a virile and active opposition, as it should have been. Certainly, it might be voted down, as every minority is ultimately voted down. Presumably, you would like larger numbers in the opposition. Even if there were larger numbers, it would be voted down. And how am I to produce the larger numbers?

What is important in a parliamentary democracy is, for certain, conventions of good behaviour to be set up and a certain adherence to principles. A small party which has firm principles, is far more important from the point of view of public education and development of democratic work, than a miscellaneous crowd of, let us say, independents who have no common thinking. A mixing together of a number of groups with entirely different viewpoints, merely on the ground of opposition, is again not helpful to the development of clear thinking.

You have quoted Acton in referring to the Congress and said that power corrupts and absolute power corrupts absolutely. I really entirely fail to understand how much a statement could be made with any relevance or truth. You know well in what context Lord Acton used that phrase. He was referring to autocracies. He might have referred to authoritarian governments of the modern variety, if he had known them. But, to apply this to a parliament or a legislature merely because one party has got a big majority, is, if I may say so, the height of absurdity.

Apart from opposition parties in the legislatures, everyone knows that in India there are all kinds of disruptive and reactionary forces. There is also the inertia of ages. And it is very easy for this inert mass to be roused by some religious or caste or linguistic or provincial or like cry, and thus to come in the way of all progress. That is the real opposition in the country, and it is a tremendously strong one. And that is what you seem to ignore completely. We have constantly to battle against it, as we have to battle against various world forces which threaten us. Whether in the domestic sphere or the international sphere, we fight for survival, and when I say that, I am not referring to the Congress only.

Evidently, you are not of this opinion. As you say, you are not worried by the cry of political instability in the country. I could not disagree with you more. I think that there is grave danger of political instability in this country and of disruption. Whatever the failings of the Congress, and they are many, it has done, I think, inestimable service to the country in checking these tendencies to disruption and instability and trying to bring about cohesion in the country. This has nothing to do with the Congress being good or bad, important as that is. What I am referring to is the grave danger of disruption and political instability which we have to face. The various courses you have suggested, might harm the

Congress, but they would certainly tend to produce this instability in the country and, therefore, injure the country as a whole. I would suggest to you to look round outside the borders of India, and see what is happening in the other countries of Asia. I would leave out China because that is under Communist rule. I think, every other country whether in Western Asia or South East Asia, lacks stability. In Western Asia, nearly all the countries are very far removed from democracy, parliamentary or other. Often there are feudal regimes and their governments are unpopular and kept up by foreign aid and, sometimes, armed forces. East of India, there is Burma which I admire very much for their brave efforts in spite of great difficulties. But the fact of these difficulties is there. There is Indonesia, which is cracking up and deliberately trying to give up its democracy such as it was. I need not refer to Thailand and such like countries.

Look at the world, hovering at the brink of catastrophe. I do not know if you would appreciate the dangerous situation in the world. In spite of us, of course, we may be blown up because of world happenings. But, at any rate, our first objective should be to have cohesion and unity in this country, so that we can face any trial, internal or external, with some measure of strength. Your various suggestions would, in my opinion, weaken the country and encourage the forces of disruption.

You say that the verdict is inescapable that the present political system has proved a failure. That may be so. It might also be said that the world as it is constituted today, is a failure because it is rapidly marching to its own destruction. We may also say that democracy has completely failed in a country like France, not to mention other countries. In other words, you are of opinion that parliamentary democracy in India is a failure. If that is so, we must face that issue clearly and try to change the system basically. I do not agree with you, and I do not think the present system has failed, though it might fail in the future for all I know. If it fails, it will not fail because the system in theory is bad, but because we could not live up to it. Anyhow, what is the alternative you suggest? I have failed to find it in any of your utterances. To say that the opposition should be strengthened within the structure of this system, seems to be neither here nor there. I take it that you are not in favour of some kind of an authoritarian approach. What, then are we to do, in your opinion.

You suggest that the leaders of the country should get together to find out if there is a better alternative. Surely, it is up to you or anyone who has clear ideas on this subject, to put them forward for consideration. What exactly are a group of people, representing the various parties as well as Independents in India, sitting around a round table, likely to produce? Such a suggestion is, it appears to me, a way of escape from thinking and merely hoping that something will come out of nothing. About you and me, as I have said above, it appears that we disagree about many important matters in both domestic and foreign policies. How exactly do we agree about these policies or to any policies, and how much less will the round table agree to any policy? We shall drift to chaos, and every disruptive tendency in India will have full play, and every reactionary force will come to the fore.

We have seen in these recent elections, how easy it is for our people, belonging to all parties, to degrade themselves and forget all standards of behaviour. It might be that this is the fault of democracy or is our own fault. We have seen, not only in the elections, but in the course of the last year, violence, arson, hatred and every kind of misbehaviour raise its head. You have often criticized police firing, and you are perfectly entitled to do so. I myself am deeply distressed by this business of firing. But I do not remember your condemning the terrible behaviour of people in regard to violence and arson and the propagation of hatred. Every ill, according to you, emanates from Government. Whether you are right or wrong in this matter, surely you will agree that what we have seen in this country during the linguistic provinces agitation, is most disgraceful and terribly harmful to our country. I am referring to the methods adopted, not to any objective aimed at. The Praja Socialist Party has taken a lead in this, including the violence and the propagation of hatred.[4] It has been often their deliberate policy to prevent meetings being held by violence and the throwing of stones. I do not know if this is considered a part of democracy or is justifiable from any standpoint. Yet, I have seen very little condemnation of it and, if there has been some condemnation, it has been in the mildest language, which has almost been a justification for it.

I do not justify or approve of many things that have been done in these elections on behalf of the Congress. I have many sources of information, apart from Government, and I have also seen many things for myself. I am convinced that in these general elections, the worst behaviour came from the PSP and, sometimes, from Lohia's party.[5] I know this from my own experience in Allahabad. I was ashamed to see and hear what had been done there by the PSP.[6]

I have always thought that there are some basic propositions on which it is not possible to agree. I am not prepared to agree with any policy which is based on violence or hatred or disruption of the country. It is because of this that I cannot agree with communal organizations like the Jana Sangh or the RSS or

4. See *Selected Works* (second series), Vol. 31, pp. 153 & 209 and Vol. 32, pp. 180-181.
5. A section of the left wing of the Praja Socialist Party that broke away under the leadership of Rammanohar Lohia, former general secretary of the PSP, founded the Socialist Party on 28 December 1955.
6. See *ante*, pp. 101 & 106-107.

political organizations like the Communist Party. I do not mind accepting, on a theoretical basis, some Communist economic theories, not all. But I cannot accept the methods of the Communists, which are full of violence and hatred, are disruptive and, I think, often anti-national and based on some outside considerations. Equally dangerous, I think, are the communal organizations which, if they have their way, would disrupt India and drench it with the blood of its people.

For these reasons, I could not conceive of any kind of alliance with either the Communist Party or the communal parties. In theory, the Praja Socialist Party was nearest to the Congress, as I told you previously. But, in practice, the Praja Socialist Party appears to have given up almost every principle for which it stood and has become a negative opportunist organization, often indulging in violence and basing itself merely on condemnation of the Congress and Congressmen. Your passion for strengthening the opposition has led you to make proposals which have resulted, directly or indirectly, in the Praja Socialist Party becoming quite rootless in so far as any principle or firm policy is concerned. They may win elections. But, what lead do they give to the country?

You refer to my reference to the Bhoodan movement.[7] I had said that I hoped that the Bhoodan movement would not become associated with a particular brand of politics, as that would, I thought, be harmful to it. I did not say that the people in the Bhoodan movement or Sarvodaya should not express their opinion or indeed take any other part in politics. But it did seem to me odd that you, who had completely devoted yourself to the Bhoodan movement, should rush out into the fray repeatedly to criticize and condemn, and then again retire to your shell. It seemed to me very illogical. Everyone has a right to express his opinion or indulge in any peaceful action. But, from a leader, a measure of responsibility is expected, and not merely an angry reaction to events, without finding out what all the events are.

You indicate that you have eschewed party politics and, therefore, do not wish to take up a partisan stand. I am afraid we must attach different meanings to words. I would not describe your incursions into politics as anything but the most active partisanship, and a partisanship which seems to be coloured by violent dislikes and has little reason or logic behind it. I do not object to partisanship and even strong partisanship. I am a partisan, that is to say, if I believe in something, I hope to stand by it and to proclaim it. I do not pretend,

7. Nehru was reported to have said at Nagpur that if the Bhoodan workers acted against the Congress, their movement would suffer. These remarks were taken as a warning and a threat by the workers. For Nehru's reference to the Bhoodan movement, see *Selected Works* (second series), Vol. 36, p. 157.

however, to be above the fray and, therefore, somehow wiser than everyone else and to consider myself justified in condemning others.

I have written to you at some length and frankly. It is not my purpose to hurt you. But, there would have been no point in my writing to you and slurring over the basic issues that you have raised.

Yours,
Jawahar

5. To U.N. Dhebar[1]

New Delhi
7 April 1957

My dear Dhebarbhai,

Your letter of April 6th. I am glad you have written to Dange.[2]

More and more I feel that something is utterly wrong with our organization and that we have to think anew and afresh. This matter perhaps could be discussed by a few of us. Nothing could be more foolish, I think, than trying to find scapegoats, as many Congressmen are now doing. The fact is that our organization hardly exists, except in some places at the top-layers. Further, that it is full of faction and intrigue. Also, that people have lost respect for it. We have no real hold on the public mind and young people have drifted away from us.

I wrote to you the other day about Prithvi Singh.[3] I think that he can be of considerable help, given the opportunity. Mauli Chandra Sharma[4] came to see me today and told me about Jammu etc. He said, and I believe him, that if he had been sent to Amritsar and Jalandhar, the results of the elections there might have been different. The AICC wanted to send him there, but Partap Singh and Musafir[5] were obviously not keen on having him, and so he did not go.

1. JN Collection. Also available in AICC Papers, NMML.
2. S.A. Dange, one of the founders of the Communist movement, was Member, Lok Sabha at this time.
3. Prithvi Singh Azad, a follower of Mahatma Gandhi, was Director of the Institute of Physical Culture in Saurashtra.
4. He was President, Bharatiya Jana Sangh, in 1953 but resigned and joined Congress in 1954.
5. Gurmukh Singh Musafir was President, Punjab Pradesh Congress Committee, and Member, Lok Sabha.

I think, Mauli Chandra Sharma also can be of considerable use, because of his past knowledge of the Jana Sangh mentality.[6]

Yours sincerely,
Jawaharlal Nehru

6. Nehru again wrote to Dhebar (not printed) on 13 April and recommended the case of Mauli Chandra Sharma who, according to him, might be of considerable help against communal organizations like the Jana Sangh and the Hindu Mahasabha. Sharma also had a lot of influence with young people who had been somewhat attracted by the RSS and other communal organizations.

6. To Nirmal Kumar Bose[1]

Flagstaff House
Chakrata
27 April 1957

Dear Friend,[2]
I have your letter of 23rd April. Also your pamphlet on planning and programme of Liaison Movement.

I have read this pamphlet, and I find many ideas in it which are good. There can be no doubt that the Congress organization has in many places lost touch with the people, and this has to be developed.

But what you have suggested is in effect to build up some kind of a new organization or a movement, and you have made various other suggestions in regard to this which seem to me not at all feasible. But the main thing is that your note, though containing good ideas, is vague and does not come to grips with the subject. I presume you have sent your note to the Congress President.

Yours sincerely,
Jawaharlal Nehru

1. JN Collection.
2. Anthropologist and secretary to Mahatma Gandhi, 1946-47.

6
PARLIAMENTARY AFFAIRS

1. To P. Kodanda Rao[1]

New Delhi
21 March 1957

Dear Shri Kodanda Rao,[2]

Thank you for your letter of March 19 with its enclosure.

What you have suggested would involve a complete change of our Constitution. To endeavour to have a unitary government now is to put forward a highly controversial issue which will split the nation into bits and put an end to all our constructive work. Personally, I do not think that in a big country like India a unitary government can be really successful. It is failing in Indonesia. What is necessary, of course, is a strong Centre.

As for a national government, I am a little surprised at your saying that the differences in the main policies of the various parties in India are negligible. I should have thought that both in domestic policies and in foreign policies the differences are very considerable and the whole conception of a homogeneous Cabinet would have to be given up. As a matter of fact, a great deal of unity in working can be devised and our attempt has been to do that in planning which is, after all, the most vital thing.

Yours sincerely,
Jawaharlal Nehru

---

1. P. Kodanda Rao Papers, NMML. Also available in JN Collection.
2. Editor, *Servant of India*, a weekly from Pune.

2. To Govind Ballabh Pant[1]

New Delhi
24 March 1957

My dear Pantji,

I understand that some people are going about asking members of Parliament to sign a petition to be sent to me requesting me to re-nominate Rajendra Babu for the Presidentship. Apparently, some of the South Indians were approached to sign this, but they declined to do so.

I am afraid this matter is getting more and more complicated and is likely to cause a considerable degree of ill will all round. The sooner some kind of a private decision is arrived at, the better.

Yours sincerely,
Jawaharlal Nehru

1. JN Collection.

3. Change and Continuity Essential in Parliamentary Democracy[1]

Mr Speaker,[2] Sir, you have been pleased to say many generous things about the Members of this House and, to my great embarrassment, about me. You have spoken in generosity but, anyhow, so far as I am concerned, I should like to offer you my grateful thanks, and I am sure I speak on behalf of the House also, when I offer you their thanks for your kind words.

It is befitting that on this occasion, when this Parliament stands at the edge of its own dissolution,[3] there should be some valedictory references to our past.

1. Speech in the last session of the first Lok Sabha, 28 March 1957. *Lok Sabha Debates*, Vol. 1, Part II, cols. 1289-1294.
2. M. Ananthasayanam Ayyangar.
3. The Lok Sabha was dissolved by the President on 31 March 1957.

Since you have been good enough to make a reference to the work of this Parliament, I am taking the liberty of saying also a few words on this occasion, certainly on my own behalf and possibly reflecting the views and ideas of other Members also here.

We have gone through, during these five years, a tremendous amount of work and, as you have said, speeches have covered, I do not know how many millions of pages; questions have also been asked and, altogether a vast quantity of paper has been consumed. Yet, the historian of the future will probably not pay too much attention to the number of speeches or the hours which the speeches have taken or to the number of questions, but rather to the deeper things that go towards the making of a nation.

Here, we have sat in this Parliament, the sovereign authority of India, responsible for the governance of India. Surely, there can be no higher responsibility or greater privilege than to be a Member of this sovereign body which is responsible for the fate of the vast number of human beings who live in this country. All of us, if not always, at any rate from time to time, must have felt this high sense of responsibility and destiny to which we had been called. Whether we were worthy of it or not is another matter. We have functioned, therefore, during these five years not only on the edge of history but sometimes plunging into the processes of making history.

We have lived here, as indeed people have lived all over the world, at a moment of great change, transition, and sometimes of vast upsets and revolutionary processes. We have not only been part of that world drama but we have had our own drama also. And it would be interesting for someone to take a rather distant view of this drama of these five years and more so as not to be lost in the innumerable details which confuse, but rather to see this broad current of history in motion in this country, how far has it moved, what changes has it wrought, how far has it laid stable the foundations of this Republic of India which we created, which the people of India created a few years back. That is the important question; not so much how many speeches we have delivered or how many questions we have asked, important, no doubt, though speeches and questions are, as bringing out the method of our working the parliamentary process to which we are addicted.

We choose this system of parliamentary democracy deliberately; we choose it not only because, to some extent, we had always thought on those lines previously, but because we thought it was in keeping with our own old traditions also; naturally, the old traditions, not as they were, but adjusted to the new conditions and new surroundings. We choose it also—let us give credit where credit is due—because we approved of its functioning in other countries, more especially the United Kingdom.

So, this Parliament, the Lok Sabha, became, to some extent—not entirely, but to a large extent—rather like the British Parliament or the British House of Commons whether it is in regard to our questions or our rules of procedure or methods of work.

Now, parliamentary democracy demands many things, demands of course, ability. It demands a certain devotion to work as every work does. But it demands also a large measure of cooperation, of self-discipline, of restraint. It is obvious that a House like this cannot perform any functions without the spirit of cooperation, without a large measure of restraint and self-discipline in each Member and in each group. Parliamentary democracy is not something which can be transplanted in a country by some wand or by some quick process. We talk about it but we know very well that there are not many countries in the world where it functions successfully. I think, it may be said without any partiality that it has functioned with a very large measure of success in this country. Why? Not so much because we, the Members of this House, are exemplars of wisdom, but, I do not think, because of the background in our country, and because our people have the spirit of democracy in them.

We have to remember then what parliamentary democracy means. In this world of change and tremendous ferment, more so than in ordinary times, change is essential; change and adaptation to new order. Even when the old order was good, it has to yield place to new lest one good custom should corrupt the world. It has to change. So, change there must be, change there has to be, in a country like India which was more or less changeless for a long time, changeless not only because of the country being a subject country under the imperialist powers, I do not mean to say that there was no change then, but basically the dynamic aspect of the country was limited, restricted, cabined and confined by foreign domination—changeless also because we had fallen into the ruts of our own making, in mind, in social framework and the rest. So, we had to take our souls out both from the ruts and from the disabilities and restrictions caused by alien rule. We had to make rapid changes in order to catch up. So, change was necessary even for survival and, of course, for progress.

But, while change is necessary, there is another thing that is also necessary; that is, a measure of continuity. There is always a balancing of change and continuity. Not one day is like another. We grow older each day. Yet, there is continuity in us, unrestrained continuity in the life of a nation. It is in the measure that these processes of change and continuity are balancing that a country grows on solid foundations. If there is no change and only continuity, there is stagnation and decay. If there is change only and no continuity, that means uprooting, and no country and no people can survive for long if they are uprooted from the soil which has nurtured them and given them birth.

Now, this system of parliamentary democracy, therefore, embodies, I think, these principles of change and continuity, both. And it is up to those who function in this system, Parliament, Members of the House and the numerous others who are part of this system, to increase the pace of change, to make it as fast as they like, subject to the principle of continuity, because, the moment that continuity is broken we become rootless and the system of parliamentary democracy breaks down. Parliamentary democracy is a delicate plant and it is a measure of our own success that this plant has become sturdier during these last few years. We have faced grave problems, difficult problems, and solved many of them; but, many remain to be solved. Indeed, there is going to be no end of the problems that will come to us, because problems are inevitable when you grow. It is only those who are stagnant that have few problems, and if there are no problems, that is a sign of death. Only the dead have no problems, the living have problems and they grow with problems, fighting with problems and overcoming them. It is a sign of the growth of this nation that not only we solve problems, but we create new problems to solve.

So, these five years have passed and we are at the end of this chapter of our history; and, the very end suddenly merges into a beginning and we begin afresh, because ends and beginnings are only of our own conception. There is only continuous life of a nation. We may pass out of this House or pass out of our lives, but the nation goes on. Therefore, here when we stand at this end, which is also a beginning, we indulge in retrospect and we indulge in prospect. Again, standing on this edge of the present, we look back on the past, but we look forward even more to the future. We may think of many things that we have to do to carry on the great work that we have undertaken and undertake new labours; but, above all, we have to remember how stable, how deep, are the foundations of this democracy that we have sought to serve and to build up in this country, because ultimately it is on the strength and depths of those roots that we will prosper, not by the number of laws we pass, not by our external activities, but on the strength of character and grit and the capacity of service that we develop in this country.

Parliamentary democracy involves naturally peaceful methods of action, peaceful acceptance of decisions taken and attempts to change them through peaceful ways again; it is no parliamentary democracy otherwise. It is essential that we, who talk and who believe in the quest of peace so much, should remember that the quest of peace and the quest of democracy can only be made through methods of peace and not through any other. We have a great united country, a country which is dear to us, and of which we are proud. But being proud of it does not mean that we should close our eyes to the grave problems we often have to face in the country and the disruptive tendencies that raise their heads and challenge the democratic process which this Parliament represents. It is in the measure that we put an end, even in our thinking, to these disruptive tendencies which divide us and which tend to break up the unity of India that we will have strengthened our country and laid sound foundations for the future. So, Sir, I would like to thank you again.

May I, as Leader of the House, express my respectful thanks to all the Members of this House for the great courtesy and consideration which they have shown me during these past five years.

4. To S. Radhakrishnan[1]

New Delhi
20 April 1957

My dear Mr Vice-President,

At a meeting of the Cabinet today, a constitutional point was raised in regard to the election of the Vice-President. I have stated what the point is in the attached paper.

As there was a difference of opinion in regard to the interpretation of the Constitution and the Acts and Rules framed for the election of the President and Vice-President, it was decided that the Attorney-General's advice should be obtained. I have consulted the Attorney-General. His own first reaction was that in an uncontested election, a joint meeting is necessary in accordance with the constitutional provision for it. But he wanted to consider this matter further. I have, therefore, given him a copy of the paper attached to this and he has promised to let me have his opinion tomorrow.

Yours sincerely,
Jawaharlal Nehru

1. JN Collection.

5. To S. Radhakrishnan[1]

New Delhi
20 April 1957

My dear Mr Vice-President,

Thank you for your letter of the 20th April.[2]

It is true that in 1952 there was no contest and we held no joint meeting. I do not think that any question can arise about that procedure not being constitutional. Only the Supreme Court can decide this issue if it was raised before them. It cannot be raised now.

The question is now that we should not only follow the Constitution, whatever its interpretation might be, but also lay down definitely for the future what the correct and dignified procedure should be. I do not yet know what the Attorney-General will finally recommend.[3] We shall have to follow his advice. When such question is raised in this way, it cannot be ignored.

Yours sincerely,
Jawaharlal Nehru

1. JN Collection.
2. In his letter, Radhakrishnan suggested to Nehru that the conventions set up in 1952 for the election of Vice-President had been accepted by the people and it should be maintained. He further added: "If we upset the convention now, perhaps it may be thought that my holding the Vice-Presidentship all these five years was not strictly constitutional and an ordinance may have to issue ratifying all my acts, legislative and executive, during that period."
3. In his letter written to Nehru on 21 April, M.C. Setalvad opined that it would not be possible "to maintain that Clause (a) of section 8 of the Presidential and Vice-Presidential Elections Act of 1952 is consistent with Article 66 of the Constitution and that I take it, is the immediate point at issue. In the circumstances mentioned in section 8(a) of the Act, where there is only one nominated candidate for the Vice-Presidency, the election takes place without the Members of Parliament assembling at a meeting and an essential requirement of Article 66 is not complied with in the procedure laid down in the Act. It will be noticed that the power given to Parliament by Article 71(3) to regulate any matter relating to or connected with the election of a Vice-President is expressly made 'subject to the provisions of the Constitution.' He further said that from a practical point of view, "I would not advise the holding a joint meeting in the present case."

6. Election of the Vice-President[1]

Article 66 of the Constitution of India, Clause 1, is as follows:-

The Vice-President shall be elected by the Members of both Houses of Parliament assembled at a joint meeting in accordance with the system of proportional representation by means of the single transferable vote and the voting at such election shall be by secret ballot.

2. Article 324, Clause 1, states that:

Superintendence, direction and control of the preparation of the electoral rolls for, and the conduct of, all elections to Parliament and to the legislature of every State and elections to the offices of President and Vice-President held under this Constitution,. . . .shall be vested in a Commission (referred to in this Constitution as the Election Commission).

3. The Presidential and Vice-Presidential Elections Act, 1952 (No. 31 of 1952) regulates certain matters relating to the elections to the offices of President and Vice-President of India. In section 8 of this Act, it is stated that :

If after the expiry of the period within which candidatures may be withdrawn,

(a) there is only one candidate who has been validly nominated and has not withdrawn his candidature in the manner and within the time specified in that sub-section, the Returning Officer shall forthwith declare such candidates to be duly elected to the office of President or Vice-President as the case may be.

4. In the case of a contest, a poll is taken, votes shall be counted, etc. When the counting of votes has been completed, the Returning Officer shall forthwith declare the result of the elections in the manner provided by the Act or the rules made thereunder.

5. Rule 10 of the Rules for the Presidential and Vice-Presidential Elections states that:

1. Note on the election of the Vice-President, sent to Rajendra Prasad with Krishna Menon's note dated 10 April 1957 and Attorney General's letter dated 21 April 1957 on the same subject. New Delhi, 20 April 1957. File No. 64/57-PMS. Also available in JN Collection.

(1) At a Vice-Presidential election, the poll shall, where necessary, be taken at a joint meeting of the members of both Houses of Parliament which shall be held in the Parliament House at New Delhi.

(2) The Election Commission shall fix the hours at which the joint meeting shall begin and end and give due publicity thereof in such manner as it thinks fit.

6. The Act of 1952 and the Rules made thereunder lay down in detail the procedure to be followed for the Vice-Presidential election and state clearly that in the case of only one candidate, the Returning Officer shall forthwith declare such candidate to be duly elected. In the case of a contest, as soon as the counting of votes is over, the Returning Officer also declares the result of the election. Further, it states that the poll in a Vice-Presidential election shall be taken "where necessary" at a joint meeting of the Members of both Houses of Parliament. In other words, such a joint meeting need not be held if there is only one candidate.

7. Article 66 of the Constitution, however, states categorically that the Vice-President shall be elected at a joint meeting.

8. The question, therefore, is whether it will be in accordance with the Constitution not to have a joint meeting in case there is only one candidate. Even if, for all practical purposes, the single candidate is to be considered elected, should not a joint meeting be held in conformity with the express provision of the Constitution? At such joint meeting, the Returning Officer may declare the result of the uncontested election himself or report to the Chairman of that meeting who can then announce it.

9. In the case of a contest also, would it be right for the Returning Officer independently to declare the result of the election or to report to the Chairman of the joint meeting who will then announce it?

7
DEFENCE

1. To Ghanshyamdas Birla[1]

New Delhi
2 April 1957

My dear Ghanshyamdasji,

Mathai has shown me your note on your talk with Mr and Mrs Bunker.[2]

What Bunkar said about the US military aid to Pakistan, was not correct.[3] That is to say, it is completely wrong to say that India is two or three times stronger than Pakistan either in the air or in the Army. We have quite adequate and fairly correct information about this matter, and the fact is that Pakistan's Air Force is rapidly becoming as big as ours and better from the point of view of quality of aircraft. In regard to the Army too, their mechanized wing is in many ways much better and stronger than ours as they have got the latest type of tanks. It is, however, the Air Force that causes us much concern. I need not go into details but it is a fact that it is a very serious threat to us, and it is under this tremendous pressure from Pakistan we have been forced, much against our will, to spend a large sum in buying military aircraft. You can appreciate how difficult this has been for us when our financial situation, chiefly in regard to foreign exchange, is so bad. Yet we had to do it, because there is a limit to the risk we can take.

Having done so, even then we cannot keep pace with the flow of bombers and fighters from the US to Pakistan. Obviously, we cannot compete with America in this matter.

1. JN Collection.
2. In his talk with Ellsworth Bunker, G.D. Birla discussed several issues. He asked Ellsworth about the ambiguity in the press conference in which he had denied that the atomic weapons were provided to Pakistan by the USA. Ellsworth reaffirmed his denial and also said that India was three times stronger than Pakistan. Birla drew his attention towards the "mad venture" which was being pursued by the Pakistan Government and wanted to know in what way America would stop it. Ellsworth replied that primarily through moral pressure and ultimately by military force. Birla enquired, "whether he meant that America would use force against Pakistan to stop their aggression." He replied "certainly." Birla also explained India's position regarding Kashmir. At this Ellsworth said, India had a strong case on Kashmir on many points such as (i) plebiscite was agreed on certain conditions which were never implemented by Pakistan; (ii) the legal position was strong and India had agreed, if necessary, to go to the interpretations of the World Court; (iii) any plebiscite at this stage would disturb the stability of the country in the sense that there may be large-scale exodus and communal disturbances.
3. Bunker had said that atomic weapons were not being provided to Pakistan by the USA.

I am pointing this out to you for your own personal information of course, and not for others. But the fact is that this American military aid has completely changed the position of India vis-à-vis Pakistan, so far as defence is concerned, and has at the same time cast an enormous burden on us, which affects all our development schemes. This is the direct result of American aid to Pakistan.

In regard to Kashmir, you apparently said that India had agreed, if necessary, to get the interpretation of the World Court. This is not quite correct. The question of our agreeing or not has not arisen because no such proposal has been made, although some vague references have taken place. What our attitude might be in this matter, will depend on the nature of the proposal.

Yours sincerely,
Jawaharlal Nehru

2. Understanding the Nature of Modern Warfare[1]

I have read the summary dated 14th March 1957 and the Home Minister's note dated 28th March. I have also read, with a feeling of numbness, the two statements attached to the summary, giving a list of subjects and equipment.

I am all for being prepared for any emergency that might arise. But there should be an adequate understanding of the possible emergencies. There should also be some understanding of the nature of modern war. It is clear that all these beautiful statements that have been prepared are based on the type of training that was given during the last war. Much of that training even then was found to be wholly inadequate to meet the situations that arose. Some of the training was unnecessary. In any event, whatever the nature of the last war might have been, it is clear that old methods of warfare are as dead as the dodo. That is the first lessen to be remembered. I fear that neither our military officers nor our civil personnel quite realize this and they continue to think along the old set grooves of thought.

I realize that if we have to face a war emergency in India, we shall probably not have to deal with the latest development of modern warfare. It is more likely

1. Note to A.V. Pai, Home Secretary, New Delhi, 4 April 1957. JN Collection.

that we shall deal with something in between the old ways and the latest new ways. Anyhow, even that will be different from the old and any preparations made along the old lines will not be much good. Unfortunately, we take as our models the British people in this respect, as in many others. The British army machine, including civil defence, etc., is known to be backward, static and rather out of date. It is for this reason that I dislike undertaking anything, at considerable cost, and then merely producing some out-of-date training and procedure.

Having said all this, I would like to add that I agree that emergency training should be given. This may be done at Nagpur or Delhi. The real training is of disciplining human beings to face emergency, whatever its nature, without fear and with as little confusion as possible. I would suggest that the list of subjects and equipment given should be revised very considerably and old and out-of-date ideas in regard to it should be discarded.

3. Keeping Defence Matters Secret[1]

It is rather difficult for me to advise on this. I am inclined to agree that chapter 4 [of the Estimates Committee report] relating to aircraft production should be omitted for security reasons. The Estimates Committee, however, should be informed that whatever they have written in this chapter, as in the rest of the report, will of course, receive the careful consideration of the Ministry of Defence. But it would not be desirable to give publicity to certain matters contained in this chapter.

The Defence Secretary[2] suggests that the entire report should be regarded as secret. I do not quite know how far this is feasible. There are bound to be questions and enquiries in Parliament about the Estimates Committee report on HAL. It may, of course, be said that this report is considered secret. Whether that would be considered satisfactory by Parliament, I do not know.

If it is possible to submit the report to Parliament omitting Chapter 4 and possibly making some other changes in the body of the rest of the report, this might be done. It might also be possible for some brief reference to be made for

1. Note to Minister of Defence Organization and Defence Secretary, New Delhi, 6 April 1957. JN Collection.
2. M.K. Vellodi.

aircraft production without divulging anything that we wish to keep secret. I do not know if this is at all a feasible proposition. Defence Secretary might discuss this with the Chief of the Air Staff and later he could discuss this matter with the Chairman of the Estimates Committee.

8
KASHMIR

I. IN THE UN

1. Message to Habib Bourguiba[1]

My dear Prime Minister,
I am grateful to you for your letter of the 12th February[2] which was given through your Ambassador in London[3] to our High Commissioner there and has only just reached me.

You refer to the Resolution of the Security Council passed on the 24th January 1957. Presumably you are under the misapprehension that some step has been taken by India subsequent to that Resolution. No such step has been taken here. Our case is and has been throughout these nine years that the Jammu and Kashmir State acceded to India legally and constitutionally in October 1947. Subsequently a Constituent Assembly, elected in the State under adult suffrage, drew up a Constitution and gave effect to parts of it in the course of the last four or five years. This was finalized some months ago. No other step has been taken since then, except that the Constituent Assembly dissolved itself.[5] Therefore, the

1. New Delhi, 22 February 1957. JN Collection. Also available in File No. P.V. 303(1)/63, p. nil/corr., EA. This message was sent through India's High Commissioner in London with a request to convey it to the Tunisian Ambassador for forwarding it to his Prime Minister, Habib Bourguiba.
2. Bourguiba referred to the Kashmir question and the Security Council Resolution of 24 January 1957. He stated that as the conflict about Kashmir could not be solved by direct negotiations between India and Pakistan for the last nine years, a plebiscite under the auspices of the UN remained the best alternative.
3. Taieb Slim.
4. The five-power Resolution, sponsored by Australia, Colombia, Cuba, UK and USA, reminded the Governments of India and Pakistan of the principles embodied in the earlier UN and UNCIP resolutions, and that the final disposition of the State of Jammu and Kashmir would be made in accordance with the will of the people expressed through the democratic method of a free and impartial plebiscite, conducted under the auspices of the United Nations. It reaffirmed the Resolution of 30 March 1951 which declared that the convening of the Constituent Assembly and any action taken by it would not constitute disposition of the State in accordance of the above principle. It also stated that further consideration of the dispute would follow.
5. On 26 January 1957.

question of our not acting up to the Resolution passed by the Security Council, which you had mentioned in your previous message and to which apparently you refer again, does not arise. I have been pained at any such assertion being made without due enquiry of the facts. Kashmir State is at present governed by an autonomous Government responsible to an elected Legislature.

Perhaps you are not fully acquainted with the course of events in regard to Kashmir during these nine years. The whole trouble began by a sudden and unprovoked aggression by Pakistan. It would be a sad day if aggression is tolerated and approved by the United Nations or by any country. We have asked the Security Council to deal with these essential matters and they have thus far not done so. The Pakistan army occupies illegally one third of the State of Jammu and Kashmir in spite of the United Nations Resolution asking them to withdraw. We have not made a single international commitment which we have not honoured and it naturally distresses me that you should make a public statement accusing India when in fact India is a victim of aggression and deserve support.

We would be happy to send you all particulars of the Kashmir affair should you so wish to have them. I would have hoped that no statement would be made without full consideration of this intricate problem.

You have been good enough to refer to the moral aspect of this question.[6] It is with this very moral aspect that we are concerned and we are distressed that it should be ignored. The peace of the world has not been threatened by us but by Pakistan's aggression and by its continued threats of war.

With my regards and good wishes,

Sincerely yours,
Jawaharlal Nehru

6. Bourguiba deplored that, "India, listless to the Security Council recommendation, declared Kashmir as already part of India." Though he admired Nehru as a champion of liberty and democracy, whose high moral position had helped in solving some of the most controversial problems threatening world peace, this attitude on Kashmir was likely to create a precedent for opposing the colonial people's right to self-determination.

2. Meetings with British Leaders[1]

I have seen Vijaya Lakshmi Pandit's personal message to you No. 0638 of February 21.[2] This relates to Krishna Menon meeting Selwyn Lloyd. I do not know what other steps have been taken in this matter. I am not keen on Krishna Menon meeting him. Indeed I would personally dislike meeting Selwyn Lloyd. But probably Krishna Menon has mentioned to Pierson Dixon[3] about meeting both Macmillan and Lloyd and the message must have been conveyed to London. Also this meeting is not to discuss any matter but rather to make clear in forcible language what India's position is. If Selwyn Lloyd does not trust Krishna Menon, neither do we trust Selwyn Lloyd. But he happens to be the Foreign Minister and cannot be ignored because of that position.

I am merely sending this message to you, to indicate my broad approach to this question. You will take such steps as you think proper.

1. Note to N.R. Pillai, Secretary General, MEA, Hyderabad, 22 February 1957. JN Collection.
2. Vijaya Lakshmi reminded Pillai that Krishna Menon's meeting with Selwyn Lloyd might further aggravate the stand taken by the UK Government against India as Lloyd had repeatedly said in very clear language that he did not trust Krishna Menon. She suggested that Krishna Menon meet Prime Minister Harold Macmillan only, though she would arrange the other interview also as desired by Pillai.
3. Pierson (John) Dixon (1904-65); entered British Foreign Office, 1929; served at British Embassies at Madrid (1932), Ankara (1936), Rome (1938); transferred to Foreign Office, 1940; served on staff of Resident Minister at Allied Force HQ, Mediterranean, 1943; Principal Private Secretary to Foreign Secretary, 1943-48; Ambassador to Czechoslovakia, 1948-50; Deputy Under Secretary of State, Foreign Office, 1950-54; Permanent Representative of the UK to UN, 1954-60; Ambassador to France, 1960-64; author of *The Iberians of Spain*, *Farewell, Pauline: Napoleon's Favourite Sister.*

3. Message to V.K. Krishna Menon[1]

Your telegram 207 February 22nd.[2] I have seen your statement[3] which has appeared rather fully in the press here.

2. I agree with you that you should inform the President that:

"The Government of India have received the Resolution[4] and will give it consideration along with the statements made in the Council during the debates.[5] At present they are fully engaged in the general elections and the

---

1. Bangalore, 23 February 1957. File No. 14-KU/57, Vol. II, p. 374/corr., MEA. Also available in V.K. Krishna Menon Papers, NMML.
2. Krishna Menon wrote that the general result of the debate in the Security Council was that Pakistan was very discomfited, the position was altered and India was no longer on the defensive. He also wrote that the battle was suspended for the present and the general opinion was that India had foiled Pakistan's attempt and the Resolution (of 21 February) merely represented a continuation of Security Council interest. In his opinion, India could now proceed with Gunnar V. Jarring, the President of the month of the Security Council, only on the basis of "our fundamental position. The British have suffered a bad reverse here. The Americans keep telling us that they were pushed into this position by the British and the British say the other way."
3. Krishna Menon emphasized that first step toward any solution must be the end of Pakistan's "war of hatred" against India. He said that "India cannot afford to disregard the internal and external security of her land." He referred to the enormous war material coming to Pakistan through US military aid which included the possibility of the use of "atomic tactical weapons." He also drew attention to the "Azad Kashmir" Government's statement of 6 February that its forces were 35,000 strong and could easily be increased to over 80,000.
4. Introduced in the Security Council by UK, USA and Australia on 21 February, the Resolution involved the Resolution of 24 January and the previous ones. It urged the President (i) to examine with the Governments of India and Pakistan any proposals which, in his opinion, were likely to contribute towards the settlement of the dispute, having regard to the previous Resolutions of the Council and of the UNCIP; (ii) to visit the subcontinent for this purpose; and (iii) to report to the Council not later than 15 April 1957. This resolution was adopted on 21 February by 10 votes to 0, with USSR abstaining.
5. Pakistan Foreign Minister, Feroz Khan Noon, stated that the sole purpose for introduction of a UN force, as suggested in the 20 February Resolution, was to facilitate withdrawal of Pakistani troops so that demilitarization could take place, and that it was never intended to be utilized for the holding of a plebiscite. This would amount to "merely an augmentation of the UN observers in Kashmir." Arkady A. Sobolev, the Soviet representative in the UN, said that he would not oppose the 21 February Resolution as the idea of Jarring's mission was acceptable.

Prime Minister and all the other Ministers are on tour. The polling in the elections will last till about the middle of March. Full consideration of the Resolution of the Security Council will have to be given by the Government.

The President of the Security Council will naturally receive the hospitality and the courtesy of our country in view of his high position. Regarding the terms of any talks with him, the Government of India will have to give full consideration to this matter."

3. I see that you have asked to see Selwyn Lloyd in London. As he is Foreign Minister, it is normally right for you to see him. But he has behaved so badly that I feel reluctant for you to ask for an interview with him. I would have preferred your asking for an interview with Macmillan. If, however, Selwyn Lloyd wishes to see you, then you should naturally see him. Also, if arrangements have been made for an interview, then you should abide by them.

4. This telegram is being sent from Bangalore. I am going to Cochin tomorrow.[6]

5. I do hope you will take every care of yourself.

6. Nehru was on the election tour at this time.

4. Instructions to Indian Missions Abroad[1]

I agree with you. We may consider all these points when Shri Krishna Menon returns.

2. As a matter of fact, all this is a question of emphasis. We cannot leave out the legal accession part. The moment we weaken on this, we have to proceed on grounds of expedience and desirability, which, of course, are important and should be stressed. So far as the UK Government is concerned, they attach great importance to the legal and constitutional aspect of accession as, in a sense, they are themselves involved in it. Also, because Pakistan challenged that aspect

1. Note to N.R. Pillai, Secretary General and M.J. Desai, Commonwealth Secretary, New Delhi, 27 February 1957. JN Collection.

SELECTED WORKS OF JAWAHARLAL NEHRU

and calls it a fraud. That accession again is tied up with the aggression of Pakistan on Kashmir.

3. What Mr Myrdal[2] says is, of course, very important. All these facts have been stated in Shri Krishna Menon's speeches.[3] They can be emphasized more in private approaches.

4. As for Shri Krishna Menon's telegram about Moulik's letter,[4] there is some slight justification for his criticism.[5] It is true that, while Bakhshi Ghulam Mohammad, Pantji and many other important persons have stated definitely that there can be or will be no plebiscite under any circumstances, I have not taken up that attitude, nor, so far as I can see, has Krishna Menon. What I have stated is that, while we cannot say categorically that there can be no plebiscite, in fact, a plebiscite is not at all a feasible proposition for a variety of reasons and, secondly, that we are not bound by various statements made by us because of other developments. These were our instructions to Krishna Menon also. The difference between the two expressions may not be very great. Yet, there it is.

5. I do not think we can criticize Dr Moulik for his letter, even though he laid a slight stress which we would have preferred him not to do. It is not easy for our Missions abroad to remain silent on these vital issues, and there is some

2. (Karl) Gunnar Myrdal (1898-1987); Swedish economist and politician; Professor, Political Economy and Financial Science, Stockholm University, 1933-50; Government Adviser on financial, economic and social questions, 1933; conducted investigation on American Negroes for Carnegie Corporation, 1938-43; Minister of Trade and Commerce, 1945-47; Executive Secretary, UN Economic Commission for Europe, Geneva, 1947-57; Professor of International Economy, Stockholm University, 1960-67; awarded Peace Prize of Federal Republic of Germany (with Alva Myrdal), 1970, Nobel Prize for Economics, 1974, and the Nitti Prize, 1976; author of *A Problem for Democracy, Economic Theory and Under-developed Regions, The Negro Problem and Modern Democracy, Beyond the Welfare State, Challenge to Affluence, Asian Drama* among others..
3. The reference is to Krishna Menon's speeches in the Security Council on 23 and 24 January 1957.
4. Moni Moulik, Public Relations Officer in the Indian High Commission in London, wrote a letter which was published in *Manchester Guardian* on 20 February.
5. Krishna Menon wrote that all Public Relations Officers should be told not to go too much into the future of the Kashmir question but "merely to confine themselves to contradiction of falsehoods or misstatements as we cannot have an official putting it on record that we are against a plebiscite." According to him, a directive should be given, "as it would be harmful to have a number of official statements in different countries either contradicting each other or which can be picked upon and used against us as indeed the leading article in the *Guardian* has done." He also thought that Moulik's letter had missed the main issues. If an expression of opinion against a plebiscite, as Moulik had put out, was desirable in England, then a non-official should have signed the letter as it could not then be quoted as an official view of the Government of India.

slight risk always of some point being stressed unnecessarily. We have to take the risk.

6. I think that a note should be drafted for all our Missions abroad about our present position in regard to the Kashmir issue. They should be asked to read Krishna Menon's speeches in the Security Council on this issue, which no doubt have been sent to them, and generally to follow the same argument though, of course, briefly. Copies of Krishna Menon's speeches should be given to the Foreign Offices concerned.

7. Our Missions should be asked not to enter into elaborate arguments but (1) to contradict falsehoods and misstatements, and (2) to lay stress on some major aspects of the case. In regard to the question of plebiscite, what I have stated above might be clarified for the information of our Foreign Missions.

8. This applies to any written communications. In private conversations, the argument could be more detailed.

5. To K.M. Cariappa[1]

New Delhi
27 February 1957

My dear Cariappa,[2]

Thank you for your letter of the 24th February.

The discussions in the Security Council on the Kashmir affair[3] and, even more so, press comments abroad, have been distressing.[4] I doubt if this has much to do with ignorance of the facts. These facts have been placed quite clearly before everybody who is interested. You would no doubt be helpful in

1. JN Collection.
2. Cariappa was former High Commissioner in Australia and New Zealand and former Commander-in-Chief, Indian Army.
3. For discussions in Security Counil, see *ante*, pp. 397-401 and *Selected Works* (second series), Vol. 36, the section on Kashmir.
4. For example, the *Daily Mail* reported on 27 February that Nehru had outlined a plan to end the Kashmir controversy to Malcolm MacDonald, The British High Commissioner in India. Accordingly, India would waive her claim to the whole of Kashmir and accept the existing boundary line provided the United Nations did not insist upon a plebiscite.

regard to the early facts of Pakistani aggression and what steps we took in regard to it, but real discussion is about subsequent developments in the Security Council, the UN Commission and meetings between Prime Ministers, etc. All this is contained now in about a dozen or more fat printed volumes. The whole thing is a maze.

Anyhow the present phase in the Security Council is over and I do not know when and in what form it will come back to it.

I am sending you a copy of Krishna Menon's speeches on Kashmir in the Security Council. You will find from these speeches that every relevant point has been brought out.

Yours sincerely,
Jawaharlal Nehru

6. Developments in "Azad Kashmir"[1]

The Soviet Ambassador[2] came to see me this morning. He spoke first about the accident of the Illyushin aircraft day before yesterday and said that they would be glad to help in any way, such as by sending their engineers. I agreed with this and told him that it would be desirable for their engineers to see this aircraft, as it is now, and help our people in enquiring. I mentioned further that the Illyushin cannot be moved till a new engine is put in. He said that he would immediately communicate with his Government on the subject and no doubt they would send the engineers and the engine.

2. He further said it would be desirable for the Illyushin aircraft to be sent to Tashkent later for a complete overhaul. I agreed.

3. He then went on to give me a confidential message he had received from his Government about Pakistan activities. The Soviet Government have received reports to the effect that disturbances might be organized in Kashmir as a pretext for asking UN forces to be sent there.

1. Note to Secretary General, Foreign Secretary, Commonwealth Secretary, Defence Secretary, and Vishnu Sahay, Secretary on Kashmir Affairs, New Delhi, 28 February 1957. JN Collection.
2. Mikhail A. Menshikov.

4. The President of "Azad Kashmir", Abdul Qayyum Khan,[3] had put forward a plan of action before the Pakistan Government. This was that Pakistan should recognize the "Azad Kashmir" Government for the whole of Jammu & Kashmir and should withdraw its forces from "Azad Kashmir". When this was done, the "Azad Kashmir" Government would take necessary measures to recover and occupy the rest of Jammu & Kashmir State. They would ask for volunteers from Pakistan and other countries to help them.

5. A meeting of Pakistan senior officers considered this plan and were not in favour of its acceptance. They pointed out that this would involve a military conflict with India and East Pakistan could not be held. This would lead to internal troubles and divisions.

6. It is not known what the Pakistan Government's decision has been on Abdul Qayyum Khan's plan, but the leaders of "Azad Kashmir" continue to deliver speeches asking the people to get ready for fighting. Muslim organizations have been directed by Pakistan to carry on a campaign for volunteers for the liberation of Kashmir.[4]

7. There has been a concentration of Pakistan troops in regions adjoining Jammu & Kashmir State.[5] Military manoeuvres took place recently in these regions. After the manoeuvres were over, two divisions were left in that area. Some other military detachments have also been sent there.

8. Pakistan may try to provoke disturbances in Jammu & Kashmir State if Security Council's decision does not favour them.

3. Abdul Qayyum Khan remained President of "Azad Kashmir" Government till April 1957.
4. In the same vein, Abdul Qayyum Khan told a *Daily Telegraph* correspondent on 9 February that "it is coming to a fight in Kashmir, whether people like it or not. We have no alternative left, and I have told the Pakistani Government... I think that it is certain that there will be fighting this year, perhaps even in a few weeks.... Kashmir wants to see some results at last, if not by diplomacy, then by war.... In Kashmir we can give the Indians hell. We are much better equipped now than in the former fighting." He insisted that "Azad Kashmir" had not been a party to the ceasefire agreement and was, therefore, not bound by it.
5. According to the "Azad Kashmir" authorities, as told to the same correspondent on 6 February, its forces numbered 35,000 men and would be increased overnight to 80,000 of whom 70,000 were trained ex-soldiers. Earlier in January, a spokesman of the Indian Government stated that Pakistani troops were stationed within a few miles of the Indian border, and that the "Azad Kashmir" forces had been increased to nearly 45 well-equipped battalions.

7. Pakistan-USSR Correspondence on Kashmir[1]

The Soviet Ambassador came to see me at midday today. He read out to me a letter dated the 11th February 1957, which the Prime Minister of Pakistan had sent through his Ambassador[2] to Mr Bulganin. This was delivered on the 13th February. He also read out Mr Bulganin's reply to the Pakistan Prime Minister, dated the 27th February.

2. The Pakistan Prime Minister in his letter expressed his satisfaction at the neutral stand taken by the representative of the USSR in the Security Council on the 24th January regarding Kashmir.[3] He further said that the Pakistan Government had gone as far as possible to secure a just settlement. Their wish was to allow the people of Kashmir to decide for themselves by a free and impartial plebiscite. India had agreed to this at an earlier stage but insist now on withdrawal of Pakistan forces from "Azad Kashmir". No such condition had been laid down previously. But Pakistan was ready to withdraw her forces provided security was guaranteed by UN force or otherwise. If India objects to the UN force being sent to India-occupied Kashmir, then the UN force should remain in "Azad" territory only, provided there was demilitarization on the part of India on the other side. Alternatively, local forces could be recruited by the Plebiscite Administrator on the spot.

3. Pakistan was also not anxious to have foreign troops. Out of respect for the feelings of the USSR Government, they would agree to the foreign troops coming from neutral countries. The Pakistan Prime Minister hoped that the USSR would continue her impartial role in this matter.

4. Mr Bulganin's reply dated the 27th February was as follows: As Pakistan Ambassador had already informed the Pakistan PM, there had been several talks on this subject in the course of which the Soviet Government had explained their views on the Kashmir issue clearly. This was a matter for the Kashmir people themselves to decide, and they had already expressed their views on it and decided that Kashmir should be an integral part of India.

1. Note, New Delhi, 1 March 1957. JN Collection.
2. Akhtar Husain was Pakistan's Ambassador in Moscow.
3. The Soviet delegate to the Security Council, Sobolev, said that the adoption of the Constitution by the Jammu and Kashmir Constituent Assembly showed that the question was settled by the people of Kashmir who regarded themselves "to be an inalienable part of the Republic of India," and that the draft resolution failed to take into account of the real situation in Kashmir. But he abstained when the resolution was put to vote.

5. The Soviet Union consider that disputes must be solved by peaceful means and negotiations, without outside interference. The Soviet Union could not agree to mediate in this matter as there were no grounds for this, in view of the total disagreement of India and Pakistan on this issue.

6. The recent discussions in the Security Council had further convinced the Soviet Union that outside interference would not only produce no good results, but would be harmful. It would only be to the advantage of certain countries associated with military blocs and colonialism. On the pretext of giving support to Pakistan, these countries were attempting to gain a hold in Kashmir and have some kind of an international administration there.

7. No outside interference could lead to any positive result. The Soviet Union will hold to its objection on such interference in regard to the Kashmir issue. As pointed out by the Pakistan Prime Minister, the Kashmir issue did not directly infringe on any interest of the USSR, but this does not mean that the Soviet Union will remain indifferent to any attempts to provoke tension in areas immediately adjoining the USSR by use of arms or the threat of the use of arms.

8. I thanked the Soviet Ambassador for this message. He said that the Pakistan Ambassador in Moscow had been particularly active during the past few weeks.

9. Copies of this note should be sent to President, Vice-President and members of the Foreign Affairs Committee.

8. British MPs in Kashmir[1]

The Prime Minister said that in our reply to a communication from the Security Council, it had been stated that our policy decision with regard to the Security Council's Resolution would be taken only after the return of Shri Krishna Menon, but Mr Jarring would, in any case, be welcome as a visitor to India.

2. The Prime Minister referred also to the impending visit to India of two Conservative Members of Parliament from Great Britain who were first visiting

---

1. Minutes of the Cabinet Meeting, 1 March 1957. File No. KS-29/57, MHA. Also available in JN Collection.

Pakistan and "Azad Kashmir". These gentlemen desired also to visit Kashmir.[2] Although their views were known to be anti-Indian with regard to Kashmir, the Prime Minister suggested and the Cabinet agreed that no objection should be taken to their Kashmir tour.

2. Two Members of British Parliament, Reginald Bennett of the Conservative Party and Frank Tomney of the Labour Party, visited Srinagar on 13 March 1957. They were also members of the Anglo-Pakistan Parliamentary Group.

9. Cable to Ali Yavar Jung[1]

Your telegram 135 March 4.[2] It is rather odd for Tunisian invitation to be sent so late. Obviously it is not possible for me or indeed any other Minister to leave India immediately after elections and just when Parliament is meeting. I should like you, if possible, to go to Tunis on this occasion to represent us. Your going will be helpful also in many ways as you can have talks there and explain our general policy in regard to various matters. As you know, Tunisian Government has been playing a rather doubtful role recently. Let me know if you think you can go.

2. For your information. Early in February I received message from Bourguiba through our High Commissioner in London about Kashmir. Even before I received this, it was given to the press. This message was a very objectionable one and accused us of falling from our high pretensions. I sent reply through High Commissioner, London, asking Bourguiba to inform me on what basis he had come to that conclusion.[3] It was rather extraordinary for Tunisia of all countries to address us in this way and, what is more, give publicity to their message. Two or three weeks later, Bourguiba replied. He was somewhat

---

1. New Delhi, 6 March 1957. JN Collection. Ali Yavar Jung was India's Ambassador in Cairo.
2. At the request of the Tunisian Ambassador in Cairo, Jung had telegraphed in advance the formal invitation of the Tunisian Government for Nehru to grace the ceremonies in Tunis on 20 March 1957 to mark the first anniversary of Tunisian independence.
3. See *Selected Works* (second series), Vol. 36, pp. 373-374.

apologetic but nevertheless maintained that, whatever the facts, so many countries had expressed their opinion against India in regard to Kashmir and this itself counted. To this again I had replied.[4] No answer to this has come yet.

3. I must say that I was greatly hurt by Bourguiba's attitude and statements in this matter. No other country, including those openly hostile to us, has functioned in this way. It is obvious that he had done this under pressure, possibly from USA or UK or France. For some years we arranged financial and other help to his representative in Delhi so that he could carry on Tunisian publicity from here. This representative, Taieb Slim,[5] is now their Ambassador in London.

4. See *ante*, pp. 397-398.
5. Taieb Slim (b. 1919); Tunisian politician and diplomatist; Head, Tunisian Office, Cairo, 1949; established Tunisian offices, New Delhi, Jakarta, Karachi; Head, Foreign Affairs, Presidency of Council of Ministers, 1955-56; Ambassador to UK, 1956-62, also accredited to Denmark, Norway and Sweden, 1960-62; Permanent Representative to UN, 1962-67, concurrently Ambassador to Canada; Secretary of State, Personal Representative of President, 1967-70; member, National Association, 1969; Ambassador to Morocco, 1970-71; Minister of State, 1971-73; member, Political Bureau Destour Socialist Party, 1970-74; Ambassador and Permanent Representative to UN, 1973-74; Ambassador to Canada, 1974-76; Minister of State, 1976-77; Permanent Representative to UN, 1981-84.

10. India's Public Relations Work[1]

The Maharaja of Patiala[2] came to see me this morning. We discussed the work of the last session of the UN General Assembly which was in many ways a more important and significant one than the preceding ones.[3] Crisis followed crisis and the delegation attending the UN, according to the Maharaja, learnt more in

1. Note to Secretary General and Foreign Secretary, New Delhi, 9 March 1957. JN Collection.
2. Yadavendra Singh.
3. The Suez crisis, the Hungarian question and the Kashmir issue dominated the discussions during the eleventh regular session of the United Nations General Assembly, held from 12 November 1956 to 8 March 1957, and the two emergency sessions held from 1 November to 10 November 1956.

this one session about world problems than they would have normally done in two or three sessions.

2. The main point he made with me was that, as he said, "our public relations work was nil". This may be an exaggeration, of course, but it would represent what he thought. He was talking not only of New York but more or less of the United States. So far as the Assembly itself was concerned, the big debates in which India took prominent part certainly helped in educating the delegation.

3. He went to the West Coast during the recess and found there too almost complete ignorance about India. In fact, he said most people were talking about Pakistan and what was being done there and seemed to him ignorant of what was happening in India.

4. In the UN, he said that not all the members of our delegation developed contacts with other delegations. Partly, this may be due to lack of finances. Such contacts, of course, are useful.

5. The Pakistan delegation indulged in the crudest form of propaganda and vilification and part of this at least went down.

6. I am just putting this down for record.

11. To Bakhshi Ghulam Mohammad[1]

New Delhi
13 March 1957

My dear Bakhshi,

....When Jarring was in New York, he had suggested reaching Delhi on the 21st, after spending a few days in Karachi. We had more or less accepted this. Later, however, it struck us that the 21st is rather inconvenient, as I shall be very busy with Parliament on those two/three days. So, I sent a message to him that, if it was convenient to him, he might come after the 25th. To that, he replied that he has already fixed his visit to Pakistan and he will be reaching there in a day or two from now. He does not want to extend his stay in Pakistan too much. He has suggested, therefore, reaching Delhi on the 23rd March afternoon. That, I think, is Saturday. He has suggested his resting here on the 24th and then meeting us

---

1. JN Collection. Extracts.

on the 25th. I am agreeing to this. Probably, we shall meet him on the 24th, Sunday.

Jarring has indicated that he does not wish to visit Kashmir or the Pakistan-occupied part of Kashmir, and he, therefore, will only go to Karachi and Delhi.

Krishna Menon arrived here last night, and I have had a brief talk with him. We shall have further talks as to the line to be adopted with Jarring. Broadly speaking, we do not intend putting forward any proposals.

The situation in Egypt is a very difficult one, and President Nasser wants Krishna Menon to go there for two days for consultation. It is possible that Krishna Menon might go there on the 16th, returning on the 19th or the 20th. He must be here when Jarring comes.

In my last letter to you, I had suggested your coming here for consultations. For the present, you need not trouble to come. If necessary, I shall let you know later.

There is one thing, however, that I should like to tell you. It does no good for any of us to run down Jarring or his visit. This will merely irritate him. Therefore, I would suggest to you not to say anything about him or his visit. You may, of course, always say that our position is quite clear and we are prepared to tell anyone about it.

Perhaps, you have noticed that at no time have I said that under no circumstances will there be a plebiscite. What I have said is that a plebiscite is not a feasible proposition after all that has happened, and that Pakistan has not fulfilled the conditions necessary for it. When I have been asked if we will be agreeable to a plebiscite if every condition was fulfilled, my answer has been that this is a hypothetical question which can only be considered when such a situation arises.

I know that you and Pantji and some others have often said that there can never be a plebiscite in Jammu & Kashmir State. I think that that kind of a statement is not helpful at present, certainly from the point of view of people in the outside world, though it may be helpful in Kashmir.

Yours sincerely,
Jawaharlal Nehru

12. To C.C. Desai[1]

New Delhi
14 March 1957

My dear C. C.,[2]

I sent you a telegram this morning about Jarring's visit.[3] The more I look at my engagements during the next fortnight, the more alarmed I am. Here, we are still in the midst of our general elections. The final picture will not be available for another few days. Immediately, the necessary consequences of these elections arise, that is, the formation of a new Government at the Centre and new Governments in the States. The President and the Vice-President have to be elected. A little later, new Governors have to be appointed in some of the States.

Meanwhile we have to face the last session of the old Parliament, and there are going to be debates in both the Houses on the international situation which means chiefly Kashmir. Also the Middle East situation.

On top of all this comes the visit of the Polish Prime Minister[4] and the German Foreign Minister.[5] The Polish Prime Minister reaches here on the 24th March afternoon and stays on till the 27th afternoon. Two hours after his departure comes the German Foreign Minister and he stays for two or three days. While he is still here, the King of Nepal[6] comes to Delhi for a brief visit. These eminent dignitaries take up a lot of time in banquets, receptions and talks.

Meanwhile, I have to draft the President's Address to Parliament and all that. There are questions in Parliament. There are meetings of the Congress Working Committee to consider the situation after the elections, and so on.

It is in this context that Jarring is arriving here. Nevertheless, we shall find time, of course, to meet him and talk with him. But this is about the most difficult time he could have chosen to come. We do not wish to appear to be obstructive as he has to function within a time limit.

1. JN Collection.
2. India's High Commissioner in Pakistan.
3. Besides discussing Gunnar Jarring's programme in Delhi in this telegram (not printed), Nehru told Desai not to be "drawn into discussion with Jarring or to express yourself about the merits of the question" and avoid any reference to internal politics or personalities in Pakistan. Nehru wrote that the Kashmir problem was delicate and complex and "we shall have to feel our way about his approach after meeting him."
4. Josef Cyrankiewicz.
5. Heinrich von Brentano.
6. Mahendra Bir Bikram Shah.

Jarring, I understand, arrives in Delhi at 6.30 p.m. on the 23rd March. I had hoped to see him that evening, but it will be too late then. So I have suggested that he might call on me at 7.30 p.m. on the next day, Sunday 24th March, at my house. This is rather a late hour, but I cannot help it as the Polish Prime Minister is calling on me at 6.30 p.m. All that day I shall be busy with the meeting of the Congress Working Committee. That evening (that is, the 24th), N.R. Pillai is arranging a dinner for Jarring.

I am not fixing any other time for meeting Jarring now. We shall do that when I see him. Please explain this to Jarring. Also tell him that we shall welcome his presence at the banquet being given to the Polish Prime Minister on Monday, the 25th March, at Rashtrapati Bhavan.

I have suggested to you in my telegram that it would be advisable for you to avoid discussing the Kashmir matter with Jarring, and more particularly not to talk to him about Pakistan personalities and what they may be saying to each other or to diplomats in regard to Kashmir. These things are repeated and may create difficulties. This subject of Kashmir has become quite extraordinarily complex, though essentially it is a simple one, and we shall have to listen to Jarring when he comes here. I do not propose to commit myself in any way. Our broad argument, of course, has been stated by Krishna Menon in the Security Council. I thought I might give you this hint because Jarring may well try to get something out of you.

I gathered from a message which Inder Chopra[7] sent us that Jarring does not intend going to Kashmir or the Pakistan occupied part of the State. He will spend some time in Karachi and then in Delhi and go back.

To add to our difficulties, Krishna Menon is really very ill. How he carries on, I do not know, but he insists on doing so.

Yours sincerely,
Jawaharlal Nehru

7. Inder Sen Chopra (b. 1909); First Secretary, Indembassy, Washington, 1947; Deputy Secretary, MEA, 1949; Joint Secretary and Chief of Protocol, 1950; Minister and later Ambassador to Sweden, 1955-58, Iraq, 1958-61, Lebanon, 1962, Kuwait, 1963; and Argentina, 1964.

13. Kashmir Issue in the Security Council[1]

The Prime Minister said that the Foreign Affairs Committee of the Cabinet had discussed the Kashmir issue on 14th March, 1957. The view taken by the Committee was that India's position had already been fully stated in the United Nations Security Council by the Minister Without Portfolio and that position should be adhered to.

2. Tracing the sequence of events regarding Kashmir from 1947, the Prime Minister explained that India's commitments related only to two Resolutions of the United Nations Commission on Kashmir dated August, 1948 and January, 1949. According to these Resolutions, there had to be (1) a ceasefire followed by the creation of a peaceful atmosphere; (2) a truce followed by the withdrawal of the Pakistani troops from Kashmir territory and (3) after the first two conditions had been satisfied, consultation between India and the United Nations Commission as to the best method of consulting the wishes of the people of Kashmir. Pakistan had not fulfilled the first two conditions, but had continued to occupy the invaded territory and strengthened her forces in that area. India could not, therefore, take any steps with regard to the third part of the Resolutions. Moreover, during the last eight or nine years, conditions had changed greatly.

3. The Prime Minister added that Sweden had made a suggestion that the legal side of the Kashmir dispute might be referred to the International Court of Justice. India had no objection provided it was a proper reference.

4. The Minister Without Portfolio supplemented the Prime Minister's statement by clarifying one or two points and, in particular, the fact that India's relations with Kashmir were established in 1947; Kashmir had become Indian territory at that time and India had done nothing so far in violation of any of the Resolutions of the United Nations. Pakistan, on the other hand, had included in her Constitution the portion of Kashmir still forcibly occupied by her.

---

1. Minutes of the Cabinet Meeting, 15 March 1957. File No. 314/CF/47, Part IV, Cabinet Secretariat. Also available in JN Collection.

14. Pakistani Raids into Indian Territory[1]

Shri Krishna Menon drew my attention to an item of news appearing in the *Hindusthan Standard* of today, page 1. This refers to a large band of armed Pakistanis attacking and looting the border town of Kamalpur in Tripura State two days ago.[2] In this connection he suggested that we should prepare a list of Pakistani raids into Indian territory ever since the ceasefire in Kashmir or, at any rate, during more recent years. This was to be done to be given to Mr Jarring.

2. These lists have been prepared from time to time in answer to Questions in Parliament and it should not be difficult to collect them.

3. I feel however that mixing up of the major and minor incidents would be confusing. Therefore, attempts should be made to separate the major incidents from such as involve cattle lifting and the like. Such a list of more or less important incidents might be prepared and it might be further stated that there have been hundreds or thousands of other incidents—of a minor nature—the figure should be given. These would apply not only to the ceasefire line but to the whole of the Indo-Pakistan border in the East and the West. The idea is that Mr Jarring could get some notion of the aggressive character of Pakistan in this respect and the consequent trouble we are having on our long frontier.

4. In preparing the list, violations of the ceasefire line in Jammu & Kashmir State should be kept separate.

---

1. Note to Secretary General, Commonwealth Secretary and Joint Secretary, 18 March 1957. New Delhi. JN Collection.
2. It was reported on 17 March 1957 that over 400 armed Pakistanis attacked Kamalpur during the midnight on 15-16 March.

15. To Kwame Nkrumah[1]

New Delhi
18 March 1957

My dear Prime Minister,[2]

I have received your telegram of 14th March conveying the hope of your Government that the differences between India and Pakistan over Kashmir will be settled amicably and that we will renew our attempt at peaceful negotiations to settle this most difficult dispute.[3] I thank you for this message and appreciate your friendly approach.

I understand that our acting High Commissioner in Ghana[4] has already acquainted you and your colleagues with the basic facts of the Kashmir question. So far as we are concerned, I need not tell you that it has been our desire, throughout these troubled years, to seek a peaceful solution of this difficult question. We will continue to strive to this end. We are always willing to discuss this matter with the Pakistan Government, but we cannot be a party to accepting anything which directly or indirectly casts a slur on our honour and ignores the fact that we have been the victims of aggression. Further, we do not want anything to be done which leads to upheavals and misery all round.

It is not possible for me to give you all the basic facts of the Kashmir question in a letter but I am asking our acting High Commissioner in Ghana to see you and hand over to you full reports of the speeches of our representative in the Security Council on this issue as they give most of the facts on the Kashmir question in some detail.

M.J. Desai[5] has just returned and given me a glowing account of the success of the independence celebrations and the excellent arrangements made and the kindness and consideration shown by you and your colleagues in giving him so much of your time during the independence celebration days when all of you must have been very heavily occupied.

With kind regards,

Yours sincerely,
Jawaharlal Nehru

1. JN Collection.
2. Prime Minister of Ghana.
3. Nkrumah felt distressed that the two friendly nations, India and Pakistan, differed so violently over Kashmir. He hoped that an amicable settlement would strengthen the Afro-Asian solidarity.
4. B.K. Kapur.
5. Commonwealth Secretary, Government of India.

16. India's Stand on Kashmir[1]

Feroz Khan Noon is a bumptious bounder and we need not attach too much importance to what he says.[2] I do not think anyone in Pakistan attaches much importance to it. As a matter of fact, he has stated publicly that he did not take the Kashmir issue to the General Assembly because Pakistan would have lost there even at that time.[3] The position has changed since then somewhat to our advantage.

2. Feroz Khan Noon has some reasons to congratulate himself for the support he got and for the widespread condemnation of India by many other countries and the press there. But the reasons for this were not the brilliant advocacy of Feroz Khan, but entirely different.

3. I am afraid, the reactions of our High Commissioner in Karachi are not always wise.[4] Obviously, we are not going to publicize what Feroz

---

1. Note to Commonwealth Secretary, New Delhi, 19 March 1957. JN Collection.
2. India's Deputy High Commissioner in Lahore, N.V. Rao, reported that Feroz Khan Noon told him on 11 March in Lahore that Pakistan had won the first round in the battle of Kashmir and listed following losses for India: (i) USA was convinced that India was in the communist camp and her neutrality was a pretence; (ii) India had lost her friends in Western world; (iii) Pakistan was collecting comments and cartoons in the world press condemning Nehru, for using them to their advantage when they take the Kashmir issue to the General Assembly; (iv) India had lost her moral position in the world and her leadership of the Asian-African group; (v) India stood in the Middle East as an anti-Muslim country opposed to the rights of Kashmiris to determine their future. Rao also wrote that a favourite theme with Pakistani propagandists at this time was that India's "present Pakistan policy is based on personal whims and fancies" of Nehru, who was also a Kashmiri. But the Indian people did not want their resources to be spent on a territory "which they could never hope to keep" and even Vijaya Lakshmi Pandit did not support her brother's policy. Rao reported that later at a public meeting there, Noon repeated these points and added that Pakistan delegation worked hand in hand with UK and US delegations in all the moves that were made in the Security Council.
3. Noon told Rao that Pakistan could have taken the Kashmir issue to the General Assembly "where every country would have voted for us except the eleven communist countries," but they wanted a friendly settlement with India. C.C. Desai felt worried, as Pakistan was confident about a verdict in their favour by two-thirds majority.
4. Desai referred to Rao's comments and wrote that it might be desirable to confront Malcolm MacDonald regarding the collusion between the British and the Pakistanis. He hoped that the Americans were conscious of the indifference shown by Pakistan to the development of communism in this part of the world.

Khan said in a private conversation about his unconcern for Indian Muslims.[5]

4. I think that many of our foreign missions are still not clear about our attitude on this Kashmir matter. They should realize this clearly. The other day I saw a letter from Shri C.C. Desai in which he reported a conversation that he had with somebody in Karachi. In this he almost accepted the fact that Junagadh's case was the same as Kashmir. This is not a fact. The two cases are completely different.[6]

5. You say that you are going to issue a circular letter. You may do so, of course. But it seems to me that in spite of our previous circular letters our missions do not seem to function as they should in this matter. Indeed, they do not seem to have grasped the essential aspects of the problem as it exists today. Because during the past eight or nine years we have slurred over the essential aspects of this problem and discussed various matters and made many suggestions, most people have forgotten about these basic facts. We intend to stick to these basic facts as indeed Shri Krishna Menon did in his speeches before the Security Council. These basic facts are :-

(1) Accession of Jammu & Kashmir State to the Indian Union.
(2) Invasion by Pakistan of Indian Union territory.
(3) Continued occupation of nearly one-half of this Indian Union territory in Kashmir State by Pakistan uptil now.
(4) The only Resolutions to which we are committed in the Security Council are those of the 13th August and, I think, the 5th January. These Resolutions lay down certain action to be taken. So far as we are concerned, we took the preliminary action. Pakistan did not do so and has not done so till now and has thus violated not only the ceasefire agreement, but other parts of this Resolution by not withdrawing its forces.
(5) We have carried out every commitment that we have made.
(6) The various discussions and proposals that have been made by us in the course of these eight years and rejected by Pakistan one after the other were no commitments by us.
(7) Confusion has arisen because people have discussed these intermediate

---

5. Noon told Rao that the internal repercussions in India "following a plebiscite are no concern of ours. It does not matter to me even if every Indian Muslim is murdered or converted." Desai suggested to the Commonwealth Secretary, M.J. Desai, that this point should be brought to the "notice of some of our prominent Muslims." He also suggested that this talk of Noon should be exploited by India to the fullest extent "during the present crisis."
6. For details of Junagadh case, see *Selected Works* (second series), Vol. 4, p. 430.

talks forgetting the basic facts and the express directions of the Security Council.

(8) Pakistan has continued to propagate hatred and religious bigotry in violation of Security Council directions which aimed at peaceful and normal conditions being established. Because of this hatred and violent propaganda it was impossible to settle down. This is continuing and nothing can be done in this context.

(9) Pakistan has committed aggression and it must vacate this aggression and purge itself of it before anything else can be considered.

(10) We do not propose to make any proposals or suggestions except on the basis of Pakistan vacating this aggression.

(11) We are not worried by threats of what Pakistan will do whether this is in the Security Council, in the General Assembly or on the field of battle. We are going to hold to our position.

6. Our missions should realize the importance of this matter and what our views are and should make them clear not only to the Governments concerned, but should reply to the press propaganda by articles and cartoons etc. They should not remain silent under this barrage, and they should bring out the basic facts. It is Pakistan that has ignored and defied the Security Council Resolutions.

7. Another fact should be stressed. It is absurd and fantastic for anyone to say that we have not carried out the Security Council Resolution, passed I think on the 24th January 1957 and that we have annexed Kashmir on the 26th January. This is patently false. We have done nothing on the 26th January in regard to annexation or in non-compliance of the Resolution of the Security Council. We cannot annex our own territory. The accession took place in October 1947.

17. On Discussions in the Security Council[1]

Jawaharlal Nehru: Mr Deputy Chairman,[2] the Chairman[3] was pleased to advise the House that it might be better in this debate on the President's Address not to lay too much stress on matters affecting international affairs, because there was going to be another and a separate debate. But, of course, it is open to Members to do so, and perhaps it is difficult to avoid even in this debate references to international affairs which form such an important part of the President's Address. Normally, of course, Sir, the President's Address is always, not only partly but largely, concerned—that is, in accordance with precedents elsewhere—with international affairs, and so it was natural for this particular Address by the President to concern itself with them, more specially when many matters today in international affairs cause us great concern.

I am trying at the present moment, rather briefly I hope, to deal with some points in regard to some of these matters like Kashmir,[4] Goa[5] and the like, and not to deal with many other points that honourable Members raised. There is just one thing I should like to say right at the beginning. The President's Address deals with a period of a year and deals with that naturally in a small compass both in the domestic field and in the foreign field. The Address may be a brief one, but this period is a period full of happenings and occurrences, in fact full of the makings of history, and I should like this House, whether in this debate or in the next, certainly to pay attention and to criticize individual points here and

1. Speech in the Rajya Sabha on the motion of thanks on the President's address, 20 March 1957. *Rajya Sabha Debates,* Vol. XXVI, cols. 232-245. Extracts.
2. S.V. Krishnamurthy Rao.
3. S. Radhakrishnan.
4. Algu Rai Shastri, Congress Member from UP, said that Jarring should be taken to Kashmir to see how much the State had progressed and how well it was being run. This could be contrasted with the account given by Margarate Bourke-White, of the tribal invasion of Kashmir. He said that unsettling a question, which had already been settled, as stated by Nehru on 29 March 1956 in the Lok Sabha, would mean uprooting of things that had been fixed legally, constitutionally and practically. Kazi Syed Karimuddin, Congress Member from Bombay, questioned the legal right of Pakistan to demand a plebiscite in Kashmir when the Head of the Government, the Maharaja, and the Constituent Assembly had acceded to India. Reopening this question would be disastrous for different communities who were living peacefully, he stated. Jaswant Singh criticized the Indian Government's policy in regard to Kashmir.
5. Kazi Karimuddin said that a survey of the work done by the Government of India regarding the liberation of Goa should be presented in the Parliament.

there, and we welcome that criticism and we hope to profit by every criticism that is offered. But nevertheless I should like this House and the country, if I may say so, to try to take in the full sweep of events, these historical events both in the world and in our own country, more specially in our country, because world events impinge upon us, and sometimes we realize that they are important, sometimes we do not. But living in our own country as actors and parties to this drama that is being enacted in this country, we are apt to forget this full sweep of events and perhaps lose ourselves in some particular thing that we like or we dislike. But after all, they are all interconnected. Not only is there a connection between the domestic and the international policies of the Government—it may occasionally not be wholly apparent, but obviously there has to be some connection—but also within this country in regard to our domestic policy there has to be some connection between the various things that happen. I do not say that that connection is complete or absolute but nevertheless there are connecting links and strings, and it would be profitable for us, as it would be for outsiders, to try to understand all these things in some perspective so that the sweep of the history being made might come before us, because I have no doubt that, whether we have erred or we have performed rightly in India, the people of India and in a small measure, the Government of India have made history during this past period. The Government of India could have done little but for the people of India, that is obvious. Nevertheless, it has been the high privilege of the Government of India to have been associated during this period with this great undertakings of India.

Now, it is important that we should remember this connection between the external world and the internal affairs of our country. We cannot follow one policy in one place and another and a totally different policy elsewhere. That would not only tend to undermine and wreck the country in the public mind outside India but in India also there will be confusion and no understanding of the basic urges that move us. Again, in considering those basic urges, whether they are domestic or whether they are international, we have to keep in view the background that conditioned us and the people of India in the course of the last generation or two, and before of course, but more particularly in the course of the last generation or two; because I do claim—we may take either the foreign policy or the domestic policy—I do claim that both are natural growths from that background in which we functioned in the course of our struggle for freedom—not in exact detail, not in regard to every point, but the broad approaches and the broad pledges that we gave ourselves to the country we had sought to fulfil. Whether we have succeeded in a large measure or in a small measure, that is for you to judge. It is in this perspective again that I should like this House to look at all these matters which are so intimately connected.

421

Now, in the course of this debate much was said about Kashmir, something was said about the Commonwealth connection,[6] something about Goa and about some other matters. I would have preferred not to say much about Kashmir because a great deal has already been said about it not only in this House or in the other House, but also in the Security Council. And I should like to join my friend, the mover of this motion,[7] in his expression of high appreciation of what was done in the Security Council by our representative and a Member of this House. I am sorry I was not here all this time, but I have taken the trouble to read many of the speeches delivered here yesterday. I found an honourable Member[8] objecting to those remarks which fell from the mover of this motion in regard to the presentation of the case in the Security Council, and putting forward the argument, which I find has been put forward elsewhere in other countries and by various newspapers elsewhere, that the length of the speeches that our representative delivered there was some proof of the weakness of the case. Now, I can forgive those people who live outside in other countries, who have little time to give to the understanding of anything and who are moved by their urges or likes and dislikes, but it is a little difficult to understand an honourable Member of this House making a statement which can only be due to the most utter ignorance of what has happened. Here I would advise him and suggest to him respectfully to read those speeches and then tell me what part of them should be left out or what part of them was irrelevant or what part of them went against our case. The fact of the matter is, Sir, that right from the beginning of this Kashmir issue we have—if I may use the word—suffered from our extreme desire to follow the path that our country should follow, the path of peace, the path of decency and the path of cooperation, and maintaining, of course, our legitimate interests. It is possible—and I am prepared to admit that indictment— that we were too reasonable and we tried to be too decent. Maybe, that is true. But I would rather err on that side then on any other. I think that India has tried with some success to function in that way, and I am quite sure that in the end that way is not only a good way, but it also pays. It may be that for a short while some other policy might pay.

Now, Sir, one major criticism which is often made in regard to Kashmir is— and it has been made almost *ad nauseam* here and on the public platform outside, and it is repeated year by year—why this issue was referred to the Security

6. Kazi Karimuddin asked why India should not sever her connections with the Commonwealth and what was common between Britain, India, South Africa and Pakistan. He also spoke about recent British attitude towards India in regard to Kashmir.
7. P.N. Sapru, Congress Member from UP.
8. Kishen Chand, PSP Member from Andhra Pradesh.

Council and why this question was taken to the Security Council. Well, apart from the fact that it is ten years ago—and I would respectfully suggest that it does not help much repeating an argument which applied ten years ago, because we have to apply ourselves to the situation today—I shall tell the House that we referred it to the Security Council, because at that time in our view the only and the immediate alternative was a full-scale war with Pakistan. We may have been right or wrong, but the situation was such that we thought—the small war was, of course, going on in Kashmir between our forces and the Pakistani forces—it would develop into a full-scale war with Pakistan. And here again I would remind the House of our background, our background for generations past, with all that we had said about peace, *ahimsa* and non-violence. We wanted to avoid plunging into a big war a couple of months after Independence. In spite of our problems and all that had happened in Pakistan and India and on our borders—the terrible happenings—we did not, in the slightest degree, like the idea of a war. It went against our grain. That was a major reason. Of course, there were other reasons too. But whether we went there or not, the matter might still go there in the Security Council. However, I am trying to bring back to my mind and to place before this House what the major reason for that reference was. If honourable Members take the trouble to look at the papers of those early days or some weeks after Pakistan's aggression or invasion of Kashmir, they will see how concerned we were, how distressed we were at all those happenings, not because of any fear of what had happened, but because it seemed to upset everything that we had cared for and the way we had functioned in the past; and for us, immediately after Independence, to plunge into a war seemed to us a tragedy of an extreme type. We thought then that the way to avert that war was this. Before that I had suggested to the Prime Minister of Pakistan this joint reference, after withdrawal, of course. I had asked him to withdraw his forces and then "let us refer the matter". Refer the matter. What matter? Also remember that we did not refer the question of Kashmir's accession and all that. We did not refer that matter. We merely went to the Security Council asking the Security Council to call upon the Pakistan Government to withdraw. That was the reference. Either we get them out by war or make them withdraw—which was a civilized way— by referring the matter to the international organization. The question of accession etc., was not an issue. We never put it there. That was something apart, and that was something complete. Anyhow, that was the main reason. And I wish to make it perfectly clear—because all kinds of suggestions and sometimes insinuations are made—that this was a decision of our Government. Insinuations are made that Lord Mountbatten, who was the Governor General then, pushed us into taking this action. It has also been said, I believe, in the course of speeches here, if I am not mistaken, that he refused to allow our forces to go and delayed our forces to be despatched to Kashmir. All these statements are completely untrue. Lord Mountbatten throughout that period acted completely as a constitutional Governor General of India. It is true that we sometimes asked his advice, especially in military matters, because he happened to have a very great experience in such things. But in this matter there was no question of Lord Mountbatten pushing us into this action. It was our decision independently taken by those who formed the Government of India in those days. So, we went because of that urge to avoid an immediate major war which we thought was coming, and it was our misfortune that the Security Council, instead of considering the issue that we had placed before it, went off at a tangent, and year after year, it went on discussing other matters which were not strictly relevant to the issue that we had raised. I do not wish to go into that matter here.

Now, as the House knows, the President of the Security Council in the last month is going to come to Delhi within a few days, and naturally we are going to welcome him as a distinguished representative of the Security Council and of his nation, and we are perfectly prepared to talk and discuss any matter with him, and if he has any doubts about our position in regard to it, to make them clear.[9] Our position has been made perfectly clear in the Security Council in the speeches of our representative, and in a few sentences, in the President's Address. It became necessary for our representative in the Security Council to deliver lengthy addresses because during the past eight or nine years, so much confusion had been caused, so much irrelevant matter had been discussed in the press, in the public and elsewhere, that the major facts had been rather covered up, and it therefore, became necessary to put everything on record so that there should be no difficulty for any person who wanted to know the facts to know them. We have got now—I really do not remember but I should imagine—about a dozen fat printed volumes of Kashmir papers, each one of them running into thousand pages or eight hundred pages. It is a jungle of papers collected, and it is not surprising that people who have not been intimately connected with this matter should forget important events and happenings and should advance arguments which have no real relevance. Therefore, it was necessary to clear all this jungle up even at the cost of fatiguing the members of the Security Council. Remember, the Security Council, no doubt, are there to find out facts. They are not there to be amused and to think that it was no one's business to put the case before them. It was put and I have not a shadow of doubt that the putting of that case had a very considerable effect on them and others. The honourable Member who criticized said, "Look at the Resolution adopted!" That is true. I would say that,

9. Jarring held discussions in India from 24 to 28 March and from 6 to 9 April. He also held discussions in Pakistan from 15 to 20 March and from 2 to 5 April.

if you examine the Resolution, it has nothing to do with what has been said there. It is an independent Resolution. They did not even seek to answer any of the points or even to consider all the points that had been raised. That has been our difficulty not today but throughout. There has been an attempt to avoid facing the issues, an attempt to by-pass them, and to consider something else which may have been relevant at some stage or other but was not relevant at that particular stage. However, so far as we are concerned, our case has been completely and clearly stated and by that we stand.

One thing I should like to make clear, and that is, there has been an amusing—shall I say—exhibition of ignorance in some newspapers abroad and elsewhere which have stated that we have violated some commitments that we made, some international commitments. It is all right for the representatives of Pakistan to say that because they are in the habit of making rather irresponsible statements, but for newspapers abroad and people who ought to know better to go on repeating that did seem to me to be rather extraordinary. I do claim that there is not a single international commitment that we have made, that we have violated or that we have not fulfilled. Now here, I make that definite and precise statement.

Then, I would like the House to remember another thing. This matter was brought up before the Security Council this time in January, about the middle of January, and there was a tremendous outcry that something was going to happen in Kashmir on the 26th of January which must be stopped before that date. We made it clear to the Security Council that nothing was going to happen on the 26th January except the dissolution of the Constituent Assembly which had performed its functions and was going to be dissolved giving place to a legislative organ. Now, the dissolution of the Constituent Assembly was not an act of the Government of India. It was an automatic thing at the end of its work. It did not add to or subtract from the relationship of Kashmir to the Indian Union. It made no difference. Nothing was going to happen on the 26th January which would have the slightest effect on this, and yet there was this tremendous outcry raised all over, and newspapers who ought to know better also indulged in it. Then this Resolution was passed by the Security Council, I think, on the 24th January, a Resolution which said that nothing should be done in regard to this matter till it had considered it further. Nothing was done. We did nothing. The Government of India did not move its little finger. In Kashmir nothing was done except that they delivered some speeches and dissolved the Constituent Assembly. And yet, after that, there was another outcry that we had violated the Resolution of the Security Council of the 24th January. I confess I even wondered if my mind was failing me or the minds of other people were failing them. It is not a question of opinion. We may differ. But here is a simple question of fact. Yet all these newspapers, some of repute and others of considerable disrepute, both of these

425

joined in this outcry that we had violated the Resolution of the Security Council. I do challenge anyone to show me where and when India had not stood by its international commitments. Why was all this done, I do not know, but the whole world knows that we attach some value to standards of political behaviour and therefore they wanted to hurt us where they thought that we were rather tender, without even satisfying themselves as to what the facts were, and telling us "Oh, what is the good of going back to something which happened eight or ten years ago?" That was amusing. The accession happened then, the aggression happened then and the only things that we hold by, the only commitments that we had entered into happened ten years ago—the two Resolutions of the Security Council. No, all that is to be set aside, "Why go that far? Let us look at the matter now." It is a most extraordinary situation whether we look at it from the legal point of view, constitutional point of view, practical point of view, any point of view, decent point of view, and human point of view. So, unfortunately, as the House knows, this question got entangled with other matters with which it has nothing to do. The embattled legions of the Baghdad Pact and the SEATO are thought of in this connection. I do not say that. It is the honourable Ministers of the Pakistan Government who say this, who are repeatedly telling us how the Baghdad Pact has helped them in this Kashmir matter. Now, the Baghdad Pact has nothing to do with Kashmir. The Baghdad Pact does not come into the picture at all; it does come into the picture only to vitiate the picture, just to mislead us and confuse the issues. So, this question has become complicated. Maybe that we should function differently from how we functioned in the past. I do not say that everything that we said or did in the last ten years is what should be said or done. It is a complicated matter, but as I said, if we err at all, it is on the side of our extreme desire to have peaceful settlements, because we try to take a long view. India tries to take a long view. India is not a kind of, well, unreal or artificial country without roots. We have roots in the past; the fact of our Independence has not made us new. Those roots have continued and those roots will go on into the future, yielding place to flower and fruit. We look ahead, and in looking ahead, it is our basic policy that we should be friendly with all the countries of the world and certainly with our neighbouring countries and certainly with Pakistan. We cannot carry this feud with Pakistan into the distant future. It vitiates us and them, of course. Therefore, we try to be soft. We try to be reasonable and all that. I can very well understand, not only some honourable Members here, but the public generally, sometimes getting a little irritated at our policy. They say, "Why don't you hit out? Why don't you show greater strength?" But ultimately, the strength that comes to a nation is not the strength of strong language, as some people in other countries apparently believe. Strength comes in other ways, by building up the country, materially, industrially, and building up the character of the country, the unity of the country, and thus facing the problems that afflict us. More especially has this become important, this peaceful approach, in this world of today which seems always to hover over the edge of disaster.

Then as a result of this matter and some other matters like the Middle Eastern crisis, many people have turned to talk on the Commonwealth connection. Here again, I can very fully understand the feelings that have been roused, not only among the Members of this House or the other House, but in our people generally the strong feelings that have been aroused in them at recent happenings and events and they ask, "Is it worthwhile for us to continue the Commonwealth connection? What good does it do?" and so on and so forth. But while I completely appreciate that reaction, I do not think it is a wise reaction. I cannot say, nor can anybody say, what the future may hold, about this matter or any other. But I do not think it is a wise reaction and therefore, my own humble submission would be that we should not mix up things and we should not act in irritation or anger and change our basic policies because some thing has happened which annoys us and irritates us greatly. That will not be a wise thing. So far as the Commonwealth is concerned, honourable Members know that even in recent days, in weeks and days, changes are taking place. The independent, sovereign State of Ghana has been created[10] and it is a member of the Commonwealth. And in two or three months' time, Malaya may also be an independent member of the Commonwealth.[11] The whole picture is changing. The only two tests that I have in this matter are these. One, of course, is that any connection that we have should in no way impair our ability to carry out the policies that we desire. If it does, then it is a bad connection and the matter ends. If it does not come in the way of any policy, political, economic, social or call it what you like, then there is no question of our considering it as automatically bad. The second aspect is—and, I think, I have mentioned this previously in this House or elsewhere— that I am reluctant in this world where there are so many disruptive tendencies at work, to break any kind of relationship which can lead to friendly contacts, whatever that relationship may be. I want more such relationships and not less. We have relationships of various kinds. We have relationships with, let us say, our neighbour country Burma. They are close and intimate relationships, closer and more intimate and more friendly, if I may say so with all respect, than with many of the countries of the Commonwealth. It does not make our relationship with Burma any less close because Burma is not in the Commonwealth. We have relationships with other countries. We have fairly intimate relationships

10. On 6 March 1957.
11. Malaysia (Malaya) became independent on 30 August 1957.

427

with Egypt and so many other countries of Asia and some of Europe. We want to add to our relationships. We do not want to break or subtract them, unless they come in the way of our policy. And I wish to submit that whatever the Commonwealth connection or relationship does or does not, it has been patently shown that it does not come in the way of the policy that we wish to pursue. Commonwealth countries have differed very greatly and gone against each other in their policies and in their activities....

18. Talk with Gunnar Jarring—I[1]

I met Dr Jarring yesterday and had a talk with him for about an hour and a half. The usual arguments were repeated by me and by him. He said at the end that he had hoped that some approach could be made on the basis of the Resolutions of August 1948[2] and January 1949,[3] which we had accepted. He did not expect some agreement to come out quickly, but this might at least have postponed a further bitter and prolonged debate in the Security Council.

2. I told him that it was true that we had accepted those Resolutions and we wished to honour any commitment that we had made. But those Resolutions

1. Note to V.K. Krishna Menon, Secretary General, and Commonwealth Secretary, New Delhi, 27 March 1957. V.K. Krishna Menon Papers, NMML. Also available in JN Collection.
2. The UNCIP Resolution of 13 August 1948 provided for immediate cessation of hostilities, and formulation of a truce agreement based on withdrawal of tribesmen and Pakistani nationals; and a synchronized withdrawal of all Pakistani troops on the one hand, and the bulk of the Indian forces, on the other. The Government of India was to begin to withdraw the bulk of its forces after (i) the tribesmen and Pakistani nationals had withdrawn, and (ii) Pakistani forces were being withdrawn.
3. The UNCIP Resolution of 5 January 1949 envisaged the holding of a plebiscite in the State and the details connected with it. The resolution stated: "The question of accession of the Jammu and Kashmir to India or Pakistan will be decided through the democratic method of a free and impartial plebiscite after the ceasefire and truce arrangements set forth in Parts I & II of the 1948 Resolution have been carried out and arrangements for plebiscite have been completed."

stood as a whole and the first two parts had not been given effect to by Pakistan.[4] In the event of their having been given effect to, we could have discussed the third part with Pakistan. Much had happened since then and every attempt of ours to find some way had not only failed but had been used against us. Thus, the basic issues were forgotten or set aside. We were not, therefore, prepared to make any proposal. The basic issues about invasion and accession had to be clearly accepted. Thereupon we could discuss the future on those terms. Any other course would entangle us still further without leading to any satisfactory result.

3. Dr Jarring reminded me of what I had said that we would not take any military action against Pakistan for the recovery of the Pakistan occupied territory of Kashmir State. This meant that there were only two courses open to Pakistan, if our approach was adhered to. One was Pakistan withdrawing completely from that area without any assurance as to what will happen in the future and the other was for Pakistan merely to remain where they were because we would take no action against them. It seemed to him that it was hardly conceivable that Pakistan would agree to withdraw on this basis. It might perhaps have been conceivable, though he was not certain of this, if some future assurance presumably of a plebiscite was given. I said that I had never ruled out a plebiscite, though this was no way of settling the question. But I was not prepared to give any assurance beyond what I had said. If the two major questions were settled and Pakistan withdrew, we would gladly meet the Pakistan leaders and discuss the form of some friendly settlement. We could not possibly continue to ignore the basic issues I had pointed out, as this course had led not only to failure during the past eight years but also to the strange development that we were considered almost the aggressors and Pakistan the aggrieved party.

4. In the course of his talk, Dr Jarring referred to some kind of a partial plebiscite, that is, in some areas only. I said that this was the old Dixon proposal which Mr Liaquat Ali Khan had rejected although we were then prepared to discuss it.[5] This question does not arise now in the new context of things.

---

4. Pakistan had been violating the ceasefire line and a list of such incidents was prepared for Jarring. See *ante*, p. 415. The issue of vacating the Pakistani aggression had been raised repeatedly by Nehru and Krishna Menon, both in national and international forums.
5. In 1950, the UN representative, Owen Dixon suggested two alternatives: (a) a plan for taking the plebiscite by sections or areas and allocation of each section according to the result of the vote therein; (b) a plan by which it was conceded that some areas were certain to vote for accession to India and some to Pakistan and by which, without taking a vote therein, they should be allotted accordingly and plebiscite should be confined only to the uncertain area—i.e., the Kashmir Valley.

5. Dr Jarring said that as there was nothing much more to be said, he would return. He asked me if I had any objection to his going to Pakistan on his way back. I told him I had no objection whatever. He added that in fact he had a return ticket via Karachi. He indicated that he would be leaving on Friday, the 29th.

6. This morning, the 27th, I happened to meet him in the corridor of the External Affairs Ministry. He was somewhat agitated at the report of Shri Krishna Menon's speech in the Lok Sabha yesterday. Apparently what had troubled him was the headline that the plebiscite offer had lapsed. Just then Shri Krishna Menon came there too and he said that the headlines were wrong and full report would be sent to him.[6] I understand that Shri Krishna Menon will be seeing him tomorrow. I shall probably also see him tomorrow afternoon to say goodbye to him.

P.S.

After dictating this I saw CS's note of today.[7]

JN

6. Krishna Menon had said that "....just because we speak about a plebiscite, it does not mean that we undertook a plebiscite....the plebiscite cannot be triggered, cannot come into operation—whatever arrangements you can make, but you cannot have the operation of it—until those two parts (of 13 August 1948 Resolution) are performed."

7. M.J. Desai wrote that Jarring and Engers saw him on urgent request and said that he must go back to Karachi early as Menon's Lok Sabha statement would be published in bold headlines all over Pakistan. He said that the statement closed the doors to any further negotiations—it mentioned as reported that offer of plebiscite like various other offers made in previous negotiations lapsed and "could not keep us bound for ever." Jarring wanted an authorized version of Menon's speech.

19. Talk with Gunnar Jarring—II[1]

Dr Jarring came to see me this evening at 6.30 p.m. He was with me for about half an hour. He said that he had had long talks with Mr Suhrawardy and explained to him our position with which he did not agree. Dr Jarring said that he was trying to find some way of postponing an acrimonious discussion in the Security Council or the General Assembly. Mr Suhrawardy had said something about taking the matter to the General Assembly. He (Dr Jarring) had, therefore, thought that perhaps we might confine ourselves to Part I of the Resolutions of 1948. While he had explained fully our position to Mr Suhrawardy, he had concentrated on our contention that even Part I of the Resolution had not been implemented by Pakistan. Mr Suhrawardy had maintained that it had been implemented.

2. Perhaps, therefore, it might be worthwhile to get this preliminary hurdle cleared in regard to the implementation of Part I before proceeding to Part II etc. Dr Jarring said that he knew well our objection to referring the whole Kashmir matter to arbitration. But this small reference in regard to the implementation of Part I only would stand on a different footing and perhaps our other objection would not apply to this.

3. He gave me a paper, copy of which I enclose. In this, it will be noted, it is proposed that the Governments of India and Pakistan agree to go to arbitration over the question whether Part I of the 13th August 1948 Resolution of the UNCIP has been implemented or not. Dr Jarring told me that this was not an official paper.[2] It was just an idea which had occurred to him and which he had put down for our consideration. If we did not approve of it, the matter would end there.

4. I asked him if he had put it to Mr Suhrawardy and what his response was. Dr Jarring said that Mr Suhrawardy was apparently agreeable to it.

5. I told Dr Jarring that any proposal that he put forward would naturally receive our consideration and we would give thought to it. But my first reaction was that this suggestion was very odd and, isolated as it was from other matters,

---

1. Note to Commonwealth Secretary, New Delhi, 6 April 1957. V.K. Krishna Menon Papers, NMML. Also available in JN Collection.
2. It was also suggested in the paper that the arbitrator would be authorized to spell out the obligations of the parties under the terms of Part I of the Resolution in general and of Part I Clause E in particular and to fulfil within a specified period such obligations as the arbitrator might declare had not been fulfilled till then. After the expiry of the specified period the arbitrator would certify whether the obligations under Part I had not been carried out.

it would not help. I understood his wish to avoid getting entangled in all the aspects of the Kashmir issue and, therefore, to keep Part I separated even from Part II etc. of the Resolution. But our experience during these past years was that the discussion of some detail by itself had led to the wholly wrong impression that the basic matters did not matter. Throughout these past years we had laid stress on the basic matters, but had agreed to discuss some details of implementation. There had been no agreement about these details and this led people to forget these basic issues and later we were put in the dock as if we were to blame. I did not see any harm if any approach to this issue could be made, provided there was a clear understanding about those basic issues. Only the other day, Mr Suhrawardy made an attack on India and on me personally in regard to Kashmir and accused us of aggression and invasion.[3] Either Mr Suhrawardy was right or he was completely wrong and me in the right. Unless this thing was cleared up, I saw no advantage in picking out Part I and proceeding with it in the way indicated. Mr Suhrawardy's accusations and charges would hang over us and we would no doubt be told later that we had passively accepted a certain position and we had no business to go back upon it.

6. We agreed to meet again on Monday, 8th April, at 4 p.m. in my house.

7. Please show this to SG and FS. I am sending a separate copy to Shri Krishna Menon who will probably reach here tomorrow, Sunday evening.

3. In a public meeting in Lahore on 3 March, Suhrawardy said that Nehru's spell on the Kashmir issue was broken once for all. He said that Pakistan's membership of the Western sponsored military alliances, such as the Baghdad Pact, had made a "favourable turn in the Kashmir dispute possible." He advised people "not to run down Britain and forget the past...If Pakistan also start abusing Britain as Mr Nehru is doing now, Britain will naturally again turn to India." Suhrawardy reiterated that Pakistan's alliance in the regional pacts would come to the aid when aggression came from a communist or a non-communist country.

20. Talk with Gunnar Jarring—III[1]

Dr Jarring and Dr Engers[2] saw PM at 4 p.m. on 8th April 1957. Minister (W.P.)[3] and myself were also present.

2. During the discussions PM made the following points:

(i) The generally aggressive tone of the Pakistan press[4] and the false propaganda put out in the recent speeches of Prime Minister Suhrawardy demanding Kashmir at any cost and threatening war.[5]

(ii) As regards Dr Jarring's proposal, dealing with bits and pieces, without regard to the basic issue of Pakistan's aggression will cause further complications and misconstruction by Pakistan.

(iii) India did not like the way India and Pakistan were put on the same level, though it was India who went to the Security Council with a complaint and is the aggrieved party, Pakistan continuing to hold over one-third of Kashmir with no other right except that of naked aggression.

(iv) Arbitration suitable in some cases; not suitable in others. Our offer of arbitration in the case of settlement of Evacuee Property claims not accepted by Pakistan. We resorted to conciliation procedure in the case of Canal Water dispute and proposed arbitration procedure also. Latest position in the case of Canal Water dispute negotiations under the aegis

---

1. M.J. Desai's note of Nehru's meeting with Gunnar Jarring, New Delhi, 8 April 1957. File No. 25-KU/57, Vol. II, pp. 53-55/Note, MEA.
2. J.F. Engers was Adviser to Gunnar Jarring.
3. V.K. Krishna Menon, Minister Without Portfolio.
4. For example, according to a report of Pakistan President, Iskandar Mirza's speech to Pakistani Air Force cadets on 11 January, he told them to be "always ready" as India had "sinister designs" on Pakistan. Their Information Minister, Amir Azam Khan alleged that Indian troops were massed on Pakistan's borders. Pakistan radio declared on the same day that tribal chieftains, impatient about the slow progress of the Kashmir question, were ready to march to Kashmir if the Security Council did not satisfactorily solve it. The Government of Pakistan published a booklet titled *Cartoons on Kashmir—Gleanings from World Press* in February 1957, featuring Nehru in poor light. Indian High Commissioner in Karachi, C.C. Desai, informed that this was circulated to different embassies and other interested persons.
5. On 1 February, Suhrawardy said that there was real danger of "undeclared war" breaking out in the tribal territories; telegrams pledging support for armed operations were pouring into Karachi from tribal leaders, and "no one could say what would happen if no effective action was taken."

433

of the World Bank, since the last three years and yet, in both cases, no progress towards settlement—only Pakistan using each procedure to vilify India and carry on hostile propaganda.

(v) Concentration on Part I of the 13th August Resolution welcome, but arbitration procedure not exactly suitable. Security Council can satisfy itself as to whether Part I is fully implemented and tell the party concerned as regards items not implemented but one cannot see where the proposal to prescribe remedies and review subsequent performance would ultimately lead. India willing to consider any measure of conciliation but, in view of past experience, unwilling to try procedures which would be misapplied and used against India as commitments. Discussion on plebiscite procedure picked up and misused by Pakistan as plebiscite commitment and similar misuse bound to occur about Dr Jarring's present proposal, particularly in view of the consistent efforts of Pakistan during the last nine years to have arbitration on Kashmir. No sovereign Government would agree to refer the question of its sovereignty to arbitration.

(vi) People in both India and Pakistan quite friendly. Visits by Polo Teams, Football Teams etc. But religious excitement deliberately worked up and Indo-Pakistan differences exploited by Pakistan leaders for internal reasons.

(vii) Pakistani leaders also aligning themselves with Portugal on the Goa question, just to spite India, though they have no interest in Goa question.

3. Dr Jarring again repeated the suggestion he had made earlier in the discussions with MWP to have a fact-finding commission to see whether Part I was fully implemented and drop the arbitration proposal. MWP repeated what he had said in the morning that this is a matter for the Security Council. They should inform themselves of the implementation and inform India, Government of India, as such could neither accept nor reject any proposal regarding fact-finding by the Security Council, as it was a Security Council affair.

4. Dr Jarring said that he understood Government of India's position and that he will be leaving tomorrow evening (9.4.57), stop in Karachi for a day and will spend three or four days in Geneva to draft his report. On the question of meeting of the Security Council, Dr Jarring said that Pakistan will press for an early meeting and it is up to the President of the month, the UK Delegate and the other members of the Security Council to decide whether and if so when a meeting of the Security Council should be held to consider his report. He himself did not see the need for an early meeting of the Council, but all depended upon the Chairman and the amount of pressure Pakistan could put on the Chairman

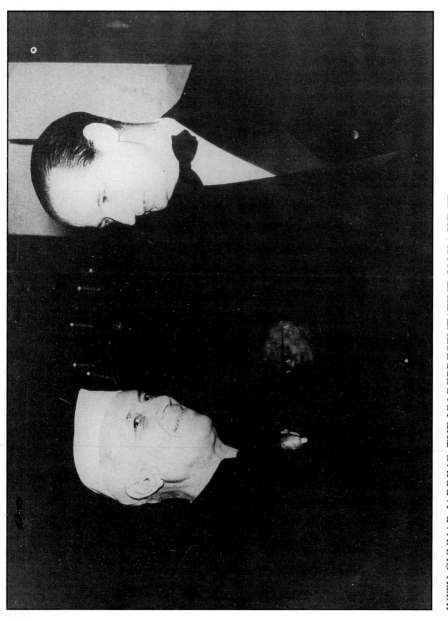

WITH GUNNAR JARRING, THE UN REPRESENTATIVE ON KASHMIR, NEW DELHI, 25 MARCH 1957

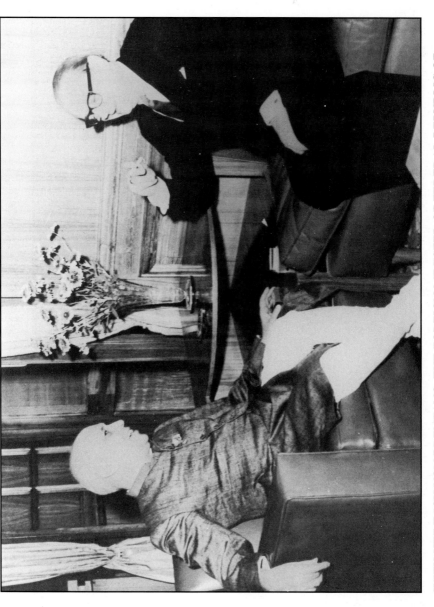

WITH HEINRICH VON BRENTANO, THE FOREIGN MINISTER OF FEDERAL REPUBLIC OF GERMANY, NEW DELHI, 28 MARCH 1957

and other members. Minister (WP) said that a meeting towards the end of May or early June will suit us. Any earlier meeting would be difficult because of formation of the new Government in the middle of May and the meeting of the new Parliament on the 13th May.

21. Talk with Australian High Commissioner[1]

I have had an hour's talk with the Australian High Commissioner.[2] I told him that I was much distressed at the attitude of the Australian Government and their representative in the Security Council in regard to the Kashmir discussions.[3] It seemed to me that the statements made on behalf of Australia in the Security Council and outside were more hostile to India than the statements of any other member of the Security Council. For any country to say that would have distressed us, but for a Commonwealth country to do so was even more distressing and it produced unfortunate consequence in India.

2. I went over the broad features of this Kashmir affair and how unfairly we had been treated by many members of the Security Council in recent debates who ignored the basic points. I referred, in particular, to the proposal to send UN forces to Kashmir, a proposal which was persisted in in spite of my stating categorically that on no account would we permit such forces to come here. This was mentioned in the Security Council Resolution, although every member of the Security Council knew what our attitude was and the fact that this was contrary to the provisions of Chapter VI of the Charter. Now, I found Mr Casey again suggesting that Australia would be prepared to send forces if the parties agreed. He knew very well that India not only did not agree, but entirely objects to it. Why then was he going on saying these things which angered our people?

1. Note to V.K. Krishna Menon, New Delhi, 12 April 1957. File No. 25-KU/57, Vol. II, p. 33/corr., MEA. Also available in V.K. Krishna Menon Papers, NMML and JN Collection.
2. P.R. Heydon.
3. The Australian representative, Ronald Walker, raised various questions during the debate on Kashmir. He sought clarity on India's stand on plebiscite, status of Kashmir with the new Constitution coming into force from 26 January 1957, perceiving the Constitution as a new obstacle in the way of a plebiscite. He said that this could be "inimical" to the previous Resolutions of the Security Council and the attention of all parties should be drawn to it.

3. I spoke to the High Commissioner about the background of the Muslim League politics, two-nation theory etc., and the fact that the leaders of Pakistan were people who had opposed our struggle for freedom in the past and chiefly consisted of big landlords and had no constructive or economic policy. They could only think of keeping their people's minds occupied with hatred of India. This was probably the main reason for keeping alive the Kashmir issue as this was and the manner of their propaganda and their appeals to religion and jehad.

4. The High Commissioner told me that he had reported to his Government that, in his opinion, a plebiscite would be unfortunate as this would let loose dangerous forces.

5. I referred to Shri Krishna Menon quoting in one of his speeches in the Security Council from a document containing the gist of some talks which I had had with some Prime Ministers in London. I suggested to him to meet Shri Krishna Menon to discuss the Kashmir matter and also find out the facts about this document.

22. To Habib Bourguiba[1]

New Delhi
23 April 1957

My dear Prime Minister,

I write to acknowledge your letter of the 1st April which was handed to our High Commissioner in London by your Ambassador there and has been forwarded to me.[2]

I am glad to note that Your Excellency understands and welcomes my explanation of our lawful position in Kashmir and that you agree that it is not open to challenge. I am surprised, however, that Your Excellency still continues

---

1. JN Collection.
2. Bourguiba wrote that he understood and welcomed the legal point of view, pointed out by Nehru (see *ante*, pp. 397-398), yet the impression remained that the Kashmir question had not been solved by the two parties concerned. He wrote that the UNO was the best resort in such cases of dispute and ascribed much hope to the presence of Gunnar Jarring in the region who would contrive to find a peaceful solution.

to approach this question as though Pakistan and India were two contestants with equal or similar and valid claims and as though the sovereignty of the Union of India over her entire territories was in doubt. Your Excellency will no doubt appreciate that this affects the integrity of India.

Let me make the present position in regard to Kashmir clear once again. The entire territory of the former Princely State of Jammu & Kashmir is a constituent part of the Union of India which is a Federation. Half of Jammu & Kashmir, as a result of invasion first by irregulars and afterwards by the Pakistan Army, is unlawfully and forcibly occupied by Pakistan. Here, may I say that Pakistan denied the fact of this invasion and concealed it from the Security Council until the Commission was about to discover the facts itself.

We did not go to the Security Council to decide our title or the issue of sovereignty in regard to the former Princely State of Jammu & Kashmir which acceded to the Union of India not only in accordance with law but in full conformity with arrangements which both Pakistan and India accepted with the British Government. It is the same procedure as was followed both by Pakistan and ourselves in regard to the other Princely States. We went to the Security Council because we were invaded and we wanted to obtain the termination of this invasion by the good offices and machinery of conciliation of the United Nations rather than by waging war and invading Pakistan territory.

I hope Your Excellency will appreciate that, in our anxiety to avoid bloodshed and conflict with our neighbour, we refrained from invasion of Pakistan in 1947, though this would, in the circumstances, undoubtedly have been legitimate action on our part. At all times, we have maintained that the soil of our territory must be cleared of the invader. Pakistan has no rights whatsoever in Jammu & Kashmir, and her presence there is the result of invasion and is illegal occupation.

Perhaps, to Tunisia as an Arab country, our position in Kashmir will strike with a greater sense of reality if I mentioned that Kashmir was invaded in the same way as Egypt was invaded by the Anglo-French-Israeli forces. In the latter case we all demanded vacation of the aggression. We do the same in regard to Kashmir, and I fail to understand how Tunisia, of all countries, can have two views on this question.

In regard to Your Excellency's own country, we have both before our own Independence and after, firmly and without reservation supported the demand for the integrity of an independent Tunisia, the removal of foreign occupation and the restoration of Tunisian sovereignty to her people. We cannot be expected to feel or do less in regard to our own country.

Your Excellency referred in your previous letter to your pride in your friendship with Pakistan and India and to your earnest wish for a peaceful solution of the conflicts between our two countries. No country is more anxious than India, and no one is more anxious than I am that conflicts between nations should be solved peacefully. This is also known to Pakistan and we have made many attempts and many sacrifices to this end. We have some achievements too to our common credit.

In view, however, of Your Excellency's friendship with Pakistan, to which you have referred, I would regard it reasonable for us to expect that your country will use her influence with Pakistan in asking her to bring her actions in conformity with the Charter of the United Nations, with international law and neighbourly relations and in furtherance of the promotion of Asian unity and strength. I hope, hereafter, we can look to Your Excellency's good offices being used in that direction, as any other, particularly the approach that you are now making, is a challenge to our sovereignty and a condonation of invasion. It causes us no little surprise that an appeal should be made to us on the basis that the invader is to reap the fruits of his aggression and that the active invasion gives him legal and even moral rights on our sovereign territory, and that he can as a result of his occupation of the neighbouring country, thereafter claim from other nations the right to be regarded as having an equal position in regard to the sovereign territory of India.

I earnestly hope that a clear statement not merely of our position but of the factual situation and the moral issues involved will induce Your Excellency to make an approach to this problem far different from what you have done.

Yours sincerely,
Jawaharlal Nehru

II. ASSEMBLY ELECTIONS

1. To Bakhshi Ghulam Mohammad[1]

New Delhi
10 March 1957

My dear Bakhshi,

I have received your letter of March 8 today.[2] In this you ask me to go to Jammu in connection with the elections.[3] I am afraid it is not at all possible for me to do so. Apart from anything else, you are asking me to go at a time when our Parliament is meeting in its final session, and I cannot be away for even a few hours. Our vast elections have taken place, new Governments have to be formed, here, the President has to deliver his Address, and Parliament has to discuss the President's Address and later separately international affairs. This will naturally include the Kashmir developments also. I am personally concerned with all these matters, and it is inconceivable for me to go away for anything, much less for any electioneering. In fact, no Minister of ours ought to leave Delhi then. But apart from others, I cannot possibly do so, when all our old MPs come here and I have to meet them from day to day.

You will also remember that this is just the time when Jarring is going to come to Delhi.

You know that I have not been to Jammu and Kashmir State for more than three and a half years. It would be odd indeed if I went to Jammu for the first time after this long period on an election campaign.

I agree with you that it was very unfortunate that nearly all the opposition

1. JN Collection.
2. Bakhshi requested Nehru to visit Jammu for a day before 24 March, as polling was scheduled for 25 March in Jammu.
3. Under the new Constitution of Jammu and Kashmir, 75 members were to be elected to the Legislative Assembly from 71 constituencies, four of them being double-member constituencies. Polling was held on 25 March in Jammu and on 30 March in Kashmir. Due to snow-bound conditions, voting was postponed for seven seats in Doda and Ladakh districts.

candidates in Kashmir proper had been practically eliminated even before polling.[4] This has had a bad effect in other countries.

In view of Jarring's visit to Delhi, which is likely to take place round about the 20th or 21st March, we should naturally like to consult you before our talks with him. Krishna Menon has not come here yet. He is in Bombay. He will probably come here on the 13th. After consulting him, I shall communicate with you again.

I am sorry to learn that you are not feeling well. You have a heavy burden to carry, and you should look after yourself.

Yours sincerely,
Jawaharlal Nehru

4. Bakhshi informed Nehru that while there were only eight contests in Kashmir, most of the seats in Jammu were being contested by the Praja Parishad. Bakhshi wrote that many of the candidates opposing the National Conference were eliminated owing to the omissions in nomination papers.

2. Elections in Jammu and Kashmir[1]

Elections will be held soon in Jammu and Kashmir for the Assembly. I hope that voters in this State will vote for the candidates set up by the Jammu and Kashmir National Conference. This organization has represented the fight and the urge for freedom in this State. It represents also all sections of the people of the State, and is not a communal body representing only one religious community. The freedom and the constitution of any country today can only be based on all the people having equal rights and privileges. To limit it to one particular community or to give that community special privileges over others, is not freedom for all and means reverting to some medieval conception, which is completely out of place in the world today. India has, therefore, adopted a Constitution which gives equal rights and equal freedom to all its citizens and

1. Message for the electorate in Jammu and Kashmir, New Delhi, 17 March 1957. JN Collection. Nehru sent a similar message in Hindi. These were published in the newspapers on 19 March 1957.

440

while the State is secular, every religion has full opportunities of functioning according to its rights and customs. Communal organizations, whether they are Muslim or Hindu, strike at the root of freedom and unity. No stable state can be built up on this basis.

The Jammu & Kashmir State acceded to India nearly ten years ago, in October 1947. Much has happened since then, but that basic fact governs the situation.

Elections in a parliamentary democracy have to be fought on the basis of parties following certain principles and programmes and not on the basis of individuals. The only party in the Jammu & Kashmir State which has not only struggled for and achieved freedom for the State, but has also consistently stood by the principles laid down in the Constitution of India, is the National Conference Party. I trust, therefore, that the candidates of this party will receive the support and the votes of the people of this State.

3. Permits for Foreign Correspondents[1]

I have consulted the Home Minister also.[2] We realize the difficulties of the Jammu & Kashmir Government in this matter and some foreign correspondents have undoubtedly behaved badly and even maliciously. Yet to refuse foreign correspondents generally is bad. I would unhesitatingly refuse permit in policy to the *Daily Telegraph* and *Daily Express* correspondents—possibly also *Daily Mail*. I am prepared to say publicly and to inform the Foreign Correspondents' Association that these people have functioned maliciously and we see no reason why we should encourage them.[3]

But, such exceptions apart, I would not come in the way of foreign correspondents going to Kashmir even though their going there at election times is a nuisance.

1. Note to Deputy Secretary (XP), New Delhi, 25 March 1957. Also available in File No. 32/16-XP(P)/57, pp. 2-3/N, MEA. File No. KS-8/57, p. 3, MHA.
2. P.N. Haksar of the External Publicity Division submitted a note about difficulties in securing permits for foreign press correspondents who wished to visit Jammu and Kashmir.
3. Haksar wrote that the President of the Foreign Press Correspondents' Association in New Delhi, Felix Naggar told him that the Association was exercised over the delays and uncertainties attending grants of permits for Kashmir.

So far as Rosenthal of *The New York Times* is concerned, we think he should be allowed to go to Jammu & Kashmir State.[4] Home Minister agrees.

4. Haksar noted that A.M. Rosenthal did not fall into the "malicious" category. He also felt that it would not be a pretty situation to contemplate if Rosenthal were to write a despatch in *The New York Times* about the refusal of the Government of India or of the Jammu and Kashmir Government to let him go to Kashmir.

4. Granting Permits to Visitors to Kashmir[1]

I enclose a letter[2] from Shri Farid Ansari[3] and a copy of my reply to him. I have given a copy of my reply to him.[4] I have given a copy of Shri Farid Ansari's letter to Shri Krishna Menon who is going to Kashmir. I have also sent a copy to Shri Vishnu Sahay.

1. Note to Foreign Secretary, New Delhi, 3 April 1957. File No. KS-35/57, MHA. Also available in File No. 32/16-XP(P)/57, p.6/Note, MEA and JN Collection.
2. A Joint Secretary of the PSP, Farid Ansari, wrote to Nehru on 2 April 1957 about his unhappy experience during his visit to Jammu and Kashmir for election work. First, the Defence Department of the Government of India granted reluctantly the necessary permit after a delay of two days. Then the manager of a hotel in Jammu, where a room had been reserved for Ansari, refused to accommodate him for fear of being harassed by the local police. Ansari wrote that "it is strange that a citizen of India be treated as a persona non grata in the territory of Indian Union." He stated that the internal conditions in the Kashmir Valley and in the interior of Jammu, as reported to him, indicated that all was not well there.
3. Faridul Haq Ansari (1895-1966); Jawyer and politician from UP; member, AICC, 1927-48; founder-member, Congress Socialist Party, 1934; imprisoned during freedom movement; member of National Executive, Praja Socialist Party, 1948-58; Joint Secretary, PSP, 1954-58; Member, Rajya Sabha, 1958-66.
4. Nehru agreed with Ansari (letter dated 3 April not printed) that difficulty in finding accommodation was very undesirable and that he was referring the matter to the Kashmir Government. Regarding grants of permits, the Defence Department of the Government of India was not at fault. Nehru explained that unfortunately some complicated procedure had been evolved which delayed matter greatly. Nehru assured Ansari that delay in his getting permit was not due to any particular reason personal to him or to the Praja Socialist Party, but due to this procedure.

2. I understand that there was some talk about this procedure of giving permits to newspapermen this morning. Shri Krishna Menon mentioned this to me. I am sure that we are harming our cause greatly by these complicated procedures and references to I & B and Intelligence, not to mention the Kashmir Government. This must be simplified. So far as newspapermen are concerned, if we accredit them here, no question of further enquiry here should arise. The only difficulty might be with the Kashmir Government. I feel that in the balance, we should allow every accredited newspaperman to go there, and the Kashmir Government should agree to this.

3. Some little time ago, I wrote a note on this subject of newspapermen going to Kashmir and sent it to Shri Vishnu Sahay.[5] In that note, I said that normally every newspaperman should be allowed to go there but in the case of newspapermen who are known to be malicious, we should not allow them to go.

4. On reconsideration, I feel that even in the case of these people whom we consider malicious, it does little good to prevent them from going and it may do harm.

5. I have asked Shri Krishna Menon to speak about this matter to the Prime Minister of Jammu and Kashmir. But, anyhow, so far as we are concerned at this end, we must straighten out this procedure.

5. See *ante*, pp. 441-442.

5. To Bakhshi Ghulam Mohammad[1]

New Delhi
5 April 1957

My dear Bakhshi,

Jarring has come back to Delhi this evening, or I suppose he has. I have not met him yet. I shall meet him tomorrow evening. I shall keep you informed of our talks.

1. JN Collection.

443

This morning, Maulvi Saeed Masuodi came to see me to bid me good-bye.[2] During the last three years, I have met him very rarely, perhaps once a year or so. I have seen him occasionally in Parliament from a distance.

I know that he has acted in a way which has not been right and, perhaps, not straight. But, as a personality, he has always struck me as a person of note. He is quiet and well-behaved and thoughtful. I have always felt that in any work that we might undertake, his help or cooperation would be of great use.

I do not know if it is possible for you to gain his cooperation at all. But, I would suggest to you still that it is worthwhile toning down his opposition. That is always helpful. Also, in any future developments, we should always try to keep some links. I would suggest to you, therefore, that it will be a good thing for you to meet him in Srinagar and have friendly talks with him. Do not isolate him completely or make him feel that there is no chance at all of any possible cooperation between you and him. In any event, this course of action is not only right, but advisable. It can do no harm, and it can do much good.

I would, indeed, go a step further, though perhaps in this matter you will not agree with me. I suppose that your newly elected Assembly will be choosing their representatives to our Parliament.[3] You will naturally want to push out some of your representatives here, who have been doing a great deal of mischief. I wonder, however, if it will be desirable to push out Moulvi Saeed Masuodi also. It might well be a wise policy to have him elected again, even though you push out the others. That will show your wide tolerance and, I am sure, will create a very good impression in Kashmir as well as outside. Masuodi cannot do much harm to you here. Whatever harm could have been done, has been done, and if he is one among others who support you fully, his capacity for any wrong-doing will be very strictly limited. On the other hand, the fact that you have gone out of your way to get him elected, will strengthen your position both in India and, I imagine, in Kashmir.[4]

Maulvi Saeed Masuodi, whatever he may have done in private, has behaved very well in public and in Parliament. He is popular with our MPs because of this decent bahaviour. He has not said a word in Parliament or even in informal gatherings against you, so far as I know. He has, of course, felt strongly about

2. A former General Secretary of the National Conference and a supporter of Sheikh Abdullah, Masoudi was a nominated member of the First Lok Sabha from Jammu and Kashmir.
3. Six members of Jammu and Kashmir State were nominated to the Lok Sabha by the President on the recommendation of the Jammu and Kashmir Legislative Assembly to the Second Lok Sabha.
4. Masoudi was not returned to the Lok Sabha.

Sheikh Abdullah's imprisonment and, no doubt, continues to feel that. Even that he has not brought in publicly.

I hope, therefore, you will consider what I have suggested.

Yours sincerely,
Jawaharlal Nehru

6. Refusal of Permits to Kashmiris[1]

I think I referred to you some requests made to me by letter and telegram about the refusal of permits to go to Kashmir. This related to some Kashmiris in India. Apparently there are twenty of them who have been so refused and all or many of them are in Delhi. If they are outside Delhi, they are told to come here to get the permits. Among them, I am told, there are some students, about fourteen. The persons who approached me are Pir Afzal, Maqdooni, Isanuddin and, I think, Kashyap Bandhu, also. There is also one Mir Ghulam Rasul, who is said to be an Engineer in the Planning Department.

These people say that they are in great difficulties here and they do not know why they have been refused permission to go back to Kashmir.

Could you please find out and let me know if it is true that permits have been refused to Kashmiris in Delhi to return to Kashmir and, if so, why this is done? Is there also any ban on these people coming to India from Kashmir? Some of these people are apparently traders or labourers.

---

1. Note to Vishnu Sahay, 13 April 1957, New Delhi. JN Collection.

9
EXTERNAL AFFAIRS

I. FOREIGN POLICY

1. Object of the "Inner Line"[1]

This question of a fresh demarcation of the "Inner Line"[2] has been pending for a very long time. It was in 1954 that I suggested that this should be examined and a fresh line should be fixed. After much labour and consultation of various State Governments concerned, some proposals were made in November 1956. The file was sent to me then but unfortunately I could not deal with it for some time and I returned it to the Ministry suggesting that it might be put up later. I have thus been guilty of this latest delay.

2. I have now looked through these various papers. This present note is a provisional one intended to draw attention to certain points that are not clear to me. I should like to discuss this matter with FS after his return and with others who have been dealing with it.

3. The whole idea of the "Inner Line" is presumably to prevent foreigners from entering that area without specific permission. In the note, it is said that "The object of the Inner Line is to deny foreigners knowledge of areas close to our border and to prevent any troublemaking in these areas either directed against India or against the interest of friendly foreign powers adjacent to our borders. In achieving this object, allowance has to be made for the fact that both Tibetans and Burmese, our nearest neighbours, have been granted certain freedom of movement; the first by the provisions of the Sino-Indian Agreement, 1954 and the second by a general understanding that there would be freedom of movement on either side of the frontier upto 25 miles."

4. The type of foreigners we have to deal with, apart from Tibetans or Burmese, are (1) missionaries, (2) those going on scientific or mountaineering expeditions, and (3) just enterprising tours or questionable persons who may come in the guise of missionaries, scientists or tourists.

5. So far as missionaries are concerned, the question is of not permitting the

---

1. Note, New Delhi, 8 March 1957. JN Collection.
2. The Inner Line Regulation was enacted in 1873 in order to bring under more stringent control the commercial relations of the British tea planters and others with the hill tribes of the North East.

establishment of missions in that area. There are, I believe, even now some missions functioning there. Presumably, we allow them to continue but we will not allow any fresh areas to be covered by them or any branch mission to be established.

6. So far as scientific or mountaineering expeditions are concerned, no expedition can go there without permission. We thus have an odd individual who may wish to go there in the guise of something else but possibly for espionage or creating trouble otherwise.

7. I do not understand the need for any special legislation for the "Inner Line" or in order to prevent any of these categories of persons from going to that area. Possibly legislation is necessary if we intend to proceed against anyone crossing the "Inner Line" without permission and to convict him of an offence. Such cases are likely to be rare and I would normally be satisfied by deporting any foreigner who does not carry out instructions or enters the area without permission. It is seldom necessary to send these people to prison. Of course, if they misbehave in other ways also, the question of punishment can arise.

8. Anyhow, I see no necessity for having any fresh legislation or even amendment to the Foreigners' Act for this purpose. If the Foreigners' Act is to be otherwise amended, this may be done. It is a very old Act and rather out of date.

9. Thus, the "Inner Line" is a notional line for our guidance and the guidance of our officers and for public information that no one can go there without express permission. Further that normally permission will not be given except for very specific and necessary reasons. Normally, we will not give permission to foreigners to go there on expeditions, scientific or mountaineering, and certainly not to tourists. The fact of the existence of this notional "Inner Line" will help us in dealing with applications for permission to go in those areas. We can simply say that those areas are not open for this purpose. Therefore, it seems to me quite enough to lay down an "Inner Line" and make this known to all concerned. No further legislative or other action appears necessary.

10. In the map that has been sent with the file, while the proposed "Inner Line" is marked, there is no indication of the old and existing line. This should be indicated clearly in this or some other map so that we can know what the changes are.

11. The desire for uniformity and continuous line is understandable, but there is no urgent necessity for this. Thus, I do not see any necessity for having such an "Inner Line" in the Jammu and Kashmir State. The whole State is an area governed by special rules and regulations and in fact nobody is supposed to go there without a permit. It is exceedingly difficult for anyone pressing to go to the Ladakh area. The only practical way of going to the Ladakh area is by air

WITH JOSEF CYRANKIEWICZ, THE PRIME MINISTER OF POLAND, NEW DELHI, 27 MARCH 1957

WITH ANEURIN BEVAN, THE BRITISH LABOUR LEADER, NEW DELHI, 25 MARCH 1957

and this is very much under control. I see no purpose, therefore, in extending this "Inner Line" right across the Jammu and Kashmir State and practically including four-fifths of the State in the area beyond the "Inner Line".

12. It is not quite clear to me from the map whether Sonamarg and the Amarnath Caves are on this side of the "Inner Line" or beyond. Both these places attract people in considerable numbers and there should be no difficulty placed in the way of pilgrims or tourists going there. The whole conditions of travelling are so difficult beyond Amarnath Cave that the question of stopping anyone does not arise. As for the Ladakh area, Zoji La beyond Baltal is a clear line of demarcation. But as I have said, I see no necessity at all for this "Inner Line" to be extended to Jammu and Kashmir State. It will serve no special purpose and it may perhaps have some undesirable consequences.

13. So far as Nepalese border is concerned, this matter has been held over for further consideration. I should like to know what difficulties the UP Government have had about foreigners going into this area near the border. Perhaps they have in mind some missions. It should be easy to lay down that we will not allow any missions to be established within a certain area regardless of the "Inner Line". I am for the present inclined to agree with our Ambassador that we should not demarcate any "Inner Line" there. But for our own purposes, we may have a notional line beyond which we will not agree to the establishment of missionary activities, subject perhaps to existing missions continuing.

14. In the map attached to this file, our international boundary is shown on the Tibetan side of Nepal. Surely this is not correct.

15. The Himachal Pradesh Government has referred to the Sangala Valley which apparently has good skiing slopes. This Valley is not marked in the map. I can hardly imagine that anybody is going to ski somewhere near Chini which is almost inaccessible for an average person.

16. On the UP border, all the famous places of pilgrimage are beyond the "Inner Line", like Badrinath, Kedarnath, etc. I agree but I hope that it does not affect the pilgrimage. Then there is the Pindari Glacier which should certainly be open to visitors, whether from India or abroad.[3]

17. I am not very happy about the whole of Sikkim and specially Gangtok as well as Kalimpong etc., being put on the other side of the "Inner Line". In fact, I do not understand how practically we can treat Kalimpong in this way. This place is full of foreigners. It has big institutes, schools, etc. It is a fine hill station. It is perfectly true that it has been and is a nest of spies, but how can one improve the situation by dealing with Kalimpong in the way proposed. Security

3. The issue of American missionaries operating within the Inner Line in UP was also discussed in the Lok Sabha on 18 May 1954. See *Selected Works* (second series), Vol. 25, pp. 411-412.

in some ways is demanded, but there are other important considerations to be borne in mind.

18. Then again the placing of the whole of Manipur on the other side of the "Inner Line" also requires more justification than has been given. Manipur is famous not only for its dancing but for its weaving and in many other ways. As a frontier area it is important no doubt but, nevertheless, I do not understand this approach of cutting off Manipur as well as the Lushai Hills.

19. Reference is made by several Governments to Central aid to establish checkposts. I do not think any question arises for any large number of checkposts to be established on the new "Inner Line" that may be fixed. In fact I do not mind if there are no checkposts at all except in some particular places. We must not think of this "Inner Line" as a kind of physical barrier. Very few persons are likely to go there. Those who ask for permission will be refused except in special cases. The only question, therefore, is of somebody creeping in without permission. I would like to take the risk and not spend large sums of money on checkposts all over this "Inner Line". Foreigners, as a rule, cannot get away with this. Thus, my idea of the "Inner Line" is not one of a succession of checkposts but a notional line beyond which we do not give permission to foreigners to go. If any odd individual does so, we shall take action against him. If he escapes such action, well, we take the risk. It will be absurd to spend large sums of money to prevent an odd individual creeping in.

20. I agree that there should be no question of fees for going beyond the "Inner Line".

21. These are some odd suggestions that have come to my mind on a first reading of these papers. Other points may arise on further consideration. But the main thing is that the approach need not be a legal one and should rather be an executive one.

22. I suggest that the Foreign Secretary, the Joint Secretary and others concerned might give further thought to this matter in view of what I have said in this note and then we can consider it together. Additional copies of this note are being sent so that they might be forwarded to FS, Home Ministry and Defence Ministry.

2. India's Policy—A Restrospective[1]

Jawaharlal Nehru: Mr Speaker, Sir, the President's Address which this House has been discussing deals with a period of about one year. But, perhaps, in a sense, we are discussing this address that is before us as covering even a longer period, i.e., the period of the life of this present Parliament, this being the last occasion when this Parliament will consider such an address, so that, a longer perspective is opened out to us, and perhaps even a longer period than five years, i.e., the period since we became independent.

It is right that honourable Members should scrutinize, criticize or condemn if they like, any particular aspect of our domestic or international policy or any event happening now or anything. But, at the same time, perhaps it is more important that we should have an overall view of this period to see how the main forces at work have been functioning shaping this country's destiny, whether in the political field, the economic or the social. It has been the high purpose and destiny of this House to lay the foundation and to start this new chapter in India's history to build democracy on a firm basis, to work and to labour for the advancement of the Indian people towards what we call socialism, to increase their standards of living in the near future as much as we can and step by step go towards the ideal we have placed before us. So, I would appeal on this occasion for this larger view to be taken, not because I want the smaller view to be put aside, but still even a small part of a picture is understood more if we have this broad and perspective view of the larger picture.

It is not my intention to go through the history of the last ten years or five years at this stage of the debate. Merely I wish to draw the attention of the House to this larger view. We are apt often to lose ourselves in the trees, we forget the wood. In doing so again, and in considering our policy, domestic or external, it is perhaps profitable to look round the world and see what has happened elsewhere, how the world has shaped itself during this tremendous period of history since the last War ended, what has happened not only in the world at large, but in individual countries, what has happened in Asia, which, since the War, has shown a tremendous vitality and a tremendous ferment; and what has happened in our neighbouring countries or the other countries of Asia. Because, then perhaps, we will have a better yard measure to see what we have achieved or we have failed to achieve.

It is easy, and perhaps right, for all of us to be impatient, to want to go faster,

1. Speech in the Lok Sabha on the motion on the President's Address. 21 March 1957. *Lok Sabha Debates*, Vol. I, Part II, cols. 226-246. Extracts.

to be impatient of the many evils that surround us, to be impatient of the inertia, to be impatient of inefficiency and all that. It is right that we should be impatient all the time. We should never be complacent. And yet, to balance that impatience, one should see this larger picture and see what has happened in other countries round about. Because, by and large, similar problems are faced by other countries; not entirely, each country has its own problems, its roots and its objectives. But, the world becomes more and more knit together and has to face the same problems and the same diseases overwhelming the world.

I put this thought before honourable Members of this House because, speaking with all modesty, and looking at this broad picture, I do feel that the achievements of this Parliament during the last five years, and of the preceding Parliament too, that is, during the last ten years, the achievements of India and the people of India have been not only very considerable, but rather striking. I do not, for an instant, forget the lack of achievement during this period. But, I think it would not be right for us to lay stress on the lack of achievement or to lay stress only on the achievement. One must see both sides of the picture. Looking at both sides of the picture, I think, it may be said with justice that we have advanced on the political plane, on the economic plane and on the social plane. Because, I do believe that a country today cannot really go far unless it advances on all these fronts together.

Most of us here, whether on the other side of the House or on this side of the House, were engaged for long years in the struggle for India's freedom. We were engaged in the Indian revolution and it was, as the world recognizes, a major revolution even though it was a peaceful one. Even though it took another shape and its methods were different, we were engaged in a revolution. A certain political aspect of it having been concluded, we did not, I am glad to say, imagine that the work of the revolution had ended. We always thought of the revolution extending to the economic and the social sphere. Maybe our approaches were different; maybe our line of thinking did not agree. Broadly speaking, we did all agree and I believe we did carry on this old political revolution to the economic and social fields. Most of us, not all, were conditioned by these past events as the country was conditioned. When we pledged ourselves to our present tasks, however lacking in worth we might have been, we had this basis of a revolutionary or semi-revolutionary background in the country. I am saying this merely to point out something that the people seem to forget—people not so much in India perhaps but people outside—that we in this country are still the children of revolution. We have been conditioned by it largely. We may forget it, we may become weak and falter or slip. That is another matter. There is some difference between a country which has gained its freedom by some revolutionary process, peaceful or not, and a country which has by chance, you might say, attained a certain objective, because the revolutionary process conditions the people, their character, their ability to resist, to go ahead, their capacity for sacrifice and all that. It is true that after every outburst of revolution, one has so often seen that very revolution sometimes eating up the people who made the revolution, sometimes going back upon it, action and reaction. Anyhow, these are major conditioning factors. We have gone through that. When other countries judge us, let them remember this that we are children of the Indian revolution and not merely persons who, by some automatic occurrence, gained freedom and who can be dealt with in a casual way as other countries sometimes are dealt with, because they gained their independence, if I may say so, rather accidentally and as a result of India's struggle for Independence.

There is this major difference which governs not only the past, but the present and the future for which we work. Because, we want changes. We work hard for them. Our attention, by and large, is concentrated on the economic and social changes that we want, on the growth and building up of a new India. Everything else is secondary to us. Everything else really comes in so far as it affects the primary purpose of ours. We cannot cut ourselves off from the innumerable foreign developments because they have a most intimate connection with what we do. We cannot be isolated. Nevertheless, our main object is to carry on this process of building India socially and economically as rapidly and as quickly as possible, knowing full well that this requires hard work, labour, sacrifice and time. It cannot be done by a stroke of the wand.

It would be interesting to look at other countries with whom we are friends and to whom we wish well. We started building democracy. We aimed at socialism. We aimed at higher standards. We aimed at a welfare state. How far have we succeeded in preserving the democratic structure and yet gone on ahead fairly fast, not so fast as some honourable Members think was desirable, nevertheless as fast as any country that I know of, in the circumstances? Look at even the countries that claim to be democratic. How many of them have even the trappings of democracy, leave out the inner content of it. They are not many in the world, certainly not many in Asia; they are very limited in number. Our neighbour with whom we have tried to be friends in spite of it, Pakistan, finds it very difficult to carry on with any democratic process.

Only this morning's news is that the whole Constitution of West Pakistan has been suspended by the President.[2] It has been suspended under Section 193 and

2. President Iskandar Mirza suspended the Constitution of West Pakistan on 21 March 1957 and took over the Government after Dr Khan Sahib's Ministry lost its majority. The crisis was caused when the Muslim League Party in the Provincial Assembly demanded the breaking up of West Pakistan into fully autonomous provinces. During the debate on this issue, about 30 members of the ruling Republican Party joined the opposition, reducing the Government to a minority.

there is no Constitution functioning in the whole of West Pakistan. It is the rule under Section 193. Now, I sympathize; I am not criticizing it, I sympathize with the people of Pakistan and the Government of West Pakistan. I am merely pointing out the difficulties they have experienced in maintaining even the trappings of democracy. I am not going into the inner content which is a much more difficult thing to have.

Two years ago, or was it three years ago, there was a great election in East Pakistan with a very big majority of one party and then within two or three months of the election, the Constitution was suspended.[3] That may have been justified or not it is not for me to say. I am merely pointing out how difficult it has been for this neighbour country of ours to function in a democratic way, even in a most elementary sense. Indeed, it is stated there that they want what is called a controlled democracy, whatever that might be, something different from normal democracy. Look at other countries round about, good countries, good people, struggling against fissiparous and disruptive tendencies, struggling inside the country; various groups wasting their energies in fighting each other; and some countries receiving a good deal of foreign aid—military and other—but in spite of that aid not, shall I say, finding roots in democracy or in free government. We talk about the free world. How many countries which presume to belong to the free world have the trappings of democracy or freedom in them? We all see this, and if you look at India, in spite of all these failings, I do submit that the democratic process has worked—not worked perfectly, because there is no perfection in this world, but worked nevertheless with remarkable success, and at the same time the progress on economic and social lines has been very considerable. I am not for the moment going into the amount of progress that we have achieved. The House knows and the House can have different opinions, but I do submit that any comparison made, that any consideration of India, should not only bear India in mind, but these major forces at work in the world and how they have functioned in various countries which have had to face more or less similar problems. That comparison is, I feel, a revealing one in so far as our achievements both in democracy and in economic and social achievements are concerned. I add 'social' specially because it is no easy matter for a country like India to advance far in the social field by the democratic process. The laws that this Parliament approved of in regard to Hindu Law Reform were, I think, among the more remarkable things that this House has done, remarkable in the

---

3. The United Front Ministry headed by Fazlul Huq was dismissed on 30 May 1954 by the Governor General, Ghulam Mohammed, after some industrial centres in East Bengal witnessed a succession of riots. The United Front had won 223 seats in a House of 309 in the elections held in March 1954.

sense that a subject like that touches people intimately. It brings out all the inertia of a people who have lived long in an inert stage, socially speaking in an inert condition. It is difficult to get over that inertia.

People talk here about opposition and the like. The real opposition in India is not the opposition of honourable Members sitting opposite; that of course is there, but it is the opposition of all kinds of disruptive tendencies, fissiparous tendencies, inertia, reaction, which in a great country like this is there, which we have to fight—all of us. So, I would beg this House to have this broad picture of these last ten years, to see what we have achieved and also what we have failed to achieve, because we must learn, we must always be prepared to learn by our own experience, errors of omission or commission.

Now, in this picture foreign affairs plays a considerable part, though not the most important part. It was understood that it would be better to deal with the foreign affairs aspect during a later debate. I shall not say much about it, but some honourable Members referred to it at some length and I should like, therefore, to say a few words and to correct a few misapprehensions which have arisen.

One of the major points for consideration and for discussion has been the question of Kashmir. I do not wish to say much. We have said enough about it and so far as the Government is concerned, it has stated its policy with clarity.

An honourable Member—I think, Shrimati Renu Chakravarty—referred in this connection to Lord Mountbatten, and I think, her words were something to the effect that he had delayed or that he had come in the way of sending our forces to Kashmir when this trouble arose.[4] May I inform her and this House that that is not a true statement? I speak, naturally, with personal experience of those difficult days.

Lord Mountbatten, as I have said elsewhere, far from delaying,—he didn't function completely as a constitutional Governor-General. In matters of defence and other matters we often sought his advice because he was a very experienced man. In fact, I may say something which is not perhaps wholly relevant. In the days of Partition trouble here, that is immediately after the Partition, when we had to face, and Pakistan had to face on the other side a fantastic situation and a horrible situation, Lord Mountbatten's experience was very helpful to us. We had formed a Committee, a kind of Superior Staff, which met every morning— some Ministers of the Cabinet, some of the Heads of Departments, some of the Heads of the Army, the Police etc.—and it met every morning as if it was

4. Renu Chakravarty said that the British officers and agents egged on Pakistani nationals in 1947 to invade Kashmir and Mountbatten delayed the despatch of Indian troops during those critical days.

conducting a kind of military operation all over India, with maps and charts and everything—what the situation was—the internal situation, Pakistan situation, with regard to that problem—huge convoys coming, of hundreds of thousands on foot, etc. It was an amazing situation. We could not deal with it in the normal way of Government and so we dealt with it in a way a war is conducted—with a rapidity of decisions and action—and we found that Lord Mountbatten with his experience was of extraordinary help during those very, very difficult days and things went through which may have taken weeks and months. Every morning we met for two or three hours and every person had to report after twenty-four hours that the thing had been done. Somebody was made responsible. So, it is quite incorrect to say that Lord Mountbatten delayed. In fact, there was no delay. It was quite extraordinary, in fact it is quite a feat which our Air Force which was in a very incipient stage then could be legitimately proud. I think, 48 hours elapsed since our knowledge of the first trouble in Kashmir, the first invasion of Kashmir.[5] We were much upset by it, we did not know what to do. We tried to get some information. We sent some people there and they came back. Ultimately, on the evening of the second day we had to come to a decision as to what to do. We sat in our Defence Committee for several hours because it was a very difficult decision, difficult from many points of view including the practical point of view because it is extremely difficult for us to reach there, and at 6 p.m. that day—I forget the exact date, whether it is the 24th, 25th or 26th October[6] but round about that in 1947—we came to the decision that we must take every risk to save Kashmir from falling into the hands of those raiders who had killed and massacred and looted and committed rapine. We decided at 6 p.m. as I said. Before that we had no intimation of this. An entirely and absolutely false charge is made on the Pakistan side that this kind of thing had been long prepared. We had not enough aircraft, we had to stop our civil air line planes coming that evening, commandeer them, and in the morning[7] we just managed to raise about 250 or 260 men to send by these civil airline planes, and these people reached the air field of Srinagar, the *kutcha* air field, when the raiders were within seven or eight miles of it. It may be if they had reached three or four hours later, the air field would have been in the possession of the raiders. So, it was a remarkable feat. Having decided late in the evening, at 5 o'clock in the morning these people went off. There was no question of delay. The moment we came to a decision there was no delay, and the decision was taken as rapidly as possible, as far as I

5. On the night of 21/22 October 1947.
6. On 26 October 1947. For a note on the meeting of the Defence Committee of the Cabinet of Government of India, see *Selected Works* (second series), Vol. 4, pp. 276-277.
7. Of 27 October 1947.

remember within 48 hours of our first knowledge of any trouble in Kashmir, that is invasion. I shall not say anything about Kashmir.

We have made it clear that the basic issues in regard to Kashmir are accession and aggression and everything has to be considered on that basis. These are the basic facts, nevertheless it is a very important thing what happens to Kashmir, apart from law, apart from Constitution, important as they are, because we are concerned not only with Jammu and Kashmir State as a part of India, as a constituent unit-State of India, but apart from that we are concerned with the welfare of the people of Kashmir, of that State. Any impartial observer, any observer partial or impartial I say, who goes and looks at the State and sees how the people are there and has a look, if he has a chance, at the people on the other side of the ceasefire line, will realize the enormous difference between the two. I have been convinced that any upset of this would bring, apart from other major consequences, ruin to the people of Kashmir. That becomes a major factor too. It would bring many other major consequences too, but we see what has happened to the people on the other side of the ceasefire line, we see what is happening in regard to the functioning of Government etc., in the whole of Pakistan. Governments come and go rapidly, the democratic process goes and all that.

Then, there is talk of our having in Kashmir done something against the decision of the Security Council. May I deal first with the criticism made very often that we were wrong in taking this matter to the Security Council? Whether we were right or wrong I do not think it does much good referring to it again and again ten years afterwards. If that is the sole argument, it does not help us in the present stage. But I do not think we were wrong because the alternative at that time for us was war with Pakistan. Well, deliberately we did not want war with Pakistan if we could avoid it and we did this. Apart from that, it is not a question of our going or not going. Others can go there too. So long as we belong to the United Nations, we have to function as a member of the United Nations. So long as we believe in the processes of the Charter of the United Nations, we have to function that way. We cannot say that when it affects us we shall ignore the United Nations and when it affects somebody else we will believe in the United Nations. Surely, that is not a legitimate position or consistent position to take up.

And we went there. Why did we go there? We did not ask the United Nations to decide on accession etc. That was a fact that had been done, we did not want anybody's authority to tell us accession is there or not. We went there to ask the Security Council to call upon Pakistan to withdraw, to take away its forces from Indian Union territory. That was the main object.

Now, we are told, sometimes we are criticized that we have done something, we have ignored the Resolutions of the Security Council, that we have violated them—I must confess that after the deepest study I do not know what this means, and I have asked people to tell me, and nobody has been able to point it out— more particularly the last Resolution of, I think, the 24th January which was passed apparently under some misapprehension, though why anyone should misapprehend the situation I do not know—it was adequately explained to them by our representative. There was some misapprehension that something was going to happen on the 26th January. Nothing was going to happen except the dissolution of the Constituent Assembly of the Jammu and Kashmir State.

Much is made about what is called the annexation of Jammu and Kashmir State. I do not know what the word "annexation" means. Anyhow, if it means accession, Jammu and Kashmir State had acceded to us nine and a half years earlier. You cannot annex something that is already with you. But there is another important aspect of it. Nobody talks, I would not say nobody, but the people who accuse us seem to ignore completely the fact that nearly half of Jammu and Kashmir State territory has been practically annexed by Pakistan whatever rights or wrongs there may be in regard to India being there—we think we are completely right—nobody has even remotely suggested that Pakistan has the slightest right to be there, under what right it is there. It is patent that it has no right, and yet for nine years it has been occupying that territory.

So, our position in regard to these matters is quite clear, but it being clear, in regard to the wider approach to various problems, world problems, we have always put forward the peaceful approach, the approach of peaceful settlement. We cannot adopt a different approach in Kashmir or, if I may say so, in Goa without violating that major approach of ours. Well, that has been both our strength and our weakness. I admit that. But, in the final analysis, one cannot ride two horses or follow two contradictory policies. We had to do that. Of course, if we are attacked, it is a different matter. Some friends have thought this is a weakness of our policy; it was weakness only that we insisted on following a policy of peace, always thinking not of the immediate moment but of the future also, because we have to come to live in peace with our neighbours and with the world.

But, look at the broader picture of the world. In this world, we live on the verge of disaster with atomic and nuclear weapons constantly being produced, experimental explosions taking place and suddenly crisis arising which bring the world to the verge of war. No one can forget this major fact. And remember one thing also, if I may venture to say so, that for the first time in the world's history we are faced by a new possibility and a new contingency. There have been wars in the past, there have been disasters in the past, terrible disasters, they occurred either in one part of the world or another, a great part of the world, but even where they occurred, something survived: some civilization, some culture, some history, the accumulation of human experience survived. And after the war was over, it grew again from that thing that has survived.

Today, we have to face a contingency that all history and all human experience might be wiped off leaving nothing behind to survive. Now, that is the first time that such a contingency has arisen. And this has arisen because of these terrible weapons of mass destruction which not only destroy outwardly and suddenly, but which are something infinitely worse, gradually destroying our bones, your marrow, and everything, due to radiation going in. It is not immediately obvious. It may take weeks, it may take months, it may take years. That is the major thing that you have to face today. And all your problems, and all the hard work that you put in in solving your problems, and all the conflicts that you may have of ideologies and everything pales into insignificance before this major fact that if somehow we go on over this brink, then all history and all past experience of humanity might be wiped off.

I repeat this, and I seek the indulgence of the House to do so because I myself feel that people do not realize it. They talk about the atomic bomb as a joke, and they talk about nuclear weapons and all that, and radiation. They do not realize the extreme danger that faces the world. And I confess that the prospect depresses me, because ultimately this danger can only be held back by the character of human beings and nothing else, by the peaceful approach, by the compassionate approach. You may make terms with each other, but if you are full of hatred and violence, I have not a shadow of doubt that this danger will break out and submerge everybody.

Therefore, I think that the approach, the cold war approach, if I may say so, is an exceedingly bad approach. I say so with all respect. And I am not moralizing. Who am I to tell anybody else? I do not think that we in India are in any sense better than other people in other countries. I do not boost up my own people. I like my people, I love my people, because I am one of them, but I do not boost them up and say they are better, more spiritual, more moral. I do not believe that. Every country has a spirituality, a morality. Every country has its periods of growth and decay. I do value what India has, I think it is something wonderful. Maybe, I am partial to India; maybe, all of us are partial to our country. But let us not forget this, let us not assume a superior pose about it.

I say this with all humility that this business of cold war which is based essentially on violence and hatred—the essence of it was hatred headed against the other party—is a thing which is bad and is a thing, which, if it is not controlled, will lead to all manner of disaster.

Take again this fact. As a result of this cold war, armaments go on and go on;

461

experimental explosions of nuclear weapons take place. The other day, there was an explosion. I think, somewhere in the Soviet Union.[8] Soon, there is going to be an explosion in the Christmas Islands in the Pacific.[9] We have received pathetic complaints from organizations and people in Japan about these explosions.[10] They have had experience of them. And they dread a repetition of that experience. But what can we do about it? But it does seem to me tragic, a tragic circumstance that these experimental explosions should take place, when even according to scientific advice, each explosion adds to the vitiation, making the atmosphere more vitiated and more dangerous. Nobody can say to what extent that poison spreads from each explosion. But every scientist knows that poison is there. Some people say that the poison is not so great as to kill you or to affect you very much, it is only in a small quantity, but others say it may affect you a little more. Nobody knows, because we are on the verge of the unknown. And suppose there is doubt about it. Even apart from certainty, suppose there is doubt about it. Then, certainly there is one aspect that it may be very dangerous to the human race. In view of that, that experiments should still be carried seem to be tragic in the extreme.

Why is this done? We come back to the cold war. We come back to this policy of believing in arms and latest armaments, in military alliances and the like. The other day, someone said, speaking about SEATO. I hope I am correct, I think it was something to this effect—that SEATO will preserve peace in South East Asia for a thousand years.[11]

8. There were reports of tests of nuclear weapons in the Soviet Union on 19 January and 8 March 1957. Another nuclear test was carried out in the USSR on 3 April.

9. According to a note issued by the British Government on 7 January 1957 to all diplomatic missions, an area of the Pacific Ocean 900 miles north and south of the Christmas Islands and 780 miles east and west was declared dangerous to shipping and aircraft between 1 March and 1 August 1957 owing to the British nuclear weapon tests.

10. These projected tests aroused nation-wide agitation in Japan. The Japanese Parliament passed a resolution in February calling Britain, USA and USSR to suspend all tests of nuclear weapons. Another resolution denouncing nuclear and thermo-nuclear tests, adopted by the Upper House on 15 March, was sent by the Japanese Government to the UN Secretary General for transmission to all UN member-countries. Large-scale demonstrations were held and a mass protest rally was organized on 1 March, supported by all political parties. Similar protests were made by many private organizations—180 Japanese physicists, fishermen's organizations and students. The Japanese Council against Atomic and Hydrogen Bombs asked for convening of a world conference in Tokyo to demand the abolition of all nuclear weapons.

11. Robert Menzies, Australian Prime Minister, said this while inaugurating SEATO Executive Council meeting on 11 March in Canberra.

Dr Rama Rao (Kakinada): With a few atom bombs.

JN: But, whether it is a thousand years or a hundred years, that meant, I suppose, the continuation of cold war for a thousand years, or whatever the period may be. With all that, it also reminded me of something rather unpleasant. Hitler had said that Nazism would last a thousand years, the Nazi regime in Germany.

So, this whole approach of cold war and military alliances, if persisted in sometime or other, I suppose, will lead to that final catastrophe. Now, I do not venture to offer advice. Who am I to offer advice to any country? I know that many things that we would like to do in this country we cannot do, for fear of having our country weak and unprotected. We dare not take that risk, and if I dare not take that risk, I cannot ask other countries to take that risk, obviously. At the same time, it is equally obvious that this race in armament and this continuation of cold war is an even greater risk than anything else.

I would very respectfully suggest to the great countries who have to shoulder these heavy responsibilities that the time has come—the time is always there, in fact—for some kind of a step in another direction to be taken. I realize that you cannot suddenly reverse big policies; you cannot, as I said, take steps which make you face risks which you are not prepared to face. But even if the step be small, it should be in the right direction, and no step should be taken which adds to this cold war business.

I think—I have often said so—some people do not like our criticizing these pacts. So far as we are concerned, whether it is the Warsaw Pact or SEATO or the Baghdad Pact, they are all, I think, dangerous things in the modern world which add to hatred, fear and apprehension. Somehow each one thinks that because of the other, he has to keep going, just as many countries say that they will stop nuclear explosions provided everybody else stops them. Everybody says so and nobody stops, and so they go on.

We have seen recently how the Baghdad Pact and SEATO were dragged in in regard to the Kashmir issue. You see how one affects another and how a wrong step leads to innumerable other wrong steps. The other day the Prime Minister of Pakistan, describing the Baghdad Pact, used rather striking language—I would not dare to do so. He said—zero plus zero plus zero plus zero equals zero.[12] His point was that unless some powerful country like the United Kingdom or the United States was in the Baghdad Pact with its big defence apparatus, all the other members of it, from the point of view of armament, were relatively zero. That means that there is another aspect to it: When a country considering itself

12. Suhrawardy defended this statement during a debate on foreign affairs in the Pakistan National Assembly from 22 to 25 February 1957.

zero attaches itself to some figure, it is the figure that counts, not the zero; obviously, it is the other figure that must count because the zero does not count. So not only policy but everything is determined by the other factor, not by this.

Whether it is Kashmir or whether it is some other country, recent events have shown us that one cannot build a country which has no roots in its own past. You cannot ultimately impose anything on a country; it may grow into it. You cannot impose anything and you cannot uproot a country from its nationalist roots. We saw in Central Europe, some months back, in the case of Hungary, how ten or eleven years' attempt did not succeed in imposing something, and the nationalism of Hungary was strong and tried to resist. There are many other factors; I am merely pointing out the major factor, that it was an extraordinary example of how strong nationalism is in a country, for it has deep roots. Nationalism may become socialist, may become communist, may become anything—that is a different matter—as, I believe, in some countries it has. But it cannot be imposed; anything cannot be imposed upon it, and a country which has not got these nationalist roots in its past life and culture and all that, will be a rootless country.

Now, I venture to point out that this theory—or call it what you like—the two-nation theory, which was advanced in India some years before Independence and about which reference is still made in our neighbour country, is a theory which makes a country rootless. It ignores the real life of the country, the roots of a country in its past, and tries to impose something without those roots, with the result that difficulties come in. We can see these things in recent history. And if I may, in all humility, say to the people and to the leaders of Pakistan, I have sympathized with them in their difficulties; but their major difficulty has been their having uprooted themselves from their own past—I am not talking about India—and tried to develop something in the air on the basis of the two-nation theory. The result is that they cannot get a grip and they have to rely more and more on external force and external aid, because they think in terms of transplanting religion to nationalism and to statehood. That is a medieval conception. In the old, medieval days, it might have succeeded because communications were not there, because many things happened which cannot happen today. But the conception of joining statehood to a religion is so out of place that no amount of repetition of it can make it real; it is unreal, and it becomes still more unreal when it is sought to be applied to, let us say, Kashmir. It is fantastic. It is not there—the two-nation theory—in Kashmir. Our friends, some in Pakistan and more so in some other countries, always talk about it to us.

So, we see in this Kashmir issue not only the basic facts to which I have referred but a basic conflict between the modern age and medievalism, a basic conflict between progress and reaction, a basic conflict between the welfare of the people of Kashmir and their ruination. Sometime back, the Prime Minister of Pakistan himself said that he did not believe in the two-nation theory. I was glad to read that because I hoped that from that other things would flow. I still hope that might happen, but unfortunately, it is not apparently easy even for him to give this new direction. Perhaps gradually it may come. Meanwhile, it is this two-nation theory, again, which has led, in the final analysis, to this tremendous and alarming exodus continuing from East Pakistan.[13] If that theory is there, whether there is exodus or not, there can never be really contentment and satisfaction among those who, inevitably, become some kind of an inferior race....

13. Total displaced population from East Pakistan at the end of the year 1957 was approximately 2.64 lakhs. These people had been living in 168 relief camps distributed in the States of West Bengal, Tripura, Bihar and Orissa.

3. On International Situation—I[1]

Jawaharlal Nehru:[2] Mr Speaker, Sir, I beg to move:
"That the present international situation and the policy of the Government of India in relation thereto be taken into consideration."

In the course of the last few days, when we were discussing the President's Address, many references were made to foreign affairs and, I also, in the course of my remarks, replied to many questions put. In a sense, therefore, we have partly covered the ground of international affairs in that previous debate.

It is now, I think, about four months since we had a debate on international affairs in this House. It was at the end of November last,[3] I believe, when we had that debate, that we were confronted by a very serious situation which had arisen in the Middle Eastern region, in Egypt, because of a military invasion of Egypt. Also, in Central Europe a serious situation had been created in Hungary. On

1. Speech in the Lok Sabha, 25 March 1957. *Lok Sabha Debates*, Vol. I, Part II, cols. 651-671.
2. Nehru was also Minister of External Affairs.
3. On 19 and 20 November 1956. Printed in *Selected Works* (second series), Vol. 35, pp. 351-388.

that occasion, in November, I ventured to deal with these two matters.[4] Many things have happened during these four months and considerable progress has been made in some matters, but I do not think I would be justified in saying that the general atmosphere in the world can be viewed with any optimism, indeed there are many factors in it which are very disturbing.

So far as the situation in Egypt, in the Suez Canal and round about is concerned, we have had the privilege of being in consultations with the Egyptian Government on the one side, and in the United Nations with others, intimately connected with these matters, and we have tried to serve, in so far as we could, the cause of peaceful settlement, a settlement which would not only guard the rights of nations or sovereignty of nations concerned, but also be fair to the interests of the international community.

I am not in a position to say anything very much about what is happening in Egypt now except that, I think, there are indications that a satisfactory solution may be arrived at in regard to the Suez Canal, the working or the functioning of the Suez Canal.[5] Probably, in the course of a few days, a few weeks or a week or two, the Canal will be open to traffic. Now, the House will remember that much of the trouble of the last five or six months arose in connection with the Suez Canal and, therefore, if it is settled satisfactorily as to how it should work to the advantage of the international community and safeguarding the sovereign rights of Egypt, that will be a great gain.

I do not say that that will solve the problems of the Middle East. But, certainly, that will go a considerable way in easing tensions there. There are difficulties, as the House knows, in regard to Gaza, in regard to the Gulf of Aquaba and, generally, in regard to conditions in the Middle East. But, I suppose, you cannot expect them to be solved altogether; one has to go slowly step by step.[6]

Possibly, looking at the world picture as it is today, the Middle Eastern region might be said to be the most difficult and potentially explosive region. Inspite of the progress made towards a possible settlement of the Suez Canal issue and other matters, inspite of the fact that the invading forces were withdrawn from Egyptian territory, this area and the Middle East still continues to be a very difficult area. I do not mean to say that the area is difficult, inherently difficult,

---

4. See also the sections on Suez and Hungary in *Selected Works* (second series), Vol. 35.
5. See *post*, pp. 523-525.
6. The Israeli forces in Gaza strip and Sharm-el-Sheikh area, the west coast of the Gulf of Aquaba, were withdrawn and these areas taken over by the UN Emergency Force simultaneously. Israel sought adequate guarantee for free navigation of her shipping in the Gulf of Aquaba and the security of her territories contiguous to the Gaza strip. General Hassan Abdul Latif was appointed Civil Governor of Gaza on 11 March by Nasser.

but it becomes a difficult area because of, I may say so with all respect, certain conflicts extraneous to the Middle East which are projected there.

Unfortunately, in a great part of the world real trouble arises partly from some local difficulties, partly from some distant difficulty which is reflected there in that particular part of the world. This House knows very well our general views about military pacts, which are called 'defensive' but, which inevitably have a certain offensive or aggressive look to others. The moment one has a defensive pact aimed at certain other countries, the result is something more than 'defensive', and we have, therefore, ventured to say, and repeat again and again, that these pacts, whoever may make them, do not tend to preserve peace, or further the cause of peace, or assure security.

Indeed, one of the obvious things that anyone can see, that has happened in the last few months in this Middle Eastern region or Western Asia, has been the disturbing factor of these pacts. If I may refer to another place, Central Europe and Hungary, it is the pacts that came into the way; so that we have had enough evidence that these military pacts by one group of nations, presumably against another group of nations, do not help the cause of peace or security.

Unfortunately, however, the pacts continue, and are even added on to. Only recently we have heard a great deal about the SEATO Pact, about the Baghdad Pact. These two affect us, India, naturally much more intimately and directly than any other pacts. The NATO alliance or the Warsaw Pact we can view distantly on grounds of certain principles and the approach we make to questions of world policy, but the Baghdad Pact and the SEATO, as everyone knows, have a direct effect upon India and, naturally, we have viewed them with suspicion and dislike.

In considering this question of military pacts, I am not, and I do not wish the House to consider that I am trying to run them down, and to be presumptuous enough to criticize the policies of foreign countries in the past, or to a large extent in the present. It may be that at one time something was necessary. What I am venturing to suggest is that in the present context of events, these pacts do not help the cause of peace. In fact, they have the contrary effect and this has been borne in upon us lately with greater force than ever. But we saw how these pacts, notably the Baghdad Pact, and to some extent, the SEATO arrangements also were utilized against us in connection with the Kashmir issue.

Now, presumably, the Kashmir issue has nothing to do with the Baghdad Pact or any other pact, but it was dragged into this picture and the members of these pacts functioned, well, as members of those pacts in regard to a particular issue which had nothing to do with it. Thus, we see how these pacts which were meant presumably for some other purpose are used for different purposes and create, therefore, greater difficulties. And thus, because of these pacts, cold war comes and impinges upon the borders and frontiers of India. That is a matter of concern to us. We do not want the cold war anywhere, much less on the borders of India. I am quite convinced that the cold war approach is an approach which will continue to worsen international understanding for a certain basic reason, and that is, if the international situation is, bedevilled today by fear, by suspicion, by dislike and hatred even, then you do not get over all these by the cold war. The cold war creates all these things or continues them. Some other approach has to be made, as I ventured to say.

I cannot say that in this country or any other, we can give up, abandon, our defensive apparatus or do something which will involve us in grave risks. No country can do that. Nobody suggests to any country that they should be prepared to take risks and hope that all will be well. But there is something in between these two policies. One is of just taking risks and hoping for the best. The other is taking no risks and yet working in the direction of peace.

Take even one of the major issues of today. What is going to happen to hydrogen bombs and the nuclear weapons and the like? I suppose it is the fear of attack by other party that drives those countries which possess these weapons to go on enlarging them, everybody knowing that if once they are used, they may be destructive to both as well as to a great part of the world, everybody realizing that they should not be used. Yet, they go on using them for fear that the other might have more of them. And so, we go on moving in this vicious circle and we do not get out of that vicious circle by the methods of cold war. It is obvious some other method has to be adopted, at the same time, protecting yourself against any possible danger or risk. I admit that. Great countries or small countries, both have to do that, but I do submit that the protection has not come in the past and will not come in the future by the systems of military alliances, whether they are with the Soviet Union or the United Kingdom or the United States of America or any other country, because, the whole effect of it is the other party has them too and they go on balancing these nuclear weapons and other forms of armaments.

Take the question of disarmaments. Lately, there have been some indications, some slightly hopeful indications, that this question of disarmament might perhaps yield some results. There is the disarmament conference. But, during the past months and years, there have often been some such indications which have not yielded any result that we hoped for. So, I do not wish to be too optimistic about it, but anyhow, I do feel that there is something today which if pursued in the right way might lead to some substantial step later on. More I cannot say, because we have been disappointed so often in the past and it has become a little frustrating experience to hope too much.

Yet, the real reason for disarmament remains there, namely, that any other course really leads to something which may end in utter disaster and that it does not, in the present stage, ensure security. In fact, it has the opposite effect; apart from the vast sums of money that are spent on armaments, so much is required for developing the countries of the world for achieving higher standards for the people.

Recently, two of the great men—of the biggest and the most powerful nations in the world, United States of America and Soviet Union—made certain proposals. The President of the United States made some proposals which are called the Eisenhower Doctrine now.[7] They are referred to like that. The Soviet Union made some independent proposals.[8] I do not presume, at this stage, to discuss or criticize any of these proposals. I have no doubt that both were meant to advance the cause of security and peace. But, what I ventured to suggest on another occasion was this: that proposals being drawn out from a distance in this atmosphere of suspicion and fear, even when they are good proposals, do not take one far, because nobody accepts them or few people accept them as bona fide proposals.

I venture to suggest that the situation in the world is difficult and serious enough for these questions to be tackled face to face by the great leaders, more particularly by the great President of the United States and the leaders of the Soviet Union, as well as others if necessary, but more particularly those two. It is just possible that that might lead to something better than we have seen in the last few months. On the one occasion that they did meet—it was about two

7. The Eisenhower Doctrine, delivered to the US Congress on 5 January 1957, embodied the US Administration's proposals for a new Middle Eastern policy. It aimed at (i) a programme of US economic aid/or military aid to any nation or group of nations in the area desiring such aid; and (ii) employment of US armed forces "to secure and protect the territorial integrity and political independence of nations requesting such aid against armed aggression from any nation controlled by international communism." These measures would be "consonant with the treaty obligations of the United States" and "subject to the overriding authority of the Security Council."

8. The Soviet Foreign Minister, Dmitri Shepilov, proposed in the Supreme Soviet on 12 February that the Soviet, US, British and French Governments should join in a four-power declaration based on the following six principles: (i) settlement of outstanding issues solely through peaceful negotiations; (ii) non-intervention in the domestic affairs of the Middle East countries, and respect for their sovereignty and independence; (iii) dropping of all attempts to involve the Middle East in Great-Power military blocs; (iv) abolition of foreign bases and withdrawal of foreign troops from the Middle East countries; (v) mutual agreements not to deliver arms to those countries; and (vi) economic assistance to the Middle East countries without political, military or other terms incompatible with their sovereignty.

years ago, I believe—that meeting resulted in a change in world atmosphere and the first hopes of some kind of peace.[9]

This is not a question of favouring any particular proposal or not favouring it. I have no doubt that a great deal in President Eisenhower's proposals, more especially those dealing with economic help, are of importance and of great value. I have no doubt that many of the proposals that were put forward by the Soviet Union, on the face of them, are helpful. How they are carried out is a different matter.

But there is one approach that troubles me, and that is this idea of thinking that areas in Asia, say in West Asia, are vacuum which have to be filled in by somebody stepping in from outside. That, I feel, is a dangerous approach, and I think an unreal approach when you say that every country which has not got sufficient armaments is a vacuum. At that rate, if you think in terms of armament, then there are only two countries which have an adequate supply of hydrogen bombs—the United States of America and the Soviet Union. You may say, all other countries are vacuum, because they have not got hydrogen bombs, which would be, of course, an absurd thing. What is the test then? Military power? Two countries stand out above all others. There are other countries, powerful military nations, great powers, two, three, four or five whatever the number may be. Are all the smaller and militarily weaker countries vacuums, apart from these six or seven? What is the test of this vacuum idea? It is a dangerous idea, especially for Asian and African countries. It seems to me really to lead to the conclusion that where an imperialist power gradually withdraws, or circumstances compel it to withdraw, necessarily you must presume that it has left vacuum. If so, how is that vacuum to be filled? Suppose there is a vacuum in power. How is it to be filled? Surely if somebody else comes in, it is a repetition of the old story, maybe in a different form. It can only be filled by the people of that country growing and developing themselves economically, politically and otherwise. Another difficulty is, when there is a conflict in the world, if one country wants to fill a vacuum, if I may use that word, or to have an area of influence, immediately, the hostile group suspects the intentions of this country and tries to pursue a policy in which it can have its area of influence there or elsewhere. So, you get back into this tug-of-war of trying to capture as areas of influence in various parts of the world, which are not strong enough, if you like, to stand by themselves or to prevent this kind of thing happening.

This thing happened, you will remember, two years ago, or probably more,

9. A summit conference of the Heads of Governments of USA, USSR, UK and France was held in Geneva from 18 to 23 July 1955 to discuss disarmament, European security, German unification and contact between East and West.

three years ago, in Indo-China, where war was in progress. Ultimately, an Agreement on Indo-China was reached at the Geneva Conference, which was essentially based on this fact that those Great Power groups should not push in aggressively in the Indo-China States, but leave them to function for themselves.[10] In effect it meant that those Indo-China States should follow an independent and unaligned policy. They may have their sympathisers. Of course, they have them; nobody prevents that. But, there should be no military intervention, pacts etc., of a military kind, because the moment one State had it, the other State wanted to have its own pact somewhere in that area and that upset the whole thing. In Indo-China they had a war for six or seven years before this Agreement was arrived at and there was a ceasefire, some kind of peace, only on the basis of acknowledging some kind of a mutual agreement that we should not interfere in a military way or anything that might lead up to it. I do not say that everything in Indo-China has turned out to one's entire satisfaction since then, but I think, it is true that that agreement not only stopped a war in Indo-China, a terrible war which had devastated parts of it, but also step by step has helped in keeping peace and in improving the situation. There are great difficulties still. We have to shoulder our burden there, as the House knows, because we have been and continue to be the Chairman of the International Commission there. It is a difficult and complicated task, a rather thankless one occasionally, but we could not possibly run away from it. We have been there and we have helped. As soon as we succeed in solving some small problem, others arise. Well, all I can say is that I hope gradually the situation will improve. One cannot do this by some sudden decision or sudden step that you might take. That thing which applied to the Indo-China area in a sense might be considered in other areas too. Why interfere? If you are afraid of the other party interfering, surely the safer course is not to interfere oneself and thus prevent the other party interfering. If the other party interfere even so, well the matter can be considered and dealt with; arrangements can be made to deal with it. In other words, instead of spreading the area of pacts, the way of peace lies in coming to agreement in having less and less of these military pacts on both sides. After all if the military pacts balance each other, the lack of them also will balance each other and will not endanger one country more than the other. I do not say these issues are simple. Of course, they are not, they are complicated and the men of goodwill in every country think about them, want to solve them and yet find them difficult.

I mentioned it previously and the House knows that we have got a force at present in the Middle Eastern region, mostly I believe in the Gaza strip of the Egyptian territory. It was made perfectly clear at the time when this force was

10. See *selected works* (second series), Vol. 26, pp. 318-319.

first of all sent that it was sent after obtaining the permission of the Egyptian Government. We did not wish to move in at all, because it was Egyptian territory. Anyhow, we did not wish to take any step in the matter without their permission. Secondly, this force was sent there on the express understanding that it was not to take the place of the invading forces, i.e., it did not go there as an occupying force, occupying other territory. It went there to help in keeping peace on the border on the armistic line and it has been serving there in this capacity. At first it was near the Canal; then it was sent to the Gaza area, where it is, and I believe, the work of our officers and men there has met with the approval of all the people concerned there. I am particularly glad that the people there—I am not talking of the authorities—have also looked upon them with favour and they are popular with them.

Since the last debate we had here, some important developments have taken place, which would have been welcome anyhow, but which were doubly welcome because of the frustration we suffer from in other parts. One of the most important development was the emergence of the old Gold Coast colony as the independent and sovereign State of Ghana.[11] It was my earnest wish to go there myself on this happy occasion, but it coincided with the last days of our elections and the meetings of this Parliament. So, I just could not go, but naturally we sent our best wishes to the leaders and the people of Ghana. The emergence of Ghana as an independent State is, I think, of great importance and great significance not only because any such thing would be important, but because it is rather symbolic of Africa and the trends in Africa. I am particularly glad that a number of internal conflicts that they had in Ghana—party conflicts and others in regard to their Constitution and in regard to their other matters—had been resolved in a spirit of statesmanship and cooperation,[12] which is of the happiest augury for their future. As the House well knows, the difficulties of a country come after independence and, no doubt Ghana will be faced with those problems and is facing them today. The real problems that they have to face come after independence. I have little doubt that with goodwill and the wise approach that they have shown, they will overcome these problems.

11. Gold Coast attained independence within the British Commonwealth with Queen as sovereign on 6 March 1957 under the name of Ghana.
12. The opposition parties in Ghana—the National Liberation Movement and the Northern People's Party—demanded on 20 November 1956 "separate independence for Ashanti and the Northern Territories and a partition commission to divide the assets and liabilities of the Gold Coast among its four component territories". This was preceded by an all-party conference to discuss the Gold Coast Government's draft proposals for a constitution, which opened in Accra on 16 October 1956.

The other day, only yesterday, I think, I had occasion to meet a Minister of the Malayan Government. Malaya is also rapidly forging ahead towards independence, and provisionally, I believe, it has been fixed that the date for Malayan independence would be somewhere towards the end of August.[13] All these are happy signs which give one some hope for the future in spite of the other disappointments that we have to experience. Then, there is Nigeria adjoining Ghana which also, I hope, is on the verge of independence.[14] Thus, on the one side, the colonial picture of the world is changing and yet, unfortunately, on other sides, it is getting stuck up and movements for freedom of colonies are met with the stern opposition.

Honourable Members will know that at present we have an eminent visitor from abroad, the Prime Minister of Poland, in this country.[15] I believe Members are going to have a chance of meeting him and listening to him. We welcome him specially not only because Poland is a country with a fascinating tradition of struggle for freedom, with a very powerful nationalism which has moved it throughout history, but also because of the terrible sufferings they had in the last War and the way they have built up their city of Warsaw and other cities which had been reduced almost to ground level. Apart from all these, Poland has been an example in the last year—a few months of the process of liberalization and democratization in the East European countries which has been welcomed by us and by many others. Because, we feel that that is the natural way of bringing about changes, relaxations and less rigidity and that to bring them about by some kind of compulsion from outside fails and in fact, leads to greater rigidity. Therefore, Poland is also a symbol of certain powerful and very valuable trends in the western world which have a larger significance.

We have also in Delhi, at the present moment Mr Jarring, who was last month the President of the Security Council, and who has come here at the instance of the Security Council in connection with the Kashmir issue. I had the privilege of meeting him yesterday and having a talk with him. No doubt we shall have further talks before he goes away. I need not say anything about our general position in regard to Kashmir because that has been made quite clear. Even in the President's Address it was made quite clear in a few sentences. In the course of the debate on the President's Address also many references were made to it. There were, I believe, quite a number of questions which honourable Members put, and the Speaker was good enough to suggest that instead of those questions being answered seriatim, perhaps, I might deal with them or most of them in the

13. On 31 August 1957.
14. The Nigerian Constitutional Conference opened in London on 23 May 1957 to discuss the proposals for granting of independence to Nigeria.
15. See *post*, pp. 545-547.

course of this debate. Perhaps some of them have already been answered. However, I shall refer to them briefly presently.

There is a problem which affects all our people here very powerfully and very deeply and that is the question of Goa. On the occasion of the debate here a few days ago on the President's Address, an honourable Member of this House who had a good deal of personal experience of Goa and Goan Portuguese administration and Goan prisons, gave us some account from his personal knowledge and experience.[16] I was not present in the House then, unfortunately. But, I read a report of his speech; others have, no doubt, heard or read it. No one can read that account without feeling a sense of horror as to what has been happening and is, no doubt, continuing to happen in Goa. The other day, some of our nationals were released by the Portuguese Government, and among them, is an honourable Member of this House who has spent a long time there under those very bad conditions. I want to make it clear that the fact of the release of some Indian nationals from there, welcome as that is—we wanted them to be released naturally—brings little satisfaction to our mind. I do not want any one to imagine that we are in any sense toning down our demands and our opinions in regard to Goa and that this chapter is closed or anyhow postponed for the present. Goa is a live and vital issue. The House may criticize us for the type of policy we adopt or may wish to change it. That is a different matter. We may discuss that. But, it is for all of us, to whatever party we may belong, a live and vital issue and we feel deeply on it. I particularly want to say that—welcome as the honourable Member is here, he has come back from prison and the others will come back—we must remember that hundreds and hundreds of Goans are in prison there and continue to be in prison and continue to be treated worse even than the Indian nationals who were there. I do not know if my voice can possibly reach them; probably not. Anyhow, I should have liked to assure them that this question and their fate are very near our minds and it is a matter of deep unhappiness to us that circumstances should be such that this problem cannot be solved easily and quickly. As with other problems, it becomes tied up with world issues, with international problems and one cannot touch a single problem

---

16. Tridib Kumar Chaudhuri, who was imprisoned in Goa for 19 months, spoke about the physical repression and human suffering of about 200 Goan political prisoners in Aguada Fort prison and about 100 in the Fort of Reis Magos, their sentences ranging from 6 to 28 years. These included nine lady political prisoners including Sudhabai Joshi, who was a Goan national and the wife of an Indian citizen, Mahadev Shastri Joshi. Chaudhri said that during the previous three years at least 10,000 people had been arrested merely on suspicion and kept in police lock-ups for periods ranging from six months to one and half years with periodical beatings.

which is tied up with other issues without, may be, creating all kinds of reactions to it. One cannot isolate this problem, and therefore, we have tried to follow there the broad policy which we have enunciated before the world, the broad policy in regard to foreign affairs or internal affairs, and I do not myself see how we can depart from it basically without giving up that broad policy, and without really launching out into an unknown course of action of which we do not know the results. At the same time, I do feel—in fact, we have been feeling it for some time past—that we must give the most careful consideration to the various aspects of our policy; I am not referring to the broad approach to the problem which, I believe, is correct and should be pursued, but I do think that we should give the most careful consideration to the various other aspects of our policies relating to Goa. In fact, we are in the process of doing that. These elections had come and they rather came in the way—and other matters—but I hope that in the course of the next few weeks we shall be able to consult not only our own people who have been dealing with them, but others too; I hope we should be able to consult honourable Members of the Opposition too in regard to these matters, and try to evolve courses of action which can be as effective as anything can be in the present circumstances.

May I refer to some of those questions, chiefly in regard to Kashmir and one or two other matters which the Speaker was good enough to keep over for this debate?

There were questions about Mr Jarring's visit. I need say nothing about it. As the House knows, he is here. The Resolution under which he has come here, the Resolution of the Security Council, is a simple resolution—it was passed after much debate, I need not refer to that—it is a simple one, reminding him of previous Resolutions and asking him to come here and to meet representatives of India and Representatives of Pakistan in their respective places and discuss this matter with them and to report by the 15th April. He has been to Pakistan, spent about a week there. He is here now. That is all I can say.

Then there were several questions about atomic weapons in Pakistan. References had been made about this matter both by my colleague, Shri Krishna Menon in the Security Council, and by me occasionally here in some connection. Both our references were based not on any secret information—we leave that out—but on certain official statements or speeches by the Pakistan Commander-in-Chief. We did not say—I did not say and Shri Krishna Menon did not say— that they had atomic weapons, but we only said what he, the Pakistan Commander-in-Chief, had said, that in their military exercises in last December, the use of tactical atomic weapons was envisaged and exercises were carried out from that point of view. That is a preparatory stage—preparation for the use of atomic weapons, I did not say they had them, I do not know—and since then the United States Government has denied the fact of their having given any atomic weapons to Pakistan, or, indeed, to any other country. Naturally, we accept that denial, but the fact remains that these preparations and exercises and the possible use of them are matters of some concern to us, more especially when all this is tied up with this large-scale military aid which comes from the United States to Pakistan, and which has made a great deal of difference, I believe, to many problems, between India and Pakistan. It has been my conviction—it was and is—that it would have been far easier for Pakistan and India to solve their problems, difficult as they were, after the Partition, if other countries—outside countries—had not interfered so much, whatever the problem might be, whether it is Kashmir or any other. I am not for the moment criticizing outside countries because often they have acted with goodwill in this matter—though not perhaps always—but goodwill or not, the fact is that this interference has come in the way of these two neighbour countries solving their problems in some measure, if not with immediate goodwill, anyhow solving them.

Then there were some questions, I think, enquiring if Pakistan had annexed the area of Kashmir in Jammu and Kashmir State occupied by them. Well, the answer to that is "Yes". Even by their Constitution they have stated that all the administered area is part of Pakistan—and undoubtedly this is one of their administered areas—so that they have for some time past, and practically speaking for a long time past, and later even constitutionally treated this as an area which is part of Pakistan. It has been surprising that little reference has been made to this annexation of part of, insofar as area is concerned nearly half of Jammu and Kashmir State area, while a great deal of discussion has taken place about what is called the annexation of Kashmir State by India. There has been no annexation. The word itself is completely wrong, inappropriate. There was accession, as the House knows, in October, 1947; the circumstances leading to it may have been different, but it was an accession in exactly the same way as was applied to the hundreds of other States in India, the same legal, constitutional way. True, the circumstances were somewhat different, but it was an accession. Nothing has happened since then to lessen that factor and nothing was necessary to add to it.

There were also questions about Gilgit and a story that was published in the press, a story emanating from Brigadier Ghansara Singh. We, of course, had known this story for a long time. Brigadier Ghansara Singh was sent by the Maharaja of Kashmir, the Ruler then, under an agreement with the British just prior to Partition. They had handed over Gilgit to the Jammu and Kashmir Government, and this Brigadier was sent there to take charge. Some very extraordinary things happened when he went there. Soon after the arrival, after two or three days, he was arrested by the Gilgit Scouts who were under the command of British officers, and the British officers of the Gilgit Scouts informed the Pakistan Government that Gilgit had acceded to Pakistan. I am not going into the merits, but the story was a very odd and curious one. Brigadier Ghansara Singh was kept in prison there or in detention for a considerable time. When he came out, we had met him, and he had given us this story then. Now, it was given out to the public.

I should like to make clear another thing. We have been asked as to the Government of India's position in regard to the Pakistan-occupied territory of Kashmir, and what we propose to do about it. Now, it is clear that in every sense, legally and constitutionally, by virtue of the accession of the Jammu and Kashmir State to India, the whole State acceded, not a bit of it or a part of it only; and, therefore, according to that accession, the whole State should form part of the Union of India. That is the legal position.

We may have, in the course of these nine years, in our extreme desire to come to some peaceful arrangement, discussed various suggestions, proposals etc. But those discussions did not lead to any result. There they ended, although, sometimes, something that we said in the course of discussion, some idea or proposal or thought that was thrown out is held up to us as a kind of commitment. Anyhow, in law, that is part of the Jammu and Kashmir territory, which is an acceded State of the Union.

But it is true that we have stated in the Security Council and outside too—and in fact, this has been our position for a long time past; we have often said—that we for our part are not going to take any steps involving the military, involving Armed Forces, to settle the Kashmir problem. Of course, if we are attacked, we shall defend, and indeed we have made it clear that if we are attacked in Kashmir, we consider it an attack on India, which it is. We have made it clear. But we have also made it clear that while we consider the Pakistan-occupied part of Kashmir as legally and constitutionally a part of India, of the Indian Union territory, we are not going to take any military steps to recover it or recapture it. We have given that assurance and we shall abide by it.

There were also questions about some messages that had come to me from the Prime Ministers of Ceylon and China in regard to the Kashmir issue. As for those messages, the House will remember that the Prime Minister of China went to Ceylon; and they issued a joint statement there. In the course of that statement, there was reference to the Kashmir issue, a friendly reference saying that they hoped that this would be settled by mutual discussions or contacts between the two countries concerned, and hoping that other countries would not interfere. That was a friendly wish from two of our friendly countries. And, so far as I know, there is nothing more that followed from it or was intended to follow.

So, I have dealt with most of these questions which were put to us. One thing more I should like to refer to, which may be in the honourable Members' minds, and about which—I had not seen them—presumably some amendments may have been sent, because whenever there is a debate on foreign affairs in this House, there are always some amendments dealing with India's association with the Commonwealth of Nations. I have dealt with this matter in the past on many occasions, and pointed out....

Ananthasayanam Ayyangar: There is no such amendment now.

JN: I hope that my suggestion need not be considered as an amendment-invitation. But whether there is an amendment or not is immaterial. The question is an important one. And I can very well understand honourable Members, not only on the other side of the House, but on every side of the House, thinking about this matter much more now than they did previously, and enquiring from me, as they have done, sometimes in writing, sometimes orally, as to why in spite of all that has happened, whether in the Middle Eastern region or whether in regard to Kashmir, that is, the attitudes taken by some Commonwealth countries in regard to Kashmir, which were certainly not impartial or neutral, which were siding with one party, and which were siding with a party which we considered the aggressor party, we still think it is right for us to continue this Commonwealth connection. They put this question to me, and we discussed it with them, but even more so, I have discussed it with my own mind and with my colleagues and others, because this is not a matter which I can settle just because I feel one way or the other. Indeed, we cannot settle any matter that way. It can only be settled, not only after the fullest consultation, but without doing violence to public feeling. Sometimes, it may be that public feeling has to be restrained or even opposed for the time being, because people may get excited, and they may think differently somewhat later. But in the final run, public feeling cannot be ignored, much less violated. So, this was a serious matter, and is a serious matter.

But I have felt, and for the first time I felt, the first time in these many years, that it may some time or other require further consideration. But in this as in other matters we are not going to act in a huff or in a spirit of anger merely because we dislike something that had happened. I feel, as I said here, that in spite of these occurrences that have happened and that have distressed us, it is right for us to continue our association with the Commonwealth for a variety of reasons which I mentioned then, among them being primarily the fact that our policies, as is obvious, are in no way conditioned or deflected from their normal course by that association. So, nobody can say that there has been this conflict in our policies, that these policies have been affected—affected every policy might be by consultation; that is a different matter. We consult other countries. We have close relations with other countries. But the decision is ours, and is not affected by the fact of our being in the Commonwealth.

Secondly, at this moment, when there are so many disruptive tendencies in the world, it is better to retain every kind of association, which is not positively harmful to us, than to break it. Breaking it itself is a disruptive thing. It does not add to that spirit of peaceful settlements and peaceful association that we wish to develop in the world.

Therefore, after giving all this thought, I felt—and I felt clearly—in my mind, that it would not be good to break up this association in spite of the painful shocks that all of us had experienced in these past few months.

But, again, no decision that we can take in these or other matters for today can be said to be a permanent decision for ever. All kinds of things happen and one has to review these matters from time to time in view of changing conditions. And I would remind the House that the Commonwealth itself is undergoing a change. Ghana is a member of the Commonwealth. Possibly Malaya will be a member of the Commonwealth. Possibly a little later Nigeria might be. Its inner composition and content is changing, and changing, if I may say so, in the right direction. Therefore, keeping all these things in view and well realizing the strong reactions that have been produced in the country in regard to this matter, I would still respectfully submit to the House that it is desirable, in the present context, to continue this association with the Commonwealth.

That is all I have to say on these subjects now. At the end of this debate, I hope that my colleague, Shri Krishna Menon, might be able to deal with the points raised in this debate and with questions that might be asked. He has been, as the House knows, very intimately connected not only in the Security Council with the various international questions that have arisen there, but also in our discussions with the Egyptian Government.

4. On International Situation—II[1]

Jawaharlal Nehru: Mr Chairman, I beg to move:

> "That the present international situation and the policy of the Government of India in relation thereto be taken into consideration."

Only a few days ago this House considered or rather debated on the President's Address and the debate consisted largely of questions relating to international affairs. There have been other debates too in the other House and it is rather difficult to cover new ground within such a short space of time. Nevertheless, I am glad that this House, which takes so much of interest in international affairs, should have frequent opportunities of considering this question. I think, it is important not only that Parliament but our country also should take this interest in international affairs, not at the expense, of course, of our domestic problems, which are and must always remain our primary consideration, but even the domestic problems are affected so much by international events that it helps to have this larger perspective. I shall endeavour not to say too much at this stage because I think, it is due to Members of the House that they should have as much time as possible to express their own opinions and other suggestions and advice for Government's consideration.

One problem which often comes up before honourable Members—and it is no doubt in their minds—is that of Kashmir. Much has been said about that in the course of the last few days, and honourable Members know that Dr Jarring has been here for some days at the instance of the Security Council of which he was President last month. And we have had talks with him, frank and friendly talks, in which we have endeavoured to place before him the views of the Government of India in regard to this matter. Those views are not secret, they are well known. More I do not wish to say about Kashmir itself.

In considering foreign affairs, naturally we consider specific problems, specially those problems that affect us or that might affect us, and yet the situation all over the world becomes more and more an involved one, each problem leading to the other—it is very difficult to separate them. In the old days people talked about roaming about from China to Peru, presumably considering China and

---

1. Speech in the Rajya Sabha, 27 March 1957, *Rajya Sabha Debates*, Vol. XVI, cols. 723-741.

Peru as two remote outposts of the world. Well, neither of them is very remote either politically or even, if I may say so, geographically. In some sense Peru might be, but even geography has altered its outlook so much because of the development of communications. China, of course, is our neighbour, and China is something more than a mere neighbour. It has grown into a great country with great influence and increasing capacity to influence affairs. Peru may be on the other side of the world, but even Peru today, as every other country, is a kind of neighbour. Every country is a neighbour of the other today, we cannot ignore that. It happens in South America or anywhere, but I mention China just now. The House knows that the question of China has exercised us, that is to say, the position of China in regard to the United Nations more especially. It has exercised us a great deal because we have felt that in this after-War world in which we are living, one of the major things that has happened is the changes in China, where a great united powerful country has arisen. They follow a policy which is not our policy; we follow our policy. But it would be as wrong for us to interfere with their policy as it would be wrong for them to interfere with our policy and the way we function here. That is the only way in which I feel that nations can function without coming into conflict and unnecessary conflict. Therefore, we have developed friendly relations with China and we cooperate in some ways and I hope we will cooperate in more ways, each following its own way. But the fact that there has been this difficulty about China's representatives finding a place in the United Nations has undoubtedly added greatly to the tensions in East Asia and to some extent in the world, because obviously China is a country which counts in the world, whether we like it or dislike it. We have often said this before in this House and elsewhere, but unfortunately for various reasons this question is postponed, put off in the United Nations year after year, and I do not think that this postponement helps in easing the situation at all. We continue to think that it is of the highest importance that China, that is, the real and legitimate representatives of China should find their place in the United Nations. In a sense it is there and if you look at the United Nations list you will find that China is represented. Of course China is; it is not a question of China being taken into the United Nations; it is there. Only somebody else is called China, which seems rather peculiar. So, here on this occasion again I should like to lay stress on this point, on the importance of it, not only from China's point of view, not only from our point of view but from the world's point of view, that facts should be faced. One cannot solve problems if one started on an artificial basis or if one closed one's eyes to the real objective facts of the situation. No one, I take it, anywhere, in any country can imagine that China, as it is today, will fade away or the People's Government of China will cease to function there. If that is so, it is inevitable that that has to be recognized, if not today, then tomorrow, or the day after; it seems to follow naturally. If it has to be recognized in that sense by other countries, as we do, and if everybody knows this had to be done, then what purpose is served in delaying it and thereby helping to add to the tension or continue the existing tension? I submit, Sir, that this is important. The issue is not being argued hotly today as sometimes, but it comes up from time to time and it is a basic issue in regard not only to South East Asia but the world and the United Nations. Whatever step the United Nations may take, if it ignores a vast country like China with a tremendous population, that step cannot be very effective—let us say, a step relating to disarmament. Suppose the United Nations comes to some agreement, as we hope it will, and suppose the Great Powers come to some agreement about disarmament and China is left out. Well, it will be a dangerous kind of disarmament in which one of the biggest powers with the largest population in the world is left out, where possibly it may be free to arm itself as much as it likes while other countries seek to disarm. In fact that very thing would prevent others from disarming. So, we go round and round.

Take another question which has nothing to do with normal political matters— atomic energy. There is the Atomic Energy Commission, which I am glad to say has resulted in the formation of the Atomic Energy Agency on which our representatives have played some part. Now again this Atomic Energy Agency wants to know facts, scientific data about the world, about uranium and other atomic minerals all over the world, about power resources and a hundred and one things, and China just does not know what is happening there. So, every day we face these difficulties arising from this incongruous position. I hope, therefore, that other countries will consider this matter from the strictly practical point of view. I am not making any appeal from any sentimental point of view, there is no question of sentiment about this. Sentiment may sometimes be good, but it does not help in considering political problems. Unfortunately, it is sentiment that comes into the picture, which prevents reality being looked at. Now, we may consider our problems here and there in the world, but it does help a little perhaps to try to think of the broad world picture, this dynamic revolutionary picture, which has arisen out of the last World War. All kinds of big changes have happened including our own Independence. We tend to think of countries or groups of countries, a great country like the United States of America, another very great power, the Soviet Union, and other great countries, the United Kingdom, France, China, Japan and so on, and we tend to think of each country as some solid body which is this way or that way. Of course that is not a fact with regard to any country. Every country has different types of opinion coursing through it, some clashing with each other, and we normally consider the opinion of a country, the one which is represented by the Government of the day. Naturally that is so but it is rather misleading to think of these countries as solid individuals having this view or that view and that is apt to mislead us whatever country it may be, the biggest or the smallest, the most authoritarian or the most democratic. We see in all these countries progressive forces at work, reactionary forces at work and, well, just negative inertia at work and it is as well to recognize this because this prevents us from falling a victim to disliking a country as a whole or in the alternative to liking a country and swallowing everything that country has to offer. Both are not very correct attitudes because every country has these various forces at work, fine human beings, idealistic human beings working for noble objectives, others tied up with vested interests, others again, maybe, having some peculiar approach of their own. Here is this jigsaw puzzle of humanity spread out all over the world represented by Governments here and there, but nevertheless gradually changing the pattern of things. Therefore, one should avoid thinking of a country as bad because one dislikes its present policy, or as wholly good in the sense of thinking that everything they do is right. That may not be very helpful to us because that would be a kind of approach for which—whether Members of this House and I are fitted for it or not, I do not know—but for which our Chairman is peculiarly fitted, being a philosopher and a thinker who is not swept away by momentary gusts of sentiment. Nevertheless, one should try to do that and not be led away in this way in this rapidly changing world. Now, in this changing world again where do we come in? Yesterday, if I may be permitted to say so, you, Sir, Mr Chairman, made a reference in another place to what happened 17 or 18 years ago when Poland was invaded by the Nazi forces. And the matter, I think, was that Gandhiji was asked about it, what his opinion was and what India should do about it, and you reminded us of what he said. I do not exactly remember the words but, I think, more or less he said that a fallen and subject nation cannot serve humanity. India or any other country can only serve humanity or any cause if it is free enough to serve it. Now of course, when that is said it sounds an obvious statement, though many people do not see the obvious in these things. Well, we became free and independent and in a sense our capacity to serve ourselves and others increased. Naturally, it is limited; there are many conditioning factors to it. We are involved in innumerable economic and other problems. We tend to get involved in international issues however much we may keep away and we tend to get involved in these international issues partly because of the circumstances of the case and partly because of our own inheritance of thought and of how we had considered these problems in a different context in the past, and so we get involved. Apart from that, no country can escape involvement when we have international organizations like the United Nations or its many subsidiary bodies. In the old days a country's involvement usually was through its neighbours or through a country with which it might have an alliance. Today, first of all, we are all neighbours, as I said, and secondly in these international organizations we have to deal with every country in the world. This was involvement enough for us and so we decided, also in keeping with our own thinking, not to get further involved or in any way involved with military alliances and pacts. Every military alliance or pact is not only an involvement but it is a promise to do something under certain circumstances, and thereby a certain commitment and thereby a certain limitation of your freedom of choice when an occasion to decide that question arises because you have become committed to it. However, for a variety of reasons we adopted this policy of non-involvement, of not entering into any pacts, military or the like. We have friendly pacts and treaties about trade and other matters for our mutual advantage but none has anything to do with the military aspects, with defence or offence. To some extent, of course, we are involved in the United Nations, in the broad policy laid down by the Charter of the UN. This policy of ours is called sometimes a neutral policy. I have often said that it is not neutral. Of course, it is an independent policy of non-involvement and it means that we decide issues in so far as we can on the merits as they appear to us. But apart from that it also means that in this world of ours today when there is so much tension and fear of war and nuclear and thermo-nuclear weapons round the corner all the time, what basic policy should a country may pursue, inevitably it must be a policy to its interest. Well, no country pursues a policy against its own interest, against its own national interest, and national interests can be viewed in a longer perspective or a shorter one. One may think of some immediate gain that the country may get and yet that immediate gain may result in some ultimate harm. Or one may think more of building up a country so that it may go step by step in the right direction, even though the process may be slow and even though there might be some injury or harm for the time being, apparent injury—it is not real injury. Now, in the present context of the world when we are so much intimately allied with other countries, any policy, first of all that obviously leads to war, and secondly which leads to an atmosphere which might create war and, if I may add to it, any policy which leads to continuing hatred, tension and fear between nations is a policy, well, always in the short run which is bad; but certainly it is bad in the long run obviously. Now, this is a statement with which I imagine everybody will agree, not every body here only but in any country, and yet the fact is that policies are pursued apparently in the national interest which tend to push the world in a direction where disaster may overwhelm it. There is something wrong about the logic or the reason. It is thought, I suppose, that by the addition to a country's military might, it might control other countries which might, misbehave, and so this process of adding to armaments and all these nuclear explosions, experimental tests and others go on. Yet it is very well known that we have arrived at a stage, more specially in regard to some of the major countries, the very few which are in possession of these nuclear and thermonuclear weapons, a stage when no country can even wipe out the other without suffering grievous injury itself and the world suffering it. So that leads us nowhere, and almost everyone is satisfied that we should not go in for doing anything which would lead to a major war. If that is so, why then is everything done which creates an atmosphere for it, which it does today? All these questions arise.

Some people say, it has been said elsewhere the other day, that we, that is the Government of India, should not adopt a sanctimonious attitude. Well, I do not know what a sanctimonious attitude in regard to foreign affairs is. I dislike a sanctimonious attitude in regard to everything, foreign, domestic or personal. It is an irritating attitude. There is no question of the Government of India doing that. We are further reminded that we must remember the type of world we live in, that it is not a world of Gandhiji's creation or a world which Gandhiji would have liked. That is perfectly true. In fact, few of us like this type of world, and therefore, one cannot follow in this world as it is the policy which one might follow in a better world, which is perfectly true. Nevertheless, I hope and try to follow a policy which might lead to a better world. We are not pacifists in the Government of India. We may talk about peace and non-violence. We maintain an army, a navy, an air force, etc., police force, because no responsible Government, so far as I can see, can do otherwise, but nevertheless we dislike these trends to war. We think that they are dangerous. We think that these experimental explosions, nuclear and thermonuclear, are not only bad in the sense that they take us in the wrong direction but they actually, according to scientists, do tremendous injury—tremendous, I am sorry for the use of the word—anyhow they would do injury to the whole of mankind today, gradually. But if that is considered moralizing, well, I do not know what to say. It is the hard fact that we have to consider. I think that many of our friends in other countries, and maybe in this country, who consider that they are following a practical policy, are as far from following anything practical as anybody can be. It is not a practical policy if you are going on a journey just looking at the tip of your nose. You have to look further ahead, otherwise you would stumble and fall. But there is another aspect to this question of what India can do and should not do. Many honourable Members often tell us that the Government of India must do this or that, whatever it may be, whether in the world, whether in regard to Kashmir, whether in regard to Goa, things which on the face of it may be desirable or not. But we can only say things and do things which we are capable of doing. It is no good striking up brave attitudes which may elicit applause from our people or elsewhere, and then we are unable to follow them or, if we try to follow them, we get involved in putting greater difficulties.

Take this question of Goa which those people imagine should be very easy of solution because Goa is a very small area, tiny area in India, because even the so-called metropolitan power behind Goa, that is Portugal, well, by any manner of reckoning, is not a strong power. That is so. Nevertheless, this question becomes involved in all kinds of international issues. It gets involved there and therefore to do something wrong there involves us in many other things and creates difficulties for us. Quite apart from the major issue that if we adopt a policy in regard to Goa which is in opposition to our broad approach which I would call a non-military approach, well that broad approach, of course, ends. Then, of course, we are neither here nor there in regard to our major policies. I am not for the moment defending what we have done or not done in Goa—that is a separate issue. But I should like honourable Members to realize that the question is not a question of that little tract of territory, important as it is, but it involves all kinds of international issues and our broad policies.

The other day I said in the other House that we feel that this whole policy of Goa, not the broad policy but rather the narrower interpretation of this broad policy should be given careful consideration, and I further said that in this matter we should like to consult with Members of Parliament not only of one particular party but all parties. I do not wish people to go away with the idea that we have evolved some big weapon to be wielded by us in the near future. That would be a wrong notion. All I said was that this matter is a national issue of course, and it is an irritating issue, and it is a human issue. A Member of the other House who spent two or three years in Goa prisons gave a horrifying account of the Goa prisons—he has just been released a little while ago—and that applied to the Indian nationals who were prisoners there, because the condition of the Goans themselves who have been there—hundreds of them are there in prison and thousands have passed through prison—is much worse. All this human aspect and national aspect is important for us, and yet the major policies that we have pursued are also important, and we do not think that by giving up that major approach we will be doing the right thing by India or Goa. Nevertheless, as I said, this is a matter requiring careful consideration and, as far as possible, consultation with others so that we may have advantage of other people's advice and opinion. We propose to proceed on those lines. What exactly we shall do and how far it would produce any kind of results, I cannot say at this stage. To quote, Sir, you referred yesterday to what Gandhiji said in connection with the invasion of Poland—a fallen and subject nation cannot serve humanity. That idea may be extended somewhat. A country which has tied itself up to powerful nations even though it may get help from them, has not only reduced its capacity for independent action and any service that it may render, but is also strictly limited in scope. To that extent, it becomes a projection of some other country's policy. It may vary in small matters slightly, but in the major things in the world it is merely a projection of some other country's policy, and that is not, I think, a kind of thing which I should like India ever to do—to project some other country's policy. We have seen this happening in Europe and in Asia. I do not wish to criticize any countries, but many a country which is called independent, so far as its foreign policy is concerned, hardly follows or can follow a policy of its own choice. I admit that no country can follow a policy of its own choice completely. It is conditioned by events, it is conditioned by its own strength or weakness. That is true. But nevertheless, to give up the right to follow one's policy by being tied up in this way, and just to spell a shadow of somebody else's policy, is not my idea of independence or of developing the capacity to serve ourselves or humanity. That is why we have regretted this development of military pacts in the world. They may have been necessary somewhere. I am not here to judge as to what fears and apprehensions of the countries might lead them to, because after the last War there was a great deal of fear and apprehension, and that fear and apprehension continues in Europe. The whole of the question of German unity is hung up because of that.

I suppose only a few persons can oppose the idea of German unity. And yet, while everybody in theory agrees with it, the consequences of it make people afraid, and make people on every side afraid, whether it is the so-called West or the so-called East, because Germany is not a country which can be trifled with. It is a very great country, great in its capacity in war and peace both. And so, many people are afraid that if in a new context German unity is achieved, as I hope it will be, in the context in which it is achieved, many results may follow which may not be desirable to this side or that. Now, the future of the German people, therefore, is governed, not so much by what the German people want, but by the fears of others. The whole of Eastern Europe including the Soviet Union remembers very vividly those repeated invasions by Germany. The whole of Eastern Europe and Southern Russia were reduced almost to ruin by those invasions, twice at least in our lifetime. The whole of Western Europe is afraid that the great strength of the Soviet Union might be exercised against it, and so they go in for military alliances, and each tries to protect itself against the other, with the result that a greater insecurity takes place, and there is a greater race in building up nuclear and other types of armaments, which, of course, leads again to greater fear; and so, you get into this vicious circle. The way of military pacts, one against the other, surely is not the way out. It might have been a way out if one side was so powerful that the other would collapse. Not that we want any side to collapse, but when, both sides are strong enough to do injury to each other—whatever happens—and a vital injury, then some other way has to be found and facts have to be accepted. And the only other way can be that of peaceful coexistence and the prevention of any aggression. Well, we tried to put these four or five principles in the *Panchsheel* which still seem to us to be a good code of international behaviour. But then unfortunately, however good the words that are used or the phrases that are used may be, gradually they become hackneyed and are used for wrong purposes. A good word and a good phrase is used for something entirely different. Peace is bandied about in accents, in tones and in looks of war, which changes its very nature. Security, which is a good thing—countries should have security—becomes a reason for armed alliances which threaten somebody else's security, and so we debase our fine words and phrases. Then we have to search some new words which might not have been so debased.

There is this Middle Eastern situation which is perhaps a little better than it was, and we hope that in the near future the Suez Canal will be functioning again. I cannot be definite about the precise date or the precise conditions in which it will function. But we are all interested—India is even more interested than many Western countries—in the proper functioning of the Suez Canal and in free navigation through that canal. We have tried, in our own small and humble way, to help by sorting out these difficulties, and all I can say is that I hope that those difficulties will be overcome in the near future. But the whole situation in this Middle Eastern region has been governed by two major factors. One, of course, is oil. Oil is a very necessary thing in this world, and a very wicked thing. It has created a great deal of trouble. Now, there is no reason why peaceful settlements about the supply of oil should not be made, and why a country is required to dominate over another country in order to have oil. In fact, in the final analysis, it will not get the oil if it has a hostile population there. We have tried all the time, but this rather novel argument, not novel perhaps, but anyhow, it has been given a novel turn of vacuums which have to be filled, appears to be really a repetition of the old approach to these questions of spheres of influence— that the world being divided up into the spheres of influence of some countries. Long ago, many hundreds of years ago, the then Pope issued a Bull dividing up the world between Spain and Portugal; some kind of line or parallel was set; "You have this part of the world and the others will have the rest." Of course, that ignored certain factors, and it was not given effect to, although even a few years ago, I should say some five, six or seven years ago, the Portuguese Government reminded us of that as part of the origin of their authority in Goa. This sphere of influence is obviously an extension or part of the colonial idea, whether it is a colony of the old type or the new type. Sphere of influence necessarily means a kind of domination, indirect if you like. Sometimes indirect domination is as bad as direct domination over a country. So, we are opposed to that vacuum idea or these power alignments.

I am not venturing to say much about specific problems, because much has been said already, but only one thing I should like to say about our neighbour, Pakistan. We talk about Kashmir, talk about other issues too, and the world talks about some of them too without knowing what the facts are, but the real difficulty—difficulties are there of course, I am not going into them—but the basic difficulty about our relations with Pakistan is the attitude of Pakistan. They have not yet apparently got over that basic attitude which some of them, the people and leaders, had even before the Partition. How can there be any settlement of any problem at the point of the sword or threats which are all the time being hurled at us? It is a simple fact. If people want to settle any problem, they should be in the mood for settlement, they should use the language of settlement and peace. They should approach us as friends and not with threats. Any country, even a small country, would react strongly against such an approach, and India is neither a small nor an ignoble country to submit to threats and bullying. It may have been thought that recent developments in which very strong language has been used, in Pakistan of course—and it continues to be used—but even in some Western countries, would tend, well, to frighten us. They forget that normally speaking it has the opposite effect, and it has had that opposite effect. It surprised us that people should think of India in this way, that they could use such language to us and hold out such indirect threats as to what might happen. That is not the way to settle problems. I do not pretend that we are always in the right; I do not pretend that there are no people in this country who tend to use wrong language or make the wrong approaches, but I do submit that, so far as the Government of India is concerned, ever since Independence and Partition, it has been our definite aim and policy to have friendly relations with Pakistan, not of course giving up our vital interests, because giving up vital interests does not promote friendly relations; it only encourages the other party to open its mouth wider, claim more and shout more. It has been our policy to have friendly relations with Pakistan—we have, of course, accepted Pakistan and accepted Partition—and to proceed on the basis of two independent nations having friendly relations, cooperative relations, with each other. We are neighbours; we have a history in common; we have a hundred and one things in common; we have thousands of persons whose families are split up, and it will be a tragedy for us to aim at anything but friendly relations. We have done that in spite of some misguided persons in this country who come in the way of such a friendly policy. Why have we done that? Surely I need not say why, because any person who at all thinks about the future must come to this conclusion that there is no other valid policy. That policy, friendly policy, does not naturally mean our giving up our vital interests or our submitting to something that we consider wrong. Subject to these two conditions, we have pursued a friendly policy, because it can only harm us and harm Pakistan, if we continue this conflict, psychological conflict, and take it into the future. It is totally immaterial whether we are stronger than Pakistan or not. That can be considered in another context. The very weakness of Pakistan is injurious to us. I do not want Pakistan to be militarily armed so much that it becomes very strong and threatens us. That is why we have not taken kindly to the vast military equipment and help that is coming to Pakistan from the United States of America; but I am not talking about that. But we want Pakistan to be a healthy, flourishing and progressive country. Even for our own safety, even for our own good, you must have this. The more you succeed with your Five Year Plans and the less Pakistan succeeds with her Five Year Plans—it is a danger to our own Plans, to our own progress. You cannot keep these walls between countries, so that apart from the historical, cultural and other reasons, practical reasons lead us to seek good relations with Pakistan as with other countries, and in fact more so with Pakistan. But unfortunately during these past years, we have had a continuous current of ill will in Pakistan, sometimes at a somewhat lower level and sometimes breaking out into extraordinary threats of war and denunciation of India, based on excessive hatred. It is a most painful thing to have to face all this, and yet to maintain one's calm and composure which one must, because the moment we do not, we are doing exactly what others want us to do, those who do not wish good to India. We cannot give way, whatever the strain and stress might be. We have pursued that proper policy, always protecting our interests and, I hope, maintaining decent standards of behaviour. We have done so in the hope that the people of Pakistan whom I can never forget—they have been our people in the past, have taken part in our freedom movements, they certainly helped us in gaining the freedom of our country although they separated from us—will react to this, in the hope that ultimately our goodwill will create a good, friendly atmosphere in Pakistan among the people and among others. I believe it has basically, but unfortunately it is covered up and swept away by the appeals, by the spread first of all, if I may use the word, of falsehood and appeals to narrow-minded bigotry and hatred. It is fear on which our neighbours have been fed. It does not produce health in nations, apart from their relationship with India. So, whatever happens, I hope that we shall continue that broad policy. Again I repeat that this should not be understood to mean—and we have made that perfectly clear—that we follow that policy through weakness or that it is a prelude to any kind of surrender on any vital issue. It is not that. We have made that perfectly clear. Maybe, it is a bit difficult to distinguish between the two, but we have to do it. On no account are we going to surrender because surrendering to what we consider wrong is bad because surrender again creates a position of future demands for surrender and so it goes on step by step. Where are we? All these questions between Pakistan and us are really parts of this major approach to each other, however big these questions may be. I am quite certain that if any one of these questions were solved or apparently solved without that major background changing, it will not improve the situation at all. That may be just used as a jumping-off ground to something else.

Sir, I have ventured to say these few words about our relations with Pakistan because I do not wish people to look at one problem, even the Kashmir problem, in its isolation and imagine that there is nothing else. It is the other things that count. It is amazing that in this context here we see, the Security Council dealing with the Kashmir issue. Even in the Security Council and a great deal outside, continuous threats are being used: 'If this does not happen, armies will march into India and then it is war' without any thought of what kind of reaction this kind of talk would produce in India, because normally it produces an angry reaction in people. The national reaction is there. It so happens that in our country, to a large extent, we have been conditioned in trying to restrain these reactions, conditioned for a long period under Gandhiji. We try to restrain them but the reactions are there. We restrain them no doubt and do not allow ourselves to be swept away.

So, I would like this House and this country to consider these in this broader aspect—these problems and others too outside this House, in our country and in Pakistan also, because it is a tragedy that when so much has got to be done in our country by us and so much in Pakistan by the people of Pakistan, that our energies should be wasted in this kind of continuous ill will and conflict and this propaganda of hatred from Pakistan.

II. PAKISTAN

1. Visit of British MPs[1]

This letter from our High Commissioner in Karachi does not fill me with enthusiasm.[2] The note of the Deputy High Commissioner (T. Sanghani) is even less to my liking.[3]

Both the letter and the note exhibit a certain lack of nerve as well as lack of judgement.[4] We have decided to treat these two MPs with courtesy and I have promised to meet them.[5] You will no doubt also meet them. There is no reason

1. Note to Secretary General, New Delhi, 6 March 1957. JN Collection.
2. C.C. Desai wrote to N.R. Pillai, the Secretary General, on 3 March 1957 about his discussions with Reginald Bennett and Frank Tomney, the British MPs of the Pakistan lobby in the House of Commons, on the Kashmir issue, and Indo-British and Indo-Pakistan relations.
3. In a note to C.C. Desai on 4 March 1957, T. Sanghani wrote that the two MPs were spending 10 days in Pakistan and 3 days in India. Sanghani suggested that "we should press" them to spend more time in India to meet all sections of public opinion. In his view, their meetings should be arranged with a few Cabinet members like Abul Kalam Azad, Syed Mahmud, and members of opposition like N.C. Chatterjee, A.K. Gopalan, Jayaprakash Narayan; and also with eminent Muslims and Christians such as Nawab of Chhatari, Mirza Ismail, Jerome D'Souza, Cardinal Gracias and Amrit Kaur. Sanghani also suggested that the two MPs should be taken round some of the cottage industries in Kashmir and shown the convent desecrated by raiders.
4. During their meeting with Desai, the British MPs hypothesized that in the event of failure of the Jarring Mission and expected Soviet veto of yet another Security Council resolution, the Kashmir case would go to the General Assembly where two-thirds majority would be forthcoming in favour of a plebiscite. What would be India's attitude then, they asked. Desai told them that if the UN had the authority to land troops in India, they could hold the plebiscite and carry out the resolution. They also discussed the possible consequences of a plebiscite—law and order situation in both countries, communal propaganda and canvassing, unsettling of minds of minorities, migrations etc. The British MPs also mentioned a possible reference to the International Court of Justice on the question of accession and desirability of a third party mediation to avoid any armed conflict. Desai wrote that the Conservative Member, Bennett could not divorce Kashmir from Suez; and the Labour Member, Tomney was prejudiced against India largely because of "our attitude in the Hungarian case".
5. Bennett and Tomney arrived in Delhi on 10 March and visited Srinagar on 13 March.

why we should fawn at them or be excessibly worked up about their visit here. Nor is there any reason why we should arrange for them to meet all our senior Ministers, Leaders of the Opposition etc. We should take them in our stride, dealing with them courteously but without showing too much eagerness to please them.

I agree with the High Commissioner that an attitude of superiority or virtue is not a good one at any time. But I regret, I cannot approach them "with humility, cordiality and mutual understanding". I am not humble so far as they are concerned, nor do I propose to go out of my way to be cordial to people for whom I have no feeling of cordiality. As for mutual understanding, this is to be mutual and not one-sided.

The explanation that our High Commissioner has given about Junagadh exhibits a lack of knowledge of the facts. The case of Junagadh is completely different from that of Kashmir. They are not parallel.[6]

6. While discussing the validity of accession of Kashmir, the two MPs raised the Junagadh case. Desai explained to them the circumstances in which India went there but agreed that there had never been any consent of the Government of Pakistan to India's position in Junagadh and they might have a case against India. Desai also told them, "if Pakistan wanted to rest its case on the Instrument of Accession in Junagadh, she would have to vacate occupied Kashmir and only then she could ask us to respect the Junagadh accession and get out of Junagadh."

493

2. To Sampurnanand[1]

New Delhi
20 March 1957

My dear Sampurnanand,

Thank you for your letter of March 19th.[2]

I had not previously seen the letter dated 31st January, a copy of which you have sent me.[3] That letter was addressed to the West Bengal Government which was most concerned with the question of Pakistani nationals. That letter was no doubt sent to prevent any precipitate action which might have led to greater difficulties even from the point of view of security and sabotage.

This is a difficult question. Unless we proceed cautiously, we actually aggravate the danger. If we make it known that we distrust large numbers of people, they are likely to behave even worse than otherwise they might do. At the same time we have to be careful.

You can certainly take quiet action in the way you think it necessary.

We would, of course, gladly take you into our confidence whenever any such

---

1. Sampurnanand Collection, NAI.
2. Sampurnanand, the Chief Minister of Uttar Pradesh, reported the presence of a large number of Pakistani citizens in India, some of whom were urging Muslims to adopt a course of action which was likely to weaken the future Congress Governments. Regarding sabotage he wrote that on enquiry it was found that important key positions such as in power houses and waterworks were occupied by Pakistani citizens who could throw lives of whole cities out of gear temporarily and create panic, if they so wished. There were Pakistani nationals in Central Ordnance Depot, Posts and Telegraph Department, and in key positions in some private concerns. He wrote that a large number of posters which emanated from Pakistan were recently found in different cities, and asked Muslims to act in a certain manner. He observed that in spite of legislation enabling the postal authorities to prevent the dissemination of such matter, they came through postal agency and feared about the tapping of telephonic communication.
3. The letter, written by R.S. Chavan, an Under Secretary in the MEA, to the Home Department of Government of West Bengal, conveyed that optees for India who adopted Pakistani citizenship subsequently, should not be considered ineligible for continuance in service merely on this ground. However, in case of adverse and objectionable reports about their activities, their services should be terminated after proper enquiry. The State Governments should promptly refer these cases to MHA for further enquiry before such action.

matter arises. The Home Ministry, I thought, kept in touch with you in such matters.

I hope you are keeping well in spite of the burden of the elections.

Yours sincerely,
Jawaharlal Nehru

3. False Propaganda against India[1]

I entirely agree that this false propaganda should be contradicted by an official spokesman.[2] It should be stated quite clearly that the allegations made in the APP message to various Pakistan newspapers regarding arrangements for the supply of atomic weapons to India from the Soviet Union, are entirely false, without foundation and appear to be deliberately mischievous. No such arrangements have been made, nor indeed was anything of this kind discussed at any time with any Soviet or other representatives. India has not received any kind of arms from the Soviet Union and there was no talk even with Marshal Zhukov or any other person from the Soviet Union about the supply of arms, much less of atomic weapons. It is not the intention of the Government of India to acquire any atomic weapons from abroad. They are only interested in the development of atomic energy in their own country for peaceful purposes.

2. I think the APP man should be sent for and asked why he sent such false and mischievous messages.

3. Our principal missions should also be informed.

---

1. Note to M.J. Desai, Commonwealth Secretary, New Delhi, 30 March 1957. File No. 5/18-XP(P)/57, p 2/note, MEA.
2. Between 6 and 15 March 1957, various stories appeared against India in *Jang, Dawn* and *Pakistan Times*, some of them filed by APP. It was emphasized that Soviet Union had strategic interests in Kashmir; that Indian neutrality was far from genuine; that India had offered use of air bases in Gilgit, Ladakh etc., to China; that a military commission of Russia, Czechoslovakia and China had reached Kashmir; that India's plans for a war against Kashmir were being rapidly prepared; and that Russia had entered a secret pact with India for supplying atomic weapons to India during Soviet Defence Minister G.K. Zhukov's recent visit to Delhi.

4. Personnel for Indian High Commission in Karachi[1]

I think that the state of affairs prevailing at our High Commission in Karachi is scandalous and disgraceful. Even a person of moderate intelligence should know that care has to be taken about domestic servants and all employees in foreign missions. In Pakistan this care is doubly necessary. And yet we find that all kinds of people from domestic servants upwards and including persons who deal with secret papers have been totally unreliable and have passed on our papers to others.

I really am amazed at this astonishing inefficiency and carelessness. It seems to me that we get tied up in some routines and details and forget major issues. That an Intelligence man is supposed to be kept at Karachi. If this happens in his presence there, one can only say that our Intelligence men have not been gifted with the least degree of intelligence. Any normal wide-awake person would probably have done better. Apparently, in this respect, there are no wide-awake persons in our High Commission there. In their efforts to get some odd bit of information and gossip from talks with various people, they forget that they are being undermined constantly.

The first thing we should concentrate upon is security in our offices. This is far more important than getting information about the other side. We get this so-called information about the other side in long rigmarole reports which seldom give any important news. I am really very disturbed.

Our Intelligence man who is in Karachi, should be withdrawn. Whether another person is sent in his place or not, is another matter and can be considered later. But on no account should incompetent men be allowed to remain there.

I can conceive of an occasional leakage, though even that should not occur. But the systematic way in which we have been fooled in Karachi for long periods does credit to nobody there from our High Commissioner downwards.

I think, in future every single person who is sent to Karachi or to Lahore or to Dacca should be vetted very carefully, whatever his grade might be. He should be told that it is his business to be wide-awake and not to rely on anybody else.

No Pakistani servants or others should be employed in any of our offices there. This matter should be remedied immediately. I think that our officers should learn never to give any paper to a servants. They should carry it themselves and not trust a servant even though he might be India-based. This habit of sitting

1. Note to Commonwealth Secretary, New Delhi, 2 April 1947. JN Collection.

in armchairs and using servants is out-of-date in civilized countries and there is
no reason why we should continue it.

As for servants used for domestic purposes, they should be as few as possible
and should of course, be from India. We must reduce the number of servants
everywhere.

5. Impact of US Aid to Pakistan[1]

Shri Krishna Menon suggested to me on the telephone this evening that you
might send for the United States Ambassador[2] tomorrow. He himself wanted to
meet him, but this could not be arranged as the Ambassador was not in Delhi at
the time.

2. You should talk to the Ambassador about the situation in regard to the Suez
Canal on the lines of Shri Krishna Menon's talk here. It should be pointed out
that we have done our utmost to bring about a reasonable situation which should
be satisfactory to all parties concerned. We have pleaded with the Egyptian
Government for a moderate approach, and the Egyptian Government has agreed
with many of our suggestions. We feel that the memorandum presented on behalf
of the Egyptian Government offers this reasonable solution. If this is not accepted,
then the deadlock will continue, which will not be to the advantage of any party.

3. It is true that the question of Israeli ships going through the Suez Canal has
not been settled. In existing circumstances, there is no chance of any of the
Arab Governments agreeing specifically to allow Israeli ships to pass through.
But, we feel sure that the solution will come, though it might be delayed
somewhat. Egypt has agreed to abide fully by the 1888 Convention. The question
is about the interpretation of that Convention. If an interpretation is given by the
International Court of Justice in favour of Israeli ships passing through, and this
is very likely, then Egypt will abide by that interpretation. But it is not likely
that any Government in Egypt or any other Arab country will take the
responsibility on its own initiative, of allowing Israeli ships to pass through the
Canal. Not only is public opinion in the Arab countries very strongly against
this, but difficulties might arise in providing adequate security for those ships.

1. Note to Foreign Secretary, New Delhi, 4 April 1957. JN Collection.
2. Ellsworth Bunker.

4. We hope, therefore, that the Egyptian proposals will be accepted by the United States Government, with such minor modifications as may be agreed to.

5. When the American Ambassador sees you, you might also mention another point. I am attaching a press cutting, giving a PTI message from New York about an article by Sulzberger in *The New York Times*. The attention of the Ambassador might be drawn to this, and he should be told that what Sulzberger has written, is not only true but it describes the situation created by the ever-flowing American military aid to Pakistan in moderate language. We are greatly concerned about this matter. Some people say that India need not worry because India is much stronger. (The American Ambassador said the other day privately to a friend that India was two and a half to three times stronger). This is wholly incorrect. We have reliable information about most of the American supplies to Pakistan. Even last year, when Mr Dulles came to Delhi, I told him of the information we possessed at the time. He accepted the correctness of that information. Since then, we have had further information which indicates that American supplies have come to Pakistan in ever-increasing measure. The Pakistan Air Force now is stronger than the Indian Air Force. In quality, the American aircraft supplies to them are superior than any of the British or French aircraft that we possess or are likely to possess.

6. Some four or five years ago, we have decided to reduce our armed forces progressively. We had, in fact, done so year after year. Ever since the question of American aid came in, we had to establish reduction. Later, we had to consider whether we should not revert to the old size. These were painful decisions for us.

7. So far as our Air Force as well as the Army are concerned, we have been compelled by the circumstances produced by American military aid and much against our will, to order British and French aircraft. Even so, we preferred getting these from the UK or France at a much higher price than we might have paid if we had got them from the Soviet Union. This has hit us very hard and upset all the calculations we made for our Second Five Year Plan. We have stopped some of our schemes and have indefinitely delayed some others.

8. All this indicates the danger to us of this continuing flow of American military aid to Pakistan and the serious affect which this has on our economy and our development schemes.

9. For us to be told that American equipment cannot be used against India, only means that the United States does not want it to be so used. We accept that. But, we do not believe that any such restriction will come in the way of Pakistan using that equipment when it so chooses. Anyone at all acquainted with the Pakistan press and with the statements made by important persons in Pakistan as well as the general condition in that country, will realize how the cry of jehad

or holy war is constantly being raised, and that this is not an empty threat. No responsible government in India can ignore this threat, because defence must necessarily be the primary consideration. In fact, we are pressed to add to our defence expenditure. Our Parliament criticizes every expenditure but not that on defence, simply for this reason.

10. Obviously, we cannot compete with the continuing supplies from the US to Pakistan. But, at the same time, we cannot allow India to become a prey to the religious bigotry of Pakistan. And we have to try in the best way we can, to prepare for any possible emergency and to get military equipment from such sources as can supply it.

11. We cannot obviously interfere with the policy of the United States. But, we feel that they should at least realize quite clearly the consequences of that policy in so far as the military aid to Pakistan is concerned. Those consequences have already become very serious for us and they are likely to become graver.

6. False Reports in Pakistan Press[1]

I attach a cutting from *Dawn*.[2] It contains a message from the Associated Press of Pakistan. On enquiry from Indira Gandhi as well as others who were present in Jammu, I am informed that this whole story is absolutely without foundation. My information from several sources is that far from any stones or shoes being thrown, there was no demonstration or act of discourtesy even towards her. And, in fact, the Jammu meeting was the biggest ever held in Jammu ever since I addressed a meeting there some years ago. The whole story as given in *Dawn* is absolutely false.

2. We may, of course, ignore this. And yet, I feel we might informally do something. Thus, you could send this cutting to our High Commissioner in Pakistan and tell him that it is completely false. He might draw the attention of

1. Note to Commonwealth Secretary, New Delhi, 7 April 1957. JN Collection.
2. The *Dawn* published an APP report on 5 April 1957 that during electioneering, Indira Gandhi was hooted out of the pandal, and stones and shoes etc., were thrown at the dias in a meeting at Nawan Shehr on 19 March. It was also reported that she "was, however, successful in addressing sparsely attended public meetings" on 18 March at Jammu and nearby Damana.

Dawn to it or some other responsible person in Pakistan. He need not do this in writing.

3. Perhaps, also, the Pakistan Associated Press correspondent in Delhi could be told by Haksar[3] or somebody how these wholly false stories are sent by the APP to *Dawn*.

3. P.N. Haksar was Director, External Publicity Division, MEA.

7. US Policy towards Pakistan[1]

I agree with Shri Krishna Menon that the extract from the Bengali paper issued by the USIS is not something which should be casually dealt with or ignored.[2] The last sentence in that extract is an assurance to Pakistan that the US will come to her aid. It is true this is said in the context of India attacking Pakistan. Even so, it is highly undesirable. But, apart from this, the effect of such a sentence can only be to encourage Pakistan in her aggressive attitude and threats to India.

2. We are entitled to know formally from the US Government whether this represents the US policy.

3. In this connection, Mr Richards's[3] recent statements in Pakistan[4] and Pakistan being brought under the Eisenhower Middle East Doctrine,[5] are also evidence

1. Note to Foreign Secretary and Commonwealth Secretary, New Delhi, 8 April 1957. JN Collection.
2. In a USIS weekly in Bengali issued from Dhaka on 16 March, it was suggested that India might attack Pakistan and that the Kashmir issue was to be settled by the UN. Krishna Menon's view was that the Indian Government should take the US-Pakistan issue more seriously and take it up with the US Government.
3. James P. Richards (1894-1979); American lawyer and politician; served in the First World War, 1917-19; Judge in the Lancaster county, 1923-33; Democrat Member, US Congress, 1933-57; delegate to Japanese Peace Conference; special assistant to Eisenhower for the Middle East, 1957-58.
4. Richards said in Karachi on 30 March that he had made tentative allocations for Pakistan from the funds approved for putting into operation the Eisenhower Doctrine. Richards had made limited commitments for the USA to supply aid to four Middle East nations under the Eisenhower Doctrine prior to his arrival in Karachi on 27 March 1957.
5. For details of Eisenhower Middle East Doctrine of 5 January 1957, see, *ante*, p. 469 fn 7.

of some definite policy against India. This taken together with the various statements made by Mr Hildreth,[6] who was lately US Ambassador in Pakistan, indicates a certain policy,[7] and we should request the US Government to clarify this matter. I think, it would probably be desirable for a brief aide-memoire to be prepared, which can be handed to the US Ambassador here (copy sent to our Ambassador in Washington[8]).

4. Then, there is the question of Mr Dulles's reported answer to a question about Kashmir.[9] We have already asked for a correct report of this. If the report we receive, is on the lines of what appeared in the press, we shall have to have this up also, though I think, this should be taken up separately.

5. We have already drawn the attention of the US Ambassador to the very considerable military aid from the US to Pakistan. He goes on repeating that this is not much and that India is far stronger and need not have any apprehensions. I think that we should now give him a concise statement, based on the information we have received, of the military aid to Pakistan in the course of the last year or so. FS has got a note on this, which he received from Intelligence. A summary should be prepared of this, giving the important factors in regard to armour, aircraft, airfields, etc., and this should be handed to the American Ambassador.

6. Minister Without Portfolio should see this note.

---

6. Horace A. Hildreth (1902-88); American lawyer and politican; Governor, Maine 1944-48; founded Diversified Communications in 1949; US Ambassador to Pakistan, 1953-57.
7. For example, Hildreth said in Peshawar on 8 March, as reported in *Dawn*, "America has helped Pakistan in her demand for a fair plebiscite in Kashmir and supported her in all her legitimate demands." *The Times of India* (Bombay) reported Hildreth's view, expressed on the same occasion, that Pakistan had the "unqualified support" of the US and UK for her demand for a plebiscite in Kashmir. On 18 February in Dhaka, Hildreth expressed his appreciation of Pakistan's growing military strength.
8. G.L. Mehta.
9. According to a Reuter report, at a private meeting of a Congressional sub-committee on 29 January 1957, Dulles was asked whether India had closed the door to a satisfactory solution of its dispute with Pakistan over Kashmir. He replied that he did not think so and "nothing irrevocable had happened yet with regard to the annexation of Kashmir."

8. To B.V. Keskar[1]

New Delhi
8 April 1957

My dear Balkrishna,[2]

In the course of the last few days, it has been pointed out to me by different persons that we ought to make some effort to broadcast for Pakistan. I was told, especially by people coming from Lahore, that there is a great desire to listen in to Indian broadcasts, specially music but often the language of our broadcasts is utterly incomprehensible to them. It is true that this does not apply to music but even the description of the music is not understood by them.

It is odd that in spite of all the shouting and cursing of India in Pakistan, there is still a basic looking up to India by the common people. I think that we should make some effort to meet this demand. I do not mean any political broadcast to Pakistan and indeed you need not call it a broadcast to Pakistan specially. The whole point is that the text of it should be more in Urdu, mostly in music. Any such broadcast will also be welcomed by the large number of Urdu knowing people in the Punjab, Delhi, North UP, etc.

I do not quite know what broadcasts you give. I believe, you give a news broadcast in Urdu. That is good so far as it goes. I suggest, therefore, that you might add some kind of a musical broadcast with some commentaries etc., in Urdu. No mention of Pakistan need be made in it but it should be so regulated that it suits Pakistan from the point of view of time etc. I think this may well have a much wider effect than we might imagine.

Yours sincerely,
Jawaharlal Nehru

---

1. JN Collection.
2. Union Minister of Information and Broadcasting.

9. To Eugene R. Black[1]

New Delhi
24 April 1957

Dear Mr Black,[2]

Thank you for your letter of 11th April 1957, recommending a formal extension of the cooperative work until September 30, 1957.

You have stated that a situation has now arisen in which it is important that the Bank and the Governments of India and Pakistan should have an opportunity of reviewing the work which has been accomplished in the course of the cooperative discussions. While agreeing to the extension of cooperative work until March 31, 1957, Government of India had expressed the hope that a sufficient measure of agreement will be forthcoming within the next few months in order that a final settlement could, with the assistance of the Bank, be reached by March 31, 1957. I am seriously concerned at the absence of any progress during this period. You will appreciate that, in the absence of any indication by the Government of Pakistan of their intention to accept the Bank Proposal of February 1954,[3] it is difficult for us to make any useful appraisal of the situation.

It was envisaged in the Bank Proposal that, after a transition period, roughly estimated to be about five years, it would not be necessary to continue any supplies to Pakistan from the Eastern rivers. Three of these five years have already elapsed. During this period, in view of our acute problems of food shortage and rehabilitation, we have been proceeding with certain development plans in areas which depend for their water supply on the Indus system of rivers. The Bhakra canals were opened in Kharif 1954, the Bhakra Dam and the Sirhind Feeder will soon come into operation and work has been taken in hand on the construction of a canal from the Headworks at Harike to feed the arid areas of Rajasthan. These schemes form part of an integrated development plan and, you will appreciate that they cannot be held up because Pakistan Government have delayed indication of their attitude to the Bank Proposal for over three years.

You have expressed the view that the Bank should have some further period of time in which to complete the appraisal envisaged in paragraph 11 of the

1. JN Collection. Also available in File No. 6(11)-Pak-III/57, pp. 13-14/corr., MEA.
2. President, International Bank for Reconstruction and Development.
3. For details of the Bank Proposals of 5 February 1954, see *Selected Works* (second series), Vol. 26, p. 466.

aide-memoire of May 21, 1956, i.e., to consider whether the employment of its good offices could make any further contribution to a solution and to determine, in the light of this appraisal, what future course of action might appropriately be proposed to each of the Governments. I agree to the formal extension of cooperative work, as recommended by you, until September 30, 1957. I hope, however, that the Government of Pakistan will give an early indication of their policy with respect to the Bank Proposal as, obviously, this is necessary to assist the appraisal contemplated by the Bank and also for the appraisal by the Government of India of the cooperative work done so far.

During this period of formal extension of the cooperative work, our Representative will, as before, keep the Bank Representative informed of our views on various technical and financial problems relating to the cooperative work, in order to assist in every way the efforts of the Bank towards a final settlement of the question, which efforts my Government and I highly appreciate.

With kind regards,

Yours sincerely,
Jawaharlal Nehru

III. CHINA AND TIBET

1. Religious and Cultural Ties with Tibet[1]

Premier Chou En-lai did mention to me something about India and Tibet having direct relations in regard to religious and like matters. I do not remember his wording, nor can I say exactly what he meant. I did not press the matter with him. But, I think, he did say something about Tibetan scholars coming to India to study religion and Sanskrit, etc., and I told him that they would be welcome.[2]

1. Note to Secretary General, Jabalpur, 26 February 1957. "Revolt in Tibet, Dalai Lama's Arrival in India 1959", MEA, Government of India. Also available in JN Collection.
2. For Nehru's talks with Chou En-lai, see *Selected Works* (second series), Vol. 36, pp. 583-619 and 623-638.

Any move in this direction should, of course, have to be referred to the Chinese Government. We should not do anything without their consent. Otherwise, as you say, this might lead to disillusionment.

About my going to Lhasa, I would indeed like to go there. But I am wholly unable to say anything definitely at this stage about my plans for the summer. Also, of course, if there is any such idea of my going there, I would have to refer it to Premier Chou En-lai first. I would do so rather informally, to begin with.

The various matters referred to in the Dalai Lama's letters might be examined and I can consider sending him an answer.[3]

I am returning the original letters from the Dalai Lama unopened to you. They might be opened and kept in the Ministry. Presumably there is nothing more in them than what is given in the translations already placed before me.

You might refer to my notes on my talks with Premier Chou En-lai. Perhaps I made some reference to his telling me about our religious contacts with Tibet.

3. In two letters Dalai Lama wrote that India being the source of Buddhist Dharma, a strong religious and cultural bond existed between India and Tibet. He referred to Chou En-lai's view that India and Tibet deal directly in the matters of religion and culture, and establish a permanent relationship on firm foundations. Dalai Lama sought the Indian Government's help for the development of Bodh Gaya Tibetan Monastery, and for establishing a new organization of Tibetan Sangha and monasteries at suitable holy centres in India. Dalai Lama informed that a new Abbot, well-versed in spiritual knowledge, would be accredited to Tharpa Choling Monastery at Kalimpong. He also hoped that Nehru would find time to visit Tibet in the following summer.

2. To Shriman Narayan[1]

New Delhi
2 March 1957

My dear Shriman,
Your letter of 2nd March about the India-China Friendship Association. I think that we might adopt a cooperative attitude with this association and you can inform MPs and others accordingly.

1. JN Collection. Also available in AICC Papers, NMML.

You might, however, inform Dr Zakir Husain[2] that while we shall be cooperative, we shall naturally expect the Association not to take any step which may be opposed to the Congress policy or the policy of the Government of India.

Yours sincerely,
Jawaharlal Nehru

2. Noted educationist and a nominated Member of Rajya Sabha.

3. Harnessing Brahamputra Water[1]

I have long been interested in this part near the India-Tibet border where the Brahmaputra enters India. What Dr Krug[2] has said was pointed out to me by Shri Kanwar Sain.[3] In fact, I referred to this matter in some public addresses.[4]

The real fall takes place in Chinese (Tibet) territory and not actually in Indian territory. Of course, it may be possible to bring the water through channels to Indian territory and have the power house there. In any event, it would require the full cooperation of the Chinese authorities. China, if it so chose, could utilize this power itself without associating India. India cannot do so by itself and without the association of China.

It is obvious that at the present moment it will not be easy to use much electric power either in Tibet or in the North East Frontier Agency. But the Chinese are

1. Note to Commonwealth Secretary, New Delhi, 12 April 1957. JN Collection.
2. Julius A. Krug (1907-1970); Research statistician, Wisconsin Telephone Company, 1930 and 1931; Chief, Depreciation Section, Wisconsin Public Service Commission, 1932-35; Public Utilities Export, Federal Communications Commission, 1936-37; Technical Director, Kentucky Public Service Commission, 1937; with Tennessee Valley Authority in various capacities, 1938-41; served with War Production Board on loan from TVA, 1941-44; Chairman, Office of Production Management and War Production Board, 1944-45; Secretary of the Interior, US, 1946-49; Leader, UN Flood and Water Control Mission to Pakistan, 1956-57.
3. Chairman, Central Water and Power Commission.
4. Nehru also wrote notes to officials of MEA regarding flood control in the North East. See *Selected Works* (second series), Vol. 26, pp. 116-118 and Vol. 30, p. 395.

people who look far ahead. If their attention is drawn to this matter, they might well begin to think of some major scheme there, though even for them this is likely to be rather a distant scheme, in view of the conditions in Tibet.

Obviously, the proper use of this great fall would be for some joint Indo-China venture. I do not myself see where Pakistan comes into the picture. Geographically, it is far away. Burma is nearer; but for Burma too, it is not likely to be of much use in the foreseeable future.

Shri Kanwar Sain also told me that there is a similar fall of a river in Indo-China at the spot which is near the meeting place, I think, of Vietnam and Cambodia. Laos is, I think, also not far. There also an enormous amount of electric energy could be produced which would be enough for all the countries of Indo-China. I think, he has mentioned this fact in the report he drew up for the United Nations.

4. To U Nu[1]

New Delhi
22 April 1957

My dear U Nu,[2]

I have received today your letter of the 17th April 1957, with its enclosures. Thank you for it.

I shall have the matters referred to in your letter examined by the Historical Section of the External Affairs Ministry. In case I can give you any useful information about them, I shall do so in a later communication.

I am sorry that there has been some difficulty in your arriving at a settlement about border problems with the Chinese Government.[3] I confess that I do not very much like the attitude of Premier Chou En-lai in this matter. The impression created upon me is that he was not fully adhering to what he had told you or U Ba Swe[4] previously. But this is for you to judge.

1. JN Collection.
2. Prime Minister of Myanmar.
3. For China-Myanmar border problems, see *Selected Works* (second series), Vol. 35, pp. 506-514.
4. Deputy Prime Minister and Minister of Defence of Myanmar at this time.

I am writing to you immediately so as to inform you of one particular development which took place here when Chou En-lai came to India on the last occasion. In your letter you say that while Premier Chou En-lai was prepared to accept the McMahon Line in the north, he objected to the use of the name "McMahon Line", as this may produce "complications vis-à-vis India", and therefore, he preferred to use the term "traditional line".

When Chou En-lai was here last, we discussed many matters at great length. He referred to his talks with you and U Ba Swe and indicated that a satisfactory arrangement had been arrived at.[5] In this connection he said that while he was not convinced of the justice of our claim to the present Indian frontier with China (in Tibet), he was prepared to accept it. That is, he made it clear that he accepted the McMahon Line between India and China, chiefly because of his desire to settle outstanding matters with a friendly country like India and also because of usage etc. I think, he added he did not like the name "McMahon Line".

This statement that he made to me orally was important from our point of view and so I wanted to remove all doubts about it. I asked him again therefore and he repeated it quite clearly. I expressed my satisfaction at what he said. I added that there were two or three minor frontier matters pending between India and China on the Tibet border and the sooner these were settled, the better. He agreed.

I entirely agree that the use of the word "McMahon Line" is not right and should be put an end to. It reminds one of British incursions and aggression. We are, therefore, not using these words any longer. Indeed, so far as we are concerned, we have maintained all along that our frontier with China, except for the two or three very minor matters, was a fixed and well known frontier and there was no dispute about it. We had never raised this question with China, but I had stated in Parliament here and also to Chou En-lai in Peking that there was nothing to discuss about our frontier as it was fixed and well known. We have now our check-posts all along this frontier.

Thus, so far as we are concerned, this frontier (known previously as the McMahon Line) is not a matter in dispute at all and Chou En-lai has accepted it. It is true that his acceptance was oral, but it was quite clear and precise.

As regards the two or three minor matters, we are expecting some Chinese representatives to come to Delhi fairly soon to discuss one of them. The territory involved is a very small one in the high mountains. We do not propose to raise the other two small matters at this stage. After one question is settled, we might, if we think proper then, refer to the other two.

5. See *Selected Works* (second series), Vol. 36, p. 614.

I am writing to you immediately in answer to your letter so as to keep you informed about this so-called McMahon Line between India and Tibet and what Chou En-lai said to me on this subject. This has some relevance to your own McMahon Line.

Thank you for what you have written about our elections. I am afraid I am not very happy about these elections. So far as our Parliament is concerned, we have got a very big majority. In some of the State elections, we did not do so well and, as you must know, in Kerala, our smallest State, Communists have formed a Government.[6] This is the first case, one might say, in history when a Communist Government has been formed as a result of democratic elections. It will be interesting to watch developments there. For the present, the Communist Government there is behaving with caution and apparently does not wish to create trouble.

But what has worried me greatly in regard to these elections, is not the measure of success or failure that we had but rather the inner weaknesses that came out. Somehow these democratic elections, good as they are, encourage human weaknesses.

I have been feeling very tired and rather stale. In another two days' time, I am going to the mountains for three or four days rest. That is not much. I am afraid I cannot remain away for much longer. Our new Parliament will be meeting early in May.

Bandaranaike,[7] has been pressing me to pay a visit to Ceylon for the Buddha Jayanti celebrations. As a matter of fact, we had specially fixed the Buddha Jayanti Day as an auspicious day for the first meeting of our new Parliament. I hope, however, to pay a brief visit to Ceylon soon after, going there on the 17th of May and returning to Delhi on the 20th.

With all good wishes,

Yours sincerely,
Jawaharlal Nehru

6. See *ante*, pp. 106, 118-119 & 334-339.
7. S.W.R.D. Bandaranaike was Prime Minister of Sri Lanka.

5. Message to Chou En-lai[1]

I am grateful to Your Excellency for your message of good wishes. I hope you will be good enough to convey my gratitude to your Government also.

The growing friendship between India and China has been a matter of the greatest satisfaction to me. I believe firmly that this friendship and cooperation are good for both our countries as well as for the peace and progress of Asia and the peace of the world. It was the happy privilege of our two countries to enunciate first the Five Principles of peaceful coexistence. As Your Excellency knows, these Principles have been accepted by a large number of countries. I am convinced that these Principles should form the basis of international relations.

I send you all my good wishes.

1. New Delhi, 24 April 1957. JN Collection.

IV. IRAN

1. To B.F.H.B. Tyabji[1]

New Delhi
2 March 1957

My dear Badr,[2]

I have just received your letter of the 24th February. Thank you for it.

It is true that we have had a hard time in connection with Kashmir. If I had not been sure in my mind about our policy and what was good for the people of Kashmir as well as the people of India and, if I may say so, the people of Pakistan also, I might have wobbled. But, I am quite clear in my mind that it is not possible for us to change our policy or to give in to this clamour. As a matter of fact, from such reports as we have from Pakistan, it appears that even the Pakistan

1. JN Collection.
2. India's Ambassador in Tehran.

510

leaders and, more so, the people do not believe much in what they themselves say. Suhrawardy's position as Prime Minister has been a wobbled one and this Kashmir issue has come to his rescue. He has, I suppose, shown some courage in taking up a definite line, that is of throwing in his lot completely with the Western Powers, even at the cost of angering Egypt and one or two other Arab countries. But, I am sure this is not going to prove a wise policy for Pakistan in the long run.

The other day, I saw some message from you about Iran's annoyance with us because of our criticism of the Baghdad Pact. It was suggested to you by some Minister there that if we toned down our criticism of the Baghdad Pact and recognized the special difficulties of Iran in this matter, they on their part, would tone down the press criticism of India in Iran.

We can obviously not enter into any such bargain, which would be completely unprincipled. I realize the difficulties of Iran and I have not gone out of my way to criticize Iran. But, I certainly have criticized and propose to go on criticizing the general system of pacts and military alliances and, in this connection, to refer to the Baghdad Pact.

Whatever may happen to us, there is no hope for countries like Pakistan and Iran and also Iraq, which maintain their feudal and reactionary character and subsist on military help from outside. Even the aid given from outside for civil development is largely wasted. The other day, a high-powered American observer in Pakistan spoke publicly about the way Pakistan had not properly utilized the aid given to it by the US. He was speaking especially about agricultural conditions and how every year less and less land was cultivated. He said, I think, that in ten years' time, a great part of Sind will be a desert, that is the part which is irrigated. This was because nothing was being done to prevent the soil becoming too saline.

All this military approach and reliance on military aid from outside, with no real attempt to improve the social and economic conditions of the people, can obviously lead nowhere.

We are in the middle of our elections, and every day brings some news which is either pleasant or, sometimes, unpleasant. Indira has hardly been traceable for weeks. She has been wandering about all over the country at great peril to her health. I had, as you must have heard, a novel and interesting experience when my aircraft caught fire. This was a close shave because a fire is a bad thing in the air. However, we escaped unhurt.

All good wishes to you and Surayya.

Yours affectionately,
Jawaharlal Nehru

511

2. To B.F.H.B. Tyabji[1]

Circuit House
Kanpur
4 March 1957

My dear Badr,

I wrote to you a day or two ago. I left Delhi this morning for Kanpur for my last election meeting.[2] As I was leaving Delhi, I saw a telegram from you about your meeting with the *Shahenshah*[3] in which the same arguments were repeated about the Baghdad Pact which had been previously placed before you by the Ministers there. There was again a suggestion that we should understand Iran's position and should, therefore, moderate our opposition to the Baghdad Pact. If we did so, Iran would also take steps to moderate criticism of India.

I have already written to you about this matter. I am now writing again to make it clear what our position is, and I should like you to explain this to the *Shahenshah* or to the Ministers when occasion offers. Naturally, you will do it in polite and courteous language, but the fact should be clearly stated.

We have not, I think, ever referred to Iran in this connection or criticized Iran as such. But it is true we have often referred to the Baghdad Pact as an evil thing, both from the larger point of view of peace and, more particularly, in relation to India. So far as its impact on India is concerned, if there was any doubt, the Pakistan Prime Minister Suhrawardy has made it perfectly clear. Only yesterday, in the course of his speech in Lahore, he stated that all their foreign policy and, in particular, their adherence to the Baghdad Pact was conditioned by India and the Kashmir question. They wanted the support of other countries in regard to Kashmir, and, therefore, they joined it. He expressed his fulsome thanks to the United Kingdom and the USA for their support on the Kashmir issue.[4]

Suhrawardy explained his foreign policy fully in this context and further said something which is not very complimentary to the other powers of the Baghdad Pact, apart from the UK. He said that without a Great Power like the UK and the backing of the USA, the Baghdad Pact was just a collection of military zeros. Zero plus zero plus zero was equal to zero. Therefore, they had to rely on England

---

1. JN Collection.
2. For Nehru's speech in Kanpur, see *ante*, pp. 93-96.
3. Mohammad Reza Shah Pahlavi.
4. For Suhrawardy's speech see *ante*, p. 432.

and the USA from a military point of view. Thus, in his expressed view, the sole purpose of the Baghdad Pact, in so far as Pakistan was concerned, was to put pressure on and threaten India and, in the final analysis, even to utilize it for war against India.

If that is so, as it obviously is, then it is natural for India to object to this Pact and to state her objection quite clearly before the world. The fact that Iran does not like our saying so cannot obviously make us give up both our basic position and what we think is to India's interest.

We have no quarrel with Iran though we do think that Iran's present policy is harmful not only to us but to Iran herself.

Our foreign policy is, as you well know, an independent one and one of non-alignment with Power blocs. Therefore, we do not approve of military alliances. We think that they do not bring peace nearer and do not even bring security in the areas concerned. We object, therefore, to all military alliances, whether they are NATO, Warsaw Pact, SEATO, Baghdad Pact or any other. NATO and SEATO affect us directly, the others have no such direct effect.

So far as the Baghdad Pact is concerned, it has brought confusion and insecurity in the Middle Eastern region. It has opened the door to Soviet intrigues and intervention in the Middle Eastern politics. It has split up the Arab world. It was one of the factors leading, I think, to Egypt getting arms from the communist countries, which again led to all kinds of other developments. Thus it increased the danger of war and, more especially, the danger to these countries, including Iran.

If Iran wants security from possible Russian aggression, this was a very unwise step to take. It seems to me patent that in case of obvious Russian aggression against Iran, there would be widespread war and the USA would come in. I do not think any country, big or small, wants that war. Certainly the Soviet Union does not. As a consequence, there is not the least likelihood of such Soviet aggression on Iran. There might, of course, be some kind of penetration and encouragement of elements hostile to the present Government in Iran. That can take place anyhow, and indeed there is greater likelihood of this kind of internal interference if relations are bad and if the Soviet Union thinks that Iran is lined up against it and is made a base of action against it. The only way to avoid it is to have a strong popular Government which gradually solves the difficult economic problems of the country, and also avoids entanglements in these Big Power politics. I am quite sure that the Soviet, for its own opportunist reasons, would then avoid any interference with Iran. But if Iran deliberately lines up with Powers hostile to the Soviet, this is almost an invitation to the Soviet to create trouble there. The trouble may be limited because of the fear of war.

If, by any chance, a major war occurred, there can be little doubt that Iran as well as Iraq would be the first sufferers from it. Whatever the other results of the war might be, Iran would be a casualty for the simple reason that Iran is supposed to be a base of operations against the Soviet. Indeed, the Soviet Government has publicly stated that any country having such bases would be a target for attack. In such an attack, Iran's little army would not count for much. The war would be on a bigger scale and in many theatres, but Iran would suffer anyhow.

I do not, therefore, understand at all how these military pacts bring any sense of peace or security to Iran or any like country. I realize its difficult position. Indeed, because of that difficult position, wisdom dictates that it should keep out of these pacts. In a sense, one might say that, pact or no pact, Iran would rely upon American power to prevent any Soviet aggression.

Take the case of the Indo-China States. There the two Power blocs came into conflict. The only way to solve that conflict was the one adopted by the Indo-China Conference held at Geneva two years ago. This accepted the neutrality of these Indo-China States. If China took any aggressive step forward there, the other party would do likewise, and there would be conflict, and vice versa. It is true that the problems of the Indo-China States have not been solved, but, at any rate, there is some kind of unstable equilibrium based on a measure of neutrality, in Laos and Cambodia especially.

The only real reason, so far as I can see, for Iran or Iraq joining the Baghdad Pact and lining up with the Western Powers is to be strong enough to deal with their own peoples' discontent. There can be little doubt that the Iraqi Government under Nuri el-Said would topple over but for the arms and equipment and help of the Western Powers. This is obviously a very unstable equilibrium, and no one quite knows how long it can last. It is conceivable that in spite of the Western help, the Iraqi Government may collapse as its Prime Minister is very unpopular there. The basic weakness of the Western Powers in these countries is their support to very backward and reactionary regimes and thus they get the ill will of the people.

During the last ten years, we have seen all these countries, Pakistan, Iran, Iraq, etc., relying only on a measure of military strength derived from arms aid etc., from the Western Powers. They have largely ignored developing their country and thus creating a basis of internal strength. In fact, the moment you become a client of another big state, you not only lose real independence, but the capacity to develop. This is very obvious in Pakistan, and I suppose it is much the same in some other Middle Eastern countries. Nothing is more revealing than a statement by an American high official who recently passed scathing remarks on Pakistan's economy and the way they had wasted the help given to them. Apart from lack of any real development in any sphere, even the basic food position is very bad there. What is worse is that this food situation is progressively deteriorating. Thus, instead of catching up, they are losing ground because of large-scale American help and especially arms equipment. They may put up a brave show, but how long can this last?

Apart from these general considerations, the fact remains that the Baghdad Pact is being utilized against India. If so, it is absurd for anyone to imagine that we are going to put up with this tamely. We do not propose to do so. If Iran imagines that it can make us change our basic policy and forget India's interests simply to please its present Government, then it is mistaken. We want to have good relations with Iran, but we are not going to throw away everything we value for the sake of those relations. Indeed, there can be no good relations on that basis. Iran's anti Indian policy may do us a little harm, but ultimately it is likely to injure Iran much more.

We propose to continue our friendly policy towards Iran as such though, certainly, we shall go on attacking the Baghdad Pact as an evil thing and injurious to our interests and the interests of world peace and security. We could easily retaliate in many ways. Thus, there are, as you know, a large number of Iranians in Bombay and round about. But, we do not propose to do so.

All these questions have to be looked at from a broader and long term point of view. We try to do so. As a matter of fact, we are intensely concerned with our internal development and our five year plans. We do not wish to get entangled in external affairs, but to some extent we do get entangled and there is no help for it. In the present context of events, we have close relationship with Egypt and some other countries in the Middle East. Are we to put an end to this relationship because the Iranian Government does not like it or does not approve of our policy? So far as I am concerned, we shall adhere to our non-alignment and independent policy and criticize military pacts, whoever makes them.

Yours affectionately,
Jawaharlal Nehru

3. Attitude of the Iranian Government[1]

You might please acknowledge this letter from our Ambassador in Tehran[2] and tell him that we do not wish to pursue this matter any further. Indeed I had no desire for this matter to be taken up with the *Shahenshah*. I wrote to our Ambassador at some length to explain to him what our policy was so that, if occasion arose, he could explain it to the Iranian Government. Since the *Shahenshah* and the Iranian Government have sent us a communication which is on the verge of being offensive, there the matter ends.

I am seeing the Iranian Ambassador[3] tomorrow at his request. I propose to speak to him with some force about this attitude of the Iranian Government.

Shri Tyabji suggested some time ago that we should invite a number of Iranian *Maulvis* or Divines. We should certainly not invite them or anyone from Iran. In fact, our attitude towards Iran should be strictly correct and no more. We need to throw no flowers at them.

1. Note to Secretary General, Foreign Secretary, and Commonwealth Secretary, 9 April 1957. File No. 52(4)-IA/57, p. 18/Notes, MEA.
2. Tyabji had written on 3 April 1957 that Iran's self-confidence had greatly risen in the previous months due to assiduous wooing and flattery of their Western allies and the Soviet Government. This was apparent by their truculence and readiness to counter-attack India "on the score of our alleged pro-Communist policy and attitude".
3. A.A. Hekmat.

4. India's Policy towards Iran[1]

The Iranian Ambassador came to see me this morning at his own request which had been conveyed to me some days ago. He had sent word to me that he had some message to convey to me, although there was no hurry about it. As a matter of fact, there was no particular message that he gave me.

2. He congratulated me on his own behalf and on behalf of his Government on our success in the general elections in India. He said they were very happy that democratic forces had been successful. There was some concern in Iran, however, over the situation in Kerala. I told him that believing in democracy as we did we had to accept the full consequences of that democracy.

3. He mentioned that he had not seen me for a long time and that was why he came. Further, that a new Government had been formed recently in Iran[2] and so far as he knew, this Government would follow the same foreign policy as the previous Government and would continue friendly relations with India.

4. I told him that I was glad he had come to see me, as I had been distressed at certain recent developments in regard to our relations. It had always been our basic policy to have friendly relations with Iran. Indeed, this was not merely a question of policy, but something which drew its inspiration from the long past.

5. Some months back, however, we noticed that the press in Tehran was attacking India bitterly. There were all sorts of statements by responsible authorities there against India. Also, a specific statement on the Kashmir issue in which they accepted the Pakistan viewpoint. We had hoped that Iran would remain neutral on this issue and so we were distressed.

6. When our Ambassador in Tehran drew our attention to the press campaign there against India and also to some conversations he had there with Ministers, I wrote a long letter to the Ambassador explaining our policy.[3] This letter was a personal one to the Ambassador and was meant for him only. But the Ambassador decided to send a copy of it to His Majesty, the *Shahenshah*. This was unusual procedure. As a matter of fact, there was nothing in the letter which could not be placed before the *Shahenshah* or the Iranian Government. But I had not meant the letter to be forwarded to the *Shahenshah*.

---

1. Note to Secretary General, Foreign Secretary, Commonwealth Secretary, and Minister without Portfolio, New Delhi, 10 April 1957. JN Collection.
2. Manouchehr Eghbal formed a new Government in Iran on 3 April 1957 following the resignation of M. Hussein Ala.
3. See *ante*, pp. 512-515.

7. In this letter of mine I had discussed and explained our policy which had been, for many years, opposed to military pacts. This was so even before the Baghdad Pact came into existence. All along since Independence, and even before, that had been our broad approach. This had nothing to do with any feeling against Iran or Iranian policy. We had never mentioned Iran in this connection or criticized it. But we had certainly criticized the Baghdad Pact as well as other pacts like the SEATO, Warsaw Pact, etc. It was true that SEATO and the Baghdad Pact affected us particularly and therefore, apart from our theoretical objections to military pacts, these pacts were of immediate concern to us. Under these pacts and especially the military aid agreement, Pakistan had received vast quantities of military aid. We could not remain unconcerned about this as this was a danger to India,

8. Our Ambassador had been told in Tehran that the criticism in the Iranian press would stop if we stopped criticizing the Baghdad Pact. This seemed to me rather extraordinary. We were called upon to change our basic policy which obviously we could not do and did not propose to do. We realized the special position of Iran and its fears. But we were convinced that the way of military pacts was not the right way to deal with the situation and, in any event, we had not criticized Iran at all.

9. Some ten days ago our Ambassador in Tehran received a note from the Court Minister of Iran[4] which was supposed to be a reply to the note that had been sent to the *Shahenshah* forwarding my letter to the Ambassador. I had read this note of the Court Minister with surprise and distress. It was not a friendly note and it made various charges against India which I did not consider justified. While at no time we had criticized Iran, we had criticized very strongly the United Kingdom on grounds of policy on various occasions and, more especially, after the invasion of Egypt. But even the United Kingdom had not sent us any kind of a note like the one which we had received from the Court Minister of Iran. Nor had they suggested that we should change our basic policy to please them. The extensive military aid given to Pakistan was a danger to India and we could not remain silent when not only our national security was threatened, but

---

4. In a note received on 1 April 1957, the then Court Minister of Iran, Manouchehr Eghbal, wrote that India's repeated attacks on the Baghdad Pact were also directed against the Iranian Government as Iran was a member of the Pact. He stated that while the Baghdad Pact became a victim of calumny, attacks and accusations, Warsaw Pact was never mentioned. He further wrote that there were ancient and strong ties between the peoples of India and Iran, and the Government of Iran could not even contemplate an anti-Indian policy. He felt that the slightest deviation from the path of friendship and sincerity might bring undesirable results for all concerned.

there were trends in the world which we thought were dangerous. At the same time we had always wanted to maintain friendly relations with Iran.

10. The Iranian Ambassador said that he was distressed to learn all this. His attention had been drawn to the Iranian press comments against India sometime ago. He had immediately taken this matter in hand and the Iranian press had now changed its tone in regard to India and was better. He was sorry that my letter to our Ambassador in Tehran had been sent to the *Shahenshah*. Our Ambassador, Shri Tyabji, was a good man but he was a newcomer there and perhaps he had not yet developed the necessary contacts which the previous Ambassador Dr Tarachand had.

11. The Ambassador said that he quite understood our general policy which was based on Mahatma Gandhi's adherence to peaceful methods. He thought that there were persons in Iran who were interested in creating trouble between Iran and India and these people indulged in provocative and malicious propaganda. It was true that there was anxiety in Iran over this question of the Baghdad Pact which was attacked not only by India, but by Egypt, Russia etc. But that was no reason why our friendly relations should be affected or for Iran not to understand our policy. We must not be led away by the provocation of some people. The Ambassador said that as the Court Minister of Iran had sent a note to our Ambassador, he would write to His Majesty, the *Shahenshah*, direct on this subject. He hinted that what the Court Minister might write did not necessarily represent the Government's view.

12. The Ambassador then said that he had recently been to Thailand where also he found some concern at India's opposition to SEATO and other pacts.

13. The Ambassador appealed to me not to attach too much importance to this note or to recent developments. I told him that I agreed with him. The old friendship between India and Iran was far too important and old-established to be affected by temporary aberrations. Nevertheless, I thought it necessary to explain to him how distressed we were at the attitude exhibited in the note of the Court Minister and in a number of statements which had been made previously.

14. A copy of this note should be sent to our Ambassador in Tehran.

V. INDONESIA

1. Situation in Indonesia[1]

The Indonesian Ambassador[2] came to see me this afternoon. He gave me the attached letter.[3] He then expressed his distress at the report from Djakarta that some of our Embassy premises had been attacked and looted.[4] He said he had not received any report about it and had asked for one. But in any event, he wished to express his deep regret.

2. He then spoke to me about the distressing state of internal Indonesian politics.[5] The two top men, namely President Soekarno and Vice-President Hatta,[6] were pulling against each other and the whole structure of Indonesian independence was being shaken up. Speaking as a non-political army man, he said that while he regretted what was happening in the Armed Forces, he felt sure that they did not mean any ill to Indonesia. They had been very unhappy about the state of affairs in the country and how it was gradually disintegrating through internal causes. And so, apparently, they wanted to bring some pressure for unity. There could be no unity unless President Soekarno and Vice-President Hatta pulled together. President Soekarno was a man very popular with the people, a great speaker and he had fine ideas. But these ideas were broad ideas forming a framework which he did not fill in. In fact, he was not good at working

1. Note to Secretary General, New Delhi, 16 March 1957. JN Collection.
2. Abdul Kadar.
3. Letter not available.
4. A house, occupied by some staff members of the Indian Embassy in Jakarta, was required by the Government of Indonesia for some other purposes. While the staff were awaiting allotment of alternative accommodation, a mob attacked the house on 15 March 1957 and caused considerable damage. Alternative temporary accommodation was then provided for the Embassy staff.
5. Indonesia was facing difficulties due to military and political revolts in Central, North and South Sumatra in December 1956, and subsequent withdrawal of support by some smaller parties from the Government. In early March further regional revolts under the military leadership occurred in East Indonesia and Borneo. On 14 March 1957, Ali Sastroamidjojo resigned and Ahmed Soekarno proclaimed martial law.
6. Mohammad Hatta.

out details, and so he threw out ideas and they remained in the air. Evidently, the Ambassador thought that Vice-President Hatta was a much more practical person.

3. The Ambassador told me that Vice-President Hatta issued a statement opposing "the conception" of President Soekarno.[7] The Vice-President had more or less retired to his hill retreat. All this was very bad and the Ambassador was greatly agitated at these developments.

4. The Ambassador told me that he had been sent here as a non-political, non-career diplomat because they attached importance to India. At first Dr Ali, the Prime Minister, wanted to send a career man here, but under pressure from Vice-President Hatta, the present Ambassador was chosen for India.

5. The Ambassador said that he was so disturbed at these developments that he had decided to go to Djakarta soon on his own initiative. He had sent a telegram to his Government to this effect. He hoped to leave Delhi on Wednesday next, 20th March. A number of Indonesian officers under training at Wellington, including apparently the Military and Air Attaches, had come to Delhi and the Ambassador had conferred with them also about this distressing and disruptive situation in Indonesia. They had all agreed that the Ambassador should go there. He is respected in military circles in Indonesia as well as by others.

6. The Ambassador said that as a personal friend of President Soekarno and Vice-President Hatta, I might write to them and appeal to them to unite and cooperate in dealing with this present situation. He realized that this kind of thing is not normally done on the official level. He appealed to me, however, on the personal level both because of India's intimate contacts with Indonesia and my friendship with these two leading men in that country. He added that he would not like these letters to be sent through our Ambassador in Djakarta as this would give it an official flavour. He would like to take the letters himself and privately and personally deliver them.

7. I told him that naturally we are deeply interested in Indonesia and we would like to do everything in our power to help. As for his proposal that I should write these letters, I should like to think over it and would let him know.

8. In the course of our talk, the Ambassador told me that when he was Minister in the Lebanon, Bokhari[8] was Minister there for Pakistan. Bokhari said one day that they knew well that the real headquarters of the Indonesian Government were in New Delhi. To this, the Ambassador replied that they also knew that the headquarters of the Pakistan Government were in Washington.

7. Soekarno had put forward a proposal of "guided democracy" on 21 February 1957 to meet the crisis. It would be an all-party government advised by a National Council of functional groups such as youth, workers, peasants, religions, regions etc.
8. Lal Shah Bokhari.

9. The Ambassador was much agitated and greatly distressed at developments in Indonesia.

10. I should like you to show this note to Shri Krishna Menon on his return from Bombay. We can then have a talk. I myself feel that it would be desirable for me to write personal letters to President Soekarno and Vice-President Hatta. They will have to be rather brief letters without going into any matter in dispute, but expressing my distress at the difficulties they were facing and hoping that they would face and overcome them in a united way.

2. Cable to G. Parthasarathi[1]

I have seen your telegram 12628 March 28.[2]

2. Indonesian Ambassador General Kadar called on me and expressed great concern over developments in Indonesia. He told me he was going there and suggested that I should give him letters to President Soekarno and Vice-President Hatta. He particularly wanted to carry the letters himself as he thought this would be informal approach and did not want me to send them through you.

3. I told him that naturally we were concerned with these developments in Indonesia as we were anxious that Indonesia should be strong and prosperous country. I hoped very much that these difficulties would be got over. I had the privilege of friendship with both Soekarno and Hatta, but I said that it would not be proper to write about the internal affairs and, more particularly, to give any letters to him.

4. It is not correct to say that I asked General Kadar to go to Indonesia from here or to convey any message from me. He himself decided to go there and informed me of it. I asked him to convey my greetings to Soekarno and Hatta.

5. This is for your information.

1. New Delhi, 30 March 1957. JN Collection.
2. Parthasarathi, Indian Ambassador to Indonesia, had informed M.J. Desai that during a talk, the Indonesian Secretary General, Subandrio appreciated India's stand on Kashmir and was aware of the cold war aspect of the problem. Subandrio said that the Indonesian Government was embarrassed by Pakistan Ambassador's propaganda activities who had been telling everyone that though Pakistan would fight for her rights but Asia would go down in that war. Parthasarathi also wrote that General Kadar, who had gone to Jakarta, told him about his talk with Nehru.

VI. EGYPT

1. Message to Gamal Abdel Nasser[1]

Your Ambassador[2] here handed over to me your kind message today.[3] I am grateful to you for it. Since Krishna Menon's return to India, I have not met him, as he is conducting his election campaign in Bombay. I have, therefore, not been fully informed about his talks with you. I have, however, had a talk with him over the telephone, but this could not be a full discussion.

2. He had already informed me that it was discussed in Cairo between you and him that if possible we would meet your desire for him to visit Cairo prior to the 20th for further discussions in regard to a statement which could not be delayed longer. I hope to meet Krishna Menon on the 13th March and to have fuller talks with him. My present answer is based on a brief telephone talk with him.

3. As you know, our position in regard to Egypt's sovereign rights has never been in doubt and we have never hesitated to express ourselves on this matter. Obviously no solution can be based upon the sacrifice of Egypt's sovereignty or self-respect. At the same time, it is in our view necessary to take into account the fact that now that the invaders have withdrawn as a result of international pressure under US initiative and also in view of the development of other policies in regard to the Middle East and the Pact countries generally, there is grave danger of the machinery of international opinion being used against Egypt.

---

1. New Delhi, 10 March 1957. JN Collection. This message was sent through Ali Yavar Jung, India's Ambassador in Egypt.
2. Moṣṭafa Kamel.
3. Nasser wanted Nehru's comment on a draft statement that he wanted to issue in regard to the Suez Canal. Nasser proposed to declare that, (A) despite tremendous sacrifices, Egypt was still willing to collaborate with all Canal users; (B) pending completion of principles for said collaboration, Egypt would continue to implement 1888 Convention and Canal Code; (C) existing tolls system would suffer no alteration; (D) tolls must be paid to the Egyptian Canal Authority, and as 1888 Convention prohibited discrimination between ships, non-payment of tolls would be an act of discrimination violating the Convention; and (E) passage of British and French ships would be allowed under above conditions. Nasser also wrote that Krishna Menon's proposal could not be accepted as it implied some sort of trusteeship unacceptable to Egypt.

There is obviously a desire to isolate Egypt and Syria in the Middle East and India in South East Asia. There is talk of sanctions and boycotts against Egypt.

4. The Baghdad and SEATO groups will be utilized and thus many countries in the Asian-African bloc, possibly including Japan, may line up with these Western countries against Egypt. There have also been remarkable advances in the technique of transportation and pipelines are being used in the United States even for transport of coal and other commodities. Thus it may be possible that efforts will be made not to use Suez Canal as far as possible.

5. Neither your country nor mine can yield to threats or compromise our sovereignties. But you will agree that we should try to avoid conflict and find solutions which are helpful and beneficial to our own peoples and to the world. This is my approach to this problem.

6. I agree that it is highly desirable for Egyptian Government to take the initiative by putting forward some constructive proposal in regard to the Canal. Some statement from you, is therefore, necessary. Perhaps it would be better to issue a brief statement now and to follow this up with a more detailed one some days later. The brief statement should be such as not to lead to an immediate break and yet will assure the sovereignty of Egypt. Our former proposals are not applicable now, especially as this brings in whole question of Canal Users Association. Krishna Menon informs me that his new proposal to you does not in any way involve "trusteeship". But he feels, and I agree with him, that it is necessary to put forward something that the bulk of the nations would accept or, at any rate, which would prevent them from joining groups hostile to Egypt, as they did in the London Conference. This aspect, therefore, requires full consideration.

7. Some parts of the draft declaration that you have sent are not likely to be accepted by Western countries and latter may create trouble and reopen whole question as after London Conference. Other issues may also be brought up to embarrass Egypt. I would, therefore, suggest for your consideration following amendments to your draft proposals.

8. Paragraph (A): It appears unnecessary at this preliminary stage to make references given in the first part of this paragraph. Also the use of the words "Canal Users" may lead to difficulties as it may reopen whole issue of Canal Users Association. We suggest, therefore, "world community" instead and shorter and less provocative phraseology. Thus you may simply say "despite her tremendous sacrifices, Egypt was still willing to collaborate with the world community."

9. Paragraph (B): I agree. Following words may be added at the end "and other arrangements which the Egyptian Government through the Suez Canal

Authority and in exercise of their sovereignty and in accord with the Convention, would make".

10. Paragraph (C): It may merely be stated that there is no intention at present of altering the level of tolls and no apprehensions need arise in the world in regard to this matter. To say that existing toll system would suffer no alteration would be ambiguous as at present some users do not pay dues to Egypt but into blocked account. It may also be interpreted to mean that it is some kind of threat on the part of Egypt to ships of countries that argue about toll payment. This issue has to be considered, but it may be unwise to raise it just now in a preliminary statement.

11. Paragraph D appears to be satisfactory. So also paragraph E. It may be better to say in E "will be allowed in the same way as ships of other countries, despite recent events".

12. I would suggest further addition to statement that the Egyptian Government has always had under consideration the problems of the development of the Canal to such modern needs of navigation and progressive developments and sound maintenance and ensuring that these developments are satisfactorily carried out. Finally, it may be stated that "this statement is only preliminary and a fuller statement setting out the basis of the Egyptian operation of the Canal in accord with the 1888 Convention, the needs of the world community and the sovereignty of Egypt, will be made by the Egyptian Government in due course".

13. These are my suggestions for your consideration. I am apprehensive that any provocative statement at this stage might lead to a conflict again and United States and many Western countries would then take a different attitude from what they took in regard to the invasion. Internationalization and all sorts of other problems may be brought up and sought to be debated in the UN General Assembly.

14. If you still wish Krishna Menon to go to Cairo for two days, I shall ask him to do so, leaving here probably on the 16th. Jarring (last month's President of Security Council) is coming here to discuss Kashmir and may arrive on the 21st March. I would like Krishna Menon to be here then.

15. In view of the serious nature of the situation in Egypt and the Canal, which might lead to grave crisis, it would be wise to take steps which are not only in consonance with dignity and self-respect of Egypt but also meet reasonable considerations of other countries.

2. Situation in Egypt[1]

The Egyptian Ambassador came to see me at 10.30 p.m. tonight. I gave him a copy of my message to President Nasser.[2] Subsequently, I told him that I was sending this to our Ambassador in Cairo with instructions for immediate delivery to President Nasser. The Egyptian Ambassador is not going to send my message as a whole to Cairo. He will probably make some kind of a summary and inform the President that the full message will be delivered from our Embassy in Cairo.

2. While the Ambassador said that he broadly agreed with the content of my message, he did not think that it would take matters far. According to him, the US and other Western Powers are bent on having a showdown with Egypt. I pointed out to him that that may be so, but it makes a big difference if they are given an easy excuse for it or are put in some dilemma. Also, whether some of the Western Powers agree or not to a proposal made by President Nasser, it is important that other countries should agree and thus a joint front against Egypt be broken. He said he agreed.

3. He discussed the position of Saudi Arabia, and he frankly said that he did not trust them at all, nor indeed did he trust any of the Arab leaders. He only trusted his own country. But he added that King Saud must know that if they deserted Egypt now, they would put themselves completely under the domination of the US and other Western Powers and will be dealt with summarily by them later. Therefore, from a purely opportunist point of view, he could not understand how King Saud could line up wholly with the US in this matter.

4. I pointed out to him that this consideration may be before King Saud. But, at the same time, he must have been told of the dangers of communism as also about his losing his oil royalties. He had thus to balance between these various considerations. I added that our own information was that he had probably given some assurances to the US Government. What exactly they were, I could not say.

5. In this connection, I referred to the alleged message by King Saud to the Prime Minister of Pakistan in regard to Kashmir, which had been denied later by the Amir Feisal.[3] The Egyptian Ambassador said that he had sent large numbers of messages to his Government in regard to Kashmir, because he had felt strongly that on this subject Egypt should support India completely. If India was disabled

1. Note to Secretary General, New Delhi, 10 March 1957. JN Collection.
2. See the preceding item.
3. Feisal was the Prime Minister and Minister of Foreign Affairs of Saudi Arabia.

in any way by the Western Powers, this would mean a terrible blow to Egypt. He said that when President Quwatly of Syria[4] was going from Delhi to Karachi, he (the Ambassador) sent an urgent message to President Nasser about Kashmir. He asked Nasser immediately to impress upon Quwatly not to weaken in any way on the Kashmir issue and to take up a strong pro-India line in regard to Kashmir in Pakistan. Nasser sent such a message to Quwatly, and Quwatly acted accordingly.

6. I am sending you various papers for record. These include the original message from President Nasser given to me by the Egyptian Ambassador, and the notes and draft sent by Shri Krishna Menon. I am not enclosing a copy of the telegram I have sent to our Ambassador in Cairo[5] as you will receive it from CCB and I have got no extra copy with me. I have limited circulation of this telegram to you and to Shri Krishna Menon.

4. Shukri Al Kuwatly (1891-1967); Syrian politician; participated in the Syrian independence movement; member, King Faisal's Syrian Government, 1919-20; exiled in Egypt, Europe and Palestine, 1921-30; one of the leaders of the Syrian rebellion against the French rule, 1925-27; returned to Syria under amnesty, 1931; Minister of Defence and of Finance, 1936; resigned in 1937; President, Syrian Republic, 1943-47; re-elected in 1948 but had to resign, and was exiled in Egypt, 1949-54; again became President, 1955-58.
5. The reference is to the message to Nasser, see *ante*, pp. 523-525.

3. Message to V.K. Krishna Menon[1]

I have received first six paragraphs of your telegram 24 of March 10th.[2] Remaining part not yet received.

2. We have to face very heavy work during the second half of March. Parliament meets on 18th. Before that there is preparation of President's Address

1. New Delhi, 10 March 1957. JN Collection.
2. Krishna Menon referred to urgent and grave position in regard to Egypt. He wrote about the reported threats by Louis St Laurent, Canadian Prime Minister, of use of force in case Egypt did not agree to the opening of Suez Canal according to UN Resolutions. He also wrote about Dulles's suggestion of boycott of the Suez Canal by the substitution of the Cape route with big tankers. Menon said that the next ten days would be crucial as the Canal would be near opening by that time, and Egypt should publish her terms on a practical basis.

to Parliament. There will be a debate on President's Address in Parliament and subsequently debate on foreign affairs. Exact date has not been fixed. I expect this session of Parliament to last about ten days.

3. As a result of elections many important consequences follow which we shall have to deal with.

4. Arthur Lall[3] sent us message from Jarring about probable date of his arrival here. He said that Jarring was likely to reach Karachi on about 15th and spend a week there and then come to Delhi. He promised to inform our High Commissioner in Karachi about date of his arrival here. Broadly, we accepted this. I am having telegram sent to our mission in Stockholm to convey to Jarring that we shall be very heavily occupied here from 18th onwards with Parliament and we would prefer his coming here after the 25th if that is convenient.

5. Your presence here is, of course, essential when Jarring comes and indeed before and after for other important purposes.

6. It is very inconvenient for you to go to Cairo during these days, but if Nasser is very anxious for you to pay a brief visit, I suppose you have to do so. Probably it would be better for you to go sooner rather than later, say, about 16th and returning by 19th at the latest.

7. It saves time if you send messages to me by telephone.

8. I have now received remaining part of your telegram No. 24.[4]

9. If you wish to come to Delhi on the 12th evening, you can certainly do so. As you know, I shall not be here then. I shall return on the 13th morning.

10. Journey to Cairo only takes a night from Bombay. Therefore, it need not take you more than three days altogether to go there and come back.[5]

---

3. India's Permanent Representative to UN.
4. Menon wrote that the Suez issue was so crucial at this time that unless some solution was "midwifed at this stage", Western countries would turn the tables on Egypt—propose sanctions or boycott against her. He reminded Nehru that the American policy basically "is to isolate Egypt and Syria in the Middle East and India in South East Asia."
5. Paragraphs 8, 9, 10 were added later.

4. Cable to Ali Yavar Jung[1]

Your telegram 201 March 26.[2] It is not possible for me to spare Krishna Menon and let him go to London as suggested. We have just got over our elections and new Government has to be formed and all manner of other difficult problems are facing us. Also, I think, that it will be very inappropriate for Krishna Menon to rush up and down in this way. We are anxious, of course, to help Egypt in every way, and we are trying to do so from here. But Krishna Menon going suddenly to London may have other consequences which are not desirable and lead to all manner of speculation.

2. This is for your personal information.

1. New Delhi, 27 March 1957. JN Collection.
2. Ali Yavar Jung had informed that it had been decided to delay the publication of declaration till 2 or 3 April and Canal opening till 9 April or 10th. A copy of the text of declaration was given to Dag Hammarskjold, and American, Russian and Yugoslav Ambassadors. Jung wrote that this delay gave more time for tackling London about which Egyptians were still anxious and Nasser enquired whether Krishna Menon would be able to go to London or not.

5. Cable to Ali Yavar Jung[1]

Your telegram 193 March 25.[2] I have enquired from our Defence Ministry and Air Force. They tell me they are very short of flying instructors and are unable to meet their own commitments for their expansion programme. For this reason it is not possible to spare eight additional instructors for Egypt. Some time ago they were asked to provide three flying instructors for Egypt and two for Syria.

1. New Delhi, 28 March 1957. JN Collection.
2. Egyptian Air authorities had requested for eight flying instructors and three navigation instructors to be provided to Egypt by 1 July 1957. The Egyptian Government did not wish to request any other Government due to political and other reasons.

They could only spare two and it was suggested that they should be sent to Syria. This matter is still pending.

Four Egyptians are due to come to flying instructors' course commencing 1st August 1957. If six or eight Egyptian pilots could come immediately, we could organize a special course for them which would be of four and a half months' duration. They could thus go back to start their school in August or September instead of July. This will in the long run be cheaper and more advantageous to Egypt and would suit us better.

As regards navigation instructors, three have already been selected and we are waiting for Egypt's concurrence before they are sent.

6. Distribution of Relief Material in Egypt[1]

Rajkumari Amrit Kaur, who recently attended the Red Cross meeting in Geneva, has told me that the Egyptian Representatives at the Red Cross spoke to her about the gifts we had sent there. They said that no one quite knew what had happened to these gifts or how they had been distributed. The Red Cross was not put in charge of this distribution. There were some reports that our blankets went into the black market.

I think, you might ask our Ambassador in Cairo if he knows anything about this matter. A secret letter can be written to him. Naturally, we do not want him to go about enquiring into this and to rub up the Egyptian Government in the wrong way. But, if he can have some idea of how our gifts were distributed, it might be useful.

1. Note to Foreign Secretary, New Delhi, 24 April 1957. JN Collection.

VII. GHANA

1. To Kwame Nkrumah[1]

Camp: Rama Nilayam,
Trichur
24 February 1957

My dear Prime Minister,[2]

It is a matter of deep regret to me that I am unable to participate personally in the Independence Day celebrations of Ghana.[3] I have long wished to go there to meet you and, if I may say so, to make more intimate acquaintance with the people of Ghana. The coming of independence would have been a particularly appropriate occasion for me to do so, so that I could join in the rejoicings on this historic occasion. Unhappily, our general elections are taking place exactly at this time and it has become impossible for me or for any of my Minister colleagues to leave India. We are continuously touring about all over this great country separately. I am indeed writing this letter to you from a place far in the South of India in the State of Kerala.

I need not tell you how happy we all are at this coming of independence to Ghana. I consider this an occasion of great significance not only to the people of Ghana but also to the whole of Africa. Indeed it is a development of great importance to the world.

Independence brings freedom, but as we know and you no doubt realise, it brings great responsibilities also. Ever since India became independent, we have had to work harder than ever before in order to give economic and social content to our political freedom. I have no doubt that you and your people will now dedicate themselves to this great task of raising the standards of the people so that they may have a free and full life. In this task, you will have the fullest sympathy from the Government and people of India and our cooperation will ever be at your disposal.

---

1. JN Collection.
2. Kwame Nkrumah was Prime Minister of Ghana.
3. Ghana became independent on 6 March 1957.

On behalf of the Government and the people of India, I offer to you, Mr Prime Minister, and the people of Ghana, our heartiest good wishes for a prosperous future and service in the cause of peace and freedom.

With kind regards,

Yours sincerely,
Jawaharlal Nehru

2. Dawn after the Dark Night[1]

Mr President,[2] friends,[3]

I am indeed happy to be present here today. I would have been happier if I could be present today at Accra, the Capital of Ghana. I wanted to go there very much, anyhow, and more specially on this memorable occasion, but unfortunately, elections and the like here, came in the way and it became impossible for me to leave India, but my mind, the minds of many of you, no doubt, have been full of this great event for which we have met to celebrate here today.

The independence of any country is a thing to be celebrated and welcomed and as the years go by, or a new country celebrates its independence, that is a matter for not only rejoicing but something more, because I feel, and I have no doubt that you also feel, that so long as this process is not complete one major element of trouble in the world will continue. But there is something more about independence of Ghana, then perhaps of some other countries. It symbolises so much for the whole continent of Africa, as the President just said, has had a peculiarly tragic history for hundred of years and to see Africa or a part of it, an important part of it, turn its face towards the dawn after the dark night, it is indeed something, the sort of which is exhilarating. There is, therefore, about

---

1. Speech at a meeting organized by African Students Association (India) to celebrate the Ghana Independence Day, New Delhi, 6 March 1957. AIR tapes, NMML.
2. C. Mboijana, President of the African Students' Association (India).
3. J.C. De. Graft Johnson, Professor of African Studies in Delhi University, and W.A.W. Clarke, Acting High Commissioner of the United Kingdom in India, also spoke on this occasion.

this event today something of the break of the dawn which moves us not only intellectually but emotionally, always, I am sure if we look back on the past of Africa, unfortunately not many people are acquainted with it. I confess that my own knowledge till recently was largely limited to some kind of recent history, I mean, the last two, three hundred years, more or less, the history of the colonial period in Africa. Gradually, I learnt some thing of its previous history and found as I expected that that history was, far from being a blank, was a rich history, rich in cultural achievements, rich in political organization and rich oddly enough, in forms of democracy and state socialism. And yet people have talked about this dark continent as if it had no past, no background, no culture not knowing all this history. It is unfortunate. I hope that people will get to know more about it, and I hope at any rate in our country, the efforts that we are making in our school for African studies here in Delhi University will prosper and people in India will know more about the past of Africa and the present, and that we shall welcome here, ever more, students from Africa who will, maybe, learn something about India, but more specially, will teach us something about their own country because inevitably we shall be thrown more together, not only we, but other countries also, because today, every country is the neighbour of the other country. The world has become so, that no country is really far removed from any other, in so far as India can cooperate, in being able to help the people and the state of Ghana, I am quite sure nothing could give us greater pleasure, but I realise and I have become more and more convinced of the fact that each country has to find its own feet, has to find its own thinking, no doubt it can and must learn from others, it must open its mind to what is happening elsewhere, and learn from it, but while learning, it must adapt that learning with its own genius, with its own past and present conditions and thus fashion its own destiny. I am convinced that unless a country has its roots in itself it cannot really go far, it may make some material progress, but that will be rather superficial, unless it has those roots in its own cultural and other traditions, not in a sense, isolating it from the rest, because no country can live a life of isolation.

So, I hope that now that the chance has come to the people of Ghana, and indeed to other parts of Africa also, they will rediscover their roots and a depth of the modern conditions and grow accordingly. I was reading recently something about this past of Africa, about the kingdom and the empire of Ghana, I am not much enamoured of empires and the like but nevertheless, in those days kingdoms and empires and more specially the organization of that kingdom and empire, even I remember that one person about whom I have read, and even written a little about long ago—was to my surprise the great African. He was that wonderful traveller who came to India many hundreds of years ago, Ibn Batuta,[4] and probably one of the biggest travellers that history knows who came from the west coast of Africa all along, right across Africa and went, I believe, to Turkey and a bit of Russia, Southern Russia, then travelled by land to India came to the city of Delhi and spent many years here, saw strange happenings here. A ruler here who was a very great scholar, but quite mad, as sometimes scholars are, and ordered one day that he will shift his capital from Delhi to Aurangabad which is Daulatabad,[5] and so the order went that everybody in Delhi, not a question of secretariat shifting, but everybody in Delhi must pack up and go and nobody must remain behind or pay the heaviest penalties, so everybody apparently had to pack up and march in a procession to Daulatabad. Having gone two or three stages the King thought he might come back and see if anybody had been left behind here. Naturally, a good few had been left behind who had hidden themselves, and he went and Delhi used to be a very prosperous city, he ruined it completely by this move. The best description of this we have is in Ibn Batuta who was here then and who has written about it in some detail. And then Batuta travelled all along India, went to China, roamed about China, came back to India, went to Ceylon, and went back ultimately to Africa, most amazing journey. So, I am most interested to find that this man whom I had admired was a very great traveller for long, was one of the great Africans of the day, and that somehow link up in my mind many things, and the past of Africa became a little more vivid in my mind than it was previously because I could associate it with events which had already found some place in my mind.

Anyhow, this is a day of rejoicing certainly, but always when there is a certain fulfilment of long sought objective or dream, this brings great responsibilities and new problems and I have no doubt that the people of Ghana and their great leader Dr Nkrumah will face these responsibilities and problems, and they will face them bravely, because in the last few years, to some extent, they have prepared themselves for this task, they have been conditioned by events which they themselves have shaped just as to some extent, many of us here were conditioned in our long struggle for Independence. Nothing is worth having, if one does not pay the price for it. It slips away, it is not respected or valued and in

---

4. Ibn Batuta (1304-77); Moroccan scholar, historian and adventurer; came to India in 1333; travelled in India extensively and held several posts during Muhammad bin Tughluq but he was critical of the Sultan; his travel diary, published under the title *Tuhfatun Nazzar fi Gharaib il Amsar wa Ajaib il Asfar*, gives useful and interesting information about almost all the aspects of Indian life; left India in 1344.
5. Muhammad bin Tughluq (1290-1351).

the course of paying that price one will condition oneself and become more and more prepared to hold it and to advance afterwards. Now, the people of Ghana have completed one important stage of their journey, but there is no end to this journey in a nation, and now they have to go ahead themselves across various ways, economically and in other ways, but what is more, they have to do this thinking always that the eyes certainly of the whole of the Africa have found them but also of the rest of the world also, and that is a great responsibility, I am sure, they will discharge it well. We should congratulate naturally the people of Ghana and their leaders and specially Dr Nkrumah. There are many things in Africa that have happened and are still happening, which are rather painful to contemplate, there are many dark shadows in Africa and so it is our peculiar pleasure that out of that darkness this light has come, which I hope will spread and those responsible for this, deserve our congratulations, certainly the people of Ghana, but also the Government and the people of the United Kingdom, who deserve credit for this. We may criticise them for other things, as some of us sometime do, but undoubtedly this has been something for which they deserve congratulations, and I hope that this example will spread. So, on my own behalf, and on behalf of the Government and the people of India, and if I may say so on behalf of all of you, we offer our hearty and respectful congratulations to the people of Ghana and their leaders.

3. No Roving Ambassador for North Africa[1]

I have read your report on Ghana.[2]

2. I agree with what you say in Paragraph 10.[3]

---

1. Note to Commonwealth Secretary, New Delhi, 20 March 1957. File No. 19(8)/57-AFR-II, p. 1/Note, MEA.
2. M.J.Desai spent seven days in Ghana participating in the independence celebrations. His note described the conditions in Ghana and its position in Africa. To deal with the immediate problems of administration and organization, Nkrumah had enquired if India could loan the services of some officials of the Army and External Affairs for six months or so to organize their Army and new civil and foreign services.
3. Desai expressed the desirability of appointing a career diplomat as Indian High Commissioner of Ghana who was familiar with the administrative and organizational aspects of the Government of India so that he could give guidance and assistance on various minor problems.

3. It is not quite clear to me what a Roving Ambassador will do.[4] The problems of the various countries of Africa are different from each other although, no doubt, there is bound to be some similarity. Such a Roving Ambassador will have to be a senior and experienced person.

4. I doubt if our Ambassador stationed at Khartoum can be suitable for the purpose you have suggested. He is not likely to be a senior man and merely to place a senior man at Khartoum for this purpose hardly seems feasible.

5. I suppose there will be no difficulty in our giving them a few military and civil officers to organise their defence and civil services.

4. Desai suggested that in the larger North African context, it seemed important to consider the appointment of a Roving Ambassador or Commissioner General or some such official who would coordinate the work of Indian High Commissioners, Ministers, Ambassadors and Consuls in the newly independent North African States. It would go a long way in keeping the Indian Government closely in touch with the political trends and developments in the North African Region as a whole. He suggested that Indian Ambassador in Sudan with headquarters in Khartoum could be the best coordinating authority in North Africa.

4. To Kwame Nkrumah[1]

New Delhi
20 April 1957

My dear Prime Minister,

Our High Commissioner at Accra[2] has informed us of your Government's wish that our Government should represent the interests of Ghana in Egypt, Saudi Arabia and Syria till such time as Ghana makes other arrangements. He has also forwarded the letters addressed by your Ministry of External Affairs to the Governments of Egypt, Saudi Arabia and Syria. These letters have been forwarded to the Governments concerned.

I need not assure you that we shall be happy to perform this service for your

1. JN Collection.
2. B.K. Kapur.

Government. We are deeply interested in the progress of the new Ghana and we welcome everything that brings us in closer association with it.

With regards and all good wishes,

Yours sincerely,
Jawaharlal Nehru

VIII. UK

1. To Shriman Narayan[1]

New Delhi
6 March 1957

My dear Shriman,[2]

In the March 1st Number of the *Economic Review* issued by the AICC, on page 11 there are notes and comments. The first one is "On a Queen on a 'Civilising Work'".[3]

I think, this is written in particularly bad taste and is wholly opposed to our expressions of opinion in such matters. Apart from this, I do not think it is correct. It does not help to compare Portugal with England. The two are very different in spite of Cyprus and Malaya. But, apart from facts, the language of this note is most distressing and further it involves almost a personal attack on the Queen of England. The poor Queen of England is not responsible for the

1. Shriman Narayan Papers, NMML. Also available in JN Collection.
2. General Secretary, AICC and Chief Editor, *AICC Economic Review*.
3. The note quoted from Queen Elizabeth II's speech in Portugal: "The world is now living in more anxious days than it did 50 years ago and the civilising work which we (obviously Britain and Portugal) pursued has not always met the understanding which it would have been right to expect in view of the results achieved." The note referred to Cyprus and Goa as "concentration camps" and "scenes of torture and human degradation". The note further said that "India knows to its cost what this 'civilising work' has been" and the results of British civilising work were very much visible in Cyprus. The note concluded by saying that all these "civilisers" were near extinction and like birds of the same feathers had flocked together on the eve of their doom.

537

British policy in Cyprus or anywhere. Any such personal attack, therefore, can only anger people who read this.

Soon I am going to the celebration of the independence of Ghana. That also is a part of British policy. One may say that this policy is two-faced, but anyhow it is something we approve of.

I think that in the next number a small note might be put in the *Economic Review* expressing regret at the reference to Queen Elizabeth in this connection. Surely, the *Economic Review* should be above this kind of low language.

Yours sincerely,
Jawaharlal Nehru

2. Cable to Vijaya Lakshmi Pandit[1]

Your telegram 0807 March 6.[2] This afternoon my attention was drawn to the article you mention in the *Economic Review*. I was much distressed to read it and immediately wrote to Shriman Narayan who is the Editor. Shriman has been away from Delhi and this appeared in his absence and without his knowledge and was written by some assistant.[3]

2. In the evening at the Ghana Independence Celebrations, *Manchester Guardian* correspondent asked me about this. I told her that this was in very bad taste and I was distressed about it.

3. I am issuing a note to the press expressing my deep regret at this article and more especially my distress that the Queen's name should have been brought in and offering my apologies to her.[4] Shriman Narayan, who has just returned to Delhi, is also issuing a note to the press.

1. New Delhi, 6 March 1957. JN Collection.
2. Vijaya Lakshmi Pandit expressed shock and distress at the personal attack on the Queen in the Reuter's report of *Economic Review* article. She sought Nehru's advice about the action she needed to take as this matter was certainly going to be pursued in Britain.
3. This note was written by Harsh Dev Malaviya, while Shriman Narayan, the Chief Editor, was away.
4. Nehru's statement offering his apologies to Queen Elizabeth appeared in the newspapers on 7 March 1957.

4. You can certainly explain that we are greatly distressed at this note for which a junior Editor was responsible, the Editor being away. On his return today, the Editor has expressed his deep regret. You can specially offer apologies to the Queen on your behalf as well as mine. Of course I have nothing to do with this *Economic Review*, but since it is issued by the Congress Party, we feel a certain responsibility.

5. In the same number of the *Economic Review*, extracts are given from newspapers in 1945 relating to police atrocities then. I have taken strong exception to this also as we do not wish to rake up old quarrels and reports and thus spread an atmosphere of hatred.

3. To Shriman Narayan[1]

New Delhi
6 March 1957

My dear Shriman,

After speaking to you on the telephone, I issued a message to the press expressing my deep regret and apologies to the Queen. I hope you have also issued your note to the press. I have also sent a telegram to Vijaya Lakshmi Pandit on these lines.

This business has been bad enough and most harmful to us. I am greatly concerned about the future. The *AICC Economic Review* is an official periodical and we have to take very special care as to what is written in it. I do not see why any political comments should appear in it at all. It should deal with economic matters and that too within the broad purview of our policy. Of course signed articles can certainly appear in it even though they are opposed to our policy. We should keep an open forum.

1. Shriman Narayan Papers, NMML. Also available in JN Collection.

The *Review* should keep a high level and not indulge in recrimination or abuse of anybody and specially of any foreign country or Government.

Yours sincerely,
Jawaharlal Nehru

4. Cable to Vijaya Lakshmi Pandit[1]

Article in *Economic Review*. In conveying my personal apologies to the Queen and to the UK Government, I hope you will make it clear that neither our Government nor I personally have anything to do with the Economic Review, which is independently published. But because it is connected with our Party, I have been particularly distressed at this article as well as references to old incidents of twelve years ago which we are trying to forget. Also I am distressed that anyone in India, whether belonging to our Party or not, should write in this way and thus give wrong impression to public and do harm to Indo-British relations.

2. Our President is also deeply pained at this publication and more especially at the attack in it on the Queen. It was suggested that he should send a personal message to the Queen expressing his deep regret. But I feel that it is not desirable to drag him into this matter as he has nothing to do with odd publications. As you perhaps know, he has recently had an eye operation and is now recovering. You may, however, convey to the Queen our President's pain and regret at publication of wrong, improper and intemperate attack on the Queen. Please inform UK Government of this also.

1. New Delhi, 7 March 1957. JN Collection.

5. To Vijaya Lakshmi Pandit[1]

New Delhi
9 March 1957

Nan dear,

The *Economic Review* article affair has practically blown over. As you know, the moment we saw this article by Harsh Dev Malaviya,[2] we went all out to express apologies etc. In fact, we did more perhaps than we need have done. There is some reaction in India. No one justifies what Harsh Dev wrote but our newspapers and others point out that when India and Indian leaders are vilified in some of the British newspapers, this is taken as a matter of course and nobody thinks of apologising. Also the reaction of the British press as a whole to this article was so bitter that it surprised people here.

All this shows that there is this great feeling of resentment and bitterness below the surface, both in England and in India. There is a feeling here that we in India have tried hard to be friends with England during the past few years but this has not been adequately appreciated on the other side. It is true that on the Suez issue we were against them because not only of broad policies but because of our own special viewpoint in regard to such questions. We have tried to help in other matters like Cyprus and even in regard to Egypt. Our influence has been to some extent a moderating one. The attitude of the UK in regard to Kashmir has been deeply resented here. We knew, of course, that the UK had been partial to Pakistan throughout these years and was always trying to put us on the level with Pakistan. But none of us expected the blatantly partial attitude that was actually adopted by the UK, ignoring many of the well known facts.

For the first time during these nine years, there is a fairly widespread feeling that the Commonwealth connection is hardly worthwhile for us. There is no doubt that if I weakened on this issue at all, there would be a big outcry all over the country to put an end to this Commonwealth connection. I do not, however, propose to encourage this. I do not think that one should deal with such matters

---

1. JN Collection.
2. (1917-89); Congressman from UP; participated in freedom movement; Secretary, UP Zamindari Abolition Committee, 1947-48; Secretary, Economic and Political Research Department, AICC, and editor of AICC Journals, 1948-57; Member, Administrative Reforms Committee, Kerala Government, 1957-58; Indian Representative on Afro-Asian Solidarity Organization at Cairo, 1958-60; Editor, *Socialist Congressman*, 1961-70; Member, Rajya Sabha, 1972-78; author of several books.

in a huff. In the course of the next ten days, we are having our Parliament meeting and there will be a debate on foreign affairs when probably great stress will be laid on our severing our relationship with the Commonwealth. I shall not accept this, of course.

The elections are proceeding and will be over in another four days. The results, though broadly in favour of the Congress, have not been as good as we had hoped for in some areas. Anyhow, we shall have to face new and difficult problems very soon.

Last evening I received your confidential cover containing a bunch of papers. I shall write to you about that separately. Probably I shall write to Ajit[3] also and send that letter to you for delivery.

Yours,
Jawahar

3. Ajit Hutheesing.

6. British Jurisdiction over Indian Nationals in Muscat[1]

I do not remember ever having had to consider this matter previously[2] and I am a little surprised that what I consider vital decisions, affecting our sovereignty, should have been disposed of by various Ministries without any reference to me. As a matter of fact, this was important enough, if necessary, for a reference to the Cabinet.

I am quite clear that we should never have agreed to put ourselves under the jurisdiction, for some purpose, of the UK Consul. I think, this is derogatory to India and very unbecoming in present circumstances.

1. Note to Secretary General and C.S. Jha, Joint Secretary, MEA, New Delhi, 25 March 1957. JN Collection.
2. This referred to the decisions made in 1948 and 1951-52 regarding legal jurisdiction of British Consular authorities over Indian nationals in Muscat. C.S. Jha wrote in a note on 20 March 1957 that it "does sound like a hang-over from our previous colonial status" and there was no reason why Indian nationals should not be subjected to the jurisdiction of the local courts. He suggested that unless there was any technical objection, this arrangement should be discontinued.

This may be examined, but whatever the result of the examination, I have no doubt that this arrangement should end and we should inform the Sultan of Muscat[3] and the UK authorities that we do not wish to continue it any longer. Please, therefore, have this examined expeditiously.

3. Said bin Taimur.

7. Message to Harold Macmillan[1]

I am grateful to you for your letter of the 6th March which was delivered to me by your High Commissioner[2] on the 19th March.

2. I told your High Commissioner that it was a little difficult for me to give a definite reply just then as the dates of the meeting of the new Parliament had not been fixed and it would not be easy for me to be away when Parliament was sitting.

3. I agree with you that the stresses and strains of the past months and the differences of opinion that emerged deserve full consideration and our meeting together would be appropriate.

4. As you know, I have valued our Commonwealth relationship and have spoken repeatedly in Parliament and elsewhere on the value of this association. We have often been criticized on this issue by political groups and individuals from different quarters. We have met these criticisms hitherto by pointing out that this relationship was not only to our common advantage but also served the larger causes which we serve and support.

5. I should tell you, however, in all frankness that there have been powerful reactions in India in regard to Commonwealth relations as a result of recent events and developments not only in the Middle East but arising also from the

1. New Delhi, 27 March 1957. JN Collection.
   Maurice Harold Macmillan (1894-1986); British politician and publisher; Conservative Minister of Housing and Local Government, 1952-54, of Defence, 1954-55; Secretary of State for Foreign Affairs, 1955; Chancellor of the Exchequer, 1955-57, Prime Minister and First Lord of the Treasury, 1957-63; Chairman, Macmillan (Holdings) since 1963; Chairman, Macmillan Company Limited, 1970-74; author of *The Middle Way, Planning for Employment, Economic Aspects of Defence*, and *Winds of Change*.
2. Malcolm MacDonald.

position taken up by some Commonwealth countries in regard to other issues in which they appear to our people to have taken sides. While we have not encouraged these public reactions and resentments, we cannot ignore them or fail to inform you about them.

6. We have continued to defend our position on this issue in Parliament and elsewhere and maintained that the relationship was in no way a derogation of our Independence and freedom in the choices and judgments each country makes and that, like all other matters, it must be considered calmly and on merits. I thought I should let you know both our difficulties and the reactions here.

7. I agree with you that an early meeting of Commonwealth Prime Ministers is desirable. It would give us, as it does you, particular pleasure to welcome the new State of Ghana as an independent State in the Commonwealth and to meet the Prime Minister of Ghana.

8. The date you have suggested, the 15th of July, presents difficulties for me. A new session of Parliament opens on that day and it would be difficult for me to be away from India just then. I would, therefore, request you to consider whether a date which enables me to return here by the 15th July would be convenient to all concerned. A date earlier in July would suit me much better and enable me to come, which I would like to do. I shall be grateful if you can consider this.

8. British Recruitment of Gurkhas in India[1]

This note makes sorry reading. It is now nine years, I suppose, when we first agreed to some kind of facilities being offered to British recruitment of Gurkhas.[2] Even then, I think, I made it clear that this was temporary. About five years ago, we decided to terminate those temporary facilities,[3] and still we are more or less

1. Note to Foreign Secretary, New Delhi, 9 April 1957. JN Collection.
2. A tripartite agreement on recruitment of Gurkhas was concluded between the United Kingdom, India and Nepal on 8 August 1947. Accordingly, the existing Gurkha regiments were divided, four were allotted to Britain and six to India. See also *Selected Works* (second series), Vol. 1, p. 431.
3. On 25 August 1952, the Government of India informed the British and the Nepalese Governments of its intention to discontinue the existing arrangements. See also *Selected Works* (second series), Vol. 20, p. 485.

where we were then. I think, this is very unfair of the UK Government authorities. It is all very well to say about their difficulties. They cannot go on sitting in our territory year after year because of some local difficulty in construction. One thing is quite certain in my mind, and that is we cannot wait for another two years. I cannot understand why they are unable to make some temporary arrangements. I think, we should continue to pursue this matter. On our part, we have been rather dilatory and allowed things to remain where they were.

IX. POLAND

1. India and Poland[1]

The visit of the Prime Minister of Poland, Mr Josef Cyrankiewicz,[2] to India is a notable event for both our countries and we are greatly looking forward to it. At any time such a visit would have been welcome. At the present time it is even more so because of various developments that have taken place in Europe and the world in some of which Poland has played an important part.

We in India are working hard to raise the level of our people. In doing so we have adhered to the methods of democracy and individual freedom. We have also tried to develop towards socialism on lines which are suited to our conditions and the genius of our people. We have felt that only thus can we build up an enduring structure which will give full play to the creative ability of our people.

I am sure that the visit of the Prime Minister of Poland will be of mutual advantage not only in promoting better understanding between the two countries and promoting closer association, but also in our learning much from the experience of Poland.

1. Message to the Polish weekly, *World and Poland*, New Delhi, 9 March 1957. JN Collection.
2. The Prime Minister of Poland was in India from 24 March to 3 April 1957.

545

2. Indo-Polish Relations[1]

Prime Minister, Excellencies, Ladies and Gentlemen,

Two years ago I visited your country,[2] Sir, and I carried with me various recollections of the warm friendship and cordiality which I felt everywhere there. I also carried with me many memories, some pleasant, some unpleasant. The unpleasant memories were of the concentration camps, the old concentration camps that I visited, and more particularly those chambers of horror where large numbers of people were done to death in the early days of War. The pleasant memories were many, the exhilarating sight of the great city of Warsaw and other places which had been reduced almost to shambles, built up and the vitality I found everywhere. Today, that you are here, Sir, and your wife, I am very happy and indeed all of us are happy that you have returned this visit and you will have noticed already even in your brief stay here how welcome you are and what the feelings of the Indian people are towards you and your country. When I went to Poland I found much that was akin to us, if I may say so, and I found some other things which were somewhat different, but we have been brought up to believe that it is the function and business of each people in each country to develop according to their own genius. And it is our endeavour always to lay stress on the many common points, rather than on points of difference. Ultimately, the points of difference are relatively few and the common points are always more. It is unfortunate that sometimes the differences between nations are stressed much more than the numerous common points not only of humanity, but of many other things that modern life gives us. Anyhow, I felt, if I may say so, very much at home in Poland because of the many common things and the ways that we found there.

You have, your country, Sir, adopted a path of socialism and you worked hard for it. In our own way, which is somewhat different, we also made socialism our ideal and we worked for it in our own way and in keeping with our past struggle of freedom and the ideals that we held then. There may be differences in approach, in ways of achieving but I believe that those differences too will gradually lessen in the world if the world is given the chance to lessen them. And we believe in India in a certain democratic structure, in our politics and in our Constitution,

1. Speech at a State banquet given in honour of Josef Cyrankiewicz, the Prime Minister of Poland, New Delhi, 25 March 1957. JN Supplementary Papers, NMML. Also available in External Affairs (PIB) files.
2. Nehru arrived at Warsaw on 23 June 1955 and had talks with Polish leaders on 24 June. See also *Selected Works* (second series), Vol. 29, pp. 232-237.

we believe in individual freedom which is very precious to us and we believe, above all, in raising our people and giving them higher standards. Many of these things, I am sure, your country also believes and works for it. We were very happy to notice various powerful urges which I have no doubt have their roots in Polish history and the great struggles for freedom for which Poland is famous. I was happy to see those urges taking shape in Poland, creating no doubt grave difficulties as all such urges do. But your country, Sir, and the leaders of your country faced these difficult problems with the courage which we admired and respected, and I am quite sure that they will overcome other difficulties that come their way because not only of your great past, but the great vitality of your people.

I am happy that you have come here with Madame and with your other colleagues because that will bring to me, not to me only, but to large numbers of people in this country, a closer idea and conception of Poland and her people and thus encourage our close and cordial relationships. I do believe that this relationship can be of great advantage to both our countries and to another thing which is dear to you and your country and dear to us in our country, and that is, the cause of peace which is of such vital importance today.

So, we welcome you and Madame Cyrankiewicz cordially and I ask you, Your Excellencies, Ladies and Gentlemen, to drink to the health of the Prime Minister of Poland and Madame and to the welfare of the Polish people.

X. OTHER COUNTRIES

1. Direct Air Services between Delhi and Moscow[1]

As consultations and discussions are taking place on this matter, we should await the result of them.

2. It seems to me that some time or other, we shall have to come to an agreement with the Soviet Union about direct flights from India to Moscow.[2] To go to

1. Note to Communications Ministry, New Delhi, 27 February 1957. JN Collection.
2. Negotiations for establishment of air services between Delhi and Moscow started in September 1956 when the Soviet Ambassador made a proposal for an air transport agreement.

547

Moscow from India via Prague is obviously a round about and much more expensive route. Also, I think, there is some advantage in going through Central Asia, Tashkent etc. I should like some contacts to develop between Central Asia and India.

3. The Soviet Union have suggested a route via Chinese Turkistan, obviously to avoid overflying Pakistan. Normally, we can have no objection to this. The difficulty, of course for us, is that we have not got suitable aircraft for flying over the high altitudes involved in this route.

4. I suppose that in the event of an agreement being arrived at, the service would not be very frequent. It might be once a fortnight or, perhaps, once a week.

2. Indian Experts for Ethiopia[1]

We should certainly help the Ethiopian Government and give them the experts they require if we can find them or spare them. But the list they have supplied is a formidable one, and I doubt if we can send them all these men.[2]

2. There is no question of our being worried about criticisms from other countries to the effect that India was penetrating into Ethiopia through technical experts. I do not know how the Emperor got this idea.

1. Note to Commonwealth Secretary, New Delhi, 19 March 1957. File No. 17-17/57, AFR-1, p.6/Note, MEA.
2. The Ethiopian Government had requested for qualified and experienced Indian specialists for various spheres of social and economic life. Their list included personnel for almost all the Ministries.

3. To K.M. Panikkar[1]

New Delhi
30 March 1957

My dear Panikkar,[2]

I have received today your letter of March 26[3] and the note attached.[4] Also the book *Contre la torture.*[5] I have read occasional reference in newspapers and periodicals about horrible methods practised by the French Army in Algeria. Cairo, of course, talks about this all the time. But one does not always take Cairo statements as gospel truth. The note you have sent gives a more connected idea not only of what is happening in Algeria but of reactions in France. This is, of course, important and I am glad you have sent this. I shall read the book.

Yours sincerely,
Jawaharlal Nehru

1. JN Collection.
2. India's Ambassador in Paris.
3. Panikkar wrote that a very grave crisis of conscience had been developing in France as a result of emerging evidence of large-scale torture and other Nazi methods of dealing with civilian population in Algeria.
4. Panikkar wrote that the note (not available) would give a general idea of what had been happening, of the evidence of this strange reversal to the extremes of Nazism among certain circles of the French Army.
5. *Contre la torture*, written by Pierre-Henri Simon, had been to a large extent responsible for the shaking up of public opinion. For the first time, it posed moral issues very clearly before the French public. Panikkar wrote that something similar to the Dreyfus agitation was developing in France.

4. Indian Repatriates from Sri Lanka[1]

Thanu Pillai, an MP from South India, who is very much interested in the Indian question in Ceylon, came to see me the other day. He said that 50,000 Indians had already been sent back from Ceylon and were round about his district in South India. Many of them were in considerable difficulties. He recognized that it was not possible for us to say that we could help these people. Nevertheless, he asked me if something could be done. He was not thinking, I think, in terms of money doles but rather of some more permanent type of assistance or opportunities for employment. I do not know what we can do about it, but I thought I might draw your attention to this.

1. Note to Commonwealth Secretary, New Delhi, 2 April 1957. JN Collection.

5. Indian Business Ventures in Nepal[1]

The papers that Shri G.D. Birla has sent should be examined by the Finance Minister and also the External Affairs Ministry.[2] So far as we are concerned, it is the third proposal that we have to consider, that is, that one of the Birla concerns should open a branch in Nepal, starting with a textile mill and later a cement

1. Note, Flagstaff House, Chakrata, 27 April 1957. JN Collection.
2. G.D. Birla had enclosed a letter from his son, Basant Kumar Birla, who visited Nepal in April at the invitation of the King to discuss the prospects of starting industries there. The Nepal Government promised to give facilities such as exemption from Income-tax, reasonable Excise duty, nominal cost of land and water etc. Three proposals emerged from these discussions: (i) the Nepal Government to hold 51% of the capital in the new project and 49% capital to be held by the Birlas; (ii) the project to be started under the proprietorship of one of existing Birla concerns and Nepal Government to give 50% of the finances as loan and/or debentures; (iii) the project to be under one of existing Birla concerns, but 50% finances to be arranged by the Government of India as loan and/or debentures. B.K. Birla also wrote that the third proposal had the maximum chances of success, and the Indian Ambassador in Kathmandu, Bhagwan Sahay, had agreed to recommend this.

factory and perhaps also a sugar mill, fifty per cent of the capital for this branch concern to be arranged by the Government of India in the form of loan or debentures.

2. Our Ambassador in Nepal has apparently sponsored this proposal and has given the impression that the Government of India are likely to agree to it. I do not understand what grounds our Ambassador had for giving this kind of an assurance. I should imagine that, in view of our financial stringency it will be exceedingly difficult, and indeed hardly possible, for us to find money for such a venture, when we are cutting down our expenditure in regard to our approved projects under the Second Five Year Plan. However, this is a matter for the Finance Minister to consider.

3. It is also not at all clear to me why the Nepal Government should object, on political grounds, to proposal No. 2, which was put forward by the Birlas, and be prepared to accept proposal No. 3. The political objections they have raised to proposal No. 2 apparently are that it will be criticized in Nepal as the profits will go to India. This objection applies equally to proposal No. 3.

4. Apart from this, the Government of India being directly associated with a venture in Nepal has greater political significance than if a private industrialist did so. The only advantage that the Nepal Government has in proposal No. 3 is that they are not asked to put in money, and all the necessary finances are supposed to come either from the Birlas or the Government of India. In fact, the whole concern will be completely in the hands of Birlas except for a loan which the Government of India give.

5. I have merely indicated some of my immediate reactions. The Finance Minister may be requested to consider this matter and advise us. External Affairs Ministry also should consider this.

1. To Ralph C. Epstein[1]

Camp: Lake View Guest House
Hyderabad
22 February 1957

Dear Mr Epstein,[2]

Thank you for your letter of February 15, 1957, which I have just received.

I remember well meeting you, but I have no clear recollection of the conversation we had. I, therefore, can only tell you how I feel now and not what I might have said then, though probably there would be no difference between the two. I do not know much about the proposed Atlantic Union except what you have said in your letter, that is, a Union of democratic countries for economic purposes and possibly political also. I cannot object to any such union of independent countries, if they choose to bring it about. The test I would apply would be its effect on the world situation. Would it tend towards a lessening of world tensions and thus make the path to peace easier, or with it add to those tensions? It is difficult for me to give an answer to these questions, as they have to be considered in the context of so many other events. A political union would presumably have its military aspects. In fact it would be an extension of the NATO alliance to include, apart from its military character, a close political association also. That would naturally have certain consequences which may not have far-reaching effects on world tensions.

In effect, this means that such a union should be considered in the context of international events. If it follows as a result of a lessening of tensions, then it may be a good thing. If, however, it is superimposed on a "cold war", then it may have the opposite effect. At the present moment, we are unfortunately facing

1. JN Collection.
2. Ralph C. Epstein (d. 1959); joined as Professor of Economics, University of Buffalo, 1926; Dean of the School of Business Administration, 1935-47; Chairman of the Economics department for over twenty-five years; member, American Economic Association and National Bureau of Economic Research; Fellow, Royal Economic Society of England; author of several books and articles.

a revival of the old cold war in its acutest form. I should think that it would be desirable to take some effective steps to reduce this tension and cold war and then proceed with other forms of organization.

Economic unions stand on a different footing. Indeed we see some kind of an economic union developing in the countries of Western Europe, excluding the United Kingdom. There are, I believe, many people in France, Italy, Belgium and Holland who would welcome a closer union, including Germany. Probably, however, Western Germany is not so keen on this because it may come in the way of the reunification of Germany which it desires so much. Thus this question is related to the reunification in Germany, which is closely connected with a lessening of tensions and some kind of understanding between the present rival blocs of countries.

I suppose ultimately there is bound to be a movement towards a closer economic and perhaps political association of groups of countries. Apart from powerful countries, the others feel weak by themselves. France, though weak, lives in hopes of developing the Sahara and thus becoming much more powerful. But for this purpose it requires the help of others.

There might also be an apprehension in the minds of some Asian countries that a powerful European or Atlantic Union might come in the way of their own development and might also delay the coming of independence of some colonial territories at present under the control of some European countries.

These are some odd thoughts which occurred to me. They are perhaps not helpful. But then the world situation is very far from helpful or clear.

Yours sincerely,
Jawaharlal Nehru

2. Separate Identity of Pondicherry[1]

I have made it clear on many occasions that we do not propose to merge Pondicherry in any of the neighbouring States and that it will maintain its separate identity. I said this only a few days ago when I was in the South. This was partly in relation to Goa also. What I have stressed is that it is entirely for the people of Pondicherry in future to decide about this matter. When occasion arises, I shall again make this clear. The Chief Commissioner[2] can do so on his own part, both informally and formally, on suitable occasions.

2. Today's newspaper says something about a Committee of the French Chamber not accepting our draft Treaty on the ground that the French nationals have not been adequately protected.[3] All this delay is unfortunate, but I do not know what we can do about it.

3. I agree that the question of fines referred to in paragraph 10 should be dealt with with greater expedition.[4] Whatever the French law may be on the subject, I do not see any difficulty in stopping immediately the levy of any outstanding fine. Further, surely even refunds can be granted by executive action.

4. I think, it is important that officers sent to Pondicherry should learn French. Also, we need not confine our recruitment to Madras State.

1. Note to Secretary General, Foreign Secretary and Azim Husain, Joint Secretary, New Delhi, 3 March 1957. JN Collection.
2. M.K. Kirpalani.
3. The French Union Assembly, an advisory body of elected representatives from France and her overseas territories, voted against ratification of the Indo-French treaty of 28 May 1956 on the cession of the French settlements of Pondicherry, Karaikal, Mahe and Yanam to India by 88 votes to 44 on 1 March 1957 on grounds of inadequate safeguards and guarantees to French subjects and interests.
4. A note by M.K. Kirpalani to Azim Husain, Joint Secretary, MEA, mentioned that fines imposed in political cases continued to be collected because under the French law there was no provision for writing them off. Kirpalani had advised suspension of further collection of fines in cases where no violence was committed. He also wrote that some way had to be found to write off the fines in consultation with the French authorities.

3. A Commonwealth of Afro-Asian Countries[1]

The proposed resolution is wholly impracticable and a discussion on it will not only yield no result, but might lead to some misunderstanding among other countries. It hardly seems to me proper for Parliament to consider the establishment of special relations with Afro-Asian countries. This may not only embarrass the Government of India, but also the other countries concerned.

2. The Bandung Conference was an attempt to bring these countries together, and it was a success, in so far as it went, because it dealt with broad principles. But even there it was clear that there were rifts. Subsequently, these cleavages have widened. There are some countries closely attached to military alliances with Western Powers. Other countries are not so attached. Then there is the third group which might be said to be mid-way and, though not attached, inclines in some direction. Because of these difficulties, even a proposal to hold a second Bandung Conference has not been considered as suitable at this stage. To talk about a Commonwealth of Afro-Asian countries goes much further, and is thus completely impracticable. In the present stage of the development of the cold war, which has extended to Asia, a discussion on this resolution would be unwise.

3. The above note may be communicated to the honourable Speaker.

1. Note to Joint Secretary (W), New Delhi, 9 March 1957. JN Collection.

4. To Norman Cousins[1]

New Delhi
16 March 1957

My dear Norman Cousins,

Thank you for your letter of the 4th March, 1957.[2] I have read with great interest your article in *The Saturday Review*,[3] which you sent me.

I am not, I think, a pessimist. Indeed, I do not think that any person can function effectively if he has no hope for the future. I have hope both for the world and for my own country, India, which I seek to serve. And yet, as I indicated to you in my previous letter, I have a feeling of depression growing within me, a feeling that the good things of the world are gradually being pushed out, that some slow disintegration is taking place in the collective mind of man in spite of the great advances that we see.[4]

You refer in your article to this new possibility of our present generation having the power to put an end to everything that history has achieved. That is a terrible thought. What is worse, I think, is a creeping sickness of humanity which gradually leads it to this final destruction. Ultimately, this is of the mind, as I think the UNESCO Constitution says. Wars begin in the minds of men. In spite of the patent fact that a nuclear war may well end everything that humanity stands for, most people take preparations for it for granted, even though they wish to avoid it. Why do they do it? We go back to this all pervading fear, which appears to them to make it incumbent on them not to be left behind in the race for the latest type of death-dealing machinery. The whole approach is patently illogical, and yet there appears to be no escape from it.

1. JN Collection.
2. Editor of *The Saturday Review* and Co-Chairman, National Committee for a Sane Nuclear Policy, 1957-63, Norman Cousins wrote about the possibility of Albert Schweitzwer, who was awarded Nobel Peace Prize in 1952, making an appeal from Oslo for world peace. He appreciated Eisenhower's October 31, 1956 statement calling for withdrawal of invading powers in Egypt. He said that it was unfortunate that in the last American Presidential campaign the question of hydrogen bomb testing became a political issue.
3. In an editorial, titled "Think of a Man" in the issue of 4 August 1956, Norman Cousins expressed his concerns about the dangers of nuclear explosions. He spoke about the power to protect the great works and ideas of all past ages or shatter them beyond recognition or expunge them. He advocated that all states take the pledge "to take no measure in the cause of our own protection that will jeopardize the safety of the world community."
4. For Nehru's letter of 19 February to Norman Cousins, see *Selected Works* (second series), Vol. 36, pp. 468-471.

Essentially, the problem becomes one of psychology or of some kind of moral or ethical approach.

Politicians, however good they may be, do not frame their policies on this basis, even though they talk a great deal about morality. An individual might and does sometimes rise to high levels. But the mass thinks chiefly in terms of self-preservation and is much more prone to fear and anger and violence. Even the great advance of education has not got rid of these ever-present dangers, so far as the mass mind is concerned. Fear feeds upon fear, as violence feeds upon violence.

Oddly enough, in a democratic society, while the dangers of any sudden and terrible action are limited, the leader's ability to control the mass is also limited. There may be occasional exceptions for limited periods.

Any political leader has to function under these limitations. Occasionally, he may override them. But, we seldom have a single leader with that power. So, a leader must not only feel what is right, but has also to convince masses of people about it. Thus, he tends to compromise or else he would cease to be the leader. The only example in current history that I know of a leader who refused to compromise with what he thought was right, is Gandhi, and Gandhi was assassinated in the end, as prophets often are. He was a rare combination of a political leader who had something of the prophetic instinct in him.

I suppose the approach to the great problem of today has to be twofold. There should be the moral approach or the prophet's, and there has to be the political leader's approach. The latter should be in tune with the former, though it may not go that far. At any rate, every step taken, however short it may be, should be towards that moral goal preached by the prophet. It depends on the leader and the circumstances he has to face, as to how big the step he takes is. But, in any event, he should not go back or take a step in a wrong direction. It is not feasible to ask the leader to take a step which he cannot give effect to, because public opinion is not ripe for it. In educating public opinion, both the prophet and the leader have to help in their respective ways.

All this is very well. But, time is short, and disaster hangs over us. Two Great Wars have brutalised humanity and made them think more and more in terms of violence. What progress, scientific and cultural, and in human values, that we have made, is somehow twisted to the needs of violence. I think that the major disservice that Marxism and communism have done to the world, is the encouragement of violence to achieve political or economic ends. But, of course, it is not Marxism alone that has done this. Fascism was, I think, even worse in this respect because it did not have the ideological element of communism. But, apart from communism and fascism, there is quite enough of this violent approach to problems even by others. I know that, the world being what it is, it is not

557

possible to do away with some violence or coercion. At the same time, I have become more and more convinced that the way of violence and hatred is not the way of solving any problem. That is why, I think, that the "cold war" is something that is essentially bad, whatever the reasons of expedience that might be advanced for it. It takes us in a wrong direction.

Taking a practical view of things as they are, we see these two very powerful countries, the USA and the USSR, opposed to each other. Regardless of right or wrong, although we cannot, of course, ignore them, it seems obvious to me that the cold war only aggravates their conflicts and spreads fear more and more. Some other approach other than that of cold war has to be found, some approach other than that of military alliances.

As a politician, I cannot suggest, as Gandhi might have done, that a country should be brave enough to do away with armed forces for its defence. I recognise the inevitability at present of providing for defence and not leaving a vacuum which might tempt an evil-doer. Even so, I do not understand how defence is helped by the tactics of cold war or by the propagation of hatred and fear. It should be possible to take adequate steps for defence and yet seek for a removal of tensions and a friendly atmosphere in the world. After all, the great masses of people everywhere want that friendly atmosphere and to avoid all horror of war.

This leads one to the question of disarmament. Again, it is not feasible to talk about this in absolute terms. But, there may be progressive steps, the main value of each step being a lessening of fear. Disarmament must inevitably take into consideration nuclear weapons. What can we do about them? I would suggest that two things can be done. One is stopping any further experiments, the other is stopping any further production of atomic or hydrogen bombs. This may be difficult now, but it is going to be much more difficult in the future, when a number of countries can produce them. At present, there are apparently only three, the USA, the USSR and the UK. Within a few years, it is likely that the process will become simpler, though the products will remain equally terrible, and a number of other countries might be able to make these bombs. Thus, delay in taking an effective step, makes the position increasingly more difficult.

In regard to experimental explosions, I am convinced that these are a crime against humanity. I have received, as others have, appeals from various organizations in Japan protesting against the proposed British experimental explosion.[5] As you point out in your article, nobody knows definitely what harm these explosions do. But, we do know that they do harm, and harm in a very vital way, which may do infinite injury in the long run to large numbers of

5. For protests against proposed British experimental explosions, see *ante*, p. 462 fn 10.

persons. If that is so, then it is surely a crime to continue them, and the least that we can do, is to try to stop these experiments.

The rival powers or groups of powers are such today that neither of them can think of defeating the other without being largely destroyed itself. If that is so, then one has to accept a policy of tolerance of each other, of live and let live, and hope that the new atmosphere that is created, may lead to a progressive lessening of tensions and fear. This, again, might and should lead to a lessening of the coercive apparatus of the State in authoritarian countries, that is greater individual freedom. We shall not get that individual freedom in these States by threatening them. In fact, this policy of threats will inevitably result in a continuation of coercion and deprivation of freedom.

Instead of military pacts aimed against each other, one would imagine that a more sensible way would be for pacts between rival powers, something in the nature of the old Locarno Treaty between Germany and the other Western countries. It is true that the Locarno Treaty did not bring peace, and Hitler came. That was not the fault of Locarno, and other circumstances prevailed. Anyhow, I see no other way except that there must be an agreement on the basis of live and let live, and that this should be backed by the United Nations. If any country breaks that agreement, then presumably the other countries will pull it back or deal with it. I know that no agreement is foolproof, and it is very difficult to trust some countries. Nevertheless, the position created by this mutual bond backed by the UN cannot possibly be worse than what we have today, and it will surely lessen tensions and fear, which will then enable the world to look at the problem in a more reasonable way.

If such an approach is made, it might be easier to solve the question of German unification, which is so vital not only to Europe, but also to the world. I do not think this reunification of Germany can be brought about by cold war methods, and presumably we rule out war for the purpose, which will mean destruction of everybody.

I hope you will forgive this jumble of odd ideas which I have placed before you. I have indulged in some loud thinking. Coming back, however, to your letter, I entirely agree that Oslo will be the right and appropriate place for an appeal by Dr Schweitzer, and it would certainly add to the value of that appeal for peace if it was made under the auspices of the Nobel Committee.

I agree with you that President Eisenhower is the one great political leader who has it in him to take an effective step. Naturally, any step that he takes, cannot be taken in repudiation of the policies he has so firmly announced in the past. But, there are many ways of doing it which can avoid that difficulty. I am sure that if he did it, there would be a mass approval all over the world of such a brave step, and very few persons will sit down to argue as to how far it was in consonance with something else. Dr Schweitzer might well approach him in this matter. Perhaps, the right time would be after his appeal from Oslo.

I am afraid I have written to you rather a long letter. I had not intended doing so. But, my mind ran away with me.

Yours sincerely,
Jawaharlal Nehru

5. US Foreign Aid Policy[1]

I am sending you a copy of a letter which Nelson Rockefeller is supposed to have written to President Eisenhower. This was published in a German newspaper and has been reproduced in the *Pakistan Times*.[2]

I have little doubt that this letter is a genuine one. It has been commented upon in some European newspapers.

This letter cannot be said to represent precisely the policy of the State Department of the USA, but I think, it does represent the broad approach of American policy. It is interesting to see the reference in it to Iran. In this matter Rockefeller himself was directly concerned. He says that "the strengthening of our economic position in Iran has enabled us to acquire control over her entire foreign policy and in particular to make her join the Baghdad Pact."

About the neutral countries and more especially India, he says that "the essence of this policy should be that the development of our economic relations with these countries would ultimately allow us to take over key positions in the native economy."

Another interesting feature is the reference to Turkey and other like countries, where it is clearly said that too much economic aid should not be given lest those countries become too independent of US control or influence.

I think that a copy of this article should be sent to our Ambassador in Iran. Also I think to our Embassy in Washington and our High Commissioner in London and perhaps one or two other places too.

1. Note to Secretary General, New Delhi, 18 March 1957. JN Collection.
2. For details, see *ante*, p. 113.

6. Drafting of Formal Documents[1]

I agree with SG and FS that it would not be desirable to ask for any formal change in the wording of the document that has been signed. It is certainly irritating for such slips to occur in our formal documents. We should not allow ourselves in future to be hustled into signing a treaty or document. We must satisfy ourselves fully that it is in accordance with our wishes.

Our Charge d'Affaires should be asked for an explanation, as suggested.

Having said this, I would add that I do not attach any very great importance to this error having crept in. Indeed I do not know what the words "will agree" mean. If it said that "contracting parties agree", the meaning was clear. "May agree" is understandable, though I would call it unhappy wording. Presumably it simply means that "contracting parties may establish....." "may agree to establish" is certainly not choice wording.

But in any event "will agree" is totally out of place. It looks, as it presumably is, to be a bad translation of some phrases in another language.

Also I do not understand the word "Commissions" in this connection. It is a most unfortunate word and it is not clear to me what it is meant to convey. I wish that the drafting of these documents should be more carefully done. Whoever has drafted this, might have his attention drawn to these matters. Here again, possibly, we have accepted some Japanese draft without much thought.

What was meant to be ensured, I suppose, was that there should be some constant supervision and appraisal of the work being done in terms of the agreement. To that, we can have no objection, provided it is done simply and not pompously in the name of commissions. Thus, someone from the Japanese Embassy here and some one from the External Affairs or from the Education Ministry may form a small committee for this purpose.[2] Some similar committee might be formed in Tokyo.

Anyhow, I am quite clear that no attempt should be made to change the wording of the cultural treaty. Such an attempt is not necessary, but if made, it will give greater attention to these words than otherwise. All that need be done, and this should be done later, is for our new Ambassador in Tokyo[3] to discuss this matter

---

1. Note to Secretary General and Joint Secretary, New Delhi, 22 March 1957. JN Collection.
2. This was in regard to the letters exchanged between India and Japan to extend upto 30 September 1957 the privileges granted to the nationals, trade, shipping, navigation and air traffic of one country by the other on a reciprocal basis.
3. C.S. Jha.

rather informally at first with the Japanese Foreign Office and point out that there was some divergence in these various drafts and in any event the English "will agree" was not a happy phrase at all. We are, however, perfectly prepared to have some simple machinery in Delhi and Tokyo for watching the implementation of the agreement. This might be done with the Japanese Ambassador[4] here also.

4. Seijiro Yoshizawa.

7. To Lord Mountbatten[1]

New Delhi
2 April 1957

My dear Dickie,

Your letter of the 15th March was handed over to me by Malcolm MacDonald.[2] Thank you for it. From all accounts, Malcolm did a good piece of work in England. This as well as other factors have, I believe, produced some considerable difference in the viewpoints of many people in England.

Our elections are over, and we have a very big majority in Parliament as also in most of the States. But these elections have distressed me greatly. This is not because of Kerala where a Communist government has been put up. I do not like that, of course, but I do not worry. What troubles me much more is what has happened in Maharashtra and part of Gujarat as well as elsewhere. In Maharashtra, there was a wave of bitter hatred and violence, on the linguistic provinces issue. This hatred has seeped down to women and children even in the villages. I am anxious about the future there.

Also, there have been many signs of disruptive tendencies growing. There is communalism both among the Hindus and the Muslims, there is caste and there is this provincialism.

I am very tired after all this election business. And now, we have to face a different type of problem, which is even more difficult.

1. JN Collection.
2. see *ante*, p. 108.

WITH H.C. HANSEN, THE PRIME MINISTER OF DENMARK,
NEW DELHI, 8 MARCH 1957

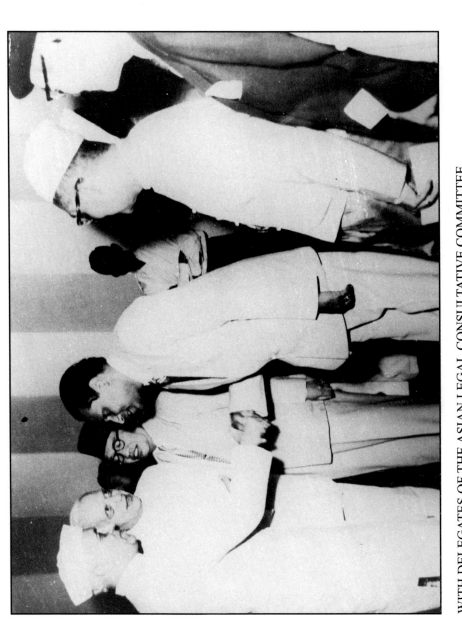

WITH DELEGATES OF THE ASIAN LEGAL CONSULTATIVE COMMITTEE, NEW DELHI, 8 APRIL 1957

Quite apart from India, I feel distressed at what is happening in the rest of the world, which includes both the UK and France. The recent revelations about the French torture in Algeria have been very bad.[3] Also, the stories coming from France, apparently based on official papers, about the French collusion with Israel before Israel started the invasion of Egypt. From these papers, it would appear that the UK Government was not ignorant of this and was at least partly involved.

The cold war is again at its height and any kind of real peace is as far as ever. Sometimes, I feel inclined to believe what H.G. Wells wrote: that there was some kind of disintegration going on in the world. Our standards fall and disruptive tendencies and hatred increase.

Pakistan is receiving continuously aid from the United States in the shape of latest type of fighter and bomber aircraft as well as other military equipment. They have already got a very large number, and not only in numbers but in quality are in many ways superior to us. You can well imagine how much concern this causes us. Obviously, we cannot compete with the United States. We have spent already far more than we can afford, on purchases of aircraft and other equipment, and this has been at the cost of our development schemes. I suppose this is what the United States calls ensuring security.

Meanwhile, Pakistan disintegrates also at a rapid pace, both in the West and in the East, politically and economically. Therein lies the danger of military adventures.

Nye Bevan is here. He spent some days in our Community Projects and came back greatly impressed. He came back also full of mosquito bites, which pained him considerably, and a violent upset inside him. He was foolish enough to eat all kinds of food in the villages. He was in quite a bad way yesterday and felt very miserable. But, he has got over it today. He is going to Bhakra-Nangal and Chandigarh and, later, to Kashmir for three days.

Yours sincerely,
Jawaharlal Nehru

3. See *ante*, p. 549.

8. Relics and Sketches of Tipu Sultan[1]

I am surprised to see these papers and to find that this matter has been hung up so that somebody's sanction might be obtained for the expenditure of £ 45/-.[2]

2. Apart from this particular matter, there is another connected with it, about which I sent a note either to SG, FS or CS. This was in regard to a large number of sketches of Tipu Sultan and others which we had received from the Duke of Wellington. I do not know what has happened to that note.

3. When I was in London some months ago, I left instructions that these relics of Tipu Sultan as well as those sketches should be sent to the Victoria and Albert Museum for renovation or restoration, whatever it is called. In fact, I went to the Museum myself and saw the head of the Indian section and spoke to him about it. Now, I am told many months after that this matter has been hung up and awaits some petty sanction. Surely this is the limit of red tape and delay. Apart from everything else it does not enhance the reputation of the Prime Minister who had personally dealt with this question.

4. I had told our High Commissioner that she should ask for an estimate because I did not want some fantastic sum to be thrown at me later. If, however, the estimate was more or less reasonable, it should be accepted.

5. Please send a telegram to our High Commissioner to go ahead with this matter immediately. Ask her as to what has happened to the several volumes of sketches of Tipu Sultan and others which the Duke of Wellington had given us. These were also to be put in proper shape by the Victoria and Albert Museum. They are very valuable.

6. Please do not wait for any sanction. If necessary, I shall pay for the renovation myself. Inform the Education Ministry of the steps you are taking.

7. These relics and sketches have nothing to do with the Education Ministry.

---

1. Note to Foreign Secretary, New Delhi, 6 April 1957. File No. 18-100/56-U.K., p. 19/Note, MEA.
2. This money was required for restoration of some relics of Tipu Sultan. These relics were obtained in exchange of two portraits of Duke of Wellington.

9. Legal Aspects of International Problems[1]

Chief Justice,[2] Attorney-General[3] and distinguished delegates,
I feel somewhat oppressed by the weight of learning represented here by the delegates to this conference.[4] I do not know that in the particular domain that you have come here to represent, and to discuss, I can say anything of value. I am really here to welcome you and to express my happiness that this conference of the Asian Legal Consultative Committee has met here for the first time and to express the hope that this meeting will, as the Attorney-General has said, lead not only to the clarification of many problems which affect us but also to closer bonds between the nations of Asia and Africa. That of course does not mean that those bonds will be limited to them because I do not think the nations of Asia and Africa want in any sense to function separately from the rest of the world. Nevertheless, it is a fact that in many matters and in matters connected with international law, probably the opinions and views of Asian nations have been given little importance in the past. Mr Attorney-General, you referred to the beginnings of international law, Hugo Grotius[5] and all that happened afterwards and pointed out that this international law was largely confined to a certain group of nations in Europe and represented their particular groupings and their views and their development. Asian and African countries did not come into the picture at all. Well, these Asian and African countries have now come into the picture in many ways, politically and otherwise, but still I believe that there is this tendency in considering these wider aspects of international law, rather to adhere to the old concept of a European family of nations, extending itself, if you like, to other countries. It extended itself in the last century or two in the form of dominating countries of Asia and Africa or many of them. Now, many of these countries are free but the old concept, I think, still governs the minds of many people, and it is desirable and indeed very necessary that lawyers and

1. Speech at the inauguration of Asian Legal Consultative Committee, New Delhi, 18 April 1957. AIR tapes, NMML. Also available in PIB files.
2. S.R. Das.
3. M.C. Setalvad.
4. This was the first session of the Asian Legal Consultative Committee of the representatives of Japan, India, Myanmar, Sri Lanka, Indonesia, Iraq and Syria.
5. (1583-1645); Dutch legal scholar and statesman, whose writings laid the basis for modern ideas about international law; his books include *Commentary on the law of Prize and Booty, Defence of the Lawful Government of Holland, Concerning the Law of War and Peace*.

jurists of Asia and Africa should look at this problem from their own point of view.

I do not myself quite understand a phrase that the Attorney-General used or rather he quoted the distinguished judge, Alvarez, I think, was his name about an Asian international law, some such phrase. I do not quite understand what an Asian international law or any other international law confined to a continent or a few countries might be. If it is international law, well it covers the world. But I can certainly understand that the concept of international law, as it has grown up, may have lost and never had, if I may say so, an international character which was confined to a group of European nations. Now, because of all kinds of developments in the world and more especially the coming into independence of a number of Asian and African countries, this aspect that is, the Asian and African aspect of it, does not form a separate part of international law, but should vary or make broader the old concept of international law.

I suppose that applies to every aspect of international relations, certainly it applies to the political aspect. Politics of the world in the old days, in the 19th century, and in the early 20th century were always governed by some countries of Europe, and Europe was a centre of political activity. It became the centre of economic activity and the politics or the economics of the countries of Asia and Africa were largely governed from that European concept of the metropolitan powers. Naturally, we do not accept that political concept now. Even in the economic domain, we do not accept it although we may be influenced by it because of various factors but gradually even in economic theory, our countries are beginning to think on their own lines because their problems are different, and we cannot solve our problems on the basis of conditions which exist in countries differently situated. In this consideration of international law also, it does seem to me important that we should bring our knowledge and experience to bear upon a wider interpretation of concept of international law which will fit in with these countries of Asia and Africa. I think, therefore, that it is of considerable importance that this gathering has met here and what is more that it will continue to meet and give consideration to these problems that arise.

I do not know very much about international law but every person who has to dabble in public affairs inevitably comes up against it and has to deal with these problems and has to take the advice of experts in regard to them and has to fit it in with his political activities in so far as that may be necessary. But I have a vague recollection that connected with this idea of international law, various times in Europe, were concepts like the holy alliance in Europe, a certain number of countries for various reasons binding themselves together against other countries or other forces which did not fit in with their thinking. Now that, of course, comes up against the very concept of internationalism. Today, we see certain tendencies and something more than tendencies of the revival of holy alliances, they are not called by that name that is a certain groups of nations functioning more or less on the basis of the 19th century holy alliances, and considering themselves more or less the centre of the world in which other countries should fit in. Now that may have some justification from some point of view, but it does put other countries in an odd and embarrassing position. Either one joins the holy alliance or one is outside the pale of international law, in a sense. Therefore, it has become very important both in the context of development of Asian and African countries as independent nations and in this return to the holy alliance idea, this mater should be considered in this wider concept—really international concept.

Take again the United Nations. I think, it was supposed to be an international organization inclusive of all independent nations of the world. There is a tendency to consider it also as something less than that, a tendency, I suppose, emanating from the holy alliance idea which has not been put in practice completely, but it has affected other problems. Individuals, usually politicians, argue about them. What the politicians and the statesmen say is always coloured by their political approach to a problem and so we do not get what might be called a scholarly objective approach or we get one side of the picture, that is to say, a non-Asian or non-African side generally. Now, I respect that side, the scholars of that side, I am not criticising them, but it is possible and conceivable that their approach might not bear in mind some aspects which would be obvious to the Asian scholars and jurists. Therefore, again, it becomes desirable and necessary that this aspect should be considered objectively and in a scholarly manner by eminent lawyers and jurists of Asia and Africa and the necessity for this gathering becomes obvious.

We hear now many words and phrases being used which have had a certain dictionary meaning and significance, but in the hands of politicians, that is the people of my tribe, they are used in all kinds of ways. We used to know what, let us say, 'belligerency' was. Belligerency, I believe, is defined as waging a regular and recognised war, it must be regular and it must be recognised, otherwise, I suppose, it is guerilla tactics which is not belligerency. I suppose everybody agrees with that and in so far as States or rulers are concerned, the opposite of belligerency was neutrality, that is, not doing that, or not siding with a power which is belligerent or which is waging an active and recognised war. Yet, delegates here must know how vaguely the word 'neutrality' or 'neutralism', as it is sometimes called, is used now. Sometimes as a term of abuse, sometimes may be not that way, but as a description of something without exactly meaning what it is. I have tried to understand this and have sometimes referred to this matter also without any person throwing light on this, because as I understood those terms, belligerency and neutrality, in relation to states, they referred to a state of war or to countries not joining a war which is taking place between other countries or states. But as everyone knows, these words are used without active war. If a country is supposed to be neutral today, I do not like the word in that sense but if it is then presumably some other country which is not neutral should be described as belligerent. It seems to follow and yet that would be a wrong description of course, because the other country is not engaged in regular recognised warfare.

So, some kind of intermediate stage has developed. I do not quite know how international law or the jurists of repute would consider it or define it something that is called cold war which presumably is some kind of suspended belligerency. Now, all these developments create problems for politicians and statesmen. I do not suppose that juristic definitions will get rid of the problems. Nevertheless, they might clear the air a little and I would hope that an eminent body of scholars and jurists would try to throw light on these terms so that at least our thinking may become straight, the politicians' thinking may become straight. So, we find today a return, to some extent, to the idea of the old holy alliance backed by military pacts and alliances and economic measures also, and not one but more than one holy alliance and behind which lies enormous danger to the world in case of war. Now, I take it that international law is meant, well, primarily to prevent war. War is an absence of law, of international or any law. Therefore, the purpose of international law or any law is to settle problems and disputes by methods other than war. It is true that international law has not that strength behind it till now of domestic law. But the main purpose is the avoidance of war. Now, how can jurists and lawyers help? They cannot, I suppose, directly help in political developments but at least help in clear thinking because after all, everybody, almost everybody in the wide world, I take it, does not like the idea of war, today at any rate, when it is so dangerous. Perhaps this concept of new holy alliances and this concept of cold war and this peculiar concept of neutrality which is something apart from war makes us so confused in our thinking and therefore in our actions that we are unable to deal with these problems satisfactorily. I hope you will help us at least in thinking clearly so that we may not be led away by the slogans of politicians and statesmen. Now, I am not going to decry my tribe of politicians and statesmen here. They have much virtue in them. And I am not going to say that jurists and lawyers are always very successful in dealing with public affairs. They may be successful, they are in dealing with matters in their courts, in giving opinions. I think some considerable time back, there was a French writer on statecraft. While discussing lawyers and in regard to statecraft he said that in general, the training of a lawyer breeds habits and dispositions of mind which are not favourable to the practice of diplomacy.

Whether that is true or not I do not know, but there is something in it perhaps, so that the politicians obviously often go wrong. But the lawyers and the jurists in their ivory towers may be thinking correctly but may also get out of touch with what is happening around them. Therefore, some of the greatest judges have been those who have not only interpreted the law but who have adapted it to changing conditions without doing violence to it, because the world changes, the social structure changes, international relations change and it would be absurd for a problem of the middle of the 20th century being considered by some textbook maxim of the 18th century or the 19th century, when conditions were entirely different. And so great judges have adapted the law, the interpretation of the law to changing social and political structures. Naturally, they cannot change the basic law. That only a legislature can do. So, these problems arise and more especially today when most thinking and sensitive persons are greatly troubled by the course of events in the world. I am not talking about political disputes but the course, the drift which leads towards conflict, major conflict and possibly great disaster. Everybody is interested in it.

There is another aspect to this, which troubles many of us. How far some recent developments can be fitted in with any conception of international law or moral law, any developments which threaten the very existence of the human race in future, which tend to poison the atmosphere and thereby imperil all kinds of things not only in regard to mass killing but what is much more dreadful to contemplate, poisoning the atmosphere so that it may have terrible genetic and other results, and diseases which may gradually sweep through any country affecting vast masses of men. Is that justifiable by any conception of international law or moral law? Surely, this is not a matter purely to be considered by statesmen and politicians. If there is any element of moral or international law—I do not know if jurists consider the moral law—but anyhow, I suppose they have it in mind even in considering the letter of the law, whatever it may be or the conventions of international law and it may be desirable for them to consider whether these developments which are taking place from day to day and in connection with nuclear warfare or the preparation for it or the test explosions, how far they are in keeping with any conception of international or moral law. These are some considerations which affect the politician, a man who has some responsibility in public affairs. But as I said, if he expresses his opinion, it is usually considered a biased and coloured opinion because belonging to the political apparatus of a country he is biased by the policy of that country. But it may be that others like jurists and others who are in the habit of considering these problems calmly and objectively, if they considered it and gave their opinion, that would have much greater weight, just as scientists who again are presumed to think of these matters objectively and in a scientific temper of mind and, if they give an opinion, they can express that opinion perhaps with greater knowledge than others. That opinion has far greater value than the pure politicians' òpinion. So, apart from dealing with the broad development of international law and how it is affected by the world becoming something bigger than the old narrow European community, apart from considering how modern developments, as the Attorney-General said, in science and the application of science in communications and in social structures—all these things affect our ways of life, our ways in relationship, international relationships as well as individual and group relations, all these must necessarily affect the concept of international law. Apart from this, there are these immediate problems which face every sensitive human being, the problem of this return to the middle of the 20th century to the concept of the old holy alliance. This use of the word and the practice of cold war and all that follows from it and this business of great nations and small nations drifting almost against their will by the force of circumstances in a direction which can only lead to terrible disaster and all that has flowed from this tremendous discovery of atomic energy which can be used for good purposes and bad.

You have referred Mr Attorney-General, to *Panchsheel*, the five principles which have been accepted by a number of countries of Asia and some countries outside Asia too. Now, I claim no special virtue for them. They are only some simple principles I submit which, if adopted by nations as regards international relationships, would not only lead us away from war but would establish healthy relationships. What are they? It is simple really and I do not know how anyone anywhere can object to any of them, the recognition of sovereignty, non-aggression, non-interference in internal affairs because if you do not do any of these things you are interfering, you are misbehaving, a country is misbehaving. It is not acting according to, I think, what should be the real basis of international law, non-aggression, non-interference, recognition of sovereignty, mutual respect and all these leading up necessarily to peaceful coexistence. Either one accepts peaceful coexistence which means coexistence of countries which differ in their policies, because there is no point in saying that two persons who agree or two countries who agree should exist peacefully. They do. There is no point in my saying that I should be tolerant to my neighbour if he and I have no reason to differ. The question of my tolerating my neighbour, his tolerating me comes in when we differ and yet we tolerate each other and the question of peaceful coexistence, therefore, comes in only when countries differ in their policies, provided always that they do not interfere with each other, provided always they do not interfere either internally or externally. If they do, then that is a breach. Therefore, I submit that these five principles which are sometimes called *Panchsheel*, are a healthy basis for international relations and I would further say in all humility, that there is no other basis unless you accept the basis which leads to conflict which, of course, I presume is not our objective. If an attempt is to compel or coerce a country to do something against its will, to fall in line with something, well, that is surely not something which international law should encourage. That brings conflicts.

We recognise that there is great variety in this world. Are we going to produce or try to produce by some measure of force whether it is military or economic or some other, a uniformity? Perhaps it would be a good thing if there is uniformity about basic principles. But anyhow that can only develop by argument, by reason, by discussion, by conversion. Otherwise, if it develops by war, then we land ourselves in the dread state of war which I am convinced does not lead to the solution of any problems, more especially in any kind of war that might unfortunately take place in the future.

I have ventured, distinguished delegates, just to place some layman's ideas before you because these matters are not of academic interest. They are of an urgency which compel the attention of every person who thinks. And I am sure they occupy your minds too. I do not suggest, I cannot suggest, that you should find remedies for the world's ills but I do hope that you will show us some way of clear thinking which will lead to clear action.

10
MISCELLANEOUS

1. To Vijaya Lakshmi Pandit[1]

New Delhi
27 February 1957

Dear Nan,

I returned to Delhi today after a heavy tour for eight days, which took me to a large number of places in a number of States. There were big crowds, of course, everywhere and, in spite of the fatigue involved, it was exhilarating to meet these people.

You must have heard of the air mishap that I had yesterday. Throughout this tour, I have been flying in the Meghdoot, the Russian Illyushin plane, which was given to me by Bulganin and Khrushchev and which I handed over to the IAF for VIP service. This plane has been serving us for a year and a half and has done very well indeed. It is solid, easy to fly and comfortable. It is of the Dakota variety but better in every way and faster. Our Air Force pilots like it. Thus far, it had given no trouble at all. But, yesterday, something odd and very unusual happened. I was flying from Mangalore to Raipur in Madhya Pradesh, a journey of about three and a half hours. When we had gone nearly half the way, there was a little smoke from one of the engines. Very soon after, probably after some seconds, this broke out into flame, and the flames grew. I suppose that a fire in a plane spreads very rapidly because of the rush of air. Immediately, the automatic danger signal gave notice. The pilot-Captain[2] took the necessary steps, whatever they are, immediately, to stop that engine and put out the fire. He succeeded. It is possible that if he had not succeeded in the course of fifteen or twenty seconds or a little more, the fire might have reached the petrol tanks and, then, we would all have been blown into the higher atmosphere.

After the fire had been put out, the only question was how we would function with only one engine working. We found that we could fly fairly easily, though nobody could be sure how long this would last and how far we could go with one engine. We seemed to be flying quite steadily and did not lose height. The pilot at first decided to go to Hyderabad, which was about a hundred miles away. Later, he discovered that there was an unused airfield only thirty miles out. So, we went to this place, Raichur, and landed there. The landing was quite successful. I spent a couple of hours there till relief planes came and then carried on with my journey to my next stopping place. The pilot and crew behaved with

1. JN Collection.
2. Squadron Leader Reginald A. Rufus.

exemplary coolness and efficiency. A little doubt or confusion or excitement might have made all the difference. Anyhow, all this was over, and, I think, we all enjoyed our experience.[3] A PTI correspondent was travelling with me, and he thus had first-hand experience. I enclose a press cutting, giving his messages.

I am a little weary of this travelling about and anyhow the elections cannot last indefinitely. My major tours are over. I am going to Gurgaon tomorrow afternoon. This is a short journey by car. The next day, I go to Meerut also by car and come back. On the 4th, I visit Kanpur[4] and Khaga, going there by air via Allahabad. Khaga in Fatehpur is part of my constituency. There will be no more touring for me I hope for some time.

The elections are going on according to schedule. I suppose there is little doubt that the Congress will do well on the whole. But, nobody can be certain about particular seats, and the position in Kerala, Orissa and West Bengal is a little doubtful.

Yours,
Jawahar

3. After the incident, Nehru received a large number of telegrams from all over India and some from abroad. In a message through the press on 27 February, Nehru said: "These messages which continue to overwhelm me are full of affection and good wishes and I am deeply moved by them. May I, through the courtesy of the press, offer my sincere thanks to those friends and comrades who have sent these messages. It is difficult for me to acknowledge them separately and, I hope, I will be forgiven for this inability."
4. For Nehru's election speeches at Gurgaon, Meerut and Kanpur see *ante*, pp. 76-96.

2. To Rajiv Gandhi[1]

New Delhi
27 February 1957

My dear Rajiv,

If you read the newspapers, you must have learnt that I had an interesting experience yesterday in the air. Or, even if you do not read the newspapers, you may have heard about it.

I was flying from Mangalore on the West coast of India to Raipur in Madhya Pradesh. We were in the Meghdoot, the Russian Illyushin plane. We started from Mangalore at 8 o'clock in the morning. At 9.30, one of the engines gave some trouble. Some smoke came out, and then this broke out into a fire. Of course, a fire in the air is very bad because if it reaches the petrol tanks, there would be a big explosion.

Our IAF pilot immediately took action to put out the fire and stop the engine. After that, we flew with one engine. The pilot decided to land on an unused airfield at Raichur. The landing was quite a good one. We left the Meghdoot there, and another plane came to fetch me.

When an accident like this happens, some people get excited and then forget to do the right thing. Fortunately, none of the crew or passengers got excited, and the pilot and his crew were very calm and cool and did the right things. I was happy at this because it is a pleasure to see people remaining cool and calm under difficulties.

The Meghdoot has to remain now on that unused airfield at Raichur till a new engine comes for it.

Mummy is in Allahabad still and will not return to Delhi till the middle of March.

At Jabalpur this morning, I was presented with two tiger cubs. They were about two months old. I have asked the people there to send them to me here. We can keep them for some months perhaps, and then send them to the Delhi Zoo.

Yours,
Nanu

1. JN Collection. A similar letter was sent to Sanjay.

3. Disinclination to send Messages[1]

You sent me the attached letter from Ellen Roy some days ago.[2] She wants a message from me for her paper, *The Radical Humanist*.

Apart from my disinclination to send messages of this type (though sometimes I send them), it would be a little embarrassing for me to send a message specially to *The Radical Humanist*. Apart from other matters, it has been criticizing our Kashmir policy and rather supporting Pakistan in this matter. I can hardly enter into an argument with the paper on this subject and merely to commend it may well lead to misunderstandings.

You need not enter into this argument with her, but tell her politely that I shall not be able to send her a message.

1. Note to M.O. Mathai, Private Secretary, New Delhi, 27 February 1957. JN Collection.
2. Ellen Roy, wife of M.N. Roy, wrote to M.O. Mathai that the weekly paper *The Radical Humanist* was going to celebrate its twentieth anniversary in the first week of April 1957 with a special anniversary number. She enquired whether it would be proper to approach Nehru to send a message to the weekly.

4. To Shyam K. Pandit[1]

New Delhi
2 March 1957

Dear Shri Pandit,[2]

I have received today your letter of the 28th February. I have also received the typescript which you have sent.

1. File No. 9/8/57-PMS. Also available in JN Collection.
2. A resident of Jaipur.

It is not possible for me to read through all this typescript as I am wholly unable to find time for reading manuscripts. I have just rapidly glanced through it. In doing so, I have found numerous mistakes. Whether these are due to typing or something else, I do not know.

I have no objection to your publishing this collection. But you should remember that my books are supposed to be copyright, and any lengthy extract from them will probably require the permission of the original publisher. So far as I am concerned, you can have my permission. But, that may not be enough.

As I have said above, there are many mistakes even in the few pages that I looked through. Even a small mistake may sometimes affect the sense or spoil a sentence. Thus, the addition of an 'a' or a 'the' where they are not necessary, or the leaving of an 'a' or a 'the' where they are necessary, makes a difference. But, apart from this, there are many other mistakes also, which I cannot refer to here. Punctuation is also often wrong. In so far as quotations from my books are concerned, you can verify them carefully. But, where you have taken some passages from speeches in newspapers, these will require very careful editing. Newspaper reports do not always give the exact words. When the speech has been, as it often is, in Hindi, you get the newspaper translation.

Then, again, quotations should always have a reference. The book reference is, of course, enough. But, quotations from speeches have no reference except a date. That is not, as a rule, enough. Where possible, the place and occasion should be mentioned.

My book *Glimpses of World History* is sometimes referred to as *The Glimpses of World History*. This is not correct. It should be simply *Glimpses of World History*. So, also, *Autobiography* should be just that and not *An Autobiography*.

"Kamala" should be as I have given it and not "Kamla".

I imagine that somewhat shorter collection might be a little better, more especially in so far as speeches are concerned.

I have given you some ideas that strike me immediately. I am returning the typescript to you.

Yours sincerely,
Jawaharlal Nehru

P.S. I might also add that I do not like the title you propose for this collection of extracts. "Nehru's Wisdom" is pompous and not suitable at all. I would suggest some simpler title.

5. General Appeal to Students to join Bhoodan Movement not Right[1]

Please reply to this letter[2] and say that I have not seen the report of Indiraji's speech. According to the writer, she asked students not to give up their studies in order to join the Bhoodan movement. Indiraji is very much of an adult person and has her own opinions which she expresses. They may or may not be right.

2. I do not think that her expressions of opinion could have been meant to be anything against Shri Jayaprakash Narayan, much less Acharya Vinoba Bhave. Presumably, she feels that students should not leave their studies for the purpose and has said so. There are many people of that opinion.

3. So far as I am concerned, I would say that any student who feels like leaving his studies to join the Bhoodan movement should certainly do so, but any general appeal to large numbers of students to do so may lead to a great deal of frustration later. They may, in an emotional upsurge, feel like doing it and then later feel unhappy about it.

4. I do not understand what Gandhiji meant by saying that religion is politics, and I am not competent to attach any particular meaning to it. In a very wide sense, religion may be everything. In another sense, it has a limited meaning.

1. Note to Private Secretary, New Delhi, 6 March 1957. JN Collection.
2. Letter not available.

6. Tribute to B.G. Kher[1]

I have learnt with deep sorrow of the death this morning in Poona of Mr B.G. Kher.[2] Only two or three days ago I received a letter from him in which he

1. Message on B.G. Kher's death, New Delhi, 8 March 1957. From *The Hindu*, 9 March 1957.
2. B.G. Kher, who was Chief Minister of Bombay (1937-39 and 1946-52), Chairman, Official Language Commission (1955) and President, Gandhi Smarak Nidhi, died of an heart attack in Pune.

discussed the various schemes of the Gandhi Smarak Nidhi of which he was the President and in whose activities he was deeply interested.

Balasaheb Kher was one of the great men in India of our generation, a man of the highest integrity and devotion to the cause of India and the Indian people. In the struggle for freedom as also in the high offices he occupied since Independence came, he was a tower of strength and he gave quality to whatever he did. The whole of India suffers from this loss which is all the greater for those who were privileged to work with him as comrades.

7. An Appeal to All Men and Women of India[1]

1. In spite of political differences, everyone should unite for the defence and well-being of the country and cooperate with others to implement programmes for the common good.

2. The unity and good of the nation should be given first importance, and people should, therefore, rise above differences of caste, creed, language and province, and think more of the country as a whole.

3. Violence of any kind must be shunned and avoided. Violence creates hatred and is disruptive.

4. Religion is meant to raise an individual and to make him tolerant to others. Narrow prejudices and intolerance do not create respect for one's own religion in the eyes of others. We should honour not only our own religion but the religion of others also.

5. We should aim at equality of treatment and avoid feelings of high and low, and touchable and untouchable.

6. We should aim at becoming good citizens, subordinating self-interest and aiming at the common good.

7. Women should be treated with respect and as comrades. They should not be kept in purdah or seclusion, but given opportunities to participate in national activities.

8. Children should be treated with affection and gentleness and not beaten or scolded.

1. Issued by Nehru as President of the Bharat Sevak Samaj, New Delhi. Published in newspapers on 11 & 12 March 1957. Also available in JN Collection.

9. Liquor and all other intoxicants should be avoided.

10. Cottage industries should be encouraged and, as far as possible, khadi should be worn.

11. Adulteration of foodstuffs and other articles must be prevented.

12. The giving or accepting of bribes is bad both for the giver and the taker, and must be rigorously dealt with.

13. The house, street and village or town should be kept neat and clean.

14. We should try to understand the great developmental work that is going on in the country, such as the Five Year Plan, the Community Development Schemes, etc., and cooperate in furthering and implementing it.

15. Manual labour should be respected and everyone should endeavour to engage himself in some form of manual labour for constructive work.[2]

---

2. This signed appeal was handed over to Ram Narayan Chaudhary, Information Secretary of the Central Bharat Sevak Samaj.

8. To John Foster Dulles[1]

New Delhi
13 March 1957

My dear Mr Secretary,[2]

It was very good of you to send me your letter of March 3rd about the little rug which we gave you as a souvenir.[3] I am happy that Mrs Dulles and you like it. We are rather proud of our handicrafts in India for their quality, variety and beauty.

---

1. JN Collection.
2. Secretary of State, USA.
3. Dulles wrote that the rug which Nehru presented to Mrs Dulles, was lovely and added beauty to their home which they would always associate with Nehru. Regarding the troubles and events that came up during recent weeks, he wrote that he was confident that they would not efface the basic understanding on fundamentals that emerged from Nehru and Eisenhower talks.

You are perfectly right in saying that troubles have descended upon us during the past weeks. I do earnestly hope that they will not embitter our minds or divert them from our efforts to promote peace and mutual understanding on basic issues.

With all good wishes,

Sincerely yours,
Jawaharlal Nehru

9. Nehru and the Socialists[1]

I met Jawaharlal after a long time. I found him looking tired but completely relaxed and free from tension. This is, I think, responsible for his ability to maintain good health and put in an enormous amount of work.

I showed him copies of the letter I had addressed to him in 1951 suggesting a rapproachement between the Congress, the Socialist Party and the KMPP, his reply to me[2] and the letter addressed to me by Acharya Narendra Deva giving his views on this proposal. I asked J.L. if I could refer to this correspondence in my proposed book. He went through the correspondence carefully and told me that I was free to publish it as there was nothing in it which needed to be withheld. He then told me how he had taken up this thread in initiating talks with Jayaprakash Narayan which unfortunately came to nothing. He had felt that there was a large area of common ground between the two and there was some possibility of cooperation on all levels. It was to explore this possibility that he had invited J.P. for a talk. The question then arose whether there could also be cooperation on the governmental level and this too, was explored but unfortunately no agreement could be reached, although, out of the points which

1. Raghukul Tilak's record of his talk with Nehru, New Delhi, 14 March 1957. JN Supplementary Papers, NMML. Raghukul Tilak was a well known Congressman from Meerut who joined the Socialist Party in 1948.
2. For Raghukul Tilak's letter of 21 September 1951 and Nehru's reply on 29 September, see *Selected Works* (second series), Vol. 16, Pt. II, p. 198.

J.P. had suggested, about 50% could be accepted without any controversy and about 25%, there could be some sort of compromise. It was only about the rest that an agreement was found to be difficult.

J.L. told me that he had been associated with Narendra Deva since about 1915 when they were both interested in the Home Rule League Movement. J.L. had himself started a branch of the League at Allahabad and N.D. had started one at Faizabad. As far as he remembered, it was Shiva Prasad Gupta[3] who had asked him to persuade N.D. to join the Kashi Vidyapith and he had been able to do so. He had also a vague recollection that N.D. had participated in the agrarian upheaval of 1920-21 which was mostly confined to Faizabad, Pratapgarh and Rae Bareli districts. As for any letters of N.D. with him, J.L. told me that he was not sure if he could find them but he would look up his files and, if necessary, later on I might also look into these files for any letters or other papers on the subject. He remembered that Tendulkar[4] had sorted out some letters for publication but these were mostly from Pandit Moti Lal Nehru and dealt with domestic matters and he did not feel it would be any use publishing them. I told him that Tendulkar had informed me that in the files which he had gone through there were some letters from N.D. also. J.L. said that, if that was so, he would certainly let me have those letters. He also said that, at a later stage, I could go through these files myself. He also gladly agreed to contribute a foreword to the book when it was ready. He was also good enough to permit me to see him again whenever I found it necessary to consult him.

3. A rich landowner from Varanasi who worked for the Congress.
4. D.G. Tendulkar was a freedom fighter, biographer and writer; well known for his eight-volume biography of Mahatma Gandhi.

10. Congress Still a Movement, Not a Party[1]

When I returned to New Delhi, coming from South India, I found myself invited to lunch by Prime Minister Nehru. We spoke about the impressions we had had in the South of India, and when we took coffee, our talk changed over to the

1. This article, based on an interview with Nehru by Giselher Wirsing, was published in *Die Welt* (Hamburg) on 18 March 1957. File No. 7(2)-EUR(W)/57, MEA. No other record of this interview is available.

political sphere. The election results are now arriving gradually from all the corners of the country, and the outlines of the victory of the Congress Party are becoming visible more clearly. "The Congress", Nehru said, "is frequently criticized because it unites different trends. But the Congress is still more a movement rather than a Party. It is the continuation of the great movement which liberated India from British rule." He smiled. "The Pantheon of the Hindus has always been large and wide and had always space for many things which seems to contradict each other. The overwhelming majority in this country tends to a new social society. Outsiders are only to be found in the religious groups which claim exclusive rights, and of course the communists." I have been told that Nehru had sometimes been asked by Americans in a rather provocative way about the communists, and that he did not like this subject. Now, he had taken up the subject himself, and how vehemently!

All his softness has gone, and we see a very ironical Nehru. He says that communism is always connected with violence. "India needs a pragmatic socialism in her own form, no dogmatism which lives from dusty books."

With regard to China, the Prime Minister says: "China is the power with whom India and her Congress is competing." It is known that Chou En-lai's visits lately, have set Nehru thinking a great deal.[2] He speaks with great respect about China, but also with a certain reserve. "There is no question of power-policy between China and India. Two very different centres are forming themselves here in Asia. In some respects following the same aims, but yet different in their methods. We can learn some or the other thing from one another, but the ways are different. The essential difference is the view on the development of the peasants. China follows her definite way. You are acquainted with our way. Approximately, half of our villages is now under the National Extension Service. In the Second Five Year Plan, we will have penetrated to the most remote village. When we obtain the voluntary cooperation of the peasants—and they are more than 300 millions out of our 380 million people—this will not be a turning point for India, but for the whole of Asia. This also explains some contradictions in the Congress. We are the greatest peasants' party of the world."

Nehru very often uses the term "flexible" in this connection. This word fits him excellently, because Nehru embodies relaxation, tension and energy. As to Russia, he seems to be less interested in the old communist system than rather in the changes it has undergone. The relation between India and Russia is a

---

2. Chou En-lai visited India from 25 to 28 June 1954. He was again in India from 28 November to 10 December 1956 and from 30 December 1956 to 1 January 1957. For more details about his visits see *Selected Works* (second series), Vol. 26, pp. 365-414 and Vol. 36, pp. 583-619.

function in the great play of Powers. The relations to China, however, is a question of the substance of the new Asia. In Nehru's eyes this is a struggle for the future of uncounted millions. And the dice must be thrown anew everyday.

When during these weeks, eight million people attended Nehru's meetings, they did not only wish to hear him, they also wanted to see him. Nehru embodies the most modern India. They do not seek any dogma behind Nehru—this would be entirely un-Indian. They seek behind Nehru the nobility of his appearance and the sacrifices which he made in his ascetic life, a sacrifice which convinces them. Nobody in this world could rule more absolutely than Nehru could in India. He does it because he is conscious of the necessity of limiting one's power. This is the great doctrine of which he gives a model to the whole of Asia.

When we discussed Congress and the elections, I said the first results showed that everything would remain as it was. "Not at all", he said and smiled, "Sometimes the votes for Lok Sabha and for the State Parliament are different in the same place. When you take the trouble of finding out why certain personalities lose in the State-elections, you have a key for many things." In the elections, Nehru sees his people—who are partly a little too much privileged—exposed to the fresh wind of free competition. He seems to appreciate these judgements rendered by the people, though in some or the other case, they may be of a tactical disadvantage to his own Party.

This bright summer-day was not the right time to discuss controversial questions like Kashmir or India's attitude towards the West. What appears to me to be more important than everyday-politics, is the fundamental question why the West does not show full confidence in this unique personality of Asia. I do not mean blind approval, but that profound confidence into the intentions of the other partner which only creates the common ground which is durable.

It is not difficult to criticize Nehru in this or the other point, such as with regard to his legalistic argumentation about Kashmir. But is this really important? Have we in the West taken the trouble to study these fundamental intentions with great care? Have we realized what this competition with China which occupies Nehru so much, means in the historical connection. Have we tried to take his and not our point of view into account, when we judge about this? The point of view of Asia which is imbued with the fervent desire to get out of social backwardness, poverty, hunger and illiteracy? Should we suppose Nehru who combines the noble traits of an ancient culture with the knowledge of a Cambridge-man, that he reacts like us in all the points?

One must ask these questions because they are Nehru's questions. He shows derision to our simple arguments just as I show derision when I hear in India superficial arguments about Germany's fundamental problems, like reunification (notwithstanding the open sympathies which we Germans, and above all West-

Germans enjoy here). Does everyday-policy not get into dangerous paths when it tries to destroy this fundamental confidence which should be shown towards Nehru, by interfering in an unconsidered way with Asiatic matters?

When we rose from the table, Nehru said a friendly word about Germany and folded his hands in farewell. Our visit to the Prime Minister is terminated.

Three profoundly serious and yet happy hours under the shady trees in the garden and under the gay spring-sky will accompany us for a long time. I begin to understand why the mighty kings of India were painted in the style of finest miniatures.

11. To U.N. Dhebar[1]

New Delhi
20 March 1957

My dear Dhebarbai,

I am writing to you about Rajkumari Amrit Kaur. As you may remember, we had suggested to her to go to the Rajya Sabha. This was not a definite promise but it was some kind of assurance.

Anyhow, I think that she should go to the Rajya Sabha. In spite of many criticisms made of her work, I think, she has given a great impetus to our health programme. She is probably among the best known five or six Indians, in so far as foreign countries are concerned and she has done very good work abroad. To leave her out of Parliament would not by fair and this will hurt many people.

I do not quite know how or from where she could be taken in. I am merely writing to you to keep this mind.

Yours sincerely,
Jawaharlal Nehru

1. JN Collection. Also available in AICC Papers, NMML.

587

12. To Amrit Kaur[1]

New Delhi
31 March 1957

My dear Amrit,

Your letter of March 29[2] enclosing a letter from Miraben.[3]

I really do not quite know how to help her,[4] much as I would like to do so. Obviously I cannot use the Prime Minister's Relief Fund for such purposes. For the rest, I have some limited non-Government funds at my disposal from which I can give small grants. It would not be at all easy to give a grant for the building of a house. Anyhow, what I can give would not take us far. As far as I can see, I could give her Rs 1000/-. Perhaps I could give her a little more. But I fear I cannot find Rs 5000/- from these small and limited funds. I do not wish to touch Government funds for this.

Yours affectionately,
Jawahar

1. JN Collection.
2. Not available.
3. Miraben nee Madeleine Slade, a disciple of Mahatma Gandhi, had lived at the Sabarmati Ashram for many years.
4. Amrit Kaur wrote to Nehru earlier also on 12 March and sent a copy of Miraben's letter in which the latter requested for "a little capital" that could enable her to settle down permanently. In his reply on 15 March, Nehru wrote that it would not be possible to provide that capital, but that the Gandhi Smarak Nidhi might be mobilized to give Miraben a monthly allowance.

13. To Edwina Mountbatten[1]

New Delhi
5 April 1957

My dear Edwina,[2]

Some days ago I received your letter of the 8th March, with which you sent me a letter from a girl in Vienna. Also a golden bangle which she had sent.

I was a little surprised to get this from you. Why should you have been troubled with this matter? You say that you sometimes receive such letters, which is surprising.

I cannot make out this young woman, because evidently she has learnt Hindi and has written a few lines in it. She also knows about this old custom of ours, called sending or tying a *rakhi*, which is any kind of bracelet from a cotton or silken string to something in jewels.

There is a special day in the year which is devoted to this business of tying these *rakhis*. Both men and women do it. But, more particularly, it is true that a woman by tying it round the wrist of a man, asks him as a brother to protect her from some peril. There are many romantic stories in our history about this. Once a Rajput Princess, who was in trouble with some neighbouring ruler, sent a bracelet by a messenger to the Mughal Emperor.[3] The Mughal responded immediately by taking an army to protect her and there was quite a war.

\Evidently, the young lady in Vienna has some other sentiments.

Yours,
Jawahar

1. JN Collection.
2. Edwina Mountbatten was the Chairman, St John and Red Cross Services Hospitals.
3. This refers to the story of Humayun and Rani Karmavati of Chittor.

589

14. To S. Abid Hussain[1]

New Delhi
7 April 1957

My dear Abid Hussain,[2]

Your letter of the 5th April.

You know that I would gladly do anything in my capacity which you ask me to do. Normally I do not write prefaces to books, but I could stretch this point in your favour, given the time. But you have not apparently understood my real difficulty. I cannot possibly write a foreword to a book of the kind you have written, that is, *The Way of Gandhi and Nehru*.[3] I have all along refused to write a preface or a foreword on a book on Gandhiji for reasons which would be obvious to you. But to write about myself or *The Way of Nehru* is quite out of the question for me. If I may say, this kind of thing would not be appropriate at all. I cannot write discussing myself or my ways or thoughts in the form of a foreword to a book dealing with those matters.

If, however, I have the time and the inclination, I might write a continuation of my autobiography and discuss directly or indirectly how my thinking or action have been conditioned. To write a brief foreword to a book of this kind would put me in a most embarrassing position. The only way I could deal with the situation is to write something which is bigger than the book, and that too, in criticism of what has been written in the book. This is not only beyond me but, as I have said, is not supposed to be done.

Yours sincerely,
Jawaharlal Nehru

1. File No. 9/2/57-PMS.
2. Syed Abid Hussain (1896-1978); Urdu scholar and writer; taught philosophy at the Jamia Millia Islamia for several years; member, Official Language Commission, 1954-56; translated classical German and English works into Urdu; also translated Nehru's *Glimpses of World History* and *An Autobiography* into Urdu, wrote several books including *Hindustani Qaumiyat Aur Qaumi Tehzib* which won him Sahitya Akademi Award in 1956.
3. The book was published in Bombay in 1959 by Asia Publishing House.

15. Royalties from Other Countries[1]

I signed a cheque today for royalties from, I think, the Romanian edition of my book.

2. A few days ago, you sent me a note in which you mentioned that some royalties were due to me from other places also, notably from China. You would, however, not call them in.

3. I think that all royalties due to me, more especially from abroad, should be called in whenever they fall due. They should not be held up there, because they might affect my current income-tax statement. I do not think this is a proper approach to this problem either from the personal or the national point of view. From the personal point of view, it makes little difference as royalties will be coming in from time to time in the future, and the same problem will constantly arise. But, from the national point of view, it is, I think, definitely improper to hold up these. We want all kinds of foreign exchange in India. I should take it whenever it comes, and not delay this process. The whole idea of delaying it has a bad flavour about it.

4. Only in the case of the Soviet royalties, I had said that half of them might be left there and half should be realized here. I decided this not because of any income-tax reason, but because it is not the usual practice of the Soviet to allow money to be taken away from their country. They had shown a special indulgence in this respect, and I felt that I should only take advantage of it partly. Therefore, from the Soviet also, half of the royalties should be realized.

5. I think, therefore, that all foreign royalties, subject to what I have said about the Soviet above, should be realized as they fall due. This should apply to Indian royalties too, though a little delay there does not make much difference. It is important for foreign exchange purposes that everything due to us abroad should be brought into the country. Of course, I pay the full income-tax on it when it falls due.

6. My current income-tax will be based on income derived till the end of March last. Anything that comes in now, will go into next year's income-tax, which means nearly a year hence. It would be absurd to hold up these sums for a year. There is no point in it, apart from the impropriety I have pointed out above.

1. Note to Private Secretary, New Delhi, 12 April 1957. JN Collection.

16. To Ram Narayan Chaudhary[1]

New Delhi
18 April 1957

Dear Ram Narayanji,

I have received your report of my interview with the Editor, *Bharat Sevak*. I have thought about this matter and I do not like an interview about my personal habits and, more especially, about what you call my mental health. As for the reference to Sir Winston Churchill, I do not think this will be at all proper. I must not repeat private remarks in public. At the most you can say something about my physical habits and that too in the third person, and not exactly in the form of question and answer. For instance, you can say that, as a rule, he goes to bed at half past twelve at night and sleeps for six hours. Whenever possible, he rests for half an hour in the middle of the day. His food is light and simple. He has no special diet, but he avoids chillies completely and hardly takes any spices. He takes some very simple exercises in the morning for a few minutes. These include *Shirsasan* for about two minutes. Health, however, does not depend only on such matters, but on a combination of many things, more especially the avoidance of worry. It is difficult to avoid worry completely when one has heavy responsibilities, but, on the whole, he tries to avoid it and, more particularly, he tries not to have any ill will against anyone, although he might be irritated for a time. Usually his irritation passes.

Yours sincerely,
Jawaharlal Nehru

1. JN Collection.

17. To Dorothy Norman[1]

New Delhi
19 April 1957

My dear Dorothy,[2]

Thank you for your letter of April 8th.

About the projected "book" or "Reader", I really have nothing to suggest to you or advise you. You are the best judge, and I am content to abide by your judgement. So far as royalties are concerned, you can certainly take the advance which is necessary. I leave these matters entirely to you. I fear I lack the business instinct, in such matters at least.

You mention my early book on Russia. This was really a series of articles which I sent mostly to *The Hindu* of Madras, articles hurriedly written.[3] The most that can be said about them is that they conveyed some impressions fresh in my mind at the time. I have found a copy of it in my library, and I am sending it to you separately. It is not easily obtainable anywhere here, and it has little value.

Both Indira and I feel very tired after our election labours. I am feeling rather flat and stale. Next week, I am going to the mountains for four days for some kind of rest. That is the most I can steal from my other occupations. Early next month, the newly elected Parliament will begin its work.

Yours,
Jawahar

1. JN Collection.
2. American civil rights advocate, writer, photographer and a patron of the arts.
3. The articles, mostly published in *The Hindu* and one in *Young India* in 1928, were written by Nehru after his visit to the Soviet Union in November 1927. They were brought out in a book form with the title *Soviet Russia, some random sketches and impressions*, and was first published by Lala Ram Mohan Lal at Allahabad in December 1928. The articles were also printed in *Selected Works* (first series), Vol. 2, pp. 379-451.

18. To Subimal Dutt[1]

New Delhi
21 April 1957

My dear Dutt,

Mrs Nellie Sengupta[2] came to see me this afternoon with the Secretary[3] of the Prabartak Samgha.[4] They gave me a letter which I enclose. They told me of the work they had been doing. Apart from putting up these buildings, they have extended their scope of activities considerably. During the famine period, they gave free food to considerable numbers of people. The East Pakistan Government is now friendly to them and they have appreciated the good work done by the Prabartak Samgha. They have even given them some money, though not much. Generally, there is a much better atmosphere for them to work and the Members of the East Pakistan Government, including Fazlul Huq[5] and Mujibur Rahman[6], have spoken highly of their work. I have no doubt that they have done and are doing very good work. More especially, they are a haven of refuge to the minority community round about.

You will see that they want to expand their educational and other activities by building hostels for boys and a hospital. Apart from this, they have not quite

---

1. JN Collection.
2. Nellie Sen Gupta, Member of the East Pakistan Legislature and a former President of the Indian National Congress, was actively involved in the social service activities of the Prabartak Samgha, Chittagong.
3. Birendralal Chaudhury.
4. Prabaratak Samgha was established in 1914 in Chandernagore. Since 1929 its Chittagong branch was engaged in constructive activities. See also *Selected Works* (second series), Vol. 32, p. 307.
5. A.K. Fazlul Huq was Governor of East Pakistan.
6. Sheikh Mujibur Rahman (1920-75); Founding Father of Bangladesh; Councillor, Muslim League, 1943-47; Co-founder of Awami (People's) League in East Pakistan, 1949, its General Secretary, 1953-66, and President, 1966-73; Member, East Pakistan Assembly, and Minister, 1954; Member, National Assembly, and Minister, 1954-57; political prisoner, 1966-69; won absolute majority in Constituent Assembly elections, 1970; declared Independence of Bangladesh, 1971; elected President by Government-in-Exile; charged with treason, March 1971; tried in camera and sentenced to death, August 1971; after the liberation of Bangladesh in December 1971 was released in January 1972; Prime Minister of Bangladesh, 1972-75; was killed in a coup in Dhaka on 15 August 1975.

finished the structures they put up for the girls. The roof is still lacking and apparently they have no money left. They have asked for a contribution of Rs 2,00,000/-.

I told them that they have come here at a time when it is very difficult for us to help because of our own precarious situation which has made us cut down our expenditure on many good things. They were disappointed of course and then asked if we could help them even to some extent. I said that we all appreciated greatly their work and would like to be of assistance to them to the best of our present ability. But I could not say exactly how far we could go. I suggested that they might see you.

Please, therefore, arrange to see Mrs Nellie Sengupta and her colleague. They are staying with K.M. Raha,[7] 12 Ashoka Road. You might get in touch with them on the telephone or perhaps they would telephone to you and fix sometime to meet them. Afterwards you could have a talk with me on this subject.

Yours sincerely,
Jawaharlal Nehru

7. Kshetra Mohan Raha (b. 1905); appointed Aerodrome Officer, Civil Aviation Directorate, Government of India, 1931; Representative of India on the Council of the International Civil Aviation Organization, Montreal, 1946-47; Deputy Director General of Civil Aviation, 1947-58.

19. Interview with Derek Holroyde[1]

Derek Holroyde:[2] Mr Nehru, now that India's second general election is over, and the Congress is back in power, would you say that you were surprised in any way by the results?

Jawaharlal Nehru: Of course, there are many surprises in the elections as there always are, but broadly speaking, the elections were always entirely in favour of

1. New Delhi, 22 April 1957. AIR tapes, NMML.
2. Derek Holroyde was BBC's representative.

595

the Congress so far as Parliament is concerned, and the surprises came in the States, which shows that the broad policy of the Congress is approved of by the people, whether foreign or internal or economic but that, there is a good deal of discontentment about local causes and local organizations.

DH: Well, now that you have a new Congress Government, a new Central Government in office, how do you see the priority problems facing it?

JN: The first problem for our Government is obviously, the economic problem—the Second Five Year Plan, and all that goes under it. There are problems of foreign exchange, of development of internal resources, because the Second Five Year Plan puts a heavy burden on us, which is increased due to subsequent happenings and we hope to shoulder that burden and we propose to do so.

DH: Can you see a way through the present foreign exchange difficulties? Is there any particular direction, for example, in which countries like Britain could help more than they are doing.

JN: Well, I cannot give you any detailed analysis of this situation. We are exploring every avenue in regard to foreign exchange, and I am sure, that Britain can also help in that. We want the greatest help we can from such countries which are prepared to help and I feel that Britain can help also.

DH: Now, before leaving the domestic scene one question I would like to ask is about the communist victory in Kerala, and the formation of a Communist Government there. Do you consider, these events will have any effect on India's democratic development?

JN: I do not know, I do not think they will have any major effect. But naturally, every such development has produced some effect on both sides. It is interesting to watch those effects. Kerala is too small a part of the country to produce a major effect in India, also it is quite clear, that the elections in Kerala, were won on internal State issues, dissatisfaction with the previous Governments there, unemployment and the like, and had almost nothing to do with the major issues for which we stand.

DH: Do you see an Indian brand of communism emerging?

JN: I suppose communism by the very nature of things, is basically one brand; that major brand itself may tone down, and, I think, it will, as every revolutionary brand does tone down. It is toning down in spite of some outbursts in this or that direction. I expect communism as a whole in the world, just like any other revolutionary movement, to tone down.

DH: Now you will be going, I believe, to the Commonwealth Prime Ministers' Conference in London, at the end of June?[3]

JN: Yes, I intend to.

DH: And would you agree then with critics who said that the Conference is being called too soon after recent stresses and strains within the Commonwealth.

JN: It is not for me to say that it is too soon but in a sense, it is always good to meet and discuss problems and perhaps when difficulties arise, it is better to discuss them than not to do so.

DH: And then how do you evaluate Indo-British relations at the moment?

JN: Well, as you have just said yourself, we have gone through a period of strain. Relations between India and Britain, or for that matter any other country, depend on, well, development of things that happen. Two things that affected our relations mostly recently, were developments in regard to the Suez and on Egypt etc. And on the Kashmir question, on which we thought, the British press as a whole, and some British leaders otherwise too, took up an attitude which was mostly unfair to India, and which was, if I may say so, with all respect, wholly uninformed.

DH: How does that fit in now with India's present relations with Pakistan?

JN: I do not know what you mean by Pakistan? Do you mean the Government or the people, or what? If you mean the Government, then our relations are not, at the present moment, very friendly. Certainly, from the Pakistan side they have said strong things about us and the press talks about 'jehad' and 'holy war'.

3. The Conference was held from 26 June to 5 July 1957.

597

Nevertheless, I am quite convinced, that the broad relationship, between the people of India and the people of Pakistan is better than it was a few years ago. There is little of the old ill will left. It can be roused up occasionally on some religious cry. But basically, I think, we still are friendly countries.

DH: And you are hopeful of settling down permanently.

JN: Obviously, I am hopeful, because without that, it will be very very unfortunate for both India and Pakistan.

DH: Now, can we turn to the world as a whole, for a moment? Do you say that the prospects of peace have improved or deteriorated in the last few months?

JN: I should think they have deteriorated somewhat, there are some hopeful elements in the situation, but broadly, I think, they have, they are not in a good way at all.

DH: And do you think the Middle East is being the centre of world tension?

JN: I do think so, that the main trouble is at present in the Middle East. I do not like to look at the Middle Eastern countries, at all at present moment.

DH: No sign of clearing up it all?

JN: Well not there. The only rather good sign slightly is, well, in regard to the Disarmament Conference Committee.[4] There has been some slight improvement there, and I believe there is some realization also, that this nuclear armament race, is a very bad thing, and it is upsetting people in large number everywhere.

DH: Yes, well, you have spoken frequently against these test explosions and Russia just had five and Britain plans a major one near Christmas Islands. This you have called it a 'mad race'. Can you see any signs of an end to it, other than perhaps, a little improvement of Disarmament Conference?

4. The sub-committee of the UN Disarmament Commission convened its meeting in London on 18 March 1957 and agreed to discuss various aspects of disarmament, including the nuclear tests.

JN: It is very curious, that almost every country that possess it, says that if you are sure, the other party will not do it, we won't do it. Well, surely if that is so, let them all meet together and say we won't do it.

DH: And that is the way you would advocate the call of halt. You don't advocate unilateral renunciation.

JN: Is not a question of my calling for unilateral renunciation, if anybody did it, it is good, it is not practical to suggest it, therefore, let them meet and do it together.

DH: So, that means, you are now really in favour of Four Power talks in the near future, if not immediately.

JN: These questions can only be solved by an approach to each other, preferably a Round Table Conference to begin with. Therefore, I would welcome these Four Power talks.

DH: And you think the atmosphere now is conducive to a meeting, I mean the people concerned could get along?

JN: The atmosphere is not too good at the present moment, but I imagine that if such a proposal was made, that itself would improve the atmosphere.

DH: Thank you very much Mr Nehru.

JN: Thank you.

20. To Govind Ballabh Pant[1]

New Delhi
23 April 1957

My dear Pantji,

Your letter of the 22nd April about Nila Nagini alias Mrs Cook. I know something about her. Indeed, I have had reports about her ever since she first came here in 1931. The reports were not at all favourable to her.

I do not think any question arises of her being made an Indian national. The only question that did arise, was whether she should be allowed to stay on in India to do some literary work. Her ability and knowledge of many classical and modern languages is remarkable. She is now engaged in writing a book about Kashmir—not the political side of it, but chiefly dealing with the literary aspect, with a dash of past history. I am told that this book she is writing, is of high quality. I think, therefore, that she should be given facilities for writing this book and remaining in India. As I have said above, there is no question of her adopting Indian nationality.

I understand that Fyzee,[2] the prospective Vice-Chancellor of Srinagar University, has asked her to continue with this work and has promised her help in it.

Yours affectionately,
Jawaharlal Nehru

1. JN Collection.
2. Asaf Ali Asghar Fyzee was member, Indian Public Service Commission at this time. He later became the Vice-Chancellor of Jammu and Kashmir University, Srinagar, in 1958.

21. To Padmaja Naidu[1]

New Delhi
23 April 1957

Bebee dear,[2]

I have just seen your letter of the 19th April, with which you have sent me Mridula's[3] newsletters, I had long ago given up receiving or reading these. Mridula has probably done us more harm in regard to Kashmir than almost anyone else. I do not think she can do anything more than what she has done and no one takes her effusions seriously. We have often thought what to do about it and have not succeeded in finding out any effective method. I have not spoken to her for many months. I think she has lost her mental balance completely.

I am glad you are at Darjeeling and I hope that you will soon recover from the effect of the rapid ascent. The house is delightful and I am sure you will see Kanchenjunga one day and be overwhelmed.

There is not a chance of my being able to go to Darjeeling in May. I shall probably go for two or three days to the other end of the world, Ceylon, in the middle of May.[4] About the Middle of June I go to Europe.[5]

Meanwhile, I am going for four or five days to Chakrata and Mussoorie.

Love,
Jawahar

1. Padmaja Naidu Papers, NMML. Also available in JN Collection.
2. Governor of West Bengal.
3. Mridula Sarabhai was a freedom fighter and organized relief and rehabilitation of refugees including abducted women after Partition.
4. Nehru left on 17 May for a three day visit to Sri Lanka.
5. Nehru visited Syria, Sudan, Egypt, Denmark, Finland, Norway, Sweden, Netherlands and Britain between 15 June and 14 July 1957.

22. Second Hebrew Edition of *An Autobiography*[1]

Many years ago, a Hebrew edition of my *Autobiography* was published. When this book first came out in English, it was banned in Palestine. I was, therefore, happy to learn of the publication of a Hebrew translation. I am glad that a second edition is going to be issued.

This book was written by me more than twenty years ago in prison. These twenty years have seen many changes in my country and the world. Some of the problems of the middle thirties have been solved. A Great War, with all its horror, has taken place and new independent nations have arisen. But even as we solve old problems, new and more difficult ones have arisen and the burden on humanity grows heavier.

I do not know how far this book, written in the solitude of prison cells, is at all helpful in the world today where we live under the dread shadow of the hydrogen bomb. Not even the terrible experience of two World Wars have made us learn the lesson that violence and wars do not solve problems. Surely some other approach is necessary, some approach which is based on humanism and compassion and the spirit of cooperation between nations.

In the prevailing atmosphere of cold war, it is difficult to hold on to intellectual integrity or to objective thinking. All of us become, to a greater or lesser degree, the victims of forces utterly beyond our control. Yet, I believe that it is only through intellectual integrity and the absence of hatred and violence that we can solve the problems that face us.

This book was written when we in India were in the middle of our struggle for freedom. That struggle was long drawn out and it brought many experiences of joy and sorrow, of hope and despair. But the despair did not last long because of the inspiration that came to us from our leader, Mahatma Gandhi, and the deep delight of working for a cause that took us out of our little shells.

All of us are older now and our days of youth are long past. Yet, even now, when we face the troubles and torments that encompasses, something of that old memory of our leader gives us strength.

1. Foreword to the second Hebrew edition of *An Autobiography*, New Delhi, 24 April 1957. JN Collection.

23. To G.P. Hutheesing[1]

New Delhi
24 April 1957

My dear Raja,

I have your letter of the 22nd April.

It is not necessary for you to remind me of my close relationship with Krishna, a relationship not only that of a brother, but even something more. Because of the considerable difference in our ages, I had naturally looked upon her as someone who was not only my sister, but one for whom I had a kind of parental responsibility. I have always felt that way and feel so now. I have no doubt that I shall continue to feel so. You need not worry about that or about Harsha[2] and Ajit, who are fine boys and whom I like.

But I have to realize more than ever how difficult it is for one person to understand another and how bad it is for one person, even a parent, to impose his will on another. A gap between children and their parents becomes ever greater in spite of the love and affection they might have. Parents seldom realize it and get angry with their children for doing something that they do not like. We live in different overlapping worlds. The misunderstanding is not only between nations, but between individuals and even in a family. That is why I refer to *Panchsheel*, which does not replace affection, but which is very important, because it teaches tolerance.

I have also found that nothing is more futile than explanations and arguments, more especially about personal matters. A person either understands another or does not do so. If the latter, then it is best to allow matters to rest and not to argue, for arguments only make matters worse.

Love and affection are always there, but even these become rather irritating if the mood is not receptive. So, one has to wait for that better mood.

Yours affectionately,
Jawaharlal

1. JN Collection.
2. Harsha Hutheesing.

24. To J.H. Adam[1]

New Delhi
24 April 1957

Dear Mr Adam,

This is in continuation of my letter to you of the 16th April, 1957.

The Prime Minister has had no time to read the manuscript of Sir Francis Tuker's book[2] that you have sent him. He read, however, some part of it and was surprised to note how full of inaccuracies and entirely false interpretation of events these parts contained. He asked the book to be read by a person acquainted with both the past and recent history of Nepal, who has pointed out that the book is so full of false statements that it is a little difficult to take it seriously. The early history of Nepal contains many statements which are contrary to well known facts. Anyone with even a moderate acquaintance with Nepal could point these out.

The account given about the more recent history of Nepal is even more fantastic and has hardly any relation to fact. It is evident that Sir Francis Tuker is so obsessed by his own notions and eversions and these lead to gross mis-statements and perversions of fact. He refers repeatedly to the Indian Congress Party engineering troubles in Nepal after India became independent. As a matter of fact, one of the earliest acts of independent India was to recognize the independence of Nepal and to have a treaty with the then Rana Prime Minister.[3] By this treaty, Nepal for the first time was recognized as a fully independent nation.

The reference to Shri Rafi Ahmad Kidwai, who is described as "the Muslim Home Member of the UP Ministry" is wholly wrong. Shri Kidwai was a Member of the Central Government as Minister of Communications soon after Independence. It is also wholly incorrect to say that there was any Muslim reaction in India against the Ranas because of the Nepalese laws forbidding

---

1. Drafted by Nehru, New Delhi, 24 April 1957. This was to be issued by the Foreign Secretary to J.H. Adam, Managing Director of Orient Longmans Ltd., Calcutta. JN Collection.
2. *Gorkha: The Story of the Gurkhas of Nepal* was published in 1957 by Constable and Co., London.
3. Padma Shumshere Jung Bahadur Rana signed a tripartite agreement with the Governments of Britain and India on 9 November 1947. See also *Selected Works* (second series), Vol. 4, p. 482.

marriages between the Muslims in Nepal and Hindu women. This fact was hardly known anywhere and have not the slightest effect on anybody.

References to Shri C.P.N. Singh, Indian Ambassador,[4] are also not correct.

It is wholly wrong to say that the Bihar Government sent insurgents to Nepal in their State lorries. As a matter of fact, the only step the Bihar Government took was to prevent people from crossing the border when the revolution had broken out in Nepal.

Sir Francis Tuker's sole argument appears to be that there was some kind of an Indian invasion, or an invasion from India, of Nepal and that the Nepalese Congress was an Indian political party. Both these allegations have no basis in fact. There was a widespread revolt in the hills of Nepal and there were large-scale army and police desertions. The Rana Prime Minister was totally unable to control the situation and appealed to the Government of India for help. It was owing to the efforts of the Government of India that an agreement was arrived at between the popular forces and the Rana Prime Minister.

Ever since then, India has fully accepted the independence of Nepal and it was largely due to India's efforts that Nepal was admitted to the United Nations. India is naturally interested in the stability and security of Nepal for geographical and other reasons.

Under the directions of the Prime Minister, I am pointing out to you a few of the numerous mis-statements and mis-representations that abound in Sir Francis Tuker's book. Even apart from Sir Francis Tuker's perversion of fact, the whole tenor of the book appears to be full of hatred and malice for India as well as the popular movements in Nepal. Sir Francis Tuker apparently believes in unadulterated autocracy and feudalism and, as he says, in denying education to people lest they might get wrong ideas. He has even been at pains to find excuses for the notorious Kot Massacre.[5]

The Prime Minister has no intention of entering into an argument with the author about his statements but he must express his surprise that a firm of Messrs. Orient Longman's standing should decide to publish a book containing such gross mis-statements and perversions of fact.

4. C.P.N. Singh was Indian Ambassador to Nepal from 1949 to 1952.
5. The Kot Massacre of 1846 was the result of court politics where the casualties were staggering both in the number and the rank of the persons involved.

GLOSSARY

Akhand Bharat	undivided India
anna	16th part of a rupee, in circulation in India till 1957
Bharat Mata	Mother India
Bharat Mata ki Jai	victory to Mother India
chaitra	first month of Hindu lunar calendar
chaprassis	peons, official messengers
gram	a village
gramsevak/gramsevika	a voluntary village worker
halal	lawful, slaughter of animals according to Muslim religious rites
Hindu rashtra	Hindu nation
jagirdari	a system of assignment of a tract of land and its revenue
Jai Hind	victory to India
jhatka	slaughter of animals according to Hindu religious rites
kisan	peasant
kowah	a low caste like *mehter*
kutcha	temporary
lokpal	a village official
maulvi	a Muslim learned person
mehter	cleaning worker or manual scavenger engaged in manually carrying human excreta or any sanitation work
maund	a measure of weight around one hundred pounds

mujtahid	an interpreter of Islamic doctrine or law
panchsheel	five basic principles of international conduct
shahenshah	emperor
shirshasan	a yoga posture, standing on head
taluqdari	a system of land holding
ulama	plural of *alim,* scholar of Islamic law and theology

(Biographical footnotes in this volume and in volumes in the first series are italicized and those in the second series are given in block letters.)

Hyderabad city, 15, 31 fn, 59, 107, 575
Hyderabad State, 3 fn
Hydrodynamic and Hydromagnetic Stability (S. Chandrasekhar), 273 fn

Iberians of Spain, The (Pierson Dixon), 399 fn
Ibn Batuta, 534 & *fn*
Ibn Saud, Abdul Aziz Bin, (VOL. 18, P. 207), 526
Imperial Bank of India, 6 fn
Imperialism in International Politics (Govind Sahai), 364 fn
India, Government of, 12 fn-13, 28-30, 38, 70, 78, 83, 105, 109, 129-130, 134-135, 138, 146, 158, 167-168, 170-171, 174, 176-177, 180 fn, 187, 199-201, 203, 215-216, 220-221, 224-225 & fn, 229-230 fn, 238, 244, 251, 257, 259 fn, 272-273, 292, 294, 303, 305-307, 309, 322 fn, 335 fn, 367, 400-401, 402 fn, 405, 420 fn, 424-425, 428 fn, 431, 434, 442 fn, 457-458, 465, 477, 480, 485, 489, 495, 500 fn, 503-504, 505 fn-506, 532, 535 & fn-536 fn, 540, 544 fn, 550 fn-551, 555, 596, 604 & fn-605
Indian Air Force, 247 & fn, 312-313, 498, 529, 575, 577
Indian Airlines Corporation, 274, 311
Indian Conference of Social Work, 242, 291
Indian Council of Agricultural Research (New Delhi), 215-216
Indian Institute of Public Administration (New Delhi), 305-306
Indo-China, 471, 507, 514; Geneva Conference on, 514
Indo-French Treaty (28 May 1956), 554
Indonesia, 26, 314, 371, 379, 520 & fn-521, 522, 565 fn; Government of, 520 fn-521, 522 fn
Industrial Finance Corporation, 241 & fn
Industrial Revolution, 16, 18, 58
Inner Line Regulation (1873), 449 fn
Inquiry into the Nature and Causes of the Wealth of Nations, An (Adam Smith), 184
International Affairs, 270, 303
International Atomic Energy Agency (Vienna), 482
International Bank for Reconstruction and Development (Washington), 434, 503-504; Proposal (February 1954) of, 503 & fn
International Civil Aviation, 313
International Commission for Supervision and Control (Indo-China), 471
International Conference of Social Work, 242
International Court of Justice (The Hague), 392, 414, 492 fn, 497
Iran, 113 fn, 511-516 & fn, 517 & fn-518 & fn, 519, 560; Government of, 513, 515-517, 518 fn-519; Shah of, *see* Pahlavi, Mohammad Reza
Iraq, 511, 514, 565 fn; Government of, 514
Isanuddin, 445
Ismail, Mirza, (*Vol. 4, p. 557*), 492 fn
Israel, 563
Italy, 553

Jabalpur, 70, 577
Jain, A.P., (*Vol. 8, p. 205*), 153 fn, 212, 214 & fn-215, 282, 327 & fn
Jaiswal, Saligram, 350
Jakarta, 520 & fn-521, 522 fn
Jal Mahal Palace Hotel (Jaipur), 346

State Bank of India, 6 fn
State Bank of India Bill (April 1955), 6 fn
States Reorganization Act (August 1956), 47 fn, 112 fn
States Reorganization Commission, 322 fn; report (30 September 1955) of, 114 fn
Stockholm, 528
Strategy for Agricultural Development (S.R. Sen), 283 fn
Subandrio, 522 fn
Subedar, Manu, (VOL. 8, P. 188), 314 & fn
Subramaniam, C., (VOL. 17, P. 103), 182 & fn, 341 & fn
Sudan, 536 fn, 601 fn
Suez Canal, 10, 33, 466, 472, 488, 492 fn, 497, 523 & fn, 524-525, 527 fn, 529 fn; 1888 Convention for, 497, 523 fn, 525; Canal Code for, 523 fn; UN Resolution on, 527 fn
Suez Canal Conference , Second (London, 19-21 September 1956), 524
Suez Canal Users' Association, 524
Suhrawardy, H.S., (VOL. 30, P. 387), 92 & fn, 94-95, 108, 406-407, 423, 431-432 & fn, 433, 463 & fn-464, 465, 511-512 & fn, 526
Sukhadia, Mohanlal, 346 & *fn*
Sukthankar, Y.N., (VOL. 21, P. 264), 275 fn, 297-298
Sulzberger, A.H., 498
Sumatra, 520 fn
Supreme Court of India, 140, 337, 385
Swe, U Ba, (VOL. 34, P. 216), 507 & fn-508
Sweden, 414, 601 fn
Syria, 524, 528 fn-529, 530, 536, 565 fn, 601 fn; Government of, 536

Tamilnad Congress Reform Committee (1957), 136 fn
Tamilnadu, 112 fn, 136 & fn
Tarachand, Dr, (*Vol. 1, p. 331*), 519
Tata Institute of Fundamental Research (Colaba, Mumbai), 272 & fn
Tata Nagar, 73
Technical Cooperation Mission, 215
Tehran, 517-519
Telengana, 3 fn, 239-240
Tellicherry (Kerala), 35 fn
Tendulkar, D.G., (*Vol. 4, p. 317*), 584 & fn
Thacker, M.S., (VOL. 29, P. 141), 268 & fn-269, 273
Thailand, 284, 371, 519
Tharpa Choling Monastery (Kalimpong), 505 fn
Theory of Moral Sentiments, The (Adam Smith), 184 fn
Thimayya, K.S., (VOL. 4, P. 13), 246 & fn, 251 & fn-252, 254, 259-260, 262
Tibet, 504-505 fn, 507-509
Tilak, Bal Gangadhar, (*Vol. 1, p. 41*), 56
———, Raghukul, (VOL. 7, P. 379), 583 fn
Times of India, The, 501 fn
Tipu Sultan, 564 & fn
Tokyo, 462 fn, 561-562
Tomney, Frank, 408 fn, 492 fn
Travancore, 47 fn
Travancore-Cochin, 47 fn
Travancore Tamil Nad Congress, 36 fn
Trichur, 35 fn, 246 & fn, 281
Tripartite Agreement of UK, India and Nepal (8 August 1957), 544 fn
Tripura, 414, 465 fn
Trivandrum, 38 & fn
Trivedi, C.M., (VOL. 3, P. 5), 228 & fn, 239, 296
Trombay (Mumbai), 326 fn